PREACHING
from the
LECTIONARY

PREACHING
from the
LECTIONARY

❧ ❧

AN EXEGETICAL COMMENTARY

with CD-ROM

Gerard S. Sloyan

Fortress Press
Minneapolis

To Myles M. Bourke
Priest, Preacher, Scholar

Cover design: Jessica Thoreson
Cover image: Veer
Book design: City Desktop Productions

The paper used in this publication meets the minimum requirements of American National Standard for Information Sciences—Permanence of Paper for Printed Library Materials, ANSI Z329-1984.

ISBN 0-8006-3606-6

Manufactured in Canada.

08   07   06   05   04   1   2   3   4   5   6   7   8   9   10

Contents

❧ YEAR A ❧

Season of Advent

Season of Christmas

Season of Epiphany

Season of Lent

Season of Easter

Season after Pentecost (Ordinary Time)

❧ YEAR B ❧

Season of Advent

Season of Christmas

Season of Epiphany

Season of Lent

Season of Easter

Season after Pentecost

Sundays of the Year

❧ YEAR C ❧

Season of Advent

Season of Christmas

Season of Epiphany

Season of Lent

Season of Easter

Season after Pentecost (Ordinary Time)

Feasts of Jesus, Mary, and the Saints

❧ Abbreviations ❧

1QH	Hymn Scroll *(Hodayoth)* from Qumram Cave 1
1QM	War Scroll *(Milḥamah)* from Qumran Cave 1
1QS	Community Rule *(Serek ha-Yaḥad)* from Qumram Cave 1
AB	Anchor Bible
Aram.	Aramaic
AV	Authorized Version, popularly known as KJV
b.	Babylonian Talmud *(Babli)*
B.C.E.	Before the Common Era
BCP	Book of Common Prayer
C.E.	Common Era
D	Deuteronomist source in the Pentateuch
DRC	Douai-Reims Version, ed. R. Challoner
E	Elohist source in the Pentateuch
Heb.	Hebrew
J	Yahwist source in the Pentateuch
j.	Jerusalem Talmud *(Yerushalmi)*
JB	Jerusalem Bible
KJV	King James Version
Lat.	Latin
lit.	literally
LM	Lectionary for Mass
LXX	Septuagint
m.	Mishnah
MS/S	manuscript/s
MT	Masoretic Text
par.	parallel Gospel passsages
NAB	New American Bible
NEB	New English Bible
NIV	New International Version
NJBC	*The New Jerome Biblical Commentary,* ed. Raymond E. Brown, Joseph A. Fitzmyer, and Roland E. Murphy (Englewood Cliffs, N.J.: Prentice-Hall, 1999)
NRSV	New Revised Standard Version
OBT	Overtures to Biblical Theology
P	Priestly source in the Pentateuch
//	parallel Synoptic Gospel passage
PC	*Peake's Commentary on the Bible,* ed. Matthew Black and H. H. Rowley (London: Nelson, 1963)
Q	Sayings Source in Matthew and Luke
RCL	Revised Common Lectionary
REB	Revised English Bible
RSV	Revised Standard Version
t.	Tosefta
TEV	Today's English Version
Tanakh	*Tanakh: A New Translation of the Holy Scriptures according to the Traditional Hebrew Text*

❧ Preface ❧

Preaching from the lectionary readings is a long and venerable tradition. But every pastor who does it regularly knows that it is difficult to bring something fresh to sermons year after year. This resource is structured to aid the pastor in identifying the central issues, struggling with the difficult elements, and suggesting new insights in the lectionary passages. The searchability of the CD-ROM also enables the reader to do keyword and biblical passage searches when looking for related topics.

Depending on when that greatest feast of the Church falls in the West (determined by the new moon), there will be more or fewer Sundays of the year before Lent and after Pentecost. The present work attends to all the Bible portions in *Lectionary for Mass* (1969) to which a few were added as alternatives in 1981 and the *Revised Common Lectionary* (1992). Its comments are exegetical and only derivatively homiletical. When the prescribed readings in the two lectionaries are identical RCL frequently proposes additional verses before and after those of LM. To avoid listing the two separately they are here conflated, giving the widest compass of the lection. The readings of the *Book of Common Prayer* can be found by consulting the Appendix.

The designation of the Sundays and the naming of the feasts constitute another difference. RCL employs for the former the term "Proper" and numbers them beginning with the Baptism of the Lord as one (1). LM speaks of a "Season of the Year" and similarly reckons what follows the baptismal feast as the Second Sunday of the Year *(in anno)*. "Ordinary Time" was the term devised for the English translation of the Latin LM, and RCL continues the usage in two of its seasonal headings, of Epiphany and after Pentecost. RCL places a bracketed numeral indicating the LM Sunday after its designation in each case; thus, for example: "Proper 6 [11] C." The difference in enumeration is invariably five. In this book brackets usually indicate the LM naming of the feasts after those of RCL; thus: Annunciation of the Lord [Annunciation]; Holy Cross [Triumph of the Cross]; Reign of Christ [Christ the King]—but occasionally the titles are conflated.

A much larger difference is the introduction of First Testament readings by RCL between Trinity Sunday (First Sunday after Pentecost) and the Reign of Christ (always the last Sunday of the Church year, Proper 29 [34]). These are taken from Genesis through Judges in Year A; 1 Samuel through Job, then Ruth and a return to 1 Samuel in Year B; and 1 Kings through Jeremiah in Year C. The distinctive feature is that RCL prescribes biblical readings on twenty-five Sundays that are important in Israel's story, hence the Church's, which are not chosen in relation to the day's Gospel. This represents a departure from the traditional principle of lectionaries that goes back to the patristic period (roughly 100–700) that saw foreshadowings of Jesus Christ on every page of the First Testament. Often the correspondence between Old Testament type and New Testament antitype is easy to discern, as in 1 Kings 17:17-24 and Luke 7:11-17 (Proper 5 [10] C), the resuscitations of the sons of the widows of Zarephath and Nain respectively; or Joel 2:1-2, 12-17 and Matt 6:1-6, 16-21 (Ash Wednesday, A, B, C), that are linked up by fasting as a penitential practice. Frequently, however, the Gospel lection has sent the framers on a difficult search, as for example, on Trinity Sunday (Year B of RCL), where *God* is described as so loving the world as to send the *Son* with the promise of the *Spirit* to energize the waters of rebirth (John 3:1-17), a text perceived to be foreshadowed by the "Holy, holy, holy" of the six-winged seraphim (Isa 6:1-8). More tenuous still, but necessarily so because revelation of the triune God was reserved for the mystery of human redemption, is the choice of Deut 4:32-34, 39-40 by LM as an intimation of the triune God in the formula of baptism (Matt 28:16-20). The Deuteronomist speaks of "the *voice* of God" (v. 33) and repeatedly of Israel's *God* as the Lord (vv. 34, 35, 39, 40), three words or names for the All Holy. This may serve as an example of RCL's desire to improve on LM where it thinks it can in relating the first lection to the Gospel reading of the day. In any case, it frequently makes the attempt by proposing a different first reading. The lectionary of the *Book of Common Prayer* of the U.S. Episcopal Church may still be widely in use at the diffusion of this volume, hence consulting the index of biblical texts should yield a commentary on most if not all of the readings.

There is no commentary on the psalms in the pages that follow. RCL cites these sacred songs by number in response to the first lection, leaving to church musicians the task of arranging them or any part of them in song. LM chooses as an antiphon a verse that echoes the main point made by the portion of the psalm to be sung or spoken as a recitative. It aids this effort by dividing the verses of the psalms into pairs—again, for musical treatment—but it was not thought necessary to provide these divisions in print. Nothing is given in this book of the directions given by the two lectionaries although the dates within months for the readings provided by RCL (LM has far fewer such indications) are given. The division of a psalm into paired verses and half-verses of LM has likewise been omitted because some settings for song already contain them. Here they have been brought into uninterrupted unity.

It would be tragic if the omission of exegetical treatment of the Psalter were to lead to its total omission as the subject of preaching. A trio of helpful titles is Irene Nowell, *Sing a New Song: The Psalms in the Sunday Lectionary* (Collegeville, Minn.: Liturgical Press, 1993), 303 pages; Roland E. Murphy, *The Gift of the Psalms,* with a brief verse comment on each (Peabody, Mass.: Hendrickson, 2000), 178 pages; George A. F. Knight, *Psalms* (Louisville: Westminster John Knox, 1982 and 1983), 336, 369 pages. See, too, W. P. Brown's *Seeing the Psalms* (Louisville: Westminster John Knox, 2000. RCL does not provide Alleuia verses before the Gospel; LM does, with a wide variety of choices for musicians.

A final comment is in order on the book's approach to its task. It attempts to achieve the *sensus literalis* (Aquinas) or "plain sense" (Luther) of each lection; namely, what the sacred author might have meant by what he wrote in his time. Needless to say, this is by no means easy to be sure of. The modern critical, i.e., historical method, is the tool employed. Preachers or other users of the book are likely to have done their study of the Bible by this method. Almost none can be presumed to have mastered the typological exegesis of the Patristic period on which Christian liturgies including their lectionaries have been based. Pointing out why a First Testament passage is thought in every case to have been a *typos* of the Gospel reading as *antitypos* is a task this volume does not take on. The attempt at discovery will, however, richly reward the preacher or public reader. A clue may be that on the Church's major Sundays and feast days all three lections cohere, not just in a relation between the first and third. On most Sundays the second, normally epistolary reading, goes its own semi-continuous way.

This book is in part an updating of *A Commentary on the New Lectionary* (1975), with numerous changes and the addition of the Sunday readings not commented on there. The latter omission was owing to the varying occurrence of Easter and the fact that the book commented on the readings of a limited span of years.

The book's primary principle is that "Scripture is to be interpreted by Scripture." The multiple cross-references within the Bible, if followed up, will abundantly confirm the truth of this axiom. The New Testament has rightly been called a commentary on the Old in the light of God's deed in Jesus Christ, just as the Mishnah ("oral instruction") and Gemara ("completion") together make up the Talmud(s), similarly a commentary on *The Tanakh* in the light of post–Second Temple Jewish life. This means that preaching on any text or texts in the lectionary, if preceded by prayer and study, can convey the spirit of the entire written word of God, the book of the Church.

A word of gratitude must go to the three persons who transformed this torrent of words from manuscript to typeface by sleight of hand and eye. They are my sister Virginia Sloyan who has edited so much writing on the Bible in the liturgy for the Liturgical Conference; to the lynx-eyed Marshall D. Johnson; and to the ever-generous Daniel Kuntz, word-processor extraordinaire.

YEAR A

❧ Season of Advent (A) ❧

❧❧
First Sunday of Advent (A)

ISAIAH 2:1-5

This justly famous oracle contains ideas of a universal peace in the future made familiar by writings of the postexilic period. Since its content is found also in Isaiah's contemporary Micah at 4:1-3, however, it probably is not to be denied to the eighth century. Later Isian poetry has a similar vision of peace with justice (e.g., 11:1-9). While the streaming of the Gentiles to the mountain of the Lord creates the suspicion of later authorship (cf. 56:7), the preexilic Ps 2:10f. expects homage to be paid to the one God by the pagan rulers of the earth. Psalm 72:8-11, 15ff. celebrates God's rule from sea to sea, with all kings paying homage to and all nations serving YHWH.

From Zion, the highest mountain (v. 2), the peoples of the earth are to be instructed (v. 3). Judgment among the nations is to come from there; the terms of peace are to be dictated (v. 4) from Jerusalem. The nations shall have peace because they will follow the instruction of the LORD, who is to be the arbiter in disputed cases. But they will turn their weapons into farm implements. And, in perhaps the best known rendition of v. 4f., they "ain' gonna study war no more." Recent Christians in Germany, Protestant and Catholic alike, have been wearing a pin on their clothing crafted of the hilt of a sword surmounting the tongue of the plough. The Advent liturgy always has two horizons: perfect peace at the end of days and the birth of Jesus, "prince" of peace (Isa 9:5b). Verse 5 appears in a fuller version in Mic 4:5.

PSALM 122[1-9]

"I rejoiced when I heard them say: Let us go to the house of the LORD."

ROMANS 13:11-14

The whole tenor of Romans 12–13 is eschatological, starting with the warning to the Roman believers in Christ that they should not be conformed to this eon (12:2) but transformed by the "renewing of your minds" to the realities of the age to come. Needless to say, Paul's concern is for present—not future—moral behavior. In this passage the current epoch is characterized as darkness, sleep, night—the time or moment (v. 11) of excess through drunkenness, debauchery, and envious quarreling (v. 13). "Salvation"—not the personal salvation of a later theology so much as rescue from God's wrath in the just judgment—is drawing closer. Believers in Christ are to live honorably; that is, perform none of the shameful deeds typical of the former eon. They must put on not merely the figurative "armor of light" (v. 12) but its fullest expression, the "Lord Jesus Christ" (v. 14). The verb for donning clothing is employed here, found also in Col 3:12 ("clothe yourselves with compassion, with kindness, humility, meekness, and patience") and in Gal 3:27 in a baptismal context ("as many of you as were baptized into Christ have clothed yourselves with Christ"). No quarter is to be given to "the demands of the flesh" (v. 14), meaning not sexual passion particularly but all the unruly desires characteristic of the present, unredeemed age. Verses 13-14 are the text St. Augustine's eyes lighted on when he randomly read from "the book of the apostle's letters" in response to the little child's chanting from the house nearby, "Pick it up and read" (*Confessions* 8.29).

ALLELUIA. PSALM 85:8

LORD, show us your kindness, and grant us your salvation.

MATTHEW 24:36[37]-44

These brief pictures from Q of sudden and unexpected change (vv. 37-39), the world "corrupt and filled with violence" swept away by the waters (Gen 6:11), and the workaday peasantry reduced to half by catastrophe (Matt 24:40b) are succeeded by a warning to be on guard for the end. "You do not know on what day your Lord is coming" (v. 42). The thief who obviously does not give the householder notice is an image of the Son of Man who will come without warning.

The parallel to vv. 37-41 is Luke 17:26f., 30, 34f. The small differences are that Luke speaks of the Son of Man as "revealed" (v. 30) rather than of his "coming" (v. 39) and has two men in one bed—a straw tick, not a four-poster—rather than in a field. Matthew has a linking verse not found in Luke: "Keep awake, therefore, for you do not know the day your Lord is coming" (v. 42), taken from the parable of the gatekeeper in Mark 13:35, while Matthew's vv. 43f. are paralleled by Luke 12:39f. Again there are slight differences: Matthew's characteristic "therefore" (12:39), specifying an exact moment; and different words for "would not have let" and "house."

The story is used as a vehicle to warn of the general need for watchfulness. Since the coming of the Son of Man was expected to be a joyous and not a disastrous event for believers in Christ, the application of the parable to readiness for Jesus' return is puzzling. The Gospel of Thomas has two sayings about a night burglar (21b; 103) but neither makes a comparison with the coming of the Son of Man.

Jesus' reported use of the flood story (Matt 24:37ff.; Luke 17:26f.) and the destruction of Sodom (Luke 17:28-32) to warn his contemporaries of impending disaster probably accounts for the primitive Church's similar use of this parable in connection with his coming. The story of the thief by night (cf. 1 Thess 5:2, 4; 2 Pet 3:10) was applied by the Church to its own altered situation, which was characterized by the delay of the *parousía*.

This Gospel, like that of the traditional last Sunday of the year (before the recent insertion of the Feast of Christ the King), came in the sequence Matthew 24 and Luke 21 before there was a distinction between the end of one Church year and the beginning of another. Now, God's coming in final judgment and Jesus' coming as an infant are fused.

☜ ☞
Second Sunday of Advent (A)

ISAIAH 11:1-10

By common consent this oracle is thought to occur in a division of the first part of the prophetic collection ("The Book of Judgment," chaps. 1–39, as contrasted with "The Book of Consolation, chaps. 40–66). The oracle is made up of the opening twelve chapters. The NAB editors further subdivide these chapters into an "Indictment of Israel and Judah" (1–5) and "Immanuel Prophecies" (7–12), while the *HarperCollins Study Bible* contents itself with twenty-seven headings for shorter segments of the same twelve chapters. NRSV has fewer—sixteen—while NIV provides numerous headings for chapters and groupings of chapters. Today's pericope sketches the ideal Davidic king, a shoot from the stump of David's father, Jesse, a branch blossoming from his roots. This future king shall have an outpouring of the divine spirit *(rûaḥ)*, connoting power, that is sixfold and listed in three pairs.

The first two convey the notion of comprehension or insight, the second two the will to act, and the last two docility or openness. The echo of "fear of the LORD" (v. 2) found in v. 3 resulted in the listing of a seventh gift of the Spirit in the LXX and Vulgate, two nouns for the same phrase. This yielded the "seven gifts of the Holy Ghost" of the Carolingian era, "piety and fear of the LORD." The characteristics of a judicious king are spelled out in vv. 3b-5: he disregards non-evidence such as appearance and hearsay, uses courageous speech and takes action against the wicked, and wears justice and fidelity as close to him as a belt and waistband. Psalm 72:1-4 paints a similar picture of a just monarch who defends the afflicted, the poor, and the oppressed.

Verses 6-9 are well known for their description of the myth of the return to a trouble-free Eden. The tranquil pose of predator and prey, reconciled opposites, is important here. The "little child to lead them" (v. 6) and the "weaned infant by the adder's den" (v. 8) are figures of the nonviolent character of all nature at ease. It was the Christian identity of Jesus as the just sovereign of the prophecy, coupled with the infancy narrative of Luke, that gave this Isaian bestiary a firm place in medieval literature, in Handel's *Messiah*, and in the modern Christmas card. Nothing in the poetry of vv. 6-10 requires that the "little child" be identified with the offspring of Jesse of vv. 1-5. "Knowledge of the LORD" is the inundating balm of a future earth that shall have a peaceful Zion as its central peak.

Verse 10 constitutes one brief oracle, vv. 11-16 another, both on the theme of the future restoration of Israel. Isaiah was summoned to the work of prophecy in the year King Uzziah died (6:1; 742 B.C.), a sovereign whose reign was the final gasp of Israel's early splendor (both kingdoms). From Ahaz of Judah and Pekah of Israel onward, it was a downhill progression of defeats at the hands of Assyrians, Chaldeans, Persians, and Greeks. "On that day" in v. 10 refers to the future age when the Gentiles shall seek out the royal dwelling place of Jesse's scion. He shall be a banner or a "signal to the Gentile nations" (v. 10). This phrase, *Nes Ammim*, is the name chosen for the small village near Haifa in Galilee where a community of Dutch Protestants gives witness by its presence in reparation for the Nazi holocaust. It is without proselytizing intent, hoping to say something to fellow Gentiles by simply being there.

PSALM 72:1-7[8, 12-13, 17] 13-19

Justice shall flourish in his time, and fullness of peace forever.

Romans 15:4[9]-13

These remarks on perfect harmony in the community (v. 5) end with praise for God's purpose in Christ with regard to Jews and Gentiles (vv. 8-9). Their immediate context, however, is the discussion in all of chap. 14 and 15:1-3 of the "strong" and "weak" in faith, i.e., the robust and delicate of conscience. They have been thought by some to be the Jewish and Gentile Christians respectively, but this categorization is over-facile and surely wrong. The two groups are the nonscrupulous and the scrupulous over eating meat of any kind (14:2) and presumably meat that has been sacrificed to false gods, as in 1 Cor 8:1-13. [The Christians should no more have as the sole canon of their choices pleasing themselves than did Christ in dying, but rather, like him, the mutual building up of spirit (vv. 2-3).]

The praise of the Jewish Scriptures contained in v. 4 that 2 Timothy echoes in 3:15ff. makes those writings a series of lessons on hope through present endurance. The stress in this passage falls on patience and encouragement (v. 5), unity of heart and voice (v. 6) in the one Spirit of Christ. First Timothy 4:4 takes the thought of Romans in another direction than 2 Timothy when it praises all creation as good rather than all Scripture as instructive. Mutual acceptance in the Roman community is stressed in Rom 15:7–9 but here between Jews and Gentiles rather than strong and weak. The two pairings are interrelated in that eating together in house churches might require sensitivity to the dietary scruples of some Christian Jews by others and even by Gentiles who are now alerted to the prohibition of acknowledging false deities (for Paul, "idols"). Paul nowhere says that since Christ accepted all and became the servant of all (vv. 7-8) to the point of death, abstention from foods prohibited under the Law might at times be incumbent on Gentiles, but such might be his principle. The scruple against meat offered to idols is more likely in question here. There were also the abstainers from wine, whom Paul presumably was not willing contemptuously to dismiss as proto-gnostics.

Jesus was the servant of the Jews (of "the circumcision," v. 8) because God's fidelity to the divine promises required it; of the Gentiles because God's mercy suggested it (vv. 9-12). The supporting quotation is woven from Ps 18:50 [49]; Deut 32:43a; Ps 117:1; and Isa 11:10. If Jesus had no trouble dying for the circumcised as such, believers in him could certainly endure living close to his scrupulous fellow Jews. The same was true of Jewish proximity to the totally nonobservant Gentiles.

Paul is evidently acutely conscious of the cheek-to-jowl situation of his Jewish friends (16:3, 6) and kinsfolk (7, 11) and his beloved Gentiles (16:1-15 et passim) in the community at Rome. He either suspects that they may be finding it hard getting on at close range or has positive word to that effect.

ALLELUIA. LUKE 3:4, 6

Prepare the way of the LORD, make straight his paths. . . . All flesh shall see the salvation of God.

MATTHEW 3:1-12

The Second and Third Sundays of Advent choose Gospel passages that describe the Baptist's preparation for the coming of Jesus. The commentary on the parallel accounts of John's preaching—Mark 1:1-8 and Luke 3:1-6, 10-18—should be consulted. John, who goes in another direction, is also of interest (1:6-8, 19-28). All are concerned to relate the Baptist to Jesus, but Matthew especially so (cf. 3:13ff.; 11:17-19; 14:1f.; 17:9-13). Matthew, unlike Luke (3:1f.), does not date the events by the governor (governorship [hēgemonenontos] is Luke's word) and priests in office and instead contents himself with "in those days" (v. 1). He calls John the "Baptist," a noun, while Mark uses the participle "the one baptizing." This detail leads some translations to render the two "Baptist" and "Baptizer" respectively. Matthew's "desert of Judea" is simply "the desert" in Mark and Luke, which the latter expands to "all the region around the Jordan" (3:3).

John comes proclaiming the nearness of God's reign (v. 2). The exact meaning of the verb employed is disputed, namely, whether it means "draws near" or "has arrived," but despite the certainties expressed by some scholars there are no conclusive arguments for either. John demands a sense of urgency in response to the impending appearance of God's dominion. This requires an about-face in the thinking of his hearers (their "mind" is to be reversed, "turned backwards"). The Greek *metanoeîte* corresponds to the Hebrew verb *shubh* in its accommodated sense "repent" (more basically, "turn about"). This verb was a turning point for Luther when he learned from Erasmus's Greek New Testament that Jesus was saying "Repent" rather than "Do penance." Isaiah 40:3, which Mark quotes in altered form, reads in the Hebrew text: "A voice cries out: In the desert prepare the way of the LORD! Make straight in the wasteland a highway for our God!" Matthew refers the quotation to "him," John (v. 3), whereas Mark and Luke apply it to his preaching activity; Matthew will put the same charge, "Repent . . ." on Jesus' lips (4:17) while the others do not. Mark conflates Isa 40:3 with Mal 3:1, omitting mention of the latter's name. The LXX of Isa 40:3 suited Matthew's purpose of messianic fulfillment better than did the Hebrew. Even so, he seems to understand the LXX's *Kyrios* as Jesus, the one whose way and path must be made straight, rather than that of Israel's LORD.

The description of John's rough dress (v. 4; cf. Mark 1:6) is patterned on the sketch of Elijah found in 2 Kgs 1:8. Grasshoppers are probably meant by the Greek noun, but it also serves for locusts; they were both edible and eaten. The wild honey was not that of bees but sweet gum from plants. The description of the Jerusalem and Judaean crowds confessing their sins and asking for immersion in the river Jordan (vv. 5f.) follows Mark 1:5 closely, while vv. 7-10 are a Q passage (see Luke 3:7-9) not duplicated in Mark. In v. 7 Matthew narrows the recipients of John's blistering charge to "many of the Pharisees and Sadducees." Their presenting themselves for baptism is noteworthy in light of their usual avoidance of each other's company. Luke may have found the combination incredible but more likely wished to broaden the scope of the petitioners, for he speaks of the "crowds" that came to be baptized by John (3:7). Matthew and Luke both give the same explanation for the request for baptism by those of ill will. They call it a precautionary measure to escape the end-time wrath. Deeds alone are what matter (Matt 3:8). Birth from Abraham's stock is of no avail in itself (v. 9). The fire that will consume fruitless trees (v. 10; repeated in a parabolic statement, 7:19) is the final conflagration of judgment (cf. Mal 3:19 for the figure of stubble consumed in a blaze).

Verses 11f. are closer to the Q of Luke 3:16 than Mark's shorter 1:7f. Jesus is "stronger" than John, according to the latter (v. 7; so, too, in Luke), in his imminent baptism "with Holy Spirit and fire" (Mark: "Holy Spirit" only). When Mark in a later parable makes a thief the binder of "a strong man" in order to plunder his house, Matthew (12:29) and Luke (8:21f., with notable differences in phrasing) follow him. John the Baptizer's subjugation to Jesus as sandal-bearer, i.e., disciple or willing slave, and his subordination as preacher of repentance who brings no gift of the Spirit or separating power of fire, is a constant in the New Testament. Not only do these motifs reflect early rivalries between the disciples of the two but they convey the Christian conviction that John announces the imminence of the final epoch while Jesus achieves its inaugural. Preaching on this Advent Sunday should withhold mention of Christ's nativity. School pageants and the religious culture generally do not know what else to do with Advent. The theologically educated proclaimers of the Scriptures, however, know the appearance of Jesus to mark the onset of the final days, so central to both Testaments.

ᕇᕇ

Third Sunday of Advent (A)

ISAIAH 35:1-6[A], 10

The previous chapter of Isaiah featured the doom of Edom, the sword filled with blood and the land of Edom greasy with fat. In contrast with the cartoonlike picture of this wasted land, which is said to be the doing of the LORD performed out of wrath, the present chapter paints a balancing picture of God's salvation. This will be accomplished in terms of the total transformation of nature. When coming to vindicate Israel, God will overcome the handicaps of the blind and the deaf, the lame and the mute, which are classes of disadvantaged with respect to participation in Temple worship. If, for whatever reason, the judgment of God on them has been assumed unfavorable until now (only perfect specimens may apply!), it will in the future be wildly favorable, as the Israelites burst into dancing and song.

The chronically dry desert to the south and east will be richly irrigated. All this leads up to a picture of the high and holy way on which a ransomed people will return singing to Mount Zion.

The modern state of Israel is a secular state like the United States, but it does not hesitate to use the Bible freely for education in the schools as part of its national purposes. Thus young agricultural workers in the still remaining kibbutzim (early Zionist labor settlements) are frequently pictured on posters reaping harvests of grain on reclaimed desert land, and at times Isa 35:6b-7a will be inscribed beneath.

The "highway" (v. 8) and "holy way" is the LORD's own way, the path on which the ransomed will return. Only they shall pass over it, not fools or the unclean. Wild beasts are not to be a threat along the way. In joy and delight shall the ransomed proceed along it to the holy mountain.

PSALM 146:[7]-10 OR LUKE 1:47-55

LORD, come and save us.

JAMES 5:7-10

This reading echoes the previous one, with its metaphor of growth from the soil as a result of moisture. Its theme is patience while the Christian community awaits the presence (*parousía*, vv. 7, 8) of Jesus its Lord. The prophets waited patiently, suffering hardship (v. 10). So must new believers (lit.: "brothers"). Grumbling in the community that can only lead to adverse judgment (v. 9) is ill-advised, because the judge, God or Christ acting for God, stands at the gate poised for judgment.

The urgency that marks this passage argues for an early date of composition. Like all of James, made up largely of proverbial wisdom, it is open to the interpretation that it was a Jewish original revised by Christian hands, but that is not likely to be its origin. The themes of end-time readiness, the model of suffering provided by the prophets and Job, and the paraenetic tone throughout, could well have marked Hellenist Christian Judaism. As a collection of hortatory wise sayings, James much resembles Sirach, Wisdom, and Proverbs.

ALLELUIA. ISAIAH 61:1 OR LUKE 1:47-55

The Spirit of the LORD is upon me; he has sent me to bring good news to the poor.

MATTHEW 11:2-11

The Q parallel to this material is Luke 7:18-28, where the similarities are close except for some duplication and brief expansion by Luke (vv. 20f.) after Matthew's v. 3.

The "works of the Messiah" (v. 2), surely a church phrase, sums up the miracles of healing, control of nature, and exorcism that have been related in chaps. 8–10. Q conceives them in messianic terms and thus speaks of Jesus as "the one who is to come" (v. 3; not a known Jewish title) by applying Isa 61:1 in a general way to him—the Nazareth synagogue text of Luke 4:18 that Jesus reads aloud and declares "fulfilled in your hearing." The Trito-Isaiah's set of deeds to be performed by the one on whom the LORD's spirit rests is only partially reproduced here. Missing are mention of captives, prisoners, and a year of favor from the LORD. The risen dead appear in Isa 26:19; the deaf and blind in 29:18; 35:5; the lame one who will leap like a stag in 35:6.

Verse 6 is a macarism or beatitude supplementary to those listed in chap. 5. It praises people who are not put off by Jesus' right to the title "the one who is to come" (the same as the "anointed one" of Isa 61:1). Jesus will later say that John "came to you preaching a way [i.e., a path] of righteousness" (or justice, Matt 21:32). Here he warns John's disciples to walk on that way and not be "thrown" by obstructions on it such as his fulfillment of signs of the last age. Jesus' phrase here is "who takes no offense at me." Later he will say to Peter, when he finds him to be a *satan* or adversary, "You are a stone to make me stumble" (more familiarly, "stumbling block" or "obstacle," Matt 16:23). There is a reference to disciples of Jesus who falter when trouble or persecution arises involving his message (13:21) and another to a group scandalized by him, namely, his townsfolk and relatives (13:57). It must not be that way with the well-prepared disciples of John.

The son of Zechariah does not sway in the wind like the sedgegrass along the banks of the Jordan (v. 7). Neither is he recognizable as royalty or part of a prince's retinue (v. 8), a possible reference to Davidic messianism. He is a spokesman for God (*prophētēs*, v. 9) and more; he is the messenger of preparation for the LORD spoken of by Malachi (3:1). Later Matthew will identify John with Elijah (17:12f.), as Mark does in the parallel (9:12f.). While Luke applies the Malachi passage to the Baptizer (7:27), he never puts him in the role of a modern Elijah. (See his silence at 16:16, where Matt 11:14 makes the identification.) This role he reserves for Jesus. In context, Malachi's divine messenger will be a purifier of Temple sacrifice (3:1, 3) through his testimony and his judgment on a variety of sins against society. In modern parlance, he will bring a class action suit.

Verse 11 applies the verb, "there has not been raised up," to John, a mode of speech confined to the prophets and the risen Christ. He prepares for God's reign in that, despite his human greatness—he is exceeded by no mortal—the new epoch that follows is populated by a progeny in which the least believer outruns him. Conzelmann is well known for his use of Luke 16:16 as the verse that signals the onset of "the midpoint of time," which for Luke was the era of Jesus. The case can be made against Conzelmann that, while Luke omits Matt 11:12f. from Q (because he does not wish to separate the eons of salvation history at this point in his narrative, waiting for 16:16), Matthew retains the watershed of history just as effectively.

The puzzling saying in v. 12 is probably a reference to military uprisings calculated to bring on God's reign in Israel, and is related to "the prophets and the law until John" only in the sense of contemporaneousness of epoch. With his preaching, John brought on a right understanding of the new age and hence prepared for Jesus' coming—the reason for the choice of this pericope in Advent.

Fourth Sunday of Advent (A)

ISAIAH 7:10-14

Quaking with fear at the threat of invasion by the Arameans under Rezin and the northern kingdom, Israel or Ephraim, led by Pekah (7:2), King Ahaz (735–715) is counseled by Isaiah to take heart (vv. 4ff.). The prophet is inspired by the LORD (v. 3) to quote an oracle to the king, the gist of which is that both Aram and Ephraim will have collapsed within sixty-five years if Ahaz's trust in the LORD is firm (vv. 7ff.). He had previously refused an alliance with them (cf. 2 Kgs 16:5) that brought them to the brink of war waged on Jerusalem. They besieged him and all Judah but they could not conquer him. The present incident takes place near a reservoir "on the highway of the Fuller's Field" (v. 3). Isaiah has brought along his little son whom he has named Shear-yashub ("a remnant shall return," or "a remnant shall turn back" [to God]). Taking with him the lad so named must be intended as a message to the king.

The oracle of today's pericope was probably delivered shortly after the encounter. The king's pious response (v. 12) refusing Isaiah's proffered sign (v. 11), which is met by the prophet's instantaneous anger (v. 13), indicates that Ahaz has already decided to go the collaborationist route with Assyria against his northern neighbors (cf. 2 Kgs 16:7ff.). He hopes to stave off the threat of that major power, and Isaiah suspects that he has already decided to do so. As it happened, Assyria conquered Damascus (Aram) in 732 and Samaria (Israel or Ephraim) in 721. The conquering Sennacherib arrived at the border of Judah, then mysteriously withdrew, in 701. But at the time of the "sign of Immanuel" none of this had taken place.

Isaiah's confidence in the power of YHWH is such that he puts no limit on the sign the king may ask (v. 11). The truth in Ahaz's response may be that, since he has already decided what he intends to do, he would be tempting the LORD by naming a sign at this late date.

The exact significance of the sign escapes us, because we do not know the identity of the young woman (v. 14). The word is rendered "virgin" in KJV, NAB, and NIV, whose translators followed the LXX (parthénos) quoted by Matthew (1:23). The MT has 'almah, which may have described a virgin bride, just as parthénos could have been a young woman of marriageable age, her virginity assumed in that culture. There is no reason to suppose, however, that King Ahaz was unmarried at the time, hence his future wife, Abi, a virgin. Her being simply a young woman would have suited the hypothesis that their son Hezekiah was the "Immanuel" of the prophecy (cf. 2 Kgs 18:1f.). The identity of the child of the sign as Hezekiah is probable, but a careful reading of chap. 8 could lead to the alternate conclusion that Isaiah's next child by his wife, "the prophetess" (8:3), is the "Immanuel" of the sign, a descriptive title if not the child's actual name. The son Maher-shalal-hash-baz ("Quick spoils, speedy plunder," a pointer to the expected Assyrian invasion), has his name recorded in an attested document (8:1, 16, 18) before his conception. Isaiah and the children the LORD has given him are the signs and portents to make the claim "With us is God" (Immanuel) a reality. The waters of Shiloah that flow gently (8:6), a quiet pool in Jerusalem, city of the LORD, are rejected by the decision of Ahaz. Therefore the waters of the Euphrates shall flood Judah, "the full breadth of your land, O Immanuel" (8:8).

Identifying the child who is the sign of today's reading is by no means essential to comprehending its impact. It has been theorized above that the son of the young woman may not be in the royal but the prophetic line.

Any impending birth will do, however, since the force of the sign lies in what may be expected in the realm of political events by the time the boy reaches puberty (the meaning of "refuses to do evil and chooses the good," 7:15, 16). The significance of a diet of "curds and honey" in his early years is uncertain. While it was rich fare to the desert nomad, it has also been interpreted as an austerity diet for city dwellers. If the latter, then a time of adversity rather than prosperity is indicated. All theories of the identity of the child in his day aside, the pericope is an obvious Advent choice because of the fulfillment of prophecy Matthew saw in it.

Psalm 80:1-7, 17-19[24:1-6]

Let the LORD enter, who is king of glory. Let your hand be upon the one at your right hand whom you made strong for yourself.

Romans 1:1-7

Like most of Paul's introductions, this one underscores his calling (v. 1) as a slave of Christ Jesus (cf. Phil 1:1) and an apostle (vv. 1, 5) set apart to preach the gospel (vv. 3f.). His greetings here are more extended than in most letters. Since he is not acquainted with "all . . . in Rome" (v. 7), he may simply be using his opening remarks as the occasion for an impersonal—but priceless—development of Christology, probably a creedal formula already in use. The "gospel of God" (v. 1) is Paul's work and challenge. Its content is Jesus Christ (vv. 3-6), a man of David's line (v. 3), "declared" or "established" Son of God with power and by his resurrection Jesus Christ our Lord (v. 4). "Son of God in power" is set against Davidic descent "according to the flesh" and is contrasted with "according to the spirit of holiness," a phrase unfamiliar in Jewish writing until it appeared in a Qumrân scroll to describe the all-holy God. This distinction is one between Jesus' Jewish humanity and his special divine calling. He was constituted Son of God by his resurrection from the dead. From that point on he was Christ the Lord. A human principle, *sarx*, and a divine principle, *pneuma*, are joined in him.

The greeting in v. 7 is the familiar one of grace and peace, which has the advantage of being meaningful to both Jewish and Graeco-Roman worlds. The gift is invoked by Paul as coming from his familiar dyad, God and Jesus Christ.

Alleluia. Matthew 1:23

A virgin will give birth to a son; his name will be Emmanuel: God is with us.

Matthew 1:18-[24]25

Luke's birth story is about the conception of a child by a virgin through the Holy Spirit's coming upon her and the power of the Most High overshadowing her

(Luke 1:35). Matthew knows of the tradition but tells instead how a pious man scruples to consummate marriage with the one to whom he is betrothed after he discovers her pregnant but not by him. Joseph is called by the angel "son of David" (Matt 1:20), meaning that the child is to have Davidic sonship. (The modern difficulty of Mary's being the sole human begetter of Jesus does not exist for Matthew; Jesus' "house" and "family" come through the paternal line). Joseph is instructed by an angel in a dream not unlike that of the patriarch Joseph in his youth, whose name he bears. Here the divine agency of conception is, as in Luke, "from the Holy Spirit" (1:20). Mary's son will save his Jewish people from their sins; hence for Matthew the Immanuel prophecy is fulfilled in him. In a profound sense the adult career of Mary's son will mean "God is with us." The oracle in its LXX form, which employs the word "virgin," is peculiarly suited to Matthew's interpretive contemporary purpose.

Matthew seems to display in his narrative a knowledge of disputes about Jesus' legitimacy. His dream-story has as its chief purpose to set at rest the mind of Joseph, the legally "just" man (v. 19). The conception of the child is God's doing; hence Joseph need have no scruples. Joseph can bestow Davidic sonship on the child by taking Mary as his wife in the second stage of Jewish marriage (v. 24). Her virgin motherhood of Jesus means here what it does in the Immanuel oracle and is similar to the divine intervention in the motherhoods of Sarah, Rebekah, and Hannah, namely, that by God's special action Jesus is the elect firstborn. Church tradition later took it to mean that and more, namely, physical virginity. Since Matthew operates in biblical categories, he cannot be demonstrated with certainty to have had this marvel in mind (even though later interpretation might well be right that he did). He concentrates on another marvel, that of divine election.

Whatever prompted the LM (1969, 1981) to eliminate v. 25 (fear of its raising problems in the hearers' minds?), it is included by the RCL and should not be omitted. It reaffirms that Joseph is not the child's father and that by giving the child his name (cf. v. 21) the providential plan of Jesus' Davidic sonship is given full scope. It says nothing about the sex life of the couple in their marriage since the adverb "until" is nonindicative of what may follow. The tradition of Mary's perpetual virginity, which emerged in the fourth century, took a position, but without biblical warrant either way. The verse is a summary statement that rounds off the pericope, recording the birth of the child to Mary and Joseph's naming of the child Yeshúa ("YHWH shall save"), conveying the action of God to be accomplished through him.

❧ Season of Christmas ❧

❧ The Nativity of the Lord / Proper I (A, B, C) Mass at Midnight

ISAIAH 9:2-7[1-6]

This oracle sets a great light (v. 1) in contrast to the gloom and darkness that it puts to flight (8:23). The people's rejoicing—likened to that of merrymaking harvesters or spoilers in war—results from YHWH's release of his people from the burden of oppression (yoke, pole, rod, v. 4) and the boots and cloaks of battle (v. 5). Assyria has invaded "the land of Zebulun and the land of Naphthali" (733–32), but the fall of Samaria (722–21) is nowhere mentioned. Candidates for "the seaward road, the land west of the Jordan, and the District of the Gentiles" are the three provinces of Dor, Gilead, and Megiddo, into which the conquering Assyrians under Tiglath-Pileser III divided the humiliated northern kingdom. In any case, that tragic scene of oppression will yield to one in which a Davidic offspring is enthroned, to whom the four titles of v. 6 are to be attributed. His rule will be peaceful. Judgment and justice will mark it, "both now and forever." Israel's LORD, not any cleverness on the part of the people, will achieve this.

In brief, the passage is a dynastic oracle not unlike those of 2 Samuel 7; 23:1-7, and royal psalms like 2; 21; 89; and 110.

PSALM 96:1-3, 11-13

Today is born our Savior, Christ the Lord.

TITUS 2:11-14

The passage immediately preceding these verses has offered counsel to various classes of persons: older men, older women, younger men, and slaves. Verse 11 underlines the fact that God's grace in Jesus Christ has been made manifest to all, even slaves. This age may be an evil one, the Pauline disciple writes, but there is no reason why Christians should not live temperate, just, and devout (NRSV, self-controlled, upright, and godly) lives.

These are not far from three of Aristotle's four cardinal virtues. Our blessed hope is the "manifestation of the glory of the great God and of our Savior Jesus Christ" (v. 13). It is not so much the epiphany of Christ that is spoken of as the epiphany of grace (v. 11). God's word has been revealed and it has come to hearers through "proclamation" (1:3, described by the same verb as "being revealed" or "appearing" in 3:4). God's grace trains people (v. 12) in the ways of faith, i.e., educates the uninstructed. (Cf. *1 Clem* 59:21, which says that through Jesus Christ, God's beloved child, God has brought us "from ignorance to the recognition of his glorious name.") In Tit 2:12 we are educated out of godless and worldly ways into those of saving grace.

Christ is called Savior (v. 13) but, while most modern translations read "the glory of our great God and Savior Jesus Christ" (NRSV, NIV, REB, JB), others "of the great God and our Saviour Jesus Christ" (KJV, DRC), only NAB renders it, "the great God and of our savior," thereby understanding the epistle not to be calling Jesus Christ the Lord [our] "great God." At the level of christological development represented by the pastoral epistles (1 and 2 Timothy and Titus), soteriological functions are transferred from God to Christ. Whether a clear distinction and subordination of Christ to God is maintained or he is being spoken of as God cannot be proved on the basis of absent punctuation. That he sacrificed himself in order to purify and redeem us and make us a "people of his own" is entirely clear (cf. Deut 14:2; 1 Pet 2:9f.). Verse 13 contains a Hellenistic soteriological statement; "zealous for good deeds." That a title of the people of Israel ("of [God's] own,") from the LXX is included here indicates the easy harmony that characterized early Christian cultic language.

The excesses of the pagan Saturnalia festival are the probable reason for the first inclusion of this reading in the liturgy of Rome: a plea to renounce impiety and curb worldly passions (v. 12).

Alleluia

Good news and great joy to all the world: today is born our savior, Christ the Lord.

Luke 2:1-14 (15-20)

Luke's chief concern is to certify the Davidic origins of Jesus. The historical tradition that Jesus comes from Nazareth in Galilee is evidently available to him. He also wishes to set the birth and the career of Jesus in a wider setting than the Jewish one of his first chapter. There was a census held around 6 C.E. when Quirinius was legate to Syria and Coponius prefect of Judaea. While it is possible to hold, from fragmentary evidence, that Quirinius served in Judaea earlier or that an earlier census preceded the one we know about, it is wiser to say that Luke's interest is in theological symbolism, not accuracy of detail. He wishes to set the event in the context of the Roman Empire, making Jesus a Jewish king but one whose reign (1:32f.) would be without political consequences. He establishes Jesus' Davidic messiahship through Joseph's lineage while at the same time maintaining that God is the child's father.

Joseph "goes up" to Jerusalem as one does to Mount Zion from all directions, traveling south from Galilee. He goes to enroll in the company of his "betrothed" (v. 5; a weak manuscript tradition has added "wife" *[gynaiki]*, no doubt to allay the fears of Gentiles who do not know the two stages of Jewish marriage). The question has been raised of the historical likelihood of an imperial census that would send people to their town of ancestry. Luke's symbolic interest, rather than historical concern, is very much to the fore. Jesus must be born in David's city and the evangelist has the problem of getting the Galilean couple there.

Mary comes to term in Bethlehem (v. 6) and bears her firstborn. The word says nothing about subsequent offspring, apologetics quite apart. A firstborn is the child to come forth first from the womb (see Gen 25:25; Exod 22:29; Num 18:15ff.). Elsewhere in the New Testament Jesus is the "firstborn among many brothers" (Rom 8:29, a theological statement; not "the firstborn within a large family" of NRSV); "of all creation" (Col 1:15); "from the dead" (Col 1:18). Israel is the LORD's firstborn son (Exod 4:22; cf. Jer 31:9). Benjaminites bear names like Becher (Gen 46:21), Bichri (2 Sam 20:1), Becorath (1 Sam 9:1), in the sense of "beloved." "My beloved *(agapētós)* son" of Mark 1:11 is thought by many to be a rendering of a Semitic original *bechor*, derived from the Old Testament texts above.

The "manger" of v. 7 has created the Christmas scene, ox and ass being contributed by Isa 1:3 (which also has a manger). Luke gives as the reason for these unusual circumstances a crowded caravansary *(katályma)*, the Greek word that will likewise describe the guest room of the Last Supper. There can be little doubt that he has in mind the contrast between the hospitable shepherds (a despised class in Talmudic writings because of their nonobservance of oral Torah) and the inhospitable local accommodations for travelers.

Once their fear is dispelled by an angelic message, shepherds receive Jesus (vv. 9f.). Bathed in light, they receive a gospel—tidings of great "joy"—proper to the final age. The infant in a manger constitutes a sign for them (v. 12). Matthew does not use the shepherd/manger motif and so has the wise men (*magoi*, connoting learning in astronomy) enter the "house" (2:11) where the child was.

The heavenly "host" (literally: an army in array; here, massed angelic choirs) sings a song in two members: to God in highest heaven glory and to human beings on the earth peace. The gift of heavenly peace is given those of *eudokías*, that is, on whom "God's favor" rests. The word is in the genitive case and describes the condition of humankind that is God's gift to them. The less authentic reading in the nominative case provided the "good will to men" of KJV, and ten million greeting cards.

⟍⟋

The Nativity of the Lord / Proper II (A, B, C)
Mass at Dawn

ISAIAH 62:6[11]-12

See 2 Epiphany [2] (C).

PSALM 97:[1, 6, 11-12]

A light will shine on us this day: the Lord is born for us.

TITUS 3:4-7 (SEE 2 EASTER [A])

This briefest of the three "Pastoral Epistles" by an anonymous disciple of Paul is addressed to a coworker (see Gal 2:1; 2 Cor 2:13; 7:6, 13f.; 8:16) who is instructed to appoint presbyters in every town of Crete. This tells more of the spread of the gospel on that island than of Paul's interest in establishing ministers by that name and their qualifications (1:1-9; cf. 1 Tim 3:1-13; 5:17-23). The term "sound doctrine" (Tit 1:9) is another indication of a development in vocabulary beyond Paul's lifetime. But today's lection has been chosen for none of those reasons. It occurred in the Mass at Dawn in the Roman Missal of 1570, which means it went back to the Middle Ages in the Church of the West. The passage is clearly a hymn or a snatch of early catechesis, although it is not treated that way typographically in NRSV. Its choice for the Feast of the Nativity needs no explanation: "But when the goodness and loving kindness of God our Savior appeared, he saved us" (vv. 4f.). Those attributes of God are a commonplace in the Jewish Scriptures, as is the idea of God as Israel's Savior. Titus 3:5 echoes Deut 9:5a, important for any who may have thought that Paul initiated the primacy of God's gift ("grace") over human deeds or merits.

The phrasing of Tit 9:5, 7 resembles Eph 2:4-5, 8-9 and 2 Tim 1:9, an indication of the way Paul's teaching that God's gift of faith in Jesus Christ needed no complement from observance of the special "works of the Law" (Gal 3:5-14; Rom 3:21-31 et passim) was being transmitted faithfully by his disciples. The hymn goes on to specify the rite by which the gift of saving faith is given: rebirth, *paliggenesía*, the word's only New Testament appearance) and renewal (*anakaínōsis*, likewise, in the genitive case. Compare Matt 19:28, where the former word refers to the end-time, and Col 3:10, where its participial form is a reference to baptism. What better subject for preaching on the birth day of the Savior than the rebirth of the baptized it made possible, confirming them as "heirs in a hope of eternal life" (v. 7)?

ALLELUIA. LUKE 2:14

Glory to God in heaven, peace and grace to his people on earth.

LUKE 2:(1-7), 8-20[15-20]

See January 1, below.

✒.✒
The Nativity of the Lord / Proper III (A, B, C) Mass during the Day

ISAIAH 52:7-10

"Your God reigns!" (v. 7) is the announcement of the messenger of "good news" (*bᵉśorah*, the biblical word that underlies the New Testament *euaggelion*). Peace, salvation—all these things will come to holy Zion in the restoration of Israel from exile. Sentinels will hail the people's triumphant return (v. 8); a ruined Jerusalem will burst into song (v. 9). God has done a work of power in the sight of all the nations (v. 10), the literal salvation of this people. The Christian liturgy employs these verses in a transferred sense to describe the birth of Jesus, while in Romans (10:15) Paul will quote v. 7a to describe the work of proclaiming salvation in Christ in which he is engaged.

PSALM 98[1-3AB, 4-6]

All the ends of the earth have seen the saving power of God.

HEBREWS 1:1-4, (5-12) [1:1-6]

This work of Hellenist Christian piety (cf. 13:22) and theology views Christ as God's Son who is at the same time the wisdom of God "through whom he also created the universe" (v. 2). As "the reflection of God's glory" (v. 3; better, "radiance" or "refulgence"), "the imprint of God's being," the Son sustains all by his powerful word. These opening phrases may have had their primitive existence as a Jewish hymn to God's wisdom. The writer gives his paean a historical cast by speaking of Christ as enthroned on high once he had "made purification for sins" (v. 3). The thrust of the biblical texts (v. 5: 2 Sam 7:14; Ps 2:7; v. 6: Deut 32:43a; v. 7: Ps 104:4; etc.) is to establish the superiority of Christ to the angels. They are ministers and adorers, he is a Son. Undoubtedly the background to these remarks, which may have introduced a Christian sermon, is a certain polemic within the Christian community or with those outside on the mediatorial office of Christ. The author places him high above angelic creatures and intimates a preexistence of this Son with God as God's wisdom and word. The development is not unlike that of the Johannine prologue.

JOHN 1:1-18

The riches of this pericope have inspired volumes. They are not readily captured in a few lines. A preexistent Jewish hymn to wisdom is hinted at but not established by the verse form opted for by NAB in 1970 (following Raymond Brown in AB). This hymn shows signs of editing, e.g., at v. 14 where the Word becomes flesh and dwells in our midst, the glory as of a father's only son. The author of the Gospel as we have it either composed the poem or took a Hellenist Jewish poem or a poem from a circle of the followers of John and connected it to Jesus and history rather than leaving it in a timeless context. The Word's becoming flesh in the midst of humanity (v. 14) is the chief departure from any pattern of gnostic or angelic speculation, if such there had been. There is also inserted a lively disclaimer of the importance of John (vv. 6-8, 15) which is continued from v. 19 onward, when the Gospel begins to be fully "historical" in its narrative fashion.

Four figurative modes of speech about divinity are used to describe the relation of God to the man Jesus: in his human existence Jesus is "as if" Word, Life, Light, and Son with respect to God. God can be or have none of these in a strict sense. All are "as if" (v. 14). A dynamic quality in God—viewed variously as speech, life, illumination, and parenthood—is bodied forth when Jesus lives as a human among others. That Word is what God is (v. 1). John does not say, either here or in his Gospel, for which the introductory eighteen verses are programmatic, that

Jesus is God. The better translation of v. 1c is: "and what God was the Word was." Jesus is Word come forth from God, Light, Life, Son (all "of God," understood) in a human existence.

The manifestation of God in Jesus outruns anything experienced heretofore, says John. With Moses came the Law, a genuine gift. Through Jesus Christ came the fullness of grace and truth, the loving kindness and fidelity of the God of the covenant but now enduring love in eminent degree. Divine favor and fidelity, it is claimed, have reached new heights in God's manifestation in Christ.

The notion of preexistence is clear in this hymn, but it is God's preexistence as Word to this man, indeed to all creation. The author searches for images to convey the divine riches that lately have come tumbling out (v. 16), "grace upon grace" or "grace in place of grace." "At the Father's side" or "close to the Father's heart" (v. 18)—God having no "bosom" (KJV, DRC) any more than God is a parent—is John's last try at intimacy of relation. As a child snuggles in a father's arms so is Jesus to God, who is the revealer to the Son of intimate secrets.

See also the commentary on John 1:6-8 at 3 Advent (B).

❧✿❧

First Sunday after Christmas Day (A, B, C)
Sunday between December 26 and January 1

ISAIAH 63:7-9

See 1 Advent (B).

PSALM 148

HEBREWS 2:10-18

See Proper 22 [27] (B).

MATTHEW 2:13-23

See below.

The Holy Family / Sunday in the Octave of Christmas (A)

SIRACH 3:2-6, 12-14

These verses are a commentary on Exod 20:12: "Honor your father and your mother, so that your days may be long in the land that the LORD your God is giving you." Doing honor to one's father is said to be a means of atoning for sins (vv. 3, 14), revering one's mother a way of storing up riches (v. 4). Failure to keep this commandment is the equivalent of blasphemy (v. 16). The reward promised for filial piety is the same here as in Exodus, namely, a long and prosperous life (v. 6). Service to one's parents is a proof of obedience to the LORD and of a respectful fear of him. When old age or signs of senility overtake one's father, he is not to be chided by those who happen to have retained their youth and vigor (v. 13). Kindness toward a parent in adversity will always redound to the credit of a son or daughter (v. 15).

The answer to one's prayers or being gladdened by children (v. 5) is not so certain a matter as Sirach seems to think, except in the global sense that respect for parents is bound to bring blessings to a household, especially in the next generation.

PSALM 128:1-5

Happy are those who fear the LORD and walk in his ways.

COLOSSIANS 3:12-21

The admonition given here is couched in direct address, a change from the preceding observations in the third person about the "new reintegrated self" (v. 10) undistinguished by particularities of nationality, religion, or social status. *Because* you are God's chosen ones, the Colossians are told, "therefore" clothe yourselves with every virtue. The community is addressed (v. 12) as if it were God's special possession or heritage (cf. Deut 4:37; 7:7; Ps 33:12) in terms like those of 1 Pet 2:9. It has been chosen and therefore should respond with the love (v. 14) that binds all the other virtues together. The five virtues listed in v. 12 should characterize the dealings of Christians with their fellow believers and others. Forbearance and forgiveness are equally important (v. 13), while love is the perfect bond (v. 14).

Christ's work in those who believe in him is peace (cf. John 14:27; Eph 2:14) and thankfulness (v. 15). Expression of the latter in response to the words Christ preached should take the form of joyful songs, a Greek word that gives us the English "ode." Everything is to be done gratefully (v. 16) in Jesus' name, but the work of giving thanks to God takes precedence over all (v. 17).

The general norms of Christian life are followed by specific ones for the family circle. The injunction to wives to be subject to their husbands can be found in Plutarch's *Conjugalia praecepta* (Marital Precepts) and other writings of the time. This understanding was characteristic of the prevailing social order, which now is to be fulfilled "in the Lord" (v. 18). Love of wives and abstention from all harshness is enjoined on husbands (v. 19), obedience on children (v. 20). Fathers must not provoke their children to anger, presumably by nagging or picking on them (v. 21) lest discouragement follow.

Except for the important social changes in many cultures that have rendered subjection in one direction archaic, the proposals sound like a perfect pattern for domestic peace.

ALLELUIA. COLOSSIANS 3:15A, 16A

May the peace of Christ rest in your hearts and the fullness of his message live within you.

MATTHEW 2:13[15, 19]-23

The dream motif of Matt 1:20 and 2:12 is found again in 2:13 and 2:19. Herod was "searching for the child to destroy him" (v. 13) much as the Pharaoh of old had given a murderous command regarding the males born to the Hebrew women (Exod 1:16, 22). Matthew's account of Jesus' infancy is a midrashic one similar to Philo's *Life of Moses*. It is at the same time in the tradition of employing biblical texts in aid of preconceived interpretation. Verses from Isaiah (cf. Matt 1:23) and Micah (cf. Matt 2:6) have received such treatment. So now will citations from Hosea (cf. 2:15) and Jeremiah (cf. 2:18). Matthew must get the young family to Egypt if the Masoretic reading of Hos 11:1 is to refer to Jesus, a text that in Micah has to do with the call of the people Israel ("my son") to freedom in the exodus. For Matthew Jesus is that people typically or in fulfillment. The holy family had to remain in Egypt until Herod's death, Matthew writes, so that the child could return to conditions of safety (see vv. 19f.). Actually, getting him to his traditional place of origin in Galilee is even more the intention (v. 23).

According to Josephus, Herod died around the feast of Passover in 4 B.C. (by our calendar). Archelaus, one of his three surviving sons, received from the emperor the title of ethnarch of Judaea, Samaria, and Idumea. He held on to power there for ten years when, having experienced repeated embassies to Rome by Jews and Samaritans to protest his barbarism, he was removed by Tiberius in disgrace. Joseph's fear of returning to Judaea (v. 22) may reflect Matthew's knowledge of Archelaus's earliest days in power. According to Josephus, he put down a grievance of his new subjects by slaughtering 3,000 of them before he could appear in Rome to solidify his appointment. There is even some suspicion that, in order to get the lion's share over his brother Antipas (the Herod of Jesus' adult years) and half-brother Philip, he altered his father's will days before the old king's death.

Matthew's knowledge of the house of Herod is not at issue here, although his account squares with the known facts. He is much more interested in explaining why the followers of Jesus are being designated *notsrim* in his day (the modern Hebrew word for Christians). Jesus' home town Nazareth seems to provide the adjective *Nazōraios* to describe him (as also in 26:71; Acts 24:5; in Mark 16:6; in Luke 24:19, *Nazarēnos*). Matthew, however, may be playing on the word *netser*, the "shoot" of Isa 11:1. But if "Nazareth" derives from a word meaning to "guard" or "protect" *(nātsar)* Matthew's meaning cannot be sustained in this way. "Consecrated to God" *(nāzîr*; see Judg 13:5, 7) is a remote possibility.

The synagogue of Ben Ezra in old Cairo not far from the Nile contains a pool from which the Pharaoh's daughter is said to have drawn out the boy Moses. Not surprisingly, it is not far from a cluster of seven Christian churches, on the site of one of which (in Greek Orthodox hands and dedicated to Mary) the holy family reportedly stayed.

✧✧

Holy Name of Jesus / Solemnity of Mary, Mother of God (A, B, C) / Octave of Christmas

NUMBERS 6:22-27

The first twenty-one verses of this chapter are concerned with the regulations laid down for Nazirites, that dedicated class whose existence is attested in every period of Israel's history. It has been conjectured that they got their start as protesters against Israel's having passed from a nomadic way of life to a settled, agricultural one in the land of Canaan. The taboo in favor of sacred hair, however—much stronger than that against wine from grapes (which they can drink when the period of their vow is over, v. 20)—may tell against this theory. In this Priestly account, the regulation of the vowed Nazirites (the *nāzîr* means "untrimmed" with respect to vines in Lev 25:5, 11) is in the hands of the priests (cf. Num 6:10f., 16, and 19f.). This is the only visible connection with the blessing that "Aaron and his sons" are instructed to give (v. 23) in the concluding verses of the chapter.

In its present form the blessing is postexilic, but it goes back to ancient times. Fragments of it that occur in Pss 4:7 and 67:1, the latter a harvest prayer in its final verses, testify to its antiquity. Sirach 50:20f. tells of the custom of the high priest Simon's raising his hands and the congregation with his lips in which "the name of the Lord would be his glory" (NAB). That is the way it is in the formulary of Num 6, where the divine name thrice repeated is the matter of the greatest significance. *Tamid* 7:2 in the Mishnah (literally "oral repetition," the collected materials of the first two centuries C.E. which are at the core of the Talmud) required pronunciation of the blessing every morning at the hour of sacrifice while the Temple stood. In the Temple the divine name YHWH was spoken, whereas in the synagogues in all services "Adonai" (my Sovereign Master) was said in its place. This means that Mary of Nazareth, celebrated in today's feast, would have heard the blessing many times.

Psalms 77:19b and 97:4, where "his lightnings light up the world," have been suggested as places to account for v. 25, but no such direct literary dependence seems called for. In its own rich language the formula is a simple invocation of protection and peace, one of the great treasures of the Jewish inheritance of Christians.

Psalm 8[67:2-3, 5-6, 8]

O Lord, our God, how wonderful is your name in all the earth.

Galatians 4:4-7

Galatians 4:4 is often cited as the sole biographic fragment on Jesus that Paul attempted short of his frequent reference to the last three days of his life. It says only that Jesus was a Jew because born of a Jewish mother—but this is already quite a lot. It is also the reason for its selection for this feast. The passage has more to do with our "adoption as children" (v. 5), however, than with Jesus' birth as a Jew. His being "born under the Law" (v. 4) is far from a title of liberty for Paul. He thinks Jews and Gentiles are each in their own condition of servitude, the Gentiles as slaves to "beings that by nature are not gods" (v. 8), the Jews in their subjection to the Law as now the sole condition of being saved on the last day (see v. 5). In its original form this passage may have been a creedal hymn into which Paul inserted his special concerns (viz., vv. 4c-5a).

It is a much argued question how Paul could have got himself into the state of mind whereby he thought the Law repressive when other rabbis of his time found perfect observance possible (as he confesses in Phil 3:6b he himself did) and even liberating (as he did not). Paul seems to have felt perfectly equal to its demands (see Gal 1:14) but that is not the question at the moment. He wants to establish to a mixed audience of Galatians, some of them perhaps Jews and most Gentiles, that enslavement was the condition of them all and that all are in danger of slipping back into it.

This passage is evidently directed to new Gentile believers who are heeding fellow Gentiles or Jewish teachers now Christian, insistent that portions of the Law ("works of the Law," 3:10) be kept. The phrase in 4:3 about the "elemental spirits of the world" is puzzling, because it does not fit into a Jewish context. It is more properly a reference to pagan dependence on astral bodies and the powers directing them, as is the case in v. 9. It may be that Paul, who declares his solidarity with Jews by the repeated "we," wishes to put calendar-conscious Jewish observants in the same class. In any case, "when the fullness of time had come" (v. 4) God had worked out both redemption in the sense of ransom or purchase for Jews and Gentiles alike and adoption as divine offspring.

Modern women may well be offended at Paul's vocabulary of sons and sonship (vv. 5-7) since redeemed status is meant to include all. This literal rendering is gone from NAB and NRSV but remains in NIV. The figure is from the realm of property inheritance (v. 1). In that culture, possessions were passed on to sons only, who then had to look after the women in their families.

Returning to a theme he first took up in 3:2ff., the inheritance Paul speaks of is the gift of the Spirit. Possession of the Spirit—with its power enabling the believer to call on God as "Abba"—is proof for Paul that slave status is in the past for the Galatians and adoptive sonship upon them. Paul is acquainted with the form of address to God that uses the Aramaic rather than the Hebrew "Ab," followed by the translation in Greek. This was probably Hellenist Jewish usage of the time. The matter of gender-specific language is not as important for Paul, however, as the inherited gift of God that makes it possible, namely, "the Spirit of his Son" (v. 6).

Alleluia. Hebrews 1:1-2

In the past God spoke to our ancestors through the prophets; now God speaks to us through his Son.

PHILIPPIANS 2:5-11

See Proper 21 [26] (A).

LUKE 2:15[16]-21

The shepherds are in that group of seven witnesses to Jesus' birth whom Luke introduces in his first two chapters and does not call on again: Zechariah, Gabriel, Elizabeth, Joseph (apart from mention in 3:23 and 4:22), the shepherds, Simeon, and Anna. It is the "manger" of v. 16 that has fixed Jesus' birth in a cave or shelter for animals. Matthew localizes the place where the Magi visit as a house (Matt 12:11). Amazement (v. 18) is a standard response in the Gospels to the wonders performed by Jesus, in this case to what has been reported of his birth. Mary's response to the marvelous events is to store them up for reflection, while the shepherds "glorify and praise God" over them (v. 20).

The narrative in v. 21 continues the parallel with the story of John by describing circumcision on the eighth day (cf. 1:59-79). Reference is made back to the naming of the child as "Jesus" by Gabriel in 1:31. In neither place does Luke explain the derivation of the name as Matthew does (1:21).

❧❧
January 1—When Observed as New Year's Day (A, B, C)

ECCLESIASTES 3:1-13

God has made everything appropriate to its time, the Teacher observes in eight verses whose very banality may account for their popularity. People's busy routine keeps them from reflecting on what God is up to, but at least they can see that God means them to be happy in their work while he pursues his awesome routine.

PSALM 8

You gave your Son authority over all creation.

REVELATION 21:1-6

See under January 1 (B) for a commentary; also 5 Easter (C).

MATTHEW 25:31-46.

See under Reign of Christ the King, Proper 29 [34] (A)

❧❧

Second Sunday after Christmas Day (A, B, C)

JEREMIAH 31:7-14

See Sunday 30 (B).

SIRACH 24:1-12[1-2, 8-12]

See on Sirach 15[16]–20, Sixth Sunday after Epiphany [6] (A); Proverbs 8:22-31, Trinity Sunday (C); Proverbs 9:1-6, 20 Sunday (B).

WISDOM OF SOLOMON 10:15-21

For a commentary see under Year B.

PSALM 147:12-20[12-15, 19-20] OR
WISDOM OF SOLOMON 10:15-21

EPHESIANS 1:3-14[3-6, 15-18]

See 15 Sunday (B); Ascension (A).

JOHN 1: (1-9), 1-18[10-18 OR 1-5, 9-14]

See The Nativity of the Lord, Mass during the Day (A).

❧ Season of Epiphany ❧

❧❧
Epiphany of the Lord (A, B, C)
January 6 (celebrated in some churches
on the nearest Sunday)

ISAIAH 60:1-6

This visionary poem is spoken in praise of Jerusalem, "city of the LORD," "Zion of the Holy One of Israel" (60:14c). Chapter 49 on which it is patterned was concerned with the return of the exiles from Babylon. This chapter is more taken up with the ingathering of the dispersed sons and daughters of Israel (v. 4). They will return not only to the homeland but to the holy mountain, "my altar" and "my house" (v. 7). In their coming, the light and glory of Israel's LORD will shine upon them (v. 1), hence upon the city. The whole people is conceived as a woman lying prostrate who is summoned to "Rise up!"—an ancient call to worship.

Darkness and thick clouds (v. 2a; derived from the Sinai theophany, Exod 20:18, 21) evoke the image of YHWH enthroned as king (Ps 97:2). Here, however, they are a prelude to that great glory of the LORD that will dispel the darkness (v. 2b). The people will shine with that radiance (vv. 3, 5). Nations and kings will bask in their light. More than that, the latter's treasures ("the wealth of nations") will be brought in tribute from distant coastlands (v. 5b) and far-off deserts. The queen of Sheba had brought gifts to Solomon from southern Arabia (see 1 Kgs 10:2). In the poet's vision dromedaries will come from Midian and Ephah (below modern Elat, east of the Sinai peninsula). Kedar is the desert of northern Saudi Arabia lying just under the Fertile Crescent.

Taken together, we have in the various images a vision of Israel triumphant through its God. Psalm 72:8-11 paints much the same picture. Foreigners shall pay tribute and do homage to the LORD for deeds of might, while the hearts of the

Israelites throb with pride (v. 5a). It has been noted that chap. 60 has verbal allusions to or quotations from the following verses in chap. 49: 1, 3, 5, 6, 7, 8, 10, 12, 14, 18, 22. So skillfully are they reworked, however, that it is a new composition to fit new circumstances.

Those circumstances are the expected assemblage of all, Israel and the nations alike, to holy Zion. The dream of the new Jerusalem was still alive when John recorded in his Revelation the vision of a city that had no need of sun or moon, into which the treasures and wealth of the nations should be brought (21:23-26). It is the perennial vision of the epiphany of God to his people, and theirs to other peoples who will share in their reflected light.

PSALM 72:1-7[2, 7-8], 10[-13]14

LORD, every nation on earth will adore you.

EPHESIANS 3:2-3[A], 5-6

The writer of these verses is convinced that in Christ Jesus a measure of the vision of Isa 60 is already fulfilled. Jews and Gentiles together are "coheirs, members of the same body, sharers in the promise" (v. 6). The preaching of the Gospel has made a reality of what before was only a hope. The mystery (vv. 3, 4) unknown to former ages has been revealed to apostles and prophets (v. 5) who are accredited ministers of its diffusion (v. 2). Paul is surely one of them (v. 1), thanks to God's unmerited grace (v. 2). The *mystērion* spoken of in v. 3 is what God had long meant to do, namely, bring Jews and Gentiles together into one.

This conviction about a divine plan hitherto concealed is held by the author of Colossians 1, although only Ephesians uses *mystērion* to signify the Jewish-Gentile union. (See the commentary on Eph 1:3-6, 11-12, feast of the Immaculate Conception.) The Qumrân hymns contain a similar sentiment: "In the mystery of your wisdom you have opened knowledge to me." The previous phrase had said: "I . . . have known you, my God, by the spirit which you gave to me. I have listened loyally to your wonderful secrets through your holy spirit" (*Hodayoth*, 20.11–13, F. Garcia-Martinez, ed. [Leiden: Brill, 1994], 356).

ALLELUIA. MATTHEW 2:1-12

We have seen his star in the East and have come to adore the Lord.

MATTHEW 2:1-13

John attests the tradition that the Messiah is to be Davidic and come from Bethlehem, David's city (John 7:42). Matthew fulfills the expectation literally as a demand of Mic 5:1. He quotes Micah in a way that derives from neither the Masoretic nor the Septuagint version, changing "clans of Judah" to "rulers of Judah" and "you are the least" to "you are by no means the least" to heighten the messianic effect (see commentary on Micah 5:2-5a [NAB, 1-4], 4 Advent [C]). Rabbinic writing of the time felt no compunction to alter a text in this fashion to suit the purpose of the writer's context.

The story of the Magi with its strong mythological elements is as much about the threat to kingly power that Jesus constitutes (see Matt 27:11-31) as it is about Gentile homage (v. 11) or the wonder of the traveling star in the heavens (2:2, 9f.). The astronomer/astrologers became three in subsequent Christian legend because their gifts were three (v. 11); they became kings by association with Ps 72:10 and Isa 49:7; 60:10. This was legitimate enough, since they may have been created by Matthew out of those passages.

Matthew's narrative genius is nowhere more evident than in this chapter and the one that precedes it. By the time the tale of vv. 1-12 has been told, the origins of Jesus and God's design for him have been underscored thoroughly.

The Magi return to their places, their "kingdoms," but are no longer at ease, said T. S. Eliot. They had witnessed a birth that was more like death—their death.

Baptism of the Lord [1] (A)

First Sunday after the Epiphany / First Sunday of the Year / Sunday after January 6

ISAIAH 42:1-9 [1-4, 6-7]

This is the first of the four Servant Songs. "The Servant is conceived as an individual figure, but he is the figure who recapitulates in himself all the religious gifts and the religious mission of Israel. . . . He incorporates the dominant features of Israel's past; he has some of the traits of a new Moses, he is the spokesman of divine revelation, is the witness of the divinity of YHWH to Israel and the nations, he is a prophet" (John L. McKenzie, *Second Isaiah* [The Anchor Bible, Garden City, N.Y.: Doubleday, 1968], LIII). The Servant is chosen for a mission by the LORD who, having decided upon him, holds fast to him (v. 1). He has been given a measure of Spirit, i.e., divine impulsion to act. The gift is for the purpose of holding out "just judgment," understood as the whole Sinaitic revelation, to the Gentiles. Unlike the loud proclamations of military and civil authority, the Servant's message will be quietly spoken (v. 2; cf. 58:1 for a contrast in manner). Verse 3 contains figures describing the powerless whom the Servant will not crush by coercion. Oppression will be no part of his activity as he delivers divine revelation to the farthest coastlands (v. 4), meaning either the Mediterranean shores to the north and south or distant realms never explored. The concept of a deliverance of *torah* ("teaching," v. 4) to the nations and not only to Israel occurs elsewhere in Second Isaiah. The Servant is envisioned as a proclaimer of covenant Law outside the boundaries of Israelite peoplehood.

Verses 5-9 are a reworking of some of the ideas of the song in simpler fashion and are often designated a response to it. Verse 5 appeals to the power of God in creation and moves on to declare the divine intent to assist and strengthen ("I have taken you by the hand and kept you . . . ," v. 6), an echo of 41:10b. The servant represents Israel under the figures of a "covenant to the people" (here *'am* is not the people Israel, as customarily) and a "light to the nations" (the LXX's phrases that Luke employs in Simeon's song, 2:32). He stands for all that judgment and teaching can mean to a Gentile world if it accepts them. The light of v. 6 does not so much go with the Servant's revealing mission as deliver from figurative darkness and blindness (v. 7) those captive to ignorance of the LORD or the service of false gods.

PSALM 29[1-4, 9B-10]

The LORD will bless his people with peace.

ACTS 10:34[-38]43

The sermon of Peter that Luke inserts here corresponds in outline to the speech of chap. 2 (especially vv. 22-24, 32-36). Today's pericope includes only the link with the situation (vv. 34f.) and a portion of the kerygma (vv. 36-38) that goes on to v. 42. Peter began to speak (literally: "opening his mouth, said," v. 34), as Philip had done in 8:35, a Semitic phrase that, like the "truly" of his opening utterances, underlines the solemnity of the moment. This is for Luke nothing less than the official disclosure of the Gospel to the non-Jewish world through Peter. That God "shows no partiality" here translates the word for a respecter of persons, literally one who favors some faces over others and denies that God is such a one. The phrase has a history of biblical use to describe God's strict justice and imperviousness to bribes (cf. Deut 10:17; 2 Chron 19:7; Job 34:19) but without the connotations of even-handedness with respect to Jews and Gentiles. "The author is not thinking of Israel's past, but of the challenge now posed by the gospel" (Ernst Haenchen, *The Acts of the Apostles* [Philadelphia: Westminster, 1971], 351).

From v. 36 on, Peter's speech parallels the presentation Luke puts on Paul's lips in Pisidian Antioch, particularly the twofold audience of Jews and "others who fear God" (13:26); compare "the sons of Israel" of 10:36 (NAB, "Israelites; NRSV, "people of Israel") and the God-fearers who made up Cornelius's household. The "message" of v. 36 is a word that proclaims peace between God and the Jewish people. Jesus Christ, the "Lord of all," is the intermediary who brings about salvation; he can proclaim peace because he has come to effect it. The proclamation referred to in v. 36 follows in v. 37. The widespread character of "what has happened" all over Judaea, beginning in Galilee, is assumed, however, throughout Palestine, even to Caesarea. The story of Jesus began with John's preaching of baptism (v. 37) as in the Markan account, not with his infancy as in Luke's first book. God anointed him (v. 38), just as he is reported to have done in Luke 4:18, which tells of the initiation of his ministry in the Nazareth synagogue. Jesus' "doing good" places him in the category of Gentile rulers who are hailed as "benefactors" (Luke 22:25). When he heals "all who were oppressed by the devil" we have an echo of the cosmic struggle in Mark, the mythos whereby he interpreted the historical reminiscences he had access to. The phrase "and God was with him" recalls Matthew's title "Emmanuel" (1:23).

ALLELUIA. SEE MARK 9:6

The heavens were opened and the Father's voice was heard: This is my beloved Son! Listen to him.

MATTHEW 3:13-17

The baptismal narratives of Mark and Luke will be read on this feast in Years B and C, respectively. The chief differences between this pericope and that of Mark on which it is patterned (1:9-11) are the insertion by Matthew of John's demurrer on the grounds of his inferiority to Jesus (vv. 14f.) and the change of the voice from heaven from the second person ("You are my beloved son," Mark 1:11) to the third ("This is my beloved son," Matt 3:17). Jerome in his *Against Pelagius* (3.2) has an interesting quotation from the *Gospel according to the Hebrews* that changes Matthew's statement of John that he should be baptized by Jesus to a scruple of the sinless Jesus at accepting a baptism of repentance. M. R. James provides this quotation in *The Apocryphal New Testament* (accommodated [Oxford: Clarendon, 1953], 6): "The mother of the Lord and his brothers said to him: 'John the Baptist baptizes for the forgiveness of sins; let us go and be baptized by him.' But he said to them, 'In what have I sinned that I should go and be baptized by him? Unless, perhaps, what I have just said is a sin of ignorance?'" (cf. Matt 3:13ff.). Both Matthew and this lost Gospel appear to be wrestling with the problem inherent in Mark's presentation of the sinless Jesus as a candidate for John's baptism. Matthew views the difficulty as one of superiority-inferiority and settles it in terms of a divine imperative: "Thus it is fitting for us to fulfill all justice" (v. 15), probably meaning the way of life appropriate to one baptized by John. "Recognizing the superiority of his own baptism, Jesus nevertheless pledges to act in accord with John's baptism" (Daniel Harrington, *The Gospel of Matthew* [Collegeville, Minn.: Liturgical, 1991], 60, n. 15).

The *Gospel of the Ebionites* (cited in Epiphanius, *Against Heresies* 30.13.8) adds these details to the canonical account: "And immediately a great light shone around the place; and John seeing it, said to him, 'Who are you, Lord?' And again a voice from heaven said to him, 'This is my beloved Son, with whom I am well pleased.' Then John, falling down before him, said, 'I beseech you, Lord, baptize me!' But he forbade him, saying, 'Let it be so; for thus it is befitting to fulfill all things'" (James, 9). The same concern to keep John in a position subordinate to Jesus is evident here. Jerome quotes from the *Gospel according to the Hebrews* in another place (*Commentary on Isaiah* 4.11.2), to the following effect: "When the Lord ascended from the water, the whole fount of the Holy Spirit descended and rested on him, and said to him, 'My son, in all the prophets I was waiting for you, that you might come, and that I might rest in you. For you are my rest; and you are my firstborn son, who reigns forever'" (Hennecke-Schneemelcher, *New Testament Apocrypha* [Philadelphia: Westminster: 1963], 1:177).

Matthew does not give any reason for the Baptist's attempt to dissuade Jesus (v. 14), having portrayed a Jesus who "came" (v. 13) from Galilee for the express purpose of submitting to the rite. He is more explicit than Mark in this, who treats the event matter-of-factly. "John would have prevented him" is the imperfect tense of attempted action. The Matthean reason why the baptism of Jesus should go forward is the justness of God which underlies the entire careers of John and Jesus (cf. Matt 6:33; 21:32). It is interesting that, while Mark 1:4 and Luke 3:3 have John preaching "a baptism of repentance for the forgiveness of sins," Matthew omits it from the two parallel places (3:1, 4), seemingly because he wishes to identify this work of forgiveness of sins exclusively with Jesus (cf. 26:28; Matthew's usage of the phrase there does not occur in the eucharistic words of Mark, Luke, or 1 Corinthians).

For a commentary on vv. 16f. (par. Mark 1:10f.; Luke 3:21b-22), see Baptism of the Lord (C), where Luke follows Mark, "You are my beloved Son," rather than, "This is. . . ," which may be his departure from Q.

Second Sunday after the Epiphany [2] / Second Sunday of the Year (A)

ISAIAH 49:1-7[-3, 5-6]

The first six verses make up the second of four Servant Songs of Second Isaiah (the others are 42:1-4; 50:4-9; 52:13—53:12). It has been observed that in chaps. 40–48 (at 41:8, 9; 42:1, 19; 43:10; 44:11, 21, 26; 45:4) the term "servant," or "servants" (in the ancient world, "slaves") is a designation for righteous Israel or its individual members. This people is chosen for the role of messenger, but as messenger to whom is not clear. Beginning at chap. 49 and continuing through chap. 55, a remarkable distinction is found between an Israel that is the servant or messenger of God and the rest of Israel (cf. 49:3, 5, 6; 50:10; 52:13). This servant of the LORD would prosper, but not without being marred in appearance (52:14), stricken, smitten, and afflicted (53:4). The vocation is a corporate one, not to a specific individual, despite the wording of 43:1f. The mystery of the servant's identity lies in the later distinction between the pious Israel, which recognizes its call from the womb (the Servant), and faithless Israel, which does not heed it.

The mission of the hidden arrow in the LORD's quiver, the sword concealed in the shadow of God's arm (49:2), is that it must come out of obscurity and proclaim the glory of the LORD (v. 3). YHWH has formed his *ebhedh* Jacob (Israel) from the womb. He is to bring Israel back to himself now, in a reconciliation of son to father; glory and strength are to be the new guise of the reconciled son (v. 5). The LORD asks the faithful among the Jewish people if they find their calling too modest, their role too confining (v. 6). Raising up the survivors of exile and debilitating wars is no less than seeing that Israel serves "as a light to the Gentiles" (*l*^e*or goyim*) and "my salvation" (*y*^e*shuati*) to the ends of the earth.

Arthur Waskow put the vision of Second Isaiah well in a review of Meir Kahane's *Our Challenge*, a book perhaps long forgotten that Waskow characterizes as unbiblical in spirit: "The Prophets in their most ecstatic calls for a return to the Land and for the great triumph of Torah throughout the world never forgot that universal peace and justice are an integral part of that triumph. Jewish particularism, certainly; Jewish nationalism perhaps; Jewish chauvinism, never." Christians, take warning!

Today's reading is a prophetic call for universal peace through its emissaries, a chosen segment of a chosen people. Christians may not forget that all of them, not just some, belong to peace churches, however imperfectly some have fulfilled their role.

PSALM 40:1-11[2, 4, 7-10]

Here am I, LORD, I come to do your will.

1 CORINTHIANS 1:1-9[-3]

"Grace and peace" (v. 3), a hybrid Greek and Jewish greeting, is a constant in Paul's letters (cf. Rom 1:7; 2 Cor 1:2; Gal 1:3; Phil 1:2; 1 Thess 1:2; 2 Thess 1:2; Philem 1, 3). So, too, is mention of his call as an apostle, someone "sent." The recipients at Corinth are designated as "consecrated in Christ Jesus" and "called to be saints" (*hagiois*, v. 2). Paul then extends his greeting to all in whatever place who call upon the name of the Lord, the Jesus Christ who is not only "our" Lord but "theirs and ours" (vv. 2, 3). In his familiar binitarian fashion, Paul invokes grace and peace upon all believers from "God our Father and the Lord Jesus Christ" (v. 3).

The greeting is a summary of those blessings that Paul is convinced have been made available to humankind through God's action in Christ.

ALLELUIA. 1 SAMUEL 3:9; JOHN 6:69B

Speak, O LORD, your servant is listening; you have the words of everlasting life.

JOHN 1:29[-34]42

John's "the next day" (v. 29) may be part of a week in a new creation patterned on Gen 1:1—2:4 (cf. 1:35, 39, 43; 2:1) but if so the exact sequence is impossible to determine. We do not know why John the Baptist describes Jesus as "the lamb of God" (v. 29), i.e., whether he has in mind the paschal lamb, a lamb of daily sacrifice, the Yom Kippur goat of Lev 16:20ff. who was to "bear on itself all their iniquities . . . into the desert," the lamb led to slaughter in Isa 53:7, or the messianic lamb (the word-form indicates a young lamb) who is the leader of the 144,000 in Rev 14:1. C. K. Barrett opts for the symbolism of the Passover lamb, a Pauline usage (cf. 1 Cor 5:7), but says we cannot know whether 1:29 influenced John 19:31-37 (Jesus' death at the hour of slaughter on Preparation Day) or vice versa. One theory has it that an Aramaic word for servant, *talya*, underlies the Gospel word for lamb, but the evidence is not compelling. The lamb is the "bearer" on his back or "carrier off" of sin, probably the latter in the sense of the remover of human guilt. The Vulgate's *tollit* is ambivalent in the same way as the Greek. Choir members of all the churches who sing Latin Masses in whole or part will recognize the direct address to the Lamb, "qui tollis peccata mundi."

C. H. Dodd contends that "after [me]" (v. 30) never has a temporal sense in the New Testament but always a spatial or relational, hence that Jesus is being described as superior in importance (see, "ranks ahead of me," "was before," which are Luke's prepositions, v. 30); therefore it has nothing to do with their respective ages as described in Luke's prologue. The precedence of Jesus to John as to all creation, in the spirit of the Johannine prologue, however, cannot be ruled out. It may even underlie the two adverbs of v. 30, above.

The testimony of the Baptizer mentioned in 1:6ff., 15 proceeds in vv. 32ff. At first the son of Zechariah did not "recognize" Jesus (vv. 31, 33; cf. v. 26), a knowing that for John connotes acceptance in faith (cf. 7:28, 29). Verse 31 expresses the paradox of the revealer to whom the subject of his revelation must first be revealed. The Spirit's descent as a dove (v. 32) is a tradition John has in common with the Synoptics (Matt 3:16; Mark 1:10; Luke 3:22), probably deriving from the dove of the subsided flood waters (Gen 8:11f.). The dove identifies for the Baptist the one who, unlike himself, is to baptize with the Holy Spirit (v. 33). Having received this testimony, he gives his own. REB, JB, and NAB (1970) follow the third-century papyrus (p[5]) and the Sinaiticus of a century later that read *eklektos*, the "chosen one" of God rather than the easier reading, "son" of God (v. 34).

❧·❧

Third Sunday after the Epiphany [3] / Third Sunday of the Year (A)

ISAIAH 9:1-4[8:23–9:3]

See The Nativity of the Lord (A).

PSALM 27:1, 4-9[1, 4, 13-14]

The LORD is my light and my salvation.

1 CORINTHIANS 1:10-18[-13, 17]

The community of "believers" (*adelphoi*, which in the New Testament always means both sexes) is asked by Paul to come to agreement and desist from "divisions" (v. 10). He begs for perfection in "mind and purpose"—unanimity, as we would say. Paul identifies his informants regarding the dissension (v. 11) at Corinth. Chloe (lit.: "a blade of green grass") is not otherwise mentioned in the New Testament. She may own a large house where her "people" labor.

Paul grows specific about the factionalism. There are parties in the Corinthian church claiming the names of Paul, Apollos (cf. 3:6; Acts 18:24-28), Cephas (Peter), and Christ. The first two have doubtless been the teachers of some. The citation of Cephas inclines certain scholars to think that he visited Corinth, but his representatives from the mother church of Jerusalem would satisfy the terms. As to the naming of Christ (v. 12) in a list of apostles, Paul may be speaking scornfully or else be referring to an actual Christ party of authoritarians who claim the highest source possible. The absurdity of the Corinthians' fragmented outlook is underscored by the three rhetorical questions (*diatríbe*) of v. 13. A divided Christ is unthinkable to Paul, as is the substitution of an apostle's name like his own for that of the only Lord.

In vv. 14f., Paul seeks to dissociate himself from the bickering of the Corinthians by naming the few he has baptized (for Stephanas, see 16:15, 17). He does not think poorly of the rite; his is another ministry, that of preaching. One suspects, however, that Paul conceives his preaching as the nobler and more unifying role, with the ritual activity of baptizing its follow-up. As soon as he has mentioned the strife over ministers of baptism, he is reminded of another folly that has reached his ears (his eyes by letter?). A portion of the church seems hot in pursuit of a "wisdom" with which he has little sympathy. The gospel for Paul is chiefly the cross, not a philosophical rhetoric that comforts seekers after *sophia*. It is a call to suffering that unsettles all who hear it. This leads to the apostle's striking antithesis between wisdom and folly, a paradox in which the world's wisdom is God's foolishness while the foolishness of the world, the cross, is supreme wisdom in God's eyes. Compare 2:7, 9; 3:18-20; 4:10, 19; 5:12f; 8:1-3.

ALLELUIA. MATTHEW 4:23

Jesus preached the good news of the kingdom and healed those who were ill.

MATTHEW 4:12-23[12-17]

Matthew (v. 12) follows Mark (1:14) in placing the beginning of Jesus' ministry in Galilee immediately after John's arrest. Both situate it after his temptation in the desert. Luke, in doing the same as they (4:14), is alone in having him return to Galilee "in the power of the Spirit." For Matthew, Jesus "withdrew" (v. 12; the noun "anchorite" is derived from this verb) to Galilee while for Mark he simply "came" (1:14) there. The expansion of vv. 13-17 is peculiarly Matthean. He omits the exorcisms and healings in Capernaum (Mark 1:21-38), including that of Simon's mother-in-law (1:29ff.), and retains only the call of the early disciples (4:18-22; Mark 1:16-20). The several wonders performed by Jesus in Galilee according to Mark are summarized in v. 23 of Matthew, where the latter reports all the teaching, proclaiming, and healing of every disease and illness accomplished there.

Matthew immediately places Jesus in Capernaum rather than Nazareth as the focus of his Galilean activity (v. 13; cf. 2:23), something that Mark gets around to only in 1:21 and Luke in 4:23 and 31, in what has to be an altered sequence. The ancient "territory of Zebulun and Naphthali" is not clear in its outlines for Matthew (Capernaum would have been in Naphthali, Nazareth in Zebulun), but for his purposes it encompassed Capernaum, for he wishes to cite Isaiah 8:23—9:1 as part of his compromise-resolution technique. That book of prophecy contrasted the degradation of darkness that fell upon the region around "the seaward road . . . and the district *(galil)* of the Gentiles" (Isa 8:23; KJV, NRSV: 9:1) when Tiglath-pileser III ravaged it in 733–32, with the "great light" (9:1[2]) that would dawn on it at the accession of the child proclaimed in oracle form in 9:1-6. Isaiah had intended to signify by "the way of the sea" the Mediterranean but Matthew takes it to refer to the Sea of Galilee. The familiar Matthean rubric of fulfillment "so that" (v. 14) is here, indicating that Jesus' settling down in Capernaum was indeed the Isaian light shed upon that dark region. The people living (lit.: "seated," v. 16) in darkness and the land overshadowed by death saw the light of God, namely, Jesus, rise on them.

Matthew (v. 17) shortens Jesus' proclamation from Mark's longer, "this is the time of fulfillment. The reign of God is at hand! Reform your lives and believe in the gospel" (1:15). *Metanoeîte* renders the Hebrew word for "turn away from," not precisely "repent," which is its meaning in the New Testament (and not, "do penance," the rendering of the Vulgate).

The changes made by Matthew in Jesus' call of the two sets of brothers (vv. 18-22) from the Markan prototype (1:16-20) are negligible, the most significant addition being "Simon who is called Peter" (v. 18). "Come after me" (v. 19) is a technical term for discipleship, a literal following of one's teacher. "Fishers of men" had only an eschatological meaning and a threatening, judgmental one at that until the milieu of the gospel gave it a favorable meaning. See Wilhelm Wuellner, *The Meaning of "Fishers of Men"* (Philadelphia: Westminster, 1967).

"Fishers for people" is well intentioned but rhetorically weak, a matter Wuellner did not get into in his book of thirty-six years ago.

ℛ☙

Fourth Sunday after the Epiphany [4] / Fourth Sunday of the Year / (A)

MICAH 6:1-8

The prophet's reproaches to Israel (vv. 3-4 [2-3]) served as the opening "reproach" *(improperium)* to the Church for crucifying the Lord with its sins, but was early understood to be—and may have been intended as—a piece of polemic against the Jews. Its text was altered after Vatican II but the correct exposition by homilists often does not occur. They are still saddled with nineteen centuries of anti-Judaic sentiment. Neither the reproaches nor the now-sanitized prayer for the Jews (unless recast in an entirely different form) should be recited or sung on Good Friday because of this sorry history.

PSALM 15

Keep me safe, O God; you are my hope.

ZEPHANIAH 2:3; 3:12-13

This prophecy, written during Josiah's thirty-two year reign (whether before or after the Deuteronomic reform of 621 we cannot say; some even think in Jehoiakim's time, 609–598) emanates from court circles and is akin to the writings of Amos and Isaiah. It predicts a day of the LORD (1:7) that will be a day of anger (2:2, 3). Only justice and humility will afford protection from it. The court is oriented toward Assyria, hence there is much apostasy from the worship of YHWH, no doubt concerning divine power, and much social corruption. The prophet does not foretell the destruction of all but the sparing of some—a holy remnant (3:12, 13). Princes and judges, prophets and priests have grown predatory and insolent (3:3f). Not so the humble and the lowly. They shall take refuge in the name of the LORD and speak no lies (vv. 12f.). This is the beginning of a theology of election in which not the whole people, as in former days, but the faithful, however few, are seen as the beneficiaries of the covenanted promise to Israel.

PSALM 146:7-10;
(MATTHEW 5:3)

Happy the poor in spirit; the kingdom of heaven is theirs!

1 CORINTHIANS 1:18[-26]31

This passage continues the theme of vv. 17-25 (see the commentary of last week) that God's folly is wiser than humans and God's weakness more powerful. The fact that the Corinthian Christians have received a call (v. 26) has not altered the social fact that they number few who by a worldly standard are wise, powerful, or well-born (v. 26). The elements reckoned foolish and weak (v. 27) have been divinely chosen to humiliate the world's wise and strong. God's categories of acceptability include the low-born, the despised, and those who count for nothing (v. 28). Through the latter God means to reduce to nothing the world's "some-bodies" (v. 28). The incarnation of God's wisdom and strength in Christ Jesus should keep humanity from foolish boasting (v. 29).

Jeremiah of old (9:22f., 23f) had cited knowing the LORD as the sole justification for a person's glorying in riches, strength, or wisdom. God has made the Son our wisdom and our justice, our sanctification and our redemption (1 Cor 1:30). In Christ Jesus alone, therefore, may we boast (v. 31) in the spirit of the text of Jeremiah. This pericope continues Paul's polemic against the strutting of partisan-minded Corinthians who are claiming various lofty spiritual pedigrees (cf. 1:10-13). The claim of some to superior knowledge or influence has divided many congregations since, and even resulted in new churches.

ALLELUIA. 1 SAMUEL 3:9; JOHN 6:69B

Speak, LORD, your servant is listening; you have the words of everlasting life.

MATTHEW 5:1-12[A]

Both Mark (3:13) and Luke (6:13) have Jesus going up a mountain to select his disciples. Following the choice he makes of them in Luke he enunciates two sets of four headings under which they will experience beatitude or woe according as they are faithful to him or not. The connection of the beatitudes with the naming of the first four disciples is just as prominent in Matthew (4:18-22) as the naming of all in Mark and Luke. He assembles various catechetical materials in the collection known as the Sermon on the Mount, presenting them as a discourse on the effects of answering the call to discipleship.

Matthew's mountain is usually a place apart (cf. 14:23; 17:1; 28:16) where Jesus goes to be with his "disciples" (a term first used in 5:1), not a site for public promulgation. The Moses topology of the sermon, long the conventional interpretation, has been challenged by two scholars as far apart on Matthean matters as W. D. Davies and Krister Stendahl. "Matthew presents Jesus as giving a Messianic Law on a Mount, but he avoids the express concept of a New Torah and a New Sinai; he has cast around his Lord the mantle of a teacher of righteousness, but he avoids the express ascription to him of the honorific 'a new Moses'" (W. D. Davies, *The Sermon on the Mount* [Cambridge University Press, 1966], 32).

Jesus uses the poetic form in this first teaching recorded by Matthew. A catalogue of blessedness ("happy the man") is familiar from the Psalms (e.g., 1:1; 40:5; 84:6) and the wisdom literature (Prov 3:13; Sir 14:1, 20). Matthew's emphasis is more ethical ("who show mercy . . . are single-hearted . . . are peacemakers") than Luke's, who confines himself to states of deprivation and persecution (6:20–23). The stress is nonetheless on the bliss of life under God's approaching rule rather than on an improved life (vv. 8, 9, 10). Matthew's "poor in spirit" (the *'anawi rûaḥ* of Qumrân's 1QM, 14.7), his "lowly" and his "single-hearted" (the "pure" or "clean of heart" of KJV and DRC) are not economic classifications, least of all is the last-named concerned with chastity. All are ways to describe generous openness to the LORD in the tradition of Jewish *'anawim* piety. It is the standard Pharisee vocabulary of self-abasement.

Verse 5 bears an allusion to Ps 37:11, v. 8 to Pss 24:4; 73:1. "Seeing God" (v. 8) means final bliss in the kingdom, although in Ps 24:4 access to the mountain of the LORD is spoken of. The key concept in all the beatitudes is the "holiness" of v. 10, not an acquired virtue but God-given righteousness *(dikaiosýnē)* which for Matthew, as Krister Stendahl says in one of his writings, is "the vindication of God's people as the goal of history."

The beatitudes culminate in vv. 10-12. There, as in v. 3, God's reign is what matters. A stance of humility may lead to insult, persecution, and even martyrdom. The persecution of disciples for the sake of or because of the upright conduct that flows from God's uprightness and "because" of (v. 10) "me" (v. 11), placed thus in close conjunction, indicates that persecution for behavior and for the disciples' relationship to Jesus, who is the source of their way of life, is the same thing. There is, in other words, no additional understanding of the causes of persecution in v. 11 over v. 10. The martyrdom of the prophets (cf. 23:34, 37) was a Jewish tradition not recorded in the Scriptures. None of the three major and twelve minor prophets of the canon died a violent death, but the slaughter of others, e.g., Zechariah (2 Chron 24:20f) and Uriah (Jer 26:20-23), is reported. Elijah attributes to the Israelites (see 1 Kgs 19:10, 14) rather than to Jezebel (1 Kgs 18:4) the slaying of certain unnamed prophets. Jeremiah generalizes. "Your own sword devoured your prophets" (2:30). Josephus (*Antiquities* 9.13.2) and later rabbinical writings show how lively the tradition of Israel's rejection of the prophets was. In Matt 5:12 (as also 22:6; 23:29-39; Acts 7:52) the Christians interpret the persecution of their missionaries as "the contemporary manifestation of the 'law of history' that Israel continually persecutes the messengers sent by God" (Douglas R. A. Hare, *The Theme of Jewish Persecution of Christians in Matthew* [Cambridge Univ. Press, 1967], 139).

❧ ❧

Fifth Sunday after the Epiphany [5] / Fifth Sunday of the Year / (A)

ISAIAH 58:1-9A, (9B-12)[7-10]

The earlier part of this chapter takes a strong stand against religious acts like fasting that bring no relief to the oppressed, the hungry, the naked, and the homeless. Verses 8 and 10 employ the theme of light and darkness from chap. 9 but modify it notably. Here the distress is caused by the sins of the people, not the Assyrian conqueror. The brightness of dawn (v. 8) or midday (v. 10) shall come not with a victorious king but as a result of repentance and an about-face in social conduct (vv. 6f.). The corporal works of mercy will bring vindication from the LORD (v. 8) and an answer to heretofore unanswered prayers (v. 9).

Verses 9b and 10a in Lawyer Jaggers's phrase "put the case that" the conditions of vv. 6f. shall be fulfilled. In this case-law form, as opposed to the apodictic form of laws, a hypothesis is stated rather than a condition demanded. Given the removal of false accusation (lit.: "extending the finger") and malicious speech (lit.: "uttering vain nothings"), given likewise the feeding of the hungry and the satisfying of the afflicted, darkness and gloom shall yield to the brightness of noonday.

PSALM 112:1-9(10)[4-9]

The just one is a light in darkness to the upright.

1 CORINTHIANS 2:1-12, (13-16)[1-5]

The latter part of 1 Cor 1 is important background for today's reading, because in it Paul sets up important pairs of opposites: wisdom versus folly (absurdity);

signs-wisdom versus Christ crucified; weak versus strong; lowborn-despised versus "somebodies." In a word, the cross is the polar opposite of all that this world esteems, yet this sure symbol of weakness in human eyes is the very strength of God. The experience of salvation (v. 18) is normative in Paul's argument. The only proper subject of a human boast (v. 29) is God's gift: Christ Jesus, our wisdom, our justice, our sanctification, our redemption (v. 30).

Paul then moves on in this reading to what seems to be troubling him. He brought to Corinth the only message that is of any lasting worth, namely, God's gracious action through the cross, and now he finds the Corinthians engaged in vainglorious boasting over their apostolic pedigrees—in modern terms, their "spiritual directors" or "former pastors." He is heartily sick of it. We know from 2 Corinthians in particular how deeply hurt he was to be by the repudiation of his person, but here he tries to keep the argument on the plane of principle, not person. What is at issue is his message and his preaching (v. 4). Paul grants the shortcomings of his mode of presentation, giving us some idea of why he thinks he is being discounted as a preacher and teacher ("weakness," "fear," "trepidation," v. 3; lack of "persuasive characteristics" of "wise argumentation," v. 4). The Corinthians have things all wrong by Paul's standards. For him, their values were nonvalues from the outset. He had brought them something different, namely, the "convincing power of the Spirit" (v. 4) and they had not recognized it, as their subsequent foolish boasting showed. The power of God, not the wisdom of men, has literally been the underpinning of their faith (v. 5) but they have not known this, even up to the time of the distressing reports that have reached him from Chloe's household (cf. 1:11).

Is Paul piqued by the claims made in favor of the eloquence of the Alexandrian Jew Apollos, whom Acts 18:24 describes as "learned" or "eloquent"? We would be able to answer in the negative, so studiously does Paul avoid any personal reference in his tirades against false wisdom (1:20, 22; 2:6f; 3:18ff, etc.), but for one detail. In citing Isa 29:14 in 1:19—and not following the LXX closely—he cannot be unaware of the force of the play on words involved:

"*Apolō* (I will destroy) *tēn sophían tōn sophōn kai tēn sýnesin tōn synetōn athetēsō* (the wisdom of [their] wise) and the understanding of their prudent I will obscure." Paul has preached divine wisdom embodied in the person of the crucified Christ. He has known the power of God as one among those who are "being saved" (1:19). The reports that have reached him on the misconceptions among the Corinthians, including the childish claims they are making in favor of eloquence and learning (Apollos) and an apostolic link to Jerusalem (Cephas), confirm Paul in the rightness of his course.

In 2:1 the reading, "the mystery" (*mystērion*) of God found in p[46], a third-century Chester Beatty papyrus at Ann Arbor, seems preferable to the "testimony" (*martyrion*) of the later Sinaiticus and Vaticanus, thus "proclaiming the mystery or plan of God hitherto kept secret" rather than "the testimony of God," as in the KJV.

ALLELUIA. JOHN 1:14 AND 12B

The word of God became a man and lived among us. He enabled those who accepted him to become children of God.

MATTHEW 5:13[-16]20

Salt sayings are related to wisdom in rabbinic literature, a detail that ties this reading in with the first two. In common modern parlance, an insipid person (lit.: one without taste or tang) is, in the rich vocabulary of Muhammad Ali, just a chump. Similarly, *mōranthēi* (v. 13), rendered "loses its taste" in NRSV, NAB, can also mean "is foolish," i.e., is characterized by the *mōría* (folly) that Paul reprobates and commends in two different senses (1 Cor 1:18, 21). The "you" (pl.) of v. 13 are the disciples of Jesus who presumably have not gone the way of the conventional wisdom of the emerging Iavneh school of Rabbinic interpretation. Reams have been written on "tasteless salt" as some granular compound mistaken for sodium chloride, but an impossible contradiction seems to be intended—real salt that no longer has taste. Hence Jesus' followers are by definition those who provide wisdom in interpretation of the Law, not folly, just as they must be agents of light if they are to fulfill their calling.

Various salt and light sayings found in Mark and Q have been woven into this twofold short parable (i.e., v. 13; vv. 14ff.) by Matthew (cf. Mark 9:50; 4:21; Luke 14:34f.; 8:16; 11:33).

If the sayings are not to be understood in praise of the faithful disciples of Jesus, Matthew may be couching them as he does to threaten the hearers of his church with the dire consequences of infidelity.

๛

Sixth Sunday after the Epiphany [6] / Sixth Sunday of the Year / Proper 1 (A)

If this is the Sunday before Ash Wednesday, this Proper may be replaced, in those Churches using Transfiguration readings on this day, by the readings for the Last Sunday after the Epiphany.

DEUTERONOMY 30:15-20

Surprisingly, this passage does not occur on a Sunday in LM but on a weekday, although vv. 10-14 are read on Sunday 15 (C). The people of Israel, new in the land to which their God has led them, are enjoined to keep the commandments if they would live and prosper there. The alternative is to disregard the LORD's statutes and decrees, a program that has about it the smell of death. All human history supports the relation of sin to mortality, despite the repeated observations of Job and the psalmist that the wicked prosper and the just languish. Numerous psalms, however, observe that while the good and the bad alike go down to *sheol* they do so in two quite different conditions. "Life and death" are the options held out, "the blessing and the curse" (v. 19). Some of the options for life are having children, caring for the aged, feeding the famished, being solicitous for the sick, taking no human life on any pretext, and burying the dead out of respect for their life. All these are choices against dying and in favor of living. The Israelites were not brought to Canaan nor are we put on the earth to destroy or diminish others or let circumstances lay them low. It is the most sacred human trust after "loving the LORD your God" (v. 20). On second thought, these are one and the same trust; there are not two: "The love of God is this: that we obey his commandments. And his commandments are not burdensome" (1 John 4:3; cf. Deut 30:16).

SIRACH 15:15[16]-20[21]

Jesus, son of Eleazar, son of Sirach, remembered the wise instruction of his grandfather well and conveyed it in pithy proverbial form (50:27 and the preface). This collection of Israel's corporate wisdom was included in the canon of the Jews in the diaspora, the Septuagint, but the Rabbis of Iavneh and Beit Shearim (House of the Remnant) in Galilee suspected its linguistic parentage. Only since the discovery of Hebrew manuscripts of Sirach ranging from 1896–1900 to 1931 and 1956 (the latter at Masada, of pre-Christian date) have some two-thirds of the book surfaced substantially, and this supports the Greek text. Today's pericope is an example of the "re-reading" of an earlier book in a later because it so closely resembles the one from Deuteronomy above. The metaphor of fire and water touching the outstretched hand for obeying and disobeying God's commandments is one difference. So is the summary statement of God's wisdom, all-seeing eye, and knowledge of every human action (vv. 18f.). One wonders if Paul may have had v. 20 in mind when he heatedly denied the slander of some that his teaching of the justice of God meant that "We say, 'Let us do evil that good may come'" (Rom 3:8). No, God has commanded no one to be wicked, given no one permission to sin.

PSALM 119:1-2, 4-5, 17-18, 33-34

Happy are they who follow the Law of the LORD.

1 CORINTHIANS 3:1-9

Paul continues the distinction between the spiritual and the unspiritual, the mature and the immature that he has begun in 2:14ff. When he came to Corinth he taught the people there who became believers about "God's wisdom, secret and hidden" (2:7). He had received "not the spirit that is of the world, but the Spirit that is from God" (v. 12a) and this enabled him to transmit the gifts of that Spirit to all. But some have made no progress in his absence. They have returned to their unspiritual condition (2:14); they are still on a diet of spiritual milk, not having grown up to handle solid food. The contrast in this passage as elsewhere in Paul's correspondence is between *pneûma* (spirit), the gift of openness to heavenly wisdom and *sarx* (flesh), resistance to it. He writes in anger more than sorrow because their jealousy and quarreling has such a fragile foundation: human figures, the men who baptized them (3:4f.; cf. 1:12). The major split seems to be between Paul and an Apollos party with Cephas thrown in because his reputation as first among Jesus' disciples was known (he may already have been in Corinth on his way to Rome) and, in heavy sarcasm, Christ himself, made an icon of partisanship. That last, however, has a prophetic touch for all subsequent ages since the authors of schism and heresy, even of division in local congregations, will forever after claim to be "with the Lord." Their followers will echo that claim while it is in fact the human teacher who has won their loyalty. It is important to note that Paul never expresses envy at Apollos's evident gifts (see Acts 18:24f.). He can live quite at ease with the contribution to the furtherance of the gospel of this Alexandrian Jew—a powerful lesson to ministers at any level tempted to confuse their gifts with the Spirit's power.

1 Corinthians 2:6-10

For a commentary, see (previous) Fifth Sunday after Epiphany [5] (A).

Matthew 5:[17-]21-37

The bulk of this chapter after the beatitudes (see 4 Epiphany [4] A) and the figures of salt and light has been called "The New Ethic: Its Basic Legal Principles and Six Hypertheses" (Benedict T. Viviano, O.P., commenting on "The Gospel according to Matthew," in *New Jerome Biblical Commentary*, ed. R. E. Brown, J. A. Fitzmyer, R. E. Murphy [Englewood Cliffs, N.J.: Prentice Hall, 1990], 631). Hypertheses are what they are, and not antitheses as is commonly said, since the Jewish teacher Jesus would never have taken a stand against Mosaic Law nor Matthew reported it in his struggle with his Rabbinic contemporaries. Abolition of the Law was the last thing Jesus was up to. Matthew calls his teaching its fulfillment *(plērōsai)* rather than the usual Rabbinic opposite, "to abrogate," namely, "to fulfill" or "confirm" (5:17). In a quick succession of figures Matthew's Jesus speaks harshly of anyone who would mitigate a commandment or counsel breaking it (vv. 17ff.). The prohibitions culminate in a positive description of Jesus' teaching as contrasted with that of Matthew's contemporaries with whom he is in contest. Commentators of an earlier century have dubbed it "the higher righteousness" (see 5:20), although that noun does not occur. Justice as practiced by Jesus' followers obedient to the Law is one that "surpasses" or "outstrips" (aorist subjunctive, *persisseúsē*) that characteristic of scribal or Pharisee fidelity to the precepts. The Gospel proceeds to show this by examples, choosing six commandments from Torah for illustration: the prohibitions of murder (v. 21; Exod 20:13) and adultery (v. 27; Exod 20:14); divorce by a man as taken for granted (Deut 20:13f.) and later qualified (24:1-4); the command not to swear falsely (Lev 19:12), to retaliate for an injury only in limited fashion (v. 39; Exod 21:23ff.) and to love the neighbor (v. 43; the "as yourself" of Lev 19:18 is omitted). An observation about each of the last two is in order, first, that "an eye for an eye," etc., is an expression of Jewish clemency, not revenge, since neighboring pagan peoples put no limits on their retaliatory conduct; it was cruelty unbounded. Second, "and hate your enemy" (v. 43) is found nowhere in the Bible but was a popular expansion of the love command that is there. That said, the more important observation is that Jesus does not set himself against any Mosaic precept, which would be unthinkable. The phrase, "But I say to you," adversative in form, is not that but standard among the later Rabbis to signal building on the spirit of a commandment. Tons of ink have been spilled establishing that Jesus contravened the harshness of a half-dozen biblical commands, pitting Christianity against its parent Israel. Not so. Like the grain of sand in the oyster that is the irritant that makes the pearl, the teaching of the late first-century Pharisees as Matthew perceived it served as counterpoint for the Mosaic observance of the Jesus community. It is regrettable that the interpretations provided are so few. It remains for the Johannine literature (apart from Revelation) and the second century *Didachē,* Ignatius, Justin, and other apologists to tell us how the early communities were living Jesus' interpretations of the Law. In the short run Matthew's brief exposition followed by the rest of the Sermon on the Mount (chaps. 6–7) gives us a very clear idea.

Jesus' stricture against lust (5:28) means true lust, the desire to have sex with another woman or another's wife were it not for the inconvenient circumstance of a violent response by the husband. It does not mean gazing on her appreciatively at length—as Jimmy Carter took it to mean in an interview in a men's magazine while running for president. Nothing needs to be said about the Hebraic hyperbole that counsels cutting off limbs or gouging out eyes. They are ways of saying, "Don't even *think* of it!" Christians have often made the cruel mistake of supposing that Jesus' rabbinic contemporaries taught that only overt acts were sins while he introduced the idea of inner intent as potentially sinful. This view is quite wrong. The Rabbis long held the position that intention *(kavvana)* determined the sinfulness or justness of an act.

The "hell" of v. 30, *gehenna* in Greek, is not *sheol,* the grave or underworld, but the valley of Hinnom south of ancient Jerusalem. It contained the city's refuse dump that burned constantly in full view. The picture language of Isa 66:24 was further built on by this text to create the image of banishment from the presence of God. But that tragic state, if there be any self-condemned to it, can have no relation to fire. The Gentile inability to comprehend pictorial Semitic speech has kept centuries of Christians from seeing the reality behind the figure.

A second, perhaps more compelling reason is that, if the "unchastity" is taken to be the woman's ("marital infidelity" in NIV and TEV), how can this adulterous wife be then "caused to commit adultery" (v. 32a)? It makes no sense. If her marriage to another man after having been divorced is adultery in him (v. 32b), would not Matthew be mitigating Jesus' stern prohibition against all divorce initiated by men (see Mark 10:9 and Luke 16:18) by allowing it in one case? The only reason the second man could be considered adulterous would be Jesus' conviction that her first marriage was indissoluble despite her conduct. Hence there is no exception to the prohibition in the case of her infidelity. If, however, *porneía* here means something other than adultery or "fornication" (as in KJV and DRC) for which "unchastity" is an inadequate translation, namely, impermissible consanguinity, then no problem exists. The Matthew community could well have a problem in Mosaic Law over such closely related couples and declare the union terminated as no true marriage. Both new Christians could then be free to marry. (For this understanding of *porneía*, see Reginald H. Fuller on Matt 5:32, in James L. Mays, ed., *Harper's Bible Commentary* [San Francisco: HarperCollins, 1988], 957.)

As to the false swearing of 5:33–37 that Lev 19:12 proscribes (the same with vows lightly taken, Deut 23:23), Jesus reiterates the prohibition. He names four verbal dodges current in his day that fail to invoke the name of God, so that the oath-taker may later say he was not bound. Italians swear "By Bacchus," the British "by Jupiter" ("Jove" in the ablative) but with no such intent. The Society of Friends has always taken the prohibition to be of any oaths, not just false ones, so that President Herbert Hoover (a Quaker) "affirmed" on March 4, 1928, that he would uphold the Constitution, not swearing to it on a Bible. President Richard Nixon was not so impeded by his Quaker heritage.

❧ ❧

Seventh Sunday after the Epiphany [7] / Seventh Sunday of the Year / Proper 2 (A)

See the note for Proper 1.

LEVITICUS 19:1-2, 9[17]-18

This book, largely of priestly authorship, is concerned in good part with the laws and rubrics of Temple worship. Chapters 17–26 are often called the Holiness Code, the framework within which this lection occurs. The injunction, "You shall be holy, for I the LORD your God am holy" (v. 2), can be called the leitmotiv of the book. Chapter 19 contains a number of disparate precepts ranging from some of the bedrock commands of Sinai (vv. 11-16) to specific ordinances of ritual purity meant as signs of interior intimacy with the LORD. After reminders of respect for parents, Sabbath observance, the evil of idol worship, and propriety in the offering of sacrifice, some stern measures are listed demanding justice. Fields and vineyards are not to be harvested or picked bare but a surplus left for gleaners among the poor and the alien. In contemporary societies the underclass is frequently not as well provided for. The specifications against ways of theft and fraud have a modern ring (vv. 11-13), as does concern for the physically handicapped (v. 14). In the matter of total impartiality, one wonders if partiality to the poor was ever a problem, then or now (v. 15). Surely the modern outcries against welfare legislation and hiring or admissions standards that look to race or need are raised by people who would think the Bible an ancient irrelevance. The same can be said of its strong repudiation of slanderous speech (nowadays, "character assassination") and long-held grudges (vv. 16ff.). A new sin has yet to be invented.

PSALM 119:33-40

PSALM 103:1-4, 8, 10, 12-13

The LORD is kind and merciful.

1 CORINTHIANS 3:10-11, 16-23

Last Sunday's reading from this epistle ended with St. Paul's twofold metaphor of the church at Corinth as "God's field, God's building" (3:9). He continues the latter image by envisioning himself as having laid the foundation, with a veiled admonition to any who would subsequently build on it regarding the care they must take. Paul cannot help but be apprehensive about the teachers who have come after him (v. 10). He immediately regrets the inference some might draw that he thought himself to be the foundation and so he declares emphatically that the sole foundation is Jesus Christ the LORD (v. 11). The next verses, omitted from the lection, seem to be a clear warning to those who have succeeded him in Corinth to do the job well lest they barely survive a conflagration on the building site (vv. 12ff.). This threat, it might be noted, was used by some medieval theologians as an argument for a state of purgation of forgiven sinners after death. Others never espoused or abandoned it because the apostle was clearly employing the figure for another purpose.

He resumes his case with a further image, the congregation of the baptized as God's Temple, knowing full well that Jerusalem's Temple was still standing. This concept of Christ's glorified body as the new Temple must have had wide currency, as John 2:19 and all of Hebrews, with Jesus as chief offerer of sacrifice and its victim testify. Paul relates the concepts of believers in Christ as individually members of his body (12:27), the edifice in which fitting praise to God is offered (Col 1:17-19), to the Spirit's dwelling within each one's body as a temple (6:19). Departing from this imagery in today's pericope, he returns to his insistence on where true wisdom lies (and the folly that is its opposite) by a simple repetition of his theme, naming names and abetted by biblical quotations (3:18ff.; Job 5:13; Ps 94:11). Paul's conclusion is global and, in his familiar cosmic order, ranges upward. All on earth in life or death, in the now or in the yet to be, is the Corinthians' possession, and Christ possesses them, and he is possessed by God (3:22f.).

MATTHEW 5:38-48

See the commentary on Luke 6:27-38 for the Seventh Sunday of the Year, Proper 2 (C) for differences from Matthew in this Q passage.

❧❧❧

Eighth Sunday after the Epiphany [8] / Eighth Sunday of the Year / Proper 3 (A)

See the note for Proper 1, above.

ISAIAH 49:8-16A[14-15]

The second Song of the Servant of YHWH, Isa 49:1-3 (see 42:1-9; 50:4-11; 52:13—53:12), contains the continuing address of the LORD to a servant people. The servant people's task is to establish the land of Judah—actually reestablish it—by summoning the exiles ("prisoners in darkness") to show themselves and return homeward on desert paths (vv. 9f.). The better known leveling of mountains and hills and preparing of a high road in the Baptist's cry on Jordan's bank (Isa 40:3f.) is repeated here in v. 11. The returning Judahites will come from every direction (v. 12) as the heavens and earth, the mountains and hills sing for joy in praise of YHWH's compassion for the exiled sufferers (v. 13). Zion would be wrong to say—as evidently many exiles had said—that the LORD had forsaken it. The idea is unthinkable. From that day far distant from ours, when mothers did not abandon their infant children, the compassion and concern they had for them is made the image of YHWH's total care. Undoubtedly the text was chosen by the framers of LM (vv. 14f. only) and RCL as a foreshadowing of God's solicitous oversight spelled out by Jesus in today's Gospel passage. At the same time, the metaphor of a woman and her nursing child is peculiarly suitable to the season of Epiphany, as many Reformation churches designate this time before Lent.

PSALM 131

PSALM 62:2-3, 6-9

The LORD will bring light to all that is hidden in darkness.

1 CORINTHIANS 4:1-5

In the eleven centuries before Steven Langton, archbishop of Canterbury, introduced chapter divisions and fourteen centuries before Robert Etienne, a Reformed printer-publisher of Basel, introduced verse divisions, Paul had been speaking of two of his apostolic colleagues in what became 3:21ff. He then moves smoothly from the mention of Cephas, Apollos, and himself into a description of their actual role in the spread of the gospel: not as baptizing persons to whom anyone belonged (see 1:12) but as servants of Christ *(hypērétas)* and stewards *(oikonómous)* of the "mysteries" of God (4:1). That last term, *mystēría* has served the Eastern churches well for what the West calls sacraments. Trustworthiness is or ought to be the characteristic of stewards. Paul knows that all who serve the Corinthian community in any capacity are being subjected to judgment and so he says: "Hold off! The Lord's advent is the proper time for that and he will be the judge." It is good advice for today's judgmental age in which the ministers of a congregation, male and female, are often subjected to unhealthy criticism. Short of passing judgment on their immorality, on their fiscal or other incompetence or criminal behavior, holding off until Christ judges them seems to have a certain merit.

MATTHEW 6:24-34

A young colleague once mentioned to me that he was offering a graduate seminar on God's providence. The venture is not as foolhardy as it might at first sound; biblical warrant for it is found on many pages. It was a reality for the English dissident Roger Williams, late of Salem, who named a settlement at the head of Narragansett Bay and two others on an island in the bay "The Providence Plantation." The collection of Jesus' remembered sayings that make up chaps. 5–7 begins in today's lection with a warning against the divided heart in favor of the single eye. The first mutually exclusive pair are God and money ("wealth" renders the Semitic *mammon* weakly). "Devoted to" and "despise" again render the stark Hebraic "love" and "hate" less well. The familiar (to some) "Be not solicitous" is gone in favor of "Do not worry," but that is all right. Worry is what most people do about the security that money brings. Those who have meager funds can do little else, however great their trust in a providential God. For centuries Jesus has been ridiculed for his utopian view of his heavenly Father's providing food and drink and clothing (v. 31). "It is happening in *Utōpia*, they say—"No Place" on this planet earth. But Jesus' examples must be examined with care. "We have to feed the birds," said the two thoughtful children in *Mary Poppins*. But they did not really have to. You never see a flock of birds lying around dead on the ground. They manage somehow. It is the same with an acre of field flowers—probably anemones, say the experts in Israel's flora. God takes care of creatures according to their kind, and the human kind is different from that of *pájaro* or posey. We have the brains to manage. That is the way the Father cares for us, apart from wars or the natural disasters that befall the just and the unjust alike. Nature is rich and acts on our behalf. It is our fellowmen who often do not. The fabled *mañana* of Latino speech must not be taken as simply dilatory by the Northern Hemisphere that wants everything ASAP. It can be an indication, in Jesus' spirit, that today's troubles are not worth the time lost in worry. The Irish journalist who was asked if *mañana* had the same meaning in Ireland as in Spain said, "Yes, but perhaps not with the same sense of urgency."

ℕ.ℊℕ

Ninth Sunday after the Epiphany /
Ninth Sunday of the Year [9] / Proper 4 (A)

The following readings are for Churches whose calendar requires this Sunday, and do not observe the last Sunday after the Epiphany as Transfiguration. For commentaries see under Sundays of the Year after Season of Pentecost, Proper 4. [9] (A) / Ninth Sunday of the Year (A).

DEUTERONOMY 11:18-21, 26-28

PSALM 31:1-5, 19-24[2-4, 17, 25]

The earth is full of the goodness of the LORD.

ROMANS 1:16-17; 3:22B-38, (29-31)[21-25, 28]

MATTHEW 7:21[27]-29

Last Sunday after the Epiphany
(in churches where it is observed as Transfiguration Sunday)

EXODUS 24:12-18

This account is complex, and the experts are not agreed on its sources or the mode of its final editing. See The Body and Blood of Christ (B) for commentary on vv. 3-8 and their setting. The Ten Commandments have been delivered to Moses on Sinai amidst thunder and lightning, clouds and thick darkness (20:1-21). To this account a body of legislation has been appended (chaps. 20–23). The present chapter reports on the ratification of the treaty God holds out to the people. It is described as happening in two stages, a great banquet of sacrificed meats at the foot of the mountain (vv. 5, 11) and the sprinkling of blood against the altar Moses has erected. The ritual act is accompanied by the people's spoken outcry that they will be obedient to the terms of the covenant. A surprising, direct vision of God by Moses and Aaron, Nadab and Abihu in the heavenly court follows (vv. 9-11) and then today's pericope. Moses is summoned up to the mountain (v. 12) where, confusingly, he already is. He ascends with Joshua, leaving Aaron and Hur below, and is given the stone tablets—but not before a six-day wait somewhere on the cloud-covered summit. This enshrouding presence and a devouring fire represent "the glory of the LORD." Moses goes up on the mountain yet again and remains there the forty days and forty nights of Noah's deluge before the ark landed on another mountain (Gen 7:17) and Elijah's flight from Jezebel to the mountain of God, Horeb (1 Kgs 19:8). Matthew (4:2) and Luke (4:2) will assign the same span for Jesus' stay in the desert, while Luke alone in Acts has the glorified Jesus remain on earth teaching the disciples for forty days (1:3). It is the biblical span for a great event adopted by the Second Testament from the First.

PSALM 2 OR PSALM 99

2 PETER 1:16-21

For a commentary see Transfiguration (August 6) after Year C.

MATTHEW 17:1-9

For a commentary see Second Sunday in Lent (A).

❧ Season of Lent ❧

❧❧
Ash Wednesday (A, B, C)

JOEL 2:1-2, 12-17[18] OR ISAIAH 58:1-2

See Proper 1 [5] (A).

Judah's crops were devoured by successive swarms of locusts some time around 400 B.C., variously described as of the species cutting, swarming, hopping, and destroying (1:4). Joel employs the catastrophe to illustrate the impending "day of the LORD" (2:1). He sees in the predatory creatures that approached in clouds and darkness an army in battle array (2:2), again as flames over the scorched earth (v. 3) and an onset of war-horses (v. 4) and warriors (v. 7). The locusts must have flown or hopped up walls and entered the windows of houses (v. 9) in such a swarm as to darken the sun, moon, and stars (v. 10). Yet the voice of the LORD commanding the troops of faithful Judahites is stronger (v. 12), summoning them to repentance despite this plague (vv. 12-14). The prophet calls for a holy fast, a solemn assembly of people of every age and condition including the temple priests who are to weep, crying: "Parce, Domine, populo tuo" (Vulgate). The mournful melody of the chant is still heard in the churches, "Spare, O LORD, spare your people." Lent took on the character of a season of fasting and repentance when the long-baptized decided to emulate the penitential aspect of the adult candidates for baptism on the home stretch of their two- or three-year catechumenate. Lent, however, is a joyous preparation for Easter and a renewal of one's baptismal promises. It should not be thought of as a six-week retrojection of the paschal three days, or, rather, one long Good Friday.

PSALM 51:1[3]-17

Be merciful, O LORD, for we have sinned.

2 CORINTHIANS 5:20—6:[2]10

In their role as ambassadors of Christ, Paul and his team of evangelizers make an appeal in God's name, an entreaty on behalf of Christ to the recalcitrant Corinthians to be reconciled *(katallágēte)* to God (5:20). Reconciling a world out of joint to its maker is the business Christ has been up to. He has then "entrusted the work of reconciliation to us," the heralds of the gospel (v. 19). One of Paul's boldest declarations follows, namely, that God's agent of reconciliation who has no need of it has, nonetheless, in solidarity with those who do, been made "sin who knew no sin, so that in him we might be made the righteousness of God" (5:21). Lent is a season of reminder of the healing of the age-old breach; it is "the acceptable time . . . the day of salvation" (6:2, quoting Isa 49:8). The catalogue of hardships that Paul and his associates have endured on the Corinthians' behalf is not put forward as a boast (vv. 4-10). In the powerful rhetoric of opposites, Paul simply reminds the people that he and the others have a claim on their gratitude. Because a congregation's ministerial team has as its sole work reconciling its members to each other and all to God, it is fitting to remind them in this season, in no spirit of self-pity, that the setbacks and rebuffs of congregation/parish service for clergy and people alike are the coin of penitential practice.

MATTHEW 6:1-6; 16[18]-21

The Sermon on the Mount is a collection of Jesus' remembered teachings delivered on many occasions but organized according to sense. Today's lectionary portion has two such warnings about ostentation or public show, one with respect to almsgiving (vv. 2-4), the other concerned with praying so as to be seen (vv. 5-8). The latter leads into the prayer that Jesus taught with a coda on forgiveness, following which a third reprobated display of piety accompanies fasting (vv. 16-18). This brief, threefold catechism of recommended action for the Matthew church is positive in sense although negative in form. Jesus' followers are to be modest in bearing, doing nothing to bring attention to themselves in their deeds of piety *(dikaiosýnēn,* v. 6, the Aramaic *tsedaqa* that is the modern Jewish term for charitable giving). One wonders how much hyperbole is employed in the passage. Were there real trumpets in the streets or in synagogue prayer other than the shofar on Rosh haShanah or Yom Kippur? The Mishnah on fasting *(Ta'anith)* prescribes much blowing of the shofar in times of crisis. And, although standing for prayer in public places was a reality—still to be seen occasionally on a bus or plane— was the stance so dramatic as to remind Jews of the Greek theater they did not have *(hypokritaì* of v. 2, the word for actors)? A tractate of the Mishnah calls charitable deeds one of the three things by which the world is upheld *(Abot* 1.2;

cf. *Peah* 1.1), the Law and Temple service being the other two. So eleemosynary giving and fasting and prayer are to be the traditional acts of Jesus' believing Jews, but with none of the attendant drama. For them, quiet, even secret prayer is in order. They are already rewarded because their Father in heaven sees them. Their treasure is being stored up with God.

🛥🛥
First Sunday in Lent (A)

GENESIS 2:[7-9] 15-17; 3:1-7

The six days of separation of the Priestly account and what was done on each of them are matters well known, but rehearsing them should do no harm (Gen 1:1—2:4): light from darkness; the waters above from those below; the waters below from the dry land; the light for the day from that for the night; sea creatures from the birds of the sky; the wild beasts from the cattle, and humankind from all the rest. The parallel creation account of the Yahwist, containing certain Elohist elements, occurs in 2:5-25. In sequence, the things formed in it (the normal word for a potter's work) are: the man (v. 7), a garden in Eden (v. 8), various trees including two especially singled out (v. 9), wild and domestic animals and birds (vv. 19f.), and the woman (vv. 21ff.). The J–E narrative continues through chaps. 3–4, resuming with the "generations" of 5:1.

"YHWH Elohim" is used throughout, a sign of the fusion of J and E. In v. 7 God forms the man *(ha 'adam)* from the clay of the earth *('adamah)*, breathes into his nose the breath of life, and the man becomes a living being. The term for clay or soil has been less aptly translated "the dust of the ground." The cognate status of the words for "the man" and "earth" are what is important here. They are related to the Hebrew words for "red" and "to be red," qualities deriving from iron in the soil. Paul will refer to this text in 1 Cor 15:47 (see below, 7(C), Proper 2). The P author has male and female created together (1:26f.). In J the LORD makes man first, then woman out of his bone and flesh (2:21ff.). Man is not only the clay of earth, he lives by the breath of God.

Creation had succeeded a "formless wasteland" in P *(tohu vabhohu,* 1:2) which later in the same verse turns out to be a watery chaos, the abyss *(tehom).* The image employed by J is that of a parched land succeeded by an oasis with trees and rivers, a "garden in Eden, in the east." The dry earth is a Palestinian image, the lush garden probably one borrowed from Eastern mythology (see Ezek 28:12-19, where the king of Tyre is ejected from "Eden, the garden of God" by a cherub, cast to earth, and reduced to dust; observe the occurrence of the precious stones of Gen 2:12 in

28:13). "Eden" is from the Akkadian *edinu*, basically the Sumerian word *eden*, meaning "plain"; the vowel quantity of the first letter differentiates it from the Hebrew word for "pleasure" or "enjoyment" with which it was soon associated. One interesting facet of the J myth is the "stream rising from the earth" (v. 6) before the LORD God sent the rains. Some moisture was evidently needed to make the dust into clay for God to form man, as a potter might do.

The trees of the garden provide food and esthetic pleasure in the ordinary way (v. 9a). One is a mythical "tree of life" (v. 9b), of which nothing more is heard until Proverbs (3:18; 11:30; 13:12; 15:4). There it is a symbol of wisdom, the fruit of virtue, a desire fulfilled, and a gentle tongue. The other tree "of the knowledge of good and evil" (vv. 9b, 17) "in the middle of the garden" (3:3) employs a possessive construction unique in the Bible, whereas the objective "to know good and evil" (3:5, 22) is quite usual. It is supposed that the former derives from the latter.

The serpent was known for cunning in the ancient world (cf. "wise as serpents," Matt 10:16), not only because of the shedding of skin and starting afresh after hibernation but also because earth habitation was thought to have put the snake in touch with the spirits of ancestors. The ability of the poisonous asp to bite the leg of the farmer in the field, all unwary, contributed to the legend of the snake's cleverness. The Yahwist sets aside any connection with wisdom and healing (cf. Num 21:4-9, the "seraph of bronze"; the Canaanite god Eshmun, like the Greek Asklepios, healed with snakes entwined on a staff), and makes his cunning exclusively evil. Not everyone agrees that the Hebrew of 3:1a has interrogative force. E. A. Speiser (*Genesis* [Anchor Bible; Garden City, N.Y.: Doubleday, 1964], 21) has a syntactical difficulty with translating the words as a question and renders it: "Even though God told you not to eat of any tree of the garden . . ." with the woman then interrupting the serpent. The LORD's prohibition of 2:17 had only been of the "tree of knowledge of good and bad"; this the woman informs the serpent of, calling it "the tree in the middle of the garden" (3:3). The couple's knowledge of good and bad can be deduced from the outcome of shame at their nakedness (2:25; 3:7) to be something different from the general power of moral discretion. Cf. 2 Sam 19:36, where the eighty-year-old Barzillai uses the phrase to describe capacity for sense pleasure. The godlike wisdom of Enkidu in the Gilgamesh epic (tablet 1, col. iv, 11, 16ff.) is a matter of sexual knowledge, i.e., experience. Enkidu is then clothed by the woman who has seduced him, in a set of correspondences with Genesis 3 that should not lightly be set aside.

The dialogue on death concerns physical death (vv. 3f.) and recalls not only the tree of life of this narrative but also the tale of Adapa and the human being's search for immortality that is central to Gilgamesh epic. Utnapishtim survives the flood and Gilgamesh is briefly given a magic plant to rejuvenate him—which a serpent ultimately steals.

The dependence of the J author on Mesopotamian material is clearer than the precise use he wishes to make of it. This much is evident: humans are fated to death, not deathlessness, and the secret of procreation, while shared with man and woman, remains the LORD's possession. They have "knowledge" now, but their knowledge is no threat to the godlike wisdom of YHWH Elohim. Its acquisition is also used to explain the nomad's horror of nudity, the "shame" of which is a ritual taboo rather than a sexual one (Max Weber, *Ancient Judaism* [New York: The Free Press, 1952], 191ff.), in opposition to the orgiastic displays of the Canaanite priesthood.

See Proper 22 [27] B for commentary on Gen 2:18-24 and the Feast of Mary's Having Been Conceived Sinless (December 8) on Gen 3:9-15, 20.

ROMANS 5:12-19

Commentaries on the passages that lead up to this one are found on Trinity Sunday (C) and Proper 6 [11], below.

Paul's paralleling of Adam and Christ has invested "the man" of Gen 1–3 with an importance in Christian catechesis that is probably far greater than that intended by the Apostle. His stress is on "the gracious gift of one man, Jesus Christ" (v. 15)—an emphasis found everywhere in his writings—rather than on the progenitor of a sinful humanity found only here and in 1 Cor 15:22, 45. Paul has been exulting in Christ who is our reconciliation with God (v. 11). The "therefore" with which v. 12 begins is hard to justify logically; it is probably intended as a loose link with the next argument. Certainty of future salvation has just been affirmed (vv. 9-11). The same is now done in another way: we can be as sure that the grace of God will abound for all (v. 15; later, "acquittal" and "life," v. 18; "justification," v. 19) in virtue of Christ's deed, as we are that Adam's sin brought death to the world.

Some, like Bousset and Reitzenstein, have held that the Adam-Christ parallel derives from a myth of the first man as a redeemer-god. Earlier (1895) Gunkel had found traces of a Jewish belief that the events of the beginning will repeat themselves at the end. In Paul's interpretation, Christ will give life to all as Adam first brought life, then death (1 Cor 15:22). W. D. Davies presents the evidence for a cosmic conception of the "first man" in biblical, intertestamental, and rabbinic sources (*Paul and Rabbinic Judaism* [New York: Harper, 1967], 37–39), while C. K. Barrett has commented fully on Paul's analogy in *From First Adam to Last* (London: A. and C. Black, 1962).

Paul takes literally the Genesis story of death's following Adam's sin of disobedience (v. 12) as a punishment. He describes death as universal because sin is universal (cf. also 3:23). The NAB's "inasmuch as" renders *eph' hōi*, which roughly means "because" (NRSV). Had the Vulgate's *in quo* (in whom) been the *quia* (because) it should have been, the Christian world might have been spared the doctrine of original sin in the form in which Augustine, chiefly, passed it along; namely, a transmission of guilt by virtue of physical descent from Adam. Paul is at pains to grant a typological initiation of all sin to Adam; in that sense he can be said to sanction the notion of "in whom." In fact, that is not what he meant, since it is not what he said when he wrote *eph' hōi.*

Original sin is attested in Scripture in the sense that Adam the sinner begot a race that, like him, sinned but not by way of a guilt transmitted by physical descent. What is not to be found in Paul is implied in the extrabiblical 4 Ezra 4:4-34, especially vv. 21f.: "For the first Adam transgressed . . . and likewise also all who were born of him. Thus the infirmity became inveterate; the Law indeed was in the heart of the people, but [in conjunction] with the evil seed."

Paul's argument, if taken strictly, would grant immunity from death to anyone who did not sin. He does not envisage there having been any such person. *Hamartía*—the creature's spirit of rebellion against the Creator—is universal, even if a law was required for it to be "imputed" (KJV, DRC: v. 13). Such was the case in Adam's breaking a "command" (NIV, v. 14), an act that Paul in this verse and the next will call an "offense/transgression/trespass." The distinction here, in more familiar biblical English, is between sin and transgression, the former a universal state of heart, the latter a formal overstepping of bounds, which has as its result that it is "taken into account/reckoned/imputed" (v. 13).

Paul so wishes to stress the reign of death through sin from Adam to Moses that he does not pause to note the Noachian precepts (according to the later Rabbis: against idolatry, blasphemy, incest, murder, and robbery, and in favor of justice by way of the Law courts). Surely an "offense" would have been reckoned against those who disobeyed these demands traditional before Moses' time. Paul's main point is that only by the Law (v. 13) is sin to be identified. It was found worthy of the judgment of condemnation in one instance (v. 16), the trespass or transgression of the "one man" (v. 17). The opposite of Adam's act of sin was God's act of grace, a word rendered as "gift" resulting in "justification" (v. 16).

Paul's analogy is not perfect in balance at all points. His main contrast is between the acquittal and life for many achieved by the one deed of Christ and the offenses imputed to the many sinners who followed the first man, whose one deed was both trespass and disobedience (see vv. 18ff.). Sin brought its train of tragic effects, chiefly death (v. 21), but the grace of justification was its outcome, "eternal life" (v. 21). In order to remove all doubt about a perfect canceling out in his figure of the two races of humanity, Paul says explicitly that grace has abounded all the more despite the increase (v. 20) of sin that came with the promulgation of the Law. The ill effects of the totality of sin and offense from Adam through the entire Mosaic period cannot match the good effects of the grace and gift that were given in Jesus Christ.

GOSPEL. MATTHEW 4:4B

Man does not live on bread alone, but on every word that comes from the mouth of God.

MATTHEW 4:1-11

The temptation narratives of Mark and Luke will be read on the First Sunday of Lent in Years B and C respectively. Commentary on them is given below. That portion should be consulted which deals with Mark 1:12f. rather than vv. 14f. and the Lukan commentary in its entirety since it features his emphases regarding Q material in contrast with those of Matthew.

Matthew 4:4 cites Deut 8:3b; v. 6 Ps 91:11f., and v. 10 Deut 6:13. The Q source makes specific the statement of Mark that Jesus was tempted by Satan in the desert (1:13). He probably does so in terms of the messianic confrontation reported by Matthew, which Luke modifies, as the urgency of the earliest epoch yields to problems of behavior in the community.

ໜ.ഈ
Second Sunday in Lent (A)

GENESIS 12:1-4A

Abram was introduced as the son of Terah in Gen 11:26 among the "descendants of Shem" (11:10), and the chapter ends with the story of Abram's flight from Ur to Haran. Abram's saga proper begins at 11:27. No reason is given for Terah's migration from the land of the Chaldeans to Canaan, interrupted as it was by a protracted stay in Haran (northwest Mesopotamia, modern Turkey; ca. 110 miles northeast of Aleppo, Syria, on the River Balikh, a tributary of the Euphrates). Ancient Ur, excavated in 1929, lies south of the modern Euphrates near An Nāsiriyah, Iraq, not far from the point where the river debouches into the lagoon Hawr al Hammār which, in turn, feeds into the Persian Gulf beyond Ābādan.

There is no compelling reason to consider Abram a fictitious character. A date of ca. 1800 B.C. is reasonable for him. He is not an eponymous ancestor, i.e., no tribe or people takes its name from him. He is the first clearly delineated person to appear in the Bible, as contrasted with types in the strict sense like Adam and Eve, Cain, Abel, and Noah. He remains throughout the Genesis account an upright individual, a man of faith. The story of his call out of Haran upon the death of his father Terah, which constitutes today's lection, is the opening of his saga. One could not learn from this tale of the advanced state of Canaanite civilization into which "Abram the Hebrew" (14:13) came. Only chap. 14, a later insertion, gives us any remote indication of the data that a century of archaeology has revealed to us.

The Priestly classification of three main groups of peoples, the descendants of Noah's sons, Shem, Ham, and Japheth (Gen 10:1), puts Abram's ancestors in with the Semites (vv. 21f.) while the Canaanites are grouped with the largely African offspring of Ham (v. 6). The categories are clearly territorial rather than ethnic. And, as S. Goitein points out, Hebrew is a "Hamite" language in biblical categories because it was spoken by the Canaanites before the Israelites arrived.

The call of Abram (12:2f.) is the first of numerous such poetic oracles. The LORD calls him to be the father of a "great nation" that shall be a "blessing" to the peoples of the earth. Later Jewish writers would see in this designation the people Israel (e.g., Isa 51:2: "Look to Abraham your father and to Sarah who bore you for he was but one when I called him, but I blessed him and made him many"; Ezek 33:24: "Abraham was only one man, yet he got possession of the land; but we [the Israelites] are many; the land is surely given us to possess"). Paul (see Rom 4:16-22) made Abraham's fatherhood consist in his faith rather than in any ethnic primacy, specifically in his belief that the word of the LORD about aged, childless Sarah's having a son (see Gen 18:14) would come true.

Today's reading confines itself to Abram's first trustful act in response to the divine promise; namely, his proceeding with his wife and his nephew Lot (the son of his brother Haran) southwest to the land of Canaan with all the possessions and offspring that had been acquired and begotten during the stay in Haran (v. 5). The *RCL* will continue it in Proper 5 [10]. Once arrived in Canaan, Abram and his family proceed south as far as Shechem, where he builds an altar on the site of the LORD's appearance to him (v. 7). He does the same in the hill country east of Bethel, invoking YHWH by name, then moves on in stages to the Negev, the southern desert (vv. 8-9). His calling God by the proper name is a first for him, but some scribe has seen fit to insert this knowledge as far back as the days of Adam's early descendants (5:26).

PSALM 121[33:4-5, 18-20, 22]

Our help is from the LORD, who made heaven and earth.

Romans 4:1-5, 13-17

Lord, let your mercy be on us, as we place our trust in you.

For a commentary, see Proper 5 [10] A; Lent 2 (B)

2 Timothy 1:8b-10

The counsel to the disciple-recipient of this epistle not to be ashamed of his testimony "about our Lord" (1:8a) or of his model Paul seems to be based on the apostle's similar declaration in Rom 1:16: "For I am not ashamed of the gospel." As to the writer's status as a prisoner, the personal information supplied in 4:10ff. might seem to presuppose Caesarea as the place of composition, with Ephesus as the residence of the addressee (cf. the route attested in Acts 20f.). A difficulty against authenticity, however, is that in 1:17 Paul is described as having been at Rome, while from the data of chap. 4 he has not yet visited there. Nor would Timothy require the information supplied in v. 20, since presumably he was along. The pseudonymous author probably possesses Acts and some Pauline letters but is not interested in plotting Paul's career exactly. He does wish to feature a share in the suffering (v. 8) that the gospel entails and declare it to be overcome by the power of God.

For the author God is the savior who has called Christians "with a holy calling" (v. 9; cf. 1 Thess 4:7), not in response to human works but in accord with God's own "purpose" and "grace." That grace or favor was proffered in Christ Jesus before time began (v. 9) but has "now been revealed through the appearing of our Savior Christ Jesus" (v. 10). Obviously vv. 9f. incorporate a kerygmatic statement of the kind familiar from Eph 3:4f.; 3:9ff; and Rom 16:25f., in which the present age of revelation is contrasted with a former age when all lay hidden.

The term "savior" for Christ, characteristic of the pastorals, appears first in Phil 3:20. It is undoubtedly a contribution of Hellenist Judaism, in which God is described as the life-giver through personal appearance or manifestation. The influence of the cult of savior-deities like Asklepios, Isis, and Serapis is not absent. The appearing (v. 10) of hidden divinity is the operative concept: here, it is the Jesus of history "bringing to light life and immortality through the preaching of the gospel." The hidden God becomes God manifest through the resurrection which, proclaimed and accepted, becomes salvation to believers.

Psalm 121[33:4-5, 18-20, 22]

Lord, let your mercy be on us, as we place our trust in you.

JOHN 3:1-17

See Trinity Sunday (A); 4 Lent (B).

MATTHEW 17:1-9

The author of 2 Peter has gone on the assumption that the account of the Transfiguration was a historical narrative of an anticipation of Jesus' future glory and even inserted himself into it as an eyewitness. It is, however, much more demonstrably an affirmation by the early Church that Jesus was God's chosen servant well before the cross and resurrection and was anticipated as such by the great prophetic servants Moses and Elijah. The reported lack of faith in Jesus by his disciples is all but incomprehensible if they experienced divine epiphanies such as those reported at his baptism and here. Moreover, the words of God in v. 5 are almost identical with those spoken at Jesus' baptism in 3:17, telling us that the evangelist is professing the same christological doctrine in both places. His chief sources are the Old Testament and Jewish eschatology.

Matthew's version follows Mark's very closely, omitting only the phrase about the work of a bleacher (Mark 9:3) and the attribution of fear to the disciples (v. 6). Both have Peter's impetuous blurting out about booths—*sukkoth* in the autumn feast of that name. The disciples fall forward to the ground in awe and are raised up by Jesus in Matthew only (vv. 6f.). Luke is the sole evangelist to speak of Jesus' impending passage *(exodos)* which is about to be fulfilled in Jerusalem (9:31) and to anticipate the detail of the sleep of the disciples in the garden (v. 32; cf. 22:45f.). He alone, also, has the three prophetic figures enter the cloud rather than merely being overshadowed by it (v. 34).

The details of the Gospel account follow closely those of Moses' being summoned apart to the mountain with Joshua his aide (Exod 24:13), the clouds covering the mountain (v. 15), and God's calling to Moses from the midst of the cloud (v. 16) that subsequently envelops him (v. 18). The disciples, like Moses (Exod 33:18-23), experience something of God's glory. Elijah in the cave on Mount Horeb hears the LORD's voice (1 Kgs 19:9), but there the similarity of detail to the career of the great prophet of monotheism ends.

The evangelists have a keen interest in the three prime witnesses to the resurrection, Peter, James and John, who are shown by the Transfiguration narrative to have been able retroactively to discern the glory of God present in the earthly life of Jesus. Many scholars see in this passage a postresurrection appearance of Jesus projected into his earthly life but, if such is the case, it does not satisfactorily account for the details. The theme of the three booths (v. 4) indicates that the evangelists were thinking of the inauguration of the new age. Zechariah 14:16 identifies the fes-

tival of booths with the cult of YHWH as king, while its earliest significance—
the ingathering of the harvest—led to the symbolism first of the bridal bower in the
sacred marriage of the LORD and the people Israel, then of the shelters used by the
children of Israel on pilgrimage. Its conjunction in autumn with the new year in
the postexilic calendar would have filled Christian believers with thoughts of a new
epoch in which Jesus was enthroned as priestly messiah. Peter's statement that "it
is good for us to be here" (v. 4) may have to do with the resting-place of the ark
in Num 10:33 and Ps 132:8—understood as Jesus, the new covenant. The Septuagintal term for that rest is *anapausis* (Heb. *menuah*). *Second Clement* uses it in the
phrase, "rest in the coming kingdom and in eternal life" (5:5; cf. 2 Esdras 2:34-35,
"eternal rest").

❧❧
Third Sunday in Lent (A)

EXODUS 17:1[3]-7

This is one of three water stories in the story of the exodus period, the others being
concerned with the turning of bitter waters to fresh (Exod 15:22-27) and the contention of the people at Kadesh (Num 20:2-13), not Rephidim as here. All are probably the same tale describing an incident late in the wanderings. *Massah* means "test"
(here, the Israelites' testing the LORD; in chap. 15 the LORD's testing them); *meribah*,
"quarreling." Rephidim ("expanses," "stretches") is probably the modern Wadi
Refayid which has an oasis and is in the vicinity of Jebel Musa, the traditional
Mount Sinai south-central in the peninsula. Kadesh is near the pre–Six Day War,
Egypt-Negev border, 'Ain el Qadeis southeast of the town of El Quseima and forty-
five miles southwest of Be'er Sheva. The whereabouts of the desert of Sīn (v. 1) is
likewise unknown. The southern foothills of the central mountainous mass Jebel el
Tîh is one possibility, the desert plain on the coast near modern El 'Arish another.

In this narrative the quarreling is between the Israelites and Moses (vv. 2ff.)
for having brought them out into this waterless waste. The stoning of their leader
(v. 4) would be the supreme indignity and mention of it conveys Moses' state of
near-despair. The "staff with which you struck the river" (v. 5) refers to his
rendering the Nile polluted (cf. 7:17f.). The instrument that made the water
undrinkable for the Egyptians will have the opposite effect for the Israelites. The
LORD makes his promise to Moses "on the rock in Horeb" which may have been
scribally induced from the mention of Mount Hor in Num 20:22. This was probably modern Jebel Maderah some fifteen miles northeast of Kadesh. Numbers 20:23
places it "on the border of the land of Edom."

The source-identity of this passage is uncertain. The selection is as follows: 1a, P; 1b–2; 3, ? J or E; 4–6 ? E; 7a and c, J; 7b, E.

Psalm 95[1-2, 6-9]

If today you hear God's voice, harden not your hearts.

Romans 5:1[2, 5-8]-11

In Rom 4 Paul began his development of Abraham's justifying faith. Abraham hoped "against hope" that he would be the father of many nations as he had been promised (4:18). His faith in his role for the future was credited to him as justice "if we believe in him who raised Jesus our Lord from the dead" (Rom 4:24). It is conventional for some to say of the latter verse and v. 25 (e.g., Buber, Bultmann) that Hebrew *ᵉmunah* is trust in the person of the Lord, whereas Pauline *pistis* is faith in a fact, a deed that God has done in Jesus Christ. Paul would probably be shocked to learn of any such difference and say that he was incapable of thinking like a German professor. He seems to be at pains to show how the Christian believer and the patriarch Abraham are identical in all respects as regards faith in God's promise. Note that 4:24 does not praise the deed of the resurrection or ask faith in it but in the one who did it. Paul cares more—if it were possible—for the faith of Christians in a God who will yet act than in a God who has acted.

Justification by means of faith is already, however, a reality for Paul. It means peace with God for believers (cf. Col 1:21) achieved through Christ the reconciler (5:1; cf. 2 Cor 5:18f.). The present condition of the Christian is grace; with respect to the future it is hope for a share in God's glory. Christ is the person who has made both possible, faith the condition to which God has successfully invited us through him (cf. v. 2). T. W. Manson writes somewhere, "The immediate results of Christ's work are ours through faith."

The road to hope may be a rocky one. Paul traces it by means of stages, the stopping-points of which are affliction/endurance/tested virtue, then hope (vv. 3f.). The hope is not a frustrating kind, because the gift of the Spirit fills our hearts with God's love (v. 5). *Agápē* for Paul, is what to do until the Messiah comes.

The "love of God . . . poured out in our hearts through the Holy Spirit" (v. 5) is our present justification and means peace with God (v. 1). It was all God's doing at God's appointed time "when we were still powerless" (v. 6). More than that, we were "godless" (*asebōn*, v. 6) and "sinners" (v. 7)—in a word, entirely helpless to save ourselves. The "appointed time" (v. 6) indicates not only a compassion on God's part but the divine initiative to save us when we had no merits of our own. That is the whole point of vv. 7f. Rarely does anyone give his life "for one who is just" (v. 7). Paul breaks off his thought and starts afresh: "possibly someone might dare to die for your good man" (v. 7). His "perhaps even" is concessive, a mere hypothesis. In the actual case the facts are all against it. God "demonstrates" (v. 8) the divine love for us by the fact that while we were still sinners Christ died for us. This total nonmeritorious condition shows what the divine *agápē* consists in. It is prevenient, undeserved, and completely reconciling (vv. 9ff.).

See also the commentary on 5:6-11 for Proper 6 [11].

GOSPEL. JOHN 4:42 AND 15

Lord, you are truly the Savior of the world; give me living water that I may never thirst again.

JOHN 4:5-42

Jesus' northward journey to Galilee (vv. 3f.) was on the West Bank, a usual route but hazardous for the Jew because of tensions with the Samaritan population. Ancient Shechem (Heb.: "shoulder") lies within modern Nablus (Vespasian's *Flavia Neapolis*, "New City" named for himself, Flavius Vespasianus), today a sizeable West Bank Palestinian town. Jacob's well is situated within a Greek Orthodox church, across the road from what was a large Israeli jail. Some years ago a hospitable priest accompanied by his shy little daughter invited me to drop a pebble down the shaft and listen for the splash. Upon my second visit nine years later, priest and Israeli conscript—a rapid-fire weapon across his knee—sat chatting amicably across from the mouth of the well, tragically not possible after *intifada* numbers one and two.

John has portrayed Jesus as the fulfillment of ceremonial (2:6-11), liturgical (2:19), and eschatological (3:3, 5) Judaism. Jesus will now heal a breach going back many centuries (cf. Josh 8:30, with "Gerizim" bowdlerized by a later hand and emended to "Ebal" since Gerizim is obviously the mount of blessing of vv. 33f.). See Josh 24:1, 25, 32; 1 Kgs 12:25; 2 Kgs 17:24-41. "To this day they worship according to their ancient rites" (v. 35); "Thus these nations venerated the LORD, but also served their idols" (v. 41); Ezek 16:51; Josephus, *Antiquities* 12.5.5, 12; 259).

Jacob's acquisition of a plot of land in Shechem (v. 5) is described in Gen 33:19; 48:22; Josh 24:32. The Greek text refers to Sychar rather than Shechem (which the Sinaitic Syriac changes to Sichem), 'Askar in modern Arabic. John with his love of paradox has Jesus, the giver of living water (v. 10), ask a woman and a Samaritan at that for a drink at the high point of thirst of the day (v. 6). Verse 9b, "Jews do not use things in common with Samaritans," is probably a reference to the Jewish scruple over purity with respect to a dipper. "God's gift" (v. 10) will be the antitype, "flowing water" (v. 11), which fulfills the type, the standing well-water of Jacob. In taking Jesus literally, the woman engages in the classic Johannine incomprehension preliminary to an explanation of his true meaning. Jesus responds in vv. 13f. that his gift will slake thirst forever, being a fountain in him (Jesus; the better understanding) leaping up to provide the life of the final eon (v. 14). She asks for it, still not comprehending his deeper meaning. He prods her by a reference to her irregular life (vv. 16ff.), a detail conceivably based in fact but much more likely to refer to the Samaritan liaisons with the gods of Babylon, Cuthah, Avva, Hamath, and Sepharvaim, namely, Succoth-benoth, Nergal, Ashima, Nibhaz, and Tartak (2 Kgs 17:30f.). Even their veneration of the LORD was vitiated (vv. 32f.) in Judaean eyes, the probable referent of "and the man you are living with now [on Mount Gerizim] is not your husband" (v. 18).

Jesus' second sight is a commonplace in John (v. 19). The ensuing exchange transcends Samaritan-Jewish differences over the locale of official cult (vv. 21f.), as so frequently happens in this Gospel. The hour is "already here" (v. 23) with the presence of Jesus when those who worship God must do so "in spirit and in truth" (v. 24). Jesus, in other words, represents a rising above all particular forms to what is of God, John's "real" and "true."

This evangelist next makes a faith-declaration in Jesus' messiahship, something inconceivable on Jesus' lips from our knowledge of the first stratum of Gospel material. Mark does something similar in 9:41 ("a cup of water because you bear the name of Christ") and in 14:62 with his, "I am." The embarrassment of the returning disciples is true to what we know of the customs of the time (v. 27) but it is chiefly a bridge to the proclamation of faith in Jesus by a member of a religiously non-Judaean people (v. 29).

The opaqueness of the disciples over Jesus' "food" is another exchange of the kind we have come to expect in John (vv. 33f.). It leads into a discourse of Jesus about harvesting in which he takes two current proverbs (vv. 35, 37), the second one popular in Greek circles, and applies them to the situation typified by the Samaritans' new-found faith (vv. 41f.). "The reaper has overcome the sower; the time of fulfillment has come" (C. K. Barrett in *PC*). By the time the Gospel is written, everyone is indebted to the apostles. The story ends with the statement by the Samaritans that "this man is truly the savior of the world" (v. 42). Despite the historical preeminence of the Jews to whom Jesus belongs (v. 22), a new encompassing of peoples has come to prevail (cf. 3:16).

Jesus is a man on the move (v. 43); it is the Spirit of truth who will remain (cf. John 14:17). John's "after two days" are his normal transition to a biblical third day of fulfillment. Verse 44 is one of the many indications that John knew various Synoptic traditions but used them sparingly (see Mark 6:4; Matt 13:57).

🐦.🐦

Fourth Sunday in Lent (A)

1 SAMUEL 16:1[B, 6-7, 10-13A]-13

The biblical tradition on the radical social change from prophetic priesthood, represented by Samuel and his sons acting as judges, to the monarchy launched with Saul, is more than ambivalent (see chaps. 8–10). Sorting out the historical strands is impossible. The same is true of the co-regency of Samuel and Saul, if it can be so called (chaps. 12–13). The psychological inadequacy of Saul to the new role of kingship in Israel is spelled out in chap. 15, where his failure to enforce the ban (*ḥerem*, total destruction) against the Amalekites—softened by the pious priestly explanation that he had meant to offer the best sheep and oxen in sacrifice—is identified as his downfall.

The first thirteen verses of this chapter seem to be an editorial introduction to the David saga which is a composite of two traditions, one in which he is an unsophisticated tender of his father's sheep and the other in which he is, from earliest youth, a successful guerrilla fighter. Verses 1-5 place Samuel emotionally on the side of the faltering giant Saul (15:35) and have the LORD impelling Samuel to go and surreptitiously anoint David as he previously did Saul (9:14—10:8). His fears over a reprisal by Saul are stilled by a suggestion of the LORD whereby he is to present himself to Jesse, the boy's father, as the itinerant sacrificer of a heifer (vv. 2f., 5).

The son of Jesse the Bethlehemite whom the LORD has in mind has not been specified in v. 1, hence Samuel's wonderment on seeing a likely candidate in Eliab (vv. 6f.), the eldest. In the event, Eliab is not let in on the choice of the younger David, as his dismissal of him as one unfit for the warrior's role makes clear (17:28). The word of the LORD to Samuel about appearance is surely a pious comment of the author on the unsuitability of the imposing but later psychotic Saul (v. 7). The later description of the ruddy and handsome David of the beautiful eyes, however, (v. 12), serves to negate it.

The verses omitted from the public reading name two other of Jesse's seven sons, all instinctively rejected by Samuel.

David is finally produced by his hesitant father in the manner of such tales the world over (v. 11). The shepherding detail is far from unimportant. Instructed by the LORD that "This is he!" (v. 12), Samuel fulfills his clear duty and pours the oil. A large measure of *rûaḥ*—the powerful breath of God—rushes down upon David, and deserts the hapless Saul in the very next verse.

The choice of a Judahite will complicate Israel's history from this point on. Saul had been of Benjamin, Judah's neighbor immediately to the north. Despite their theoretical kinship as the two southern tribes, David's habit of victory—and Saul's defeat at his hands—will succeed in aligning the men of Judah in an uneven contest against all the other tribes.

PSALM 23[1-6]

The LORD is my shepherd; there is nothing I shall want.

EPHESIANS 5:8-14

The author of Ephesians draws freely on the Pauline light-darkness theme (cf. 1 Thess 5:4f.; 2 Cor 6:14; Col 1:12f.). "Children of light" are *tekna phōtòs* here (v. 8) but *huioùs* (sons) *tou phōtòs* in the one use of the phrase in the Synoptics (Luke 16:8). The "sons of light" of John 12:36 appear also in the Dead Sea Scrolls *Manual of Discipline* (1.9 and 3.24) as well as frequently in the War Scroll.

Darkness is the realm of shameful deeds (vv. 11ff.), a commonplace figure in the ancient world. "Everything exposed by the light becomes visible" (v. 14) seems to be an equating of the good deeds of believers with the light that is Christ. We assume that in v. 14 we have a snatch of a lost baptismal hymn. The nonvigilant sleepers of the New Testament are not praised (cf. 1 Thess 5:6ff.; Matt 25:5; 26:40; Luke 12:37). Here as in some other places they are the dead (1 Thess 5:13ff.; 1 Cor 7:39).

A series of cautions follows: against folly (v. 15; cf. Matt 25:1-13), in favor of "making the most of the time" (v. 16; cf. Col 4:5) and discerning the will of the Lord (cf. Rom 12:2; 1 Thess 4:3; 5:18), against drunkenness (v. 18; cf. 1 Tim 3:3), and the encouragement of spiritual song, thanksgiving, and praise.

GOSPEL. JOHN 8:12

I am the light of the world, says the LORD; the one who follows me will have the light of life.

JOHN 9:1-41

Robert Fortna (*The Gospel of Signs* [Cambridge: Cambridge Univ. Press, 1970]) thinks that this pericope was built up by the evangelist from a book of seven signs consisting of 2:1-11; 4:4b-54; 21:2-14; 6:1-14; 11:1-45; 9:1-8; and 5:2-9, 14, which concluded with a passion narrative. Fortna supposes that this "signs source" had as its purpose proving Jesus' messiahship by his works of power.

Clearly the narrative is an expansion of the saying of 8:12: "I am the light of the world. Whoever follows me will never walk in darkness but will have the light of life" (cf. 9:5). The Synoptic-like Sabbath healing narrative (cf. v. 14) of vv. 6f. (cf. Mark 8:22-26, including the detail of saliva; 10:46-52 where it is not mentioned) is introduced by a familiar Johannine dialogue (vv. 1-5) in which the ignorance of the disciples (v. 2) is removed by Jesus' illumining response. There was no sin committed to account for the physical incapacity, he says. Rather, the blindness was permitted "so that God's works might be revealed in him" (v. 3). Verses 8-12 represents a slight expansion of the healing narrative and vv. 13-34 the full-scale investigation and exchange in the service of which John employs the cure. Verses 35-41 complete the faith meaning of the incident.

Jesus takes the initiative, not the blind man (vv. 1, 6f.). He does God's deeds "while it is day" (v. 5), namely, before the nightfall of his death. Applied to the Johannine church ("We must work . . ."), the reference would be to a season of good deeds in Christ's eschatological presence. Jesus in the world is its light, in glory its continuing light and life.

So far as we can tell from the narrative, Jesus is still up at Jerusalem for the Feast of Booths (*Sukkoth*; cf. 7:2, 37). The water used for its libations was drawn from the Pool of Siloam (*Shiloah*; Neh 3:15; Isa 8:6), part of an aqueduct in the southern part of David's old city on Mount Ophel. The verb *shalaḥ* does indeed mean "send," and may have something to do with the etymology of the name of the pool (e.g., "sent" through Hezekiah's conduit from the Spring of Gihon, its source). This is as may be but John's intent is not in doubt, viz., to identify Jesus as "one who has been sent" (v. 7). The man is cured as a result of his obedience, a possible parallel with the obedience of Jesus to his mission.

The opponents of Jesus who challenge the validity of the cure are variously "the Pharisees" (vv. 13, 16, 40) and "the *Ioudaioi*" (vv. 18, 22), in either case the late first-century opponents of the Jesus Jews. The passage is an inquiry into Jesus' motivations by unfriendly elements among his own people in a Gospel that has only one question by the high priest ("about his teaching," 18:19) in the passion narrative. J. Louis Martyn (*History and Theology in the Fourth Gospel* [Philadelphia: Westminster, 1968]), led the way in suggesting that John is operating at two levels of time here as elsewhere, the unique occurrence of the historical cure and the subsequent challenge to a Jewish believer in Jesus in the Jewish quarter of some diaspora city decades later. The elaboration, with its question put by the Pharisees who seem to have grown in influence after Jesus' day (vv. 16, 17, 19, 24, 28f.,

34), argues strongly for a confrontation of Jesus-believing Jews of a later period by others who have not accepted him.

An especially influential detail is the occurrence of the word *aposynágōgos* (v. 22), which appears to be a technical term for someone expelled from the assembly (cf. its occurrence in the plural at 12:42; 16:2). It is nowhere to be found in secular Greek usage or the LXX. Martyn thinks it a term that arose in a period on which we have little information beyond the Gospels on tensions about Jesus within the Jewish community. He ties it in with the phrase contributed to the Eighteen Benedictions *(Shemone esre)* by Simon the Small ca. 85 C.E., which prays officially against *minim* (i.e., those who lead astray from worship of the one God), but most Jewish and Christian scholars deny any such relation. The man's having been driven out is not a bodily removal from a building but expulsion from the community. The heated argument and its phrasing if read in this setting become far more comprehensible than if it were a spontaneous exchange that took place in Jesus' lifetime. The parents, for example, seem more alerted to the possibility of a public reprisal and its nature than they would have been if the Jesus of their son's cure had appeared in their lives only immediately before. A third possibility is that of elaboration by the evangelist of a historical incident without any data from his own age. The argument against this is cumulative, however, both from what we know of Gospel composition generally and from data found elsewhere in the Fourth Gospel.

The case against Jesus is that he does not keep the Sabbath (v. 16), that it is being claimed of him that he is the Messiah (v. 22), that he is a sinner (v. 24), and that his origins are obscure (v. 29; cf. 7:27f.). The blind man in response confesses him to be a prophet (v. 22), calls him devout and obedient to God's will (v. 31), assumes that he is from God (v. 33), and concludes by stating his belief in Jesus coupled with a gesture of veneration, in a verse that is missing from some manuscripts (v. 38).

The polarization in the exchange is between disciples of Moses who are sure of what is possible under Mosaic revelation from Sinai down to the oral Law (vv. 28f.) and disciples of Jesus, an unknown without pedigree (cf. 7:41 but also 8:23.) The man blind from birth keeps alleging the miracle he has experienced as something that God would work only through a faithful servant (vv. 11, 15, 17, 25, 30-33). This was the way the believers of the Johannine church were arguing: from Jesus' "works" or "signs" to his messiahship.

Verses 35-41 disclose the meaning of the event. It was so that the healed man might come to believe in the Son of Man. His progress from blindness to sight was a parable of progress from not having faith to having faith. The paradox of Jesus is that through him the blind see and those who claim to see are sightless.

Verses 40f. become explicit: the continuing claim, "but we see," by those who do not accept Jesus is, for the evangelist John, the ultimate in blindness.

This pericope is especially persuasive in making the case that the Fourth Gospel represents an internal struggle within late first-century Judaism. It is found in the Lenten liturgy because of the catechumens' progress toward faith and baptism.

Fifth Sunday in Lent (A)

EZEKIEL 37:1[12]-14

The vision of the dry bones lying on a battlefield and summoned to life at the LORD's command by the prophetic word of Ezekiel might seem to be about the resurrection of the individual dead. The interpretation of v. 11 makes clear, however, that a restoration of hope to the whole house of Israel is at issue. The people will be brought back to their land from the grave (v. 12). Revivified by the breath (or spirit) of God, this people of the LORD will once again be settled on its own land (v. 13). God will do this for them in fulfillment of promise (v. 14).

If preachers wish to speak about hope in the future for apparently lost causes, or the power of the word of prophecy, or the necessity of God's Spirit if there is to be life, they may do so from this text. Most fittingly, it applies to the hope for liberty of a people that at present is defeated or under a conqueror's heel. For a disquisition on the dead rising again, one is better advised to turn to Dan 12:2f., which deals with that subject directly. Isaiah 26:19 is ambiguous. It may refer to personal resurrection but is more probably a hymn to faith in the people's vindication.

PSALM 130[1-8]

With the LORD there is mercy, and fullness of redemption.

ROMANS 8:6[8]-11

Just as the dry bones of Ezekiel represent a people that has not yet called on God for renewed power and restoration, so "flesh" in this passage is humanity that has not been enlivened by God while "spirit" is humanity that has. Flesh by definition is not subjected to God's Law (v. 7); it serves and suits itself, hence cannot serve God. Paul's word is "please" (v. 8). To please God (cf. 2 Thess 4:1) and one's neighbor (cf. Rom 15:2; 1 Cor 10:33) is for Paul to live selflessly or in the Spirit. Its opposite, living to please oneself (cf. Rom 15:1, 3), is living in the flesh.

The apostle turns in v. 9 to what he assumes is the situation of the Roman believers. They are in the Spirit since the presumption is that the Spirit of God—indistinguishable for Paul from the Spirit of Christ—dwells in them. This is a new definition of Christian life which does not call on eschatological categories such as "dying and rising with Christ." Through knowing Christ in faith, one receives the Spirit. A new life—lived "in Christ"—begins. Christ within one means death to the body (v. 10), namely, the self, the province of sin. (See 7:4: "You have died to the Law.") That death of the former, sinful self would be of no consequence, however, unless the Spirit who is life, because of righteousness, had created a right relation of the whole person to God.

We are not to suppose that Paul is dividing present humanity into a dead body and a living spirit. The distinction is between a pre-baptismal dead self, whole and entire, and a body and soul now spirit-enlivened. With life in Christ came the action of God's Spirit resulting in a life of spirit—being just or righteous, to use the Pauline term that is synonymous with it.

The ultimate act of God's Spirit in the last days will be to raise up our bodies as it has already raised up Christ's. But that lies ahead. The Lord may have his dwelling in the new eon but we continue our mortal existence, however much on the edge, in the old one. Nevertheless, the one Spirit is having its effect on all that lies between the two ages. Dwelling in us, it brings our mortal bodies to life also (v. 11). This will culminate in our bodily resurrection, but the present tense of the verb argues for a present spirit-quality in our lives. The Spirit in us gives a life that is spirit.

See the commentary on Rom 8:9, 11-13 for Proper 9 [14], below.

JOHN 11:25A AND 26

I am the resurrection and the life, says the Lord. Those who believe in me will not die forever.

JOHN 11:1-45

This is the fifth of the seven signs in the order proposed for a "signs source" in last week's commentary: Cana, the royal official's son, the miraculous catch of fish, the loaves and the fish at Passover, the resuscitation of Lazarus, the man blind from birth, and the man at the sheep pool of Bethesda.

Today's narrative has several points in common with last week's: the announced purpose of the illness ("that the Son of God may be glorified through it," v. 4), daylight—the time of Jesus' presence in the world—as the time for the deeds of

God (vv. 9f.), and the official opposition of the "the Pharisees," leading in this case to a session of the Sanhedrin. The chief differences from the story of the blind man are the emphasis on acceptance of Jesus as giving *life* rather than *light* (vv. 25f.) and the belief of "many of the Jews" in him as a result of the sign (v. 45); "the Judaeans" is probably better in the context, Jesus being a man of the north operating in the south.

Lazarus has not previously appeared in this Gospel. The reference to his sisters cannot presume on the reader's awareness of Luke 10:38f. (which John probably knows from a source common to him and Luke rather than from Luke's Gospel); therefore an identification of Mary is made through an anticipation of 12:3. Some dialogue is contrived in familiar Johannine fashion about the disciples' confusion between sleep and death (vv. 11-14); Judaea is identified as the region inimical to Jesus, the likely place of his dissolution (vv. 7, 16); Jesus makes his way to his dying friend after waiting a biblical three days (v. 6) to heighten the sign value of what he means to do.

The characteristics of Martha and Mary from the Lukan story are probably reflected in v. 20. Martha concurs in the Pharisee teaching on bodily resurrection on the last day (v. 24), a prelude in John's technique to some soaring transcendence of the familiar. Jesus does it by making clear the sense in which belief in him brings an end to death (v. 26). He is rewarded by a faith-statement of Martha in him as the Messiah, the Son of God, and the "one coming into the world" to save it (v. 27) which has the ring of a creedal formulary.

Verse 25 contains the best known of the Johannine "I am" sayings (cf. 6:35, 41, 48; 8:12; 10:7, 9, 11, 14; 14:6; 15:1, 5). A Chester Beatty papyrus (p[45]), various Latin and Syriac versions, and Origen and Cyprian do not have "and the life," but the great bulk of manuscript witness favors it. The force of the saying is not that belief in Jesus is a protection against death or a promise of future resurrection but that whoever believes is assured of being raised to a new life *in this life*.

Verse 32, Mary's view of Jesus' power, echoes that of Martha in 21 before the revelation was made to her. Jesus' troubled emotional condition, vv. 33, 38 (for C. K. Barrett but not for all commentators: connoting anger), is not easily explained. Mention of it encloses the idea that "Jesus began to weep" (v. 35 in its entirety) but another emotion is being described. Is it a special drain on his intercessory power to ask for resuscitation of a fetid corpse? Is Jesus' taking on of man's last enemy, death, responsible? Does he shudder at having to provide this greatest of signs to elicit faith in him as "the resurrection and the life" (v. 25)?

The "four days" (v. 39) reflects the Jewish popular belief that the spirit or breath of a person hovered in the vicinity of the body for three days; hence Lazarus's death was final.

Jesus utters a *berakah* or blessing of God spoken in gratitude ("Father, I thank you," v. 41). The only such recorded prayer is in Matthew 11:25 (Luke 10:21) where the verb, "I give you praise," is a rendering of the same Hebrew verb, *barak*. Of Jesus' blessing of God spoken at table before he suffered, all we know is that he spoke it, not what he said. Here he thanks the Father for having heard him, as he always does, but this time for the sake of the crowd and its belief in him (v. 42).

It has been asked whether John might have historicized the parable told of another Lazarus by Jesus in Luke 16:19-31. Probably not. His record of lack of fidelity to Synoptic material in other places tends to free him of the charge. He doubtless has a traditional account of a certain resuscitation (the Synoptics have two such, although neither person is long dead) and works up the story for his usual theological purposes.

The miracle is said to have had its intended effect, namely, the faith of some Judaeans in what they saw. The narrative provides a welcome exception to the usual employment of *hoi Ioudaioi* in John to describe the adversaries of Jesus.

❧ ✿

Sixth Sunday in Lent /
Passion Sunday or Palm Sunday (A)

Liturgy of [Procession with] the Palms (A)

MATTHEW 21:1-11

For a commentary see Mark 11:1-11, Year B, on which Matthew's account is based, the differences there being noted.

PSALM 118:1-2, 19-29 (A, B, C)

Liturgy of the Passion

ISAIAH 50:4-[7]9A (A, B, C)

See Proper 19 [29] (B).

Psalm 31:9-16[21:8-9, 17, 20, 23-24]

Philippians 2:5-11 (A, B, C)

See Proper 21 [26] (A).

Matthew 26:14−27:66 or 27:11-54

Despite a tradition that goes back to the middle ages in the West of reading Matthew's passion narrative on this day, LM and RCL lost an opportunity by retrieving the custom. It obscures today's primary observance, Jesus' entry into Jerusalem, but—far worse—can confirm worshipers in the wrongly held view that they have heard a historical account of the motives and actions that led to his death. In fact, Matthew wrote a "passion play" based on Mark's, not a historical chronicle, in which literary venture Luke and John were later to be engaged. All possessed already-developed historical reminiscences of the two power blocs, one the Temple priesthood and the other the occupying imperial power, that operated in concert to rid themselves of Jesus. In writing their respective dramas the evangelists meant God to be the chief actor but obscured their own primary intent by the very skill of their imagining how events, characters, and verbal exchanges must have worked themselves out. See the comment at the end of this exegesis. The Judas tradition available to Mark—which Matthew follows—was one that described his complicity with religious leadership (Mark 14:10; Matt 26:14), not civil (cf. Mark 14:43). Matthew makes Judas take the initiative for reasons of cupidity whereas Mark does not actively supply a motive. "Iscariot" is usually taken to be a Greek rendering of "man of Kerioth" (see Josh 15:25), a Judaean town, because the Codex Beza writes *apo Karyōtou* wherever *Iskariōtēs* occurs in the Fourth Gospel; Sinaiticus has the same at John 6:71. This attribution of a place name may be early interpretation, however. Torrey and Gärtner propose an Aramaic word meaning "of betrayal" or "of falsehood," in which case it would be a clear case of *nomen est omen*. Matthew derives the betrayal price of thirty pieces of silver from Zech 11:12f., from which even more of the Judas story appears to stem.

Matthew 27:3-10 is an insertion into Mark between 15:1 and 2, although the connection of Judas's death with a graveyard called Field of Blood (27:7) is probably pre-Matthean (cf. Acts 1:15-20). Matthew tells his story of Judas's regret and subsequent self-destruction as an elaborate introduction to the last of the many "formula quotations" (vv. 9f.) in his Gospel. This is a stitching together of Zech 11:12f. and Jer 32:6-15, with incidental reference to Jer 18:2f. The mention of Jeremiah when it is the Zechariah quotation that is being fulfilled (27:9) is a slip or else testimony to the casual mode of citation in this targumic (i.e., paraphrasing) procedure. Basic to Matthew's fusing of the two texts is the similarity of the Hebrew words *yōtsēr* and *ôtsār*, meaning respectively "potter" and "treasure/treasury." The result of the priests' action, for Matthew, is the unconscious fulfillment of prophecy since the thirty pieces of silver that could not be put in the temple treasury (Zech 11:13) were used to buy a field. Jeremiah had bought a field from his cousin Hanamel as a sign (Jer 32:6-15), putting the deeds in a pottery jar (v. 14). He had also spoken of Israel under the figure of a vessel on a potter's wheel in God's hands (18:2f.). Matthew gives what he thinks is the hidden meaning of the Zechariah text by an involved procedure that results in a reading of Zechariah not to be found in any Greek, Aramaic, or Hebrew text of that book.

For Matthew the Last Supper is a Passover meal eaten on the first day of Unleavened Bread (*matzoth*, 26:17). He adds as a saying of the Teacher, "my time is near" (v. 18) to Mark, as part of his conviction that everything that happens to Jesus is part of the divine decree (see 26:54: "it must happen in this way"). Matthew follows Mark closely in describing the preparation of the meal at the home of an unspecified householder (v. 18, literally "a certain someone"; he eliminates Mark's detail about meeting a man carrying a water jar). Verses 17-24 parallel Mark 14:12-21 until Matthew adds a specific question to Jesus by Judas, "Surely it is not I, Rabbi?" (v. 25, previously "Lord," v. 22). Jesus' response is the "you have said so" of the later exchange with the high priest (26:64).

Matthew's additions to the table injunctions of Jesus (vv. 26-29; Mark 14:22-25) are the imperatives "Eat" (v. 26) and "Drink of it, all [of you]" (v. 27), plus "with you" (v. 28) in his vow of abstention from wine until he drinks it "new" in his Father's reign.

The passage from the supper room to the Mount of Olives and Jesus' prediction of Peter's threefold denial, preceded by his quoting Zech 13:7 on a stricken shepherd and scattered sheep, is much as in Mark (26:30-35; Mark 14:26-31). His statement that, once raised up, he will go to Galilee ahead of them (v. 32; Mark 14:28) is important because it conveys the conviction of both evangelists that Galilee, not Jerusalem, is the site of the origins of the gospel, i.e., the proclamation that Christ is raised from the dead. Matthew eliminates "twice" (v. 34) from Mark's prediction of the cockcrow. In Gethsemane, Matthew does not include the redundant "Abba" (Mark 14:36; v. 39) in Jesus' prayer, the wording of which he alters slightly. More importantly, here and in v. 42 Jesus prays as he has taught others to pray (cf. 6:10b), "Your will be done." For the rest, the prayer of Jesus "sorrowful nearly to death," is in the same three stages and three challenges to the sleeping "Peter and Zebedee's two sons" (v. 37) as in Mark (vv. 35-46; Mark 14:32–42).

Matthew removes "scribes" from the party of captors (v. 47), possibly as out of place there, but like Mark makes Judas the leader of a band of toughs "from the chief priests and elders of the people," i.e., it is an arrest by religious not civil forces. The prearranged sign of Judas's embrace may be a practical detail (even though the moon was at the full) but is meant to underscore his betrayal of friendship. His greeting in Greek is the usual *Chaire*, although a Jew would have said *Shalom*. Jesus' challenge, "Friend, do what you are here to do," is a Matthean touch. Its declarative form will strike any who have been reared on the Vulgate's "Amice, ad quid venisti?" as strange; similarly, Protestants familiar with the KJV's, "Friend, wherefore art thou come?" But aside from the absence of an interrogative mark in the Greek codices, Jesus' command accords better with his lordly bearing throughout Matthew (cf. John 13:27 to Judas at the supper table: "Do quickly what you are going to do").

When Jesus rejects the use of the sword (vv. 52ff., not found in Mark, although Luke 22:51 has it briefly, with a healing), Jesus speaks majestically as the Son of God who can call on more than twelve legions of angels, a peculiarly Matthean concept. He also acts on his own advice in 5:39 to offer no resistance to evil. Without his capture the Scriptures cannot be fulfilled (vv. 54, 56). When the disciples forsake Jesus and flee, Matthew terminates the narrative there (v. 56). He does not include Mark's story of the young man in the linen cloth, perhaps anticipating flights of fancy like Morton Smith's in *Clement of Alexandria and a Secret Gospel of Mark* (Cambridge: Harvard Univ. Press, 1973), rather than Mark's intent.

Matthew supplies the correct name of the high priest, Caiaphas (v. 57), missing from Mark. Neither he nor Luke includes it, but John does through the Annas-Caiaphas relation (18:3) and in the taking counsel that followed upon the raising of Lazarus (11:49). Matthew implies, along with Mark, that the scribes and elders were convened in the residence (or courtyard, *aulē* of the high priest. Mark has used the verb "were assembled" (14:53) which Matthew changes to another with the same meaning, perhaps (v. 57) to bring it in line with its use in the LXX of Ps 2:2: "The rulers take counsel together against the LORD and against his anointed." Mark observes of Peter somewhat ominously that he went inside, not to "warm himself at the fire" (Mark 14:54) but to "see the end" (26:58); cf. the use of *telos*, "end," in 26:6, 14, to designate the end of the age). This reflects Matthew's certainty that this death marks the consummation of an epoch.

The Matthean account of the search for testimony against Jesus by the "chief priests, with the whole Sanhedrin" (26:59) impugns their motives even more than Mark does by calling the witness they bring against Jesus' "false testimony." He also shortens Mark, who denies that there was any agreement among the witnesses (14:55-59), by having two of them come forward to say the same thing (vv. 60f.).

The tradition that Jesus had prophesied the destruction of the Temple evidently came from an earlier period in his public life (Mark 13:2; Matt 24:2; Luke 21:6) and was introduced into the interrogation narrative as one of the chief charges against him. Matthew removes Mark's adjectives about temples "made by human hands" and "not made by human hands," no doubt finding it a "spiritualized" version less probable historically. This change accords with Matthew's interest in continuity, for he refers to "the temple *of God*" and says "I will rebuild it," whereas Mark speaks disparagingly of "*this* temple" and says "I will build another."

Whatever the historical substrate of Jesus' saying on the Temple, Matthew wishes to imply that two witnesses agreed (26:60) on what had been a true prophecy of Jesus, namely that he would destroy the temple of God and rebuild it in three days. By the time the *logion* has reached the trial narrative it has acquired for those who believe in Jesus the Johannine meaning of "the temple of his body," even if, as spoken, it had referred to the actual edifice.

We need not go beyond Jeremiah to find a paradigm for Jesus' prophecy about destruction in Jerusalem: "The priests and prophets said to the princes and to all the people, 'This man deserves death; he has prophesied against this city, as you have heard with your own ears'" (Jer 26:11).

Matthew depicts the high priest's attempt to put Jesus under oath before the living God to tell whether he is "the Christ, the son of God" (26:63). The adjuration is not historically probable in its wording (the formula is Christian), but it adds to the solemnity of the occasion and leads to Jesus' practical refusal to be bound by oath. His reply, "It is you who say it" (v. 64), is probably not an evasion; certainly it is not the formulation of an oath. Hence it is neither denial nor affirmation of Jesus' status as Messiah (with which "Son of God" is taken by the evangelist to be equivalent). It is Matthew who has changed the response away from the "I am" of Mark 14:62. Hence, in neither Gospel is the response to be confused with a declaration of messiahship by the historical Jesus. Most probably Jesus is being made, by the phrase, "You have said it," to have nothing to do with an oath, and to declare at the same time what the Church already knows: that he is Messiah and Son of God.

Matthew (26:66) follows Mark (14:64) in having the high priest ask his colleagues their opinion and in finding Jesus deserving of death because of the blasphemy they have supposedly just heard. He does, however, eliminate a word of Mark that may have been thought proper to a judicial sentence, "What is your decision?" satisfying himself with the neutral, "They answered."

Matthew omits the detail of blindfolding from Mark as if it were self-evident (v. 67). "Messiah" (v. 68) is a taunt delivered to one presumed to be a false messiah.

The alterations in the account of Peter's denial are relatively few and inconsequential. He omits the detail of Peter's warming himself (Mark 14:67) and has the slave girl call Jesus "the Galilean" rather than "the Nazorean" (Matt 26:69; Mark 14:67), inserting "Jesus of Nazareth" later at v. 71. Matthew's Peter denies Jesus "in front of everyone" (v. 70) and "with an oath" (v. 72), getting more explicit in his second denial, "I do not know the man (ibid.), than in Mark. The phrase, "Even your accent gives you away" (v. 73), is a further Matthean explication. He likewise adds "bitterly" to the account of Peter's weeping, and tidies up Mark's prophecy of a threefold denial by the time of a second cockcrow (14:72) by having a cock crow once (Matt 26:74). He then brings Jesus' prophecy into line with this change (v. 75).

Matthew's account of the morning activity by the Sanhedrin ignores what has happened the night before just as thoroughly as does Mark. The chief priests and elders "confer/conspire/plot" to put Jesus to death in the same phrase (27:1) as that used in 12:14 and 22:15. His fate is sealed before he goes off to Pilate.

The charge on which Jesus is brought before Pilate (27:11) is the only one actionable before a civil court, namely, that he is a revolutionary ("Are you the King of Judaea/the Jews?"). His answer is a cryptic "You say so," much like the response of 26:25 and 64 although using another verb. In vv. 12-14 Jesus remains completely silent before the accusations of the chief priests and elders. In all this, there is no substantial departure from Mark in substance and very little in wording.

The same is true of Matthew's account of Barabbas. He does not specify murder in an uprising but contents himself with calling him a "notorious prisoner" (27:16). It is interesting to speculate why he should have softened the charge against Barabbas, since the latter's sentence for insurrection is presumably the same one under which Jesus will shortly fall. It is true that Matthew stresses the alternative between the two, as Mark has not done (v. 17). Jesus is "called [the] messiah" in Matthew (27:17), whereas in the parallel place Mark (15:9) has Pilate designate him "the king of Judaea/the Jews." The Jewish people would not have called him by that political designation if they had written the title but "king of Israel" (cf. Matt 27:42). Pilate is as aware in this gospel as in Mark that the Jewish leaders have handed him over out of envy (v. 18).

The improbable account of the warning Pilate's wife delivers to her husband as a result of a dream (27:19c) accords with Matthew's reliance on dreams in his first two chapters. It also highlights Pilate's neutrality, something that the four Gospels are committed to, in contrast to the guilt of the priestly leaders and even of the "whole people" (v. 25; cf. Acts 3:13-15). For the genesis of the people's disclaimer of guilt, "Let his blood be on us and on our children," see the reference to Jer 26:15 and 51:35 and the phrase attributed to Paul, "Your blood be upon your own heads. I am not to blame" (Acts 18:6). The expression, far from being a self-inflicted curse, is a strong statement of innocence. It appears in later, Mishnaic form in the tractate *Sanhedrin* 37a, where in capital cases the witness uses the invocation as a proof of his innocence. If he is lying, he is willing to have the blood of the accused fall on himself and his offspring until the end of the world. Matthew has Pilate wash his hands and declare his innocence (a Jewish, not a Roman custom; cf. Deut 21:6-9; Pss 26:6a; 73:13b) so that he may set the willing acceptance of responsibility of the "whole people," i.e., all present (certainly not all Jews of all time) against it. This verse in Matthew has caused the Jewish people incalculable suffering, which a correct understanding of it in context can do little to alleviate. Because of its tragic history of misinterpretation, which may be repeated modernly, it should never be read publicly.

Pilate yielded when he saw that his offer of Barabbas was gaining nothing but bringing on a riot instead (v. 24). Matthew has him "hand Jesus over" (v. 26) as in Mark. This verb is frequent in the passion accounts (Mark 14:10; 15:1; Matt 27:26; Luke 23:25) and is heavily freighted with religious symbolism in Rom 8:32.

The place of Jesus' appearance before Pilate has been undetermined. He is now led "inside the praetorium" (v. 27) for a mocking at soldiers' hands. For long this military garrison that Pilate made his headquarters while in Jerusalem was thought to be in the fortress Antonia on the Via Dolorosa. More recently, archaeologists favor David's palace just inside and to the right of the Jaffa Gate upon entry. The royal scepter in the form of a reed (v. 29) is a peculiarly Matthean detail; so is his "scarlet military cloak," Mark having reported a (royal?) purple cloak (15:20). The mocking game of the soldiers ends in Jesus' being led away to be crucified (v. 31).

In Matthew's passion, a tendency to view the Jewish leaders unfavorably is undeniable. That, however, is not primarily what the evangelist is interested in. He wishes to convey that the one whom he portrays as innocent and just dies. This is not to be taken "in the sense of an error of justice or of an infamous judicial murder, nor even to magnify the guilt of the Jews thereby, but as a profoundly necessary event in God's plan of salvation" (G. Barth in G. Bornkamm, G Barth, H. J. Held, *Tradition and Interpretation in Matthew* [Philadelphia: Westminster, 1963], 146). The one who dies is the Lord, the Son of God. A perceptive contemporary scholar may come to this conclusion but it is doubtful Christian congregations (or Mark and Luke in Years B and C) on Passion/Palm Sunday are able to. They can only take it to be a dependable eyewitness account of the events, which it is not, rather than the proclamation of God at work that Gerhard Barth correctly perceives it to be. This and the other three passion narratives may fittingly be the subject of exploration by strictly self-selected groups in the manner above. They are not proclaimed publicly to any good purpose, because the reading gives the false impression that "the Jews" were responsible for Jesus' death while the

Roman official who sentenced him to it was innocent of having done so or, worse still, favorably inclined to the victim of "Roman justice."

✑✑
Monday of Holy Week (A, B, C)

ISAIAH 42:1[7]-9

See Baptism of the Lord (A).

HEBREWS 9:11-15

See The Body and Blood of Christ (B).

JOHN 12:1-11

Luke locates this narrative in the house of a Pharisee (7:36-50), not in the house of the resurrected Lazarus and his sisters as here. See Proper 6 [11] C. The details in John resemble those in Mark's account (14:3-9) more closely (cf. the similar Matt 26:6-13) except for the latter two's placing the event in the house of Simon the leper. Establishing any of the Synoptics as a source for John in this case is impossible, since all may have had access to the narrative in different sources. Jesus' feet are anointed by Mary in Bethany before he enters Jerusalem (see 12:12), not by an unnamed woman as in the Mark/Matthew tradition or Luke's "sinful woman in the city" in a much different setting (Luke 7:37). Mark has told of the indignation of some at the waste of ointment that could have been sold and the money given to the poor. Matthew makes the disciples the objectors; John: Judas Iscariot, whom he calls a thief (12:6; cf. 13:29 for Judas as treasurer of the group). Earlier the evangelist has identified Judas as a devil (6:70) and a little later as one whose act of betrayal was primarily the work of the devil inducing him to do it (13:2, 27). It is by no means clear whether John wishes this anointing by Mary to be symbolic of Jesus' rôle as Messiah-King. Some have seen in the omission of an anointing of Jesus' head as in Mark a calculated absence of any such intent. Does the description of nard as *pistikēs* (v. 3; cf. 14:3) mean that it should be rendered "genuine" or "pure" as cognate with *pistos*, "faithful/true"? Other speculations link it with the pistachio nut (but the first vowel seems wrong for that) or the more likely East Indian spice plant piçita. John's quotation of the first half of Deut 15:11 put on Jesus' lips may make him seem callous and self-centered, but it is a preface to the command to be openhearted toward the poor and needy. The evangelist, like Mark, wishes only to underscore the unique, symbolic importance of Mary's act.

Tuesday of Holy Week (A, B, C)

ISAIAH 49:1-7

See Second Sunday after the Epiphany (A).

PSALM 71:1-4

1 CORINTHIANS 1:18-31

See 3 Lent (B).

JOHN 12:20-36

See 5 Lent (B).

Wednesday of Holy Week (A, B, C)

ISAIAH 50:4-9A

For a commentary see Passion or Palm Sunday (A, B, C). See Proper 19 [24] (B).

PSALM 70[69:8-10; 21-22, 31, 33-34]

HEBREWS 12:1-3

See Proper 15 [20] (C).

JOHN 13:21-32

Jesus has washed his disciples' feet (13:3-11) and told them they should do the same for one another following his example (vv. 12-17). After a brief hint of who his betrayer will be (vv. 18f.) there comes a saying unusual in its multiple attestation. The one who receives/hears Jesus receives the one who sent him and whoever receives the one Jesus sends receives him (v. 20; cf. Mark 9:37; Matt 10:40; Luke 9:48). The logion may serve to introduce the identification of the friend who has decided precisely *not* to receive Jesus, who in turn is "troubled in spirit" at the very thought (v. 21; cf. 11:33—his emotional response in grieving over the dead Lazarus). Some prefer to see in *etaráchthē* "moved to anger." The solemn "Amen, amen, I tell you" precedes the disclosure of the betrayal and the disciples' puzzlement (vv. 21f.). This Peter tries to resolve by a word to the unnamed loved one reclining close to Jesus on the floor in the Greek manner proper to the Passover season. If all heard Jesus' word to Judas they must not have comprehended it or they surely would have laid hands on him. Stunned into silence, they interpret Jesus' command to depart to be a simple matter of community business. It is John's stage direction for a change of scene.

For a commentary on vv. 31-35 see 5 Easter (C).

MATTHEW 26:14-25

See Liturgy of the Passion (pages 79-80).

❧❧

Holy (Maundy) Thursday (A, B, C)

EXODUS 12:1-4, (5-10)[8], 11-14

The Priestly author's version of the Passover ritual (vv. 1-28) is here inserted between the ninth and tenth plague. It is proposed for the first month of the year (Abib to the Canaanites, 13:4; in the Babylonian calendar, Nisan) as it was before the postexilic move of the first month to autumn. Two previous rites had already been fused by the time they were made a commemoration of the deliverance from Egypt (v. 14). One was engaged in by sheep herders that centered on the sacrifice of a lamb (vv. 3-10) and the other was practiced by men of the soil who anticipated a good harvest by the symbolism of bread free of yeast *(matzoth)* from the previous year. Verses 3-13 describe in detail how the beast was to be slaughtered, the meal prepared and eaten, and the blood smeared on houses as a remembered sign that no plague struck the Hebrews who dwelt in them, even as it destroyed the luckless Egyptians (v. 13). The narrative describing abstention from all leavened bread for seven days follows that rite (vv. 15-20), and is repeated in the next chapter (13:3-8). With the destruction of the Temple in 70 C.E. blood sacrifice ceased but the ritual has continued uninterrupted "as a festival to the LORD throughout your generations" (12:14). At some undated time in the past Jews placed a shank bone on a plate at the Passover meal while followers of Jesus began to see him as the victim offered in unbloody sacrifice. As early as the mid-first century Paul could write, "Christ our paschal lamb *(tò pascha)* has been sacrificed" (1 Cor 5:7). In its rite, the Greek Church of the East began to use leavened bread for the Eucharist (perhaps as symbolic of the risen Christ) while the West followed the biblical practice of yeastless bread. This was a matter of serious contention in the eleventh century, as it has been ever since. After the breach, however, neither side abandoned its firm commitment to the change of the elements by the prayer of the Church.

PSALM 116:1-2, 12[13, 15-18]-19

1 CORINTHIANS 11:23-26

See The Body and Blood of Christ (C).

JOHN 13:1[-15]-17, 31B-35

The first verse of this narrative is probably intended as a preface to the entire "Book of Jesus' Hour," not just this chapter. The verb for "depart" has been used in 5:24 to describe his passing from death to life, which for John means Jesus' transfer from one sphere to another as in 12:31, when he will drive out "the ruler of this world," be lifted up from the earth and draw all to himself (vv. 32ff.). "His own who were in the world" recalls the usage in 10:3, 4, 12, where "his own" modifies "sheep." Jesus' love for his own "to the end" can mean either "to the outer limit" or "to the end of days," history's final consummation. In any case, assurance of this has been the Christians' consolation over the ages.

The devil's part in the handing over of Jesus has been put even more strongly in 6:70f. (see Luke 22:3 where he is called Satan). Jesus' mission from his Father (v. 3) has already been spoken of (3:35), as his coming from God and returning to God will be again (v. 3; cf. 16:27f.). The gesture of footwashing by a host to receive dusty travelers was a commonplace in the culture, but it must have been one that the disciples were not ready for at Jesus' hands. "During supper" (v. 2) is the first clue we have to the setting. Simon Peter's demurral and the exchange it brought on has been the subject of discussion for centuries. John wishes to frame a parable of love in action and in doing so has the disciples unable to grasp the gesture's meaning until the "later" of Jesus' risen life (v. 7; see 2:22; 12:16). Simon

Peter's blurted query, followed up by his demand to be washed all over (vv. 6, 9), is John's familiar technique of bringing on an explanation from Jesus of the meaning of his cryptic remark. Being bathed by him and hence cleansed is the proper disposition for participating in the drama that is to follow, the event of the cross (see Mark 10:38-39). The phrase "except for the feet" does not occur in all Manuscripts and has no special significance even if in the original reading. Readiness for a bath of pain is probably meant rather than a washing in sacrament. Such a figurative cleansing has been received by all but one disciple (v. 12). Jesus then spells out the example he has set (vv. 12-18). Maundy is an Anglicization of the old French for *mandatum novum do vohis* (v. 34). For a commentary on vv. 31b-35 see 5 Easter (C).

❧ Good Friday (A, B, C)

ISAIAH 52:13 — 53:12

For a commentary see Proper 24 [29] (B).

PSALM 22[31: 2, 5, 12-13, 15-17, 25]

HEBREWS 10:16-25 OR 4:14-16; 5:7-9

For commentaries, see Proper 28 [33] (B) on Hebrews 10; Proper 23 [28] (B) on Hebrews 4.

JOHN 18:1 — 19:42

For a commentary on 18:33B-37 see Reign of Christ the King (B).

❧ Holy Saturday (A, B, C)

For use at services other than the Easter Vigil: Job 14:1-14 or Lamentations 3:1-9, 19-24; Psalm 31:1-4, 15-16; 1 Peter 4:1-8; Matthew 27:57-66 or John 19:38-42.

❧ Season of Easter ❧

❧❧
Easter Vigil
(A, B, C, In RCL Intercalated with those of LM)

SERVICE OF READINGS

Genesis 1:1—2:4a. See Trinity Sunday (A) for commentary.
 Psalm 136:1-9, 23-26 [Psalm 104:1-2, 5-6, 10, 12-14, 24, 35c]
Genesis 7:1-5, 11-18; 8:6-18; 9:8-13 (not in LM)
 Psalm 46
Genesis 22:1-18. See 2 Lent (B) for commentary.
 Psalm 16[5, 8-11]
Exodus 14:10-31; 15:20-21. See Proper 19 [24] (A) for commentary.
 Exodus 15:1-13, 17-18
Isaiah 54:5-14 (not in RCL)
 Psalm 30:2, 4-6, 11, 12a, 13b
Isaiah 55:1-11. See Proper 13 [18] (A), Proper 20 [25] (A), Proper 10 [15] (A).
 Isaiah 12:2-6
Baruch 3:9-15, 32—4:4 or Proverbs 8:1-8, 19-21; 9:4b-6. See Proper 15 [20] (B) on Proverbs 9.
 Psalm 19
Ezekiel 36:[16]24-28
 Psalm 42 and 43
Ezekiel 37:1-14 (not in LM)
 Psalm 143
Zephaniah 3:14-20 (not in LM)
 Psalm 98
Romans 6:3-11
 Psalm 114[118:1-2, 16-17, 22-23]
Matthew 28:1-10

An expository introduction—brief and in carefully chosen words—should make clear what the Church has done over the centuries in proclaiming these biblical passages. Just as Jews at a Passover *seder* celebrate God's power and mercy in delivering Israel from Egyptian captivity, so Christians proclaim the action of the same powerful and merciful God in the death and resurrection of the Son. The paschal mystery can be recognized as a culmination only if the assembly has a sense of what went before in Israel's history.

Well read, the passages speak for themselves. Similarly, the responses from the designated psalms, whether rendered by the congregation in simple melodies or by a small group of singers, should be approached with great care. Hymnody in substitution of the psalms is not a good idea because the words are so often banal. The singers' or the entire assembly's song should be a relaxing interval between the readings. This means that each reading should first be followed by a period of silence, as on any Sunday, so that the worshipers can briefly meditate on what they have heard.

Why seven (LM) or nine/ten (RCL, BCP) readings before three from the New Testament? They were reduced from the twelve of the Roman Rite with the framing of the current lectionaries. When Greek, Latin, and Syriac were widely spoken vernacular languages there were many more readings. The meaning of the vigil was prayer through the night. Keeping people awake was an important part of it. Egeria's diary (381/384?) contains a record of the way the vigil was kept in Jerusalem, where what later became Holy Week was inaugurated and was called by the local people, "The Great Week."

The story of the human race's graced condition by God's power through Israel and Jesus Christ begins with the formless primeval chaos while the wind or spirit breath of God hovered over the waters (Gen 1:1—2:4a). The sung response is Ps 136:1-9, 23-26. The formation of the cosmos was accomplished in an artisan's work week of six days. At its conclusion the Worker rested on the Sabbath like any good Jew, a day God declared holy and blessed. This last was the whole purpose of the narrative form adopted. The first creation story is immensely impressive if read with the proper pace and dignity. LM proposes an optional shorter version (1:1, 26-31a): the creation of the human pair and all green growing things for their sustenance, and that of the newly made birds, beasts, and fish. It should be substituted only if there is a perceived need for a shorter service, although usually there is none. Psalm 104: 1-2a, 5-6, 10-14, 24, 35 or 33:4-9, 12-13, 20, 22 is the response.

The Roman Missal of 1570 had as its second "prophecy" (its term for all twelve readings) the flood story. A complete Genesis 6 and edited 7 and 8 version was given. LM proceeds to the story of Abraham's obedience in the land of Moriah

(Gen 22:1-18; Ps 16:5, 8-11); RCL and BCP retain the Noah tale, Gen 7:1-5, 11-18; 8:6-18; 9:8-13; Psalm 46. It culminates in a rainbow in the clouds as a sign of God's covenant with all the peoples of the earth. This night's celebration of baptism and Eucharist is a celebration of that covenant and the LORD's covenant with Israel (Gen 12:1-3; 15:5-12; Jer 31:31-34) renewed.

The story of the LORD's cruel command to Abraham to take the life of his late born, only son is mystifying by any standard (Gen 22:1-18; Ps 16[5-8]); Exod 15:1b-13, 17-18, [15:1-6, 17-18]). It is justified only by the storyteller's conviction that such a graphic tale was required to convey the abhorrence the God of Israel had for human sacrifice and that the divine will can demand the totally unwelcome and seemingly impossible. Here the apparent destruction of Abraham's line is asked for. The narrator, of course, knows the providential outcome, for without the sparing of Isaac the story of the Hebrews could not continue nor that of the Christians.

The accounts of covenant renewal with Isaac, then Jacob, are passed over in favor of an immediate move by the three lectionaries to Israel's passage through the sea: Exod 14:10-31; 15:20-21 [14:15—15:1]; Exod 15:1b-13 [1-6], 17-18. Moses' lengthy song of victory is not proposed (Exod 15:1-18), but RCL provides the shorter version of Miriam and "all the women" (15:20-21). The divine compassion consistently shown to Israel is nowhere in evidence for the pursuing Egyptians. That is because this is a tale of rescue or deliverance by God as through water. Such salvation (or redemption) is the reason why each story is chosen for the Easter Vigil. BCP is alone in providing Isa 4:2-6 after the song of victory at the Red Sea. "The branch of the LORD" is the remnant of survivors in a purified Jerusalem on Mount Zion resplendent as on the day of Sinai. LM proposes a reading that the others do not: the LORD is the active reconciler with the wife he has briefly abandoned (Isa 54:5-14; Ps 30:2, 4-6, 11-12a, 13b). Judah's sinfulness may be the reason for the breach but perhaps the author has in mind God's permitting the exile to occur. In any case, the predominant theme of the passage is covenant renewal in mercy and love. This eminently befits the reception of the newly baptized and the receiving back into the community of the long-baptized.

The much loved Isaian passage that the three lectionaries employ (Isa 55:1-11; Isa 12:2-6) is a symphony to a divine forgiveness (see v. 7) that many adult candidates or simple participants may require on Easter night. Drinking wine and milk (v. 1c) mixed with honey was part of some early baptismal liturgies (see *The Apostolic Tradition* 23.2). All who eat at the table of the Lord this night delight in rich fare, whether coming to it for the first time or after a long absence, that they may have life (vv. 2b-3a).

Wishing not to omit the wisdom immanent in Israel's life and that of the church, LM and RCL but not BCP choose a lengthy hymn in praise of wisdom, Baruch 3:9-

15, 32—4:4. The latter proposes as an alternative to this deuterocanonical scripture (with Ps 19 [8-11] in response) a passage from Proverbs (8:1-8, 19-21; 9:4b-6) that should be familiar to Protestants and Catholics alike. It is more direct than the wordier Baruch as it enjoins: "You simple ones, learn prudence; gain sense, you who lack it" (v. 5). It has in common with the words of Jeremiah's secretary this figure: "Come, eat of my bread and drink of the wine I have mixed" (Prov 9:5). To partake of the eucharistic meal is to ingest the Christ whom Paul calls "the wisdom of God" (1 Cor 1:24, 30).

Ezekiel 36:[16]24-28, with Ps 42[3, 5] and 43[3, 4] in response is common to the lectionaries, although only LM includes the charge of Israel's profaning the Lord's holy name in pagan lands. Both have this prefiguring of baptism: "I will sprinkle clean water upon you to cleanse you of all your impurities" (v. 29a). The promise of a new heart of flesh and a new spirit replacing a heart of stone is repeated in 36:26 from 11:19. It will remind many of the Jeremiah promise of a new covenant to be written on the hearts of all in Israel and Judah (31:31-34). The liturgy sees in the Ezekiel passage the newness of baptismal life. Similarly, that prophet's vision of the dry bones (Ezek 37:1-14; Ps 143) is viewed as a figure of new life in Christ.

RCL and BCP provide Zeph 3:[12]14-20 as their last reading. It is a shout of exultation at the presence of the Lord in Jerusalem's midst: "The Lord . . . will rejoice over you with gladness, and will renew you in love; the Lord will exult over you with loud singing as on the day of festival" (v. 17). The Episcopal lectionary includes two verses that speak of the faithful in Israel as a "remnant," a word Paul used to describe Jewish believers in Jesus (Rom 11:5).

These passages from Torah, the Prophets, and the Writings should help readers and hearers recognize certain biblical types of new life in Christ and its sacramental symbols that the vigil celebrates. The readings well executed will prepare worshipers to hear Paul on baptism from death to life (Rom 6:3-11) and the Psalm in response (114) that speaks of the sea turned back and the gushing springs from the rock, then Matthew's (28:1-10), Mark's (16"1-8), or Luke's story of Jesus gone from the empty tomb, his garments laid by (24:1-12). The succinct introduction suggested in this paragraph—no words wasted—should prepare hearers to know what to listen for and why.

ROMANS 6:3-11

Paul returns in this passage to a matter he had raised in 3:8, where he attributes the question to slanderous opponents of the Gospel: If grace in Christ Jesus is so abundant, may not a life of sin be allowed and even cultivated as a way to prove

God's power to justify? (see 6:1f.) He is resoundingly opposed to any such perverse interpretation of "grace" or "faith" (of which confused antinomian Christians may be guilty) and here he spells out the reasons for his opposition. His rhetorical questions in vv. 1 and 3 are characteristics of the style of the *diatríbē*. They may reflect questions that have been put to Paul elsewhere. He has not yet visited Rome, hence cannot know in detail the difficulties of Roman Christians.

Paul has denied flatly in verse 2 that those who precisely as Christians *(hoítines)* have died to sin can go on living in it. The first reason in his chain of argument occurs in that verse: "we died" (*apethánomen*, aorist), that is, at a specific time in the past there was death to sin. His subsequent development reveals that he has the day of baptism in mind. Continued life (*zēsomen*, future, v. 2) in sin is not a possibility for the dead. He proceeds to a second argument in v. 3 by beginning with an "Or" *(ē)* which NRSV does not translate. Barrett is so convinced that it means "secondly" that he renders it, "Or (if you want further proof) . . ."

We cannot know how much awareness (v. 3) of the effect of baptism Paul can count on in a church he has not instructed. Enough, at least, for him to assume that its members are a baptized community into *(eis Christòn Iēsoûn)*, eliptical for "in the name of Christ Jesus." Whether they are conscious before reading his epistle of a burial with Christ "into death" (the Greek does not have "his" death) which renders them dead to sin, even as Jesus' death brought an end to his human condition as "sin" (cf. 2 Cor 5:21), we cannot know. We need not take for granted here as common to all in the diaspora the concept of a mystical union of the baptized with Christ. The model of an initiation into pagan mysteries which brought about union with the god of the devotee is widely assumed in New Testament scholarly writing, especially in theological circles unhappy with sacraments. Paul may well be saying a simpler Jewish thing, namely that baptism should be recognized by all as a turning-point, a beginning of life in the new age (Heb. *ʽōlām*).

There followed upon death in Christ's case his being raised up "by the glory of the Father," in our case the "living of a new life" (v. 4; literally "walking in newness of life," a Semitic echo or practicing *halakah*, viz. Walking in the way of the commandments). The notion of baptism "in a name" has occurred in 1 Cor 1:13 and 10:2 and is sufficiently explicable in terms of the current practice of Jewish baptizing sects without turning to a Greek model. Paul must take care here, as in all such expositions, to distinguish between Christ's having entered on the life of the new age and Christians' being only at its threshold, with suffering and resurrection yet to come. This he does in the present chapter by consistently using the future tense or the imperative. His experience with the Corinthians on this point has made him chary of any vocabulary of anticipated eschatology. The new resurrection-life for the believer is both present (v. 4) and future (vv. 5, 8).

Paul's verb for "united" in v. 5 means literally" grown together" (solved by the Vulgate by the rendering *complantati*) but he uses it figuratively here. His word for likeness, *homoíōma*, seems to have a history of connoting similarity to divinity in Greek religion, although the LXX rendering of Gen 1:26 *(homoíōsis)* would suffice. The imaging in baptism is twofold, both of death and resurrection. Interestingly, the apostle does not attend here to the primary property of water as washing but only as immersing ("we were buried with him," v. 4); he does so in 1 Cor 6:11 (cf. Ac. 22:16). Elsewhere in the New Testament the washing away of sin (the footwashing of John and the references to the Baptist apart) is in the blood of the Lamb (Rev 7:14).

The "old self" of v. 6 is literally the "old human being," Adamic humanity that died with Christ on the cross. Paul calls for a consideration of ourselves (v. 11) as dead to sin in that sense. Human nature as sinful *(tò sōma tēs hamaritís, v. 6)* has been destroyed by Christ, but not necessarily for us as individuals. We must conduct ourselves in faith as members of the new, Christ-headed race. Death brings an end to actual slavery because it ends the life of the one enslaved (vv. 6f.). Death ended finally and forever Jesus' human life in the likeness of sin (vv. 9f.). It should do no less for us. The dead man is freed *(dedikaíōtai, v. 7)* from sin. He must therefore be and act like Christ, "alive to God.") In his case, this comes about through being "in Christ Jesus" (v. 11).

For additional commentary see Proper 8 [13] (A).

PSALM 114[118:1-2, 16-17, 22-23]

MATTHEW 28:1-10

Matthew probably has Mark's account of the women at the tomb before him, modifying it in light of certain discrepancies from the special material at his disposal (e.g., the names of the women at the burial and at the tomb, 15:47 and 16:1; the Markan account of burial rites completed by Joseph of Arimathea, 15:42-46). Thus, in Matthew the women come "to inspect the tomb" (v. 1) rather than "to anoint Jesus" (Mark 16:1). The angel in Matthew charges the women to "tell his disciples" (v. 7), eliminating "and Peter" (Mark 16:7). Matthew is evidently leading up to the single appearance to all the disciples in Galilee (v. 17) for the missionary charge, hence sees no need to single out the appearances to Peter and the disciples as Mark does. Furthermore, he has no interest in or perhaps awareness of Mark's theology of the messianic secret, more accurately, "the Son of God secret." This means that the detail of instructing women otherwise fearful and silent (Mark 16:9) to proclaim the risen Christ to Peter and the Twelve, as the final unveiling of the secret, is meaningless to him. Matthew's women cannot remain silent. "Fearful yet overjoyed" they run to carry the good news to his disciples. The encounter with Jesus (vv. 9f.) is a Matthean insertion into Mark's narrative. Jesus greets them, they worship him, and he repeats the angel's charge. This appearance of Christ to the women in Jerusalem is unexpected. We would have looked for his meeting the disciples in Galilee next. Matthew seems to possess the tradition from some independent source and wish to work it in. It may have been an appearance of an angel to the two Marys in its earliest form, since it does not occur in 1 Cor 15:5-7 or in Mark. The christophany of John 20:11-18 seems to be from the same tradition but independently developed. (Cf. Luke 24:22, where the women report "a vision of angels.") This christophany in Matthew is the turning point of the "relocation of the primary appearances to the disciples in Jerusalem in Luke 24 and John 20" (R. H. Fuller, *The Formation of the Resurrection Narratives* [New York: Macmillan, 1971], 79). It is also the first materialization of the appearances (viz., "embraced his feet," "did him homage"), a departure from their mere listing, as in 1 Cor 15:5f. and Mark 16:17. The borrowing of details from Mark 5:6 and 5:22, with its view of Jesus as a "divine man," indicates that while the appearances may be out of a primitive tradition the narratives are not.

❧❧ Resurrection of the Lord / Easter Sunday (A)

ACTS 10:34[A, 37]-43

The omission of 34b-36 from LM is a sensitive one. It suppresses a key concept in Lukan theology, namely, his late first-century attempt at "reconciliation" of the wolf and the lamb, Gentile Christianity and Judaism, which has the lamb ending up inside the wolf. God's impartiality is such that the message sent to the sons of Israel leaves them with no special distinctiveness such as they have in Paul (where theirs are "the adoption, the glory, the covenants, the giving of the law, the worship, and the promises . . . the patriarchs, and from them, according to the flesh, the Messiah," Rom 9:4); they are "the first fruits," "the root," "the cultivated olive" (Rom 11:16, 24). For Luke the sons of Israel, like the person "in any nation who fears God and does what is right," is merely acceptable to God (Acts 10:35). Luke overcomes the obstacle provided by the fact that God addressed his message to the Jews by citing Jesus' Lordship as the reason why anyone may now enter the messianic community of salvation.

Peter's vision in the house of Simon the tanner at Joppa (Acts 10:9-16) has convinced him that all foods are clean. Hence he is relieved of any scruple over dietary laws in eating with the "God-fearing (i.e., Jewish-oriented) centurion Cornelius and his household (v. 22). Seated at ease in the midst of this Gentile company, Peter begins to share a portion of his "message" (lit.: "word," vv. 36, 44) with them.

Peter's sermons, Lukan in authorship, bear a remarkable resemblance to Paul's in the book of Acts, while the latter seem barely acquainted with the fundamentals of Pauline theology. They do contain, however, the basic elements of Paul's proclamation, namely the crucifixion of Jesus (Gal 3:1), his death for our sins (Gal 1:4; 1 Cor 15:3), his burial (1 Cor 15:4), his having been raised from the dead (Rom 8:34) on the third day (1 Cor 15:4) and made "son of God in power" (Rom 1:4) at the right hand of God (Rom 8:34), where he intercedes for us (ibid.), at which time God will pass judgment through him on the secrets of all (Rom 2:16). For the above ideas in Paul's preaching as found in Acts, see 13; 16:31; 17:31; 26:23.

The notion of a message that brings the good news of peace and the very phrasing employed in the New Testament derive from the Septuagint versions of Nah 2:1 [NAB] (Vulgate, NRSV, 1:15) and Isa 52:7. There the context is respectively the announcement of the smashing of Assyria's brutal hold (v. 7c) and the proclamation to Jerusalem and Zion of the impending restoration of Israel from Babylonian captivity (v. 6c). For the Christian author of Acts the good news of peace is the final liberation proclaimed "through Jesus Christ [who] is Lord of all" (10:36).

A slim but influential book by C. H. Dodd published in 1936, *The Apostolic Preaching and Its Developments*, gave currency to the notion that Peter's discourse in Acts 10 provided the framework for the Synoptic Gospels, notably Mark. In this theory, Mark in his passion story deserts Acts 10 and takes his cue from 1 Corinthians 15. It is generally supposed nowadays that the literary form gospel, which Mark seems to have invented (although he may have possessed an archetype), does not depend so neatly on the form of the apostolic preaching *(kērygma)*. It simply goes in the only direction open to it. Nonetheless, the correspondence between Peter's discourse at Caesarea and the Synoptic Gospel sequence (Galilee, Judaea, passion-resurrection) is undeniable. Galilee witnesses the initiation and the greater part of Jesus' ministry after his baptism by John, inevitably a Judaean occurrence.

In his homeland he breaks the devil's grip by healings and exorcisms in proof that the reign of God has drawn near. The "Judaean countryside" (v. 39)—some of its inhabitants or "Judaea," not all Jews taken ethnically—is charged with Jesus' death. The sermon's high point is the claim by Peter to be among the chosen "witnesses" to the resurrection. This is a technical term for the sharers in the eschatological meals of the earliest believers who were charged with proclaiming Jesus' rising from the dead (v. 42; Mark and the Pauline letters have him "raised up," as in v. 40). In a sacramental sense, modern Christians who partake of the Easter Eucharist do so as witnesses to the resurrection. Like their apostolic forebears they have been commissioned to preach and bear witness to the Christ whom God has set apart as judge. The testimony of "all the prophets" to Jesus (v. 43), belief in whose person (= "name") brings forgiveness of sins, means the whole gamut of biblical texts collected into "books of testimonies" for preachers—texts in which the book of Acts abounds.

JEREMIAH 31:1-6

Why this reading for the feast of Christ's resurrection? Because it is a poem of rejoicing over a restoration. The LORD's everlasting love and continued fidelity is about to rebuild a people that has been in exile. The Judahites are already returning across the desert, even as Jesus lay in the desert of death but lives again. The joyous song and pealing organ that celebrate his risen life respond to the tambourines and dance of the merrymakers of old. But what about all the talk of Israel and the mountains of Samaria and the hill country of Ephraim? What can it possibly mean? Was it not Judah that was off in exile and is now on its way back? How can a poet of the southern kingdom rejoice for the return of the northern? The vineyards will be planted, he writes, on the mountains of a neighbor near in place but far in affection. In the hoped-for future, the sentinels will summon the poet's people of the south with a word to include the alienated north: "Come, let us go up to Zion, to the LORD our God" (v. 6b). It is the dream of a people united after Judah's return from exile. Just as Jesus in his lifetime knew that the ostracism and contempt of his people for the Samaritans was a scandal, so the divisions and schisms within schisms of those who claim to be his disciples are a particular scandal on this feast. All of divided Christianity is summoned unwillingly into one by the power of the Resurrection. See Proper 25 [30] (B) for a commentary on 31:7-9.

PSALM 118:1-2, 14-24[16-17, 22-23]

This is the day the LORD has made; let us rejoice and be glad.

Acts 10:34-43

See Baptism of the Lord [1] (A).

Colossians 3:1-4

The letter to Colossae seems to contain anti-gnostic arguments (although arguments against a type of Christian-Jewish angelology would do) which stress the superiority of Christ to angels (2:16), his role as firstborn of all creatures and the one who continues them in being (2:1), 17), him in whom "all the fullness of God" resides (1:19), the reconciler of all on earth and in the heavens (1:20). Through him as image of the invisible God (1:15) we have been rescued from the power of darkness and brought into "the kingdom of his beloved Son" (1:13; only a few New Testament phrases attribute kingly reign to Christ, e.g., 1 Cor 15:24f.; Matt 13:41; 2 Tim 4:18). The "Great Christology" of Col 1:15-23, while drawing on Jewish and possibly pagan religious writings for its vocabulary, is remarkable chiefly for its attribution of divine status to Christ at so early a period—whether during Paul's captivity at Ephesus (early 50s) or Rome (58–60), or shortly after his lifetime, as some would have it.

In any case, the assumption of the present reading is that Christians have been mystically raised up with Christ. For this reason they are to set their hearts on what pertains to the higher realms, an adverbial phrase found also in John 8:23. There the contrast is between "above" and "below." The antithesis between "above" and "on earth" in Colossians (3:1, 2) is more closely paralleled by the heaven-earth opposition of John 3:31. Gnostic terminology may be invoked but ordinary Jewish usage on the respective abodes of God and the human will do. Christ is at God's right hand for Paul (Rom 8:34) and 1 Peter (3:22); he is seated there according to the authors of Ephesians (1:20) and Hebrews (10:12).

The attention of Christians is summoned to what God has done for them in Christ, not the other-worldly as contrasted with the this-worldly. The invitation to transcendence is issued and is expected to be accepted *here*, not in some ethereal realm. The contrast is between a God-centered life and one that is selfish or trivial.

The theme of death with Christ and hiddenness with him is reminiscent of Paul's reference to mystical death and burial with him in Romans (6:4) and a death to sin that parallels Christ's (6:10f.). Life in Christ as a life of faith in the Son of God is the theme of Gal 2:19f., with an echo of the same "life" after death in Phil 1:21. The actual state of being with Christ is a thing of the future for Paul (Phil 1:23; 1 Thess 4:17). He takes a strong line against the Corinthian enthusiasts who imagine that through baptism they have "risen" as much as they are going to (1 Cor 15), a view made explicit in 2 Tim 2:18. The uncharacteristic notion of Col 3:1 of being raised up with Christ in the present (Paul makes it future in virtue of a resurrection in Rom 6:5, 8, although he does not balk at the reality of new life in him now, Rom 6:11) is balanced by the anticipation of our appearance with him in glory only when he appears (Col 3:4).

This passage cannot be made into an appeal to transcend the material order. The "spiritual" of the New Testament always embraces the material, orienting it Godward. Only when this is not done do humans become "unspiritual"—even in their intellectual and psychic powers. When the Lord appears at the end in glory, it will be manifest how committed to the Spirit faithful Christians were. This manifestation, like that of Christ himself, has nothing to do with noncorporeality.

1 CORINTHIANS 5:6B-8

Paul identifies Christ as our Passover, our *transitus* from death to life. Just as in Israel's safe passage from Egypt to the desert of freedom and from the land of Sinai to the land of promise there was escape to liberty and new life, so the believer in Christ as a sacrificial victim lives again through this commemorative action. It is a second symbol of release, the Passover meal (which is not rescinded) being the first. Paul recalls to his Corinthian readers familiar with Jewish practice the rabbinic custom of destroying every available crumb containing yeast during the Passover as a means of fulfilling literally the command of Exod 13:7. Only *matzoth*, yeastless breads, are to be used during the eight-day observance. This commemorative practice makes yeast the enemy; an otherwise neutral or even helpful agent becomes the symbol of corruption and wickedness. *Matzoth* in themselves are no more innocent than leavened bread, but they become the symbol of sincerity and truth. Jesus is reported as using the same figure of speech, "the yeast of the Pharisees" (Mark 8:15), to describe that portion of their teaching that he disapproved.

Deliverance for the Christian is spoken of in this passage as a present reality. It has often been asked why Paul inserted this reference to the Passover here. The usual response is that he was probably writing his letter at that season. What is the boasting he warns the Corinthians against (v. 6), which is the context of his remarks? It could be their arrogance in assuming that their tolerance of an incestuous union in their community is proof that they can "handle it." This corruption doubtless is the "little yeast" of Paul's severe warning. His pastoral principle seems to be that the immoral conduct that must pass unnoticed in those who do not know Christ is not to be admitted within the Christian community.

Since the ostracism of those of irregular life has caused untold pain in Christian churches over the centuries, Paul's meaning must be pondered deeply before any too hasty conclusions are drawn from his warning.

JOHN 20:1-18

See 2 Easter (A) for a commentary on John 20:19-31. Verses 10-18, which continue the earlier vv. 1-9 of today's reading, have the two disciples leave the scene of the tomb ("their homes" being wherever they were staying in Jerusalem). The weeping Magdalene is questioned by the two angels. She responds to their inquiry and then turns to see the Jesus whom she does not recognize (v. 14; cf. Luke 24:31 for a similar failure to recognize Jesus). Confusing him with the tender of the orchard, she first accuses him of tomb robbery and equally irrationally volunteers to take his body away. After a brief exchange Jesus calls her by name, at which she calls him "Teacher" in their familiar Aramaic tongue. This improbable exchange—not the evangelist's reminiscence of her presence at the tomb—is his way of conveying Mary's utter dismay but also the difference between Jesus' risen body and his earthly body. Jesus' mysterious reticence in forbidding her to continue clinging to him (v. 17) may be explained by the fact that, "since for John Jesus' true glory consists in his being lifted up from the earth in crucifixion, the glory of the risen appearances is anticlimactic . . . [t]his portion of Jesus' earthly time is [therefore] a transition from his historical existence to his heavenly glorification, hence in the nature of the case an ambiguous interval: a kind of glory but not his ultimate glory." Jesus has promised in his supper discourse to come to his disciples, but he has not yet come in the sense promised" (Gerard S. Sloyan, *John* [Interpretation, a Bible Commentary; Atlanta: John Knox, 1988], 220f.). Unlike the women at the tomb in Mark who "out of fear" did not do as commanded, Mary went to tell the disciples that she had seen the Lord and told them that he had said these things to her (v. 18).

SEQUENCE

Victimae paschali laudes immolent Christiani. (Christians, to the paschal victim offer your thankful praise.)

ALLELUIA. 1 CORINTHIANS 5:7B-8A

Christ has become our paschal sacrifice; let us feast with joy in the Lord.

JOHN 20:1[9]-18

This reading from John combines two traditions on the resurrection in the early Church, the earlier one of appearances of Christ to various persons and the later, more developed one of the empty tomb. The christophany to Mary Magdalene begins in vv. 1-2 and resumes in v. 11; v. 3, which is almost identical with v. 13 (except for its plural, which is probably a rhetorical device and does not require any other person at the sepulcher), and serves as a link to the story of the two disciples. Mary's lament to the angels is duplicated to the disciples in a transition from the more primitive discovery story (e.g., Mary Magdalene's; cf. Matt 28:1ff.; Mark 16:1ff; Luke 24:10) to an alternative one in which John features the faith of the beloved disciple (v. 8). A second development besides that from christophanies to empty tomb *may* be that from the earliest appearance in Galilee (see John 21) to those in Jerusalem, all accomplished before the first Gospel is written.

Luke has a running Peter who, alerted by the women's report, stoops down when he arrives to see the wrappings in the tomb but nothing else (24:12). In John's account, the beloved disciple outruns Peter but allows him to enter first. This preserves the tradition of Peter's primacy of discovery but leaves room for the special Johannine character of the beloved disciple: "He saw and believed" (v. 8). Mary too will stoop to look inside (v. 11). She is no more moved to believe by what she sees than is Peter. The neatness of the wrappings is an apologetic detail, hinting against the theft of the body (cf. Matt 27:64; 28:13-15) and in favor of Jesus' miraculous passage through the wrappings as through closed doors (cf. John 20:26). The beloved disciple announces his faith to no one and when the disciples assemble a week later (vv. 19ff.) none of them is reported as already believing. The race to the tomb and its outcome, therefore, is for a specific Johannine purpose: the relation between Peter and the disciple whom Jesus loved as a well-remembered figure in the author's community.

MATTHEW 28:1-10

For a commentary, see Easter Vigil, above.

Easter Evening (A, B, C)

ISAIAH 25:6-9

See Proper 23 [28] (A).

PSALM 114

Not to us, O LORD, but to your name give the glory.

1 CORINTHIANS 5:6B-8

See Easter Day, above.

LUKE 24:13-49

See 3 Easter (A) and (B).

❧❧

Second Sunday of Easter (A)

ACTS 2:14A, 22-32[42-47]

For a commentary on the earlier Acts passage see 3 Easter (A).

Joachim Jeremias is associated with the view that in v. 42 we have the shape of a primitive eucharistic liturgy in the sequence: apostolic teaching, table fellowship, breaking of the bread, and prayers. He considers "devoted themselves" to be a verb denoting cult and thinks that Luke here uses ambiguous phrases about the Eucharist to mask it from non-Christians. Against this is the difficulty that cryptic speech has not yet overtaken a community whose representative Luke elsewhere reports the formula, potentially damaging in a context of banqueting on human flesh: "This is my body. . . . This cup is the new covenant in my blood" (Luke 22:19f). Moreover, the temple is identified as the place where the apostles go for prayer (Acts 3:1) and teaching (5:21); the distribution of food—if, as is likely, this sharing is the meaning of "fellowship/communal life"—is carried out apart from a worship service (6:1); and "prayers" do not conclude a Christian worship service only. It therefore seems more likely that Luke is here using "and" to list four distinct activities of the community, one of which undoubtedly is the communal meal (cf. 2:46; 20:7, 11; 27:35). "The breaking of the bread" (cf. Luke 24:35) is already standard usage for the eschatological meal that becomes the Eucharist. The term derives from the symbolic gesture with which every Jewish meal opens, although there is no evidence from the period that it existed in Jewish circles as a usual designation for having a meal.

The summary that runs from v. 43 to v. 47, a favorite Lukan technique, anticipates those of chaps. 4 and 5 (4:32-35; 5:41f.). He uses them skillfully to separate his stories. This one features the subsequently repeated phrase "signs and wonders" (5:12). The "fear" that overtakes them all is the holy awe that marks the last age and which in turn is clearly identifiable as the milieu of Luke's Spirit-dominated Jerusalem community. Non-Christians presumably look on in wonder at the life of a Church filled with miracles.

Community members did not divest themselves of their property but sold it as there was need (v. 45). Neither did they break with their Jewish religion, the worship center of which was the temple (v. 46), but observed what was special about their new faith in Christ through "breaking bread" at substantial meals of celebration, even those eaten "with glad hearts/exultation" in homes. All is done in the spirit of gladness (*agallíasis*, v. 46) that marks the messianic hope (see Luke 1:14, *1 Enoch*, and *Testaments of the Twelve Patriarchs*). Luke often features the notion of praise of God (2:13, 20; 19:37; Acts 3:8) which he here couples with a divinely favored people (v. 47). The entire picture of the early Jerusalem community is romanticized—eschatologized, actually—a fact that has led to much peace in Christian living. It has also accounted for a multitude of sects through literalist attempts to reproduce a world that never was.

Psalm 16 [Psalm 118:2-4, 13-15, 22-24]

Give thanks to the LORD for he is good, whose love is everlasting.

1 Peter 1:3-9

The greeting that precedes these eight verses is addressed to the Christians scattered throughout the five Roman provinces that constituted the bulk of Asia Minor at the turn of the second century. Only south-central Pisidia and Lycaonia and Cilicia along the southern coast (plus Commagene to the far southeast) were omitted. Christian believers are described as having been providentially called to a life of "obedience to Jesus Christ and to be sprinkled with his blood." A triadic scheme of divine activity is present in the greeting: foreknowledge of election attributed to God the Father with consecration to obedience to Christ and purification in his blood, made a work of the Spirit (cf. 2 Thess 2:13). There follows in vv. 3-5 a snatch of a Christian hymn, probably a baptismal one. Jesus is described intimately as "our Lord Jesus Christ," a usage found as early as 2 Thess 3:18 and going back to the Aramaic "*Marána thá*" (1 Cor 16:22).

Compare Tit 3:5-7 for a common stock of ideas on which this author is drawing. God is praised as the merciful giver of "a new birth into a living hope" that is derived from Christ's resurrection from the dead. Our hope of rising is grounded on and guaranteed by his rising (cf. Rom 8:10f.; 1 Cor 15:12-22). The author will make the connection between baptism and Christ's resurrection again in 3:21. The whole complexion of life—now a matter of baptismal bath, rebirth, hope—has been changed by Christ's victory over death. Paul's phrase for this reality "walking/living in newness of life" (Rom 6:4), occurs in a discussion carried on in terms of baptism, Christ's resurrection, and ours. The birth imagery is sustained by 1 Peter in 1:23 and 2:2. It occurs throughout the New Testament (e.g., John 3:1-8; 1 John 2:29; James 1:18) and may be dependent, at least verbally, on the mystery cults of Isis, Cybele, and Mithra—all of which speak of the "regeneration" of their votaries—but in context on the Jewish expectation of a new creation. The baptismal hope is an "inheritance," a fitting enough figure for the newborn but also one with a long Jewish history (cf. Deut 19:10, where the inheritance is Canaan; it is God himself in Ps 16:5—"Dominus, *pars*" that was long recited on the occasion of clerical tonsure; in Dan 12:13 it is a rising up at the end of days). Moreover, this heritage is incapable of destruction, fading, or defilement (v. 4). No matter what vicissitudes the baptized may undergo, their inheritance will be preserved safe in heaven, to be revealed in the last days as a birth "to salvation" (v. 5). God, in other words, will keep Christians from disaster and show forth the result of the genuineness of this faith "when Jesus Christ is revealed" (v. 7).

Does 1 Peter betray a conviction, by speaking of what will happen "in the last time" (v. 5), that the final age will come soon? Those who say so cite 1:7, 13 and especially 4:7. Yet the epistle is full of practical advice for the conduct of ongoing life, so we must not too hastily assume that the timeless "suddenness" of eschatological discourse was taken by the author and his readers to be a temporal "soon."

The exchange of letters between Pliny, imperial legate to Pontus-Bithynia in 110, and the emperor Trajan make some think that vv. 6-9 speak of a real persecution and not of the apocalyptic testing or trial that will precede the end. The genuine quality of faith, more precious than fire-tried metals, recalls Paul's usage in 1 Cor 3:11-14, where the image of the construction of each one's life on the foundation that is Christ is similar. The image of testing by fire at the final judgment, like the judgment itself, seems to have come via Babylon to Israel from Iranian sources. Here the late New Testament concentrates on love of Christ rather than of God, an idea that only begins to appear in the Johannine literature. The language of vv. 8f. is that of eschatological joy, a joy paradoxically realized in this age. Verse 9 speaks of "the salvation of your *psychōn*," meaning your persons or selves, not only your souls.

ALLELUIA. JOHN 20:29

You believe in me, Thomas, because you have seen me; happy are those who have not seen me, but still believe.

JOHN 20:19-31

This account of Jesus' appearance to his disciples is parallel to Luke's in 24:36-43. Both depend on traditions which, by the time the Gospels are written, have placed the appearance to the disciples in Jerusalem rather than the earlier tradition of Galilee. John has changed Luke's "feet" to "side" (v. 20) because of his piercing narrative in 19:34. Both evangelists are interested in connecting this appearance with the inauguration of a mission, in Luke the preaching of penance for the remission of sins (vv. 36, 47) which is to be confirmed by "the promise of my Father" (v. 49), in John the forgiveness of sins (v. 23) by the breathing of the Spirit (v. 22). Luke has separated the outpouring of the Spirit (Acts 2:1-4) from any christophany.

There is much discussion as to whether John's "forgiving" and "holding bound" (v. 23) is a disciplinary injunction similar to that of the rabbinically oriented Matt 16:19; 18:18. Even though the latter may have its origins in a post-Easter saying—the Petrine confession is thought by many to belong to the risen life—the verb Matthew uses is "loose" rather than the "forgive" of John, which is cognate with Luke's baptismally oriented use of the noun form (3:3; elsewhere, Acts 5:31; 13:38). The phrasing in John is very Hebraic, hence presumably primitive: a word of the Lord circulated in the Aramaic-speaking community. Fuller thinks vv. 22b-23 may even be the earliest form of the command to baptize.

John uses Thomas, who is just one among the Twelve in the Synoptics, as a foil of misunderstanding (11:16; 14:5) and here (20:24-29) of doubt, a role that Peter tends to have in the Synoptics. The evangelist ties in his Thomas story with the appearance story that went before—with which it does not seem to have been connected—by modeling the "locked" doors (NAB; "closed" seems a better translation) of his linking passage, v. 26, on v. 19. He employs the same parallel in v. 27 with v. 20. The creedal statement, "My Lord and my God!" would be unusual for the New Testament were it not for John's previous, studied attempts to convey Jesus' equality with God (1:1; 5:18; 8:58; 12:45; 14:9). Throughout, he remains quite clear that God is God and Jesus the presence of God in act in the last age. Such is the case here, where Thomas's expression of faith (nominative; with vocative force?) comes in a risen life that vindicates all that John has claimed for Jesus in his discourses.

An interesting question is whether Thomas ever did with his finger what Jesus directed. The evangelist does not say. He is interested in the faith of believers of his time who had not seen Jesus, not so much in an apologetic against docetism.

The last two verses (30f.) are clearly the end of the book, which only heightens the puzzle of why the Galilee appearances were added in chap. 21. They were probably in a tradition that was come upon by the author of 21:24f. who is likely to have written the whole chapter, and who in any case wishes to attribute the content of the first twenty chapters to the mysterious "disciple whom Jesus loved" (vv. 20, 24).

✍✍
Third Sunday of Easter (A)

ACTS 2:14A, [22-33] 36-41

For a commentary on 2:14, 36-41 see 4 Easter (A). Peter's reported discourse to "Jews" is to the people of Jerusalem, that is to say Judaeans, along with festal pilgrims. Alfred Loisy called v. 14 "the solemn inauguration of Christianity." Verse 22 returns to Peter's more intimate speech after his self-defense against the charge of drunkenness and the extended quotation from Joel. Jesus is identified as the Nazorean, perhaps a reference to his hometown which Luke in one place calls Nazara (Luke 4:16), elsewhere using the adjective *Nazarēnos*. The Jewish Christians came to be known as *Notsrim*, possibly for this reason, although some following another derivation think it was because they were "dedicated/consecrated" like the Nazirites. The legitimation of Jesus' mission had been accomplished by God through the "deeds of power, wonders, and signs" (v. 22) with which the hearers were presumed to be familiar. The next verse combines the workings of God's plan with man's free, malicious choice. Some translations have the agents of Jesus' destruction, "those outside the law" *(nomos)*, as pagans (NRSV), others "lawless men" (NAB), a reference to disregard of Roman justice. The explanation of Jesus' death which fixed responsibility on certain Jews in positions of power acting in concert with the occupying Roman forces had been worked out by the time of the four passion accounts. Luke's antithesis is: "you . . . killed him" (v. 23) but "God raised him up again" (v. 24). Death binds man fast, but "God freed him" (ibid.). Some think the word *anómōn* means simply "of wicked men." In any case, this text of Acts (2:23), along with 2:36; 3:15; and 4:10, has done more to fix Jewish responsibility for Jesus' death in the Christian mind than anything in the Gospels, even Matt 27:25. The results have been tragic for Jews. Because of two millennia of Christian anti-Judaism based on such texts, readers of Acts' lections on the Sundays after Easter would do well to edit them severely so as to avoid continuing anti-Jewish thinking in the popular Christian mind.

Psalm 16 is attributed, in the Jewish manner, to David, God's anointed king. In context the psalmist is expressing his confidence that God will not let him die and go down to the netherworld before his time. The Christians saw in these verses a prophecy of the raising up of God's true anointed one from the grave. They were abetted in their use of these verses as a proof-text by the LXX, which rendered a word that could mean "security" (v. 26) by "hope." Acts 13:35 will use Ps 16:10, "you will not let your holy one see corruption," in the same way, in conjunction with Ps 2:7 and Isa 55:3a. This type of interweaving of texts both here and in Peter's sermon in Acts 2 argues for the existence of collections of biblical "testimonies" for early Christian preachers. "The path of life" of Ps 16:11—upright living for the psalmist—is taken by the author of Acts to mean Christ's risen life (v. 28), which is the context in which it is quoted.

The use of the LXX throughout is an indication that Luke is the author of Peter's speeches. These he derives from the Hellenist Judaism out of which he comes rather than the primitive Jerusalem community. This highlights the theologically developed condition of early Acts with its triumphalist report of growth by leaps and bounds (2:41). The actual steps by which the gospel was spread are no less remarkable. Unfortunately, they are hidden from us.

Psalm 116:1-4, 12-19[16:1-2; 5, 7-11]

Lord, you will show us the path of life.

1 Peter 1:17[21]-23

The widespread assumption that 1 Pet 1:1-4, 11 is a baptismal homily (H. Preisker, F. L. Cross), may not be correct, but it is at least contributed to by this hortatory segment that culminates in cryptic references to "having purified yourselves" (v. 22) and "been born anew" (v. 23). The passage also undoubtedly contains embryonic creedal formulas or christological hymns (vv. 20, 21). Psalm 34:[10] ("fear the LORD, you his holy ones") probably underlies vv. 15-17. God is identified in v. 17 as a Father who judges impartially, a usage that derives from coupling the notions of God's perfect justice (Deut 10:17f.) and fatherhood (Jer 3:19; Mal 1:6). Awareness of this total impartiality should result in fear of the LORD (Isa 11:2), here expressed as a command to "live in reverent fear during the time of your exile" (v. 17). The latter phrase renders *paroikía*, an echo of the author's "exiles" of 1:1. Both words connote transitory residence without a citizen's rights. The Israelites are aliens in the LXX of Lev 25:23 and elsewhere; in Acts 13:17, their stay in Egypt is but a sojourn. Such is the earthly pilgrimage of the Christian.

The epistle tells its hearers that they have been ransomed from the "futile ways of their ancestors." This is certainly a reference to their once pagan status, for the LXX version uses the word "futile" scornfully of the heathen (see also Eph 4:17). Deliverance comes to the Christian not by silver or gold but by the precious blood of Christ. The word "ransomed" in v. 18 is redolent of the similar imagery found in both Testaments, God as redeemer or buyer back (Gen 48:16; Ps 19:14[15]; Isa 52:3; Tit 2:14; 1 Tim 2:6; Heb 9:12; Mark 10:45). The blood is not paid *to* anyone as in some erroneous later Christian theology—least of all to the devil. God is the referent rather than the recipient. It is God who acts as deliverer and rescuer of the baptized, the same role exercised in delivering Israel from the hands of the Egyptians in Exod 6:6.

The author shifts easily in v. 19 from the ransom figure to one of sacrifice. Silver and gold have a price; Christ's blood is priceless because, as eternally elect, he is a "lamb without defect or blemish." These are two adjectives in the Greek, the first reflecting the ritual requirements for beasts in Exod 29:1; Lev 22:19-21, while the second has no LXX counterpart. He who, for long ages, was chosen is now revealed. The familiar creedal God "who raised him [Christ] from the dead" (v. 21; cf. Rom 3:11; 2 Cor 4:14; 1 Thess 1:10) is, through him, the author of the "faith and hope" (ibid.) of the baptized—the latter two a coordinate that means total confidence in God rather than two distinct theological virtues. Christians are reminded at Easter that they are not simply believers in God, theists, but believers in the God who raised Christ up from the dead.

ALLELUIA. SEE LUKE 24:32.

Lord Jesus, make your word plain to us; make our hearts burn with love when you speak.

LUKE 24:13-35

As they drive to Jerusalem from the Lod airport, visitors to Israel today see a sign at Latrūn pointing to Imwās. This is one identification of the Emmaus of Luke's Gospel, but unfortunately it is more like fourteen miles from Jerusalem than seven. The medieval Franciscans hit upon modern Al Qubeiba, which is the designated "sixty stadia" from the city and more sharply to the northeast. The garrison town of Vespasian called Ammous by Josephus (modern Kaloniye), is a third possibility, though the best textual witness to his mention of it in *The Jewish War* places it only thirty stadia from Jerusalem. Exact geographical reference, however, is not Luke's primary concern. There is also the question of whether the place name and that of Cleopas (v. 18) crept into the account later

The story is a model of the storyteller's art. The empty-tomb account (vv. 22f.) and that of the assembled company in Jerusalem (v. 33) have evidently been combined with Emmaus, as a reading from vv. 21a to 25 and an examining of the link constituted by vv. 33-35 will show. The last-cited verse contains mention, by way of a flashback, of the primary appearance to Simon (cf. the primitive appearance account in 1 Cor 15:5). As in John 20:7, Peter in Luke 24:12 did not see Jesus at the tomb. The longer ending of Mark (16:9-20), which is made up of portions of the canonical risen-life accounts, reports the Emmaus story in vv. 12f. Taken together, the tale reminds us of angels visiting earth in human form (see Gen 18:1; 19:1; Heb 13:2).

The latter part of v. 19 and v. 20 strongly resembles a kerygmatic speech in Acts, while vv. 25-27 conform perfectly to the Lukan theology of glory through suffering. The poignant, "We were hoping . . . ," of v. 21 has been much preached upon, echoing as it does the probable actual state of the dispirited community. Central to the story is the identity of the two in relation to Paul's listing of appearances. Since the story is one of a later appearance in Jerusalem rather than an earlier one in Galilee, it seems that they should be identified somehow with the "all the apostles" of 1 Cor 15:7. We would be surer of this if the name of Cleopas (Greek for the Jewish Clopas) meant a particular apostolic personage.

Luke sets the disciples' recognition of Jesus in the context of a meal (v. 30), using the standard cultic vocabulary fixed by his time. This joining of the narration of appearances to table fellowship is to be expected, and it occurs elsewhere (Luke 24:41-42; Acts 10:41(?); John 21:9-14).

In the dialogue on the road, the identification of Jesus as a prophet (v. 19; cf. Deut 18:15) may mean that the narrative derives from earliest Christology. That he will "redeem/set Israel free" (v. 21) is an idea that will recur in 1 Pet 1:18, commented on above. In Luke it may be a historical reminiscence of the dashed political hopes of some. Verses 25, 26, and 27 contain the idea of the fulfillment of Scripture found in 1 Cor 15:3f. All in all, the Emmaus story is a remarkable interweaving of Easter traditions made newly meaningful by Lukan theology.

Fourth Sunday of Easter (A)

ACTS 2:42-47[14A, 36-41]

For a commentary on the later Acts passage vv. 42-47, see 2 Easter (A).

Peter's "standing with the eleven," means taking a stance for purposes of speaking publicly. The numbering of the group exclusive of Peter acknowledges the recent election of Matthias. Today's reading in LM takes for granted the first reading of last week up to v. 28, hence omits the argument that David in Psalm 16 must have been speaking of Jesus as God's faithful one who will not be let undergo corruption. It also assumes that Ps 110:1 is speaking of Jesus' heavenly glorification as the Christ, not of an earthly enthronement of a Davidic king (its original sense).

The conclusions Luke has Peter draw from his citation of Joel and the two psalms is that the crucified Jesus is beyond doubt Lord and Messiah (v. 36), for in what other age has God's Holy Spirit been poured out so profusely (vv. 33, 38) and who but Jesus has escaped death and corruption? Peter is made to charge his Jerusalem hearers (whom he addresses biblically as "Beth Israel") with the death of Christ, in the phrase, "whom you crucified" (v. 36). This interpretation of Calvary is part of the tradition by this time, as the three Synoptic passion narratives demonstrate. Yet Luke uses the charge to connote personal guilt rather than vague group guilt. His damaging theological conceit that the Jerusalem populace was responsible for Jesus' death, in other words that the sins of those who were called to be believers had brought Jesus to the cross, is an absurdity. The response proper to the charge is repentance and baptism for the forgiveness of their sins, a rite which would bring the gift of the Spirit (v. 38). Baptism "in the name of Jesus Christ" (ibid.) is the formula Luke is familiar with in his own community. There is no mention of ecstatic behavior as a result of the gift of the Spirit as in 1:5; 2:4; 10:44; 19:2-6. Hence it is a misreading of Acts to understand "baptism in the Spirit" as if extraordinary behavior such as speaking in tongues were essential to it. Here as in 8:16f. the gift of the Spirit (sixty-two times in Acts) does not have such observable effects. In the account of Peter and John at Samaria (8:16f.) the gift of the Spirit is described as separable from the rite of baptism in the Lord Jesus' name.

The result of Peter's preaching—reported as if it were given only fragmentarily ("many other arguments," v. 40)—is mass acceptance of the message and of baptism. By his use of scriptural proofs derived from the Septuagint Luke establishes that he is not reporting on primitive happenings in Jerusalem, an Aramaic-speaking church. His Peter does not depend on wonders (as at Pentecost) but on careful arguments. Luke in his various sermons is probably following the typical preaching pattern of his age (ca 90?). It includes an introduction suited to the needs of the hearers, the *kērygma* of Jesus' life, death, and resurrection, stress on the witness function of the disciples, scriptural proof, and an exhortation to repentance for the *hearers'* sins. Numerous examples of it are found in chaps. 2, 3, 5, 10, and 13 of Acts. In every case there is a legitimation of Jesus' mission by the signs that accompanied it culminating in the resurrection, and an explanation of his shameful death in terms of the presumed guilt of those who executed him. The understandable horror of an early believer at this miscarriage of justice has led him to make repeated accusations of Jerusalem's Jews (e.g., v. 36), almost all of whom had nothing whatever to do with it.

PSALM 23[1-6]

The LORD is my shepherd; there is nothing I shall want.

1 PETER 2:19[20B]-25

"Putting up with suffering" is identified as the vocation of Christians, household slaves in this case (v. 18). This underlines one of the main objectives of the letter, namely, to strengthen the readers' spirit in time of adversity. The latter need not be persecution at imperial hands; petty harassment by local magistrates will do. It is not suffering in itself that is the virtue but "patient endurance" of it (v. 20). Christ's suffering "for you" is provided as the reason for the Christian's calling; the "example" (lit.: "a child's letter-tracing," v. 21) of the sinless Jesus (v. 22, citing Isa 53:9) is put forward as a motive for following in his footsteps. The use of the fourth Servant Song (Isa 52:13—53:12) identifies Christ as the supreme example of the innocent sufferer. Some commentators think this whole passage an extract from a hymn, although the abrupt switch from the second person to the third in v. 21 indicates that a tag-line from a creed (cf. 3:18; 1 Cor 15:3) has been inserted here.

The point of vv. 22f. is that Jesus left his vindication to God, hence slaves unjustly dealt with should do the same. That Jesus "bore our sins in his body on the cross" (lit.: "tree," as in Deut 21:23) has the same sense as in Isa 53:12—either to carry or take away since the verb in the LXX is the same.

The preposition *epi* with the accusative conveys the idea of motion toward. Does the author have some figure of transferred guilt in mind, like that of an offering on an altar or the symbolic deliverance of sins onto a scapegoat? Grammatically, "on" the cross is as justifiable as "to" the cross; "righteousness" here (v. 24) needs to be understood as uprightness, a high standard of moral behavior. The "wounds" of the same verse from Isa 53:5 are actually bruises or stripes, an apt figure for slaves. The main point of the use of the servant song is probably the intimation to sufferers that, just as Christ's wounds were beneficial to many, so their endurance of persecution by others may have a vicarious quality. "Shepherd" and its cognate "guardian" or "overseer" (v. 25) are coupled in Paul's speech to the elders at Miletus, Acts 20:28. God is described in various places in the LXX as "Shepherd" and "Overseer." First Peter so designates Christ. "Your souls" are "yourselves."

ALLELUIA. JOHN 10:14

I am the good shepherd, says the Lord; I know my sheep and mine know me.

JOHN 10:1-10

The first five verses of this reading are the only parable in the Fourth Gospel, properly speaking, although John calls it a *paroimía* (v. 6), a "figure of speech." Even then, it may be understood to have allegorical elements since its follow-up in vv. 7-10 is pure allegory; but without reading the subsequent elaboration back into it, it can stand by itself as a parable. Some scholars (like John A. T. Robinson) think that two parables have been fused, the first ending at v. 3a with "the gatekeeper opens the gate for him" and the second, which begins at v. 3b, following immediately without benefit of the opening it once had. In the first half the contrast is between the shepherd and a bandit/robber (v. 1), in the second half between the shepherd and the stranger (v. 5). This opposition between two characters is standard in the Synoptic parables (cf. the Pharisee and the tax collector, Luke 18:9-14; the builders, Matt 7:24-27). The introduction of a third character, the gatekeeper, is not unusual (cf. the father in the parables of the two sons, Matt 7:21:28–31 and the prodigal son, Luke 15:11-32). The shepherd figure of John is familiar from a number of places in the Synoptics (Matt 25:32; Matt 18:12f.; Matt 9:36). At all points in the Gospels the descriptions of grazing practice are true to the realities of Palestine. "Calling his own sheep by name" (v. 3) is a phrase for knowing them individually, just as the shepherds of the Synoptics are spoken of as solicitous for individual sheep. The gatekeeper of v. 3 appears in the parable of the waiting servants (Mark 13:34), where he is in a position of trust with respect to the master of the house like the shepherd, if he does not own the flock. John's "thief" (v. 1) appears as a housebreaker in Matt 24:43f. and Luke 12:39f., parables of servants waiting for their master, although the element of surprise does not figure in John. The latter is interested in the fact that the gatekeeper admits the rightful entrant.

John in vv. 1-5 calls on material from a reservoir of tradition similar but not identical to that available to the Synoptic authors. He then uses it, characteristically, as a point of departure for his own development. In it, Jesus becomes the gate and unnamed predecessors (probably the Jewish leadership in John's area, a favorite target of John) become thieves and bandits. The usage is like that of the many Johannine "I am" statements—among them way, truth, life, vine, shepherd, living water, bread of life. The thief comes to steal, slaughter, and destroy; such is his purpose. Jesus' purpose in coming is that "they may have life . . . and have it abundantly" (v. 10). Like all the I-sayings in the Fourth Gospel, this one may well have had a creedal history in the third person.

The gift is life, a common Johannine theme, in this instance a natural complement to the figure of pasturing.

❧❧ Fifth Sunday of Easter (A)

ACTS 7:55-60[6:1-7]

For a commentary on 7:55-60 see 7 Easter (C).

The revival of the permanent diaconate in the Catholic and Episcopal Churches has created an early interest in the question, "Who were the seven?" The disciples (a self-designation of the Palestinian Jewish Christians taken over by Luke in Acts but not found in Paul) were divided among Greek-speaking Jews and Hebrew-(i.e., Aramaic) speaking Jews. The former were probably settlers in Jerusalem from the diaspora. Widows among them could have been numerous because of the tendency of the aged to gravitate toward the holy city. They would also have been dependent as a class. The "daily distribution" of 6:1 is unlike any Jewish scheme of poor relief we know of from the time. Extant data tell of the distribution of food on Friday for indigent residents and daily for transients. If these accounts and Luke's are dependable, a period of time is required for some evolution to have taken place.

The term "the twelve" appears only here (v. 2) in Acts, although it may be deduced from 1:26 and 2:14. First Corinthians 15:3-5 (ca. A.D. 54) is its first occurrence in the New Testament. An assembly is called (cf. 4:23) to solve the inequity of the neglect of preaching by the twelve to wait on tables. It is not a question of fixing blame but of remedying a situation. Numbers 27:18 in the LXX provides the verbal model—Moses' choice of Joshua, a "man in whom is the spirit." Luke requires wisdom as well, understood as administrative ability (v. 3). The passage suggests the requirements for bishops and deacons in 1 Tim 3:7ff. Luke does not use the word *diakonos*, but it is fairly inferred from *diakonía* (vv. 1 and 4) and *diakoneîn* (v. 2). The group seems, from Acts 21:8, to have become known as "the seven," possibly on a Jewish community model, "the seven of the town" to describe leading figures. It is the community that chooses these seven (v. 5) but the apostles who install them ritually (v. 6). They are seen as men of prayer, as in 1:14 and 3:1, but also given to preaching and teaching (v. 4). Stephen is singled out for his fullness of faith and the Holy Spirit, Nicolaus of Antioch as a convert (i.e., proselyte to Judaism, hence probably the only ethnic non-Jew of the seven, v. 5).

In his passage of conclusion and transition (v. 7), Luke speaks of the growth of the community in terms of Jewish priests, a sign of God's blessing. These were probably the numerous impecunious priests of the twenty-four classes among whom Zechariah was numbered (Luke 1:5), not the "chief priests" whom Luke will identify as enemies of the gospel.

The Greek names of the seven—Stephen prominent among them—help identify the greater number as Jews from the diaspora. Whenever we encounter them again they are preachers, not servants at table. This means that Luke has used the story to account for a distinct Stephen party which is provoking the wrath of certain Jews in Jerusalem (v. 15) and elsewhere (11:19f.). Diaspora Jews were also among Stephen's opponents (6:9). The cause of division was evidently a considerable freedom adopted by the Stephen party with respect to the Law (see the charges of v. 13), culminating in the acceptance of Gentiles in Syrian Antioch (11:19-24). This move is described as winning the approval of the Jerusalem community (v. 22), but in Acts 6:8-15 it resulted in Stephen's being apprehended and stoned to death. Already the interpretation of the Law in Jesus' sense, reported in the Gospels, is resulting in persecution, not only by the Sanhedrin (6, 12) but by other "Jesus Jews" as well. This division would account for the poor treatment of the Hellenist widows and the separate scheme for their relief. By the time Luke comes on the tradition there has already developed in the community a segregation on the basis of language and ideology.

PSALM 31:1-5, 15-16[33:1-2, 4-5, 18-19]

LORD, let your mercy be on us, as we place our trust in you.

1 Peter 2:2-10[4-9]

The writer wishes to support his readers in their persecuted state by reminding them of their splendid vocation as the baptized. He does this through a variety of figures developed in midrashic form (i.e., through recondite elaboration on biblical texts). Having described them as newborn infants (2:2) told they should long for pure, spiritual milk, he proceeds to speak of them as living stones to be built into a spiritual house, a holy priesthood to offer spiritual sacrifices (v. 5). He is convinced of their elite status and assurance of God's special protection. Verse 4 combines Ps 118:22 (cited in full in v. 7) and Isa 28:16, two favorite texts of the early Church (cf. Acts 4:11; Mark 12:10). The first identifies Israel as discarded by the world-powers but nonetheless marvelously exalted by God. The Christians, influenced by what may have been a Jewish messianic reading of this text, saw Jesus in the place of Israel. The "precious cornerstone in Zion" of the Isaian text is the promise made to the Davidic dynasty in 7:13-16, laid in right and justice, not lies or falsehood, and consists of Yhwh's assurance of salvation against the Assyrian threat. "Living stone(s)" in vv. 4 and 5 for Christ and the baptized is not biblical in origin; it doubtless derives from the Lord's risen status (from the tomb?) and is related to the imagery of Christ as the new temple (cf. Mark 14:58; John 2:21) and believers as a similar edifice (cf. 2 Cor 6:16; Eph 2:20), a "spiritual house" (v. 5).

They are not only a temple but a priesthood offering "spiritual" sacrifices—if coupled with Rom 12:1 the "oblationem rationabilem acceptabilemque" of the Roman eucharistic canon (cf. Heb 13:15f.). The author of 1 Peter uses the texts from Ps 118 and Isa 28 as if their authors had a personal messiah in mind, which is not the case. He then employs the phrase from Isa 8:14, "an obstacle and a stumbling stone," to describe what Jesus will do to "those who do not obey the gospel of God" (1 Pet 4:17). Such is their predestined role, even as others are called by God's foreknowledge to obedience (2:1; cf. 1 Thess 5:9). Verse 9 is a conflation of Exod 19:6 and Isa 43:20f. from the LXX. The praise meted out by 1 Peter is corporate rather than individual and conveys the clear conviction that the baptized have a corporate, priestly function. Chief among God's "deeds of power" of Acts 2:11 is the raising up of Christ from the dead. God's call out of darkness into light is not only the familiar biblical antithesis of the two, here the eschatological light (cf. John 12:35; Rom 13:12; Eph 5:14), but also a probable reference to baptism, which would shortly come to be known as *phōtismós*, "enlightenment" (cf. Heb 6:4; 10:32).

ALLELUIA. JOHN 14:6

I am the way, the truth and the life, says the Lord; no one comes to the Father except through me.

JOHN 14:1[-12]14

Jesus' discourse after the departure of Judas (13:30f.) is punctuated by questions from Simon Peter (13:36), Thomas (14:5), and Philip (14:8). In familiar Johannine style, all act as foils for Jesus. The concern of this part of the discourse is imminent separation (v. 2) which is to be followed by reunion (v. 3). During the separation the disciples will be able to "know my Father" (v. 7) and do "greater works" than any Jesus has done (v. 12). One comes to the Father only through Jesus (v. 6). Seeing Jesus is seeing the Father (v. 9). Jesus is in the Father and the Father is in Jesus (v. 11). Here we have a compendium of Johannine "realized eschatology" in which the believer is already in possession of the benefits of the last age. Such a one "sees," "knows," "comes to know," and "recognizes" the reality of the Father through the Son. The futurist eschatology of the Synoptics is not abandoned in John (cf. 14:2f.) but is subordinated to the present experience of God which "faith in me" (vv. 1, 12) brings. Jesus will again speak of his return to the Father in 16:5, 7, 17 where there is mention of the Advocate, as there will be in 14:16ff. The striking parallels between portions of chaps. 15–17 and 14 have convinced many that we have here alternative versions of the last discourse placed in sequence (some would say a different sequence), unedited.

Jesus' departure will be accompanied by his return to the believer through the gift of "another Advocate" (v. 16). Since Jesus is "the way" (v. 6), to know him is to know the way that leads where he goes (v. 4). It is also to see the Father (v. 7) who speaks and works through the Jesus in whom the Father lives (v. 10).

The "many dwelling places" of v. 2 refer to Jewish belief in compartments or abodes in heaven (cf. *1 Enoch* 39:4; *2 Enoch* 61:2). Jesus' "going" for John (v. 2) is always his death and resurrection to his Father's house. This "passion and glorification . . . is the means by which believers are admitted to the heavenly life" (C. K. Barrett). Similarly his "coming back" to take his disciples with him (v. 3) means something more in John than the Synoptic *parousía*.

Verses 10a and 10b recur in 17:21 and other passages of the prayer of that chapter. Later theology will see "circumincession" here, the intimate presence and movement of divine persons to each other. For John there is never a perfect reciprocity of Father and Son. The Son always depends on the Father and can do nothing apart from him; the Father is in no such dependent condition. He lives in Jesus and accomplishes his works in him (v. 10) but merely as a mode of self-disclosure. Belief in Jesus should come first; failing that, belief in the testimony afforded by his works (cf. 2:11; 5:26; 10:18). It is always the Father who accomplishes them.

❧.❧

Sixth Sunday of Easter (A)

Acts 17:22-31, [8:5-8, 14-17]

Whether or not Paul spoke this challenge to the pagans of Athens in front of the *Areiou Pagou* ("hill of Arēs," Latin: Mars, god of war; v. 22), the phrases are those of a Hellenist Jew presenting an apologia for the one, invisible God (see 1 Thess 1:9f.; 1 Cor 8:6). The apostle uses natural theology against the pagans who have not read the creation rightly in Rom 1:18-32. Here the author Luke employs it to bastion his appeal. To capture the hearers' benevolence Paul calls them "extremely religious," although the KJV and DRC had translated the word *deisidaimonestérous* (v. 22) as "too superstitious," following the Vulgate *superstitiosiores*. The REB opts for "scrupulous," a compromise, since the word can have a good and a bad meaning. The more favorable one accounts for its use as a woman's name, Desdemona. Visitors to St. Paul the Apostle Church near Columbus Circle in Manhattan find this short phrase in Greek in a floor mosaic as they enter the narthex. The inscription in the singular, "To an unknown god," has been found in inscriptions in the plural in Philostratus and Pausanias (citations in Richard J. Dillon, "Acts of the Apostles," in *NJBC*, ed. R. E. Brown, J. A. Fitzmyer, R. E. Murphy [Englewood Cliffs: Prentice Hall, 1990], 755).

The Lord speaks of the heavens and the earth as "all these things my hand has made" in Isa 66:2 but, whereas "made with hands" *(cheiropoíētois)* is used to modify temples or shrines, it has no such occurrence in the LXX. Israel's God does not dwell in any building nor are human hands needed in the service of God (vv. 24f.). Rather, life and breath and all things come *from* God, the common ancestor (lit.: "from one") who begot a progeny that could search, grope, and perhaps find God (vv. 26f.). Aratus's *Phaenomena* influenced by a Stoic hymn of Cleanthes are the "some of your own poets" cited. God can be imaged by no human artifacts (v. 29) but only act as judge through a man appointed whom God has raised from the dead (v. 31).

Luke began his story of Stephen's *passio* as if it had been a set of legal proceedings before the Sanhedrin (NRSV, "council," Acts 6:12) presided over by the high priest (7:1). He ends it as if it bore no relation to the procedures laid out for a legal execution by stoning (on which the later Mishnaic tractate *Sanhedrin* provides detailed information: boulders were to be dropped on the condemned man from a height). What he describes instead is the action of an infuriated mob that ends in Stephen's death. He identifies the event as one that triggers "a severe persecution against the church in Jerusalem" (8:1) and brings about a psychological change in Saul, not easily believable, from consenting bystander (v. 1) to persecuting zealot (v. 3).

In the LM reading Luke, having left the apostles in Jerusalem to assure continuity, describes the spread of the gospel in terms of the dispersion of all the rest (v. 4). The "countryside" of 8:1 is the two provinces named, not the rural districts, for the act of evangelizing is centered on the town of Samaria—probably Sebaste, though perhaps Shechem—until v. 25, when there is mention of "villages" on the return journey. The Philip of v. 5 is one of the seven (cf. 6:5) who preaches to dispersed Hellenists, going "down" (north) from elevated Jerusalem. He reappears at Caesarea as the father of four virgin daughters (21:8). The confusion between the two Philips and the Philip of the twelve (see John 12:20f.) is complete by the time of the erection of the basilica of St. Philip at the site of his martyrdom in Hierapolis, Asia Minor. Parenthetically, the traditional site of Stephen's stoning is marked by the latest of several churches named for him, in the École Biblique complex on the Nablus Road in East Jerusalem.

Philip's preaching is accompanied by visible and audible ("loud shrieks") wonders—v. 7. The result is "great joy" (v. 8) and with this familiar Lukan cachet the scene closes. The episode of Simon, the practitioner of magic, intervenes. The narrative thread is resumed at v. 14. Samaria "accepts the word of God" in the New Testament sense that there are some new believers there. Apostolic presence, in the persons of Peter and John, sets the seal on Philip's evangelizing efforts, but even the apostles are subordinated to the gift of the Holy Spirit (v. 15). Here, the Spirit is distinguished from baptism in the name of the Lord Jesus as an additional gift. Its mode of transmission is the imposition of hands, a rite which will survive minimally in baptism—although it still existed in Tertullian's time (d. after 220) as witnessed in his *De Baptismo*. It will be transmitted to what is later called "the sealing" and still later "confirmation," where the minister's hand on the confirmand's head accompanies anointing on the forehead.

PSALM 66:8-20[1-7, 16, 20]

Let all the earth cry out to God with joy.

1 PETER 3:13-22[15-18]

The context of this reading is the suffering that may come to those of upright life for their very commitment to what is good (cf. vv. 13f.). They have been promised in the above two verses that no harm can come to them (cf. Isa 50:9; Matt 10:28; 8:31) and told that if their doing right brings on pain their condition is blessed (v. 14)—the word used in the beatitudes. There is no promise, however, of immunity from physical abuse. Vulnerability and the likelihood that its consequences will overtake believers have already been conceded (2:20). A person's inner integrity will be retained through all calamities if he or she remains faithful. Verses 14f. are an adaptation of Isa 8:12f., the Asian persecutors now being understood to replace the Assyrians of Isaiah's time and "Christ as Lord" proposed as the object of blessing rather than YHWH. In the Christology of 1 Peter, Christ is freely called "Kyrios," the LXX translation of "Adonai," a substitution for the divine Name. It was the LORD in early Isaiah who would be Israel's "dread," not the fear brought on by the king of Assyria. Gentleness and reverence rather than fear are to reside in the Asian Christians' hearts (v. 16). The reply they should be ready to make is an apologia, a legal term meaning "defense," the "accounting" or "reason" they give, a *logos*. Both terms have a juridical flavor, conjuring up the interrogations of Acts 25:16 and the account that must be given before God in Rom 14:12. A less formal explanation of one's position, however, is a possibility. Rabbi Eleazar in Mishnah *'Abot* (2:14) similarly proposes that students of the Law be able to answer an "Epicurean," typical of all pagan philosophers. The Christian's response is to be such in tone (the "reverence" of v. 16 being toward God rather than the challenger) that the libelous will be shamed. If Providence has suffering in store, it should at least be unmerited by evil deeds.

See 1 Lent (B) for a continuation of the commentary on this lection.

ALLELUIA. JOHN 14:23

If any love me they will keep my words, and my Father will love them and we will come to them.

JOHN 14:15-21

C. H. Dodd finds in the "asking in my name" of v. 14 immediately preceding, a similarity to the Synoptic tradition of two or three "gathered in my name." When they ask for anything it will be granted by the Father (cf. Matt 18:19f.). An important difference is that in John prayer is addressed to Christ who will grant what is asked, "I will do it" (v. 14), rather than to the Father as in Matthew; but compare Luke 24:49. In today's reading from John the best gift of the Father is "another Advocate" (v. 16), to be given on condition of love and obedience to Christ's commandments (v. 15). The "Advocate" of 1 John 2:1, namely, Jesus Christ, similarly renders the word *parákletos*. At first it seems that this counselor of John 14 will be bestowed in Christ's absence, as with the prompting of the Holy Spirit (Luke 12:12) and words (lit., "a mouth") and wisdom (Luke 21:15) for purposes of giving witness. But v. 18 seems to equate the Advocate's "remaining" and "being in you" (v. 17) with Jesus' "I am coming to you" (v. 18). The text does not say "coming again," however, only "coming." The injunction to love Jesus and keep his commandments occurs three times: in 14:15, 21/23, 24 (in the last-cited verse, "my words"). Some commentators see a threefold presence in those who love and obey: Advocate/Spirit (vv. 16f.), Jesus (vv. 18-21), and the Father (v. 23). Yet the pattern is not perfect, for v. 23 speaks of a presence of both the Father and Jesus. It has been conjectured that the three modes of divine presence stem from three different stages of the Johannine tradition, here woven together. In such a supposition, "often the sayings about God's presence through and in the Paraclete are thought to be the latest [stage]" (R. E. Brown).

Love for Jesus is not a common New Testament theme. It occurs largely but not exclusively in the Johannine writings (but see Eph 6:24; 1 Cor 16:22; 1 Pet 1:8). It has been suggested that, as Jesus comes to be seen in a covenant relation with believers, so he is portrayed as demanding exclusive love for himself after the model of the Sinai covenant (Deut 6:5). Such love and obedience toward him as was asked by Israel's God will bring, he promises, the gift of a mysterious figure (*Parákletos*; in the Old Latin and Vulgate versions *advocatus* and *consolator* respectively) who is variously witness (John 15:26), instructor (14:26), encouraging friend (16:6f.), guide (16:13), and prover of the world wrong (16:8-11). The functions of such a one derive from the angelology of the late biblical and intertestamental periods. Only in the Qumrân literature is the title "spirit of truth" found in the pre-Christian period (1QS 4.23–24, *The Dead Sea Scrolls Translated*, trans. F. García-Martínez et al. [Leiden: Brill, 1994], 7) where it denotes either an angel or a way of life. Some lines above this we read: "The nature of all the children of men is ruled by these [two spirits]. . . . Truth abhors the works of falsehood and falsehood all the ways of truth." John follows the standard Jewish usages of having two figures in a complementary relation, the second of whom completes the work of the first; the transmission of the spirit of the main figure of these two through the second one; and a personal, angelic spirit who leads others and guides them to truth as contrasted with an opposing spirit who leads to darkness and destruction. All these images John puts in the service of the ideal of the *Advocate*, who stands for the personal presence of Jesus in the believer while Jesus is with the Father.

The idea of being "orphaned" (v. 18) is found in rabbinic writings with respect to disciples at the death of their teacher.

Verses 15-17 and 18-21 can be shown to contain two sets of parallel features, as between the coming and remaining of the Advocate and the coming and remaining of Jesus (both have the necessary conditions: the recognition of this Spirit and Jesus by the disciples and the failure of the world to recognize them; the resultant "being within" the disciples of the Spirit and Jesus). The same features occur in 1 John 3:2, 15-17, 23-24. The phrases "in a little while" (v. 19) and "On that day" (v. 20) do not fit exactly either the parousia or Christ's resurrection appearances. The Johannine outlook here stresses the continued, intimate presence of Christ to the believer "forever/always," lit.: "unto the [final] eon" (v. 16) in a love on Christ's part that is self-revealing (v. 21).

❧ ❧

Ascension of the Lord /
Thursday after the Sixth Sunday of Easter (A, B, C)

Where this feast is celebrated on the following Sunday, the second reading and Gospel given for the Seventh Sunday may be read on the Sixth Sunday.

ACTS 1:1-11

Luke 1:1-4 is a preface to Luke-Acts in its entirety, addressed to the unidentified, highly placed ("most excellent") Theophilus. Acts 1:1-5 is a preface to this book only, which reviews certain materials found in Luke 24. Among these are Jesus' being carried up to heaven (Acts 2; cf. Luke 24:51); his appearing to "the apostles" over the course of forty days (v. 3; cf. Luke 24:15f., 30f., 36); his suffering (v. 3), of which he spoke in Luke 22:25ff. and 44-47; and his meeting (to eat) with his disciples (v. 4; cf. Luke 2:42-43), at which time he told them not to leave Jerusalem (v. 4; cf. Luke 24:49). The order of events in the preface to Acts is obviously different but this does not alter or minimize their importance, namely as links between Luke's "first book" (Acts 1:1) and his second. Jesus' life, death, and glorification prepare for his Father's promise to be sent down: "power from on high" (Luke 24:49) or "being baptized with the Holy Spirit" (Acts 1:4f.) which will bring power. The detail of forty days (v. 3) does not appear in Luke's Gospel. This sacred space of time (see Gen 7:12; 8:6; Exod 24:18; 1 Kgs 19:8) gives ample room for the demonstration "by many convincing proofs" (v. 3) of his state as living. Luke's Gospel, conversely, seems to describe Jesus as leaving the Eleven after having blessed them (24:51) on the evening of the day he was raised up. (Cf. vv. 9, 13, 36, 50 for indications of the sequence.) The difference is of no consequence; least of all is it to be settled by recourse to a theory of Jesus' earthly visitations from his new home in heaven. The two things being affirmed are the reality of his being taken from his friends into glory and his conversations with them about God's reign (v. 4), which for Luke will begin with the parousia. For him the life of the Spirit-directed Church is a separate matter. The affirmations against gnostic docetism (Luke 24:43; Acts 10:41) were probably later developments. "All that Jesus did and taught" (v. 1) describes Jesus' earthly life, while the risen-life instruction (lit.: "command") he gave to the chosen apostles (v. 2) corresponds to Luke 24:44. It is in their chosenness "through the Holy Spirit" (v. 2) that they have been given authority to teach in the ways that will follow in Acts.

Luke's word in v. 2 for Jesus' being taken up has already been used in its noun form in his Gospel (9:51) for the same purpose. It seems to derive from the LXX of 2 Kgs 2:11, where Elijah—for Luke a type of Christ—was taken up in a chariot of fire.

Only in Mark 13:11 and its parallel in Matthew (not Luke, interestingly) does Jesus speak of the Spirit in the Synoptics. In Acts 1:15 and again in 11:6, a saying attributed to John the Baptizer is put on Jesus' lips (Matt 3:11; Luke 3:16). Luke will later have Paul make the same distinction in Ephesus between the water-baptism of John and the Spirit-baptism of Jesus (Acts 19:1-6) as is made in v. 5.

The apostle's query about when Israel will have the *basileía* restored to it (v. 6) is answered in terms of undivulgeable mystery (v. 7) and missionary command (v. 8). Mark 13:32 (//Matt 24:36) contains a logion of Jesus like that of v. 7 which Luke had not used in his Gospel, saving it for here. It is calculated to relieve disappointment in the Christian community over the nonrealization of the parousial hope (cf. 2 Pet 3:3ff.). By Luke's time the question is not even to be raised; a new relationship to the world has been arrived at: life in the holy community. The notion of witnessing to Jesus, viz., to his resurrection, is common throughout Acts. Jesus' sending of the apostles "to the ends of the earth" (v. 8) will mean only getting Paul as far as Rome in this book, but it is at least a divine sanction on his mission. Peter and John travel as far as Samaria.

There is no final blessing by Jesus in Acts as in Luke 24:50 (cf. Sir 50:20-21). He is taken up swiftly in the apostles' sight (v. 9), a detail that constitutes them witnesses of the ascension. Livy tells of Romulus's being swept up in a cloud, while the intertestamental book of *1 Enoch* has that prophet say the same of himself. The two men in white (v. 10) resemble those in Luke's empty-tomb account (24:4). They administer a rebuke intended for the whole Church. All expectation of the imminent return of Jesus is to be reprobated. It is a reality of the future but one that has about it no precise connotation of time

PSALM 47:[2-3, 6-9] OR PSALM 93

God ascends the throne to shouts of joy; a blare of trumpets for the LORD.
    The Lord is king, robed in majesty.

EPHESIANS 1:15[17]-23

After its greeting, Ephesians begins in v. 3 with a blessing of God for the many benefactions bestowed in Christ; it continues to v. 14 with gratitude for the seal of the promised Spirit and then moves on to a thanksgiving in vv. 15-23 (see v. 16). The anonymous author, known to some as "the Ephesian continuator," includes both forms because such was Paul's practice at various times. The technique, while redundant, is nonetheless to be found in Dan 2:20, 23. The hope expressed in the present passage is that the wisdom bestowed on Gentile Christians (v. 9) may be received by them effectively (v. 17). A heritage has been given, the wealth of which (v. 18) consists in wisdom and understanding (v. 9). This inheritance is not yet fully given but exists at present as a pledge or first payment (v. 14) to be rendered in its entirety when the full redemption of "God's own people" (cf. 1 Pet 2:9) has been bestowed. Such time will be after the parousia. The acceptance of the inheritance by believers is required if it is to be a completed reality. That Christians may know the hope to which they are called, the "eyes of [their] hearts" must the enlightened (v. 18). God's power in the believer is likened to the strength shown in Christ in his being raised from the dead and seated at God's right hand (v. 20). Verse 20 importantly distinguishes between the resurrection and the subsequent exaltation of Christ, something that Paul does not do. He thinks in terms of a single act of glorification, while Luke-Acts resembles Ephesians in its division of the mystery into two episodes.

Mention of having heard of the Ephesians' faith (v. 15) betrays this excellent pastoral and theological treatise in epistolary form as not having been written by someone who lived among the recipients for quite a while (two years, according to Acts 19:10). Paul knew this congregation as well as any and did not need to learn of its faith by hearsay.

The anti-gnostic or anti-angelic-hierarchy tone of Colossians is caught in vv. 21-23 and again in 6:12. Christ is high above the choirs of angels. Four of the traditional nine are here named: rulers, authorities, cosmic powers, and spiritual forces of evil (Col 1:16 has "thrones" and "dominations"). Pseudo-Dionysius in his *Celestial Hierarchies* names three groups of three: seraphim (Isa 6:2), cherubim (Ezek 1:5) and thrones; virtues, powers, and principalities; dominations, archangels, and angels. The headship of Christ here (vv. 22-23) is over his body, the Church, whereas in 1:10 it had been over all things in heaven and on earth and over every principality and power in Col 2:10. The important declaration of faith in Christ (as in Col 2:9) is that he has been made the "fullness" of the one who fulfills everything in the universe, namely, God. Colossians says that the fullness of God dwells in Christ Jesus bodily. Both writers mean to challenge all gnostic and angelic hierarchies that lay claim to *plērōma* status and put in their place an ascended, exalted Christ and him alone (Eph 1:23).

ALLELUIA. MATTHEW 28:19 AND 20

All authority in heaven and on earth has been given to me.

LUKE 24:44-53

For a commentary, see Ascension of the Lord (C).

MATTHEW 28:16-20

This concluding section of Matthew with its command to make disciples of all the nations (a proper ending such as no other Gospel has), is a departure from the description of Jesus' ministry to Israel attributed to him in 10:5f. and 15:24. The evangelist's pattern for Christ's "all authority" (v. 18) is no doubt the dominion given to "one like a son of man" in Daniel and in the LXX "all glory." Matthew has used an earlier part of the Daniel text in 26:64. The concluding vision of the book of Isaiah cannot be far from his mind; in it, God's glory shall be proclaimed to the nations (cf. Isa 66:19) and Israel's siblings from all the nations (v. 20) shall be brought as an offering to the Lord. The "in" of v. 19 is literally "into" *(eis)*, connoting entrance into the messianic community understood as fellowship with the Father and the Son and the Holy Spirit. Matthew has spoken only of the kingship of the Son and Man and that of the Father up to this point (16:27f.). In adding the Holy Spirit he follows a lead already given by Paul in 1 Cor 12:4-6 and 2 Cor 13:13. Matthew is probably citing a baptismal formula from his church in Antioch, where it is found again in *Didachē* 7 (first or second century), in which "running water" is prescribed. The phrase "to the end of the age" (v. 20), used also in Matt 13:39, 40; 24:3, is of some help in establishing the primitive character of the tradition on which it is based.

❧✦

Seventh Sunday of Easter (A)

ACTS 1:6[12]-14

Luke's Book Two opens with the risen Jesus appearing to his disciples over forty days telling them to wait in Jerusalem until they are baptized with the Holy Spirit (1:5). Once assembled they address him as Lord and put a question natural in the presence of one who has come back from the dead. Would their hopes for the kingdom that he has preached so often now be fulfilled? Was this the time for its restoration? Jesus answers in the negative, as Luke has had him do in the Gospel (Luke 21:9). There he said that a great period of persecution must intervene (vv. 12-19). This time he tells them that God has not revealed a schedule of future events. They must await the power of the Holy Spirit to confirm them as his witnesses, both in the land of Israel and to the ends of the earth. With the abruptness that marks many Gospel narratives, since none of the evangelists has produced a polished novella by a modern standard, Jesus is immediately lifted up and enveloped in a cloud. His glorious ascent is described in a half sentence. Two men in white robes, presumably the same pair as at the tomb in Luke 24:4, charge the disciples with stargazing—time lost when they could be up and about proclaiming the good tidings of the Risen One. In a clever description not of history but of time future they predict his coming *(parousía)* as a reversal of his going *(exodos,* Luke 9:31).

Zechariah 14:4 describes the feet of the LORD as resting on the Mount of Olives on the day of a mighty battle between Jerusalem and all the nations. "The Lord" (Acts 1:6) is understood to be Jesus, not YHWH. A Sabbath's journey was the distance a Jew might travel without breaking the commandment to stay at home on that day (Exod 16:29). Much later reckoned at 960 yards, it was somewhat over the athlete's 880 or half-mile. The "eleven and their companions" who had been gathered in Jerusalem (Luke 24:33) were led out as far as Bethany (Luke 24:50) by Jesus to witness his being taken up into heaven. That town's modern site, el-'Azariyeh, is a couple of miles around the base of the Mount of Olives. Luke is unconcerned here, as elsewhere, with a topography he does not know.

Having made his point calmly about possible idle speculation concerning Jesus' coming (v. 11), he returns the eleven—whom he names—to the city and the "upstairs room where they were staying" (v. 13). Since the word is different the place may not be the large room upstairs of Luke 22:12. Luke 24:53 returns the eleven to the temple for continual prayer (notice Acts 2:46). His list of disciples is not identical in order with that of Luke 6:4-16; the three groups of four remain, but in different sequences in the first two cases, while Judas Iscariot is missing from the last. "The women" of Luke 24:10 were three who are named plus "the other women"; in 8:3 Susanna appears but not Mary the mother of James. Mark 6:3 names James, Joses, Judas, and Simon as Jesus' brothers. These, together with Jesus' mother, give us a sizeable nucleus, especially if the men's wives are included. Such was the company that devoted itself steadfastly to pray "together" or "with one accord," a favorite Lukan adverb for acting in concert). Luke is trying to identify the earliest Jewish congregation—probably made up of women of means (see Luke 8:3) and Jesus' more plebeian family members.

PSALM 68:1-10, 32-35

PSALM 27:1, 4, 7-8A

I believe that I shall see the good things of the LORD in the land of the living.

1 PETER 4:12-14; 5:6-11[13-16]

This epistle, actually a treatise, has brought home to its readers the idea that the Christian calling is one of suffering after the example of Christ (2:21), and that to have suffered in the flesh like him is to have broken with sin (4:1). Today's passage is a return to that theme. To suffer is to have cause for present rejoicing, just as at the revelation which his parousia will be there will be reason to rejoice anew. (Compare Rom 8:17; 2 Tim 2:11, for the same sentiment, a commonplace in New Testament writings.) Verse 14 is reminiscent of Matt 5:11 and uses the same word to describe the happiness of those insulted for the sake (lit.: "the name") of Christ. "The Spirit of the Father will be speaking in you" was Jesus' word to those handed over to authority (Matt 10:20). Stephen, too, "filled with the Holy Spirit . . . saw the glory of God" (Acts 7:55). The spirit resting on the early believers here (v. 14) is the "glory" of the Old Testament (as in Exod 16:10; 24:16). The God who comes now will be given to sufferers in God's fullness at the end.

The shift to vv. 15f. is puzzling in its harshness. The point made seems to be that suffering for being a *Christianós* (the word occurs elsewhere only in Acts 11:26 and 26:28) is noble, whereas a Christian's suffering for his sins is something else again. The list of heinous crimes seems to be a stock one—more rhetorical than actual as regards the community members in question. If there is a practical lesson to be learned it is that believers long adept at crying "foul" need to be sure that none of their suffering is fair.

The letter goes on to invite God's judgment on the Christian community ("the household of God," 4:17), confident that innocent sufferers will continue to do good in a spirit of trust (4:19; 5:7). Humility in the present is the key to future glory (5:6). The figure of the roaring lion as the psalmist's enemy (22:21) or the prophet's princes in Babylon (Ezek 22:25) is employed to represent the devil as adversary (v. 8), a verse used in the Church's night prayer (now only Tuesdays). He must be resisted, for whatever sufferings the far-flung "exiles of the Dispersion" (1:1) are experiencing—and the provinces named in the opening verse cover the bulk of modern Turkey—they must take comfort from the fact that all other believers (*adelphótēti*, 5:9) worldwide are undergoing the same. The knowledge alone does not console, rather the awareness that all alike, called to God's glory in Christ, know God to be their support and their strength (v. 10). A doxology is the fitting end of the letter's substance (v. 11).

ALLELUIA. JOHN 14:18

The Lord said: I will not leave you orphans. I will come back to you and your hearts will rejoice.

JOHN 17:1-11[A]

The term "high priestly prayer" goes back to D. Chrytaeus (d. 1600). Some scholars (notably Käsemann) see in the prayer of Jesus of chap. 17 the climax of the final discourse, an epilogue to his public life provided by the evangelist to match the prologue. Thus, "a glory I had with you before the world began" (17:5) speaks to the "glory as of a father's only son" which "we have seen" of 1:14. The prayer of Christ, which is the form this chapter takes, is a proclamation and a thanksgiving, not a petition. Jesus earlier uttered a prayer of thanks to God "for the sake of the crowd," for "I know that you always hear me" (John 11:42). The prayer of John 17 is at once a concluding testament and a farewell speech—like Moses' song and blessing on the tribes (Deuteronomy 32 and 33), the *Testaments of the Twelve Patriarchs*, and Paul's charge to the elders of Ephesus at Miletus (Acts 20).

"The speaker is not a needy petitioner," Käsemann writes, "but the divine revealer and therefore the prayer moves over into being an address, admonition, consolation, and prophecy" (*The Testament of Jesus according to John 17* [Philadelphia: Fortress Press, 1968], 5). Later in the chapter Jesus will pray for his disciples and for all believers. In the early portion he makes a proclamation of fidelity to his charge: "I have . . . finished the work you gave me to do" (v. 4), "I have made your name known" (v. 6), "The words you gave to me I have given to them" (v. 8). The Johannine Christ has been obedient to his Father in sharing a knowledge of the Father's glory. His obedience has been this glory incarnated and made manifest. The result of his embassy will be eternal life to believers (v. 3; the life proper to the final *aiōn*) and a resumption of glory at his Father's side. Heavenly glory has broken in upon those who believe in Jesus' teaching.

As he prepares to return to the realm from which he came, those who accepted him are invited to pass from death to life. Knowledge is their means of doing this (see Wis 15:3), a knowledge of the only true God and him whom God has sent (v. 3). Having received the entrusted words (v. 8) they continue to possess the presence of Christ. All that Jesus has is God's and all God has is his (v. 10). Those whom God gave to Jesus are likewise God's (v. 9). Their belief in Jesus' words contributes to his glory: "I have been glorified in them" (v. 10). He stakes out a portion of "the world," which by definition is *not* his Father's realm, as a place that becomes such by the very presence of believers in it (v. 11a). As Jesus comes to his Father he leaves a portion of the Father's glory behind: the community of faith. Differences between John's conception of Jesus' person and mission and that of the Synoptics is clear. For them he is a person of earth exalted to God's right hand by obedience to his calling. For John he is a visitor from above who goes back to where he was before to enjoy the (now augmented) glory that was his.

❧❧

Day of Pentecost (A)

Acts 2:1[11]-21 or Numbers 11:24-30

For a commentary on the latter passage see Proper 21 [26] (B). Commentary on Acts 2:12-21 begins on the next page.

Those who are gathered in one place are "all," in the Greek text—the one hundred twenty of 1:15. They assemble on the Jewish feast of Weeks, *Shavuoth*, which comes at the completion of seven weeks, "from the day after the Sabbath, the day on which you bring the wave-offering sheaf" (Lev 23:15f.; cf. Deut 16:9-12). This makes it the fiftieth day, in Greek *pentēkostē*. The noise heard by the gathering resembles that of a driving wind. All in the house hear it. The parted, fiery tongues (or "tons of fire," in the reading provided by a small school child) appear in *1 Enoch* 14:8-15 and 71:5. There, however, the tongues convey divinity without connoting differences of language. Individual flames rest on the believers (v. 3), filling each of them with the Holy Spirit (v. 4). Their expression in speech is solemn or inspired, not ecstatic (the verb means simply "speak"); the "other" languages are foreign rather than various, as *dialéktō* in v. 8, one's native tongue, will show. The utterance the disciples begin to engage in is proclamation rather than ordinary discourse, as shown by the participial form of *laleîn* (v. 11). There is no indication of ecstatic Spirit-language. Such speech would mean nothing to hearers who were not yet believers and hence would defeat the purpose.

Authorities differ on whether the Jews "staying in Jerusalem" (v. 5) were pilgrims (Billerbeck) or regular residents (Haenchen). A multilingual population from the diaspora of both Jews and proselytes (cf. v. 10) is indicated, whichever the case. They are attracted by the "sound" (v. 6), but whether this is the "noise" or "rush" of the wind in v. 2 or the diverse speech of the assembly of believers is hard to say.

Confusion and utter amazement are the reactions (vv. 6f.) of the crowd to the marvel of Galilean Jews being heard in the variety of languages listed (vv. 8ff.). The author inserts their query, beginning at v. 7, as a means of conveying the wonder that was taking place. He is not interested in an exact analysis of the linguistic occurrence, just as throughout he is creating the mood of the Spirit's visitation rather than writing a documentary. Yet one point that he wishes to make is that the disciples are not speaking a single Spirit-language that all could follow. The marvel consists in the variety of languages of the hearers, all of them made comprehensible.

The Medes and the Elamites (v. 10) were a historical memory by the time of the writing so they must have been borrowed from the LXX to convey the idea of remote distances. If Judaea is removed from v. 9, twelve regions remain in vv. 9-10. These undoubtedly corresponded to the signs of the zodiac, as Cumont's researches (1909) reported by Haenchen, *The Acts of the Apostles* (Philadelphia: Westminster, 1971), showed. In such a scheme, Persia was the ram, Babylon the bull, etc. (cf. Dan 8:20f.). Luke has rendered Persia as Parthia, a military threat that was on everyone's lips in his day; Aquarius was Egypt. Each country named possessed a Jewish population. Missing from the list in Acts are Armenia (unless Pontus is meant in its place) and Hellas-Ionia. Luke makes up his twelve—Libya Cyrenaica is eleventh—by adding Phrygia and Pamphylia, provinces of Asia Minor. The "Cretans and Arabs" (v. 11) fall outside the zodiacal scheme of twelve and, like "Judaea," are a later addition. Luke's ordering is presumably calculated. It begins with the specter of Parthia and ends in Rome (Italy = the scorpion), where his book will also conclude. A reason for various inclusions may be that Aquila and Priscilla came from Pontus (Acts 18:2), Apollos from Egypt (18:4), and Lucius from Cyrene (13:1) along with various unnamed others (11:20). In any event, the author of Acts wishes to make it clear that the spread of the gospel to far-flung parts existed germinally on Pentecost day through the Jews and proselytes assembled in Jerusalem. We should not look for a Gentile witness here. That is to be inaugurated, for Luke, with the conversion of the household of Cornelius in Acts 10:45.

The disciples celebrated in speech God's deeds of power (v. 11), a generic term that Peter will spell out in his description of the career and glorification of Jesus immediately following.

The disciples' amazement and perplexity is comprehensible as is the attribution of their speech in the pilgrims' many languages to having too much to drink—the handiest explanation for bizarre behavior (vv. 12f.). Peter denies that the speaking in languages familiar to others is caused by drunkenness. After all, it is on a pilgrimage feast and every language of the diaspora could be heard in Jerusalem's streets. In the first of the "Peter speeches" he begins to explain the strange happenings by quoting at length from the prophet's apocalyptic imagery (vv. 17-21; see Joel 2:28-32a, NAB 3:1-5 according to the LXX) in a book that predicts the final days. Luke is the author of the reconstructed *earliest* days in Jerusalem, weaving later frequently employed arguments from the Scriptures into his narrative, some based on the Pentateuch and Psalms.

PSALM 104:24-34, 35B[1, 24, 29-31, 34]

Lord, send out your Spirit, and renew the face of the earth.

1 CORINTHIANS 12:3B[7, 12]-13

The context of the earliest and briefest of creedal statements, "Jesus is Lord" (v. 3b), is a discussion by Paul of spiritual gifts (v. 1). The chief of these has been the progress made by Corinthian Gentile Christians from their worship of mute idols to that of the living God through Christ. The ability to proclaim Jesus' Lordship is a gift of the Spirit; nothing else will adequately account for it. In what circumstances might Christians declare him accursed (v. 3a)? These are hard to conceive. Paul may simply need a balance for his contention that faith in Jesus expressed by ecstatic utterance is a work of the Spirit. Some have thought that he had in mind the weakness of Christians hailed before civil or synagogal authority. If these were to yield to pressure and say "Cursed be Jesus!" as commanded, this could not be an utterance of the Spirit. Again, according to others, if frenzied speech in the community—the "tongues" of 13:8 about which the entire discussion of chap. 14 is concerned—should result in such a contradictory utterance, Paul is holding here that it is to be judged immediately by its content. The statement is false, hence the Spirit of God cannot be its author.

At no time does Paul deny the reality of ecstatic speech or behavior. It is assumed to have been a phenomenon of Greek paganism, unless he introduced something of the behavior of Eldad and Medad (Num 11:26-29) or Saul (1 Sam 19:23f.) into the Corinthian community—perhaps a Hebraizing of Greek behavior. Paul simply wishes to provide norms for the discernment of claims made for the Spirit. Gifts differ (12:4); so do ministries (v. 5) and works (v. 6). They are all the doing of the same Spirit. A manifestation of the Spirit to an individual is always made with the same purpose, namely, mutual profit or "the common good" (v. 7). Later theological language will speak of such gifts as *gratiae gratis datae*, meaning freely given—church offices, for example—for the purpose of further transmission of the divine gift. Paul judges all such endowments as personal but communal in God's design. He is rejecting strongly the idea that God could act in such a way for the benefit of the individual only. This brief passage provides the principle that he will later specify at length: while each member of the Church has his or her gift and none is excluded, none has received it for private use but for the good of all. As Paul will make clear in chap. 14, any contest between tongues and teaching is to be settled in favor of the latter. "Prophecy," here meaning comprehensible teaching, is demonstrably in the common interest; tongues may or may not be. The one thing that can be clearly shown about the latter is that they are a gift to the individual. Hence any speaking in tongues must yield to an intelligible exposition of its meaning.

SEQUENCE

Veni, Sancte Spiritus. (Come, Holy Spirit, send forth a ray of heavenly light.)

JOHN 20:19-23 OR JOHN 7:37-39

For a commentary on John 20:19-23 see 2 Easter (A). If 7:37b and 38a are read as a couplet, "If anyone is thirsty let him come to me / and let the one who believes in me drink," then "out of his heart" (lit., mid-section) means from Jesus, not the believer, gratuitously added by NRSV. The scripture that John has in mind (v. 38) could be Exod 17:1-6 or Ps 78:15; 105:41.

❧ Season after Pentecost ❧
(Ordinary Time)

❧❧
Trinity Sunday / First Sunday after Pentecost (A)

GENESIS 1:1 — 2:4A

A Priestly author is responsible for this prose poem which is basically an exhortation to Sabbath observance (2:2f.; cf. Exod 31:17). The Yahwist contributed another creation account, employing phrases characteristic of the Elohist (2:5-25). The verb *bārā* (1:1) does not mean created in the sense of made out of nothing but rather shaped or fashioned, in this case of a "formless void" (*tōhû, bōhû*). The idea of *ex nihilo* does not occur in the Masoretic canon of Scripture but something close is found for the first time in the LXX's 2 Macc 7:28 "did not make them out of existing things." "Began to create" is the better translation of 1:1, as given in *Tanakh: The Holy Scriptures* (Philadelphia: Jewish Publication Society of America, 1985). There are several features of the biblical account derived from the Akkadian *Enuma elish* epic and other Mesopotamian cosmogonies, but without the cosmic struggles of the separation of the gods of earth and sea from those of sky and so on. In Genesis God acts as a methodical craftsman calmly engaged in a week's work, at the conclusion of which like any observant Jew he rests. The days begin in the darkness of night with the wind *(rûaḥ)* creating a turbulence on the waters (*tĕhōm*, "the deep"). God does a work primarily of *separation* of preexistent realities on the following days: (1) light from darkness (vv. 3f.); (2) a dome called sky *(rāqîa)* dividing the waters under from those above it (vv. 6ff.); (3) the earth then separated from the seas, bringing forth seed-bearing plants and trees of every sort (vv. 9-13); (4) the sun distinct from the moon and the stars, each with the practical purpose of lighting up the land by day or by night and creating the seasons, and not to be worshiped as the pagans do (vv. 14-19); (5) the sea creatures separated from the birds (vv. 20-23); (6) the animals tame and wild from the humans of two sexes in God's image, whose charge it is to have dominion over them and subdue the earth while humankind itself increases and multiplies (vv. 24-31). God then blesses and makes holy the seventh day and abstains from all work on it, having serially declared the various effects of the creative hand good (vv. 10, 12, 18, 21, 25) and the totality very good (v. 31).

Each day begins with the evening in the Jewish manner; also, all subhuman and human species are presumed to be herbivores. Only after the flood are the animals, birds, and fish in dread of Noah's offspring because the LORD has decreed them fit for consumption on condition that their life's blood be not in them (9:2ff.). This indicates that in the postexilic period of the composition of the creation accounts the kosher laws were in place. As to the first of these public readings on Trinity Sunday in RCL (the initial lection of the Easter Vigil in LM and RCL), the passage must be acknowledged as a work of theological and literary genius. Based on ordinary observation, the groundwork of all that we call the sciences, this prose poem about the universe and the earth we inhabit would be hard to improve in the same economy of words. One can only deplore its debasement as "creation science" with its well-meant retaining of the divine creative hand at the expense of both literary genus and genius.

The "generations" *(tôldôth)* of 2:4 are literally "begettings" and are the blocks into which a final editor has organized the material. See its recurrence in 2:4; 5:9; 6:1; 10:1; 11:10 before Israel's story begins, then again five times in that people's narrative: 11:27; 25:12; 25:19; 36:1; 37:2, rendered usually by "descendants" but sometimes by "sons" or "story."

PSALM 8

EXODUS 34:4B-6, 8-9

Martin Noth reconstructs the original J (Yahwist) narrative as follows: chap. 19, then some part of 24:12-15a according to which Moses was summoned up the mountain, followed immediately by chap. 34 with its reference to the broken tablets (v. 1). The latter verse was inserted to take into account Moses' wrathful response to the golden calf episode (32:19). This chapter with its religious laws is explicit about the terms of the covenant YHWH makes with his people (34:4). The LORD has announced that he will write on the tablets (v. 1) and has told Moses to be ready in the morning (v. 2), probably by some cultic preparation like that described in 19:10f. The mountain is to be free of anyone but Moses, including flocks and herds (v. 3). The ritual sacredness (i.e., separateness) of the mountain is to be strictly preserved.

Moses makes his way to the top as instructed in v. 2, and YHWH descends in a cloud, standing next to him. It is not easy to determine whether the speaker in vv. 5-7 is Moses or the LORD. In whichever case, the sacred Name is proclaimed and God is celebrated for mercy and justice in stereotyped phrases (cf. Ps 103:8f.; Exod 20:5). The LORD's "passing before" Moses and calling out to him from a cloud (v. 6) is suspect as authentic J material, being closer to the less anthropomorphic 33:18-23. Verse 8 describes the natural, awestruck reaction of Moses to the LORD's passing by. The purpose of the account of the theophany is to underscore the common lot of the God of Israel and the people despite the latter's sins (v. 9). Moses sets the condition: "If I have found favor with you." His function is mediatory. The presence of the Lord effected by the covenant with Israel is not distant: "Let the LORD go with us . . . take us for your inheritance" (v. 9).

The Vulgate, from which LM is taken, has "Dominator, Domine Deus" in v. 6 for the Hebrew YHWH, YHWH El. One supposes that this verbal occurrence accounts for the use of the passage on Trinity Sunday.

PSALM 8; DANIEL 3:52-56

Glory and praise forever!

2 CORINTHIANS 13:11-13

Chapters 10–13 of this epistle are as severe a polemic against anyone as Paul indulges in, with the strictures they contain against the "super apostles" (11:5). The passage 13:11-13 seems to be the conclusion to an independent letter (the epistle written "with many tears" of 2:4?). A minority maintain that it concludes the one letter written in several different moods (chaps. 1–7; 8; 9; 10–13). In any case, these three verses are an unmistakable Pauline valedictory. They contain a charge to the Corinthians to "Put things in order," to encourage one another, to think harmoniously, and to live in peace (v. 11). The reward for such behavior will be a dwelling with them of "the God of love and peace" (ibid.). The holy kiss of v. 12 is the ordinary Eastern embrace, not the mouth to mouth or mouth to cheek kiss of the West. It is, at the same time, the model of the restored exchange of peace in congregations where people know each other more than casually. The "saints" of v. 12 are the baptized—standard New Testament usage.

Paul's farewell culminates in a triadic invocation in which grace is connected with the Lord Jesus Christ, love with God, and communion with the Holy Spirit. Is the threefold usage conscious with Paul? Undoubtedly it is. Does he have three gifts in search of tutelary patrons? It is much more likely that he is carried on from the mention of Christ as Lord to the God from whom the Lord comes and then to the Holy Spirit without whom nothing in the order of grace is accomplished. All three are indiscriminately tied to the three gifts. There is, however, a sense in which God is the author of a selfless *love* that he shares through the *grace* of his deed in Christ, the result being a *fellowship* in the Holy Spirit which is the Church.

Aʟʟᴇʟᴜɪᴀ. Sᴇᴇ Rᴇᴠᴇʟᴀᴛɪᴏɴ 1:8

Glory to the Father and to the Son and to the Holy Spirit: to God who is, who was, and who is to come.

Mᴀᴛᴛʜᴇᴡ 28:16-20

For commentary see 6 Easter (A).

Jᴏʜɴ 3:16-18

This brief segment of the Johannine kerygma centers on God's Son as the end-time revealer—the one sent by the Father not for the condemnation of the world but, because of God's great love for it, its salvation. The use of the first person does not occur here or in the conclusion of the discourse (vv. 31-36), unlike the usage in the solemn declarations of 5:19, 24, 25. The absence of the phrase "I am," found in all the other great discourses, does not however mean that John is not presenting a revelation of God by the Son. The evangelist's "We testify to what we have seen" (3:11) is his way of identifying himself completely with the testimony of the eschatological revealer about what goes on in heaven. He has "transposed it into his testimony as preacher" (Schnackenburg). The question whether Christ or the evangelist is the speaker would be falsely put. The latter's vocabulary of "seeing," "knowing," and "testifying" indicates that what Christ has revealed he, John, transmits unaltered.

Verse 16 sums up the whole message of redemption in memorable form. First John 4:9f. will repeat it, with the added note of Christ's uniqueness as Son supplied by the Greek word order. The giving of v. 16 is the sending of v. 17, not the delivering over of the passion account (cf. John 18:30, 35, 36; 19:11, 16). The purpose of the giving is belief unto eternal life, not rejection unto death (*apólētai*, lit "destruction," "ruin"). The "world" of v. 16 is the world of a human race separated from God and in need. It will divide itself by its response to God's revealer into an inimical world and a community of salvation. Condemnation—adverse judgment—is not what God intends in sending the Son. Lack of faith in the Son will result in it, but what God has in mind is that the world be saved through him (v. 17). The life and death may be literal life and death for John in the manner of the Jewish Scriptures, just as condemnation and rescue are literally that. The believer escapes condemnation; the unbeliever is already condemned by the fact of his unbelief. He should have committed himself over in faith to God's only Son ("the name"). Instead, judgment overtakes him here and now in a final age that has arrived.

John's basic scheme of salvation is binitarian rather than trinitarian. He is familiar with a begetting Spirit (v. 8), who in a subsequent passage will be seen as an enveloping light (v. 20) and truth (v. 21). His great concern, however, is with a Son who reveals the Father in an invitation to belief. The invitation can be accepted only if an unseen Spirit like the wind is let to blow where it will (v. 8). In such case, Spirit will beget spirit (v. 6). The alternative is a begetting of flesh by flesh which means the world, condemnation.

The apocryphal "Johannine comma" of 1 John 5:7, a third century Latin interpolation of the North African church and then the Spanish, identified the three witnesses in heaven as "Father, Word, and Spirit," a needless explication taking its lead from the threefold witness of "Spirit, water, and blood." The interpreters and copyists of the patristic age were unwise not to let well enough alone. All three witnesses are in effect testimony on the Son's behalf, the testimony possessed in the heart by the fact of belief. If Father, Word, and Spirit are all witnesses, there is nothing left to witness *to*. The Johannine triad is much more subtle—and much more clearly a dyad.

☙ ❧

The Body and Blood of Christ (A)
(Thursday after Trinity Sunday but Commonly Celebrated on the Following Sunday)

DEUTERONOMY 8:2-3, 14B-16A

"Deuteronomy" takes its name from 17:18, where the Greek word renders the Hebrew phrase, "a copy of this law." It is cast in the form of three addresses given by Moses on the plains of Moab (1:1—4:43; 4:44—28:68; 29:1—30:20), followed by a series of appendices in chaps. 31–34. He begins to speak "on the first day of the eleventh month" (1:3) and dies on Mount Nebo (34:4). A thirty-day period of mourning follows (34:8). By the tenth day of the first month the Israelites under Joshua are camped near Jericho (Josh 4:19). This works out to a forty-day period for Moses' discourse. The book probably emanated from Priestly circles in the north rather than Jerusalem and under the influence of eighth-century prophets like Hosea and Jeremiah. Critical scholarship relates the book to the reform of King Josiah in 621. The book is more likely to have been the cause of such a reform than the result (see the tradition of the discovery of the "book of the law" in 2 Kings 22–23, taken by many to be Deut 12–26, 28, but possibly even Deut 4:44—30:20). Linguistically, Deuteronomy has affinities with the E stratum of the first four books of the Torah.

Chapter 8, from which this reading is taken, is central to the book. It names obedience to God as the condition of Israel's prosperity and warns against idolatry as the path to ruin: "It is the LORD your God who gives you the power to acquire wealth. . . . But if you forget [God], and follow other gods . . . you will perish utterly" (vv. 18f.). Today's reading has Moses reminding Israel of the LORD's protective care during the forty years of desert journeying and the testing of the people's intent to remain obedient by the afflictions God has sent (v. 2). They are reminded of the manna (cf. Exod 16:15, where a popular etymology renders *man hu* by "What [is] this?" *man* doing double duty as the late Aramaic "what?" and "manna"). The mysterious "food [the generic *leḥem* which the LXX makes "bread"] unknown to you and your ancestors" (Deut 8:3) is the sweet, sticky sap of a tree (the Arabic *tarfa,* tamarisk?) that has passed through the bodies of insects. The point the Deuteronomist makes is that any contemporary of his too sophisticated to revert to idol worship as in desert days may credit himself with his own achievements (v. 17) and thereby "promote himself to the divine vacancy" (Henton Davies).

The sense of the antithesis "bread alone" and "every word that comes from the mouth of the LORD" is not material versus spiritual—the interpretation generally put on it especially since its attribution to Jesus (Matt 4:4; cf. Luke 4:4)—so much as it is between one kind of sustenance and another that is more lasting. If the latter is accepted, namely, God's words of command, then every benefit of life both spiritual and material will come to Israel.

Matthew has Jesus quoting Deuteronomy accurately according to sense, for the intent of the temptation narrative is to show that Jesus counsels living trustfully by God's word as did the Deuteronomist. This, presumably, Israel failed to do in its time of temptation.

The typology of manna for the Eucharist on the feast of the Body and Blood of Christ should be clear. The evangelist employed it with respect to the person of Christ (cf. John 6:48ff. and see commentary on it below). The Roman liturgy uses the manna/Eucharist typology in the versicle and response: "You gave them bread from heaven to eat," "providing in itself every pleasurable taste" (from Wis 16:20, which also contains the phrase "bread of angels"). The isolation of the manna theme in this truncated reading (returned to in v. 16) obscures the central point of the chapter: the very richness of Canaan, with its potential for agriculture (v. 8) and its iron and copper (v. 9), will provide occasion for the self-delusion that says, "My power and the might of my own hand have obtained for me this wealth" (v. 17). The editing of this pericope is a reminder of how unbiblical it can be to preach about bread from heaven as a type of providential care without reference to the idolatry of self, latent in certain economic patterns. The omitted portion (vv. 4-13) is important for the meaning of the whole, establishing as it does the folly of taking for granted the rich earth and the comfortable living it affords.

PSALM 147:12-15, 19-20

Praise the LORD, Jerusalem.

1 CORINTHIANS 10:16-17

Paul is counseling his formerly pagan Corinthian Christians to be wary of trafficking with demons (cf. Deut 32:17) in eating meats sacrificed to idols (vv. 14, 19-21). Such is the context of his statement that participating in the cup and in the bread means sharing in Christ's body and blood. A sharing with those whom the food represents—whether Christ or demons—is assumed. The assumption underlies his argument. The union with Christ that Paul claims for participants in the eschatological meal is more than a merely moral one; it is real in the order of symbol. "Cup of blessing" is a technical term found in Jewish sources for the cup of wine drunk at the end of a meal to close it formally (cf. 11:25). The blessing is a thanksgiving or grace addressed to God, similar in wording to the prayer spoken at the offering of the wine in several Christian liturgies. The "sharing" of v. 16 is not meant to be in the blood and in the body only. It is also a common participation among those who drink and eat. Their sharing in the one Lord is at the same time a sharing with each other.

The order cup–bread rather than the more familiar bread–cup of the Synoptics (the textual problems of Luke 22:17-20 are special) is not significant. Paul is not recording a worship form here as he will do in 11:23-26 but framing an argument. He wants the bread/body symbolism to come in second place as a lead into his use of the "one bread" (v. 17) to illustrate the fact that we "who are many" are "one body." By the shared body of Christ (v. 16) is probably meant the Church (cf. 1 Cor 12:27; Rom 12:5). The specification, "his fleshly body" of Col 1:22 does not settle Paul's meaning in 1 Corinthians since here the body could easily be Christ's glorified body, the sharing of which makes us to be one Body-Church.

Eating this loaf means having a share in the company that "has by anticipation entered upon the new age which lies beyond the resurrection" (C. K. Barrett). The question, "Is it not . . . ?" of v. 16 means that Paul is appealing to a eucharistic faith that he can count on his Corinthians to hold as a result of the teaching he brought them. In v. 17 he means to develop the tradition further—the link is "Because"—by deducing that, since one loaf is broken and distributed, those who partake of it are, despite their plurality, one body. The argument resembles that of 5:7f., where Christians become unleavened loaves, as it were, through having been united with their Passover Christ. Paul's theoretical argument is in the service of a practical purpose: he wishes to keep his new believers free from demon-worship as contrasted with the mere eating of food sacrificed to idols, which could be done inculpably. He also wishes to put the Eucharist on a basis of personal faith and loyalty to Christ rather than have it thought of as achieving anything in itself through mere eating and drinking. This insistence is the chief importance of the passage to people of this age who are unlikely to be moved by the reference to food offered to idols.

ALLELUIA. JOHN 6:51-52

I am the living bread from heaven, says the LORD; whoever eats this bread will live forever.

JOHN 6:51-59

Bultmann's lack of sympathy for sacramentalism has led him to conclude that 6:51b-58b, which he thinks refers without any doubt to the Eucharist, has been taken from a quite different circle of ideas than that of 6:27-51a and has been added by an ecclesiastical editor. The hand that has written "and I will raise him up on the last day" (v. 54) has added the same phrase, he thinks, at vv. 39, 40, and 44, as a means of imposing unity on the whole discourse. Bultmann finds the background for the present passage in the Hellenist mysteries, where the food taken is the god himself.

If we take the "ecclesiastical editor" to be the final redactor or evangelist, it is clear that this John means to interpret the foregoing discourse on Jesus as the bread of life in terms of his redemptive death ("the bread . . . is my flesh, for the life of the world," v. 51) and of the eating and drinking that characterizes the Lord's Supper. The body-blood of the eucharistic accounts elsewhere in the New Testament (Mark 14:22-25 and parallels; 1 Cor 11:23ff.) is flesh-blood in John; this will be the usage of Ignatius and Justin.

John inserts the quarreling of his familiar opponents of Jesus, "*hoi Ioudaioi*," to show that the reality of Jesus' suggestion ("the bread that I will give for the life of the world is my flesh," v. 5) is understood and rejected by them as absurd. Jesus replies solemnly with the double "Amen" characteristic of John—"very truly" in NRSV, v. 53—referring to cultic practice in his church by adding mention of the drinking of blood to the eating of flesh (v. 54). The former would be found especially revolting in Jewish circles in light of the stern prohibition of Lev 17:10ff. Partaking of the Lord's Supper is understood to be the necessary means to life (v. 54); those who eat and drink at this meal bear the power within them that guarantees their resurrection. The food and drink of Jesus' flesh and blood are "real" or "true," a familiar Johannine designation. Eating and drinking them leads to coinherence in Christ ("abiding/remaining" v. 56). "Feeds on" in vv. 56 and 58 is a different verb from the ordinary one for eating and can mean munching or gnawing, as if to stress the reality of the eating over some spiritual type of ingestion. The evangelist is affirming that the sacrament truly nourishes life; all other eating leads ultimately to death (v. 58). The transmission of the Father's life through the Son is to be accomplished sacramentally only (v. 57). The phrase describing union with Christ, "he in me and I in him" (v. 56), is found elsewhere in John at 15:4f. and 17:21ff. The living power of Jesus (cf. 5:21, 26) is made the basis of the power of the sacrament. The talk that is difficult or hard (v. 61) is not only that which features eating and drinking flesh and blood, although this seems to trigger the response. It is the total stumbling-block provided by Jesus, God's revealer "coming down" (vv. 50, 51, 58) from heaven.

Proper 4 [9] / Ninth Sunday of the Year (A)
Sunday between May 29 and June 4, inclusive

GENESIS 6:9-22; 7:24; 8:14-19

With the Trinity Sunday lection of the opening chapter of Genesis, RCL launched its three-year post-Pentecostal selections from the First Testament independent of the type-antitype pattern that has up to now marked all lectionaries of the East and West.

Today's story of Noah's flood resembles the Akkadian Gilgamesh epic that has Utnapishtim as its hero. There the gods are disturbed by the noise that accompanies the unwelcomed proliferation of the human race and punish them for it (thus W. L. Moran's theory in a 1971 article, cited by R. J. Clifford and R. E. Murphy in "Genesis," *The New Jerome Biblical Commentary* [Englewood Cliffs: Prentice Hall, 1990], 14–15). Genesis gives a different reason for the deluge decreed by the LORD, viz., the human corruption and violence on the earth (vv. 11ff.) that the righteous Noah and his three sons have escaped (vv. 9f.). The dimensions and construction of the ark of cypress wood and pitch (vv. 14ff.) into which Noah and seven family members are to enter (v. 18) are given next. The P account requires that two pairs of every kind of animal, bird, and reptile be brought on board with sufficient food for all (vv. 19-22), while J demands seven pairs of clean animals and birds and one pair each of unclean animals and birds (7:2f., i.e., prohibited by the kosher laws). Every living creature left on dry land is blotted out. Only Noah and those with him in the ark are left (7:22ff.). When the earth is seen to be dry God instructs Noah and his wife, his three sons and their wives, to leave the ark and bring with them all the beasts and birds by families (thus NRSV and *Tanakh*, translating what has become the modern Hebrew word for family) so that all can increase and multiply. The flood was evidently a long remembered tragedy that took the lives of thousands in that part of the world. P and J wove of it a tale of sin and a second chance for the just.

PSALM 46

DEUTERONOMY 11:18-21, 26-28

Verses 18-20 repeat 6:6-9, see Proper 17 [22] (B), with v. 18b containing the injunction of 6:8 to bind the words of the LORD on the wrist and wear them as a pendant on the forehead. Both are literal interpretations of Exod 13:9, where the "sign on your hand" has to do with a signet ring and the reminder on the forehead the tattoo of many middle eastern tribes. In Exodus the week-long eating of unleavened bread was to serve as the remembrance rite of the deliverance from Egypt in place of the customs of Israel's neighbors. The Passover *matzoth* prevailed, but so did the wearing of four portions of Torah in leather pillboxes strapped to wrist and forehead and in a cartridge affixed to the door post *(mezuzah)*. Whether this custom goes back to Deuteronomy we do not know. The Bible quotations enclosed were Exod 13:1-10, 11-16 and Deut 6:4-9; 11:13-21, containing the basics of Israelite religion: the uniqueness of God, loving obedience to God's commands, the deliverance from Egyptian captivity, and the redemption of the firstborn.

The choice offered to Israel between a blessing and a curse (vv. 26ff.) is of primary importance in this reading. The LORD has made choice of Israel. It, in turn, is to make choice of its God in the new land. Like Deut 11:29, chap. 27 dramatizes the election of the one God and reprobation of false gods by making Gerizim the mount of blessing and Ebal the mount of cursing (vv. 12f.). The same story is told in Josh 8:30-35, where Joshua acts out the renewal of the Mosaic covenant from atop the two hills that dominate Shechem. Surely Gerizim appeared primitively as the site of the covenant altar in 8:30 (also in Deut 27:4) in place of Ebal in the biblical text as the Samaritan Pentateuch has it. The scribal reversal in the Hebrew text was part of Judah's later repudiation of the "false worship" carried out on Mt. Ebal. The unique status of YHWH was the matter of earliest concern. The Deuteronomic hand made it a matter of commandments.

PSALM 31:1-5, 19-24[2-4, 17, 25]

LORD, be my rock of safety.

ROMANS 1:16-17; 3:22B-28[21-25A, 28] (29-31)

RCL is wise to introduce Paul's discussion of the revelation of the righteousness of God through faith as God's power for salvation to Jew and non-Jew alike. In the LM lection the hearer is brought into it *in medias res* with the phrase "apart from the law" (3:21) which is apt to create an immediate puzzle (better: "the Law," since moderns tend to think in terms of any law rather than Mosaic Torah). But how could the gospel be the cause of shame (1:16) such that the apostle needs to defend himself against a charge by a church he has never yet visited? Probably because his gospel is a "message about the cross" (1 Cor 1:18), a shameful way for any Jew to die. "Through faith for faith" translates the literal "from faith to faith" correctly, since faith is both the means and the purpose of the disclosure of the righteousness of God. Faith is God's doing from start to finish.

A further reason for the public reading of Rom 1:17 may be that since Luther and Reformation theology made so much of the quotation from Hab 2:4, some worshipers might question never having heard it from the lectern on a Sunday. In fact, the prophet in context was setting the fidelity or faithfulness of the just in contrast with the spirit of the proud. Paul knew, however, that the word *pistis* of the LXX sufficed to suit his purpose which was to signify an acceptance of or trust in God's deed in Christ. For Paul, this and no other state of mind rendered believers just before God.

The Law and the prophets do, of course, attest to God's justice (3:21). It works now through faith in Jesus Christ for all who believe (v. 22). Universal sinfulness is a fact. Its result is universal deprivation of any title to the divine glory (v. 23). God now gives a gift *(dōreán)* to all through the grace of universal redemption (*apolýtrōsis*, v. 24). The blood of Christ is the "sacrifice of atone-ment" that achieves it (Paul's word is the LXX word for the ancient propitiatory or mercy-seat). God thereby shows forth his justice in the present (v. 26) and remits all sins of the past (v. 25), in the former instance by the overlooking (v. 25) of sins, in the latter by forbearance (v. 26). The mode of remission is not so important; Paul simply needs two separate words to describe the two periods. The blood of Christ, the effective sign of God's justifying intent, is operative as expiatory for both.

Verse 28 is the great watchword of Christian faith to describe the way redemp-tion is available. Paul did not mean by it to drive a wedge between Christians and Jews forever, nor could he have foreseen one between Catholics and Protestants, but this is what has been made of it. It is a simple declaration of the need for total trust (faith) in God's action.

Verses 29-31 of chap. 3 are helpfully added to the LM reading to finish off the argument begun in v. 21. In them Paul wishes to convince Jewish believers in the Roman community that God's oneness in which they firmly believe requires unity of effect in God's action. The one faith of Jew and Gentile will bring the one justification to both. The force of the rabbinic mode of argument may escape the homilist's contemporaries, but some congregants may have heard the Law down-played as having been rendered nugatory by saving faith, hence they need to hear: "Do we then overthrow the Law by this faith? By no means! On the contrary, we uphold the Law" (v. 31).

ALLELUIA. LUKE 19:38

Blessed is the king who comes in the name of the LORD; you have revealed to lit-tle ones the mysteries of the kingdom.

MATTHEW 7:21-[27]29

Matthew's Sermon on the Mount (chaps. 5–7) sets forth the terms of a "more per-fect righteousness" for Jewish believers in Jesus than that proposed by the Rabbis of yavneh in their academy, reconstituted there after the fall of Jerusalem. The con-cluding verses (24-27) frame a brief parable about a house built on rock or sand which are a key to the discourse ("these things," 7:28) as a whole. The latter con-tains rock-solid teaching. Fidelity to these words is a practical assurance that the Law and the prophets (5:17) are being fulfilled properly.

A warning is directed in vv. 15-23 against quite another group, the charismatic "false prophets" who in Matthew's view are predatory as a class (v. 15). He will refer to them again in 24:11 and 24. Presumably they have no affinity with the patterns of community *(ekklēsía)* organization of the evangelist (cf. 16:18ff.; 18:15-18). He proposes the test of deeds as a means to deal with them (vv. 16-20). Their stock in trade seems to be the multiplying of invocations of Jesus as "Lord." This verbalizing will prove profitless on "that day" (v. 22), the day of the Lord or judgment. Jesus will be the judge for Matthew as we know from 25:31-46. Exorcisms and miracles will have no meaning then (v. 22). Whomever Matthew has in mind, their works are evil (vv. 16-20, 23). They may therefore expect to be destroyed in the eschatological fire, an obvious figure of speech.

✌
Proper 5 [10] / Tenth Sunday of the Year (A)
Sunday between June 5 and June 11, inclusive

GENESIS 12:1-9

For commentary on Genesis 12:1-4, see 2 Lent (A).

Abram is described as going with his family, his retinue and his possessions to Canaan from Haran (vv. 4b-5, of Priestly composition) and through it by stages to the Negev, the southern desert. The stopping places are Shechem, modern Nablus, nowadays the largest West Bank city, and Bethel which is the site of an Israeli army camp. At both places he builds a sacrificial altar to the one God "who had appeared to him," sanctifying the territory so to say as symbolic of later conquest (vv. 6-9 conveying the Yahwist's lively narrative style). The oak or terebinth of Moreh (v. 6) would have been a landmark of Canaanite worship, now marked out for God in the new land.

PSALM 33:1-12

HOSEA 5:15 — 6:[3-]6

The LORD is likened to a ravaging lion who takes after Ephraim in the north and Judah in the south (v. 14), even though only the former attempted an alliance with the "great king of Assyria" (v. 13b). The LORD threatens to return to his lair, awaiting repentance on the part of both kingdoms and their suing for his favor (v. 15).

Hosea was an eighth-century prophet of the northern kingdom, Israel, which he most often designates Ephraim. His chief concern was the failure of leadership during the reign of Jeroboam II (781–53) and after, down through the period of Assyrian expansion under Tiglath-Pileser III (745–27). In the first three auto-biographical chapters of the book we learn of Hosea's marriage to his wife, Gomer, of the symbolic names he gives his children, and of his love for an adulteress (3:1)—his wife or some other. Fact and figure are so interwoven in the imagery of the prophet's wife as harlot that the only thing clear is that Israel is being accused symbolically of infidelity.

The first six verses of Hos 6 for centuries provided the first reading of the Good Friday liturgy, a communion service then as now but not a eucharistic celebration. It was perhaps this passage about Israel's woes, with its phrases, "[The Lord] has struck down but will bind us up. / After two days he will revive us; / on the third day he will raise us up" (Hos 6:1f.), that was alluded to in the Pauline "gospel" of 1 Cor 15:4: "that he was buried and, that he was raised on the third day in accordance with the scriptures" (but see Exod 19:11). In the Hosean context, Israel's confession of sin is insincere. It expects God to provide relief after a short time, namely the three days that mark a divine healing (cf. 2 Kgs 20:5).

It could be that a Baal-like fertility cult is drawn upon, in which the "tearing/rending" of 6:1 is a reference to the violence done to nature by the dry summer season. The god dies and goes into the nether world only to be revived by the rain of v. 3, the "spring rain" that matures the crops. In any event the irony of the prophet in this passage—which features the cheap grace of feigned repentance as a means to swift restoration—is muted in the use made of it, out of context, by the lectionary. Here it seems to convey a sure knowledge of God and his coming ("as certain as the dawn"). Yet the sense of the reproach of the Lord is retained. Both the north and the south are addressed in v. 4, reprobating the piety of the two kingdoms as no more substantial than morning clouds or dew that the sun will dispel. The Lord's exasperated response will be to slay the people with a prophetic word (v. 5), smiting them with the demand (v. 6) for love and the knowledge of God rather than sacrifice and burnt offerings. This verse is the key to the message of Hosea. It will be picked up by Matthew in 9:13 and 12:7 to be used as a saying of Jesus. The strong statement of Hosea in favor of covenant love cannot be taken as a rejection of temple sacrifice (cf. Isa 1:11-17; Amos 5:21-24). It is a strong preference for interior disposition over external observance. "Shall I give my firstborn for my transgression, / the fruit of my body for the sin of my soul? / You have been told, O man, what is good, / and what the Lord requires of you; / Only to do justice and to love goodness, / and to walk humbly with your God" (Mic 6:7b-8).

Psalm 50:7-15[1, 8, 12-15]

To the upright I will show the saving power of God.

Romans 4:13[18-]25

This passage validates Abraham's faith, which was "credited to him as righteousness" (v. 22), just as ours will be credited to us (v. 24). The difference lies in the object of faith, not its quality. Abraham was asked to believe in God's promise that he would be the father of many nations (i.e., Hebrews and Gentiles; v. 24). We are asked to believe in God "who raised up Jesus our Lord from the dead." Paul's allusion in v. 18 is to Gen 17:5 and 15:5. The phrase in that verse, "Hoping against hope," is literally, "against hope, in hope," the first being human expectation, the second a reliance on the unseen things that God will accomplish (cf. 8:24f.). St. Paul has identified the God who creates as the reason for Abraham's faith (v. 17), not any human potential.

The advanced age of the couple represents death (vv. 19f.). The promise of God not only strengthens Abraham's faith but represents life (vv. 20f.). Abraham never doubted (v. 20); he was fully convinced (v. 21) that God would do what had been promised. Abraham's confidence gave glory to God (v. 20), as those who did not believe in God failed to do (see 1:21). Trust in God's power as God is the essence of faith. The opposite is a reliance on human possibility, whether by way of total fidelity to the Law or being intimidated by the fact of human limitation, in this case the infertility of the aging Abram and Sarai (who would be called Sarah only as a mother-to-be, Gen 17:5-15).

Faith for Paul grows stronger (v. 20) in the measure in which it is not mixed with reliance on "any thing or any one other than God himself" (C. K. Barrett). Verse 22 returns to the quotation of Gen 15:6 with which the argument began in 4:3: "It was reckoned to him as righteousness." Paul is dealing with Abraham not as an historical figure but the father of all believers; hence it is that the words from Genesis were "written for us too" (v. 24). In our case it is not faith in the son Isaac who comes forth from a dead womb but in God's Son Jesus who comes forth from the tomb.

Paul does not seem to be making use of the rabbinic theme "the binding of Isaac" in v. 25, although he may be alluding to it in 8:32. He centers his attention on Jesus and what God has accomplished through him. Jesus is the new and more effective sign of power than the one made manifest in Abraham. The pericope, and with it chap. 4, ends in what seems to be a creedal formula. We do not have any clues regarding it, nor can we be sure if the "handed over" (v. 25) is a reference to the LXX of Isa 53:12. The deed of Christ is taken as one, and as accomplishing the one effect. Thus, it is not to be supposed that Paul conceives the crucifixion as meeting the challenge of our sins while the justification we stood in need of is deferred until his resurrection, indeed, through it. The phrasing is rather a rhetorical antithesis which does not mean to separate the death and resurrection. Together they achieved the one effect, namely, our justified status.

Alleluia. Matthew 11:25

Blessed are you Father, LORD of heaven and earth; you have revealed to little ones the mystery of the kingdom.

Matthew 9:9-13, 18-26

For a commentary on 9:18-26, see Mark 5:21-43, from which it derives, Proper 8 (13) B.

The early reverses of the pericope tell the story of the calling of a tax collector named Matthew to whom this Gospel is somehow traced. He will appear in the Gospel only once again (at 10:3), in a listing of the "twelve apostles." Matthew has omitted Mark 2:13, which describes Jesus walking along the lakeshore teaching. He transmits the content of Mark 2:14 with the important change that Matthew is listed as Levi the son of Alphaeus. When Mark composes his list of twelve, Levi does not appear but Matthew does (3:18). "James the son of Alphaeus" occurs in both lists. We do not know a reason for the change from Levi to Matthew. Tradition has made Matthew Levi's name as a believer in Jesus, in a historical tidying-up process. It is much more likely that the author Matthew, using the Markan account of Levi's call, made it a story of "Matthew" (taken from Mark's list) to tie his Gospel in with the apostle most closely connected with the church to which he belonged.

Simon, Andrew, James, and John had been called to follow Jesus (Matt 4:18-22) without his giving them any reason; no more is a motive supplied here. The disciples receive a gift (10:8) which they are expected in turn to give. Merit is no part of the calling.

Tax gatherers were in the pay of Rome via the Temple priesthood, hence were assumed to be dishonest and "sinners," i.e., voluntarily outside the Law. The importance of their inclusion in Jesus' table fellowship is crucial (cf. Gal 2:12). Jesus is not concerned with observance of the Oral Law, portions of which are "works of the Law" for Paul. The messianic banquet that the meals taken with Jesus foreshadow has no such condition as this attached. Sickness is a symbol of sin in v. 12. The evangelist explains what has happened at this meal that includes tax gatherers and other undesirables by appending Hos 6:6, as he will do again at 12:7a with respect to the charge that his disciples "harvested" in plucking grain; see Exod 20:8, interpreted by the Rabbis in the spirit of Lev 24:4f. The covenant relation is held out not to the self-righteous but to "sinners," whether their offense be ethical or ritual. The conditions of acceptance as part of the covenanted people, in other words, are notably altered in Matthew's understanding of Jesus' call.

❧❧
Proper 6 [11] / Eleventh Sunday of the Year (A)
Sunday between June 12 and June 18, inclusive

GENESIS 18:1-15, (21:1-7)

For a commentary on 18:1-10a see Proper 11 [16] C.

Abraham has already laughed at the absurdity of his ninety-year-old wife's bearing a child as God has promised him [17:17], so that when she in turn hears the prediction of one of the three visitors concerning her childbearing "in due season" we are not surprised that she laughs to herself from the entrance to the tent behind him (18:12). The LORD then speaks through one of the three, challenging Abraham on his wife's behavior and saying that nothing is too wonderful for the one who is the LORD (vv. 13f.). Out of fear she denies that she laughed but the LORD says he knows that she did. The earlier chapter is from P, the later one through 19:38 from the lively, anthropomorphic pen of J.

PSALM 116:1-2, 12-19

EXODUS 19:2[-6]8A

Although the itinerary is Priestly (resumed from 17:1), a Deuteronomist hand has inserted the words of the LORD in 3b-6 into the E narrative here. The encouragement is cognate with that of the poetry of Deut 32:10f., but the prose of Exodus has a stronger beauty. Rephidim is related to the narrative of the battle with Amalek in 17:11f. It is not known where "the front of the mountain" may be. The present Jebel Musa (7,500 feet) has been identified as Mount Sinai since the fourth century. Exodus 17:1-7 and Num 20:2-13 situate the mountain near Kadesh, which would satisfy the requirement of the Amalekites' proximity (see Gen 14:7; 1 Sam 15:7; 27:8). In the Kadesh region—about 60 miles due south of Gaza on the Mediterranean—the likeliest candidate for Sinai-Horeb is Jebel Helal (3,000 feet), which is about 25 miles west of the Kadesh oasis.

The point of this pericope is God's readiness to rescue his people, as an eagle might do in swooping down to catch its little ones that have fallen from the nest. Elsewhere Israel is described as the LORD's "treasured possession" (19:5); among the passages are Deut 7:6; 14:2; 26:18f. Moreover, in all three the people is "sacred" to the LORD. This notion is similar to that of the kingdom of priests and holy people in that it means set apart or separated rather than ethically upright while including, however, the latter notion. Holiness in the biblical sense was likeness to deity, specifically to YHWH, and it consisted in being distinct from all that surrounded it. The separated character of the priests is here expanded to include the entire people. First Peter 2:5f. will contain the same idea as regards the baptized. The condition of such corporate priestliness for the Deuteronomist author is obedience to the covenant, the terms of which are shortly to follow (chaps. 20ff.).

PSALM 100[2, 3, 5]

We are God's people: the sheep of his flock.

ROMANS 5:1-8[6-11]

For a commentary on 5:1-8 see 3 Lent (A).

Paul's argument as to how early believers are made upright or just in God's sight through faith denies that supplemental adherence to certain precepts of the Law can be any part of it. Consequently he must go back beyond Moses, the champion of certain believers in Christ who are making this demand, to Abraham as the paradigm of faith. Having made this point in what is now chap. 4, he turns to its consequences with a "therefore" (*oûn*, 5:1): justified by faith, we [now] have peace with God through Jesus Christ who has given us access (or introduction) to this grace or favor. The boasting that Paul will not countenance on any human ground—least of all merit—he encourages if its object is hope, the hope of sharing the glory of God. He provides what Hellenist rhetoric calls a *klimax*: suffering, endurance, and character, one leading to the next. All three are grace-empowered and operate as one until hope is attained. This hope cannot disappoint because it resides in hearts into which God's love has been poured through the gift of the Spirit. Paul's language is not a series of abstractions. It is a concrete expression of states of mind and will and emotion to describe the indescribable, namely how God is at work to make the human creature even more Godlike than creating it in the divine image first achieved.

A people right with God by faith (v. 1) can endure much suffering because of its hope for a share in the glory of God (vv. 2f.). Israel in the previous reading is matched in this one by God's concern for the ungodly (v. 6), meaning those still "sinners" (v. 8) for whom Christ died. The "love of God" that has been poured into our hearts through the Holy Spirit (v. 5) is doubtless a subjective genitive meaning God's love for us, the idea found in verse 8. The Spirit has been given at some time in the past (v. 5) such as the first call to belief or the event of baptism. Similarly the death of Christ can be dated; it happened "at the right time" (v. 6). Its providential occurrence took place within that long period when the human race was "godless," i.e., powerless to remedy its sinful state. The appointed time is the eschatological moment that brings the wait of centuries to an end (cf. Gal 4:4). God has taken the initiative on our behalf in terms of fidelity to the divine commitment. "For us" of v. 8 employs the familiar preposition *hypēr* of passages describing the reality of the redemption (such as John 10:11; 1 Cor 11:24; Gal 2:20; Heb 2:9). Paul compares God's action favorably with that of a man who is not likely to die for his fellow humans (v. 7). Courage like this is displayed rarely enough and, when it is, the manifestation is usually on behalf of a "good type," such being the sense of the phrase, which has the article in Greek), not merely a good individual. God, acting in Christ, is undeterred by the general unworthiness of the human beneficiaries. The divine action in history is the proof of "God's love for us" (v. 8). The Holy Spirit was given to us (cf. v. 5) while we were still sinners.

Since Christ's blood was the price of our restoration to justice, freedom from God's wrath may be expected in the future (v. 9), even as peace is the effect of justification in the present. The former situation of enmity has led to reconciliation; the present reconciliation may be expected to lead to our being saved on the last day (v. 10). It was Christ's death that achieved the first. It will be his life as risen that accomplishes the second. In this discussion Paul speaks of the tension between God and the human race under two figures, reconciliation to terminate enmity and justification to terminate a legal dispute (vv. 9f.). The two, however, are one. Similarly, there are not two distinct realities spoken of as accomplished by his death and by his life (v. 10). The two steps or moments of importance are not Christ's (1) death and (2) resurrection, but (1) the manifestation of God's love in the one historical deed which includes both, laid hold of by faith, and (2) the later salvation of all believers when history shall come to an end. The second step will happen "much more surely" because, whereas our first condition was totally unmeritorious, now God may be presumed to finish gloriously what God has begun. Concluding this thought in v. 11, Paul makes God's anticipated action in

Christ the subject of a boast. Such boasting had only been a hope in v. 2. The "now" of v. 11 is the reconciled condition of Christians in the present that justifies Paul in exulting about the favorable outcome in the future.

Alleluia

Open our hearts, O Lord, to listen to the words of your Son.

Matthew 9:35[36]—10:8, (9-23)

This pericope is the introduction to the second of five collections of Jesus' sayings in Matthew, all of which end with a summary like that of 11:1. It consists of a statement about the needs of the people (v. 36) to whom Jesus, moved with pity, was proclaiming the gospel and whom he was likewise curing. It also includes Jesus' charge to pray for laborers (9:37f.), his empowerment of the twelve to exorcise and heal (10:1), and his naming of "twelve apostles" (10:2-4). Israel in the Bible is a nation of "sheep without a shepherd" (see Num 27:17; 1 Kgs 22:17; and Zech 10:2). The substitution of Jesus for YHWH is a staple of New Testament Christology; he, rather than Israel's LORD, will be the shepherd of Matt 25:32 (the judgment scene). He appears again as shepherd in 26:31 (which quotes the "Song of the Sword" of Zech 13 about an associate of the LORD of hosts, a stricken shepherd). Hosea 6:11 and Joel 4:13 use the figure of the harvest as a time when God will settle accounts with the world in judgment. Such is the spirit of Matt 13:30 and 39, whereas here the harvest is a gathering of the just. For this holy task, laborers are needed (v. 37; cf. 1 Tim 5:18 for the term; to describe false apostolic workers, found also in Phil 3:2 and 2 Cor 11:13).

The twelve apostles are almost certainly chosen to correspond to the number of the tribes of Israel (cf. Matt 19:28). Matthew derives his list from Mark 3:16-19, reordering the names slightly. Andrew is brought forward and put directly after Simon; Mark's "Matthew and Thomas" are reversed. The word "apostles" occurs in Matthew only here (10:2), just as in Mark only once (6:30). It is Luke who favors it. The term was used in the early Church to describe others than the twelve. Literally it means those "sent." "The Cananaean" (10:4) means that this Simon was a known zealot for the Law (from Aram., *kănănă,* enthusiast). The political group known as "zealots" committed to the ejection of Rome by force was a phenomenon of the '60s, not—as far as we know—of the late 20s. Iscariot (v. 4), according to the researches of C. C. Torrey, cannot mean "man of Kerioth" (Josh 15:25; Jer 48:24) or be a corruption of *sikarios,* "a dagger wielder." It has to be a Greek transliteration of some Aramaic designation. Torrey holds for *ishqaryā'*, the "false one" from the adjective *sheqaryā'*.

Jesus has been sent by his Father to preach, teach, and heal. He now sends out the twelve disciples with a similar authority (10:1).

Verses 5-7 have no parallel in Mark or Luke. They confine Jesus' missionary charge to the Jewish people. The shepherd of Israel is described as having no interest in (literally) going "toward the road of the Gentiles" (v. 5) or any Samaritan town (v. 7). This command is in marked contrast to that of 28:19, which probably reflects the actual practice of the Matthean community, however tentative, as distinct from this earlier theological construct or memory of Jesus' instructions. Matthew 10:6 accords better than 28:19 with the hesitant sorties outside Jewish circles reported in Acts 11:1ff. and 11:19, a tradition that would never have been preserved in the Jerusalem community if there had been an authentic logion of Jesus like 28:19.

The apostles are instructed to preach and heal. The command to "raise the dead" of v. 8 may be meant metaphorically for bringing life and salvation to the world (cf. Eph 2:1f.). In any case, others are to be treated as the disciples have been in receiving God's gifts without payment.

Chapter 10 goes on to describe the ways in which the earliest disciples have conducted themselves in teaching people to observe all that Jesus has commanded them (see 28:20), namely how the biblical commandments should be kept (5:17-48). They were to dress simply, expect to be offered hospitality for their teaching, and be on the alert for a hostile reception. The courts of "governors and kings" would have meant antagonism by Herodian and imperial authorities, "synagogues" the resistance of Jewish communities (vv. 17f.). Punishment in the latter would have been the thirty-nine lashes prescribed as an act of leniency relative to the unlimited floggings administered by pagans (see 2 Cor 11:24, a mitigation of the forty stripes of an earlier day, Deut 24:3). The assurance that the spirit of the Father will be given, enabling disciples to speak if and when handed over, has led to the description of an unprepared sermon—in a day when Latin was a lingua franca among the Roman clergy—as a *"dabitur vobis"* (v. 19). Matthew knows of the types of harassment fellow evangelizers are undergoing as he writes, including being turned in to authorities by grudge-settling family members (children reporting on their parents in the terror of the Maoist regime!). The prediction that the Son of Man would come before "all the towns of Israel" will have heard the gospel is an expression of Matthean end-expectation to which no time-table is attached (10:23; 24:36; Acts 1:7).

❧❧

Proper 7 [12] / Twelfth Sunday of the Year (A)
Sunday between June 19 and June 25, inclusive

GENESIS 21:8-21

For a commentary see 2 Lent (B).

PSALM 86:1-20, 16, 17

LORD, you are good and forgiving.

JEREMIAH 20:7[-10]13

The word "jeremiad" derives from the attribution of the five Lamentations to the prophet, the result of a misreading of 2 Chron 35:25 and the LXX preface to Lamentations. (The Hebrew canon does not associate the book with the prophet.) Today's reading, however, is from a poem that, with 15:15-21; 17:14-18; and 20:14-18, reveals the heart of Jeremiah in his deepest distress. In his struggle with the Temple administrator, Pashhur, which is given as the setting of his outcry, he expresses chagrin at the mockery heaped upon him for his repeated, doom-filled message, "Violence and outrage!" (v. 8). This description of the realities of the situation is too much for the optimists in residence who are, as they think, winding down the war. But the word of the LORD has become like a fire burning in his heart (v. 9). He cannot be silent. Jeremiah renames Pashhur, "Terror on every side" (v. 3), to indicate that the harassing visited by his Temple police on the prophet (v. 10) will ultimately be visited on him by the nation's enemies. Some have thought that Jeremiah's prophecy of 19:14f. was inspired by the defeat of Egypt by the Babylonians at Carchemish on the Euphrates in 605 (cf. 46:2; 36:1ff.). In any case, he knows he is being watched like a hawk at every step (v. 10) for any false prophecy, at which point he will be apprehended and dispatched. He feels totally secure, however. YHWH is his "mighty champion" (v. 11). The prophet's enemies will fail and be put to shame as a result of the vengeance taken by the LORD (v. 12). This portion of the poem ends with an expression of confidence in final vindication (v. 13), a convention in this type of writing (cf. Ps 22:23-31). In v. 14 Jeremiah will return to an expression of despair which has become classic in the world's literature, showing the alternation of moods possible in a man of great faith.

PSALM 69:7[8]-10, (11-15) [14,17], 16-18[33-35]

LORD, in your great love, answer me.

ROMANS 6:1B-11

For a commentary see Resurrection of the Lord, Easter Vigil (A).

ROMANS 5:12-15

This passage follows immediately upon that of last Sunday in LM. For a commentary see 1 Lent (A).

ALLELUIA

Your words, Lord, are spirit and life, you have the words of everlasting life.

MATTHEW 10:24-39[26-33]

Matthew's exhortation to fearless confession is not from Mark but Q (Lukan parallel, 12:2-9). The logion of Matt 10:26 occurs in Mark 4:22, that of Matt 10:33 in Mark 8:38. This preparation for persecution at the hands of "synagogues . . . rulers and kings" (10:17f.; cf. Luke 12:11, "synagogues, rulers, and the authorities") is employed in the same way, by and large, by the two evangelists. Jesus has been warning his disciples in Matthew that the pupil should not expect a better fate than the teacher nor the slave than the master (v. 24). Proclamation of Jesus' teaching is obligatory for his disciples (vv. 26f.), but it should be expected to bring the same sanctions that would be (at the time the Gospels were written) leveled at him. Three times the disciples are enjoined not to fear (vv. 26, 28, 31). Persecution may bring death but it can do nothing worse. Denial of the message can bring destruction of soul and body in Gehenna, a figure of destruction by fire taken from the Valley of Hinnom south of Jerusalem where refuse was burned—and where popular Jewish belief located the last judgment (cf. Matt 5:22; Mark 9:49; Isa 66:24).

The remaining sayings are only loosely connected, being expressions of providential care (vv. 29ff.) that the author of Q saw fit to insert in this context of persecution. The Lukan phrasing of Matt 10:32ff. is more primitive, "the Son of Man will acknowledge [him]" (Luke 12:8) and "[he] will be denied" (v. 9) having a more

authentic ring in their third person and (divine) passive voice than Matthew's identification of the Son of Man with Jesus and conversion to the active "I also will
deny" (Matt 10:33). All of this heightens the puzzle of the greater Hebraic character of certain sayings in Luke, and has led R. L. Lindsey (*A Hebrew Translation
of the Gospel of Mark* [Jerusalem: Dugith/Baptist House, 1969]) to the unusual
conclusion that Luke was written first, from a primitive narrative and Q.

❧❧

Proper 8 [13] / Thirteenth Sunday of the Year (A)
Sunday between June 26 and July 2, inclusive

Genesis 22:1-4

For a commentary see 2 Lent (B).

Psalm 13

Jeremiah 28:5-9

Hananiah prophesies falsely to please the king, as the event will prove. The date
is early in the sixth century not long after King Zedekiah's reign has begun.
Jeremiah had proposed to him that he submit to the yoke of the king of Babylon
(27:13) whereas Hananiah's prediction is that the yoke of Nebuchadnezzar will be
broken within two years and the vessels of the Temple restored to Jerusalem. The
Chaldean defeat did not come for another decade at the hands of the Persians.
Jeconiah, whose throne name was Jehoiachin, in fact never came back from Babylon (Jer 52:31-34; cf. 2 Kgs 25:27-30) but there is an elaborate account of the vessels' return to Jerusalem in Ezra 6:5; 8:24-34. The point of the passage is that while
Hananiah is in line with the prophets of a century before in predicting victory over
Nebuchadnezzar, he will be proved wrong. It will not happen. Jeremiah declares
that a true prophet is known when his prophecy comes true (v. 9). He will be shown
to be such when peace follows submission to the yoke of Persia. The lectionary
chooses it to exalt the way of peace, not war, the polar opposite of a nearly forgotten battle cry, "Better dead than Red."

Psalm 89:1-4, 15-18

2 KINGS 4:8-11, 14-16A

Elisha is one of God's prophets, a man possessed of a double portion of Elijah's spirit (2:9), hence capable of intercessory influence with the divine. Shunem is in the land of Issachar (later Galilee) at the southeastern tip of the Plain of Jezreel, about five miles south of Nain. A miracle of resuscitation was later to be reported of Jesus at Nain (cf. Luke 7:11f.) like the one (2 Kgs 4:32-37) which this passage leads up to and that related of Elijah on which it is patterned (1 Kgs 17:17-23). This is not surprising because of Luke's consistent attempts to make Jesus an Elijah-figure.

In v. 13, which the lectionary eliminates, the prophet asks the Shunammite woman through his servant Gehazi if he can speak a word on her behalf to the king or the commander of the army. She replies with some spirit, "I am living among my own people," an indication of the strength of her clan. Here was a wife who had the backing of her family, hence needed no favors from the king or the military. The prophet's promise of childbirth within a year, and a son at that, may be what prompts her to cry out in grief a dozen years or so later, when the boy has died in the fields: "Did I ask my lord for a son? . . . Did I not say, Do not deceive me?" (v. 28).

The story is one which ultimately reflects Hebrew belief in the communication of power by direct contact, but today's pericope contents itself with a prophecy of the birth of a son in response to a wealthy woman's hospitality.

PSALM 89:2-3, 16-19

ROMANS 6:12-23[3-4, 8-11]

For a commentary on the lection that immediately precedes this one see Easter Vigil (A). Paul has been holding that our injustice provides proof of God's justice (3:5) and that "through my falsehood God's truthfulness abounds to his glory" (3:7). He hears his teaching slanderously reported as "doing evil that good may come" (3:8). This has made him very sensitive concerning all matters that touch on God's Law and God's grace. In chapter 6 and the two that follow he tries to set the record straight. He is not, he must insist, in favor of continuing in sin that grace may abound (6:1). This sounds like the taunt of libertinism from his enemies; it forces him to express the Christian ethic in its fullness.

His response is that the old self of the Christian is just as dead in baptism as Jesus was on the cross, just as buried in its waters as he was in the tomb, and just as much living a new life (the familiar Hebraism "walking in newness of life") as Jesus was, raised from the dead (vv. 3f.). Moreover, both occurrences were caused "by the glory of the Father" (v. 4), meaning God's power—possibly a snatch from a creed (see 2 Thess 1:9). It is evident that Paul can count on a knowledge of this baptismal doctrine in a community he has not instructed.

The religious terminology of Middle Eastern cults is often cited in this connection, but the content of the doctrine is Jewish: an identification with the messiah in tribulation as a prelude to the age to come. Paul is careful not to suggest that the baptized Christian has come up out of the waters to the fullness of this age, only to a "new life" (v. 4). The baptismal rite is the effective symbol of the reality of Christ's death and resurrection. It achieves likeness to the former perfectly, to the latter only inchoately. The tense of our living with Christ (v. 8) is future, not present. Our rising with him is something we believe (v. 8), hence that lies in the eschatological future; his death and its finality is something we know (v. 9).

This certainty that Christ will never die again affirms his conquest of death as anticipatory of the general resurrection in the last age. The death of the obedient Christ, although in a context of sin ("God made him to be sin who did not know sin," 2 Cor 5:21), achieved his final break with sin (v. 10). His risen life was a life lived "to God" in the sense that the former identification with sin was behind him. Christians must similarly consider themselves dead to sin, but Paul is realistic enough to know that his being alive is by way of a new relation to God, even though outward appearance continues as it was. The transition from this age to the age to come is accomplished "in Christ Jesus" (v. 11), meaning that being alive to God is something that cannot be seen.

Being under grace rather than subject to the Law means for Paul that the ethnic Jews and Gentiles of the Roman community must freely keep their bodies from becoming instruments of sin (vv. 12ff.). That slavery is over; it led only to death (vv. 15-17). But now, set free from sin, obedience to the new teaching makes one a slave to God (v. 22), the happy outcome of which is sanctification and its "wages" life, not death (vv. 22f).

Those dead to sin and alive to God through baptism (v. 11; see vv. 3-8) must present their bodies in every member as instruments of upright living, not of sin. God's grace, not Law observance, must dominate their lives from this point on. Here, as so often, Paul does not denigrate the Law but uses it as a code word for the former era in his periodization of history. The baptized in Rome are being reminded that the epoch of grace is the "newness of life" of 6:4. When the apostle puts a rhetorical question in v. 15 that is almost identical with the questions he had posed in vv. 2-3, he seems to be responding to a challenge he has faced many times since he made the case in Galatians for a new order of divine graciousness. The Law was the way Jews knew right conduct from wrong. Faith is the new key to the totality of upright conduct, a kind of universal solvent of sin past and present. Because some have accused Paul of telling the newly justified they can now sin bravely he denies the allegation heatedly—on the assumption it has been made. Sin and obedience to God are mutually exclusive, he writes; they lead respectively to death and upright behavior. One cannot lead to the other. Paul uses the figure of enslavement either to obedience or sin as Jesus had to God or mammon. His tone is positive in describing the Romans' present state of "obedience from the heart" (vv. 17ff.). But he is a realist and knows that, although justified, they can sin again. That is why he warns strongly against it (vv. 12f., 19a).

Alleluia. John 17:17b, a

Your word, O Lord, is truth; make us holy in the truth.

Matthew 10:[37] 40-42

Elisha restored the Shunammite woman's son to life by God's power. God does the same for both his dead son Jesus and all those who, believing in him, die to sin. Matthew's Gospel in this passage spells out certain conditions of life in the new age. The disciple must love Jesus more than his own kinship circle (v. 37). Taking up the cross (v. 38) is figurative for risking the shame of being an outcast, for "Anyone hung on a tree is under God's curse" (Deut 21:23). The way Jesus ended is never far from the thoughts of any early believers in him. Verses 38f. are a doublet of Matt 16:24f. In the former the verbs are find–destroy; destroy–find, and in the latter, wish to save–destroy; destroy–find.

Verses 40ff. bring the discourse, which has been a charge of Jesus to his disciples, to an end. Verse 40 is reminiscent of the Mishnaic passage *Berakoth* 5:5: "A man's agent is like to the man himself." It is an identification of preachers of Christ with Christ, stress being laid on the roles of prophet and righteous one, the two types of persons held in honor in the Matthean milieu (v. 41). Church ethics are stressed here. They constitute a set of understandings about behavior that Paul might stigmatize as "works" if they were thought to be saving of themselves. But in biblical ethics good works are the fruit of a righteous life.

🙐 🙒
Proper 9 [14] / Fourteenth Sunday of the Year (A)
Sunday between July 3 and July 9, inclusive

GENESIS 24:34-38, 42-49, 58-67

The lectionary provides large portions of this chapter-length tale because it links up Isaac, the son of Abraham and the now dead Sarah, with all that is to follow, but also because of its charm. Rebekah at the well identifies herself to Abraham's servant, who has come laden with presents for her (vv. 22, 47) and her family (v. 53) to make payment for the bride should they accept. She has acted spontaneously and generously in watering the camels of the stranger's retinue. (An anachronism? Were there camels in Israel in the patriarchal era?) Her brother Laban, at the sight of the gifts, acts in a way that will prove characteristic (vv. 30-32). But the servant must explain his mission before accepting food (v. 33), so the story of Abraham's plan to find a non-Canaanite wife for his son is repeated (vv. 34-38; cf. 1-9). Intermarriage with the pagan population would later be prohibited (Deut 7:3) but Abraham's present hope is to ensure a wife for Isaac from among his kin as part of his stake in the land the LORD has promised him (v. 7). The unnamed emissary then repeats in full, in the leisurely manner of Middle Eastern narrative, what has already been told about the incident at the well and its value as a sign (vv. 42-48; cf. 12-27). He asks if the family will deal honorably with Abraham; if not he will turn and go back (v. 49). Having received the assurance he asks for (vv. 50f.), he engages in the giving of gifts; there is celebration and an overnight stay, and Rebekah is sent for and says she will go willingly. Isaac meanwhile has traveled to the Negev, the southern region, with his flocks. Rebekah on approaching does not recognize him nor he her but, upon the mutual disclosure, the consummation of their union is delicately indicated (v. 67). Three important matters distinguish this lengthy account: Abraham speaks in his own voice for the last time (vv. 2-8); the direction in which this people is to go is shown not by divine appearance or voice but by the actions of human players; and Laban, by his interest in the gifts and his delaying tactic (vv. 53-55), gives hints of how he will act later (31:14-16, 36-43).

PSALM 45:10-17 OR SONG OF SOLOMON 2:8-13

ZECHARIAH 9:9-[10]12

The king through whom the LORD is to save Israel will be a peaceful ruler, unlike other strivers after world sovereignty who attempt their conquest by force. Aram

(Syria), Phoenicia with its cities of Tyre and Sidon, the Philistine cities of Ashkelon, Gaza, Ekron, and Ashdod—all will be reduced to domesticity, according to the oracle immediately preceding this one. The pride of the nations will be broken: "I will destroy the pride of the Philistine and take from his mouth his bloody meat" (vv. 6b-7a). The prophets restored the popular figure of the king of peace from the age of paradise (cf. Isa 9:5f.; 11:1ff.; Jer 23:5f.). Judah's offspring, who shall hold the scepter and mace forever, will tether his young ass to the vine (Gen 49:11; cf. Judg 5:10; 10:4).

The ass suited Israel's poor economy. Horses, by contrast, were like rocketry next to infantry. There were brief periods of splendor, as in Solomon's time (1 Kgs 10:26-29) or when the last kings of Judah entered the gates of Jerusalem in chariots and on horses (Jer 17:25; 22:4). In the present passage the savior king of the future will do God's will and put an end to national self-seeking. This messiah will have no part in the wars and revolutions of the monarchy. He will terminate all violence with his kingdom of peace.

The collection of oracles that make up Zechariah 9–14 cannot be shown to be postexilic as clearly as can chaps. 1–8. Whatever the date of authorship, the notion of hope for the future through a kingly figure or the house of David largely ceases after the references in 9:9f. and 12:1 through 13:6. The idea of a messiah does not die entirely but he does not play a particularly central role in Jewish eschatology. Messiah and suffering servant may blend in 9:9f. (and in 12:10?—"when they look on the one whom they have pierced" [quoted in John 19:37], they shall mourn for him as one mourns for an only child") but it cannot be demonstrated, only inferred. These Zecharian oracles, indeed, are the only trace of a meek and humble redeemer we have from the postexilic period, even though Israel never lost sight of submissiveness and humility as its vocation.

Verse 9abc has a parallel in Isa 62:11. As Zech 9:9 moves on to "an ass . . . the foal of an ass" it employs poetic parallelism; the phrase does not speak of two beasts. Matthew's free rendering of this passage (21:5) adds an additional "and," thereby contributing a second animal, a colt who trails behind in Christian art. Some ill-conceived artistic literalism has even had Jesus straddling two beasts. The king and "just savior" of 9:9b will eliminate the war-making potential of both north and south (10a). His peace to the nations will be universal— from the Euphrates to the waters supposedly at the ends of the earth (cf. Ps 72:8 and Mic 5:3 for the same cosmic promise). He will strip warriors of the bow, as in Ps 46:9[10], or the better known promise of Isa 2:4 about the recycling of swords and spears.

Psalm 145:[1-2]8-14

I will praise your name forever, my king and my God.

Romans 7:15-25a

Paul's famous passage on the inner conflict experienced by religious people occurs in LM as a reading on Friday in Year A [29] but not on a Sunday. RCL rectifies the omission and begins the reading three verses earlier than its occurrence there. Krister Stendahl, retired Lutheran bishop of Uppsala and longtime professor at Harvard Divinity School, did an important service to scholars and preachers by pointing out that v. 19 is not the key to Paul's introspective conscience because there is nothing autobiographical about the passage. For centuries various schools of New Testament interpretation have taken the apostle to have been tortured by his longstanding inability to fulfill the precepts of the Torah, only to be liberated by justifying faith. By his own account, that was the case with Luther's scrupulous conscience. Paul's conscience, on the other hand, was remarkably free of self-recrimination. He reports that he was a zealot for his people's ancestral traditions (Gal 1:14) and totally self-confident, "in observance of the Law, a Pharisee" (Phil 3:5). When he acknowledges his weaknesses or the thorn in his flesh he is talking about the sufferings he has endured or an unspecified physical handicap or malady (2 Cor 12:5, 9). "I am not conscious of anything against me," describes his mental state best (1 Cor 4:4). The one sin he is acutely aware of is having persecuted the Church of God (Gal 1:13, 23; 1 Cor 15:9). Chapter 7 up to this point has been about the holiness, the justness, the goodness of the Law (v. 12). This is reiterated at the conclusion of a graphic metaphor in which sin personified uses the commandment that prohibits covetousness (Paul's chosen example) to deceive and figuratively slay the unwary sinner. Paul lays the blame on "sin" and "flesh," descriptions of the downward pull in human nature, in order to "rescue" the Law, the good gift of God. . . . Unfortunately—or fortunately—Paul happened to express this supporting argument (viz., about the goodness of the Law) so well that "what to him and his contemporaries was a common observation appeared to later interpreters to be a most penetrating insight into the nature of man and into the nature of sin" (Wayne A. Meeks, ed., *The Writings of Paul* [New York: Norton, 1972], 432, reprinting Stendahl's "Paul and the Introspective Conscience of the West," *Harvard Theological Review* 56 [1963] 199–215). St. Paul speaks for all humanity in doing what we do, not what we know not to do.

ROMANS 8:9, 11-13

In Paul's flesh-spirit opposition the sex passion of a giant of a man can be spirit and the intellect of a person of genius flesh. He is concerned with *sarx* as human resistance to God and *pneuma* as docility to God or, better, to God's Spirit. In v. 9 Paul assumes that his Roman readers possess the Spirit of God—which is the same as the Spirit of Christ. As a result their existence in its totality is in the Spirit. They are not in the flesh like those of v. 8, persons who cannot please God because they are busy pleasing themselves.

It might be better to say that the Spirit of Christ possesses them than is possessed by them. It is only through Christ that the Spirit is known and received. The effect of the Spirit's action is to make one "his," i.e., Christ's (v. 9).

The Spirit who raised up Christ as the first deed of the final age will give life to mortal bodies in this same age (v. 11). That quickening activity is a reality of now. What has been put to death for those in whom Christ dwells is their sin-prone body; what has risen to a life of justice is their mortal body as spirit (v. 10). The transformation takes place gradually—"from glory to glory"—by the action of the risen Lord who is not in the least flesh but totally spirit (cf. 2 Cor 3:18). It can occur in the baptized only through a lifetime of free choices. The indebtedness referred to in v. 12 is the obligation we are under through having been raised up in baptism. Life according to the "flesh" will bring death. Life guided by the Spirit is death-dealing to the deeds of the body (v. 13), a phrase similar to "whatever in you is earthly" of Col 3:5.

ALLELUIA. JOHN 6:64B

The Word of God became man and lived among us. He enabled those who accepted him to become children of God.

MATTHEW 11:16-19, 25-30

This chapter begins with Jesus' testimony to John in prison (vv. 2-15) and leads into a saying attributed to Jesus that contrasts him with John but deplores the failure of the crowds to heed the teaching of either of them (vv. 16-19). Luke 7:31-35 is an exact parallel to these Matthew verses except for the logion with which each concludes. The element of comparison is between little children playing two games in the marketplace and the two men. The first game is playing wedding (vv. 17a, 19a), the second playing funeral (vv. 17b, 18a). Many in the crowds have no time for Jesus with his singing and dancing, his eating and drinking. The Baptizer is sour in mien, not to say funereal. A textual divergence mentioned above is that Matthew appends to the twofold image a saying of Jesus probably spoken on another occasion: "But wisdom is vindicated in all her works" (Matt 11:19b) while Luke's version of the saying ends: "in all her children." Who were the originally meant vindicators of God wisdom? The second would seem to be the better reading if the proverb—which is doubtless pre-Christian—intends early hearers of the Gospel to understand Jesus and John as wisdom's children. The fruits of wisdom's womb, however, are all the new believers whose works give proof of God's wisdom. Some later New Testament manuscripts make the two Gospels read alike in the familiar assimilation practiced by careless copyists.

The RCL wisely includes the image from Q (Matt 11:16-19; Luke 7:31-35) about children playing wedding and funeral which LM proposes only as a weekday reading. Whether God's emissary is a desert ascetic or companionable villager, some cannot be pleased. Verses 25f. are a *berakah*, a hymn in praise of God like that described before Jesus' multiplication of the loaves and his prayer over bread at the Last Supper. Such prayers are the essence of the prayers of thanks and praise that later become anaphoras or canons. They are in three parts: thanksgiving to the Father for a revelation received, a statement of its content, and an invitation to a course of action. Chapter 11 has spoken in praise of John the Baptizer (vv. 7-15) but in reproach of the present generation whom no preacher can accept (vv. 16-19) and of the unrepentant towns of Galilee (vv. 20-24). By contrast, the "infants/childlike" (v. 25) have had revealed to them no one less than the Father at the good pleasure of the Son (v. 27).

Verse 27a closely resembles John 3:35 except for its active voice; v. 27b is like John 10:15a. This similarity of wording in two otherwise dissimilar writings leads to the supposition that Jesus' actual expression has been reworked by the two different communities or schools. The revelation of God to the simple, which the learned and clever have had withheld from them (v. 25), is entirely a matter of God's gracious design (v. 26). This sovereign freedom of the Father to reveal is a Matthean theme that will recur at 16:17. In John, Jesus is more clearly the revealer of the Father than in Matthew; nonetheless, the whole Sermon on the Mount is an instance of Jesus' teaching with authority (7:29). He is uniquely God's Son in Matthew (see 3:17) without any of the Johannine implication of divine pre-existence, yet his possession of "all things" (v. 27) in common with the Father is indistinguishable in the two gospels.

Wisdom invites the untutored to partake of the instruction of her food and drink (Sir 24, 51, NAB). It is even said: "Put your neck under her yoke" (v. 26). Jesus is personified wisdom in the present pericope, a Matthean theme that will reappear in 23:37ff., where Jesus' lament over Jerusalem "bears unmistakable traces of the idea of Wisdom's rejection by men" (M. Jack Suggs, *Wisdom, Christology, and Law in Matthew's Gospel* [Cambridge: Harvard Univ. Press, 1970], a book largely about the six verses of this reading).

Accepting the yoke of Torah was described by the Rabbis as giving rest and ease. First century C.E. Rabbi Nehunia ben ha-Kanah wrote: "Everyone who receives upon him the yoke of Torah, from him they remove the yoke of the kingdom and the yoke of worldly occupation." Verses 29c and 30 appear as saying 90 of the Coptic *Gospel of Thomas*: "Jesus said: Come to me, for easy is my yoke and my lordship is gentle, and you shall find repose for yourselves." The heavy loads that Matthew accuses the scribes and Pharisees of putting on others (23:4) are here replaced by the teaching of Jesus. He does this as the gentle one who fulfills all justice, acting side by side with sinners to bring them into fellowship with himself. The result is rest for the weary and heavily burdened (vv. 28, 29; cf. Isa 28:12; Jer 6:16). Jesus' yoke and burden (which are easy and light, v. 30) are his interpretation of the Torah, demanding yet quite endurable.

Didachē 6:2 employs these verses in a more explicitly understanding spirit than any encountered in the New Testament: "If you can bear the Lord's full yoke you will be perfect. But if you cannot, then do what you can."

☙☙

Proper 10 [15] / Fifteenth Sunday of the Year (A)
Sunday between July 10 and July 16, inclusive

GENESIS 25:19-34

The Abraham saga is over with vv. 7-11, which tell of his death and burial along with Sarah in the cave of Machpelah (for moderns the "tombs of the patriarchs" in the disputed mosque/Israeli shrine at Hebron). Of interest is the listing of Ishmael's twelve sons as the heads of tribes (vv. 13-16), proving the awareness of the biblical authors that they and their non-Canaanite neighbors were of the same stock. The *Qur 'ān*'s adoption of Abraham as Islam's progenitor by way of Ishmael, son of Hagar, whom is does not name, is not surprising, for it claims a parentage that Israel's tradition rejects for itself. Today's pericope begins with the word "generations" (v. 19, *tôldôth*) but goes no further than Isaac's sons after summarizing the Rebekah narrative in a sentence (v. 20; see 24:1-67). Her early infertility, brought to an end by Isaac's prayer, is characteristic of the narratives of the P tradition. The Isaac story that follows is brief enough, being found largely in chap. 26 and leading into the Jacob-Esau rivalry of chaps. 27–28. Isaac dies in 35:29, with little else reported of him than his sending Jacob to take a wife from among the daughters of Laban (28:1-5). The oracle of the LORD predicting the struggle of the twins in Rebekah's womb is one pole in today's narrative, Esau's selling of his birthright the other. The law of primogeniture normally prevails among Semitic peoples but, just as Ishmael was born before Isaac, even if not of a proper wife, so "the elder shall serve the younger," Jacob second out of the womb gripping the heel of Esau as he came (v. 26). The word for heel, *aqeb*, is less likely to account for Jacob's name than *yaaqob-el*, "may God protect," but Semitic writing loves such homophones. Similarly, Esau came to birth reddish in color (v. 23, *admoni*), and is called Edom because he craves some of Jacob's "red stuff" *(adom)*, probably lentils or kidney beans. The whole tale is told to explain his fatherhood of the Edomites and the red earth (cf. Gen 2:7, *adam*) they inhabited. The Jew Saul of Tarsus would employ this story of the younger brother's ascendancy of the elder (Rom 9:8-13) to illustrate God's freedom of choice in electing among Israelites "children of the promise" over those Saul describes as not true descendants of Abraham, namely non-accepters of the gospel. But well before this the Jewish Scriptures will provide other examples of God's reversing the expected order of inheritance.

PSALM 119:105-12

ISAIAH 55:10-13

This chapter is at first addressed indiscriminately to all who are thirsty (v. 1), even though it centers on covenant renewal offered to the people of David, "a leader and commander for the peoples" (vv. 3, 4) by "the Holy One of Israel, who has glorified you" (v. 5d). Verses 8 and 9 stress the transcendence of Israel's LORD and his differences from his people, yet vv. 10 and 11 suggest God's way of closing this great gap. Under an agricultural figure that would mean much to a people dependent on moisture and soil (vv. 10a, 10b), the prophet speaks of God's word (v. 11a) as effective in intent (v. 11b) and fruitful in result (v. 10c). Isaiah 45:23 has referred to God's oath regarding an unalterable word uttered. This word is to be fulfilled simply because it contains the power of God and the will of God which brooks no interference. The word and plan of God are one.

The theme of invincible intention has appeared in Deutero-Isaiah before: "Cyrus, my shepherd, / who fulfills my every wish" (44:28); "My purpose shall stand, and I will fulfill my intention" (46:10); "and the will of the LORD shall be accomplished through him" (53:10). God does not expect to utter a single word to his people without its achieving its purpose. There is the same certainty about the fulfillment of the divine design as the succession of the seasons.

PSALM 65:(1-8), 9-13[10-14]

The seed that falls on good ground will yield a fruitful harvest.

ROMANS 8:1-11[18-23]

See Proper 9 [14] (A) for Paul's understanding of flesh and spirit/Spirit.

The previous Sunday's reading ends with 7:25a, perhaps because the word "slave" is offensive to African-American worshipers. But Paul uses that image to suggest total obedience—to one master or the other. Will it be mind adhering to the law of God or flesh adhering to the law of sin? It need never be the latter, this chapter repeatedly affirms. Those who live according to [God's] Spirit have been set free from the demands of the Law weakened by the flesh if they will have it so. Paul is always conscious of the awful possibility of not going on that path. But God made it possible by the gift of the Spirit which is stronger than the flesh is weak. One can set one's mind in one direction or the other (vv. 5f.). The key to "flesh" comes late in the discussion. The apostle means by it not simple weakness but hostility to God (vv. 7f.). Having the Spirit of Christ dwelling in oneself makes the difference. It brings life—an uprightness before God—even though the downward pull of the body ("concupiscence") remains sin's last gasp, so to say (v. 10).

God has given a new liberating law of the Spirit that can accomplish what a sin-weakened law was incapable of (vv. 2f). By a kind of divine homeopathy the Son in the likeness of sinful flesh has condemned sin in the flesh, making the just fulfillment of the Law a possibility (vv. 4-8). You in whom the Spirit of God dwells will have that Spirit give life to your mortal bodies (vv. 10-11). Sin has its victories in the present age: sufferings (v. 18), subjection to futility (v. 20), slavery to corruption (v. 21), groaning and agony (v. 22). All continue right up to Paul's day despite eager awaiting (v. 19), hope (v. 20), and the Spirit as first fruits (v. 23). The latter figure (*aparchē*; Heb. *bikkurim*) describes the initial green shoots that presage a harvest; they are a pledge of all that is to follow (cf. 11:16; 16:5). The chief contrast in this passage is between the hardships of the present and the "glory to be revealed in us" (v. 18; cf. 3:23; 5:2).

If "the creation" of vv. 19f. means the human race rather than the cosmos, it becomes easier to understand the hoped for setting free of "the creation itself" (v. 21) from its bondage to decay to the full freedom of the glory of the children of God.

T. W. Manson suggests that the human race is in three stages rather than two: that segment subject to futility (v. 20) and corruption (v. 21) through not knowing Christ; believers in him who have the first fruits of the Spirit (v. 23); and an already redeemed humanity that is confident it will live in a transformed universe (vv. 18, 19, 21). It appears that Christians are not the only ones who "groan inwardly" while awaiting the redemption of "the body" (v. 23), here the body of the individual, not the Church. The whole created world is in similar condition (v. 22), having the same agony but not the same hope (See *PC*, 946).

Believers in Christ have in prospect their being revealed (v. 19) as children of God, the eschatological revelation referred to in 2:5; 1 Cor 1:7; 2 Thess 1:7. It will bring to consummation the revealing of the mystery of the gospel which has already been accomplished after long ages (cf. Rom 16:25).

The latter part of this lection may be influenced by gnostic thought-patterns, with their claimed influence of heavenly bodies on human lives. God is in control throughout, however, not locked in combat with some opposite dualistic force. It is God "who once subjected" the creation to futility (v. 20), not Adam or Satan, although the story of Adam's sin as an explanation of the world's woes is perhaps understood here.

ALLELUIA. MATTHEW 24:42A, 44

Be watchful and ready: you know not when the Son of Man is coming.

MATTHEW 13:1-9, 18-23[1-23]

The parable told in Matt 13:4-9 (//Mark 2:8) is chiefly about the confidence of the farmer who broadcasts his seed. He is secure in the knowledge that he will reap a rich harvest despite some waste of seed in the process. The details are secondary and are included to make a good story of it. The early Church, missing the simplicity of the tale with its single point, appears to have allegorized it (Matt 13:19-23; Mark 4:14-20). That single point is the conviction of Jesus that the consummation of all is God's work and that it is bound to come despite "every failure and opposition, from hopeless beginnings" (Joachim Jeremias). The superabundant return from good soil in v. 8 is a figure of end-time richness; it describes not so much a portion of the field as another point in time, the last day. Like so many of Jesus' stories this is a contrast parable, in this case between what Israel expects in view of many setbacks and what God will surprisingly accomplish.

The explanatory conclusion of vv. 19-23 can be shown to be the work of the early Church by its use of the technical term "the word" for the Gospel (cf. Mark

4:33; Luke 1:2; Acts 4:4; Gal 6:6; Col 4:3 and many other places; it is used by Jesus in this sense only in the interpretation of the parable of the sower); by the occurrence within it of a number of words that are not found elsewhere in the Synoptics but are common in the rest of New Testament literature; and by the use of the verb for sowing to express preaching, a usage not characteristic of Jesus in other sayings attributed to him. More to the point, perhaps, the interpretation appended alters the meaning of the parable from its original eschatological one to a psychological. It exhorts early believers to examine their states of mind and heart and give thought to perseverance.

Verse 12 was originally an isolated saying of Jesus, which Matthew tacks on because it seems to echo the abundant outcome reported in v. 8.

In his explanation of Jesus' use of parables (vv. 10f., 13-17), Matthew follows Mark 4:10-12, who is committed to the distinction between the mystery entrusted by Jesus to the disciples and the mystification of "those outside." This introduces the erroneous "hardening theory" which held that Jesus used parables precisely so that certain hearers of his teaching might not understand it. Mark quotes the Targum version of Isa 6:9f., which ends, "lest perhaps they repent and be forgiven," while Matthew quotes the Isaiah passage from the LXX (as does Acts 28:26f.).

Jeremias argues that targumic use establishes that the Greek word for "lest" in Isaiah and Mark 4:32 renders the Aramaic word meaning "unless," followed by the divine passive "and they be forgiven." If so, the meaning would be, "unless they turn, and in that case God will forgive them." This leads him to conclude that Mark introduced the targumic version of Isa 6:10 not to explain Jesus' use of the parable form but to account for reaction to his teaching in general, i.e., "the secret of the kingdom of God" (Mark 4:11). Outsiders find Jesus' words obscure, but if they repent all will go well: they will find forgiveness. The "secret" is the breaking in of God on people in the teaching and action of Jesus.

Even if Jeremias is right, Matthew with his "the reason is that" (v. 13) is explaining the use of parables not as a pedagogical device—which they were—but as part of the working out of God's plan. Verse 35, which quotes Ps 78:2, will do the same. Matthew's inclusion of vv. 16f. in this context (Luke 10:23f.) confirms this view. Prophets and saints from Israel's past could not have known those mysteries, a knowledge of which has been given "to you," the disciples (v. 11).

In the allegorized explanation (vv. 18-23), Matthew ties the various types of hearers in with an understanding of the word (v. 17); and it is to be noted that he does not make Jesus the sower. The evangelist's change of focus from that of Jesus' original telling to the fate of the word as seed is supported by the absence of the allegorical explanation in the Coptic *Gospel of Thomas* 9, discovered at Nag Hammadi, Egypt, in 1945.

❧❧

Proper 11 [16] / Sixteenth Sunday of the Year (A)
Sunday between July 17 and July 23, inclusive

GENESIS 28:10-19A

Jacob proceeds north from Beersheba in the desert (site of the modern Bar Ilan University) to Haran, from where his progenitor Abraham had come south to Canaan. His dream of the ladder pitched from earth to heaven (vv. 12f., used by John in 1:51 as a figure of the angels' descent on the Son of Man) identifies the place as Beit El, "house of God." First, however, God is self-disclosed to him as YHWH, reiterating the promise of the land made to Abraham and his offspring in whom all peoples shall find a blessing (vv. 13ff.). Filled with awe upon awakening—the Vulgate word for the place is *terribilis*, "awesome"—he anoints the stone that had served as his headrest and puts it in place to commemorate the theophany. The Roman Rite prescribes this reading for the commemoration of the dedication of a church, while "Gate of Heaven" has given its name to countless cemeteries. Modern Bethel is the site of a synagogue whose name is *Beit El.*

PSALM 139:1-12, 23-24

WISDOM 12:13, 16-19

The first-century B.C.E. Alexandrian author takes a view of the Canaanites in vv. 3-6 not unlike that of those "varmints" and "pesky redskins" held by citizens of the Righteous Empire. "They were an accursed race from the beginning" (v. 11), he says. Therefore YHWH's conduct could only be reckoned magnanimous as Israel gradually exterminated them.

> Judging them little by little you gave them an opportunity to repent though you were not unaware that their origin was evil and their wickedness inborn, and that their way of thinking would never change. (v. 10)

All this is a much later reflection on why the ancestors had been instructed to destroy the inhabitants of the land. The theological defense arrived at is that because God's rule is omnipotent there is no need for divine self-justification. God's conduct may be presumed just (vv. 13ff.). His might is his justice, his sovereign power his leniency (v. 16). Never so clearly does the might of the LORD shine forth as when it is challenged (v. 17). Yet it is always tempered with mercy, and justice with clemency.

The entire passage is a lesson in the noble restraint of power. Israel is to learn from its God that it can afford to be just because of its strength. God is now perceived to judge with mildness and govern Israel with great forbearance, teaching the people thereby that the righteous must be kind. There is always room for repentance.

Jacob Israel has been addressed as Yeshurun in Isa 44:2 (cf. Deut 32:15; 33:5), a term of endearment that means something like "my darling." In today's lection God is called the people's Redeemer or, better, Ransomer/Bail Bondsman *(go'el)* and their Rock *(tsur),* the word that gave its name to Tyre on the sea in modern Lebanon. Some modern bumper stickers bear the legend "No Fear," meaning trust in God who is ever trustworthy (v. 8).

For additional commentary on Romans 8:12-17, see Trinity Sunday (first after Pentecost).

PSALM 86:11-17[5-6, 9-10, 15-16A]

LORD, you are good and forgiving.

ROMANS 8:12-25[26-27]

The Spirit is the life-principle common to the Son and God's people in this final age of outpouring. This Spirit of God has led the community out of slavery into a spirit of adoption (vv. 14f.). The new condition of believers as children and heirs has enabled them, in the Spirit, to address God as "Father" (vv. 15c-17). In this lection the Spirit is not only a witness with our spirit but a strengthener and enabler in the work of prayer (v. 26). The Spirit, being distinct from God, can intercede for us (v. 26), an office that Christ will be described as performing in v. 34. The inward groaning of those who possess the first fruits of the Spirit is related to the whole creation's groaning in labor pains as "we wait for adoption, the redemption of our bodies" (vv. 22, 23). God, who is the searcher of hearts, can alone interpret the intercession for believers that the Spirit makes from within them. The Spirit speaks to God, who is spirit, from the depths of the human spirit. The thought is relatively obscure but it is evident that the "portion of spirit" bestowed on the prophets is to the fore in Paul's mind. Now, however, the gift given is godhead itself.

ALLELUIA

Open our hearts, O LORD, to listen to the words of your Son.

MATTHEW 13:24-30, 36-43[24-43]

The parable of the weeds and the wheat (vv. 24-30) occurs only in Matthew among the evangelists, although the *Gospel of Thomas* 57 also gives it. There the ending is abrupt and no allegorization follows: "on the day of harvest the weeds will appear. They will pull them and burn them." The agricultural vendetta reported, strange to us, was evidently quite conceivable in ancient times and even in modern. The weeding of a wheat field described in v. 28 was evidently a commonplace.

As it stands, this parable of Jesus was told to impress on the impatient the need for patience. The elaboration found in verse 30a beyond the phrasing of Thomas shows that Matthew is preparing the way for an allegorical interpretation, provided in vv. 37-43. The parable of the mustard seed is taken almost verbatim from Mark (4:30-32) while the presence of the brief parable about the woman with the three measures of flour is from Q (cf. Luke 13:20-21). These two parables show the future magnitude of God's realm despite humble beginnings and also the inexorable character of God's rule. God's work cannot be stopped any more than the growth of a tree or the action of yeast in the dough. The quotation of Ps 78:2 in explanation of why Jesus taught in parables is found in Matthew alone. The "parable" or comparison in terms of which the psalmist chooses to speak, his "dark sayings" from of old, are the history of Israel's desert wanderings told in detail, concluding with events down to David's day. The evangelist has no special interest in the psalm as it develops, only in its early affirmation that the speaker will teach by multiplying examples.

The vocabulary of the allegorical explanation in vv. 37-43 is distinctly Matthean, as can be seen by the more than three dozen words that are his. Jesus never speaks of his kingdom (v. 41); other terms like *ponērós* for the evil one, *diabolos* for Satan, and *kosmos* for the world are not part of the first layer of Gospel tradition. They all represent development of vocabulary in church circles. Matthew in his explanation accounts for seven categories in the story, one after the other (vv. 37-39). He then appends a "little apocalypse" (vv. 40-43) that tells us the fate of the wicked and the just to expect at the final judgment.

Matthew bypasses the point of the parable about patient waiting until the end, so intent is he on moralizing about the fact that believers (members of his church) and unbelievers must live side by side, and about the ultimate fate of each at the separation that will characterize the judgment. He warns against false security and promises those who cause others to sin and evildoers a bad end (v. 41). The righteous will fare much better (v. 43).

Thus, even as early as the year 85 the urgent note in Jesus' tales that asks the hearer to recognize an eschatology that is in the process of realization has been lost. In its place has been put a moralizing about persecution and falling away cast in apocalyptic dress.

***&.**

Proper 12 [17] / Seventeenth Sunday of the Year (A)
Sunday between July 24 and July 30, inclusive

GENESIS 29:15-28

Laban was Rebekah's brother in Haran (24:29) to whom she sent her favored son Jacob to escape his twin brother Esau's wrath (27:42ff.). In this largely J narrative Jacob has met Rachel at a well in "the land of the people of the east" (29:1), to discover that she is the daughter of his mother's brother Laban. The story of Jacob's finding a suitable marriage partner in her (vv. 9-14) much resembles that of the Isaac-Rebekah encounter in Aram Naharaim (24:11-33). Despite the effusive reception that Laban gives to his kinsman Jacob (vv. 13f.), he is already calculating how to get the most work out this prospective son-in-law. Are Leah's eyes lovely (*rak*, v. 17) or does the word mean weak, dull? NRSV and NAB opt for the former, *Tanakh* and REB for the latter as the seventeenth-century translations have done. If both women are being described as attractive there seems little reason for the expression of Jacob's preference for Rachel over Leah, especially since she is the younger. In any case, the hard bargain that Laban drives is one of the best remembered tales of the Bible (vv. 26f., 30). Even better remembered, perhaps, is the declaration of love attributed to Jacob: the seven years he served for Rachel seemed to him but a few days "because of the love he bore her" (v. 20). As to Laban's unethical behavior, it is part of the man's character (cf. his covetous glance at the nose ring and bracelets that Abraham's envoy bestowed on his sister in 24:30f.). Successful trickery or deceit is a high value in this ancient Semitic culture (see Gen 12:10-20; 20:1-18; 26:6-11 where it is a device by which the Hebrews outwitted their pagan neighbors and 27:5-38 where Rebekah schemes in favor of her son Jacob to forward the narrative's intended outcome.) Jacob's love for Rachel must have been great indeed for him to let himself be bamboozled in such docile fashion.

PSALM 105:1-11, 45B OR PSALM 128

1 KINGS 3:5-12

Solomon was a boy-king when he succeeded his father David on the throne ("twelve years old" according to the LXX of v. 12; Josephus says "fourteen"). This dream story, heavily edited by the pious Deuteronomist, is told to account for Solomon's wisdom—even though in 2:6 he is said by David to possess it natively. Gibeon, where the dream occurred, is located six miles northwest of Jerusalem in Benjaminite territory. The king had gone there to offer sacrifice at the formerly Canaanite "high place," probably to mend a few political fences with his Benjaminite and Canaanite neighbors. The Deuteronomist editor regrets his presence at this sanctuary which took the place of Nob a short distance to the south after Saul's vengeful slaughter of the priests there (2 Sam 22:18f.) and balances it off by situating Solomon at Jerusalem for sacrifice before the ark in v. 15.

The Temple had not yet been built nor had public worship been consolidated at one place only. Still, the Deuteronomist is uneasy over Solomon's presence at the Gibeonite shrine. He is more at ease in accounting for Solomon's astuteness regarding men and affairs (vv. 11, 12), which will lead to riches and glory (v. 13). The story of the two harlots (vv. 16-28) is told to illustrate Solomon's sagacity. Unfortunately, his carrying on of a blood feud with Joab and Shimei until he destroys them, attributed to his father's counsel (2:5-9, 34-46), is also cited as proof of his wisdom.

For dreams as a way by which God might communicate with a worshiper at a shrine, see Gen 28:12; 31:10f.; 1 Sam 3:1-18.

PSALM 119:129-36[57, 72, 76-77]

LORD, I love your commands.

ROMANS 8:26-39[28-30]

REB makes "the spirit" of vv. 26f. the subject of the sentence in verse 28; thus: "And in everything, as we know, he cooperates for good," the spirit having been the subject of pleading in v. 27. On the other hand "all things work [together, NRSV] for . . . good" (NAB 1987), on the supposition that God is required by the context as the subject of the following sentence (v. 29). In some MSS (including Chester Beatty p[46], Vaticanus, and Alexandrinus) "God" occurs after "works," thus "God works all things." The Vulgate makes "all things" the subject of "works" thus, *omnia cooperantur in bonum*. If, however, "all things" is an accusative of specification, we have the "in everything God works for good" of RSV.

While Paul's statement about God's providence regarding believers is subjective as regards their love, he puts the greater stress on their being objects of God's love since they are called as a result of God's purpose (v. 28). In the working out of the divine plan the stages are: God's foreknowledge (v. 29a); humanity's sharing in the image of God's Son who serves as the model ("the firstborn among many," v. 29b); and the calling of the predestined (v. 30a) who are justified (v. 30b) and will at the end be glorified (v. 30c). While the last stage lies in the future, Paul with the certainty of one who knows how the plan is meant to work out uses the aorist to describe it, which can connote past action. There is undoubtedly the notion of predestination in this passage but it is a predetermination (v. 30) to glory, not to reprobation. God's decree inspires confidence, not fear, because it is above all a saving decree.

For a commentary on vv. 31b-34 see 2 Lent (B) and on vv. 35, 37-39 see next Sunday, 18 (A).

Alleluia

Your word, O Lord, is truth. Make us holy in the truth.

Matthew 13:31-33, 44-52

RCL has opted to eliminate the reading of vv. 31-35 from the previous Sunday's lection (Proper 11 [16]) and place the brief comparisons of the mustard seed and the yeast here. The parable, actually a simple parallel, of the mustard seed is one in the "triple tradition" because it also occurs in Mark 4:30-32 where it probably originated and Luke 13:18-19. The yeast in the three measures of flour is of the "double tradition," occurring here and in Luke 13:20-21. These two appear in their respective Gospels (Matthew and Luke) in the same sequence and identical wording in the case of the yeast and near identical wording of the mustard seed, leading to the suspicion of Q as their provenance. In both cases an incommensurate result from small or invisible origins is the point at issue. And so with God's reign.

The mustard bush with birds in its branches is an echo of Ezek 17:22ff. (see also Ps 104:12 and Dan 4:10ff., 20-27). Matthew's "three measures of flour" are a huge amount, as in the parallel place in Luke (13:20f.).

The parables of the buried treasure, the pearl, and the dragnet do not occur in Mark or Luke, but *Thomas* has the first two as sayings 109 and 76. *Thomas*'s story has a parallel in a rabbinic midrash on the Song of Songs. In the former the man who finds a treasure on his land lends money at interest to whomever he pleases; in the latter, the seller of the land grows choleric at the sight of the prosperity of the buyer. Jesus in Matthew seems to be using a folktale to describe the supreme value of the reign of God, which is worth all that a person has and more. *Thomas* 76 on the pearl is substantially the same as Matthew (plus the content of Matt 6:19f.) on a treasure immune to moth and rust, in *Thomas* moth and worm. Matthew makes the merchant sell all he has to establish a parallelism with v. 44. In *Thomas* he merely sells "the merchandise." The key phrase for both parables is "rejoicing" (v. 44), the joy being eschatological as part of a true estimate of what is of worth in this life.

The parable of the dragnet (vv. 47f.) has its close parallel in *Thomas* 8, except for the detail of one large, fine fish in *Thomas*. It is much like the story of the wheat and the weeds (Matt 13:24-30) in its ending about a separation at the judgment. The "useless" fish would be those without fins or scales of Lev 11:20f. and the shellfish which Jesus' contemporaries did not eat. Again, separation is left to the end and to God's angelic agents, both because distinguishing the worthy from the unworthy is beyond human capacity (see v. 29) and, more importantly, because the fullness of time decreed by God must be reached: "when it was full" (v. 48).

The householder who brings forth new and old from his store, to whom Matthew compares the scribe learned in the reign of God, can be reckoned as the subject of a brief parable but most commentators consider it merely a simile.

Verse 53 contains the rubric, "When Jesus had finished these parables" (elsewhere "words" or "giving this instruction," 7:28; 11:1; 19:1; 26:1), with which five of his six major discourses in Matthew conclude (not 23:1-39, which ends, "After Jesus left the temple," 24:1).

❧ ❧

Proper 13 [18] / Eighteenth Sunday of the Year (A)
Sunday between July 31 and August 6, inclusive

GENESIS 32:22-31

The verse enumeration is higher in this chapter in NAB than in NRSV because the latter's 31:55 is explained in a note as 32:1 in Hebrew. This makes NRSV's v. 2 to be v. 3 in NAB, which follows the Hebrew—and so throughout. Clearly Jacob's wrestling match with a man who proves to be God is based on a folktale. Its purpose in Genesis is twofold, to explain how Jacob's name became Israel and to account for a joint of meat the Israelites did not eat that was never adopted in the Torah classification of unclean foods. The contest takes place in the darkness before daybreak (vv. 24, 31) at a place called Penuel and its variant form Peniel, "face of

God." Jacob's successful contest with the stranger who will not tell him his name lest he have power over him results in the victorious cry, "I have seen God face to face and survived." Unlike the veteran's minimal claim when asked what he did in the French Revolution, "*J'ai vecu*" (I lived through it), Jacob makes a unique claim. No one in the Bible is allowed to see God and live (cf. Exod 33:20; Deut 34:10; Judg 6:22f.; 13:22). The people that will be Israel stands alone. It is blessed by God (v. 29 or 30), has contended with God and men, and has prevailed. *Yisra'el* perhaps means, "let God rule," but in a popular etymology the first part is related to *sarita* (v. 29), "you contended."

Psalm 17:1-7, 15

Isaiah 55:1-[3] 5

This pericope occurs in the second collection of oracles of the Deutero-Isaiah (chaps. 49–55), the entire chapter serving as the climax. In it the author sees the return of the exiles to the land for covenant renewal (vv. 3b, 12), a land to which fertility shall be restored (v. 13) if this condition is fulfilled. In Hos 2:9[10] the Lord is Israel's provider. Heeding him means rich fare and life (Isa 55:1ff.; cf. Prov 9:1-6), failing to do so unrighteous and wicked behavior (v. 7). The people are summoned to return to the Lord in a new land of promise. The benefits assured to David for covenant fidelity will be theirs in this age (v. 3b) if they represent YHWH to the nations as David once did (vv. 4f.).

Psalm 145:8-9, 14-21[15-18]

The hand of the Lord feeds us; he answers all our needs.

Romans 9:1-5

Some commentators on this epistle think that its main message has drawn to an end with the stirring rhetoric declaring that nothing can separate the elect—the justified—from "the love of God in Christ Jesus our Lord" (8:31-39). But the sounder opinion is that the entire letter up to this point is preparatory to a discussion of the mystery of Jews and Gentiles living at peace in the one faith community, specifically in Rome. Paul had described the plight of both in their need for deliverance at God's hands (1:18—2:29) and proceeded to explain that only faith in Christ, a trust in God like Abraham's, could achieve the effect of a second gift, uprightness or justness before God (chaps. 2–8). Now he turns to the major disappointment of his career as an apostle, namely that so few of his fellow Jews have accepted the Gospel. The opening declaration of sincerity in the matter (9:1) must be a response to charges of duplicity in word and deed that Paul has defended himself against in his previous correspondence. His conditional wish to be cut off from Christ for the sake of his people (v. 3) is a *per impossibile* outburst like those recorded of certain saints who were more heart than head in saying: "I would willingly be condemned forever to hell if it could achieve the salvation of a single soul." This is religious nonsense and Paul knows it, but he has to convey his sincerity to those in the Roman church who have not known him. He lists the major gifts of God to "the Israelites" (here and in v. 6; cf. 11:1; 2 Cor 11:22), perhaps by that term to link himself and the Jews of Rome up to the patriarchs. The full measure of God's beneficence to this people culminates in the gift of one of them whom he and they believe to be the Messiah (v. 5).

ROMANS 8:35, 37-39

Verses 8:31-39 are a hymn of praise to "the love of God in Jesus Christ" (v. 39) that is made effective for us in the intercession of Christ, dead but now raised and "at the right hand of God" (v. 34, obviously a creedal fragment). God has predestined his elect to glory, i.e., those whom God called and who are justified, (v. 30). Neither God (v. 33) nor Christ (v. 34) is conceivable in an adversary relation, a figure from the courts of law. The suppressed personal accuser of v. 31 can be taken either as Satan (cf. Job 1:6) or the Law of Moses. No one, in any case, can make a successful prosecution, so strong will be the defense (vv. 29f.). For comment on vv. 31-34, see 2 Lent (B), below.

Persecution is a real contender for separating Christ from his chosen. Paul doubtless has his own trials in mind (cf. 5:2ff.; 1 Thess 3:3f.; 2 Cor 11:23-33). Verse 36 quotes Ps 44:24. Yet God's personal love (v. 37) is superior to death and life to all human and angelic powers (v. 38). "Neither height nor depth," a possible reference to the positioning of heavenly bodies, can defeat this love. No creature is thinkable who has the power to contend with the overmastering divine love (v. 39).

The lectionaries content themselves with three brief readings from chaps. 9, 10 and 11 on successive Sundays to convey what many are convinced is the core of this reflection in letter form, namely Paul's speculation on God's design for Israel, the people of his special love. The brief introduction to the question, 9:1-5 (today in RCL, next Sunday in LM) expresses Paul's anguish that not many of his fellow Jews have accepted his Gospel over the previous twenty to twenty-five years.

He employs a phrase of rhetorical excess that could make no sense if taken literally to describe his desire (v. 3). He then lists all that God has done and continues to do for his people. It cannot be that with the culmination in Jesus as Messiah God will disregard all that has gone before.

ALLELUIA. JOHN 15:15B

I call you my friends, says the LORD, for I have made known to you all that the Father has told me.

MATTHEW 14:13-21

For a parallel to this first feeding of the multitude, see the commentary on Luke's account (9:11-17), under The Body and Blood of Christ (C). As is remarked there, the Lukan narrative is sufficiently like Mark 6:30-44, from which today's lection is derived, that it could have come from it as its sole source (cf. in particular Luke 9:16f. and Mark 6:41ff.). The words of blessing and distribution (v. 19) are close to those attributed to Jesus at the Last Supper (26:26), which means that the eucharistic meal practice of the Matthean church is mirrored in both accounts.

The point of the story is not that Jesus has moved the hearts of the crowd to the point where they share voluntarily, as was being maintained by various gospel-as-ethics schools earlier in the last century, but that he performs a Moses-like work of power. Numerous colorful Markan elements are removed from the story (e.g., the phrase "to sit down in groups on the grass," Mark 6:39) but the specifically eucharistic usage remains ("loaves," "broke," "fragments/broken pieces"). Matthew also heightens the miraculous by reporting the detail that the 5,000 who were fed did not include women and children.

Like Mark, Matthew has the fragments gathered up into twelve baskets, symbolic of the completion of elect peoplehood.

❧❧

Proper 14 [19] / Nineteenth Sunday of the Year (A)
Sunday between August 7 and August 13, inclusive

GENESIS 37:1-4, 12-28

Abraham and Isaac have been described as aliens in Hebron in the land of Canaan (35:27), hence Jacob is the same (37:1). His "family history" (Heb. "generations,"

v. 2) which is from J up to v. 20 but also vv. 25-28a, proves to be the introduction of the Joseph story (chaps. 37–50), which concludes in the deaths of the father
and the son. Jacob's bones are to be brought back to the cave of Machpelah in
Hebron and Isaac, returning to Egypt to die (50:12f.; 26), instructs that the same
be done with his (v. 25). Today's long reading will be familiar to many hearers
who may be dismayed to hear nothing of Joseph's "coat of many colors" (vv. 3,
32). This sign of his father's favor has become "a long robe with sleeves" in NRSV
and REB but, in other translations, an "ornamented" *(Tanakh)* or "decorated" tunic
(JB) and in (NAB) simply a "long" one—all testifying to the uncertainty of the
Hebrew. The sons of his father's secondary wives, not Leah, are made the envious
schemers against their half-brother. The firstborn of Jacob by Leah, Reuben, begs
the others not to kill the younger one but to throw him into a waterless pit that
he may rescue him at a later date (vv. 21f.). This compassionate son of Jacob was
earlier described as having lain with his father's concubine Bilhah (35:22) and
thereby having lost his primacy among the sons (49:3f.). Verses 21-24 and 28b,
36 are from the Elohist source, so that the returning Reuben finds the cistern empty
and is ignorant of this brother's rescue by passing Midianite traders (vv. 28, 36).
This accounts for Judah's having proposed the plan in the Yahwist source for selling Joseph to some Ishmaelites (vv. 26-28) while Reuben is off the scene (v. 29).
Thus Joseph's life is spared but for a pragmatic reason (v. 26), not from any nobility of spirit. The ten not born of Rachel are moved by greed at the sale rather than
leaving behind a profitless corpse (vv. 26-28). The Church fathers liked to see a
prefiguring of Christ come forth from his rock tomb in the deliverance of Joseph
from the "cistern" (NAB, REB, following KJV and DRC) after being left for dead by
us, his brothers.

PSALM 105:1-6, 16-22, 45B

1 KINGS 19:9-18[9A, 11-13A]

Elijah's victory over the prophets of Ba'al is complete, and the drought comes to
a close with a heavy rain, bringing to an end the famine in the land (chap. 18).
This should have pleased King Ahab, but his wife, Jezebel, apprised of the slit
throats of her 450 co-religionists, is moved to murderous reprisal. Elijah hears of
her intent and flees for his life, discouraged. The action of the LORD in sending
rain has not made his life quite so easy as he expected. He makes his journey of
forty days and forty nights to Horeb (as it is in the D and E sources; Sinai, in J)

on the strength of the cake/bread on hot stones and the water miraculously provided (vv. 5f.).

The conversation between the LORD and his prophet in the cave reveals a state of mind not unlike that of the sulking Jonah. Elijah is far from Israel where he belongs and is reproached for his flight (v. 9b). In a burst of self-pity he complains of his reverses as if only he, of all Israel, has kept faith. "As though Carmel had never happened!" one commentator puts it.

Strong wind, earthquake, and fire supervene but none of this is the sign of God's power. Rather, a "gentle whisper/a sound of sheer silence," the "still, small voice" of KJV. Verses 13f. are an obvious doublet of 9f., with the difference that Elijah is sent back to the Aramean desert to anoint King Hazael in the second case rather than outside the cave to "stand on the mount before the LORD" (v. 11). When Elijah recognizes YHWH's speech in the sound that was barely a whisper he hides his face, as Moses had done in similar circumstances (cf. Exod 3:6). The passage is a powerful parable of the unexpected way of God's action. Popular understanding has taken the "still, small voice" as having to do with conscience. It is, in fact, concerned with God's action in ordinary ways, not the flamboyant extraordinary.

PSALM 85:8-13[9-14]

LORD, show us your kindness and grant us your salvation.

ROMANS 10:5-15

For a comment on 10:8-13 see 1 Lent (C).

ROMANS 9:1-5

Paul can be separated by nothing from God's love in Christ (8:38f.) but that does not mean that he feels no pain of separation. The great grief of his life is separation from his fellow Jews over the Gospel. He could even wish, as by way of paradox, to reverse the course of things and be separated from Christ in order to be joined with his kinsmen (v. 3), enduring the one for the sake of the other. Paul lists the irrevocable benefits to his own people (v. 4), among them "the glory." This "glory of the LORD" dwelling in their midst (cf. Exod 40:34f.) was the epitome of all the rest. Whose were Abraham, Isaac, and Jacob if not Israel's, and whose the blood line from which sprang that Messiah who, in Paul's faith, is Jesus (v. 5)? Overwhelmed at the irreversible course of history with its gifts to his own people,

Paul can only conclude with a prayer of blessing that singles out the blessedness of God responsible for it all. (NAB cuts a grammatical Gordian knot by rendering v. 5b as a distinct prayer of praise of God. NRSV and NIV assume with KJV and DRC that the Messiah is over all and "God blessed forever.")

In the first eight chapters of this epistle, Paul has been speaking in praise of God's freely bestowed love for sinful humanity. With these opening verses the epistle goes in a new direction. Paul begins to reflect that despite all of Israel's privileges of the past (and God's energies expended on its behalf), there is in prospect indeed a present reality, the refusal of the love. Paul speaks the truth of the matter not on his own but "in Christ"; his conscience bears him witness "by the Holy Spirit" (v. 1). For the phrase "separated [by a curse] from Christ" (v. 3), see 1 Cor 16:22; Gal 1:8f. To be cut off from Christ for Paul is to be consigned to destruction since the word he uses, *anáthēma*, is the LXX rendering of the Old Testament *ḥerem* or ban. His "own people/brethren" are specifically his human not yet Christian kinsfolk. Paul can no longer claim kinship with them according to the Spirit. He will make the same qualification in v. 5 as here in v. 3 with respect to the Jewishness of the Messiah; it, too, is "according to the flesh." Israel is called God's firstborn son (in Exod 4:22; Hos 11:1) as if some new status were acquired at the exodus. God's purpose in choosing Israel as adoptive offspring (*huiothesía*, lit.: "sonship," translated "adoption") seems temporarily thwarted. It is with this paradox that Paul will wrestle in the next three chapters.

ALLELUIA. JOHN 14:6

I am the way, the truth and the life, says the Lord; no one comes to the Father except through me.

MATTHEW 14:22-33

Matthew takes the account of Jesus' walking on the sea from Mark 6:45-52 but puts it to quite different use by adding vv. 28-31, the section about the rescue of Peter, and omitting Mark's v. 52. This provides an important illustration of redaction criticism, the editorial use of traditional materials to serve an overall theological purpose. Both evangelists have Jesus separate his disciples from the crowd after the feeding miracle but, whereas Mark uses the appearance of Jesus on the stormy waters to heighten their lack of understanding (in this case, about the loaves, v. 52), Matthew employs it as a confession of the Lord who has marvelously appeared to them (v. 33). It is, in other words, construed as an illustration of faith in the latter case and lack of faith in the former.

In both Gospels the disciples are described as terrified at Jesus' appearance (Matt 14:26; Mark 6:50a). Not even his comforting words in Mark (v. 50b) can dispel their fears; if anything, the latter seem to be heightened as the pericope ends (v. 51b). The disciples' early terror in Matthew, however (v. 26), is replaced by a trust in Jesus that goes as far as confessing him to be "the Son of God" (v. 33).

Matthew in his insertion of vv. 28-31 (his use of the plural "waters" as in 8:32 rather than "the lake" or "the sea" found in Mark 6:48f. and copied in Matt 14:25, plus the characteristically Matthean address "Lord" [vv. 28, 30], certifies that it is an insertion) uses the epiphany of Jesus to "set them free to exercise a fearless faith" (H. J. Held, "Matthew as Interpreter of the Miracle Stories," in G. Bornkamm et al., *Tradition and Interpretation in Matthew* [Philadelphia: Westminster, 1962], 206). Matthew understandably has Peter crying for help in words very close to the disciples' cry during the storm on the sea (8:25). The "It is I" of v. 27 is joined by "If it is you" as a faith link. Jesus has said "Do not be afraid!" in both Gospels (Mark 6:50; Matt 14:27) but only in Matthew do they heed his injunction.

Matthew uses his Petrine insertion for a double purpose. It shows the promise made to faith in a context of discipleship, a theme that runs throughout his Gospel. It also underscores the disciple Peter's inability to remain firm on his own during a time of testing. It is Jesus who gives his disciples the power to follow him. Without that there is only dismay and fear at his prowess and destruction as the fruit of misplaced trust in the self.

The scene is ecclesiological, not only christological, as is usual in Matthew. Jesus looks for a community of believers that is not, like Peter, of "little faith" (v. 31b). Jesus means to transmit his authority, signified by the power to walk on water, to those whom he sends in his name.

❧❧

Proper 15 [20] / Twentieth Sunday of the Year (A)
Sunday between August 14 and August 20, inclusive

GENESIS 45:1-15

This is one of only two selections from the Joseph cycle chosen for Sunday by the RCL (the other being on Proper 19 [24] [A]). LM has none. It does propose, however, readings from chaps. 37, 41–42, 44–45, 46, and 49–50 on 2 Friday Lent (chap. 37), then successive days on Wednesday through Saturday of Week 14, Year A. Today's narrative reports the dramatic self-disclosure of Joseph's identity to his brothers marked by loud outcries of joy on his part, dismay on theirs, and no call by him for revenge for their evil deed. Rather, Joseph the dreamer (see 37:5-11) and interpreter of Pharaoh's dream of starving cattle and withered ears of grain (that predicted seven lean years to succeed seven good ones 41:27, 54) tells them that the famine in Egypt has five more years to run (45:6). The narrator provides a providential explanation for the turn of events. God has made Joseph a "father to Pharaoh"—a title also encountered in an Egyptian inscription—and "lord of all Egypt," "greatly honored in Egypt"—so that the Jacob clan may settle in the land of Goshen northeast on the Nile delta as a remnant preserved by God to keep the sons of Jacob-Israel from poverty (vv. 7, 11). The brothers hear all this in silence. No mention is made of the several ruses and deceits Joseph has engaged in to lure young Benjamin down to Egypt and away from his father. The final scene is heavy with emotion and seems to be drawn from J and E (vv. 14 f.). Only after kisses and embraces do Joseph's brothers speak with him.

A well-remembered occurrence in the early days of Giuseppe Roncalli as bishop of Rome and no longer patriarch of Venice was his reception of a delegation of highly placed Italian Jews. He who had rescued many from the *Shoah* while posted as a Vatican diplomat to Turkey and Bulgaria came forward to embrace the group saying, "I am Joseph your brother." They had not been prepared for this, aside from knowing quite well their Scriptures from which he was quoting.

PSALM 133

ISAIAH 56:1, 6[-7]8

This chapter marks the opening of the third book in the collection known as Isaiah, which spans two centuries. The Babylonian exile is over and Judah is back in the homeland. Perhaps the Temple has already been rebuilt (520–16 B.C.E.). Deutero-Isaiah had been a gospel of promised salvation; the restored community must now be enjoined in an institutional spirit to "observe" and to "do" what is just. The author we call Trito-Isaiah tries hard to be faithful to the outlook and even the vocabulary of his predecessor. Verse 1 is like 46:13a and 51:5a as to wording but the spirit is different. The LORD's "justice" that is about to be revealed— even to foreigners and to the previously excluded eunuchs (Deut 23:2)—is a matter of observing Sabbaths (vv. 2b, 4a, 6c), holding fast to terms of the covenant (vv. 4b, 6c), and offering sacrifices and holocausts on God's altar (v. 7b). It is understandable that in exile Sabbath observance would have come to the fore, since Temple sacrifice and other cultic forms were impossible to keep (cf. 58:13). Still, the new demand for observance on priestly terms is somewhat disturbing in light of the great Isaian prophetic tradition.

Deutero-Isaiah had spoken marvelously of Egyptians, Ethiopians, and Sabeans who would come to Israel joining her in chains (45:14), of every knee bending to the LORD (45:23b) and nations who did not know her running to Israel because of its LORD (55:5). Verses 3 and 4 attempt an "opening to the left" by welcoming "foreigners" (proselyte Gentiles) and "eunuchs" into the worshiping community on condition that they keep the Sabbath and make the proper offerings in the temple on Mount Zion.

The castrated had been disbarred, probably because of their inability to have offspring. Here, their fidelity to observance is accepted in place of the impossible perpetuation of their names in their children. The foreigners "ministering" (v. 6) to the LORD, a priestly term, are proselytes who in virtue of circumcision become the mysterious "temple" of 1 Chron 9:2 and Ezra 8:17, 20.

The ringing prophecy of Isa 2:2-4 and of chaps. 40–55 is somehow fulfilled in v. 7. The bold term "house of prayer" is one of several descriptive titles to which this author is partial (cf. 58:12; 60:14, 18; 62:4, 12). All are triumphalist ways of describing the return from the exile, depressingly like modern Church pronouncements to the effect that promised reforms have now been achieved.

PSALM 67[2-3, 5-6, 8]

O God, let all the nations praise you!

ROMANS 11:1-2A[13-15], 29-32

Paul reiterates from 9:1-3 his "heart's desire and prayer for [his fellow Jews] that they may be saved . . . [by] submitting to God's righteousness" (10:1, 3). He pleads that the gospel be preached to them, for "how are they to believe in one whom they have never heard?" (10:14). Asking and answering a rhetorical question he affirms strongly that God has not rejected them. Some Gentile believers he has heard of must have been teaching this or he would not deny it so vehemently. As a token proof to the Roman community he underscores his own Jewishness. The salvation of many like him, he declares, was surely foreknown by God.

Paul's wrestling with the theological problem of the refusal of the fellow Jews of his experience to accept the gospel he has preached to them, carried on over chaps. 9–11, culminates in this reading. It begins with his firm denial that God has rejected (or repelled) a people foreknown from the time of Abraham onward (vv. 1f.). LM does not include these verses, but their importance is that they state clearly what has gone before. They also prevent hearers of the lection from assuming that the entire epistle is addressed to Gentiles only in the Roman church (see v. 13). He has expressed his conviction that there is a "remnant chosen by grace," (v. 5), a nation within a nation made up of Christian Jews. As to those who do not accept the choice made of them by grace but persist in works and their own "seeking" (v. 7)—by far the greater number—Paul's argument concerning them takes the familiar *a fortiori* form, "so much the more."

Addressing the Gentiles of Rome directly as one conscious of his special apostolate to Gentiles (cf. Gal 2:7, 9), he explains why his concern for fellow-Jews nonetheless persists. Paul puts forward the unusual explanation that the greater his efforts to evangelize the uncircumcised, the greater is the likelihood that the circumcised will be moved by envy. That expectation may strike some recipients of the letter as unreal but his purpose is perhaps to confirm former pagans in their new, Jewish-based faith. His goal with respect to Jews generally is modest: "to save some of them" (v. 14). He writes as if he realizes that, while a few may come to believe, the acceptance of Christ by all Jews is an event at the farther limit of history (see v. 26). If the Jewish rejection of his message has meant reconciliation of the non-Jewish world (or both worlds, as in Eph 2:16), how much more will their acceptance of it mean? It will be an event of the end-time, however, and the "life from the dead" it signals (v. 15) is no less than the final resurrection of all. Paul's theology here is one of happy fault. There is no telling what progress, if any, the Gospel might have made among the Gentiles but for Jewish resistance to it. That persistence in familiar, old ways has triggered a modest stage one. Consider, then, he suggests—on the hypothesis of future Jewish openness to the Gospel—the magnitude of stage two. NRSV, NAB, and NIV have left "their rejection" and "their acceptance" ambiguous, not taking a position on its meaning like that above. At least they do not assume that God's "casting away of them" (KJV; "loss of them") is Paul's meaning, which is totally unlikely in the context of his discussion.

Verses 29-32 put the argument another way. Gentile disobedience in the past has now been responded to by the divine mercy with current Jewish disobedience as the very condition of it. Since the majority of the Jews Paul has encountered have resisted his preaching he can identify their condition with that of the Gentiles. Now all are "imprisoned in/delivered to disobedience" but, marvelously, God's mercy is available to all. In fact, had the Jews not fallen to the Gentiles' low estate, there is no telling how rescue would have come their way.

The gifts and the calling of God are irrevocable (v. 29). As an elect people Israel is forever beloved despite its present enmity to the Gospel. Apparently, the failure of the Jews to believe in Christ is, for Paul, a necessary stage on their way to faith. God's mercy is the key to all human need, whatever a people's spiritual history or lack of it. Such is the main point of these three chapters. Unfortunately, because of the later conviction of the Church that all of Paul's letters are inspired of God, his musings on the meaning of the twenty-five years of his experience have been taken to be God's judgment on the Jewish-Gentile relation of all subsequent ages. Paul is more modest. He praises God in the face of a problem he cannot solve (vv. 33ff.).

ALLELUIA. JOHN 17:17B, A

Your word, O LORD, is truth; make us holy in the truth.

MATTHEW 15:(10-20), 21-28

Verses 11 and 17-20 are derived almost verbatim from Mark 7:15-23 but without the latter's editorial insertion declaring that all foods are now fit to eat (*kosher*; Mark 7:19b). Jesus' insistence that only evil thoughts expressed by the lips and coming from the heart can defile was, to be sure, his authentic teaching. The evangelist's comment on it indicated that his was a largely Gentile or at least a non-observant Jewish church. Matthew omits the comment because he does not believe Jesus had anything to say on the subject or perhaps because some in his community were still keeping kosher—if so, out of longstanding habit rather than that they have to as a condition of their faith in Christ. Verses 11 and 17-20 are taken almost verbatim from Mark 7:18-23 with the exception of 19b.

On the two previous Sundays the readings from Matt 14 were his first of two accounts of feeding a multitude and Jesus' miraculous walking on the water that followed immediately. RCL proposes vv. 10-20 as a way to lead into what follows. (See a commentary on the Markan passage that this pericope is based on, Proper 17 [22] [C].) Interestingly, Matt 15:3-6 (Mark 7:8-13) on avoiding the care of aged parents is not read on any Sunday. Mark 7 makes clear that in his church the precepts of Oral Law are not being observed and seems to be saying the same of any dietary observance. Matthew does not go that far, confining himself to lessons on the inner and outer as the locus of sin. He follows Mark closely in what comes next, beginning with v. 21.

Matthew follows Mark 7:24-30 in this pericope, omitting chiefly the characteristic note of secrecy in Mark's account, calling the woman a Canaanite rather than a Syrophoenician, and adding the detail of the disciples' attempt to be rid of her. This merits Jesus' important statement in response: "I was sent only to the lost sheep of the house of Israel" (v. 24, repeated from 10:5f.). The phrase is an addition to the Markan exchange about the woman's status as a Gentile. The remaining alterations in Matthew are small and verbal only, not substantive.

Mark's situating Jesus outside Jewish territory, namely, on the Phoenician coast, is followed by his appearance in the Ten Cities (Decapolis) region east of the Jordan (7:31). This brief "Gentile ministry" may be a Markan outreach to his Gentile audience. The overall tradition, however, does not support any such extensive stay.

The main thrust of the story as Matthew tells it does not lie in the healing but in Jesus' initial silence (v. 23a) and then the conversation (vv. 25-28a) that precedes the miracle. Jesus' answer to the woman's plea indicates that his powers are conceived by the evangelists as specific spiritual powers in aid of God's establishment of his reign among the Jewish people. The Gentile woman is described as accepting this without difficulty (the harsh term "dogs" was the ordinary religious obloquy of the times of any less favored group than one's own). She is portrayed as accepting the divine division of things as between Jews and Gentiles. By her persistence and in her speech she acknowledges Jesus as Israel's Messiah ("Lord, Son of David . . .", v. 22). The point of the tale is not only her spirited response but her seeming concurrence in the Jewish reading of the providential plan of salvation (v. 27). Jesus' praise of her great faith means for Matthew that the barrier "Israel only" has begun to be breached.

Matthew describes Jesus as having regarded his commission during his public life as confined to Israel. As a learned teacher, however, he would have been aware of the many prophecies that spoke of the Gentiles as participants in Israel's saved condition (see Isa 19:19-25; 60; 66:19f.; Mic 4:1f.; Zech 8:20ff.). That, however, was to be a matter of the last days. Any anticipation, as in Paul's reading of the data in Romans above, was an exception. The relative places of Jew and Gentile in the order of salvation were fixed.

Jesus' upraising from the dead changed this perspective of his followers but not immediately. Only the adventures of the Gospel in Jewish circles over four decades brought about serious reconsideration of this position. Meanwhile, Matthew, an evangelist to fellow Jews, tells the story of the young Canaanite woman's cure in support of the position that nothing has been changed as between Jewish and Gentile election (see v. 24). But with Jesus' healing of her daughter there is a crack in the wall. Matthew 28:19, with its command to "make disciples of all nations" as basis, brought the wall down (cf. Eph 2:14-19).

🦢_🦢
Proper 16 [21] / Twenty-first Sunday of the Year (A)
Sunday between August 21 and August 27, inclusive

EXODUS 1:8—2:10

LM does not have this as a Sunday reading but it is proposed in two parts for Monday and Tuesday in Week 15, Year A. Verses 1-7 are a link with Gen 50:22-26 and tell of the settling in Egypt of the households of the eleven tribes by name while all those of Joseph's generation died there (v. 6). The multiplication of Jacob's offspring (by now "Israelites" after his new name [Gen 35:10] but still called "Hebrews" in the narrative) intimidated the new Pharaoh who "knew not Joseph" (Exod 1:8). Setting the men to forced labor lest they band with other non-Egyptians to mount an uprising, he condemned them to work with mortar and brick in the fields. The directive he gave the midwives is well remembered in Jewish and Christian history: drown the newborn boys in the Nile but save the girls. But these pious and patriotic Hebrew women happily disobeyed the murderous command. Note the reason that the babies came to birth rather than aborted naturally as a result of their mothers' slave labor: the women were hardier than the Egyptian women (v. 19).

The stage is set for the birth of Moses and that of Aaron and Miriam. Two from the house of Levi, therefore not from any of the twelve tribes, beget this handsome child. Later we learn that they are Amram and Jochebed (6:20). His mother's clever ruse saves the baby's life while his sister, presumably Miriam, watches close by. We are not told whether the mother hid the child for safety by day or knew that the Pharaoh's daughter regularly bathed there in the river. Probably the latter, for the sister emerges immediately and volunteers the services of a Hebrew wet nurse who will be, of course, Moses' mother. When the boy comes to maturity the Pharaoh's daughter takes him as her son. What other adoptive parent should this great one have, in the Hebrew telling, but a woman of the Eygptian royal house? The young princess' name is not given nor is she heard from again. Her sole appearance in the story is to account for Moshe's Egyptian name. It means "born" or "begotten" and would have been preceded by the name of a god like Thut or Amon or Ra, dropped in horror by the Hebrews. The Egyptian-speaking Pharaoh's daughter unaccountably says the boy is Moshe "because I drew him out" (of the water), alike in sound to the Hebrew verb of that meaning, *măshāh*. Moses is mentioned 76 times between Exod 2:10 and Josh 24:5, but we know nothing of his youth aside from the murder of the Egyptian who beat his kinsman (2:11f.) and the leadership role on his people's behalf that his life as a fugitive led to.

Psalm 124

Isaiah 51:1-6

The opening verses of this long hortatory poem remind the returning people of Judah of their ancestry (see Gen 12:1-3) and their growth as a people (v. 2), the imminent restoration of the deserted land (v. 3), and this people's vocation to be a light to the Gentiles (v. 4b; cf. Luke 2:32). The Jews had learned the need the Chaldeans had of Israel's "teaching" and "justice" from their fifty years in exile. The RCL evidently thinks this passage a better foreshadowing of Jesus' constituting Simon as Rock of his *ekklēsía* than the commission of Eliakim as royalty's steward (see Isa 22:15-25) in place of the venal Shebnah. The "key of the house of David" placed on a sash on Eliakim's shoulder undoubtedly accounts for the LM's choice (see the use of the text in one of the "great O's" (an antiphon at Vespers in Advent, December 20, but December 19 in the Sarum rite). Isaiah 51:1-6 is thought to be a figure or type of Jesus' promise to Simon because of the rock and quarry from which the people are hewn, namely the patriarch and matriarch who are their ancestors (vv. 1-2). The LORD says that a teaching and a justice shall "go out from me" for "a light to the peoples" (Isa 51:4). Is "to all the peoples, teaching them to observe all my commandments" (Matt 28:19-20a) a reasonable antitype? "My salvation will be forever and my deliverance will never be ended" (51:6e) corresponded to by "the gates of Hades shall not prevail against . . . my church" (Matt 16:18)? Perhaps. But if so, the prefiguration is as tenuous as any in LM. One can only hope that RCL did not avoid the key of David as prefiguring that of Peter for fear of an echo of Petrine primacy. While the text of Matthew has little to do with the way the papal office developed, the Eliakim story (Isa 22:15-25) ends with this "peg in a sure place" later giving way, much like Peter's failure to acknowledge Jesus in his "hour" (Matt 26:69-75). It is a shame to deny worshipers that sober tale of betrayed trust.

Isaiah 22:19-23

We do not know who Shebna was (v. 15) aside from being a political upstart who had feathered his own nest, in this case a sepulcher hewn from the rock. The prophet in consigning him to oblivion has given him a surer place in history than he would have had through his career or his memorial. "Master of the household" was his title (v. 15), an office we know of from 1 Kgs 4:6. Shebna probably also served as chief cabinet minister in the court of King Hezekiah of Judah (716–687 B.C.E.). The present incident is to be dated some time before the happenings of chaps. 37–39, which are usually put at 701.

The Lord will eject Shebna from his office (v. 19), deprive him access to the government car-pool (the vehicles are chariots), and replace him by the trustworthy Eliakim. The virtues of this son of Hilkiah are specified in v. 21. The divine wrath was evidently only moderately effective against Shebna, who continued to function as the king's "secretary" (36:3; 37:2; cf. 1 Kgs 4:3; Jer 36:12), an office of cabinet rank.

The importance of the passage to Christian literature—for in itself it merely describes a faithful public servant—is the use made of it in Rev 3:7. Writing to the *"aggelos"* or presiding spirit of the church of Philadelphia in Asia Minor, the apocalyptist applies the Isaian text to Christ as "the holy one, the true." From here it makes its way into the "Magnificat" antiphon of December 20, "O David." The symbol of Peter's keys in Matt 16:19 may also be drawn from this mention of a key, a heavy wooden boxlike affair carried on a sling from the shoulder and symbolizing authority.

An appendix to the poetic oracle of vv. 15-24 written by another hand in prose indicates that Eliakim, fixed "like a peg in a secure place" (v. 23), will regrettably "break off and fall" (v. 25), a cryptic reference to one more political appointee's inability to withstand the pressures of office. It is generally assumed that the weight of the cloak referred to some offense like nepotism or trading in favors to hangers-on.

Psalm 138[1-3, 6, 8bc]

Lord, your love is eternal; do not forsake the work of your hands.

Romans 12:1-8

See the comment on next Sunday's second lection (vv. 1-2) for an orientation to today's. Verse 3 is an echo of Phil 2:3, and vv. 4-6 a recasting of 1 Cor 12:12, 27, concerning which see the comment on The Third Sunday after Epiphany [3] (C).

Romans 11:33-36

The passage prescribed for LM follows immediately that of last Sunday, which was a highly compressed version of Paul's view of God's mercy shown to Jew and Gentile alike, each of whom was disobedient in its own way. In today's reading, the concluding segment of his argument, Paul praises the inscrutable design of God.

He has already alluded to the wealth of God's kindness and forbearance (2:4) and of God's glory as contrasted with God's wrath (9:23). Compare Col 1:27, which tells how great among the Gentiles are "the riches of the glory of this mystery, which is Christ in you, your hope of glory." Here, God is rich in wisdom and knowledge (v. 33). Paul's exclamation in verse 33b has a Job-like quality. The next verses, 34 and 35, are quotations, one from the Septuagint (Isa 40:13) and the other not (Job 41:11). No one acts as the LORD's counselor; moreover no one is a donor to God in such a way that a claim can be lodged against that person. At all points the LORD is the initiator in mercy.

All things are from, to, and for God for a Jewish believer like Paul (v. 36a). There is a phrase not unlike this in Marcus Aurelius's *Meditations* (4.23), after he has apostrophized the universe and nature: "From you are all things, in you are all things, unto you are all things." Such verbal usage was probably a convention in the Hellenist Judaism from which Paul sprang.

He ends in an ascription of glory to God for the richness of the divine gifts (v. 36b).

ALLELUIA. MATTHEW 11:25

Blessed are you, Father, LORD of heaven and earth; you have revealed to little ones the mystery of the kingdom.

MATTHEW 16:13-20

As we have come to expect, Matthew adds to Mark (8:27-30) for his special confessional and ecclesial purposes. He has Jesus call himself "the Son of Man" in v. 13 (interchangeable with the "I" of Mark 8:27b), adds the name of Jeremiah (v. 14) and the phrase, "the Son of the living God" to "Christ" (v. 16), and finally inserts vv. 17-19 about Peter as the rock into the Markan account. Caesarea Philippi, modern Banyas near Dan at the northern extremity of Israel, is of no Old Testament significance, hence doubtless existed in the historical tradition as it came to Mark. It was the site of a shrine to the god Pan still clearly distinguishable by its niches in the sandstone rock face, hence its Greek name. The wall of rock rises almost sheer, if not high, as part of the foothills below distant Mt. Hermon.

Mark's parallel passage (v. 29) has the disciples recognizing Jesus as the Messiah for the first time, with Peter as their spokesman. Mark is chiefly interested in the first prediction of the passion, which culminates in the rebuke delivered to Peter (v. 33) and, through him, to all. Matthew retains this idea, adding that Peter is a hindrance ("stumbling block") who threatens to make Jesus trip and fall by his resistance to the idea of his suffering (v. 23). Jesus has previously been recognized as the Son of God in Matthew (14:33) but this is his first designation there as the Christ or Messiah.

Verses 17-19 include, among other things, a Matthean explanation of Simon's name Peter. The latter descriptive name occurs only once in Paul (Gal 2:7f.), who generally uses Cephas, as does John in 1:42; but "Peter" is frequent in Matthew, less so in Mark and Luke. Aramaic *Kēpha*, Hellenized by the addition of an "s," means rock (just as *tsur* does in Hebrew, the modern way to say Peter). In the Gospels the name says nothing about Peter's character; indeed, Matthew takes the pains to deny any special human qualification to him and attribute all to God (v. 17). The rock figure clearly has something to do with Simon's office of spiritual leadership with respect to the community (*ekklēsía*, v. 18, found again in 18:17), referred to in terms of faith in Luke 22:32f. and love in John 21:15-19.

The church spoken of as an edifice has interesting parallels in the Qumrân *Community Rule* (1QS8.7): "[The council of the community] shall be established in truth. It shall be . . . a house of holiness for Israel. . . . It shall be that tried wall, that precious cornerstone, whose foundations shall neither rock nor sway in their place" (cf. Isa 28:16). The *Testament of Levi* 2:3-5, which occurs in an Aramaic fragment at Qumrân, says that "unrighteousness had built itself walls and lawlessness sat upon towers." In a dream, Levi says, "I beheld a high mountain, and I was upon it." He had this vision while feeding the flocks in Abel-Maul (the Abel-meholah of Judg 7:22, generally situated in Samaria near the Jordan). Stendahl speculates that this fragment may provide a parallel to the country around Caesarea Philippi, "since this area played a role in Jewish apocalypticism as a place of revelation and as a meeting-place for the upper and lower world." What the geographic link with *Testament of Levi* may be he does not say (*PC, 787*).

Peter's binding and loosing under the figure of keys can refer to the ordinary judgments of a rabbi in determining the measure in which people are bound to rules in following *halakah*, "the way," or it can refer to Church order. Probably the former is intended in Matthew. An important question is, did Jesus envision in his lifetime an assembly or community of followers, or was such simply the reality from Matthew's time? The evidence of Qumrân favors the notion of organization as a Jewish reality, whereas what we know of Jesus from his other sayings tends to be against it. A community of faith in him was real, however, in his lifetime.

Peter is to be the "Rock" (v. 18) in his own person through his faith. Cullmann has shown that most attempts to have the term describe this firm *characteristic* of Peter but not his *person* stem from Protestant bias. At the same time, not every claim made for the chief bishopric in the new faith community of many decades later can be traced to the intent of Matthew in this crucial passage. Linus would have been the first in any case, since the position of Peter, like that of Paul, in Rome was unique. The name Linus heads the list for the first time ca. 180 in Irenaeus's five-book work *Against Gnōsis Falsely So Called*.

Bornkamm holds, against Cullmann and Oepke, that the saying of vv. 17ff. belongs to the period after Easter. The "church" of v. 18 is an eschatological entity but also one of future, earthly time. It "bears throughout an institutional character, characterized by the authority in doctrine and discipline of a particular apostle." Decisions about doctrine and discipline in this church will be confirmed and ratified in the coming reign of God. Matthew has changed the rejection of Peter's confession by Jesus in Mark into a confession of Peter endorsed by Jesus as the ground for making him the Rock of the Church.

🙠🙣

Proper 17 [22] / Twenty-second Sunday of the Year (A)
Sunday between August 28 and September 3, inclusive

EXODUS 3:1-15

For a commentary see 3 Lent (C).

PSALM 105:1-6, 23-26, 45C

JEREMIAH 15:15-21

Jeremiah is discouraged. He has reason to feel abandoned. The prophets lie, deceiving the people, but the people believe them (14:13-16). He has been given words with which to address them but knows they will not listen. The prophet has just expressed Job-like regret that his mother gave him birth (15:10). Does not the LORD know he has served him for the people's good (v. 11)? Jeremiah receives an answer. God has made him a wall of bronze (brass?) against the people (cf. v. 20; 1:18). They will not prevail over him (v. 20). The LORD is with him and will deliver him out of the hand of the wicked (v. 21).

PSALM 26:1-8

JEREMIAH 20:7-9

This passage immediately precedes the first reading for [12] (A) in LM, proposed as an alternative for Proper 7. See the comment on Jer 20:10-13 there for background material.

Verses 7-13 constitute a literary unit, a psalm that has as its burden the prophet's awful suspicion that he has been taken in by the LORD (see also 15:18). In context it comes after a declaration that the Temple administrator Pashhur will be captured by Babylon and carried off into exile (v. 6), much in the way he inflicts beatings and forcible restraints (v. 2) on the prophet. The psalm could serve, of course, as a more general outcry of the heart stemming from Jeremiah's anguish at having to be a prophet of doom. His role is an unenviable one. The prognosticator of impending tragedy is thought to wish it to come on, whereas those who deny its likelihood are being confused with people who have no desire for it. The prophetic stance is even more painful for the one forced to assume it if he is by nature cheerful and gregarious. His only burden is that of clear vision. He will not compromise his integrity by remaining silent.

But even Jeremiah, a truthful man, is subject to doubts. Like any popular teacher with an unpopular message, he needs some response, some "feedback," to indicate that he may be on the right track. Hearing none he begins to wonder if he may be one of the false prophets described in 1 Kgs 22:19-23. There, "lying spirits" are described by Micaiah as sent by the LORD into certain prophets' mouths, a part of Micaiah's strategy to deter Ahab from his foolish plan of attack. Jeremiah suffers the ultimate doubt. Has counsel been taken in heaven resulting in the choice of him as the mouthpiece of a lying spirit? One is reminded of the tortures of the saints who wondered if it was the devil who was acting through them.

Jeremiah concludes that he must be duped by the LORD because he is the object of such mockery and derision (vv. 7, 8). His message, "Violence and destruction!" (8a), has come true only in Pashhur's mishandling of him, not as between Judah and Babylon. The entire sequence is remarkably modern.

Then a ploy occurs to him: absolute silence about the LORD (9a). He will act the mute so as to stay out of trouble. But it won't work. Such action would make him a false prophet. He could not endure the pain of holding in what he knows to be true (9c). "Thy love is like a burning fire / within my very soul" might serve as a paraphrase of 9b. Better to wear out in prophetic truth-telling than rust out in cowardly silence.

PSALM 63:2-6, 8-9

My soul is thirsting for you, O LORD my God.

ROMANS 12:[1-2] 9-21

Although the two initial verses follow those of last week's LM reading, the epistle goes in a new direction with the opening of chap. 12. Perhaps better put, Paul begins to list the practical moral implications for his fellow-believers in Christ of the fact that God has willed to "be merciful to all" (11:32). His doctrinal teaching concluded, he proceeds to spell out its necessary ethical consequences; hence the "therefore" of v. 1.

God's mercies, the *raḥemim* or "compassion" of the Hebrew Bible, are Paul's point of appeal. The way God has expressed it has been sketched in the epistle up until now, chaps. 9–11 in particular. The proper response to these mercies is self-surrender. "Your bodies" (v. 1) means your whole selves. The vocabulary is that of formal worship, specifically a sacrifice that is holy and acceptable. The worship is to be spiritual (cf. 1 Pet 2:2, 5), that is, a movement of one's whole inner *logos* or spiritual self. The notion is familiar from the *Miserere*, which speaks of a contrite spirit as the psalmist's sacrifice (Ps 51:19). There is also the idea of loving and serving God with one's whole heart (cf. Deut 11:13). However biblical Paul's thought may be, his term translated "spiritual" *(logikē)* to describe the Christian's sacrifice is Stoic usage current in Hellenist Jewish circles.

Paul's exhortation in v. 2 is eschatological. Christians may not take the present age as their standard of conduct, "this world" being understood as an age still ruled by demonic powers despite Christ's death and resurrection. Those "in Christ" have entered upon the new age of the Spirit (cf. 8:13, 23) but Paul never speaks of the age to come as if it has arrived except by foreshadowing. The renewal of mind that will qualify believers to judge God's will for them rightly and tell what is good and acceptable and perfect in their regard is a fruit of life in the Spirit, hence of the new age. The "renewing of minds" spoken of is total, beginning at baptism and proceeding with every conscious choice throughout life. It is with this renewed *nous* that Paul serves the Law of God but with its opposite, *sarx*, that he serves the law of sin (cf. 7:25). Nothing else can pass judgment on what is good, acceptable, and perfect. The latter Greek adjective is related to the concept of Christ as the "end" of the Law (10:4).

Verses 3-8 are a reprise of Paul's teaching on the baptized as individual members of the one body of Christ (1 Cor 12:12-26) who in any given community of believers have a variety of gifts (vv. 27-31; cf. Eph 4:7-16). Verses 9-21 exhort to a humility like that proposed as the lead into the Christological hymn of Phil 2:6-11. In a series of counsels of perfection, the apostle instructs the church at Rome to hate what is evil and cleave to the good, to show mutual affection, and to be fervent in service of the Lord meaning Christ. The needs of the community members ("the saints") must be inquired into and met by hospitality if that be the need. Harmonious living is the goal. Surely Paul has knowledge of certain tensions in a church he has not yet visited, probably between ethnic Jewish and Gentile members. The former would have included some who had been banished from the capital by imperial edict. Suetonius in his *Lives of the Twelve Caesars* reports that Claudius ordered the expulsion of Jews around 49 C.E. because of disputes in their quarter over a certain "Chrestus." Acts 18:2 tells of Paul's meeting in Corinth with a couple named Aquila and Priscilla who had been the subjects of such a ban. The Jews were subsequently readmitted but the community would understandably be divided between those who had suffered for Jesus Christ and his ethnicity and those who had not. In view of this recent harassment by imperial authority, the exhortation to bless one's persecutors and not repay evil for evil would have special meaning. Since the Roman church had been recently divided but was now reunited, the plea for harmonious living and the avoidance of any lording it over others would make eminent sense. This may be everyday hortatory prose but the greater likelihood is that Paul knows why and how some are suffering and is responding to it directly.

Verses 17-21 with which the chapter closes are a strong admonition to avoid "getting even." The "wrath" of v. 19—NRSV adds "of God"—is the way God, being a just God, *has* to respond to evil at the judgment. "Vengeance is mine" (v. 19; cf. Deut 32:35) means that doing ultimate justice is not a human prerogative but divine. The watchword about treating enemies decently is from Prov 25:21f., but the ending is as puzzling there as here. Are the live coals a symbol of remorse for the harm done or of the intensity of the desire for reconciliation? Paul interprets it to mean: conquer evil with good (v. 21).

Alleluia. See Acts 16:14b.

Open our hearts, O Lord, to listen to the words of your Son.

Matthew 16:21-28

Last Sunday's reading and commentary will have alerted us to Matthew's special use of Markan material. In today's pericope he gives us the text of Peter's rebuke (v. 22), whereas Mark had been satisfied to record the fact (8:32). Matthew adds the word for stumbling block/obstacle (v. 23), and removes Mark's "crowd" (8:34) so as to constitute verse 24 a charge to the disciples alone. In v. 27 he features the repayment of faithful acknowledgment by Jesus when he comes in glory at the end, much in the manner of the later judgment scene (25:31-46). Mark is content (v. 38) to let the shame that the disciples experience over Jesus be countered by his being ashamed of them. For the rest, the two narratives are largely alike.

In both Gospels Peter's confession of faith in Jesus serves as the context of the first prophecy of suffering (Mark 8:31; Matt 16:21). Matthew highlights the relation of the two more than Mark with the phrase, "from then on" (Mark's link between the two narratives had been "and . . ."). Similarly, Matthew employs a favorite word, "then," in v. 24 to show clearly that the doctrine of the cross for disciples follows from Jesus' prophecy of his own suffering.

In Mark Jesus makes Peter's confession nothing but an occasion for an injunction to silence (8:30). Matthew on the other hand gives it an importance in itself (16:17-19). Having inserted the promise to Peter, he might well have reduced the tension caused by the rebuke of Peter by eliminating it. Instead, he heightens it by providing the wording of Peter's remonstrance, "God forbid it, Lord! This must never happen to you" (v. 22) which Mark does not do. Matthew has no special interest in Mark's deferral of a disclosure of Jesus' status as Son of God until after the resurrection, despite the penultimate cry of faith by the centurion in 15:39, even though he knows about it (v. 20). His concern is to have Jesus endorse Peter's confession of faith in him and use it as the ground for making him the Rock of the Church.

Matthew's theology is such that he does not tone down Mark's contrast between the glory of Jesus as the Christ and his sufferings as Son of Man on earth. He too wishes to place the disciples on the way of suffering imitation (cf. 16:24ff.). The judge who will come to repay them according to their fidelity (v. 27) is none other than this suffering Son of God and Son of Man.

The promise of the keys to Peter is clearly a Church tradition, one that may even go back to a post-Easter appearance. Matthew's making it a pre-Easter story, particularly in the context provided by Mark, shows his determination to teach that the Church with its power of the keys is subject to the law of suffering of the earthly Jesus. Jesus will sustain the Church's decisions in the coming judgment if its binding and loosing (v. 19) have been carried on in imitation of Christ's sufferings and fidelity to his vocation. The norm for the Church is that when he does [come] "with his angels in the glory of his Father, he will repay everyone for what has been done" (v. 27, lit. "according to his conduct").

Concern with Matthew's theology of the Church may have its thousands, but Jesus' words in vv. 24-26 (cf. Mark 8:34-37) have their tens of thousands. One is hard pressed to find their like in all literature to express the place of personal integrity in the human search for meaning, discipleship of Jesus quite apart.

☙❧

Proper 18 [23] / Twenty-third Sunday of the Year (A)
Sunday between September 4 and September 10, inclusive

EXODUS 12:1-14

This reading includes that for Maundy Thursday (A, B, C) in RCL (which see), where it makes vv. 5-10 optional and, while LM retains the details about the blood of the yearling lamb or goat smeared on door posts, the same Holy Thursday passage omits saying that they must be roasted whole and that any residue must be burned. But today the entire fourteen verses are proposed to be read. Both pericopes speak of the significance of hearing that the smeared blood is to be the sign that the children of Israel are to be saved if the door posts and lintels of their houses have received the stipulated sign.

PSALM 149

EZEKIEL 33:7[-9]11

These verses repeat 3:17-19, as part of the parallelism between the two parts of this book, chaps. 1–24 and 25–48. The beginning of the second half (chaps. 25–32) is made up of prophecies against Moab, Tyre, Sidon, and Egypt, while from chap. 32 onward there are messages of comfort and salvation for Israel.

The parable of the watchman concerns the prophet, whose favorite designation for himself is "son of man." He interprets his role as one involving heavy public responsibility. Just as the negligent guard or sentry can expect the death sentence for his failure, so Ezekiel feels he must warn his people of their perilous condition under pain of his life. Anyone who falls before the oncoming Chaldean army has only himself to blame if he disregards the prophetic trumpet (vv. 4-6). The passage makes clear that, although it is based on the imagery of a city taken by surprise, its chief thrust is ethical. The prophet is not a political or military man—even though he should prove to be one indirectly—but a moral teacher. A person's or a nation's sin is Ezekiel's concern (v. 6). Dissuading the wicked from their guilt is his task (v. 8). Once the prophet has delivered himself of his warning he is free of responsibility; it now lies with the other. The prophet, having done his work, can rest secure (v. 9).

The parable is a powerful example of Hebrew (hence Christian) morality which holds that the religious person must in some measure be a public person.

PSALM 119:33-40

PSALM 95:1-2, 6-9

If today you hear his voice, harden not your hearts.

ROMANS 13:8[10]-14

The first seven verses of Rom 13 contain Paul's theory of obedience to legitimate authority. Conceivably it was penned in a spirit of "Get this word to the Roman magistrates" to win for the Christian community the benefits, chiefly exemptions, Judaism enjoyed. It is more likely, however, that the passage represents Paul's deepest convictions on the power of the state as an arm of God's providence. The empire acts as a regulating and even a restraining force (cf. 2 Thess 2:6f.) to ensure the spread of the gospel until Christ shall return in glory. No law-abiding Christian whose conscience is clear need fear reprisals, Paul writes. His is the simplicity of one who has not yet learned how few rivals the ancient (or modern) state will endure.

Turning in v. 8 to the morality of interaction among Christians as contrasted with that regarding the government, Paul counsels that all go free of debt. The obvious exception is the obligation to mutual love, a debt that no one can be free of. This is doubtless an injunction to practice *selfless* love (*agápē*, the noun and verb forms of which Paul uses) in the community. He is on record as not being interested in Christians loving Christians only (cf. 12:14, 17, 19ff.) but he seems to understand "neighbor" here (vv. 8, 10) as Lev 19:18 did, namely fellow-countryman in a community of faith. Yet he takes pains to designate the recipient of this love as "another" (v. 8) rather than the "neighbor" of the LXX in vv. 9, 10, as if to highlight difference or distinction, not likemindedness. Perhaps not too much should be made of this, since v. 9 contains the word as "any other" commandment.

Verse 8 speaks of fulfilling the Law, a phrase that has this meaning clarified by v. 9. As was the case with Jesus when quoted by Mark on the Decalogue (10:19), Paul does not name the prohibitions in the order given in either Exodus (20:13-17) or Deuteronomy (5:17-21). He says that keeping them fulfills the Law with regard to the neighbor, a matter adequately summed up in Lev 19:18. Mark 12:31 and parallels indicate that there was contemporary rabbinic usage to this effect. Paul does not identify this usage as a "word of the Lord" as he does elsewhere (1 Cor 7:10; 1 Thess 4:15). It either has not come to him as such or else he wants to favor the sentiment without quoting Jesus, thereby running the risk of a new legalism.

One who loves cannot do wrong to a neighbor (v. 10), hence is free of any offense against ethical demand. Love is the fulfillment of the Law in the sense that it keeps it, not that it dispenses from the need to keep it. Paul's usage in v. 9 establishes this. The Christian's love fulfills Lev 19:18 and all that is summed up by it.

Verses 11-14 (on which see 1 Advent [A]) provide, as the motivation for the love that has been taught in vv. 8-10, "the day" which is near, meaning the last day. With it will come "salvation," for Paul deliverance from God's wrath on the day of judgment. Mention of that day puts him in mind of the opposition of light and darkness that marks day and night and so he rehearses the evil deeds performed under cover of darkness in a near repetition of Gal 5:4-10. Verse 13 of this chapter is what St. Augustine opened to when he practiced the *sors biblica* or random selection with a finger in response to the child's chanting: "Take up and read, Take up and read." Putting on the Lord Jesus as a garment (v. 14) will ensure that no provision is made for the desires of the flesh—here as always not sexual sin but any human resistance to the divine prompting. (Augustine's attention, understandably, was drawn to one of the nouns in v. 13, *koítais,* "debauchery," discreetly rendered "chambering" by KJV and DRC).

ALLELUIA. MATTHEW 11:25

Blessed are you, Father, LORD of heaven and earth. You have revealed to little ones the mysteries of the kingdom.

MATTHEW 18:15-20

The lectionary proceeds from the Church or Assembly-oriented passage and Jesus' need to suffer of Matt 16, read on the last two Sundays, to the only other one in his gospel that uses the term *ekklēsía*. Prevailing as the notion of the early community is in Matthew, the word occurs in these two places only (16:18; 18:17). As we might expect, there is no parallel place in Mark (Luke has a saying in 17:3 that somewhat resembles 15a, but that is all).

We are not too far wrong in seeing in this passage a portion of a manual of discipline for the community like that of Qumrân or *Didachē* 7–15, addressed to church leaders. There is indeed a striking resemblance between Matt 18:16 and the 1QS 6.1: "No one should speak to his brother in anger . . . but instead reproach him so as to incur a sin for his fault. In addition no one is to bring a charge against his fellow unless it is with reproof in the presence of witnesses." Both obviously derive from Lev 19:17. A little earlier in what served as Qumrân's community rule (v. 24) an annual review of spiritual attitudes is proposed that should end in promotion or demotion.

Matthew features catechetical elements for beginners, but it has disciplinary counsel for the leadership as well, as today's pericope indicates.

Recalcitrance is tested in three stages: as between individuals (v. 15), before witnesses (v. 16), and in the presence of the assembly (v. 17). If it persists beyond the last stage it is to end in formal expulsion, such being the force of the reference to Gentiles and tax gatherers. Matthew 18:18 is repeated from 16:19 but in a different sense. There it was the promulgation of a practice and had the force of giving Peter authority as the chief rabbi, i.e., arbiter. Here it is repeated precisely to alter its implications in the direction of disciplinary action.

The sayings on prayer, whatever their original significance, are employed by Matthew as a means whereby two or three witnesses can count on Christ's presence to support their disciplinary action. The technique proposed is not unlike that suggested by Paul against the incestuous Corinthian (1 Cor 5:4f.). Verses 21ff., which follow today's reading, exhort to an even more generous handling of community disciplinary problems than Luke 17:4 with its "seven times."

Verse 20 has a long history of being cited in Christian circles, whether in favor of community prayer, against formal liturgical prayer, or as testimony to Jesus' mystical presence. Matthew's concern that the gathered two or three are there to settle thorny interpersonal problems in the congregation does not negate its more widespread application, needless to say, although one becomes uncomfortable with interpretations the farther they depart from the Matthean context.

❧.✿

Proper 19 [24] / Twenty-fourth Sunday of the Year (A)
Sunday between September 11 and September 17, inclusive

EXODUS 14:19-31

A few observations on vv. 10-18 should prepare for the longer 14:10-31; 15:[1], 20-21, which is added to it on the Easter Vigil (A, B, C). The Pharaoh and his officials are disturbed that they let the Israelites escape and pursue them to the encampment by the sea (14:5-9). So says the P document. The livelier J takes it up with an Israelite cry of panic to the LORD at the sight of the advancing Egyptian chariots.

If the Egyptians had second thoughts, so did they. Egypt had pots for the ovens on which to prepare meat ("flesh," 16:3). It also had ample space for burial without the need for graves in the wilderness (14:11). On all counts the Israelites were finding their recent enslavement comfortable relative to their present fright before six hundred picked chariots and others besides (v. 7). Moses tries to stiffen their spines with the assurance that the LORD will fight for them (v. 14). The pillar of cloud in the night is shifted from before to behind them, obscuring the Israelites from the view of the pursuing Egyptians (vv. 19ff.). Israel's God gives Moses the word to divide the sea by stretching his staff toward it (v. 16). The bed goes dry and, when the Egyptian forces enter the sea after Israel has crossed it safely, that is an end to them. P had called on a strong east wind to push the sea back and turn it into dry ground (vv. 21f., 29) while J has the LORD give calm assurance that the Israelites should go forward because he will fight for them (v. 14). The LORD equally calmly has the sea return to its normal depth at dawn by the gesture of Moses' outstreched hand (v. 27), leaving the bodies of the Egyptian dead strewn on the shore (vv. 30f.). There is no need to deplore the LORD's murderous destruction of Egypt. It is all the stuff of saga written by the self-proclaimed victors.

PSALM 114 OR EXODUS 15:1B-11, 20-21

GENESIS 50:15-21

LM gives Gen 50:15-24 as part of the reading on Saturday 14, Year A, but Joseph's last years in Egypt, with which the book ends, are not heard on a Sunday. RCL corrrects the omission by providing it as an alternate this morning. Jacob at death had been embalmed in the Egyptian manner and brought home to be buried in Canaan (50:1-13). The cruelly offending brothers beg Joseph's forgiveness upon his return from Egypt, saying that granting it had been their dead father's wish. There is no record of that, only that he had blessed Joseph's younger son Ephraim over Manasseh so that the clan could return to Canaan and prosper. But Joseph does forgive. He goes further, saying that he will provide for them and their off-spring, which is forgiveness in act. The good that God will bring out of their evil is "the preservation of a numerous people" (v. 20).

SIRACH 27:30—28:7

Jesus ben Sirach, the author of this book, is identified as the first of the sapiental authors—the psalmists here not included—to identify wisdom with the Law (cf. 28:7). Previous biblical wisdom writers, unlike the priests, had not been concerned with institutional religion or a covenantal concern with YHWH. One achieves wisdom, ben Sirach holds, by frequenting the company of the elders (6:34) and men of prudence (v. 36) and meditating constantly on the LORD's precepts and commandments (v. 37).

Vengeance is not in man's province; it belongs to the LORD (28:1). This is the teaching of the Law (Lev 19:18; Deut 32:35, 39, 41b). The part of humans is to forgive—even injustice—and they may expect the same from God in return (v. 2). Here, as in the teaching of the later Jesus, forgiving others is the condition of receiving forgiveness (cf. Matt 6:12, 14; 18:21f.; Mark 11:25). This successor Jesus will illustrate v. 4 with a parable in Matt 18:23-35.

Perhaps the most telling advice in the passage occurs 28:7b: "overlook faults." The Bible contains few loftier counsels.

The motivation provided is the thought of death the great leveler and the covenantal relation in which the believer stands to Israel's God (vv. 6, 7).

PSALM 103(1[-4]7), 8-13[9-12]

The LORD is kind and merciful; slow to anger and rich in compassion.

ROMANS 14:1-12[7-9]

Among others, John R. Donahue, in a 1998 lecture, "Breaking Down the Dividing Wall of Hostility" delivered at Santa Clara University, holds that the "weak in faith" are most likely Jewish Christians or Gentile "God-fearers" prior to their becoming Christians, while the "strong," among whom Paul numbers himself (15:1), believe in eating anything (14:2), esteem all days alike (v. 5), and drink wine (v. 21). He criticizes both groups but especially the strong for not welcoming the weak (see vv. 1, 2; 15:1-7). Verses 6-8 indicate that the Lord, meaning Jesus, must be the center of all, including being honored on his own day (6a, Sunday?). NSRV seems to have Paul acknowledge ("servants . . . of their own lord") the pagan poets of the weak (v. 4).

Paul cannot conceive of a human situation in which the believer escapes being the Lord's, that is, Jesus Christ's. Such a one is his special possession. Whether in death or in life the believer is under God's judgment; hence is unwise to judge another before appearing at the judgment seat (v. 10). Christ risen is Lord of all (v. 9).

Paul enunciates his certainty, expressed elsewhere, that no foods defile (1 Cor 10:25), just as no diet or abstention brings us closer to God (1 Cor 8:8). Yet he is as sensitive here as he was in 1 Cor (8:9-13; 10:23-30) to the plight of the weak believer who could come to ruin or commit blasphemy at the sight of a Christian whose acts show him to be more liberated than he (vv. 15, 16). Dietary laws are not what the kingdom of God is about (v. 17) but rather the Spirit's gifts of justice, peace, and joy. ("Kingdom" is an infrequent word in Paul, occurring only seven other times in epistles that are indisputably his.) But working for peace and mutual strength (v. 19) in the community may mean staying away from certain foods that are harmless in themselves (vv. 20ff.). Paul shows no awareness here of any teaching of Jesus in similar vein (e.g., Mark 7:15).

There is a paradox in this teaching in that the judgments of others should not determine anyone's course of action; it is God alone whose judgment counts (vv. 10-12). Yet if the strong boast of their superiority and despise the weak they have fallen under judgment. So, one's conduct with respect to a fellow believer turns out to be of supreme importance. The other person both is and is not the determiner of one's actions.

Paul has already laid it down in Romans that the supreme command is love (13:8ff; 12:9f.). In this passage he suggests some practical implications of this love in a world where not all are strong.

ALLELUIA. ACTS 16:14B

Open our hearts, O LORD, to listen to the words of your Son.

MATTHEW 18:21-35

Last week's commentary spoke of the enlargement of the need for forgiveness in Matthew over the norm provided in Luke 17:4: "If the same person sins against you seven times a day, and turns back to you seven times and says 'I repent,' you must forgive him."

Only Matthew has this parable of the merciless slave. The amount he owes is so great that he must be thought of as having some large position of trust. That is not the point, of course, but rather the huge discrepancy between his indebtedness ("ten thousand talents," v. 24) and the tiny sum that is owed him ("a hundred denarii," v. 28). It is as if we should speak of many thousands of dollars and a few dollars.

The application of the parable may be Matthew's; in any event it is one that dulls its effect considerably. ("My heavenly Father" in v. 35 and elsewhere is a Matthean term.) Forgiveness is not a matter of speech only but something that comes from the heart (cf. Matt 15:8). This is a parable of the last judgment at which the merciful may expect forgiveness but the unmerciful strict justice.

❧ ❧

Proper 20 [25] / Twenty-fifth Sunday of the Year (A)
Sunday between September 18 and September 24, inclusive

EXODUS 16:2-15

See commentary on 18 Sunday (B). This passage does not recount the first or the last time God will be accused of wanton cruelty (vv. 2f.). The divine response takes the form of sending "bread" from the heavens, a fine gummy substance. "*Man hu?*" they ask, literally, "What is this?" hence "manna." See Proper 13 [18] (B).

Today's longer reading tells of the people's complaining against Moses and Aaron—actually against the LORD (v. 8)—for their literally God-forsaken plight. The LORD promises relief from their hunger via a daily miracle. The hymn known to choirs that may or may not know Latin has the adjective *caelicus*, descriptive of the *panis* that that is Christ's eucharistic body, rhyming with *angelicus*. The reference is to the "bread from heaven" of v. 4. The "glory of the LORD" (v. 7) in the narrative is the promised miraculous power about to be displayed. The double portion of Friday is a rabbinic hint that no work is to be done on the Sabbath. The repeated "what are we?" of Moses and Aaron is the people's complaint that should be lodged with God. If the tale had been told in Yiddish the question might have read, "What are we, chopped liver?" (vv. 7, 9) but this would scarcely be fitting given the people's meat-starved condition. Interestingly, they are "drawn near to the LORD" (v. 9) for the vision of his holy glory *(kabod)* in the cloud and not the LORD to them. That word would later have as its synonym in the Talmud *shekinah*, "dwelling" or "divine presence" (see Exod 25:8; Lev 16:16 for cognates). God's glory lies in the divine compassion as well as in power. The Priestly authors took the pains to work in a lesson on the prohibition of Sabbath work (v. 5) and another on greed (vv. 16-20). They also paired meat with bread, in this case exhausted migratory quail found on the ground at night (vv. 8, 12f.).

PSALM 105:1-6, 37-45

JONAH 3:10—4:11

First Testament readings in LM are chosen, in the typological mode that marks all ancient liturgies, for the way they foreshadow something in the day's Gospel. The RCL continues to move through Exodus, but at the same time offers an alternative which it finds more suitable than LM's Isaiah 55. It sees in Jonah's anger at Nineveh's repentance a type of grumbling of the day-long workers, in this case the antitype. The vineyard owner in Matthew asks why he cannot act generously if he wishes to, just as God can have a change of mind and withhold calamity from the Ninevites. Both stories show the superiority of God's justice to human justice, the very point of Isa 55:8f.

See v. 3 after Epiphany [3] (B) for this brief and amusing tale, which the LXX and Vulgate place among the books of the prophets but the MT includes with the "writings" *(ketubim)*. Jonah's anger at Nineveh's repentance when he had predicted its overthrow (3:4; 4:1) is a veiled reproach directed at the postexilic community. Mercy extended to the pagans—at the writing Assyria had long since fallen from power—may have been the LORD's project, but it certainly was not Jonah's. The bush that sheltered him, a gourd plant in NAB and one of castor oil in JB, afforded shade to the hapless schlemiel Jonah before its speedy withering. This is a parable of centuries of God's favor to Israel and its withdrawal if this people cannot abide a show of divine clemency to the Gentiles, whom Judah had experienced at close range in the exile.

PSALM 145:1-8

ISAIAH 55:6-9

The oracles of the postexilic Trito-Isaiah have opened with chap. 55 (see the commentary on 15 Sunday (A). Israel's God will summon the Gentiles, who will come running to this sole deity. But there is a condition. The LORD must first be sought by the elect people. Only its identification with this God will make him attractive to the nations.

Today's passage shows how the LORD is to be called on, namely in repentance and conversion (7a and b). The wicked think vengeful thoughts. Reprisal, "getting even," is their stock in trade. Not so the LORD, who is as different from ordinary mortals in the way they think as the heavens are far removed from the earth (v. 9).

People tend to look for repayment or at least psychic satisfaction. God offers mercy (7b).

The invitation held out in Isa 55 is to be like God, not like people. It is a message of the nearness of salvation but couched within it is a warning to turn away from sin and back to the LORD who shows mercy.

PSALM 145:2-3, 8-9, 17-18

The LORD is near to all who call on him.

PHILIPPIANS 1:21-30[20C-24, 27A]

In last week's second reading Paul had said, "whether we live or whether we die we are the Lord's" (Rom 14:8). Today's selection opens with the same thought. Christ is exalted in believers in him whether they live or die (v. 20c). Both life and death are alike under Christ's dominion. This passage is noteworthy because in it Paul faces the prospect of his own death, something he had failed to do in 1 Thess 4:17 or 2 Thess 2:1 and left an open question in 2 Cor 5:2-5. In the latter place it cannot be determined how he thinks the "heavenly dwelling" will envelop him with mortality giving way to life, whether by death or by some eschatological over-taking of the living.

In Philippians he is quite specific. Life *(zōē)* and Christ are the same for Paul; dying would put him in possession of that life much more fully (v. 21). Continued survival means that the hard work of evangelizing will continue (v. 22). Paul is ready for either and attracted to both, the former because of the immediate improvement of his personal situation and the latter for the sake of those he serves (v. 23). He ends by opting for continuing on in the body because of the Philippians' need of him (vv. 24f.). They should be prouder to have him as a live companion than a dead hero (v. 26), even though his present availability to them is minimal. (We do not know if his imprisonment mentioned in 1:13 is at Caesarea ca. 56/58 C.E. or Rome ca. 58/60). He leaves the question of his return to them open, as indeed a man in jail must (v. 27). Stone walls do not a prison make but they tend to create an impression. What he pleads for from the Philippians is continued fidelity to the gospel of Christ. In the same way, the Isaiah oracle above has asked for fidelity to the understandings of the covenant (55:3b). Paul knows who the opponents of their faith are in Philippi (v. 28) but we are not so sure. From 3:2-6, which follows 3:1 so abruptly that many think it a snatch of another letter, we can deduce that the community there is under siege to adopt certain Jewish practices like those in the Galatian churches (see Gal 2:3-5). Paul offers the Philippians the comfort of being able to suffer for Christ as he has done (vv. 29f.).

ALLELUIA

Heaven and earth are filled with your glory.

MATTHEW 20:1-16

NAB and NRSV do not have v. 16b, "For many are called but few are chosen," following Sinaiticus, Vaticanus, and other early manuscripts. Matthew alone has the parable. He inserts it after the Markan saying about the first and the last (Mark 10:31), showing that for him it represents the reversal that will take place on the last day. In its original form, however, it scarcely ended with v. 16a. This phrase is demanded by the context Matthew assigns it. The generalized conclusion mentioned above as missing no doubt made its way back in some MSS from Matt 22:14.

The details of the parable are not important. They simply reflect the agricultural labor practice of the time. It is a mistake to take the owner of the vineyard to be God or to worry over the equitable character of his action at the day's end. The proletariat of Jesus' day was familiar with such high-handed procedures. The evangelist wanted his hearers to realize that the vintner's arbitrary decision, uncharacteristically favoring the least deserving of the labor force, could trigger thoughts of the incomparable divine generosity—a higher justice.

Rabbinical literature has an almost identical parable concerning Rabbi 'Hiyya ben 'Abba (d. ca. 325 C.E.).

The lesson of Jesus' simple, powerful tale is a single one: in the reign of an openhanded and generous God there is equality of reward.

✌

Proper 21 [26] / Twenty-sixth Sunday of the Year (A)
Sunday between September 25 and October 1, inclusive

EXODUS 17:1-7

The grumbling of the people on their weary pilgrimage continues unabated, this time over thirst. Moses' suspicion that they are almost ready to stone him (v. 4) may account for similar threats against Jesus in John's Gospel (8:59; 10:31). The rock at Horeb that yielded fresh water when Moses struck it with his staff may have been in the memory of centuries a spring below sun-baked mud flats or a rocky gully that covered a hidden stream. It does not matter. The testing *(Massah)* and the quarreling *(Meribah;* cf. Deut 33:8; Ps 95:8) are the longer-lasting memory of the nurturing LORD challenged by a fractious people. The Amalekites of the southern desert first appeared as long ago as Abram's time in the battle of the five kings against four (Gen 14:7), then again several times in alliances with their neighbors against Israel in the days of the judges, finally to be defeated successively by

Saul (1 Sam 5:7f.) and David (30:13, 17-20). Today's story has Moses being told by the LORD to depute Joshua to "blot out the remembrance of Amalek from under heaven." The attempt on that occasion was partly successful (v. 13) but fated to continue for many generations (v. 16). The military engagement is subordinate to the story of Moses' needing Aaron and Hur to support his uplifted arms as the battle progresses. This needed assistance—a parable in act to convey that all leaders must rely on associates—prepares for Moses' ascent of the mountain leaving seventy elders under the guidance of Aaron and Hur to settle disputes in his absence (24; 13f.). Surely this reflects a later settlement as to where teaching authority lay, namely in the Sanhedrin or Great Council *(Beit Din haGadol)*. Early and medieval Christian art would pair it with the victory achieved by Jesus' outstretched arms on the cross. The shared responsibility of Christian leaders has developed much more slowly.

PSALM 78:1-4, 12-16

EZEKIEL 18:1-4, 25[-28]32

The prophet acts as a pastoral theologian in this chapter, spelling out a code of personal responsibility that goes counter to the theory of corporate guilt and innocence implicit in the proverb of v. 2. Ezekiel rejects the proverb utterly, viewing it as a rationalized attempt to escape responsibility for one's acts. The father is accountable for what he has done; likewise the son. Neither can have imputed to him the virtues or vices of the other. The doctrine of personal responsibility is not new with Ezekiel (cf. Deut 24:16; 2 Kgs 14:6) but he is its clearest exponent up to his day (but see Jer 31:29; cf. 3:16-21; 14:12-20; 33:1-20).

Today's passage deals with Israel's complaint that God acts unfairly whereas actually it is its own injustice that keeps it from discerning the righteousness of God. Two cases are cited in support of God's acting, the punishment that overtakes the man who departs from the path of virtue and the new life that is his who repents of his wickedness. Ezekiel does not argue the cases, he simply states them. He implies that only the person of ill will would claim that the LORD had not acted fairly in both instances. God's righteousness is self-evident for the prophet. The unrighteousness of the man who has difficulty comprehending it is equally so.

When Ezekiel speaks of life and death as the divine sanction on human behavior (cf. Deut 30:15ff.; Jer 21:8) he means it literally. He conceives continued earthly existence or its lack as the sign of God's judgment as his ancestors had done. Nonetheless, since he is making a breakthrough with respect to which acts are culpable and which inculpable, he may be expected to have new insights into reward and punishment. And he does. A man's survival or his imminent destruction are doubtless in Ezekiel's mind as modes of God's judgment, but he does not rule out life for the just and death for the unjust here and now. If a man experiences illness, suffering, or other setbacks he knows a mitigated form of death. Likewise happiness, peace, and prosperity are experienced as amplified forms of life. These are the ways in which God responds to ethical choices even when they constitute a sharp break in a person's life from what has gone before. God takes a person's freely-arrived-at decisions with complete seriousness and in doing so, says Ezekiel, is utterly fair.

PSALM 25:1[4-]9

Remember your mercies, O LORD.

PHILIPPIANS 2:1[11]-13

Paul writes from some situation of imprisonment (1:7, 17) to the first church he founded on the European continent. He asks all the people of Philippi to be of the same mind and have the same love (*agápē*, v. 2). In order to impel them "to stand firm in one spirit"—which could just as well be translated "the one Spirit" (1:27)—he cites the humble attitude of Christ as it is expressed in a hymn. Some, like Lucien Cerfaux, think that the hymn is Pauline but most find the language too unlike Paul's to wish to attribute it to him.

The sacred song of vv. 6-11 was probably of Jewish origin and may have had a prior history in gnostic circles. Some attribute its content and even its wording to the fourth Servant Song (Isa 52:13—53:12), accounting for small differences like the word *doulos* for "slave"(v. 7) instead of *pais* by recourse to Aquila's translation rather than the LXX. Joachim Jeremias, one of those who holds for the dependence of Phil 2:6-11 on Isaiah, says that its use of the Hebrew text of the servant song and not the LXX takes care of most difficulties.

Other scholars feel that this explanation does not take sufficiently seriously development in Jewish thought since the time of Deutero-Isaiah. Thus, Eduard Schweizer holds that the humiliation/exaltation theme was expressed by a fusion of the Servant with the apocalyptic Son of Man into a suffering Righteous One, who would be like to God (i.e., God's image, someone in his "form"). Still others see the Jewish hypostatization of wisdom or speculations about the two Adams, Anthropos and Kyrios, behind this hymn. For Käsemann the underlying motif is Hellenistic. There was, he thinks, a myth of the divine primal man which the Christian author took over, making it describe one who once was the same as God but has now become the same as man. For his obedience he is placed in the highest position, made lord of the cosmos, that is, set over all cosmic powers (v. 10). As enthroned redeemer he becomes the "reconciler of all" (cf. Col 1:20).

The arrangement of the hymn in NRSV and NAB is basically the widely accepted one of Lohmeyer, viz., a hymn in two stanzas (vv. 6-8 and 9-11) of three strophes each, three lines to a strophe. Jeremias favors grouping vv. 6-7a, 7b-8, and 9-11 for reasons of Hebrew parallelism of members. This would yield three stanzas, one devoted to the redeemer's pre-(earthly) existence, another to his earthly existence, and a third to his post-earthly existence.

What the "form" of God is we cannot be sure (v. 6). "Status," "stamp," and "specific character" have all been proposed. In any case, the notion is that of Christ as heavenly man. Again, when being "equal to God" is spoken of as not thought "something to be exploited," or "held on to" (the "robbery" of KJV and DRC), it is not clear whether this treasure is conceived by Paul as something to be achieved or something already achieved. The exploiting is more probably of the latter kind. That is, the preexistent Christ possessed equality with God but did not deem it something that could not be let go of should the providential design require this.

Christ's emptying of himself (v. 7) is not to be understood metaphysically but as a figure for the nadir of abasement he endured. His status as a slave is surely an echo of the Isaian Servant Song. His being "found in human form" may reflect the "one like a son of man" of Dan 7:13, LXX. The fullness of his humiliation comes with death (v. 8). "Death on a cross" is probably a Pauline addition to the hymn.

Exaltation results from this obedient self-abnegation. At Jesus' name the powers of heaven and earth acknowledge his lordship in phrases patterned on Isa 45:23. It is his resurrection that has won him this acknowledgment, the fullness of which will come with the parousia.

The divine Christ as preexistent Word is not the one who is being hymned here. It is the servant Son of Man, previously existent in some kind of equality to God, now hailed as Lord in glory.

The Christian mind, dogmatically formed, is prone to read Phil 2:6-11 as a description of an eternal, divine Son whose emptying consisted in his taking on human nature. The early hymn is not open to this interpretation, however. It knows only of a man with God who did not hold fast to the glory that was his in that association but accepted the conditions of a hard human life, then death, and was raised even higher than before for his obedient conformity to the divine plan.

Alleluia. Revelation 2:10

Be faithful unto death, says the LORD, and I will give you the crown of life.

Matthew 21:23[28]-32

This parable, found in Matthew only, may be derived from the same source that gives us the Lukan prodigal son (11:15-32). It is told against those who profess to be servants of God keeping the Law but who fail to do so, in contrast with those reckoned ungodly (the nonobservants; Gentiles) who nonetheless do the Father's will. There may be some notion here of the Law offered to the Gentiles who refused it at the time of Sinai whereas Israel at the time gave a fervent yes. Jesus tells his tale to convey his conviction that the roles are now reversed.

Verse 32 is an editorial addition, as we know from the existence of the logion as independent in Luke 7:29f. It changes the parable from one which had as its original purpose the ultimate vindication of the good news (the despised will receive and accept God's invitation which the self-proclaimed observants reject) to one that is interested in who will be saved at the end and who will not (cf. Matthew's parables of the tenants, 21:33-44, and the wedding banquet, 22:1-14).

The pious had put no trust in John (vv. 23ff.). So much the worse for them. Tax-gatherers and prostitutes did. God will know how to reward them.

🙞🙜

Proper 22 [27] / Twenty-seventh Sunday of the Year (A)
Sunday between October 2 and October 8, inclusive

Exodus 20:1-4, 7-9, 12-20

This lengthy and important passage is from the E source, as the name Elohim for God testifies (see vv. 1, 19, 20, 21). The Commandments are also found in Deut 5:6-21 and their common source is probably Deuteronomic in origin. The prohibition of idols means the image of Canaanite deities (vv. 3-5a). Blenkinsopp favors "impassioned" over "jealous" for God but has to accept the notion of hereditary guilt and punishment. "Wrongful" use of God's name probably denotes oath-taking more than casual usage. Sabbath observance requires total inaction, not action. The honor given to parents is a demand placed on adult children, while the prohibition is of murder rather than any killing. The numbering of the Commandments is catechetical, not biblical. Catholics and Lutherans reckon vv. 2-6 as containing one commandment, other Reformation era catechisms as two; the former then divide the prohibition of covetousness (v. 17) into two. This assigns a higher number to each commandment beginning with the one on taking the LORD's name in vain (v. 7a) through to that on bearing false witness (v. 16).

PSALM 19

ISAIAH 5:1-7

Psalm 80 is familiar with the image of Israel as a "vine transplanted from Egypt." Verses 8-15[9-16] of that psalm end with the plea to the LORD: "Have regard for this vine, the stock that your hand planted." Ezekiel knows the figure too. "Your mother was like a vine in a vineyard . . . it towered aloft . . . stood out in its height . . . plucked up in fury, and cast to the ground"; now it is planted in the desert (19:10-13). There is the possibility that Isaiah's Song of the Vine was originally a piece of love poetry, as testified to in the Song of Songs. There the bride says of her body, "My vineyard is at my own disposal" (8:11f). Speaking modestly, like a Hebrew maiden of ancient time or a Jew or Christian of today, she declares that its pleasures are reserved to another once they are married. She is not making a modern declaration of those on whom she intends to bestow her favors, least of all that she will abort the fruit of sexual union at will. She addresses her beloved as Solomon, saying that all the fruits of her vineyard are his to deal with, even as Israel's king had had the disposition of his extensive fields of grapes at Baal-hamon. But she means to save herself for him (actually, the one she loves) as the figures of a wall, a parapet, and a door in v. 8 attest.

As the song appears in Isaiah it is a plea to the populace, Judah itself, to pass judgment between the owner and his recalcitrant vineyard, standing for the LORD and his people. Jesus' parables similarly put the auditor in the role of judge. He even tells one (Mark 12:1-11; Matt 21:33-42; Luke 20:9-18) that seems to derive from Isa 5, although the spoilers are not the wild grapes on the vines but the tenant farmers who mistreat the collectors of produce. (See the Gospel commentary below.)

YHWH, the plaintiff, asks for judgment in his favor against the "choice vines" (v. 2a) he planted that yield only "wild grapes" (v. 2c). Literally, these *b^eoshim* are "stinking things," perhaps overripe fruit, in any case inedible. There is a play on words in the pairings "judgment–bloodshed; justice–outcry" in v. 7 (*mishpaṭ/mispaḥ; tsedakah/tse'akah*). There is no choice for Judah but to concur in the sentence against the vineyard which is itself.

This parabolic song introduces a catalogue of woes against a people guilty of injustices of every sort (vv. 8-23) and ends in a threat concerning the form the Lord's wrath against it will take (vv. 24-30). He will summon a far-off nation—Assyria—by whistling to it. It will come with bows and arrows, horses and chariots, roaring like a lion bent on destruction.

Psalm 80:7-15[9, 12-16, 19-20]

The vineyard of the Lord is the house of Israel.

Philippians 3:4b-14

A commentary on this lection is given on 5 Lent (C), except for vv. 4b-7, which RCL has wisely appended. The lengthy section made in vv. 2-21 gives evidence of being an insertion from another letter with its harsh words about "evil workers" (v. 2) who are "enemies of the cross of Christ" (v. 18) and whose "end is destruction" (v. 19). Less likely but possible is that Paul has been interrupted in his counsel to the Philippian church to rejoice in the Lord (3:1; 4:4) by news of some external threat to its practice of fidelity to the gospel. He is in any case overwrought at hearing of the demands placed by some unidentified persons on his beloved Philippians to continue with the ritual observances of Judaism as a supplement to faith. He yields to no one in the rightness of these practices for Jews like himself (vv. 5f.) in the former eon. Now, however, his boast and that of others "in the spirit of God" is in Christ Jesus (v. 3). Despite his indisputable Jewish pedigree, he no longer has confidence in the flesh, which in the context seems to be the bit of foreskin removed in infant circumcision. Now, "it is we who are the circumcision" (ibid.). He regards all that he could previously boast of as present loss.

Paul plays on the word, "flesh," denying it the meaning "foreskin" suggested by his reference to circumcision (v. 3). In the flesh in this sense he has no confidence—although he himself is circumcised—but in his flesh as lineage he has every confidence. The genealogy he claims for himself is an elaboration of the shorter one of Rom 11:1, with particular stress on his Pharisee connection (cf. Acts 23:6) and blamelessness in Law observance, which gives the lie to Rom 7:13-24 as being autobiographical in intent.

Philippians 4:6-9

This brief passage begins with the call to rejoice (v. 4), once familiar as the first word of the entrance song of Gaudete Sunday (3 Advent, *Missale Romanum*). Joy and rejoicing are recurrent themes in this epistle (cf. 1:18f.; 2:17f., 28; 3:1; 4:10). Verse 6 proposes that the prayer of thanksgiving be offered to God as an antidote to anxiety. Paul expresses the latter notion by using the verb that Jesus employed with respect to concern over clothing (Matt 6:28), worry about what to say when handed over to give witness (Matt 10:19), and anxiety about numerous details of housekeeping (Luke 10:41). Presenting one's needs to God in prayer will bring peace, says Paul. Verse 7 moved King James I to remark that "Dr. Donne's verses are like the peace of God; they pass all understanding." The incomprehensible nature of God's peace is the fact that it is bestowed in the midst of difficulties. It is given "in Christ Jesus," that is, in the mystery of our salvation through his cross and resurrection.

The list of adjectives in the neuter plural describing virtuous states and conditions that Paul recommends for serious thought in v. 8 constituted a commonplace in Hellenist ethics. He takes them over completely, here as in so many places, secure in the knowledge that life in Christ incorporates whatever is good in human life. Again, he does not hesitate to propose imitation of his own teaching and conduct as a means to ensure the presence, not of the peace of God so much as of the God of peace (v. 9).

ALLELUIA. JOHN 14:6

I am the way, the truth and the life says the Lord; no one comes to the Father except through me.

MATTHEW 21:33-46

Matthew follows Mark carefully in the parable of the tenants, where it is already an allegory. This makes it all but unique among Jesus' parables as a tale in which *he* figures. It occurs in *Thomas* 65 in the form servant-son, the latter identified as the heir. An important difference is that the details about the hedge, vat (Mark; Matthew has "winepress"), and tower, taken from Isa 5:1f. have not yet been incorporated. This shows editorial activity as early as Mark. Interestingly, Luke (20:9) omits the Isaian touches, along with *Thomas*. The use by Mark and Matthew of phrases from Isaiah's song puts beyond all doubt the thought that Israel's LORD is represented by the owner, but the killing of the son and heir as the last in a series is already enough to establish the story's allegorical character.

The succession of emissaries beaten and killed (in Mark 12:5 "many others") is an expansion of Jesus' original parable referring to the prophets and their fate. Luke tells the story with the most restraint, but whether as a result of his stylistic superiority or the tradition available to him it is hard to say.

Mark had given the story a christological twist by calling the son my "beloved son" (12:6), a detail that Matthew omits. Matthew has the killing occur outside the vineyard (21:39), probably a reference to Jesus' execution outside the city walls (cf. John 19:17; Heb 13:12f.). If in Jesus' original narration an identification was made between himself and God's son, this would not have struck his hearers as an ordinary way to speak of the Messiah. Moreover, the destruction of the central figure of the messianic age simply was not contemplated. Jeremias reports on the rabbinic form of the parable (*Sifre Deut* 32:9, §312) in which the son is taken to be Jacob representing the people Israel. The people can suffer; not the Messiah.

Verse 42 provides one of the early Church's favorite proof texts for the vindication of a rejected Christ, Ps 118:22f (cf. Acts 4:11; 1 Pet 2:7). This text referred originally to the tiny nation despised by the powerful ones, for which God nonetheless had a plan.

The explicit threat to the Jewish people of v. 43 is peculiar to Matthew, himself a Jew, in the manner of the threats of the prophets. A "people that produces its fruits" is not the Gentiles but the Church, whatever its ethnic makeup. The graphic v. 44 is textually doubtful, having crept its way in from Luke 20:18.

✍✍
Proper 23 [28] / Twenty-eighth Sunday of the Year (A)
Sunday between October 9 and October 15, inclusive

EXODUS 32:1-14

See Proper 19 [24] (C) for a commentary on vv. 7-14, with its possible explanation of Aaron's otherwise inexplicable conduct. The fact is, however, that this stalwart upholder of the covenant is portrayed as yielding to pressure by the people—nervous as to Moses' long delay on the mountain (v. 1)—to cast an image of a calf from the molten gold rings of their ears. They chant, "These are your gods *(elohim),*" or "This is your god, O Israel" (v. 4) and before the image the people offer sacrifices and engage in revels. Seemingly a memory of recidivism to pagan worship lingers, but a later editor has changed Aaron's complicity in it to worship of YHWH. Moses coming down the mountain, sees the calf and the revelry and in anger smashes the two stone tablets (see vv. 15-20), which he will refashion in 34:1.

Aaron's compliance with the wishes of the people is puzzling. Up to this point he has been portrayed neither as weak nor as doubting who God was who had delivered the Israelites from Egypt. Nothing has prepared us for his sharing the mistrust of the people in his brother, Moses. Their chant in v. 4b shows how they have lost faith in the God of Israel. Therefore, Aaron's proclamation that the next day there would be a festival to the LORD is either a scribal correction or else proof that the cultic act will mean a different thing for him than for them. The LORD knows it can mean only one thing and he wrathfully promises to destroy the people and spare Aaron. But at this point Moses intercedes successfully for the people so weak in faith in him by reminding the LORD of the covenantal promise made to the ancestors (v. 13). The LORD yields, and the people is spared (v. 14).

PSALM 106:1-6, 19-23

Give thanks to the LORD who is good.

ISAIAH 25:1-9[6-10A]

Isaiah 24-27 is known as the apocalypse of Isaiah and is probably a much later composition than the eighth century of the prophet's day. They proclaim the LORD's impending destruction of the earth and the dwindling of its inhabitants down to a few who will suffer for their guilt (24:6). All joy is dead, all gladness of the earth is banished (v. 11). Sandwiched in among these woes is a song of joy and praise (vv. 14-16a), after which the manifestation of the glory of the LORD on Mount Zion is prophesied (23b). All this leads to the song of praise in the earlier portion of today's reading (25:1-5). The ruin of the "city of chaos" of 24:10-12 is attributed to God who is the LORD (25:2). Since it will never be rebuilt, the buried city of Babylon may be meant. Who are the poor the LORD has sheltered from pelting rains and heat of the sun, and who are the ruthless and the foreigners whose conduct can be compared to a chilling winter rainstorm? Evidently these strong and fierce conquerors of tiny Israel are meant who grudgingly have to glorify Israel's God for sheltering the poor from the worst onslaughts of the elements.

This passage tells of a coronation feast for Israel's LORD provided for the Gentiles on Mount Zion. They will be served the best of food and drink. The shroud (or veil) and the sheet to be removed (v. 7) are probably those of mourning since the context is one of death, which the LORD "will destroy forever" (v. 8). One thinks of the antiphon from *Tenebrae* in the former liturgy of Holy Week: "*O mors, ero mors tua*," "O death, I shall be your death." A reference to the Canaanite god of death, Mot, similar to the Hebrew words for death and dying, may be intended (cf. Ps 49:15[14]b). There will be an end to sorrow as the Lord wipes away the tears from every face (v. 8), a phrase quoted twice in Revelation (7:17; 21:4). The hostility that God's people have experienced they will experience no more "on that day" (v. 9), an indication that the last day is meant.

The LORD will then be seen to be the savior of the people. To this the only fitting response is joy. "We looked to God to save us," who indeed will do so.

PSALM 23[1-6]

I shall live in the house of the LORD all the days of my life.

PHILIPPIANS 4:1-9[12-14, 19-20]

There is no expression of love and affection for any of the churches quite like that found in this letter (see vv. 1, 15). Whom else does Paul call "my joy and my crown"? But there is a jewel or two missing from his crown. Philippi is not paradise, as witness Euodia and Syntyche, who are *not* of the same mind. "*Sýzygē*" (4:3), literally someone yoked with Paul (but this noun, here in the vocative case, may be a man's name), becomes "my loyal companion" in NRSV (more literally "yokemate" in NAB), while we know nothing of this Clement (ibid.) except that like the other co-workers of Paul his name is in the "book of life" (see Rev. 20:12, 15). Frequently, Old Testament writers will speak of "the book," the record of human deeds of a God who never forgets a good one. We see from this and many other places how wrong it is to think of the apostle as soldiering on alone. He always works with a team. A few words on vv. 6-9 were included in last week's commentary. LM divides 4:1-14 into two parts at v. 9, omitting 10 and 11.

Paul's sentiment echoes that of Isaiah in that he acknowledges the Lord, in this case Jesus, as the source of his abundance and strength. The Philippians' assistance to him has been unexplainably interrupted but is resumed once more (v. 10). He is grateful but he wants to make the point that he can do without it.

An old saw says, "I' been rich and I' been poor, and, believe me, rich is better." Paul says that neither is better. He has learned to cope with both through being inwardly "self-sufficient" (v. 11, a Stoic term occurring only here in the New Testament). Paul can do all things in the One who strengthens him (v. 13). Despite this claim of inner divine resources, the apostle does not wish to appear ungrateful to the generous Philippians (v. 14). He seems to be using their gift as the occasion for a moral lesson. They are a source of strength to him. The Lord is an even greater one.

ALLELUIA. I SAMUEL 3:9; JOHN 6:69B

Speak, O LORD, your servant is listening; you have the words of everlasting life.

MATTHEW 22:1-14

The lector who terminates today's reading at v. 10 will have read one parable of Matthew while the LM homilist who elects the longer version will read a second one, the parable of the guest without a wedding garment. The first, the wedding banquet, occurs in this allegorized form here alone, while Luke 14:16-24 and *Thomas* 64 report it more simply as a dinner from which guests absent themselves (Matthew also has this feature) by a variety of excuses. In the latter telling it is a story of a full complement of guests assembled as a result of the host's insistence, while the invited who are disinterested must forgo the feast. *Thomas* concludes with the special allegorical ending, turning it into a parable of the last judgment: "The buyers and the merchants will not enter the places of my father."

In Matthew that is its character throughout. The host is a king. He gives a wedding banquet for his son. There are two refusals of his invitation, the second one marked by violence which he meets with murderous reprisal. Probably Matthew intends to convey the reception accorded the prophets by the first group of slaves (v. 3), that given to preachers of the gospel by the second (v. 4) including their persecution (v. 6), and the destruction of Jerusalem by the fate of "those murderers" whose city is to be burned (v. 7). Verses 9f., on such supposition, describe the Gentile mission. We know from 21:43, with which last Sunday's reading concluded, that Matthew is interested in having Jesus' stories illustrate the eschatological plan of salvation.

The second, appended parable (vv. 11-14) would then have to do with baptism (vv. 11f.), the last judgment, and hell (cf. 8:12; 25:30). Matthew's allegory of the plan of redemption is thus complete. It is comforting to know that the "weeping and gnashing" (NRSV: "wailing and grinding") of those in outer darkness is a product of Matthew's apocalyptic imagination. Gnashing, by the way, seems to be something you can only do with teeth, or so says the *Oxford English Dictionary*. (Old Norse folk were gnashing as early as 1300, the English by the late 1400s.) The aged toothless have clearly chosen the better part.

❧❧

Proper 24 [29] / Twenty-ninth Sunday of the Year (A)
Sunday between October 16 and October 22, inclusive

Exodus 33:12-23

Years ago Roark Bradford wrote a novel about life in a southern Black Sunday school called *Ol' Man Adam and His Chillun*. From it Marc Connolly wrote the better-known Broadway play and later film *The Green Pastures*. Theatergoers who did not know the Bible well were amused by the intimacy of the dialogue between "de Lawd" and characters like the angel Gabriel, who had to be restrained from blowing the last trumpet over heaven's rim. Bradford, however, knew the Bible well and elaborated only slightly in Negro dialect on passages like today's exchange between Moses and the LORD. The one who received the Law on Sinai had to know God's ways a little better if he were to continue finding favor with him but also in leading the people further. Moses was moved to challenge the LORD directly with the reminder: "You have said 'I know you by name' and you have found favor in my sight" (v. 12). "Show me your glory, I pray you" (v. 18). At this the LORD demurred, for it was well known to Israel that no one could see God and live (v. 20). A compromise is struck. All God's goodness (NAB, beauty) will be made to pass before Moses and "the Name" (*ha Shem*, i.e., YHWH) will be proclaimed before him but God's face shall he shall not see (v. 23). The leader who "brings up" this people (v. 12) is about to be placed in a cleft in the rock while God's glory passes by. God's hand will be removed and Moses will see God's back. This is surely an editorial correction of v. 10a, which has the LORD "speaking to Moses face to face."

Years after the Bradford novel an Englishman who had explored parts of sub-Saharan Africa, Negley Farson, wrote about a continent dark only because of European ignorance of it, *Behind God's Back*. Such was his insular view of a huge land whose natives could well have used the same description of the white colonial world. But both would be right to grasp the meaning of the theophany in Exodus. We see in the beauty of the world around us an image of the God we cannot see. Only we in all creation are also in the likeness of God.

Psalm 99

Isaiah 45:1, 4-6

The poetic oracles of Second Isaiah (chaps. 40–55), at least those contained in chaps. 40–48, were composed in Babylon on the brink of release from captivity in 538 B.C.E.

Chapters 49–55 may represent the work of the prophet's disciples upon their return to Jerusalem; otherwise, at a later period in the last stages of the captivity.

Cyrus, king of Persia, is hailed as the Lord's anointed (*mashiah*, "messiah," v. 1). This is the only instance in the Old Testament in which the term is applied to anyone outside the faith-community of Israel. Normally it designated a kingly figure but there are cases of its use to describe the anointed priest Aaron and priests who came after him, also the whole priestly people. The term did not at any time have the precise significance that Christianity gave it, although in postbiblical Judaism it began to describe a leading figure or figures of the messianic age. The concept of such an epoch is much more prominent in the Jewish scriptures than that of a single person who would dominate it.

The author of Second Isaiah portrays Cyrus after the manner of Abraham because he wishes to describe a return to the land of Israel from the east and the north, the route of the patriarch. The king of Persia is called the Lord's "attendant" / "summoned to his service" and "the champion of justice" / "victor" (41:2). Jacob/Israel is from Abraham, the friend of God (v. 8) who was "called from the earth's farthest corners" (v. 9). Israel, worm and maggot though it be, will be fashioned as a threshing sledge with teeth to eat mountains and hills. Cyrus, in turn, is described as someone whom "I have stirred up from the north and who "has come from the rising of the sun; he was summoned by name" (v. 25a). This chosen one shall trample down the rulers as a potter treads the clay (v. 25b).

If Israel is the Lord's servant in one sense, Cyrus surely is in another. (Some have seen a contrived antithesis between the humble Israel and the conquering Cyrus, but this is doubtful.) We have an inscription on a clay barrel, the so-called Cyrus Cylinder, that contains that sovereign's pledged loyalty to Marduk, "the great lord," who "pronounced his name [i.e., declared him] to be(come) the ruler of all the world" (James B. Pritchard, ed., *Ancient Near Eastern Texts* [Princeton: Princeton Univ. Press, 1955], 315). nrsv renders 41:25a "he was summoned by name." It is entirely unlikely that the biblical author is attributing Yahwist faith to this instrument of Yhwh's purpose. The initiative is the Lord's throughout. Both Cyrus and the servant Israel merely respond to it. Cf. 45:3d: "I, the Lord, the God of Israel, who call you by your name."

Verse 1b and c of chap. 45 echoes the prowess of the Lord through Abraham (41:2f.) and Cyrus (41:25). It is a declaration of intent to keep the promises made in 42:13ff. and 43:5 ("Do not fear, for I am with you; I will bring your offspring from the east, and from the west I will gather you"). The Lord is made to explain in 45:4b his usage of "anointed" in v. 1: "I call you by your name, giving you a title [surname you] though you do not know me." There follows in vv. 5f. a familiar declaration of the absolute uniqueness of Israel's LORD (cf. Deut 32:39; Mal 1:11a). He alone arms Cyrus, as he says to him, "though you know me not" (5b).

PSALM 96:1-9, (10-13)[1-5, 7-10]

Give to the LORD glory and honor.

1 THESSALONIANS 1:1[-5B]10

This greeting, which precedes the first of Paul's letters we have, is a summary of how he thinks divine election works. God first chose this community in the Macedonian seaport and then sent Paul and Silas (Silvanus) to work among them (Acts 17:1-9; probably Timothy too, cf. 16:3). As a result of their preaching in power and in the Holy Spirit (16:5f.) the community began to live lives of faith which led to love and were carried on in hope (1 Thess 1:3). Corresponding to these three gifts of God are the efforts of the Thessalonians, characterized as "your work of faith and labor of love and steadfastness of hope in our Lord Jesus Christ" (ibid.). This combination of the three Christian graces probably precedes Paul, who uses it also in 1 Cor 13:13. His distinction between what faith and love accomplish may be that between daily living (faith) and the spread of the gospel (love). Hope looks for the return of the Lord Jesus, hence is patient in endurance.

Paul finds the survival and fruitfulness of his gospel in this busy commercial capital a marvel. He will not attribute this success to the force of his words; his preaching derives its power from God (v. 5ab). Verse 5c proposes the generous service of Paul and his companions to the Thessalonian community as an essential part of the message of the gospel.

ALLELUIA. JOHN 8:12

I am the light of the world, says the Lord; the one who follows me will have the light of life.

MATTHEW 22:15[-21]22

This pericope follows immediately last Sunday's Gospel. Matthew alters his Markan source (12:13-17) only by an occasional change of word, notably the designation of Jesus' enemies as "you hypocrites." The latter is the familiar Matthean stigma of the Pharisees (6:2, 5, 16) which is also found in *Didachē* 8:1f. The presence of the Herodians (v. 16) heightens the notion of a political trap.

Matthew favors Pharisee teaching but not its practice in his day (cf. 23:3). In this discussion and the next two on the resurrection of the dead (vv. 23-33) and the greatest commandment (vv. 34-46), Jesus gives unexceptionable answers. He silences the Pharisees even if he does not satisfy them, and he downs the Sadducees, at least by a Pharisee standard.

The challengers flatter Jesus for his sincerity and his fidelity to *hē hodós* ("The way of God," v. 16). They then question him on the rightness of a Jew's subjecting himself to a foreign (Gentile) ruler by paying imperial taxes. Not only was the tribute exacted onerous but it had attached to it the shame of being required in coinage that bore the emperor's "graven image" and inscriptions proclaiming his cult. The coins of Tiberius, the Caesar of Jesus' adult lifetime, bore the titles *divus* (a divine one) and *pontifex maximus* (supreme bridge-builder).

Jesus makes his first point by not having such a coin in his possession whereas his opponents do (v. 19). They hand him a *dēnárion*, the coin with which the census tax is paid. He makes them spell out whose image and inscription are to be found on it (v. 20), following which they are told to repay it to Caesar. The cleverness of Jesus' response is complete. The coins are to be out of Jewish hands and into Gentile ones with all possible speed; therefore Jesus cannot be faulted as an offender against Torah (Exod 20:4f.). No more is he to be charged with political subversion. Some in Israel favored armed revolt whereas the Pharisees waited for God's good time in which Israel would be set free. Jesus in his response aligns himself with the Pharisees.

Centuries of interpretation have made this text read as a clear delimitation of the claims of religion and the body politic. But what belongs to each sphere? Primarily, Jesus holds out a choice between two forms of worship. In Tillich's term, what will be a person's "ultimate concern"? Will he or she choose money, the state, a religious establishment at ease with both? Or will there be transcendence of these extensions of the self and a choice made of God?

❧ ❧

Proper 25 [30] / Thirtieth Sunday of the Year (A)
Sunday between October 23 and October 29, inclusive

Deuteronomy 34:1-12

LM has this reading for 19 Wednesday, Year A, but not on a Sunday. RCL corrects the omission, as it so often does, by fittingly concluding its continuous reading of the Pentateuch with the account of Moses' death and Joshua's succession.

Moses is portrayed in Deuteronomy as the expounder of the Law who speaks uninterruptedly from 1:6 to 31:6. Even after that his words continue with but a few interrupted instructions from the LORD (31:14, 16-21, 26-29; 32:49-52; 34:4). Moses had been situated by the Deuteronomist in "the land of Moab beyond the Jordan" (1:5), and it is from its plains that he climbs up "Mount Nebo to the top of Pisgah opposite Jericho," from which the whole land from Dan in the north to Zoar in the south could be seen. The LORD reiterates the promise to Abraham by oath that all this land should be the Hebrews' (see Gen 12:7a; 15:8) but Moses was not to die there, rather in a valley in Moabite territory in a place unknown by the time of the book's writing. Our age has known many women and fewer men who have reached five score years, some retaining full vigor, others clear sight or hearing. It is doubtful the Deuteronomist knew the possibility or he would have ratcheted the figure even higher to impress upon the reader Moses' greatness. His unknown grave is an indication of the direction to which the paths of glory lead. A rabbinic pen has awarded him the customary month's mind of mourning. After the transfer of authority to Joshua by the traditional laying on of hands, the lawgiver receives the encomium that would be hard to match for rhetorical force and beauty (vv. 10-12). Although the LORD knew him face to face, Deuteronomy does not say he knew the LORD face to face.

PSALM 90:1-6, 13-17

LEVITICUS 19:1-2, 15-18

This chapter is made up of a variety of precepts found elsewhere in the Mosaic books. Its antiquity cannot be doubted, and it may have preceded the other codified laws rather than deriving from them. The holiness of YHWH and who he is is given as the reason for observing them (v. 2; cf. vv. 3, 4, 10, 11, 16, 18, 25, 28, 30, 31, 32, 34, 36, 37). Reverence for parents and Sabbath observance (v. 3) are to be found in Exod 20:12, 11. For parallels to the prohibitions of unjust judgment and partiality to the poor or the mighty (v. 15) see Exod 23:2 and Deut 16:19f. The commandment not to slander (v. 16) stands alone among collections of laws and so do the stern prohibitions of vengeance and holding a grudge (v. 18). These sins are reprobated obliquely in various chronicles and wisdom writings but they are nowhere so starkly forbidden as here. The command to "love your neighbor as yourself" (v. 18b) will be coupled by Jesus with the prescription to love God above all else and all others (Deut 6:5; 10:12; 11:13). The "neighbor" of Lev 19:18 is a *rea'*, while the nearby "fellow countryman" is an *amith*. Deuteronomy

10:18f. is alone in commanding the love of strangers *(gerim)* and providing food and clothing for them, giving as the reason that the Hebrews "were strangers in the land of Egypt." The frequency of the verb "to love" *(ahab)* in these texts should prompt a homily on the love command in Torah. Christians need to hear it since they have so long lived with the false notion that Jesus inaugurated love of God and neighbor by placing two commands together that are not found in proximity in the Mosaic books.

Psalm 1

Exodus 22:20-26

This portion of social morality from the law code of Israel reflects some recurrent biblical concerns. The Israelite people was constantly reminding itself of its obligation to the widows, orphans, and non-Israelites who lived in its midst (cf. Lev 1:16; Deut 10:18; Zech 7:10; Jer 7:6). From Yhwh's first call of Moses to a new covenantal relation, the setting free of this people in a rich land is tied to its release from Egyptian enslavement (cf. Exod 3:7-10). They could do no less for others than was done for them. The divine punishment for the neglect of orphans and widows would be warfare ("I will kill you with the sword," v. 23) which would convert the wives and children of Israel's offending men into widows and orphans in turn.

The prohibition of money lending is one against exploitation of people in their need, whether this takes the form of interest that is extorted unfairly (v. 24) or a man's only cloak to keep him warm (vv. 25f.). Such lending at interest, moreover, is forbidden with respect to fellow countrymen but allowed in the case of foreigners (very specifically in Deut 23:20f.). Deuteronomy gives as the reason for this the economic solidarity necessary for the Israelites to "make it" in the new land.

Money lending by Jews to Gentiles (later, for example in the Middle Ages in Europe) was something they were forced to do to survive, because land owning and the trades were closed to them. But it was always permitted within Mosaic law to lend to non-Jews so long as no usurious (in the sense of excessive) practice accompanied it. No borrower feels kindly toward the lender when he falls behind in his payments, however, no matter how upright the latter may be. Hence Christians began to persecute Jews for reasons besides the one that led to the relationship in the first place, namely, their own economic necessity. The entire matter was complicated by the scholastic teaching that departed from that of the patristic period, which had forbidden interest-taking altogether by holding that goods consumed by use (grain or oil or wine, called *fungibilia*) were unproductive, while money, which had been called "sterile" by Aristotle, began to be thought of as permitting a charge for its use—not in itself, that is, but only under some extrinsic title. Over the course of the next few centuries numerous such titles were devised such as the opportunities for profit forgone by the lender when the money was on loan. These developments meant that money-lending Jews were given additional possibilities of suffering at Christian hands.

Amos 2:7c-8a grows wrathful at those who do not keep the prescription of v. 26; "Son and father go to the same prostitute, profaning my holy name. Upon garments taken in pledge they recline beside any altar."

The compassion of the LORD (v. 26c) must be emulated by human compassion. This is the basis of the entire morality of Torah.

PSALM 18:2-4, 47, 51

I love you, LORD, my strength.

1 THESSALONIANS 2:1-8[5C-10]

See the following Sunday in LM for a comment on this passage, beginning with v. 7. As the chapter opens, Paul reminds the Thessalonica congregation of the mistreatment he has suffered at Philippi before coming to them (vv. 1f.; cf. Acts 16:16-40; 17:1-9 will report a similar ejection from the Macedonian capital). His reference to deceit or trickery is probably an indication of the slick purveyors of doubtful cults and philosophies all along the Roman *via Egnatia* that passes through Saloniki (Thessalonica) to this day. Despite varieties of opposition to "the gospel of God" (vv. 2, 8) Paul continues to proclaim it to please, not mortals, but God (vv. 2, 4). Neither flattery—human praise—nor greed, he maintains, has ever motivated him. He could have made demands on the members of this church in his rôle as apostle but he preferred to go the way of gentleness. To what male pastor nowadays would it occur to compare his solicitous care to that of a nursing mother at the breast (v. 7)? Paul is not shy. He knows he has spent his very self on behalf of these people and does not hesitate to remind them of it.

Nor does Paul hesitate to couple messengers of the gospel like himself with the Lord (v. 6) as fit models for the Thessalonian community. These Macedonians have been through numerous trials for their faith but the result has been joy. Paul keeps hearing from various places in Macedonia and Achaia, the two provinces that make up northeastern and southern Greece, how strong the faith of the Thessalonians is (vv. 7f.). Evidently large numbers of them have been pagans and not

Jews (v. 9) and are awaiting the Son's return—Jesus, the deliverer from the coming wrath. This blazing anger will be directed toward the wicked in the last age. The linking of pagan Greeks to Jewish eschatological motifs shows us that primitive Christian preaching made few cultural concessions. Jewish thought-patterns were the narrow door through which all had to enter but not adoption of the special customs that signified Jewishness.

Paul recalls to the Thessalonians the beating he had received in Philippi just before he came to them on his journey westward (see Acts 16:19-24). The suffering evidently energized him to proclaim "the gospel of God" and this he did forthrightly. No flattery for him to obtain their good will as a cover for greed (v. 5)! Acts speaks of Paul's companion as Silas but the plural usage throughout seems an editorial "we." Paul came to love this congregation so much that he did not have to "pull rank" as an apostle but shared his very self with them. He would have plied his craft everywhere he went in any case but in Thessalonica it was so that he did not have to be a public charge.

ALLELUIA. JOHN 10:27

My sheep listen to my voice, says the LORD; I know them and they follow me.

MATTHEW 22:34[-40]46

After the silencing of the Sadducees on bodily resurrection, which the lectionary omits (vv. 23-33), the Pharisees return to testing Jesus. A "lawyer" is a "scribe" and vice versa. Here he is called *nomikós*, normally a Lukan word. Matthew uses *grammateús* in every other place.

As does Mark, Matthew has Jesus bring together the love of God (Deut 6:5) and the love of neighbor (Lev 19:18). Luke (10:27) has them already combined (cf. Matt 19:19), a Jewish catechetical practice that we know about from the *Testament of Issachar* (5:2). The enumeration of the 613 positive and negative Mosaic precepts found in the Law under a few headings (v. 40) could already have been common practice in Jesus' day. It is not cited here as a matter of dispute but of agreement between him and his opponents. They ask a received question and are given a received answer. Matthew's point is that they can make no capital of his unexceptionable rabbinic response.

✿✿
Proper 26 [31] / Thirty-first Sunday of the Year (A)
Sunday between October 30 and November 5, inclusive

Joshua 3:7-17

LM will select only two narratives from this book for Sunday proclamation, 5:9a, 10-12 on 4 Lent (C) and 24:1-2, 14[15]-18b on [Proper 16] 21(B) read more extensively in RCL. Next Sunday the latter will feature 24:1-3a, 14-25, which LM proposes for Friday and Saturday of Week 20, Year A (24:1-13, 14-29). Joshua 3:7-17 provides an authentication of Joshua's leadership in succession to Moses as the people cross the Jordan from the east. Next Sunday's lection, 24:1-3a, 14-25, will tell of their promise of fidelity to God under the Sinai covenant in the new land. The crossing of the Jordan is reported in 3:8 as a stately religious procession in which the transport of the ark by the priests is paramount. A prediction of the conquest of Canaan is given in v. 10 listing a variety of tribes, some known and others unknown to Middle Eastern history, that will be driven out of the land by the "living God." The warrant claimed in that far-off day was the same as that of the "religious" settlers of Israel and Palestine of our day. They have driven the Palestinians from their homes and off their lands, saying that it was promised them by God. This has been done with the aid of a secular government whose sole basis for the claim is a dwelling in the land going back centuries, when those who are now called Palestinians may have been there before them. Many Israelis protest the settler actions of their government.

The account of the crossing is deliberately patterned on the crossing of the Sea of Reeds in Exodus 14–15. The waters of the Jordan flowing south are described as being raised up in a "heap" permitting first, the priests with the ark, then "all Israel," to cross the river bed dry shod opposite Jericho. Archeologists have identified Adam (v. 16) as situated on the east bank sixteen miles north of the ford near Jericho and placed Zarethan ten miles north of that. For these sites and the identification of some of the Canaanite tribes that could not have been aware of impending conquest, see Michael David Coogan, "Joshua," in *NJBC* (Englewood Cliffs, N.J.: Prentice Hall, 1990) 18, 114–15. The Arabah is the geological rift that is the Jordan valley as the river debouches into the Salt Sea and then continues into the Red Sea at Eilat down to modern Sudan. But geography in the tale is subordinated to the driving out of pagan worship by the presence of the ark borne by the priests, and of God's own people.

Psalm 107:1-7, 33-37

MICAH 3:5-12

Micah of Moresheth was a contemporary of Isaiah in Judah who is known to Christians almost exclusively for his prophecy of a future Bethlehemite (5:1) and his peaceful counsel to "do right, love goodness, and walk humbly with your God" (6:8). He was, however, as strident as any of the forth-tellers for God, whose only foretelling was of the destruction the people could expect (5:9-14) for the exploitation of the poor by the rich (chap. 2) and the venality of leaders, priests, and prophets (3:11). The last-named are well fed as they declare that all is well in the land while they make war on the poor (v. 5). The darkness of night must fall on them for they have no message (v. 6). Micah, contrariwise, is supremely confident that he is God-inspired to charge Jacob Israel with its crimes. The rulers have built Zion with perverse deeds not the least of which are bribery, simony, and graft (vv. 9-11). They claim exemption from divine sanction, little knowing that when God's agent, crouching Assyria, pounces it will reduce Jerusalem to rubble (see 5:4f for the foolish boast that the tyrant can be turned back by a land force of shepherds under arms).

PSALM 43

MALACHI 1:14B — 2:2B, 8-10

Not all was "life and peace" in the postexilic community. In particular, the priesthood had its sins to answer for.

Sheshbazzar and Zerubbabel had first bravely got an altar up and then the foundations of a rebuilt Temple. This was in the movement of return to holy Zion of the 530s and 520s. But the old men cried in sorrow, because the new structure was such a poor patch on the Temple of Solomon they had known. Others cried out with joy. The one sound could not be distinguished from the other (see Ezra 1–3). The inhabitants of the land provided every kind of resistance to the work of resettlement. It went ahead nonetheless. Ezra the scribe came from Babylon in 459, Nehemiah the civil servant of Persia from Susa in 446. Together they laid the foundations of what came much later to be called Judaism. Temple worship flourished though the structure was modest; the priesthood was strengthened. The scribes—the learned class—were theoretically subordinated to the priests and influential laymen.

In fact, however, when the priests grew rich through sharp practice (see Mal 1:6-14) the scribes were moved to action. By the mid-fifth century, the mid-point as well of the reign of the supportive Artaxerxes I (465–25), priestly abuses reached a crescendo. Taking the pseudonym Malachi ("my messenger"), a bold, prophetic spirit lashed out at the sins of the priesthood. He might have been a priest himself; he need not have been a scribe. He was, in any case, an anti-establishment figure zealous for the honor of the LORD.

Malachi's threat is not a novel one. All the prophets had uttered it before him. If the abuses continue, he says, the Lord will desert Israel's covenanted Levites and turn to the Gentile nations. Among them his "name will be feared" (1:14b). There the LORD can expect sacrifice and a pure offering, the acknowledgment of his name from the rising of the sun even to its setting (cf. 1:11).

The offense of the priests was twofold. They should have taught the people well but instead taught them falsely (about a God interested in generous donations, a magnificent structure, religious display?). They further showed partiality, presumably to the rich but also and above all to themselves.

The results are in full view, says Malachi. The unjust, venal ways of the priests have become familiar. The people hold them in contempt.

PSALM 131:1-3

In you, LORD, I have found my peace.

1 THESSALONIANS 2:[7B]9-13

Paul's boast is in a direction completely contrary to the practice of the fifth-century priests. While in Thessalonica, he had worked and worked hard, not *at* preaching the gospel but *while* preaching the gospel. He not only made no money from the works of religion; he supported himself while recommending them. What a nursing mother does for her baby, Paul had done for his Macedonian new believers (2:7); he supported new life from his very self. A moment later he can compare his concern for each one of them to that of a solicitous father (v. 11). The good tidings of Christ had thus imposed no burden. God's grace was *gratis*. There were no handling charges.

This self-support aspect of Paul's teaching ministry was not incidental to it but at the heart and center. He does not hesitate to remind the Thessalonians of his labor and toil among them so as not to be a financial burden. Look at my blameless conduct, he says. It bore fruit. You received my word for what it really is: God's word, at work among you.

ALLELUIA. JOHN 17:17B, A

Your word, O LORD, is truth; make us holy in the truth.

MATTHEW 23:1-12

Jesus continues the tradition of Malachi here. The offenders are not priests, eating the shoulder-cut of beef while offering blind and lame beasts in sacrifice (see Mal 2:3; 1:8). Yet, like the priests, the scribes and Pharisees are leading people astray by their teaching, Matthew charges. In his day (i.e., after the fall of Jerusalem) the Sadducees who held power in both the Sanhedrin and Temple are no longer the enemy; the scribes and Pharisees, men of learning and conviction (cf. 23:2) are. Does this teaching reflect Matthew's day only and not the conflicts of Jesus' time? Luke 11:46; 20:46; 11:52; and 11:47 lead us to believe that these sayings derive from historical tradition and not merely from the situation of the Matthean church.

The opposition between the emerging Church and the rabbinic teachers within Judaism is such as to be described as stylized by the time this Gospel is written (cf. Matt 6:16 and the "hypocrites" of *Didachē* 8:1). All the same, the resistance of Jesus to teachers who laid burdens on others while not lifting a finger to help them (v. 4) was apparently a fact of his lifetime. His sharp criticism of certain Pharisee teachers is duplicated in the Talmudic writings which that very tradition produced. Whereas the Jewish world was taught to distinguish among its Pharisees as we are among our doctors, lawyers, and businessmen, the Gospels blurred the distinctions and taught the Christian world to mistrust the Pharisees as a whole. This is as unfortunate as mistrusting all politicians and all clergymen as practicers of duplicity. The curse of Christian preaching has been to pummel the Pharisees indiscriminately as if all were like some of their sorriest specimens. That certainly is not true of Christian clergy. Only some of us are hypocrites, as I have just proved by this statement.

Moses' seat (v. 2) was a piece of synagogue furniture from which the Rabbi taught as real as a modern pulpit. Verse 3 about "doing whatever they teach you" is a puzzle in light of vv. 16 and 18, where the teaching selected serves only to highlight its untrustworthy character. The earlier verse is therefore probably a dramatic way of distinguishing between the nobility of the scribal office and the low estate to which it has fallen. Vigorous efforts to proselytize in this debased spirit (see v. 15b) only heighten the evil.

Jesus accuses the teachers of interpreting the Law to suit themselves. Vanity of office seemingly accompanied their practice in the forms of dress and behavior (v. 5; cf. 6:1-18). Phylacteries represented an interpretation of the phrases "as a sign on your hand" and "an emblem on your forehead," already literalized by the time of Exod 13:16 and Deut 6:8. Snatches of the Law (from Exod 13 and Deut 6 and 11) were encased in leather boxes "strapped to the wrists and the forehead."

Tassels *(tsit-tsit)* were prescribed for the garments of the pious in Num 15:38-41 and Deut 22:12. Jesus wore the latter (Matt 14:36), presumably with a becoming ordinariness.

The title "Rabbi," which Matthew equates with the Greek "teacher," "father," and "instructor," was evidently coming into use in Jewish circles. He repudiates them all in highlighting the uniqueness of God and Christ. Jesus is *the* Teacher, like Qumrân's anonymous "Teacher of Righteousness." Taking Jesus at his word by expunging the titles from human usage ("Call no one on earth your paternal parent") would be falling into the trap of literalism that he warned against. The early Church did not do this. Yet, following his spirit on signs and titles of office is something concerning which the Church has never had a distinguished record. The titles are not the problem so much as the overblown importance with which some holders invest them.

Matthew concludes the passage with one repeated saying on humility (cf. 20:26 for a parallel to v. 11) and a new one (v. 12)—which Luke will use twice (14:11; 18:14).

🙠🙠

Proper 27 [32] / Thirty-second Sunday of the Year (A)
Sunday between November 6 and November 12, inclusive

JOSHUA 24:1-3A, 14-25

For a commentary see 21 Sunday [16] (B).

PSALM 78:1-7

WISDOM 6:12-16[13-17] OR AMOS 5:18-24

The wisdom here personified is an attribute of God. This literary convention is found in Job (chap. 28), Proverbs (1:20-33), and Sirach (24:1-21), among other places. God's spirit, God's word and God's justice are likewise spoken of in other sapiental writings as if they were persons. Wisdom in the earlier literature resulted from possession of the spirit of God. The present, first-century B.C.E. book "the Wisdom of Solomon" makes the two identical, spirit-wisdom becoming the principle behind the universe that sustains all human life and action.

Today's passage contains echoes of Prov 1:20-22 and 8:1-36, especially the references to wisdom's crying out in the streets and appearing at the city gates. Wisdom is a feminine noun in Hebrew and Greek, but gendered nouns in languages that have them say nothing with respect to the human sexes. Her clothing is royal, since she is of God (v. 12). She goes out of her way to make herself known (vv. 13-16). Like the father of the wastrel son in Jesus' parable, she runs out to meet those in need of her. But the best guarantee of her ministrations is that one should be a seeker. She responds most generously to those who search her out.

The earliest concept of wisdom in the biblical books was one of mental skill or ability. It yielded to that of ethical discernment, with God serving as the universal moral standard to whom all could appeal. This later notion is found in the Hellenist book of Wisdom, *sophia* in the original; to it is joined the Hebraic idea of *ḥokmah* as an all-pervasive principle that confers meaning and order on the world.

The praise of heavenly wisdom parallels that found in Proverbs, with one important difference. The earlier book does not name heeding wisdom's laws as an assurance of immortality. That Hellenist concept did not replace belief in the resurrection of the just that followed on the Maccabean revolt but existed beside it in the Greek-speaking diaspora. This book from 100 B.C.E. or thereabouts is the only one in the second canon written in Greek. (See Pheme Perkins, *Resurrection* [Garden City, N.Y.: Doubleday, 1984], 47–56, 315, 331–38, on faith in the immortality of the soul and the resurrection of the body as coexisting.)

Some pulpit Bibles do not have the Wisdom of Solomon and so RCL proposes an excoriation of those who offer burnt offerings in sacrifice and not justice and uprightness (Amos 5:24).

WISDOM 6:17-20 OR PSALM 70

PSALM 63:2-8

My soul is longing for you, O LORD my God.

1 THESSALONIANS 4:13-18

Former Catholic altar-servers of a certain age may well carry around in their heads the rhythmic cadences of this passage in Latin, ending in a sonorous, "*Itaque consolamini invicem in verbis istis*," from the days when the daily Mass of Requiem figured largely in their lives. Paul's message of consolation which he proposed for regular exchange (see v. 18) was that we should be with the LORD "forever" (v. 17). Followers of John Nelson Darby, who left the Church of England ministry for the Plymouth Brethren, may know it stitched together with part of 1 Corinthians 15 to form "the Rapture."

Paul's categories are those of Jewish end-time thought, the distinctive feature being that when the living are caught up into the air with the risen dead (cf. vv. 16f.) all should "meet the Lord," namely, Jesus. Paul may or may not suppose that he will be among the living. He uses the editorial "we" because he is sure of his vocation to preach Christ until his glorious return, but apocalyptic categories do not include a time schedule.

The obvious thrust of the passage is comfort for the survivors of the Thessalonian dead, about whose fate Paul seems to have left no clear message. The "hope" (v. 13) of Christians is Christ dead, risen, and expected back again. They are perfectly free to mourn their dead, but their grief cannot resemble that of those who have no such hope. Christ, moreover, did not rise for himself alone but for the raising up of all who died believing in him. The second question raised by the Thessalonians seems to have been, Will not the living enjoy some special advantage over the dead? No, says Paul, it will all take place with each one "in proper order," as 1 Cor 15:23 has it, the dead first (1 Thess 4:16), then the living (v. 17), but not in such a way as to constitute an advantage for the latter.

Paul is sure of his response. It is not as if he had given a private opinion, like his counsel to some to remain unmarried in 1 Cor 7:25. He teaches here "on the word of the Lord" (v. 15). The fate of the dead and of the living was therefore a part of the substance of the tradition, traceable back to Jesus and the Church's earliest preaching. What is sure is the nature of Christian hope. No such claim is being made for the imaginative details. These Paul borrows freely from the Jewish picture of the end-event, simply inserting Christ as the summoner in the skies as agent of God.

ALLELUIA. JOHN 1:14 AND 12B

The Word of God became a man and lived among us. He enabled those who accepted him to become children of God.

MATTHEW 25:1-13

The Gospel parable echoes the first reading. Its stress, however, is on prudential care rather than wisdom. NRSV and NAB retain the familiar descriptive adjectives of the bride's attendants as "foolish" and "wise," calling them "virgins," thereby continuing the possibility of coarse humor based on a misconception of what their folly and wisdom consisted in. Translating "sensible" and "flighty" or even "thoughtful and "thoughtless," and "attendants" for "virgins"—since most members of a wedding were unmarried—would have obviated total misunderstanding. The two companies of maidens were not wise or foolish over the preservation of their virginity. Jesus in telling the tale was interested in something quite different. His concern was over preparedness for the final days. The tale is day-of-the-Lord oriented, like all his kingdom parables. This one is cast in the future: "the reign of God *will be* like" (v. 1), not "is like," as in the parables of chap. 13.

The marriage between the Lord and Israel (or Jerusalem or Zion), God's virgin bride, is a familiar biblical theme. We are not surprised to encounter it as a motif for the consummation of all at the end. Matthew has told a previous parable of a wedding banquet that ends unhappily (20:11-14). If he had given us a story of the return of the groom *and his bride*, as some manuscripts have it, it would be a simple tale of being on the alert. The fact that all ten fell asleep (v. 5) makes the praise of vigilance in v. 13 inapplicable.

No doubt Jesus' original story, like all that he told, had a single point: "Be ready!" As Matthew tells the story it is an allegory, the groom inevitably suggesting Christ and the two groups of women with their two outlooks those fated to enjoy the "presence" of Jesus as Lord and those not. The delay in the groom's coming establishes with certainty the allegorical nature of Matthew's version. This is fortified by the activities of the two groups of bridesmaids, who represent waiting Christians. Some take prudent measures while they wait. Others relax their vigilance.

In this case, as in so many others, the message is: "Be ready!"

❧ ❦

Proper 28 [33] / Thirty-third Sunday of the Year (A)
Sunday between November 13 and November 19, inclusive

Judges 4:1-7

This is the only Sunday lection from Judges in the RCL; LM has none, but it does provide readings from chaps. 4, 6, 9, and 11 on a succession of weekdays in Week 20, Year A. The choice was surely motivated by the presence of Deborah, a prophet and wife to the judge Lappidoth. In LM the women of the Bible are woefully unreported on at the Sunday Eucharist. If this story were to be used, it is hard to know what Gospel narrative, if any, it could be thought to foreshadow on the typological principle of that lectionary. Lydia in Acts 16, perhaps, and the three Marys standing by the cross in John 19. Indeed, there is a puzzle as to why RCL stops where it does, for the two interesting things we know now about Deborah are that she acted as a judge (important enough) and that the victory chant attributed to her celebrating Barak and his forces came as the result of a victory she engineered (chap. 5). Alas, the tent peg driven into Jabin's general, Sisera's, skull by Jael, wife to Heber, would have made a much more interesting, if blood-chilling story (4:17-23). For the headless Holofernes at a woman's gentle touch, see Jud 13:14 and any Renaissance art gallery.

Psalm 123

Zephaniah 1:7, 12-18

For brief background on this book see 3 Advent (C). Since King Josiah has gone down in Judah's history as Josiah the good (640–609), it may be asked why the people merited this harsh censure in the reign of one who promulgated the Law so vigorously (see 2 Kgs 22:8-13; 23:1-27). The answer seems to be that as a boy king he was surrounded in his court by Assyrian-tilting counselors. This allowed Judahite observance of the Law to be in relative eclipse. Zephaniah seems to have been the king's exact or near contemporary, Nahum the same, both writing before or not long after Nineveh's fall (612). But if Josiah initiated his legal reforms in 622 there was a full decade of lax living that preceded it. Hence Zephaniah could have been fulminating against the resurgence of pagan worship he saw all around him: bowing down to the stars in the heavens (1:5), an Assyrian innovation, and to Milcom, god of the Ammonites. The sin of the people is complacency; they refuse to be alerted to the coming storm (vv. 12f.). The prophet senses that three-hundred years of Assyrian cruelty are coming to an end. This being so, he paints the impending collapse in terms of the lively myth of the Day of the Lord. Distress awaits Judah on the day the LORD will vent his wrath, as all the earth's inhabitants look forward to "a full and a terrible end" (1:18c).

As a youthful altar server at many a funeral, the present writer wondered what could have been meant by the prayers over the body before its committal to the earth in the Roman Rite. The Mass of Requiem had featured Thomas of Celano's (?) *Dies Irae*. The plangent Gregorian melodies in the parish church were doleful enough. But what could a fourteen-year-old or, more importantly, the grieving family of a good person so recently dead, make of, "That day is a day of wrath, of wasting and of misery, a dreadful day and exceeding bitter when Thou shalt come to judge the world by fire" (Zeph 1:15, 18)? This reading is now placed on the next to last Sunday of the church year, while the Reign of Christ the King has been interposed between it and the first Sunday of Advent. Older worshipers may recall Gospel lections from Matthew 24 and Luke 21, Jesus' end-time discourse, on those successive Sundays. In a time long past when the two readings did not signal the end of one Church year and the beginning of another, both were lections in a longer Advent. LM has retained some sense of the End of Days with Daniel 12 and Malachi 3 in Years B and C, both of them proposed as alternates in the RCL. The latter does it best as it approaches the conclusion of the Church year with Isa 65:17-25, Proper 28 [33] (C), which calls for rejoicing in Jerusalem as the center of new heavens and a new earth.

PSALM 90:1-8, (9-11), 12

PROVERBS 31:10-13, 19-20, 30-31

It is clear what the worthy wife was giving in that male-dominated culture, not so clear what her husband's gift was. One presumes fidelity. Perhaps a great deal more. The husband's praise of her is cited (vv. 28f.), but it is neutralized by the poet's view of a good wife as a man's possession and his prize (vv. 10f.).

There are but two modern touches in this eulogy, deeply flawed as it is by its good intentions. One is the reality of the hard labor of a wife and mother. The other is the counsel in the first part of v. 31: "Give her a share in the fruit of her hands." This cannot come about contemporarily by "letting her works praise her in the city gates" (husband's shirts always starched, children neat at school clutching their lunch money). It can only come about by the whole culture's repudiating the picture of womanhood represented by vv. 10-31.

Preaching homilies on vv. 1-9 would be a good start in this direction, especially v. 8: "Speak out . . . for the rights of the destitute." Wives know something about the drinking that makes their men forget what the Law decrees (v. 5) and the vigor given to other women (v. 3). Proverbs 31, even in its abbreviated form, can be infuriating to a thoughtful woman because it depersonalizes her thoroughly and tells her (boob of a poet!) that charm and beauty count for nothing so long as the linen closet stays full. Enter the vigor bestowed on other women.

PSALM 128:1-5

Happy are those who fear the LORD.

1 THESSALONIANS 5:1[6]-11

Paul was fully committed to the biblical reality of the "day of the LORD" (which becomes for him the "day of Christ," as in Phil 2:16) but like any wise rabbinic teacher of his time he knew enough not to name specific times or seasons (v. 1) in connection with it. It was a certainty and a certainty of the future. That was enough for him. The chief feature of the onset of the last days would be its suddenness. The figure of a thief in the night and labor pains were not new with Paul but current coin (cf. Mark 13:8, 32; Matt 24:8, 43f.).

The criers of "Peace and security!" in Thessalonica are purveyors of the false assurance that was being hawked in Jeremiah's time (cf. Jer 6:14; 8:11). Paul expects a little ruin (v. 3); he just does not wish it to fall on his Thessalonian friends unaware. They are children (lit.: "sons") of light, and the day, not of the night and darkness (v. 5). He gets somewhat lost in his imagery when he says in v. 4 that "the day," meaning the day of Christ, should not catch off guard those whose proper medium is daylight rather than the darkness that shields the thief. But "the day" that will overtake the daylight is not his meaning. He simply names vigilance and sobriety as the best preparedness for any untoward cosmic occurrences—at the center of which will be the coming of Jesus as Lord.

Night and darkness are good for recuperative repose, not only for thievery and drunkenness, but Paul wishes to make sleep a figure of lack of vigilance and the daylight a figure of alertness and sobriety. He knows that Isaiah has used the metaphor of a soldier's uniform dress (59:17) to illustrate justice and salvation but he puts breastplate and helmet in the service of faith, hope, and charity with salvation from God's wrath something to be hoped for, not a present reality (see Eph 6:13-17 for an expansion of the military symbolism).

ALLELUIA

May the Father of our Lord Jesus Christ enlighten the eyes of our hearts.

MATTHEW 25:14-30

Differences could be pointed out between Matthew's parable, where the *tálanton* is the monetary unit, and Luke's, which features the far less valuable *mina* (19:12-27), but they would not be especially instructive. Suffice it to say that Luke's story seems to be our parable conflated with another about an unpopular ruler (Herod Archelaus, 4 B.C.E.–6 C.E.?), which he uses to explain why the "coming" or "presence" of Christ is delayed.

Matthew's version is clearly the earlier one but even it has undergone some development. He interprets Jesus' story as a parousia parable, although not incorrectly like Luke (cf. its setting in the context of 24:32—25:13 and 25:31-46). The watchfulness enjoined in v. 13 provides the cue, a fact obscured in English by the understandable omission of the postpositive *gar* of v. 14 (which begins, literally, "For, like a man on a journey . . .").

Without its allegorical additions the story tells of a rich man who expects the successful investment of his funds in his absence. Failure to invest by his slaves is interpreted as laziness, the offender receiving the kind of obloquy that the little man is used to from the rich and powerful: "Why didn't you take some initiative, since I never encouraged you to take any initiative?" Jesus' original tale had to do with self-preservation as the first law of life and inertia as the first step toward economic death. Matthew's interpretation (v. 29) of Jesus' meaning is not too wide of the mark: "Them as has, gits."

The evangelist cannot restrain himself, however, from adding some allegorical details about Christ and the last days. Thus, in vv. 21 and 23, in the phrase, "Enter into your master's joy!" the master in question is surely Christ, the joy the bliss of the final age. Similarly, the command to "throw this worthless slave into the outer darkness" is not the utterance of an exasperated man of means but made to be a word of Christ, the final arbiter in the final age.

Once again, the principle is sustained that Jesus told marvelous stories before he began to get a little help from his friends.

❧ ❧

Proper 29 [34] Reign of Christ or Christ the King / Thirty-fourth or Last Sunday of the Year (A) Sunday between November 20 and November 26, inclusive

Ezekiel 34:11-16, 20-24[11-12, 15-17]

This chapter contains a severe indictment of Israel's rulers under the figure of shepherds (for this verbal convention, cf. 1 Kgs 22:17; Jer 23:16; Mic 5:3). Their crime was that they fleeced and slaughtered their flocks for their own gain. Chapter 34 was probably written retrospectively with reference to the fall of Jerusalem. In the present pericope the Lord says that he himself will do what the rulers failed to do: retrieve the scattered flock from "clouds and thick darkness"—signs of the threatening "day of the Lord"—and bring them to good pastures on the mountain heights of Israel (vv. 12f.). The first 18 verses of John 10 may derive from this passage. Surely today's Gospel reading from Matthew, whatever its original form, was beholden to v. 17.

It is interesting to observe that the LORD will not judge between sheep and goats (who often pasture side by side) but between sheep and sheep, between tough old rams and kid goats. Some have seen in this passage a reference to the mid-fifth-century situation described in Neh 5:1-5. There, Jew preys upon Jew by letting the (Persian) king's tax be levied on a landless peasantry. As a result, the latter have to pawn off their own children in order to eat. In Ezekiel's image the emphasis is on predators of the same stock or kind, not two different kinds.

LM surely includes this passage in order to set the stage for the second and third readings on the last judgment. Verse 17 acts as a special cue for the Gospel pericope. RCL wisely proceeds to the cruel ravaging within the flock (vv. 20ff.) and holds out hope: a David figure of the future will pasture them as a good shepherd ought (vv. 23f.).

The stern judgment on Israel's political leaders (here not the prophets or priests) sees them as fat sheep bullying the lean and weak ones, but it is the latter the LORD shall save from being ravaged. How? By raising up a Davidic figure among them who will do the work of a prince (v. 24).

PSALM 100 OR 95:1-7A

PSALM 23:1-3, 5-6

The Lord is my shepherd; there is nothing I shall want.

EPHESIANS 1:15-23

For a commentary on this lection see Ascension of the Lord (A).

1 CORINTHIANS 15:20-26, 28

Paul has been dealing earlier in this chapter with the special problem of the Corinthian enthusiasts, namely, their conviction that they need not die and rise since, by faith and baptism, they already live "risen lives." After arguing carefully the causal relationship between Christ's having been upraised and their need to be, he moves on to today's passage.

In v. 20 he uses the agricultural figure "first fruits," the early presage of a grain harvest. Possibly he is thinking of the actual season of Passover, at which time the first fruits of grain are being offered in the Temple. It was at this mid-point of the month of Nisan that Christ rose from the dead. Paul will return later (Rom 5:12-17) to this theme of an unredeemed humanity from Adam, who fathered it in death, and a redeemed one whose begetter to life is Christ (v. 22).

The apostle's vision of the final resurrection is of an event that will be both "in proper order" (v. 23) and in stages ("Christ then," v. 23; "then," v. 24; "when" . . . "then," v. 28—a succession of adverbs of time preceded by Christ's coming). The "end" follows the destruction of all cosmic powers inimical to God (v. 25), of which death is the last (v. 26). There is evidently, therefore, a period of the intermediate reign of Christ. The "end" will bring the final and total reign of God. Verse 27 quotes Ps 8:6, while v. 25 is redolent of Ps 110:1.

The imagery contained here is very probably that of several Jewish apocalypses that envision first, "the days of the Messiah," then "the age to come" or "the end." It is clear that, at this coming, "all those who belong to Christ" (v. 23) will be raised up. There is no teaching about the fate of the reprobate, if in fact there are any—those not "in Christ."

Needless to say, vv. 24-28 had a lively history in the subordinationist controversies of the fourth century. C. S. C. Williams (in *PC*, 964) traces the creedal phrase "and of his kingdom there shall be no end" to a refutation of Marcellus of Ancyra, who held that v. 24 meant that there would be an end to Christ's kingdom.

God's being "all in all" (v. 8) is Paul's way of expressing the complete divine dominion. There is no need to deny that this will be achieved by the total interpenetration by God of the creation. What is needed to make it a final reality is the submission of "even our rebellious wills."

Alleluia. Mark 11:10

Blessed is he who inherits the kingdom of David our Father; blessed is he who comes in the name of the Lord.

Matthew 25:31-46

This passage offers a vision of God's judgment "by a man whom God has appointed" (Acts 17:31). The Son of Man, come in his glory (v. 31), is the king (v. 31) and the judge (v. 32). His action answers perfectly the problem posed by Matthew's Gospel, "What should the community addressed by it be doing about discipleship until the Lord returns?" The answer lies in helping those in need. They represent the Lord. All that Israel's rulers did not do (cf. the commentary on Ezekiel above), this segment of Israel must do. Their performance, even if totally acceptable to Christ, will be so "secular" and natural that they will not be aware of its virtuous character (cf. vv. 37ff.). The same is true of the unacceptable behavior of the negligent (v. 44). If the severe judgment on them is to be just, they must have heard another word of Jesus: "On the day of judgment you will have to give an account for every careless word you utter" (Matt 12:36).

The norm of judgment is works of mercy. It accords well with Matthew's concern for the "little ones" (18:16, 10, 14) who will find forgiveness only if "each of you forgives his brother from his heart" (18:35). The norm creates a problem for those Christians who consider faith alone as saving and are scandalized by a Jewish concern for works.

A second problem arises: Is this a vision of the final judgment of the human race or only of the judgment of Christians? Matthew intended to answer the question of what to do till the Messiah comes. He has unconsciously given God's answer concerning all. Serving one's fellow mortals is the behavior that leads to salvation, even if one happens to be in that great company that has never heard of a saving Gospel.

It seems fitting to observe how well the various lectionaries have caught the spirit of the kingship (i.e., messiahship) of Christ in biblical categories.

❧❧

All Saints [A, B, C in Lectionary for Mass]
November 1 or the First Sunday in November

REVELATION 7:[2-4], 9[14]-17

Six seals on a scroll that had been handed to the Lamb by the One who sat on the throne (cf. Rev 5:7) were opened in chap. 6. At the beginning of chap. 8 (v. 1), the Lamb opens the seventh seal. Hence the present chapter, 7, represents an interruption like the interruption between the sixth and seventh trumpet blasts of 9:13 and 11:15. The four angels restraining the earth's winds (v. 1) at its four corners (*gōnías*) are from Ezek 7:2 and 37:9. The corners, not the compass-points, are normally sources of destruction as in 7:2 rather than of life (restored to dry bones), as in 37:9. The underlying concept is the apocalyptic Jewish one of spirits charged with control of the elements. In v. 1 they achieve a calm on the earth.

This calm sets the stage for imprinting the seal (*sphragís*) of the living God on the foreheads of his servants (vv. 2-4), once the land and sea and trees have been forcibly stilled. God's enemies, represented by locusts (9:4), will be commanded to spare those thus sealed, just as the Israelites who bore the bloodmark on their houses were rendered immune from being struck down in Egypt (cf. Exod 12:13). Ezekiel 9:4 with its symbolism of the Hebrew letter *taw* on the brows of mourners—rendered in NAB by the more familiar English "X"—is probably the source of this saving sign. The "seal" of this chapter will be specified as the name of the Lamb and of his Father in 14:1 (if the reference there is to the same group) and 22:4. The word *sphragís* emerges in the mid-second century as a term for baptism, a sealing of the faith begun in repentance, according to the researches of F. J. Dölger (*Sphragis*, 1911).

The completion of God's people is represented by the squaring of twelve, the number of the tribes, and multiplication by a thousand (v. 4). In their own minds believers in Christ were the authentic Israel. The omission of the tribe of Dan is a puzzle, as is the listing of Manasseh where we should have expected Ephraim or his father, Joseph (cf. Gen 48:13f., 17-19; 49:16f, 22). Yet Hebrew literature, including the Bible, lists the twelve tribes in a variety of namings and sequences. Judah no doubt comes first (v. 5) because Jesus descends from him. It is not certain that the celibates *(parthénoi)* of 14:4, probably a figure for martyrs, are identical with the believers of chapter 7, although the number is the same.

The 144,000 are the "huge crowd" assembled from every "nation and race, people and tongue" (v. 9). The vision of vv. 9-17 is undoubtedly meant to strengthen fearful Christians against their own "great trial" (v. 14), an anticipation of the final apocalyptic engagement. The martyrs have survived in the sense that they have kept their faith and their honor. The white robes and palm branches are signs of a victory already achieved. Joining angels and others around the throne, the victors sing the praises of God (v. 12) in a phrase reminiscent of Ps 3:9 which says, "Salvation is the LORD's!"

The entire vision could very well be Jewish, with "the Lamb" substituted for "God" in vv. 9, 10, and 14, martyrdom being signified by the phrase, "made white [i.e., resplendent, glorious] in blood."

PSALM 34:1-10, 22

PSALM 24:1-6

LORD, this is the people that longs to see your face.

1 JOHN 3:1-3

Verse 1 is an utterance of joyous amazement that God should have made those who receive the Son to be God's children (cf. John 1:12). The Johannine "world" can no more recognize this sonship in us than it did in him (v. 1). Spiritual likeness to God, which is the present reality, is perhaps being identified as the cause of an even greater likeness, when full light and the vision of the Son reveal him as he is. The Son is "pure" (*hagnós*, v. 3), he is sinless (cf. vv. 5, 7, 8). That is why our hope is based on him (v. 3).

While it is certain that such claims of sinlessness are being made for Christ, it is doubtful that v. 6a means to reprobate a heretical position adhered to by some who are "in him." It is even less likely that the statement, "The man who remains in him does not sin," is itself heretical. What cannot be denied, however, is that the Johannine literature reflects the convictions of a particular group distinguished from others that do not have its faith in Jesus as the Christ.

ALLELUIA. MATTHEW 11:28

Come to me, all you who labor and are burdened, and I will give you rest, says the LORD.

MATTHEW 5:1–12[A]

See 4 Epiphany [4] (A) for a commentary.

✍✍

Thanksgiving Day
Fourth Thursday in November (United States)
Second Monday in October (Canada)

DEUTERONOMY 8:7-18

For a commentary on the symbolism of manna see The Body and Blood of Christ (A). Fidelity to the commandments of the LORD will alone befit residence in the rich land the forty-year wanderers are about to enter. It is rich not only in agricultural products but mineral deposits as well (vv. 6-13). Once settled there, the people may think they have done it all themselves and forget the God whose rich gift the land has been to them. The United States and Canada are lands more richly endowed than many on the globe. Robert Frost's *The Gift Outright*, which he recited at President Kennedy's inauguration, is an unconscious parody of this portion of Ezekiel. It assumes that we gave the land to ourselves—by conquest westward.

PSALM 65

2 CORINTHIANS 9:6-15

Many a church notice board has borne the Pauline legend, "The Lord loveth a cheerful giver" (9:7). The apostle was quoting Prov 22:8a in the LXX (v. 9a in the MT) as part of his encouragement to the church at Corinth to give to his collection for the famine-stricken Christian Jews of Palestine (v. 13). The *hilaròn dótēn* of his appeal easily became *hilárem datorem* in Latin-speaking Italy and North Africa. The biblical verse in Hebrew continues, "for [the generous] share their bread with the poor." Paul prefers to quote Ps 112:9, changing "the generous who lend" of v. 5a to God as the one who "scatters abroad, giving to the poor; his righteousness endures forever" (2 Cor 9:9). The thought continues with God as the giver of seed and bread (v. 10, from Isa 55:10), multiplying not only it but a harvest of good works (v. 8) and righteousness (v. 10). The only proper response to the divine generosity is thanksgiving for the many gifts and a matching gift-giving to supply the needs of the fellow baptized (*tōn hagíōn*, v. 12) and all others (v. 13). This passage is a remarkable interweaving of the themes of gratitude for the divine largesse and the openhandedness that must be the response in thanksgiving. Preaching on it on this day should not foster guilt for family feasting but inspire increased giving as the best mode of thanks.

LUKE 17:11-19

For a commentary see Proper 23 [28] (C).

YEAR B

❧ Season of Advent ❧

❧❧
First Sunday of Advent (B)

ISAIAH 64:1-9

Isaiah 56–66, known as Trito-Isaiah, are the work of disciples of Deutero-Isaiah, now back in Palestine from Babylonian exile. There are numerous disparate poems in the collection, with themes from various periods in Israel's history. Isaiah 64:1-9 is chosen to lead off the Advent season for two reasons: (1) its cry of repentance for sin, a motif that goes back to the days when Advent was observed as "St. Martin's Lent" (November 11), preparation for the Nativity revels (vv. 5b-9a), and (2) its demand that the LORD come down from the heavens (v. 1; cf. v. 3) to make the Gentile nations tremble at the divine presence. Advent is about a twofold coming, God's glorious descent in Christ from heaven to earth at the end of days and the commemoration/expectation of the infant Savior's coming. This is a season of waiting (v. 4)—but impatient waiting (v. 1), with the hope that our iniquities (v. 6) will not impede the hoped-for advent. Mark uses the verb for rend or tear *(schizeîn)* to describe the heavens at the descent of the Spirit-dove (Mark 1:10), a rendering of the Hebrew *kara'* in the second half of Isa 63:19. Paul's oft-quoted phrase employs 64:4 (3 in NAB) at 1 Cor 2:9a, followed by his commentary on it in the remainder of the verse, to describe what God has revealed to us through the Spirit (1 Cor 2:10). Isaiah speaks of those who "wait" on the one who performs such marvelous deeds while Paul makes it read: those who "love" God. In the spirit of the fourth week of Advent, when Jesus' conception in Mary's womb is first spoken of (Luke 1:26-38), the Isaiah lection is about an "awesome deed that we did not expect" (v. 3[2]).

PSALM 80:1-7, 17-19

Isaiah 63:16b-17; 19b; 64:2-7

This passage, part of a long prayer of intercession that runs from 63:7 to 64:11, is noteworthy chiefly for the use made of v. 4 [3bc] by Paul in 1 Cor 2:9: "What no eye has seen, nor ear heard, nor the human heart conceived, what God has prepared for those who love him." The postexilic prophet centers his attention on what God has done in recent times. Paul makes v. 64:4 refer to God's mysterious, hidden wisdom that planned all that happened in Christ not long before. The preparation God has made for all who love him includes for Paul the mystery of the cross and resurrection. Many have been invited by God's recent revelation to share in this wisdom. The verse of Third Isaiah and the use Paul makes of it are therefore not too far separated. The one plan of God has been revealed in two stages. The unintended but widely held conclusion that a life to come is being spoken of by Paul would be still a third.

The "invasion of your holy place" (NAB) and "trampling down of your sanctuary" in 63:18 could provide a valuable clue to dating the prayer if the event were able to be identified; the same is true of 64:10 [9], "Zion is a wilderness, Jerusalem a desolation." A deserted city anywhere between 586 and 620 is as close as we are likely to come.

Verse 16 praises God for faithful fatherhood even though the patriarchs Abraham and Israel (Jacob), who gave the people its name, should desert them. Compare 49:15 for the similar figure of a mother forgetting the child of her womb. No longer do "the tribes that are your heritage fear the Lord" (63:17); the prophet pleads that the hardening of hearts which "causes" this should stop.

This intercessory prayer contains not only historical reminiscence (63:11f.) but praise of God as well. The Lord is reminded by the composer of his triumphs in the past (64:2f.) so that he will wreak a little havoc in the present (v. 1). There is, however, a catch which keeps the Lord from acting. The sinfulness of the people prevents it. They have forgotten their Father (v. 8 [7]), the one who works them like a potter his clay (ibid.).

The appeal in this prayer is based on an election made long ago. The Lord is Israel's age-old ransomer (*go'el*, 63:15; cf. 43:3; 63:1) who comes to save. He does so neither by a messenger nor an angel but by coming himself (63:9b). The people grieve his holy spirit (vv. 10a, 11c) which he has sent to "guide them / give them rest" (v. 14). Nothing good can be hoped for until the Lord turns back (v. 17c) for the sake of his servants. He must "tear open the heavens and come down" (64:1/63:19b, the phrase that accounts for the choice of this pericope as an Advent reading). The Lord is pleaded with to forget his anger at the people's iniquities for, after all, they are *his* people (64:9). The first two Sundays of Advent look forward to the final days, the third to the Baptist's witness. Only with the fourth is Jesus' birth foretold.

Psalm 80:1-7, 17-19[2-3b, 15-16, 18-19]

Lord, make us turn to you, let us see your face and we shall be saved.

1 Corinthians 1:3-9

Verse 3 of Paul's introduction grows increasingly familiar to the modern ear as a greeting of presider to people in a number of revised eucharistic services.

The reason for Paul's continued expression of thanks in v. 4 (*Eucharistó* is "Thanks" in modern Greek, *Parakaló*, "You're welcome," literally, "I beg you") is the favor *(charis)* bestowed in Christ Jesus. Speech *(logos)* and knowledge *(gnōsis)* are part of the resulting enrichment (v. 5). God has followed up Paul's initial witness in Corinth with gifts of every sort (v. 6) bestowed on a community that awaits the final revealing *(apokálypsis,* v. 7) of Christ. The strength God gives will find the Corinthians blameless "on the day" (v. 8). The initial call was to have all things in common with Christ *(koinōnía,* v. 9); God's utter fidelity will ensure this.

Despite the concentration on Christ and the gifts given in him, Paul's thanksgivings, like his theology, remain theocentric.

Alleluia. Psalm 85:8

Lord, show us your love; grant us your salvation.

Mark 13:24[33]-37

This chapter is a warning delivered by Mark to his contemporaries of all that must precede the coming of Jesus in glory (cf. 2 Thess 2:1-2) under his Danielic title, "Son of Man" (Mark 13:26; Dan 7:13), a title elaborated by several noncanonical works like *1 Enoch*. No one is to be believed, Mark says, who proclaims that the Messiah has come (vv. 21ff.). The dominant theory on this chapter is that the evangelist had access to an apocalyptic scenario of the final days of the kind widely circulating in the two centuries at the turn of the millennium, into which he has inserted at v. 14 details from 2 Macc 6:2 (the "desolating sacrilege" of v. 14, echoing Dan 8:13; 9:27, the statue of Olympian Zeus set up in the Temple by Antiochus IV), and the panic that would attend the approach of the Roman army in 70 or has already done so (vv. 14-20). The occurrence of the passage on 1 Lent is related to that of Zephaniah on Proper 28 [33] (A), as explained there. Today opens the Markan year in the three lectionaries, a Gospel little proclaimed publicly in the West until LM was promulgated in 1969, on the erroneous assumption that it was an abbreviation of Matthew which had all of Mark's content. Advent 1 invites worshipers to reflect on the culmination of all human and cosmic history, in the center of which the human one Jesus Christ will come in glory. Neither the angels nor even the Son knows when that will be (nor do self-confident astrophysicists with their cosmic projections about entropy). God has kept that secret like the mystery of death itself. But that it will come to pass Christian faith is sure.

Jesus' eschatological injunction to watchfulness (cf. Matt 24:42; 25:13) is illustrated by two brief parables, that of v. 34 (cf. Matt 25:14) and that of vv. 35f (cf. Luke 12:38). The first also bears a resemblance to Luke 19:12f. Like the master's unexpected return, God's reign will come when it is least expected. That is true of the many comings of Jesus Christ into our lives and not only that of the Last Day.

❧ ✐
Second Sunday of Advent (B)
ISAIAH 40:1[5, 9]-11

The opening poem in the collection of oracles (chaps. 40–55) that hail the rise of Cyrus and the imminent liberation of Israel (538 B.C.) features the coming of God with power. His release of the people Israel from captivity is spoken of under the figures of ruling by his strong arm (v. 10), feeding his flock like a shepherd, and "carrying the lambs in his bosom" (v. 11). Salvation is imminent. Release from exile is predicted as certain.

Second Isaiah in v. 2 asks God for gentleness toward Jerusalem, meaning the people in its exiled condition. The punishment that was brought on by the LORD, "refining your dross in the furnace, removing all your alloy" (1:25) is described as twice as severe as the crime. The LORD was the sentencing judge but he is also the pardoner: "For a brief moment I abandoned you, / but with great tenderness I will take you back" (54:7). The references are, of course, to the punishment of exile in Babylon.

The voice that speaks to the prophet is that of some kind of herald from the heavenly court (40:3). It introduces the theme of a royal road *(derek)*, a highway that the LORD will traverse at the head of his people. The road-building operation of v. 4 is required for the theophany to follow, the manifestation of "the glory of the LORD" (v. 5) walking at the head of the people in their triumphal return. All humankind, despite its weak condition (vv. 6f.), will witness this glory in a display of unity and solidarity. The word of God will supply strength to human weakness (v. 8).

A portion of the people ("Zion," "Jerusalem," v. 9) is selected to transmit the glad tidings of deliverance to the whole people. There is no place for fear. The coming with power of the LORD who is God rules it out (v. 10).

PSALM 85:1-2, 8-13[9-14]

LORD, let us see your kindness, and grant us your salvation.

2 PETER 3:8[-14]15A

The author of this tract, self-consciously derivative from Jude and the latest New Testament book to be received into the canon, attempts to assure his readers ("beloved"/"dear friends," v. 8) about the delay of the *parousía*. What some call delay is not that at all (v. 9), he says, since the Lord's time-schedule is so unlike that of humans (v. 8); Ps 90:4 is quoted here. Rather than being neglectful of the world, the Lord is providing ample opportunity for repentance. His delay or slowness (v. 9) is simply an example of his forbearance.

Jesus had likened the coming of the Son of Man to a thief breaking in (Matt 24:43; Luke 12:39); the figure turns up as a staple in early catechesis (1 Thess 5:2; Rev 3:3; 16:16). When the surprise occurrence of the End takes place it will be marked by cosmic catastrophe. Only in 2 Peter in the New Testament does the idea appear that the world will be destroyed by fire (vv. 7, 10, 12), an Iranian eschatological concept found in late Jewish lore in the Sibylline Oracles and the Qumrân writings and in Stoic literature (the doctrine of *ekpýrōsis*). This impending catastrophe is held out as a motivation for living well (vv. 11f.). It will be succeeded by "new heavens and a new earth" (v. 13; cf. Isa 65:17; 66:22), the setting for a period of God's justice. The certain coming of the new order requires special efforts on the part of believers to be found without blemish and at peace (v. 14).

ALLELUIA. LUKE 3:4 AND 6

Prepare the way of the Lord, make straight his paths; all humankind shall see the salvation of God.

MARK 1:1-8

Mark is the inventor of the literary form "gospel" as we know it—sayings interwoven with a continuous narrative. He even uses the term (1:1), deriving it from Second Isaiah's use of glad tidings, in Old English *gōd spel* (see Isa 40:1-11, above) but also probably with a view to the Roman imperial cult. An inscription of 9 B.C. from Priene south of Ephesus reads: "The birthday of the god was for the world the beginning of the tidings of joy [*euaggelion*] on his account." Mark is convinced that Jesus is a person deserving divine honors, the very "Son of God" (1:1, a phrase lacking in some early manuscripts).

Mark cites Isaiah but quotes a conflated version of Mal 3:1 and Isa 40:3, probably taken from some early preacher's handbook or "book of testimonies." The messenger of preparation for the last age was popularly taken to be Elijah. Certainly John is described in terms reminiscent of the Tishbite (cf. 2 Kings 1:8; cf. Zech 13:4 for the prophets and prophets' "hairy mantle"). His message is one of repentance. The one "more powerful than I" in the struggle against the common foe is Jesus. Later (3:27, following Isa 49:24ff.) Mark will designate Satan as "the strong one" against whom Jesus struggles and whom he succeeds in binding and plundering. The plunging of penitents in the Jordan River is but a prelude, says Mark, to the baptism in the Holy Spirit of the last age.

Perhaps the most remarkable parallel to Mark's baptismal narrative is the *Testament of Levi* (second century B.C.), a Hebrew document that probably contains Christian interpolations: "The heavens shall be opened, and from the temple of glory shall come upon him sanctification, with the Father's voice as from Abraham to Isaac. And the glory of the Most High shall be uttered over him, and the spirit of understanding and sanctification shall rest upon him. . . . And Beliar shall be bound by him, and he shall give power to his children to tread upon evil spirits" (see Mark 1:10, 25ff.).

In short, Mark's opening verses convey his conviction that the cosmic struggle is joined and with it the preparation for the messianic age inaugurated.

❧ ⁊

Third Sunday of Advent (B)

ISAIAH 61:1[2A]-4, 8[10]-11

The postexilic poet-prophet views himself as one invested with God's spirit, an anointed individual who has been sent (the verb is *shalaḥ*, from which *shalíaḥ*, an "apostle," derives). The "lowly" of v. 1, *anawim*, are the pious poor rather than the economically depressed. The glad tidings brought to them are those of freedom in the ancient homeland, discouraging though the daily work of restoration may be. Third Isaiah is perhaps capitalizing on an actual year of jubilee in v. 2 (cf. Lev 25:10) to teach the true nature of redemption. Comfort is in store for the mourners in Zion. The year 538 was a year of vindication in a special way but God's continuing, providential care is such a figurative year. In vv. 10-11 the jubilant groom and bride decked out for their wedding and the fruitful earth are the symbols of salvation, justice, and peace. This lyrical outburst is different in quality from the verses with which the chapter opens, but it hymns the same reality: a release from the hardships and inequities of postexilic life.

PSALM 126 OR LUKE 1:47[46-50, 53]-55

1 THESSALONIANS 5:16-24

The apostle's invitation to rejoice is the same verb in the plural as Gabriel's greeting to Mary in Luke 1:28, *chaírete* (v. 16). This injunction to eschatological joy derives from LXX usage. Paul goes on to suggest unceasing prayer and thanksgiving as God's will for believers (vv. 17f.). He hints at trials (3:13) and the grief of loss (4:13) in the Thessalonians' lives. The counsel given about not quenching the spirit (19ff.) may be a general one but it may also hint at resistance to claims for special gifts of prophecy. Paul does not wish them to be rejected out of hand. He does propose, however, a critical spirit with regard to them.

God is faithful (v. 24). Therefore the God who first called the Thessalonians will preserve them until the Lord Jesus' return. "Spirit, soul, and body" (v. 23) was the ordinary way of the times to say "whole and entire." We would say "in soul and body."

ALLELUIA. ISAIAH 61:1 (CITED IN LUKE 4:18)

The Spirit of the LORD is upon me, who has sent me to bring Good News to the poor.

JOHN 1:6-8, 19-28

The lectionary separates out some verses (but not all; 12b, 13, 15, 17-18) which are widely thought to be prose insertions into a poem adapted by the editor of the gospel to refer to Jesus Christ (v. 17).

A distinction is made between John, son of Zechariah, as witness to the light and Christ "the true light" (v. 9). The light is real or true in the Platonic sense of a heavenly paradigm but more in the Hebraic sense of that which God has done. NAB and NRSV have the true light "coming into the world" (v. 9) but, since the participle "coming" agrees with both "human being" in the accusative and the neuter noun for "light" in the nominative, other translations have had the true light giving light to "every human coming into the world." Context alone suggests the choice. Verse 10 has the "true light" "in the world," which makes it reasonable to assume that the previous verse has described *his* coming into the world.

The catechetical exchange between John and "priests and Levites" from Jerusalem (v. 19) is an early indication that the Fourth Gospel *may* preserve the better historical reminiscence of Jesus' traditional opponents in that city. The Synoptics, beginning with Mark, feature "scribes and Pharisees," a probable echo of the later opponents of those who believe in Jesus. The questioners are *hoi Ioudaîoi*. All modern translations render this as "the Jews" but the translation is inadequate. In thirty-four cases in John's gospel it seems to mean simply that, namely, Jewish people and their customs most often, (e.g., 1:19; 11:19; 18:33). Thirty-seven times, however, it is the evangelist's syncopated way of referring to Jews in positions of authority but meaning for John "those Jews in his day who opposed the Jewish believers in Jesus." In either instance, whether neutral or hostile, *Ioudaîoi* can be rendered correctly as "the Judeans" (even in chap. 6), the people of the southern province where Bethany lay and the seat of Jewish political power, learning, and worship. The evangelist's first chapter builds up to a succession of titles of Jesus (vv. 34-51), including "messiah" (v. 41). Here that title is denied to John (v. 20), as are "Elijah" come back to life (v. 21; cf. Mal 4:5; 3:24) and "the prophet" (cf. Deut 18:15; Acts 3:22).

John is made to quote Isa 40:3 in testimony to himself, he becoming the herald's "voice." He baptizes with water (v. 26) in performance of a lesser task. After him will come the greater (v. 27) who baptizes in the Holy Spirit (v. 33).

See commentary on John 1:1-18 for Nativity of the Lord, Mass at Midnight, Proper 1.

❧ ❧

Fourth Sunday of Advent (B)

2 SAMUEL 7:1-11[1-5, 8B-11], 16

This pericope contains the so-called "dynastic oracle" that legitimated the throne and house of David for all time to come. It occurs in a chapter that stands apart from the rest of the book in which it appears. David was a commoner (1 Sam 16:12f.) who, after the murder of Ishbaal, son of Saul (2 Sam 4:7), was anointed king (5:1-5). The prophet Nathan is here described as David's intermediary with God. No priest is consulted; indeed, David himself has worn the priestly apron (*ephod*, 6:14) while dancing before the ark of the LORD.

The word for "house" has at least a twofold meaning: dwelling-place and Temple. It can also signify family line. The LORD tells Nathan that he has never had a house (dwelling place) in all the people's desert wanderings (vv. 6f.) but now he will establish a house for Nathan (v. 11b) in the sense of offspring or posterity (seed, v. 12b). David is promised that he will be God's son (v. 14a). The divine favor will never pass from him as it did from Saul (v. 15); it will somehow be permanent in character.

Texts like 2 Sam 23:5; Ps 89:28f.; and Isa 55:3 show how the tradition of the commitment of the LORD to David and his house has entered into the religious-political life of the people with the force of a covenant like that made with the patriarchs of old.

LUKE 1:47-55 OR PSALM 89:1-4, 19, 26[2-5, 27, 29]

ROMANS 16:25-27

These three verses, the conclusion of the epistle, take the form of a doxology in which glory is invoked as God's due forever through Jesus Christ, in familiar Pauline binitarian fashion. As part of the description of the God who strengthens, mention is made of the *mystērion* long hidden but now made known to the Gentiles. This is none other than the "plan," "counsel," or "will" of Eph 1:9 (where it is also called a "mystery") and the "mystery" of Col 1:26, 27; 2:2. It signifies what God long intended to do and now has done: manifest himself through a death and resurrection culminating in "Christ in you, your hope of glory" (Col 1:27).

The Pauline literature, broadly taken, has the term "mystery" in twenty-one places. This secret of God is now gloriously being revealed among the Gentiles through the preaching of the apostles.

LUKE 1:26-38

See commentary on the Feast of [Mary's] Immaculate Conception in her Mother's Womb, December 8, under Feasts of Jesus, Mary, and the Saints following Year C.

❧ Season of Christmas ❧

The Nativity of the Lord / The Vigil Mass / Proper 1 (B)

ISAIAH 62:1-5

See 2 Epiphany [2](C).

PSALM 89:4-5, 16-17, 27, 29

Forever I will sing the goodness of the LORD.

ACTS 13:16-17, 22-25

Luke has Paul proclaim Jesus, of David's posterity, a Savior, in a synagogue of Antioch in Galatian Phrygia.

ALLELUIA

Tomorrow . . . the Savior of the world will be our king.

MATTHEW 1:1-25

See 4 Advent (A).

✺✹
The Nativity of the Lord / Mass at Midnight / Proper I (A, B, C)

ISAIAH 9:2-7[1-6]

See commentary under Proper 1 (A).

PSALM 96

TITUS 2:11-14

See commentary under Proper 1 (A).

LUKE 2:1-14, (15-20)

See commentary under Proper 1 (A).

✺✹
The Nativity of the Lord / Mass at Dawn / Proper II (A, B, C)

ISAIAH 62:6[11]-12

See 2 Epiphany [2](C) for a commentary on Isa 62:1-5.

The nations shall see Jerusalem's vindication upon her people's return from exile (vv. 1-2). A crown shall she be in the hand of the LORD, a diadem (v. 3). New names shall be hers, no longer "Forsaken" or "Desolate" (vv. 4f.). The figure of Jerusalem "My Delight" as a bride means that "my delight is in her *(Hephzibah)*" and it is to the LORD that the land is "Married," *"Beulah."* Viewed as a city, she has sentinels who must remind her builder constantly that it is his business to make her renowned. Her products are not to be for export or exacted as tribute but are for home consumption (vv. 8f.). Everything must be done to let this city's own people enter it freely so that they may be a holy people, a "banner to the Gentiles" (*nes ammim*, the name of a long-enduring kibbutz in Israel, the work of Dutch Protestants). But why all this as an Advent reading? Attend! "See (v. 11b), your Salvation comes." Christians know that the name of their salvation is Christ Jesus.

PSALM 97[1, 6, 11-12]

TITUS 3:4-7

NAB sets these verses in type assuming them to be the lyric of an early hymn. It speaks of God's appearing *(epipháneia)* in Jesus Christ to be the world's savior through newness of life in baptism (v. 5b), made just by God's gift and not any human doing (vv. 5a, 7).

LUKE 2:(1-7), 8-20[14]

For Luke 2:1-14, see Nativity of the Lord, Mass at Midnight; and for Luke 2:15[16]-21, The Holy Name of Jesus/Mary Mother of God, January 1.
    See commentaries under Proper II (A).

❧☙
The Nativity of the Lord / Mass during the Day/ Proper III (A, B, C)

ISAIAH 52:7-10; PSALM 98[1-6]; HEBREWS 1:1-4, (5-12)[1-6]; JOHN 1:1-14[18]. SEE UNDER PROPER III (A).

❧☙
First Sunday after Christmas

ISAIAH 61:10—62:3

See commentaries under 3 Advent (B) and 2 Epiphany [2](C).

PSALM 148

GALATIANS 4:4-7

See commentary under Solemnity of Mary, Mother of God (A).

Luke 2:22-40

Luke has reported on Jesus' circumcision (2:21; cf. Lev 12:3) as also on that of John the Baptizer (1:59). He continues with an account of the rituals for male infancy prescribed in the Mosaic books, "everything required by the Law of the Lord" (2:39). While he is convinced of the importance of Jesus' Jewishness for his own people (v. 32b), he is no less concerned to tell of his importance for the whole human race (v. 32a). The story of the boy Samuel's presentation by his previously childless parents to the priest Eli at Shiloh is very much in Luke's mind as he makes Mary echo Hannah's song (1:46-55; cf. 1 Sam 2:1-10). Just as that priest judge and his parents were paragons of fidelity to Torah, so is this later couple and so will their son be. But Jesus' Law observance will be for Luke a way to reach out to the Gentile world. The precept requiring the consecration to God of the firstborn male, man or beast, is found in Exod 13:1-2 with no mention of how or where it is to be done. Luke conflates it with the precept enjoining ritual purification (not ethical) of a mother after childbirth (see Lev 12:2-8). The language of the Hebrew and Luke's Greek, faithfully rendered in all vernacular translations as "made clean" and "atonement," gives the impression that this Semitic people thought nature's course to be somehow reprehensible. Quite the opposite is true. The observance had to do with the marvel of menstrual flow in the production of new life, just as male seed was (erroneously) thought to be solely responsible for it once deposited in the womb. The Jews thought nothing about sex "unclean" in the modern manner.

This long pericope features who Jesus is and is to be, with the ritual observance as its setting. Luke balances out the sexes as he will do throughout his Gospel and the follow-up book of Acts. Old Simeon is a layman, not a priest. The Gospel writer sees in him a long awaiting Israel encountering the Lord's "salvation" in this tiny child. The name given to the infant means "Ya saves" (Yeshu-[y]a, 1:31). The child's growth, a matter of wisdom and divine favor, is similarly patterned on that of the boy Samuel (2:40; cf. 1 Sam 2:26). P. G. Wodehouse in one of his novels about Bertie Wooster and Jeeves mentions that no Protestant household in early twentieth century England was without its statuette of the boy Samuel bearing the legend beneath. "Speak, Lord! Your servant heareth."

For further commentary see Presentation of the Lord (A, B, C), February 2.

❧❧
The Holy Family

SIRACH 3:2-6, 12-14

For commentaries on this and Colossians see under A.

PSALM 128:1-5

COLOSSIANS 3:12-21

ALLELUIA. COLOSSIANS 3:15, 16

LUKE 2:22-40 OR 2:22, 39-40

For a commentary see 1 Christmas above.

❧❧
Holy Name of Jesus / Solemnity of Mary, Mother of God / Octave of Christmas (A, B, C)

NUMBERS 6:22-27

PSALM 67:2-3, 5-6, 8

GALATIANS 4:4-7

PHILIPPIANS 2:5-13

LUKE 2:15-21

All as in Year A.

January 1—When observed as New Year's Day (A, B, C)

ECCLESIASTES 3:1-13

The earlier part of this passage is probably a poem the author has come upon or, less likely, composed. Its continuing popularity is a mystery; perhaps this is because it says so little. One wonders when there is a fitting time for killing (v. 3) or for making war (v. 8). Ecclesiastes (Qoheleth) would surely be distressed to learn how often public readings of the passage end at v. 8, since its purpose is to underscore not the meaninglessness of human toil (v. 9) but the mystery of life itself. What, indeed, is God up to in the mystery of time and history? St. Augustine wrestled with the first in Book 11 of his *Confessions (Prayers of Praise)*. He gave up wrestling with the second when he embraced the Gospel, but later turned to it in his *City of God*.

Qoheleth does have an interim solution to his own problem. It is by no means the pursuit of pleasure or the satisfaction taken in work, as might seem to be the case (vv. 13f.). It is that we are meant by God to be happy (v. 12). But so have all the philosophers of the ages concluded. So too did Jesus when he affirmed with the Psalmist: "Happy *(asher/makarios/beatus)* is the one who . . . [does not take the path of sinners, Ps 1:1; hungers and thirsts for justice, Matt 5:6]. The Teacher is neither a pessimist nor a nihilist, as the thoughtless have sometimes concluded. He is a firm believer in Israel's God as the LORD of all human history (vv. 13f.) who is quite sure what to do about the mystery of life (12:13f.).

PSALM 8

REVELATION 21:1-6A

If the choice of Eccl 3:1-13 for public reading on the first day of a new year is self-evident, so should this one be, for it is all about newness of life (v. 1). The new Jerusalem come down from heaven (v. 2) is, of course, the Church, "a bride adorned for her husband" (v. 2; "the wife of the Lamb," v. 9). There is no need of Eph 5:25-27 to clue us in. The framers of RCL may have been motivated in their choice by v. 6, which speaks of God as the LORD of time and history. Still, the beginning of another year is an event in the life of the Church: God's dwelling in human midst in Christ the strong bridegroom and his bride the community of the baptized. Hence, this reading should be preached that way. The poem's promise of the new Jerusalem's return to heaven—where the tears of all eyes will be wiped away, where pain and mourning will be no more and as to death, there's no more dying there—should give hope to those worshipers who have just concluded a pain-filled year. There is a temple of faith that the present writer passes each Sunday on his way to and from his own eucharistic worship service. It is called the Refreshing Spring Community (see v. 6). That is exactly what life in a community of believers should be, "Let anyone who is thirsty come to me, and let the one who believes in me drink" (John 7:37).

MATTHEW 25:31-46

See under Reign of Christ the King, Proper 29 [34] (A).

See The Holy Name of Jesus/Mary Mother of God, January 1.

LUKE 2:22-40[16-21]

❧❧
Second Sunday after Christmas Day (A, B, C)

As in Year A.

JEREMIAH 31:7-14

See Proper 25 [30] (B) for a commentary on vv. 7-9.

The "land of the north" is Assyria in which a "remnant of Israel" (v. 7) has been captive but is now rejoicing in release. The LORD has shown himself a father to Israel/Ephraim (see Exod 4:22; Deut 3:6). It is called "the firstborn" because of the favor now shown it but this does not mean that the southern kingdom is put in second place. The word of Jacob's liberation must be spread far and wide— to the Gentiles, to the farthest isles. The flock scattered by an empire "too strong for it" has been gathered. Its people shall assemble on Zion to sing the LORD's praises. The land shall again yield its products from the tilled fields and its pastures shall once more be host to flocks and herds (v. 12). The sorrow of the people young and old shall be turned into dancing and song (v. 13, a rephrasing of v. 4), the priests once again receiving their rich portion from the sacrifices (v. 14).

Sirach 24:1-12[1-4, 8-12]

The attention of preachers is turned to the portion of Wisdom 6 proposed for Proper 27 [32] (A) in LM for the literary convention of Wisdom personified. It is an attribute or quality of God Most High made to speak for itself, therefore, the voice of the all-wise Lord. The "assembly" or "hosts" of v. 2 are the heavenly court of the Sovereign who fittingly hears his glory sung. This Wisdom once uttered has gone out from its place of origin as the voice of deity to govern all things on the earth and the seas below. The peoples who inhabit the earth are likewise under Wisdom's sway (vv. 6f.). But where on earth should Wisdom properly be lodged? In no better place than Jacob/Israel. The timeless aspect of godhead now dwells in the holy tent of desert days that has been brought to Zion (vv. 9f.). Wisdom has become this people's portion (v. 12; see Ps 16:5), has taken root among them and flourished like the trees and bushes of the land. The sapiental tradition as it is sometimes called is an expression of Torah observance that has its root in Psalms and Proverbs.

Psalm 147:12-20 or Wisdom 10:15-21

Ephesians 1:3-14

See Proper 10 [15] (B) for commentary.

John 1:(1-9), 10-18

See Proper 3, Mass during the Day (A, B, C), for commentary.

Wisdom 10:15-21

Here holy Wisdom is described as the deliverer of the people's oppressor who is evidently Egypt. Moses is then that "servant of the Lord" (if the people itself is not meant) made wise in the power of wonders and signs before the Pharaoh and the tribal chieftains encountered on the desert route to Canaan. Wisdom gives to this people guidance and shelter along the way, drowning its enemies in the Red Sea and despoiling the wicked. Wisdom it is who, once the reward is achieved, inspires hymns of praise from voices muted far too long and tongues of babes held bound.

❧ Season of Epiphany ❧

❧❧
Epiphany of the Lord (A, B, C)

ISAIAH 60:1-6; PSALM 72:1-7, 10-14[2, 7-8, 10-13];
EPHESIANS 3:1-12[2-3A, 5-6]; ALLELUIA, MATTHEW 2:2;
MATTHEW 2:1-12

See commentaries under Epiphany of the Lord (A).

❧❧
Baptism of the Lord [1] (B)

First Sunday after the Epiphany / First Sunday of the Year / Sunday after January 6
   All as in (A)

GENESIS 1:1-5

See Easter Vigil (A, B, C) for commentary.

ISAIAH 42:1-4, 6-7

See commentary under Baptism of the Lord (A).

PSALM 29[1A AND 2, 3AC-4, 3B AND 9B-10]

ACTS 19:1-7

This narrative describes an occurrence on Paul's third journey, as Luke reckons it, which began at 18:23 after "some time" spent in Antioch (via Caesarea). He then went back overland to the areas of Galatia and Phrygia, coming to Ephesus for a second time. His previous stay there had been brief (18:19ff.). Paul would remain in that large port city on the Aegean, long since silted in, more than two years (19:10). It is baffling to know how Apollos could have been instructed in the Way of the Lord and taught about Jesus without having heard of baptism "in the Spirit" (18:25). The same is true of the Ephesians whom Paul comes upon who do not know there is a Holy Spirit. Can both omissions be part of a narrative technique to review for the reader the successive steps in the formation of an evangelizer? Such would seem to be the case. Or is it that Luke wishes to describe Apollos as less well formed than Paul? Paul arrives in Ephesus, to discover there the alarming gap in knowledge of some disciples. Their baptism "in the name of the Lord Jesus" is clearly meant by Luke to distinguish it from that of John. The joining of the rite to the knowledge or gift of the Holy Spirit both here and in 8:16f., where the Spirit is given to the already baptized, and in 10:44, where baptism follows the descent of the Spirit, is an indication of the conjunction of the two rather than their sequence (see 1:5 and 11:16, where "baptism with the Holy Spirit" is used to describe the rite in the infant church). When the gift of the Spirit is spoken of as distinct from baptism (8:16f.; 10:44; 19:1-6) Peter and John, Peter alone, and Paul are the ones who confer it, hence Luke may be making a point of its bestowal as apostolic in origin. Baptism "in the name of the Lord Jesus" may similarly have been the formula Luke was familiar with. It did not survive in the tradition, however, having been eclipsed in the rite by the triune Name of Matt 28:19 and the *Didachē*. It was resurrected in some English-speaking circles early in the twentieth century on the supposition that Acts records the earliest practice of the Church, whereas in fact it is an ingenious Lukan reconstruction. Pentecostal practice stems from congregations in Topeka (1901) and Los Angeles (1906), where it was concluded on a literal reading that water baptism was but a preliminary to baptism in the Spirit. The latter, greater gift, it is thought, brings with it the power to speak in tongues (2:4; 10:46) and to heal as the apostles did (3:7f.; 4:22; 5:15f.). The Pentecostal conviction is that God's arm is not shortened with time. (See Killian McDonnell, O.S.B., *The Baptism of Jesus in the Jordan: The Trinitarian and Cosmic Order of Salvation* [Collegeville, Minn.: Liturgical, 1996]) for a study of the way the Church of East and West in the first five-hundred years appropriated this mystery, its lapse in popular consciousness, and contemporary efforts to restore it.

A pastor I know provides his congregation with inexpensive, half-sized plastic drinking glasses already filled with water on this feast, on which he invokes a blessing in their name. He then asks them to pour the water into any running stream or river they can find ("living water"), to remind themselves of the Lord's baptism and their own. The Cooper and the Delaware rivers are not far.

ACTS 10:34-38

See commentary under Baptism of the Lord (A).

ALLELUIA. SEE MARK 9:6

The heavens were opened and the Father's voice was heard; this is my beloved Son, hear him.

MARK 1:4[7]-11

See commentary under 2 Advent (B); also, check Matt 3:1-12 under 2 Advent (A).

❧ ✍

Second Sunday after the Epiphany [2] / Second Sunday of the Year (B)

I SAMUEL 3:1-10, [3B-10, 19] (11-20)

This reading describes an oracle of the Lord that overtakes the boy Samuel in sleep, calling him to forceful priestly leadership. He is awakened from his place near the ark where he is sleeping, close to the old priest Eli. The author underlines the fact that at this period "a revelation of the Lord was uncommon and vision infrequent" (v. 1). Exodus 25:10-22 describes the ark, a chest of acacia wood forty-five inches long by two feet wide by twenty-seven inches high, slung on poles for carrying purposes. On top of it were two cherubs of beaten gold facing in toward the propitiatory, an oblong surface of gold designated to receive the sprinkled blood of bullock and goat for sin-offering on the Day of Atonement (cf. Lev 16:1-19). The ark was made to hold the tables of the Law. Its chief characteristic was mobility: it went where the people did as a sign of the LORD's presence to them in their wanderings. For the moment, the ark was stationary at Shiloh where the sons of Eli carried on their wicked traffic (2:12-17). It was, moreover, in the temple (v. 3) of the Lord.

The story hints at the many communications in store for Samuel later in his career (v. 7). He is aroused by a call that comes to him three times, the ordinary ritual pattern. Upon instruction, he tells the Lord to speak for his servant is listening (v. 9). The message, which contains a threat against Eli for his failure to reprove his sons (vv. 11-18), is repressed in this reading. It prefers to feature noble acceptance of the Lord's sentence by the old man. The reading is made to conclude with the young Samuel's growth to manhood under the watchful eye of the Lord who (literally in the Hebrew) "let none of his words fall to the ground" (v. 19).

In its expanded form this reading will occur also on Proper 4 [9] (B). As the tale continues, Samuel learns that he will succeed Eli as the priest at Shiloh by default of his sons whose wickedness is a scandal. Chapter 3 says he did nothing to restrain them (v. 13) but the previous chapter has him reproach them; ineffectually, however (2:22-25). The sins of Eli's house will require expiation in sacrifice "forever" (v. 14) but the older man is admirable in wanting to know the content of the vision as it tells against him (vv. 15-18).

Psalm 139:1-6, 13-18

Psalm 40:2, 4ab, 7-10

Here am I, Lord; I come to do your will.

1 Corinthians 6:12[13c-15a, 17]-20

It is clear from other passages in Paul's letters that he believes that the resurrection body will be a transformed body (cf. 15:35-44; 2 Cor 5:1-5; Phil 3:21). Here he affirms his faith in human resurrection at the hands of the same divine power that raised Jesus up as Lord (v. 14).

In the present context he is inveighing against sexual immorality. Paul willingly admits the naturalness of digestive processes and the inevitability of death, quoting what seems to be a familiar saw (v. 13). The sense of the proverb that precedes it (v. 12) may be that no activities of the body can have everlasting consequences. This Paul takes special pains to deny. The body *(sōma)* means humanity as a whole for Paul, not just material organs and processes. The argument he appears to be refuting is that illicit sexual activity is no more lasting in its consequences than food intake and excretion. Since Paul allows freedom there, how can he restrict it in matters like fornication? His response is that the proper correlative of the body (the self) is the Lord; in other words, in the matter of sex there is nothing like the natural correlation that there is between humanity and digestion or disposal.

Human bodies are human persons. They are as if member of Christ's body (v. 15a). The elimination of vv. 15bc and 16 from the lectionary (out of delicacy?) makes what follows even harder for the hearer to understand. The man who lies with a prostitute is understood to become one body with her, and because the choice is wrong, one "flesh" in the pejorative sense, in the marriage image of Gen 2:24. Paul may be overestimating the character of such a union, particularly if it is transient, for rhetorical purposes. But he obviously means to contrast that *sōma*-to-*sōma* union with the *pneuma*-to-*pneuma* union of Christ and the believer in him (v. 17).

Paul's strong charge to the Corinthians to shun lewd conduct (v. 18) has as its appended reason the statement that fornication implicates the body as no other sin does. Strictly speaking, that is not so. One has only to think of suicide, alcohol and drug abuse, and self-mutilation. Yet Paul's point remains in general true. The giving over of one's body-person to a prostitute when it should be committed to the Lord subjects it (and her) to a unique indignity.

Each man is destined for the Spirit's indwelling (v. 19), not a prostitute's caresses. One should act, therefore, so as to give God the glory. This, for Paul, is quite readily done in the body since he sees no opposition whatever between the action of physical members and a life in the spirit (for him, no different than *the* Spirit).

ALLELUIA. JOHN 15:15B

I call you my friends, says the Lord, for I have made known to you all that the Father told me.

JOHN 1:43-51[35-42]

Interrupting this reading after v. 42 destroys its force since the Johannine "call of the disciples" is made the vehicle of successive titles of Jesus. The Christology of the gospel to follow is built around the designation "Lamb of God" (v. 36), "Rabbi (v. 38), "Messiah" (v. 41), "the one Moses spoke of in the law—the prophets too" (v. 45), "Son of God . . . King of Israel" (v. 49), and as a culmination, "Son of Man" (v. 51). The fourth evangelist possesses the historical tradition of Simon's change of name to Cephas/Peter. He also connects the calling of Jesus' followers with discipleship of John, vv. 28-35, as the Synoptic authors do not do (but see Luke's "one of those who was of our company while the Lord Jesus moved among us, from the baptism of John," Acts 1:21f.).

The pericope is part of complex sequence of symbolic days in a week. Note "the next day" in vv. 29, 35, 43 as preparation for Jesus' manifestation of "the third day" (2:1) perhaps patterned on Exod 19:1, 10 culminating in the Lord's coming down from Sinai "on the third day" (v. 18). The "Where do you stay?" of v. 38 has been suggested as an echo of God's dwelling with his people forever (cf. Dan 6:27). The verb *eskḗnōsen*, "made his dwelling," in 1:14, has likewise been suggested as word play on *shakaneti* of Exod 25:8, "I shall dwell (among them)"; cf. the LXX of Sirach 24, where Wisdom first dwells (*kateskḗnēsa*, v. 4) in the highest heavens, then pitches her tent (*skēnēn*; *kataskḗnōson*, v. 8) in Israel.

John is the only evangelist who gives the Aramaic original of the Greek name Peter, *Kephas* (the Greek adding a final *sigma*). Note the two-language designations of messiah and Kepha in v. 42, found elsewhere only in Matthew (16:18) in the setting of Caesarea Philippi. Jesus' identification of Nathanael as without guile/deceit may be an echo of the LORD's removal of the country's guilt as each man is seated under his own tree (see Zech 3:10; cf. Mic 4:4) but this is by no means certain. It is in any case the first instance in the gospel of Jesus' knowledge of states of heart and mind. The image of an open heaven and a ladder on which angels ascend and descend (a puzzling sequence for angels) is doubtless from Gen 28:12. It is fitting for the Johannine Word made flesh who first descended and then ascended. R. E. Brown gives no fewer than five reasons why 1:51 may have originally been a resurrection-parousia saying that fits in awkwardly in this place (*The Gospel according to John I–XIII*, AB 29 [Garden City, N.Y.: Doubleday, 1966]), 88–91.

❧❧
Third Sunday after the Epiphany [3] /
Third Sunday of the Year (B)

JONAH 3:1-5, 10

This postexilic tale challenges the earlier biblical notion that God's protective care necessarily excludes all the enemies of Israel. It is written as if the grandeur of the Assyrian capital Nineveh (destroyed 612) is still a vivid memory. The archaeological evidence is that Nineveh was about three miles wide. This size, unusual for the ancient world, has become a matter of a three days' journey across (v. 3).

Very probably the seed of this drama in miniature is the declaration of Jer 18:7f.: "Sometimes I may declare concerning a nation or a kingdom that I will pluck up and break down and destroy it. But if that nation, concerning which I have spoken, turns from its evil, I will change my mind about the disaster I intended to bring on it." The identity of a certain prophet Jonah son of Amittai, unknown except for mention in a context of the spread of the northern kingdom's boundaries in the reign of Jeroboam II (783–43), has been preempted for purposes of the tale. He preaches to the Ninevites in the name of his God, the Lord. Far from resisting the message, as Israel consistently does, they repent and put on sackcloth, man and boy. The king declares a fast so that God may relent and forgive. God in turn does as Jeremiah says he will do by reconsidering the punishment he has threatened and not carrying it out (v. 10).

Chapter 4 appears to be based on Elijah's flight in terror to the cave of Horeb, followed by his pique at the Israelites because he alone was faithful (1 Kgs 19:10, 14). The repentance of the Ninevites is the "sign of Jonah" of the first stratum of Gospel material (Matt 12:39, 41; 16:4; Luke 11:30), which a later tradition read (misread?) in terms of the whale's belly and Jesus' "three days and three nights in the bowels of the earth" (Matt 12:40).

Psalm 62:5-12

Psalm 25:4-9

Teach me your ways, O Lord.

1 Corinthians 7:29-31

As in Mark's so-called Little Apocalypse (Mark 13), where the Lord "has shortened the days" for the sake of those he has chosen (13:20), so here what Paul actually says is that the time before the end "is shortened" (v. 29). His meaning is the simple one that there is little time left. In that which remains, translated "From now on," people should conduct themselves in all aspects of life "as if they were not" married, weeping, rejoicing, owning things, or using the world. Paul gives as the reason for such detachment the fact that the world "as we know it" (meaning its outward appearance, *schēma*, v. 31b) is passing away.

He has made clear in 7:2-5 that he does not expect the married to live apart from each other while awaiting the end. Similarly, he does not counsel here a Stoic suppression of tears or laughter. (Recall Rom 12:15: "Rejoice with those who rejoice, weep with those who weep.") Least of all does he wish sham behavior: acting one way while inwardly feeling another. His point is not that marriage and family life and business are transient but that all human institutions will shortly be transformed. At the Lord's coming, people will devote themselves entirely to him. Paul is asking for a wholehearted anticipation of this now (cf. v. 31).

ALLELUIA. MARK 1:15

The kingdom of God is near; believe the Good News.

MARK 1:14-20

Mark gets John off the scene in order to launch Jesus on his ministry. The son of Zechariah has heralded the Messiah and baptized him. Now Jesus appears in order to proclaim the good news of God (v. 14). He preaches the reform of people's lives (v. 15), related to the repentance or turning about (v. 4) of his predecessor, and faith in the new tidings as well. This is Mark's programmatic statement of Jesus' ministry—an end to the time of waiting and the arrival of "the time of fulfillment" (v. 15).

The "fishers of men" story is illustrative of Christian call and response, a narrative of divine power. In rabbinic literature nets and fishermen are related to judgment, not to "catching" in a cause.

☙ ❧
Fourth Sunday after the Epiphany [4] /
Fourth Sunday of the Year (B)

DEUTERONOMY 18:15-20

Deuteronomy, the work of Levitical priests, emanated from some northern sanctuary but was connected with public proclamation at Jerusalem in Josiah's reign (621). It attempted a regulation of the duties of the king (17:14-20) and priests (18:1-8) before turning to the function of prophets (18:9-12). The part on prophets concludes with a criterion for recognizing a genuine oracle of the LORD, namely, that it be fulfilled (vv. 21f.). Verses 15-20 are set in a polemic against Canaanite priests and their magical rites. Soothsaying, necromancy, and fortune telling are declared abominations; the practice of child sacrifice is also suggested (v. 10). Opposed to all this is the proper attitude which is one of utter candor toward the LORD (v. 13). He will abide no traffic with the spirit-world (v. 14).

The LORD is made to tell Moses he means to raise up a succession of teachers like him. The Deuteronomist goes on to describe a collective prophetism

(vv. 15, 18). Subsequent generations will take this to refer to one man (John 6:14; 7:40). That a singular collective is intended by vv. 20ff. is clear. Such a one may be a true prophet or a false. In the former case he will speak as the LORD has commanded him; in the latter, presumptuously, either in another vein or in the names of other gods.

PSALM 111

PSALM 95:1-2, 6-9

If today you hear his voice, harden not your hearts.

1 CORINTHIANS 8:1-13

Earlier in this letter Paul has been contrasting God's wisdom with the wisdom of the age (2:6f.) which he calls folly (1:21, 25; 2:14). He has spoken almost glancingly of self-knowledge and a knowledge of what pertains to God (2:11) but has strongly repudiated boasting of any sort (1:29, 31; 3:21; 5:6) or being inflated with pride (4:18f.; 5:2). Chapters 5–7 deal with knowing right from wrong and doing what is right in the context of several moral dilemmas. It remains for this chapter-long discussion, however, of a problem we do not encounter—at least in this form—for him to tackle the claim to superior knowledge (gnōsis, 8:1, 10, 11) of a peculiarly Greek type. Aristotle began the treatise he called *Metaphysika* (because it came after his *Physika*, "Nature") with the statement: "All human beings by nature desire to know." He then launched on a discussion of the senses as the doorway to knowledge and memory as the storehouse of things known. The Corinthians, even those who had studied no philosophy whatever, knew they were perched on the shoulders of giants. They seem to have been convinced that knowledge was their "thing." It had evidently been reported to Paul that some knew what others did not, namely that eating meat sacrificed to idols (the Hellenist Jewish term for false gods) was morally indifferent because the deities they represent have no existence: "There is no God but one" (v. 4; see v. 6). Well and good. But if knowledge is not informed by love, Paul says, it can be harmful. Such is the case in the church at Corinth where some have been educated away from their polytheist orientation so well that they entertain no scrupulous fear that eating food previously dedicated to a tutelary god or goddess may constitute an unconscious wrong. They are quite secure in this knowledge. Paul calls them the "strong," meaning the robust in conscience. Others he calls "weak," meaning of tender conscience. The strong in his terminology are not superior to the weak. They are if anything inferior because they are not perceptive enough to realize that they are giving scandal. Paul hastens to agree that no moral wrong is being committed, there being no gods behind the idols. But he warns against this knowledge because it is being used destructively of scrupulous fellow believers "for whom Christ died" (v. 11). Paul teaches an important lesson in the danger of giving scandal. Knowledge is important only if it is harbored, and shared, with love. The way of love can at times require not acting on what one knows. Better put, *knowing* when not to act on a piece of *knowledge*.

1 Corinthians 7:32-35

This reading immediately follows last Sunday's in LM and RCL. Paul expresses the hope that his Corinthians should be anxiety-free as they wait for the Lord. He does not wish their lives to be wrapped up in family life or commerce, in possessions or relationships. Paul may be speaking in v. 32b of the form the anxiety of the unmarried man takes, in v. 33 that of the married man. He may, again, be using the verb form *merimnậ* in two different sense, "is busy with" (v. 32) and, uncomplimentarily, "is caught up in" (v. 33). In either case he is contrasting, unfavorably, pleasing one's wife with pleasing the Lord.

The Christian husband by definition is committed to pleasing both the Lord and his wife. This means that he is divided but in a good way. If he were to be devoted to the world's demands and to pleasing his wife, he would be divided in a bad way. The question is, does Paul classify a wife with "the world" and against the Lord? Not necessarily. He does think, however, that there is bound to be division of some kind. He seems unwilling to identify pleasing one's wife with pleasing the Lord, if only because they are distinct, each making personal demands. That the wife's will should coincide with the Lord's will or that pleasing the wife should be identical with doing the Lord's will is a possibility Paul does not entertain.

Rather, he goes on the assumption that, being free from marital obligations, a man (v. 32) or woman (v. 34) will be free for "holiness in body and spirit." The latter sentiment may be one held by the Corinthian ascetical party, as 7:1b undoubtedly is, hence properly set in quotation marks. In such case, Paul is identifying himself with the opinion. Yet we know from other expressions of view that he does not confine holiness in the body to the unmarried but considers it the vocation of all (cf. Rom 6:12; 12:1; 1 Cor 6:13).

Paul requires that one be detached in all matters. He never says that the unmarried or the virginal have, ipso facto, achieved detachment. He merely intimates that they have a running start on the problem.

ALLELUIA. JOHN 64B AND 69B

Your words, Lord, are spirit and life; you have the words of everlasting life.

MARK 1:21-28

According to Mark, Capernaum was the center of Jesus' ministry. It lay on the north shore of the Sea of Galilee west of the point where the Jordan debouches into it. A ruined synagogue of Capernaum is there to be visited, but this edifice did not stand in Jesus' day. Mark is not so much interested in *what* Jesus taught (he transmits little of his teaching compared to Matthew and Luke) as he is in the effect it had on his hearers. He is especially concerned to report that Jesus taught with authority (*exousía*, v. 22), not like the scribes, and that people were spellbound by his teaching. The "authority" in question is not that of the well-informed teacher, the layman who, although without rabbinic training, discourses like a master. For Mark it is rather the divine authority of one who is God's Son (1:11b).

The cosmic struggle between God and superhuman powers, which is a feature of Mark's Gospel, is first introduced in this passage. Jesus deals not merely with a sick man but with an "unclean spirit" or demon who shrieks at him, convulses the victim, and then at Jesus' sharp command leaves him. The spirit (who speaks in the plural: "Have you come to destroy us?") addresses Jesus in fear, not in respect. He recognizes him as "God's holy one" (v. 24). The adversaries are thus here joined: God's chosen one and the troubler of humanity.

The unclean spirits' search to express Jesus' identity does not include utterance of his name. The title arrived at is thought by some to be an attempt to gain power over Jesus (as in various Jewish magical papyri, where possession of the victim's name or identity gives such power). If so, it is an unsuccessful attempt. Jesus speaks a simple word of command. The Greek verbs for "rebuked" and "Be quiet" (v. 25) have a history in exorcism formulas of the time. The crowd is amazed by Jesus' authoritative stance. It is all that is needed to convince the people of "the surrounding region of Galilee" (v. 28) that God's emissary has taken up residence in their midst. Mark achieves his initial purpose by portraying Jesus as one who has come to usher in the new eon by stripping the rulers of the former age of their power.

✿✿
Fifth Sunday after the Epiphany [5] /
Fifth Sunday of the Year (B)

ISAIAH 40:21-23

The verses that immediately precede today's portion (18-20) are about the steps in the fashioning of an idol, to show what a poor patch such an object is on the seas, the sky, the mountains, and hills of the earth made by Israel's God (40:12). NAB and NEB do some critical work on the text by placing the obviously misplaced 41:6 and 7 after 40:20, where they belong. Beginning at v. 12 there is a sustained Job-like challenge, continuing to the end of the chapter, to "all the nations" (v. 17a; cf. 23) like the captor Chaldea that thinks it has won an ultimate victory over the flock of the LORD God, Israel's shepherd (v. 11a). The long poem takes the form of a disputation with any who would misperceive the situation or be foolish enough to take on this God of power. The people of Judah has served its term, paid the penalty for its sins (v. 2). Now it is being brought back to its homeland by the one who "sits above the circle of the earth" (v. 22a). The rhetorical questions of v. 21 repeated in part in v. 28 are a taunt thrown to Babylon from Jerusalem that says, in the argumentative speech of our day: "Don't you get it? Haven't you the remotest clue to the power of my liberator?" And then the effects of that power are spelled out in a poem of incredible strength and beauty. This God looks down on the earth's inhabitants like grasshoppers, stretches out the heavens like a tent to live in (v. 22), carries off despots like stubble in a strong wind (v. 24). Once one lifts up one's eyes and sees the grandeur of the many things the Holy One has created, it will be clear that this one has no equal in power, no peer in strength. And this strength the Creator gives to the weary, this power to the powerless (vv. 29f.).

JOB 7:1-4, 6-7

This chapter of Job, a continuation of the preceding one, contains Job's response to Eliphaz, the first of his troublesome comforters. Job has been describing his brothers as having no more dependability or staying power than desert streams in the summer sun (see 6:15-17). His three visitors are terrified at the adversities in his life with which he confronts them (v. 21). He wants nothing from them but a little instruction, some convincing argument about the meaning of his present distress (vv. 24f.). They can supply him with none. *Their* words they take as proof but his desperate utterance as wind (v. 26). Job plows ahead in what, for him, is the only sincere and truthful appraisal of the state of things.

Man's life, he says, is like that of the field worker who owns nothing and never will. He waits for the sun's heat to abate and the day to end, for the next payday, for the relief of nightfall. But night does not bring sleep, only restless, insomniac tossing (vv. 3f.). The days are long and the nights longer but paradoxically it is all over in an instant and without hope. The shuttle flies (v. 6), the thread is snapped, the cloth is finished. Yet nothing is done. Job's life is like the wind. He shall not see happiness again (see Eccl 1:3; 12:6-7).

Benjamin King's "Pessimist" said there was

> Nothing to do but work,
> Nothing to eat but food
> Nothing to wear but clothes
> To keep from going nude.

Job is weary of having nowhere to stand but on. He wants Eliphaz to know that there's nowhere to fall but off.

PSALM 147:1-11, 20C

1 CORINTHIANS 9:16-23

The one thing Paul most holds in horror is the boasting that his opponents in the spread of the gospel glory in. *Kauchàomai* is a verb he uses about thirty-five times, plus its cognate nouns *kauchēma* and *kauchēsis*. The sounds are onomatopoeic in their resemblance to the cawing of crows. Priding himself on externals has no appeal for Paul. If he has to boast it will be in Christ Jesus with respect to his relationship to God (cf. Rom 15:17).

The context of Paul's remarks here is that he has never exacted support from the Corinthians, even though in principle "those who preach the gospel should live by the gospel" (1 Cor 9:14). He does not press these rights lest anyone rob him of his "boast," that is, deprive him of the possibility of preaching the gospel untrammeled (v. 15). On reflection, however, Paul concludes that he is not so much free with respect to the Gospel as constrained. He *has* to preach it; failure to do so would spell his ruin (v. 16). Free or unfree, he cannot make the responsibility go away. He is Gospel-haunted, God-ridden. The recompense or reward he receives consists in presenting the gospel free of charge and thereby retaining his liberty (v. 18). Pressing the full use of his rights in the gospel on his hearers might bring an end to this, so Paul forbears.

The apostle Paul is "free" with respect to all (Fitzmyer calls his claim of *eleuthería* part of his Graeco-Roman heritage, v. 19). This liberty is a happy servitude in the cause of convincing others of the truth of the gospel.

Verses 20-21 are omitted from the reading with a commendable delicacy. The framers of the lectionary are seemingly sensitive to the long history of proselytizing directed against the Jews. Paul the observant Jew could press on fellow-Jews his convictions about his freedom from the Law in a way that no Gentile can, yet many, offensively, have.

The "weak" of this passage may be Jews of his time who cannot bear the burden of freedom from the special "works of the Law" and feel they must conform to it in every respect. Paul is sympathetic toward them. He does not bully them into a freedom which for them would be no freedom at all. His "all things to all persons" stance (v. 22) has been both praised over the ages as resiliency of spirit and reviled as a chameleon-like strategy or low cunning. It is probably neither of these. It is an open declaration of conscious motivation made specific in v. 23. Paul does all that he does "for the sake of the gospel." His interest, he admits disarmingly, is self-interest. He wants some "share," some commonality (v. 23), in its benefits. He knows no better way than to offer participation in the saving message to others on any terms that may prove congenial to them.

ALLELUIA. MATTHEW 11:25

Blessed are you, Father, LORD of heaven and earth; you have revealed to little ones the mysteries of the kingdom.

MARK 1:29-39

Jesus, for Mark, shows his power over the forces inimical to the human race not only by ejecting the shrieking unclean spirit but also by healing the fever-ridden mother of Simon's wife. The fact that she immediately begins to wait on them (v. 31) has nothing to do with the domestic role division of the times, however marked that might have been. It is instead Mark's familiar cachet signifying the return to normalcy after a wondrous deed has been performed by Jesus. The chaos in nature has been overcome. The order that speaks of God's power succeeds it.

Mark distinguishes between the unwell and the possessed (vv. 32, 34). This helps give the lie to the modern supposition that the ancient world attributed all otherwise unexplained pathologies to demonic influence. Still, Mark is insistent on the common feature in all human suffering. Humanity is under the influence of a baleful enemy so powerful that only the "holy one of God" (v. 24) can break his hold. Jesus for Mark is the man who by God's power puts the strong one under restraint in order to despoil his property and plunder his house. Satan's household is not a house internally divided (see 3:23-26). That is the false supposition of opponents of Jesus' ministry. In his holiness he is laying siege to it from without.

Jesus' reduction of the demons to silence (v. 1:34) is conceivably a historical reminiscence but more demonstrably a narrative technique of Mark. Their knowledge of Jesus is not the knowledge of faith but of hatred, just as their acknowledgment of his identity is a "shrieking" not a "proclamation," two words that sound alike in Greek but for a prefix attached to the first. Mark reserves genuine epiphanies of Jesus for later times (8:30; 9:2-7; 14:62; 16:6).

The desert for Jesus is a place of testing by inimical forces in Mark's theology that employs a geographic setting (1:13). Its solitude is also, however, a place of prayer and recovered strength (1:25; 6:31; 8:4), not to mention protection (1:45). But, as is so often reported, the crowds seek Jesus out and remind him of his vocation. He has come, he affirms, for proclamation (vv. 38, 39).

Mark's Galilee is the favorable region where the gospel is preached and demons are expelled. In Judaea, Jesus engages in polemic, is plotted against, and meets his death (see 10:32; 11:27f.; 12:13; 14:1; 15:37).

❧ ❧

Sixth Sunday after the Epiphany [6] / Sixth Sunday of the Year / Proper 1 (B)

For instructions on the readings of today and the Sundays through 9 Epiphany and Transfiguration Sunday see under (A).

2 KINGS 5:1-14

For a commentary see Proper 23 [28] (C).

PSALM 30

LEVITICUS 13:1-2, 44-46

Biblical leprosy (*tsara'ath*, literally a "striking down" or "laying low"; in Greek: *lepra*) is not Hansen's disease but something contagious, like impetigo or ringworm.

Sufferers from Hansen's disease have been caused untold anguish as a result of the false conclusion from biblical data that their disease is a divine punishment for wrongdoing. The priests are charged by the Mosaic legislation with acting as public health officers. Verses 3-44 in the Hebrew text may be repulsive and unfit for public reading in their clinical detail but they have been much praised for the diagnosis of symptoms they propose. It is as up-to-date as that of any modern practitioner in a dispensary.

The isolation technique of vv. 45-46 is primarily to provide protection for the healthy but also contains elements of a crude hygiene for the afflicted. The latter's cry, "Unclean!" had to do with the ritual impurity resulting from their physiological condition. Because of the lack of distinction between ritual and moral imperfection in the early biblical period, this warning technique, whatever its effectiveness, came to be taken in the popular mind as synonymous with moral offense. Thus, the Hebrew adjective of vv. 45 and 46 becomes *akáthartos* in the Septuagint, the same word as that used to describe "unclean spirits" in Mark 1:23, 26, 27. The segregation of those with infectious diseases (and Hansen's disease, it should be pointed out, is barely such) therefore ceases to be a public protection and takes on the character of moral stigma. Purists may say that any such notion is "unbiblical" but the popular misconception seems to be a fact (cf. 2 Kgs 5:27; John 9:2f.).

PSALM 32:1-2, 5, 11

I turn to you, LORD, in time of trouble, and you fill me with the joy of salvation.

1 CORINTHIANS 9:24-27

The Gospel portion for this Sunday is foreshadowed by the first lection on the usual typological principle but, unusually for a Sunday, the common occurrence of a theme in all three that is proper to feasts is at work: the epistolary reading is of the same character as the other two. They speak of a return to health and strength by the power of God. Paul's word for keeping fit through controlled eating (*egkrateúetai*, v. 25) is from two athletic contests, unusual for him because Jews did not participate in track and field, let alone boxing. The scantily clad athletes of both sexes discouraged their participation. Here, however, the metaphor of competition is one he could not have been unaware of in Tarsus, Macedonia, or Achaia. The winner's crown of laurel leaves did in fact wither, but then today's gold, silver, and bronze will lose their metaphorical luster in a display case in the home. Paul says he stays trim in body and spirit as he competes in two similar contests (v. 26) in proclaiming the gospel (v. 27) so as not to "be disqualified." In the latter verse, "lest I become a castaway" is happily gone from KJV and DRC. It always made readers wonder what a shipwreck was doing on the athletic field. That fate would come much later; the catalogue in 2 Cor 11:23-27 establishes that. Meanwhile, his physical stamina was evidently far from mean.

1 Corinthians 10:31—11:1

Paul here provides his new believers an overarching principle for the conduct of their everyday lives, just as in last week's pericope he had supplied one to account for all that he did in his attempts to spread the gospel. Today's passage comes as the summary of his lengthy discussion of the legitimacy of eating meat that has been sacrificed to idols (as most of that available in Corinthian markets had). His conclusion transcends all the counsel he has given in individual cases: Do all that you do for God's glory. The way to achieve that is to avoid personal offense whenever possible. The person comes first for Paul. Being solicitous for his needs, whatever his particularities (Jew, Greek, weak, strong, of tough mind or tender conscience), has the highest priority. Seeking the advantage of the other rather than oneself is the means to ensure both that person's salvation and God's glory.

Volumes have been written on Paul's final sentence, "Imitate me as I imitate Christ" (11:1). He has already hinted at a practical norm for the conduct of others (9:22). Now he makes it explicit. The suggestion that his conduct might have about it some exemplary character has come up in previous letters (1 Thess 1:6; 2 Thess 3:7, 9; Phil 3:17). Part of his special calling as an apostle is to show in an especially clear way the demands of Christian life (cf. 1 Cor 4:9-13). Paul does not hesitate to propose that people imitate Christ directly (Rom 15:2f., 5) but he is convinced that, since that is what he is doing, others are safe to follow him. There is no implication that a mediated discipleship is a necessary or even a better one, only the realistic view that the remembrance of Paul's presence provides a more accessible model than the historical life of Jesus.

Alleluia. Luke 19:38

Blessed is the king who comes in the name of the Lord; peace on earth and glory in heaven.

MARK 1:40-45

This Gospel reading, consecutive with last week's, shows why today's selection from Leviticus was chosen by LM as necessary background material. The detail of the leper's kneeling down (v. 40) is consistent with Mark's view of Jesus as Son of God. Mark has Jesus heal with a touch, thereby showing his power (v. 41); then he enjoins silence (v. 44) as part of the Markan technique of keeping Jesus' true identity secret from all except the unclean spirits until 14:62; 15:39. Jesus conforms fully to the Levitical prescription (v. 45). The evangelist may be ironical if the phrase "a proof for them" is intended to go with the phrase about the offering rather than with the ritual of the leper's presenting himself.

🕊 🕊
Seventh Sunday after the Epiphany [7] / Seventh Sunday of the Year / Proper 2 (B)

ISAIAH 43:18[19, 21-22, 24B]-25

The poet known to history as Second Isaiah (chaps. 40–55) employs the exodus theme in vv. 16-17, with the usual references to a path in the sea and chariots and horsemen lying prostrate, never to rise—only to admonish his reader to forget all this imagery (v. 18). Jeremiah 16:14f. likewise hints that in the popular mind the memory of the Exodus will fade and yield to that of deliverance from Babylon. Israel's God is doing something new, making a way in the desert and in the wasteland rivers (the Qumrân MS of Isaiah seems to read "paths," a reading followed by NEB). His own people have water to drink in the desert but Israel, instead of praising God, grows weary of him. The lesson of the new deliverance is lost on the people, the LORD complains. They weigh him down with sins and crimes instead of offering sheep and fatlings and sweet cane on their sacrificial altars. He does not respond by remembering their sins but wipes them out.

Would they have a true audit? They had better go along with his forgiveness, for they could not stand a day in court.

PSALM 41[2-5, 13-14]

2 Corinthians 1:18-22

Many scholars considers 2 Cor 1:1—6:13 to be part of a letter written in Macedonia that should follow the fragments of correspondence represented by 6:14—7:1 and 10:1—13:10. After 6:13 would come 7:2 through 9:15, with 13:11-14 constituting the conclusion to chaps. 7–9. Whatever the sequence, we have in 2 Corinthians an early edited version of several letters (although some hold otherwise).

Paul has been speaking of his sincerity in having had the intention of visiting the Corinthians twice, once on his way to Macedonia and again coming back. Only consideration for them restrained him from doing so (1:23). He insists that he keeps his word even as God himself does (v. 18). This prompts Paul to describe Jesus Christ as the great affirmative. The Greek word for a strong yes is *nai*, which strikes our ear as strange. That is what Christ is, though: the fulfillment of all God's promises. And that is why it makes sense to associate oneself with Christ at the great "Amen" of the assembly of worshipers (*pros doxan*, v. 20). "Amen" means "It is firm," a usage that prompts Paul to describe God as "firmly establishing" him along with the Corinthians in Christ. The three aorist participles *(chrísas, sphragisámenos, dous),* which speak of anointing, sealing, and depositing the first payment of the Spirit in our hearts (vv. 21f.) may be early baptismal vocabulary, although non-sacramentally oriented Christian scholars tend to refer the "Amen" addressed through Christ to God to the response to preaching, namely, faith. One thing that is certain is the legal nature of the figure of "down payment" or "pledge" (*arrabōna*, v. 22; it occurs also in 5:5). Like the agricultural figure "first fruits" of Rom 8:23, it describes the gift of the Spirit, following Christ's resurrection, which serves as the first installment of the new age that is to come.

God, the firm establisher, is likewise the giver of the gift.

Alleluia. John 1:14 and 12b

The Word of God became a man and lived among us. He enabled those who accepted him to become children of God.

Mark 2:1-12

Capernaum is the center of Jesus' Galilean activity for Mark. Crowds gather around his door (v. 2). Here, as characteristically, the reality in the onlookers that elicits the miracles is their "faith" (v. 5). The faith of the healing stories is neither faith in God (as in Mark 11:22) nor faith in Jesus (as in Matt 18:6) but something absolute— a power that is the very power of God arising from the encounter with Jesus (cf.

"faith" in the healing stories of Mark 5:25-34 and par.; 5:21-24, 35-43; 7:24-30 and par.; Matt 15:28; Mark 9:14-29; 10:46-52 and par.; Matt 8:5-13 and par.; Matt 9:27-31; Luke 17:11-19). The stories of healing are basically not stories of healing at all but exemplary stories of the power of faith, which is elicited through Jesus. The healing is not the object of faith; God is, with Jesus as the instrument.

Mark has Jesus forgive the man's sins, as the Church of his day is doing. Jesus is then charged with blasphemy and is made by Mark to use the power of healing (v. 11) to justify the possession of still greater authority.

&
Eighth Sunday after the Epiphany [8] / Eighth Sunday of the Year / Proper 3 (B)

HOSEA 2:14-20

The God of Israel has been made a fool of time and again by the adulterous adventures of his wife, the people. What no man in Israel has had to endure he stands ready, even willing, to undergo. He will take back this self-seeking spouse who callously gives as the reason she intends to return, "I will . . . return to my first husband, for it was better with me then than now" (2:7a[9]). The Lord divulges his strategy in today's pericope. He will re-create the situation in which he first won his bride by leading her out into the desert of Sinai and there wooing her afresh (v. 14 [16]). Nowhere is the Canaanite idea of the sacred marriage better made use of.

Adlai Stevenson, in conceding defeat on the night of one of his unsuccessful tries for the presidency, confused the reporters thoroughly by quoting 2:15 [17] as a comment on his loss. The morning papers went to press before any of them had located the quotation he used about making the Valley of Achor (i.e., trouble) a door of hope. Emek-Achor was a western entry into Canaan where Achan was stoned for pillage (Josh 7:24ff.). The early Zionist settlers named one of their first towns, now a thriving city, Pethah-tikvah, "Gate of Hope," out of this verse in Hosea.

The prophet looks for a response from the people such as Israel made in the days of her youth. Right and justice, love, mercy, and fidelity are all favorite words of Hosea. They are the terms of the renewed and lasting marriage which he envisions. Crowning all is a particularly sublime Hosean concept: "You shall know the LORD," again derived from the intimacy of marriage.

PSALM 103:1-13, 22

2 Corinthians 3:1-6

Throughout this portion of the letter Paul stresses the purity of his motivation. He has said that he is a noxious odor to those on their way to destruction but a breath of life to those who are being saved (2:15f.). He is no Christ-monger, with the Gospel his stock in trade. Veiled reference to other preachers is apparent. Paul knows his Corinthians so well that he scoffs at the idea of needing to be introduced to them. The letter-technique has presumably been reported to him of others. The "letter written on your hearts" refers to the new covenant (cf. 1 Cor 11:25) spoken of in Jer 31:33, although the tablets of stone go back to Exod 24:12; 31:18; 32:15f. Paul, here as elsewhere, is not proposing a new Mosaic dispensation in place of the first but is suggesting that a written form of words cannot contain the richness of God's intent. Only his life-giving Spirit can do that. The written Law "kills" only in the sense that it literally does not allow breathing-space. It informs the believer from without what he is held to. The Spirit tells him from within what he is capable of.

Here there is no question of two distinct covenants but of one that is renewed by the gift of the Spirit. Neither is there thought of a spirit that underlies written rules.

This is a Spirit who interprets and makes possible the observance of written rules, removing all despair over the inability to do so.

The "competent" of vv. 5f. ("those qualified") are described by words meaning "sufficient," that is, to the task. The Greek translations of the Bible by Aquila, Symmachus, and Theodotion rendered the divine title "Shaddai" by the same adjective, *hikanós*, relying on a doubtful etymology. Paul may have this in mind as he declares God and not ourselves our great sufficiency. God is the one who has made us ministers of a covenant of Spirit, the one covenant in which a life-giving Spirit instructs us.

Alleluia. John 6:64b and 69b

Your words, Lord, are spirit and life; you have the words of everlasting life.

Mark 2:13[18]-22

Levi son of Alphaeus is the tax gatherer who was the first one Jesus recruited in the Gospel of Mark. He is not one of the Twelve listed by Mark shortly after his call (3:16-19). Levi's importance is that he joins a company of fellow professionals and "sinners" at table along with Jesus and his disciples. Tax gathering by Jews was a despised profession because its incumbents worked against their own people for the Temple priests who served as fiscal agents of the empire. "Sinners" may have included some of disordered life, but it is the Synoptic Gospels' term for nonobservers of the Pharisees' "oral Law" as well as the written. The fact that Matthew's Gospel makes much of a tax gatherer named Matthew (9:9-13) in a similar context has led to an identification of the two, but there is no reason to do so. Both accounts culminate in the same apophthegm or epigram (Mark 2:17; Matt 9:12), a characteristic of Synoptic narrative technique.

This passage appears not only in Mark but also in Matthew and Luke, as a substantial portion of Mark does (cf. Matt 9:14-15; Luke 5:33-35). The call of Levi introduces the chasm that existed between the religious observants of Jesus' day and the company he kept. He was well remembered for having consorted with "sinners"—not moral offenders necessarily but people at the fringes of a ritually observant society. The brief narrative of v. 18 provides the setting for the saying of Jesus found in 19a: "The wedding guests cannot fast while the groom is still with them, can they?" This question is the center of gravity of the passage. Mention of fasting and the use of wedding imagery suggest that the saying originated in Jewish circumstances. Yet v. 20 indicates a break with the practice of fasting. *Today* is a wedding day; the groom is with them; there is no mention in this phrase of future expectation. These features suggest a modification of the Jewish setting.

Nothing in vv. 18-19a expresses the Church's faith in the resurrection or the theological interpretation of Jesus' mission that grew out of that faith. Hence we are right to take it, in its reflection of contemporary Judaism, as something coming from the setting of Jesus' lifetime. Verse 20 (and perhaps 19b) is a different matter. It comes from a later time, for it is evident that in it the death of Jesus is very important for Mark. Not only does his death assume a prominent place in his gospel but it occurs as a "plot to destroy him" in 3:6, the summary conclusion to all the conflict stories with Jewish authorities collected between 2:1 and 3:6, of which today's pericope is one. The slight allusion to Jesus' death in 2:20 "anticipates the more direct hint in 3:6, which in turn prepares for the definite predictions of Jesus' death which begin at 8:31" (Dan O. Via, *The Parables: Their Literary and Existential Dimension* [Philadelphia: Fortress Press, 1967]).

Verses 21-22 express the joy of newness, a break with the past. In the five verses of this reading two major matters are expressed: Mark's hinting at reasons for Jesus' death—he challenged the established order—and Mark's understanding of the significance of Jesus' death and resurrection—a new day of celebration has dawned. Believers are being told why the generation before them was free of ritual requirement, and that in Jesus' absence they may now fast or not as they choose.

❧.❧

Ninth Sunday after the Epiphany [9] / Ninth Sunday of the Year / Proper 4 (B)

DEUTERONOMY 5:12-15

Students of the Jewish Scriptures like Peter Ackroyd, Roland de Vaux, and H. H. Rowley assume that the religious observance of the Sabbath came into prominence during the exile, in default of other ritual possibilities in Babylon. This is not to say that the Sabbath originated there but only that sacred time probably took on more importance with the loss of sacred place.

While the Priestly writings tend to support this view, the evidence is by no means certain. What is clear is that the Sabbath loomed large for the P author. Genesis 1:1—2:4 reaches a first climax in the creation narrative in the account of the Sabbath, an anticipation of the final climax, which is the picture of the tabernacle as the center of a worshiping community. Again, the materials used by P in this account may be presumed to have preceded its sixth-century composition.

The Exod 20:8-11 account of the "fourth word" in the Hebrew division of verses in the Decalogue—E expanded by additions from P—connects the term "Sabbath" with the Hebrew root for "rest." *The* original meaning of the word, which is also found in the Babylonian *(šapattu),* is disputed. The latter is the fifteenth of the month, the day of the full moon. The observance of phases of the moon, hence of a period of four weeks, is very old. Assyria seems to have forbidden work to the king and priests on the seventh, fourteenth, twenty-first, and twenty-eighth days because these were unlucky. It was only in ancient Israel that work was stopped on the basis of a religious principle.

There are small differences between the Sabbath precept in Deuteronomy and that in Exodus. Deuteronomy has "observe" (v. 12) rather than the "remember" of Exodus (v. 8). There are small additions in vv. 12b and 14. Deuteronomy 5:15 links the Sabbath with deliverance from slavery rather than with creation as does the P author of Exod 20:11. This choice illustrates the relation of the fourth word, with its prohibition of labor, to the LORD's clemency in freeing Israel from its forced labor in Egypt.

Perhaps no custom besides circumcision so separated the Jewish community from the Gentiles after the fall of Jerusalem as did Sabbath observance. This means that the option of the Gentile church, as contrasted with Jewish Christianity, to worship on the first day contributed importantly to the breach with Judaism. The various sabbatarian restorations of the Reformers and those who came after them are well known—on the rest principle (Puritans like Nicholas Bownde) and on the seventh-day principle (Adventists, like the much later William Miller and Ellen White).

Religious considerations quite apart, it is clear that ancient Israel gave the globe the legacy of a day of freedom from its week of toil. This immense contribution has made prayer and re-creation possible for all who are not bound by economic servitude, a condition that too often is the result of cupidity by observants of a weekly free day.

PSALM 81:1-10[11]

2 CORINTHIANS 4:5-12[6-11]

Paul in this section of the collection of letters that has come to be known as 2 Corinthians (the unit is probably 2:14—7:4) writes as a theologian against discouragement in the church (cf. 4:1). He proclaims the truth openly; it is not veiled. He views the splendor of the gospel as a light shining out of darkness (vv. 4, 6, the latter referring to Gen 1:3 and Isa 9:1). The treasure carried in earthen vessels is an ability to proclaim the Moses-like "glory of God shining on the face of Christ" v. 6; cf. Exod 34:29-35; Heb 1:3). It is made possible, in the first instance, by the light shining in our hearts.

This is God's doing and not ours (v. 7), as the present afflictions of apostles like Paul amply demonstrate (vv. 8-10). Nothing short of divine power could send such beams of light from lamps of human clay. The master stroke is the paradox of Christ's life being revealed and made accessible by the daily mortality of those who proclaim it. The dying are themselves the life-giving principle. In Francis Thompson's words, "The Slain hath the gain, and the victor hath the rout."

Only those headed for destruction, those who actively resist the gospel, are in a "veiled" condition for Paul (v. 3). He takes his stand against any esoteric character of the message. It is a beacon in the manner of the pre-cosmic Wisdom of God in Hellenist Jewish thought—Paul's favorite exemplar for Christ.

ALLELUIA. JOHN 8:12

I am the light of the world, says the Lord; whoever follows me will have the light of life.

MARK 2:23—3:6

These are the final two conflict stories of the collection that runs from 2:1 to 3:6. Mark wants his reader to see in Jesus of Nazareth the eschatological messenger who restores true understanding of God's will in the end-time. Mark spells out this role in relation to specific issues, here the precedence of human need over Sabbath observance. The evangelist presents Jesus as one whose ministry was characterized by the work of interpreting God's Law anew. Repristination of the Law was one of the eschatological events expected in early Judaism to occur in the Last Age. At Qumrân the Teacher of Righteousness was to fulfill this role. For Mark it was Jesus.

Jesus' disciples are accused of offending against the prohibition of harvesting on the Sabbath in Exod 34:21, as interpreted in strict Pharisee circles. Jesus counters with a question of his own in approved rabbinic fashion, citing 1 Sam 21:1-6. Ahimelech was high priest at the time of the incident but his son Abiathar, better known through his association with David, is evidently the one of whom the anecdote is being told in some circles. Mark uses the exchange to show the transcendent character of human need (v. 27, a rabbinic maxim, which may well have been abroad in Jesus' day) and to identify Jesus as having the authority to set aside the venerable Sabbath law. Even if the phrase "the Son of Man" means simply a man here, which is unlikely, the power of Jesus remains Mark's main thrust.

The second story likewise arose out of Christian debates about Sabbath observance, since it is not primarily a healing story. The Christians are clearly on the side of Hillel, whose interpretation of Sabbath requirements was more humanely oriented than that of Shammai. The latter's school permitted only the saving of a life on the Sabbath. Jesus here identifies disease as incipient death.

The plot against Jesus' life reported in 3:6 is not to be thought of as being hatched early in his ministry; there are no rubrics of time in Mark. It is characteristic of this evangelist to sum up a section in such fashion. The verse sets the stage for Mark's preoccupation with the desire of the "the chief priests and scribes" to entrap and kill Jesus (14:1) of which he was convinced, historical probability apart. Its presence here is chiefly a matter of dramatic anticipation.

❧·❧

Last Sunday after the Epiphany / Transfiguration Sunday (B)

2 Kings 2:1-12

Although an Elisha healing story was told four Sundays ago, it has no bearing on today's account of the relation between him and Elijah, which is that of disciple and master. The present pericope is chosen as a type of Jesus' Transfiguration, which has as its common elements Elijah "translated" in the archaic sense from earth to heaven by a whirlwind (v. 11) and in Jesus' case "onto a high mountain." Elijah and Elisha have traveled from the memorial at Gilgal, "the circle of standing stones," to Bethel, where Jacob consecrated another stone to mark his dream. They come upon a band of prophets who seem to know that Elisha, already aware of it, is soon to be bereft of his friend (v. 3). The same disclosure is made to the pair at Jericho. Then, in the manner of Semitic storytelling, a third such incident occurs. This last is at the Jordan where the waters will be parted as at Gilgal (Josh 3:16), in turn a reenactment of the crossing of the Red Sea (Exod 14:29). On dry ground across the river Elijah is caught up out of sight in a chariot of fire, letting his mantle fall to the ground for Elisha to retrieve. With it he strikes the stream and it is parted for a second time for him to cross. Thus the nearly perfect tale concludes. The double portion of Elijah's spirit has been passed from one vessel of election to another, for Christians a type of transmission of the Gospel (see 1 Cor 11:23; 15:1).

2 Corinthians 4:3-6

For a commentary see the preceding Sunday, Proper 4 [9] (B).

Psalm 50:1-6

Mark 9:2-9

For a commentary see 2 Lent (B).

❧ Season of Lent ❧

❧❧
Ash Wednesday (A, B, C)

See the readings for Ash Wednesday (A).

❧❧
First Sunday in Lent (B)

GENESIS 9:8[-15]17

Genesis 1:29f. had described the human creature as herbivorous by nature and, interestingly, the birds and beasts as similarly created. Noah and his sons were granted a relaxation of that restriction with the word that henceforth every animal, bird, and fish will live in dread of the human species because it has become carnivorous (9:2). On the part of framers of these pre-Abrahamic tales, this would appear to be regress rather than progress, as evidenced by the rabbinic condition editorially inserted that no blood be left in meat prepared for eating (v. 4) every moving thing that lives (v. 3). The reason given is that animal life is symbolized by blood. From this is drawn the surprising conclusion that God will judge adversely not only murder but the killing of some subhuman species by others as well as by humans (vv. 5f.). These prohibitions and conditions, along with the command to be fruitful and multiply, convey a stringently pro-life Creator who is about to offer a unilateral compact to "every living creature of all flesh that is on the earth" (v. 16). There is no limitation of time on this statute. God will be in a contractual relation with all the living for as long as a rainbow appears in the sky, "the other side of never." What is evident here is that the learned Jews who assembled these long-told Middle Eastern tales, giving them a YHWH-Elohim meaning, could not imagine the peoples of the earth without an initial covenant such as they had been given centuries later, beginning with Abraham. Interesting above all is that this primordial, postdeluge covenant did not have its terms spelled out. Uneasy with the omission, the Rabbis supplied what Genesis *should* have said by designating seven conditions for acceptance of this covenant by Jews and Gentiles alike. The injunctions are derived from various places in chaps. 1–11 and prohibit: (1) blasphemy, (2) idolatry, (3) sexual immorality (including homosexual activity), (4) murder (including abortion), (5) robbery, (6) eating a portion of a living animal, and (7) a positive precept concerning the administration of justice (*b. Sanhedrin 56a*, as cited in Z. Werblowsky and G. Wigoder, eds., *The Oxford Dictionary of the Jewish Religion* [New York: Oxford Univ. Press, 1997], under the entry "Noachian Laws." These were assumed to be commandments that even the Gentiles had to keep lest they pollute the land. Up to recent times such was the totality of Jewish teaching on God's concern for non-Jewish peoples, although some, like Maimonides (d. 1204), courageously acknowledged that Christians and Muslims were monotheists and not idolaters.

This Priestly narrative contains the first biblical mention of the idea of covenant (*bᵉrith*). It is also marked by the initial appearance of a biblical "sign" (*'ôth*, v. 12), which is any event interpreted as the entrance of God into human affairs (cf. Judg 6:36-40; Exod 4:2-8). The tale is obviously designed to account for the origin of the rainbow—a sign of God's compact with all living creatures, visible after rainfalls. By it God commits himself never again to wreak the devastation of the earth by flood. The rainbow will appear as a symbol of divine splendor again in Ezek 1:28 and Rev 4:3.

The covenant made with Noah has a universality about it unlike the particular one with Abraham that is to follow (15:9-21). The Noachian covenant embraces all humanity and all living creatures. Human beings are to have complete discretion over the lives of animals, but not over human life. Human blood is not to be shed under any circumstances (v. 6). Neither is the blood of animals to be ingested. The latter cultic taboo is here validated in terms of a covenant that supposedly went back to the time after the flood, well before Abram's call. Because of its antiquity it is thought of as binding on all humanity and not just on the circumcised (Genesis 17). The rationale is that, since blood is the symbol of life, it participates in the sacredness of all life.

The LORD has committed himself to all mortal creatures, including the subhuman. No one of them, whether wild or tame, escapes God's solicitous care.

PSALM 25:1-10[4-9]

1 PETER 3:18-22

The writer has been speaking in the previous passage about persecution and the equanimity with which it should be faced. Here he turns to the reason why Christians should be confident, namely, because of the victory over evil that Christ has won by his resurrection, a victory made accessible through faith and the saving waters of baptism (v. 21).

The compression of phrasing in parts of this passage, its careful balance, and the introduction by the particle *hoti* ("for") all contribute to the impression that a liturgical hymn or catechetical formula has been inserted here. Verses 18 and 22 are evidently phrases that have been sung in praise of Christ, more clearly so than the labored figure developed in between. The author obviously wants to relate "Noah's fludde" to baptism. He does it by identifying water as the means of salvation in both cases. Noah and his wife and the three sons and their wives were the eight saved by God's patience (v. 20). The same kind of effect is possible today, says the writer: not the removal of physical stain by water but life in Christ, bestowed on condition of the pledge of a good conscience (v. 21).

The author of 1 Peter prefers the verb "suffered" to "died," which means that the latter's use in v. 18 comes as a surprise; as a matter of fact, "died" occurs as a textual variant in some MSS. Compare the similar creedal formula in 1 Cor 15:3. "Once for all" *(hapax)* is reminiscent of Rom 6:10 and various appearances in Hebrews (7:27; 9:12, 26, 28; 10:10). The author favors antithesis, as is evident from his use of just/unjust and flesh/spirit. The latter occurs in Rom 1:3f. and 1 Tim 3:16. "Spirit," of course, means the corporeal Christ in his heavenly or exalted sphere of existence as contrasted with his previous career as a man among men.

"The spirits who had disobeyed" are probably the wicked angels' of Gen 6:1-4 who lusted after the daughters of men, who in turn begot giants by them. The exploits of these perverse spirits are a commonplace in postbiblical Jewish literature, including the Dead Sea Scrolls. The dovetailing of this tale with that of the flood in Gen 6:4-5 can be seen to be very close. The "prison" of v. 19 is probably not the *sheol* or underworld of biblical literature but the second of seven heavens postulated by *1* and *2 Enoch*, up to which the risen Christ ascended to preach. Why this proclamation to wicked spirits? It is not a preaching of the gospel but a proclaiming by Christ, the new Enoch, that their power is finally broken.

MARK 1:9[12]-15

See Baptism of the Lord [1] (A), Matt 3:13-17, for differences in Matthew's account of the same inaugural incident of Jesus' public ministry. Mark's verb "drove" for Jesus' induction into the desert is too strong for Matthew, who changes it to "led" and from the active to the passive voice. Matthew also eliminates the wild beasts, adds to Mark Jesus' fast of forty days and forty nights, and prefers to call the tempter "the devil" rather than Mark's "Satan."

In Mark Jesus is driven by the Spirit into the desert. This rocky wasteland is the home of jackals and mountain lions (Isa 34:11-15) and is also the traditional dwelling-place of spirits inimical to man. Jesus' testing here described is not one of interior struggle. It is a joining of eschatological forces, the holiness of God versus all that is opposed to it. Mark has it in mind to assure his Christian readership that their resistance to hostile forces is part of the same ongoing battle. Mastery of the wild beasts was part of the equipment of the righteous man, as in the Adam story, Job 5:22, and *Testament of Benjamin* 5:2; cf. also the expectation that in the messianic age the animals would live in harmony, Isa 11:6ff.; Hos 2:20. In Ps 91:11-13 dominion over the wild beasts goes hand in hand with service by angels. "St. Mark probably means that by his victory over Satan Jesus has reversed Adam's defeat and begun the process of restoring paradise" (D. E. Nineham, *The Gospel of St. Mark* [New York: Penguin, 1963]). The forty-day period without any hunger that is being reported on is clearly eschatological. Perhaps Mark has in mind the feeding of Elijah by angels and his forty-day flight to Horeb (1 Kings 19).

Verse 14 marks the beginning of Jesus' Galilean ministry, his public declaration of himself once the messianic herald John is off the scene. Mark saves the details of the Baptizer's detention until chap. 6; here he simply has him "handed over." John's work is finished. The time has come for Jesus' mission to begin. Verses 14-15 are a manifesto or summing up of the entire ministry of Jesus. The proclamation of the good news of God (*beśorah*; Greek: *kērygma*; Isa 40:9; 52:7; 61:1) meant that the time of waiting was over and that God's reign (*malkuth*; Greek: *basileía*) had, in some form, arrived. Mark here has Jesus proclaim himself as the messianic bringer of the kingdom, but in his gospel he portrays Jesus as muting or downplaying this role. This stems from his theological conviction that Jesus is no mere wonder-worker but the Son of God who must nonetheless suffer and die as Son of Man.

He uses the language of later Christian evangelism in giving a summary of Jesus' public activity. This includes terms like "the fulfillment of time," "the coming near of God's sovereign rule," and the commands to "repent" and "believe in the Gospel." Such terms in Aramaic may well have been employed by Jesus in his preaching. We are surer of them as Markan vocabulary.

❢❢
Second Sunday in Lent (B)

Genesis 17:1-7, 15-16

The seed of the covenant offered to Abram occurs in Gen 12:7 when the Lord promises to give "this land" (Canaan) to his descendants and reiterates the promise in 12:14ff. The actual proffering of the covenant with its deed of the land from the Nile to the Euphrates comes in 15:18 as the conclusion of the traditional and to us moderns arcane rite of "cutting" it. Today's lection is quite specific as to God's gift of ancestry of a multitude to Abram and his offspring forever but it stops short of including "all the land of Canaan" as part of the gift (v. 8). Strangely, too, the lectionary omits the requirement of male circumcision if Abram is to accept the offer, skipping forward to the promise of a son by the superadult Sarah. The newly named Abraham (v. 5) finds this a cause for mirth (v. 17). The readings of last Sunday and this describing a covenant for all humankind and then a specification of it for Israel are proper to Lent, because the season leads up to the covenant renewal in baptism of adult new Christians and a renewed commitment to its terms by the long baptized. There are some who have laughed like Abraham at any such possibility as his parenthood but our God is a God of the improbable as well as the impossible.

Psalm 22:23-31

Genesis 22:1-2, 9A, 10-13, 15-18

This narrative is so rich that no amount of reflection can exhaust it. It is dear to Jews, Christians, and Muslims alike. For Jews Abraham is the first of the patriarchs, the father of an elect and covenanted people. For Christians he is the progenitor of all, regardless of peoplehood, who cleave to God in faith, understood as a spirit of complete trust. The world of Islam venerates him as *al Khalil*, God's "friend"—the name by which it knows the town of Hebron.

    Aetiologically (i.e., in the realm of causes or origins) the tale is probably rooted in polemic against Canaanite human sacrifice. The Hebrews—Jacob, to become Israel, is as yet unborn—are to sacrifice animals as burnt offerings, not children. "God himself will provide the sheep for the holocaust" (v. 7; cf. Mic 6:7). The site is important. "Moriah" is related in popular etymology to vision from a height ("the Lord will see," *yireh*, v. 14). The Elohist writer speaks of Jeruel (2 Chron 20:16), a wilderness near Tekoa that satisfies the condition of Abraham's three-days' journey. Later the mountain will be identified in folklore with Mount Zion in Jerusalem. If the better rendering of v. 14 is "on the mountain the Lord will see" or "will provide," there could already be reference to the Temple site.

Abraham's prompt obedience is consistent with his leaving his kinsfolk and his father's house in Haran (Gen 12:1). His binding of Isaac *(aqedath Yitzhaq)* and placing him on the wood of the altar (v. 9) is thought of by Jewish scholars like Hans Joachim Schoeps and Shalom Spiegel to have supplied Paul with the rabbinic paradigm that led to his development of Jesus' expiatory sacrifice. Since there had been no tradition that the Messiah would die, mention of the binding of "your own beloved son" (or "your only son") would have served Paul as the necessary bridge. Geza Vermès has proposed that an expiatory view of Isaac's sacrifice was widely held in the Jerusalem of the first century. It cannot be established that Paul originated the doctrine of the atonement on his own and neither can it be shown that he had this obedient sacrifice as his paradigm.

This is to get far ahead of the Yahwist's narrative. He is at pains to describe the high point in the spiritual pilgrimage of Abraham. The patriarch survives admirably the testing he is put to. His complete spirit of surrender is a symbolic passing through death, a sealing of the covenant that has been "cut" in chap. 15.

PSALM 116:10, 15-19

ROMANS 4:13-25

This is a continuation of Paul's argument that Abraham had faith in God's promise that he would be the father of many peoples and that this faith was reckoned to him as righteousness *before* he was circumcised. We have to remember that Paul was engaged in a polemic that has not been relevant for Christians—almost all of them Gentiles—since the second century. "Law" means largely the precepts of Torah that were the special signs of Jewishness. Paul is by no means repudiating the entire revelation made to Moses on Mt. Sinai. He is describing one epoch in Israel's history that has been succeeded, but not superseded, by another. The only idea repudiated is that justness before God can be earned by the human effort necessary to complement faith. Receiving the Jewish Scriptures in Greek (LXX) established the early churches outside Palestine in their conviction that they were in harmonious continuation with the religion of Israel if not with the interpretation deduced from it by the Rabbis. The "adherents of the Law" of v. 14 are those who claim to believe in Jesus Christ who are known to Paul to be making such an additional demand. At this point in the letter he is not concerned with his Jewish people more generally, saving that to what are now called chaps. 9–11 (i.e., since the division of the two Testaments into chapters by Stephen Langton, ca. 1210). The promise made to Abraham, "the father of us all," is grace or gift (v. 16). God "who gives life to the dead" probably refers to Sarah's womb thought erroneously to be "dead." Only here in the Second Testament is God described as "calling into being things that do not exist" (v. 17), a concept first expressed in a Jewish writing in 2 Macc 7:28 (cf. *2 Enoch* 24:2). The transmission of the guilt of Adam's sin to his seed occurs first in another apocryphal book, 2 Esdras (4 Ezra) 7:118 (cf. 4:30).

ROMANS 8:31B-34

See Proper 13 [18] (A) for the passage immediately following this one. The condition Paul puts is, "If God is for us." If it is fulfilled our salvation is assured despite difficulties and opposition of every sort. But it is fulfilled. Jesus Christ is the proof. To him we must adhere in faith. Verse 32 seems to contain a reference to Gen 22:16 above, where the LXX word "spared" is used by Paul. It may also echo Isa 53:11.

Paul's questions in vv. 33f. are rhetorical and probably ironic. God's "chosen ones" is unusual for him (cf. vv. 16, 13; also Col 3:12). The obvious answer to the question in v. 33, in the context of a law court or the final assize, is Satan. The patent absurdity of the justifying God or the resurrected and interceding Christ taking a stand against the elect on whose behalf they have labored seems to be the force of Paul's interrogative responses. He may have Isa 50:7ff. in mind here, a passage in which the innocent sufferer is confident of the LORD's support.

MARK 8:31-38

Reading the commentary on vv. 27-38, Proper 19 [24] (B), first should prove helpful.

This passage, one of three in Mark that contains a summary of Jesus' impending suffering, death, and resurrection (see also 9:31; 10:33) is the one with which the Gospel peaks and points toward chaps. 14–16. It is all part of the evangelist's literary technique. Jesus may well have shared the premonition with his friends that he would end badly, but a prophecy of his rising from the dead in such formulaic fashion is scarcely to be credited as an utterance of his lifetime. We know that the Gospels were written with the faith conviction that he had been raised up by God, a point that each evangelist tried to save to the end of his narrative but not always successfully. Mark *does* mean to have Jesus' prediction that he would die violently, followed by the sharp rebuke to Peter for rejecting the possibility, serve as a prelude to the transfiguration narrative. The Gospel goes further in spelling out the early apostolic teaching that suffering and perhaps dying with Christ could be part of the hope of rising with him. This is the very heart of the Markan Gospel: there can be no crown without the cross. It gives the lie to the agonized complaint of some of the baptized, often delivered in anger: "I've always lived a good life. Why should this happen to me?" For some it is the price of accompanying the Son of Man when he comes in the glory of his Father with the holy angels (v. 38; cf. 14:62, a similar look to 8:31 into the future, projected on the screen of the remembered past).

MARK 9:2-9[10]

Verse 1 probably reflects this evangelist's conviction that the parousia will occur in his lifetime or, if not that, that the Gentile mission will succeed sufficiently to vindicate his words. The transfiguration narrative that follows at the very least supports the claim that Jesus is the Messiah. The literary resemblance of 9:7 to 1:11 of the baptismal account is evident but it is not certain, as some hold, that this is a resurrection narrative placed back in Jesus' earthly life. Moses and Elijah represent the Law and the prophets, hence the totality of foreshadowing. Elijah was also connected with the coming of the Messiah (Mal 3:23f.). Matthew will describe the occurrence as a vision (17:9). The booths proposed by Peter are like the *sukkoth* of the autumn harvest feast of Tabernacles (*sukkos*, in much modern Jewish pronunciation of the arbors erected in many back yards and patios). Jesus' injunction to silence in v. 9 is part of the Markan design to build up to the final climax of 16:6.

Third Sunday in Lent (B)

EXODUS 20:1-17

Deuteronomy 4:13 and 10:4, also Exod 34:28, refer to the "Ten Words." The Commandments interrupt the flow of the narrative, which leaves the people at the foot of the mountain in 19:17 and returns to them, in fear and trembling there, in 20:18. The Decalogue is not a law code so much as a designation of the spirit underlying all the laws that will follow.

Jewish tradition makes v. 2 the First Word and then groups vv. 3-4 as the Second. Philo, Josephus, the Greek Church, Calvin, and the Anglican tradition reckon v. 3 as the First Word, vv. 4-6 on graven images the Second, and so on until the

Tenth Word, which is all of v. 17. The Catholic division of commandments, which Luther continued to use, derives from St. Augustine. In it, vv. 2-6 constitute the First Word, the prohibition against idolatrous images being subsumed under the command to adore only the LORD. The Second Commandment is v. 7, and so on, until Nine and Ten, which are v. 17 divided into coveting one's neighbor's wife and his goods, following the order of Deut 5:21 (in Exodus "house" comes before "wife," in Deuteronomy vice versa).

In postexilic times Israel was clearly monotheistic in the strict sense. In an earlier period, as testified to by vv. 2-6, the Israelite concern like that of its polytheistic neighbors was that its God was supreme over all the others. The command to practice monolatry led in time to a theoretical monotheism. The Lord's "jealousy" comes to have as its practical consequence the meting out of punishment and mercy according as the Israelites "hate" or "love" him.

No human image or indeed any image can be carved, including representations of heavenly bodies, the beasts of the earth, and the fish of the sea. A tradition of images continued in Israel long after Moses' time (e.g., mentioned in Judg 8:27; Num 21:8f.; 1 Kgs 12:28ff.). Mosaic floors in synagogues from the Common Era contain fish, geese, and hares but no representation of humans or YHWH has ever been found from the earliest period, nor of anything resembling a consort.

Verse 7 stresses the sanctity of God as it is represented by his name. The prohibition is not against oath-taking but against spells, incantations, and the loose invocation of the divine name in attestation of the truth. On vv. 8-11, see the commentary on Deut 5:12-15 for the Ninth Sunday of Year B. In Exodus as has been noted the LORD's six days of creative activity are given as the motive for imitating him in his rest.

Respect for parents by sons and daughters of any age comes after respect for God in Israelite piety. Cf. Exod 21:7 for the punishment of a serious breach of filial concern. The reward for decency to parents is longevity, both to the individual and to the people for its corporate fidelity to family life. "'Honor your father and mother' is the first commandment to carry a promise with it," says Eph 6:2.

What is proscribed by v. 13 is murder, killing in war being specifically allowed in this culture (Deut 20:13)—no cruder than ours, surely—and capital punishment as well (Exod 21:12-17). The commandment not to kill is concerned with the sanctity of human life, the next three with the sanctity of marriage (cf. Lev 18:20), property, and good name. The terms of perjury in the law courts, a matter prohibited by v. 16, are spelled out in Deut 19:16-21.

Israel's ethical requirements, unlike those of its neighbors, are rooted in God's will. They are apodictically addressed to individuals in the second person singular, not couched casuistically as in the common law of other ancient peoples: "If a person should . . . then thus and so." There is no magical component to these commands. It is a simple matter of fidelity in behavior. If there is moral lapse, no curses or plagues are promised, but the Lord will desert this people as he has said he will do.

Psalm 19[8-11]

1 Corinthians 1:18[22]-25

Paul continues in this letter where he had left off in v. 17 (for which see 3 Epiphany [3]), by recalling again what folly the message of the cross is to some in Corinth. Those "who are perishing" and we "who are being saved" does not mean the Christian hell and heaven but going on the wrong path or the right one once having heard the Gospel proclaimed (v. 18). At this point a few lines from Isa 29:14 suit Paul's purpose. The nearby v. 13 is quoted more than fourteen times in the New Testament (Mark 7:6f.; Matt 15:8f.), but the whole Isaian passage is the same kind of Jewish irony as in the frequently cited Isa 6:9f. In the present case, Isaiah had no wish to destroy wisdom or thwart discernment, hence was made by the poet prophet to say quite the opposite. Here, however, Paul *does* want to see the worldly wisdom that cannot accept the cross destroyed, yielding to what is folly to the world: acceptance of the cross as God's deed. The apostle doubtless knew many who were reckoned wise in the rabbinic circles of his youth (the "sages"). These learned men of writing ("scribes") and debaters of the fine points of Torah (v. 20) may not be the ones identified as purveyors of "the wisdom of the world" (ibid.) but Paul's next statement is that some Gentiles and a Jewish peasantry innocent of such wisdom have been given the gift of true wisdom (v. 21). Throughout the passage this wisdom is faith in Jesus Christ crucified and raised up.

Paul describes the proclamation of the gospel (v. 23) as satisfactory to neither Jews nor Greeks in the states of mind he ascribes to them. Like most epigrams, this one derives its power from generalization. Putting God to the test or retreating skeptically into gnostic categories cannot be met satisfactorily with the *skándalon* of the cross. Paul in vv. 24f., as in 31, draws on Jer 9:22f. but adapts the passage considerably. God's address to "those who are called" (v. 24) makes all the difference in what is real power and wisdom, real folly and weakness. We must prescind from what seems to be a slur on two ethnic groups (v. 22) to arrive at Paul's real meaning. He is describing the powerlessness of God before egocentric concern, wherever it may be found. God's action in Christ is such that it goes against all conventional wisdom. We would err grievously if we thought that the apostle were addressing himself exclusively to two peoples long since dead. He is speaking to a mentality alive in every age.

JOHN 2:13-22[25]

Robert Fortna in *The Gospel of Signs* (Cambridge: Cambridge Univ. Press, 1970) develops the view that the source used by the fourth evangelist was composed of seven sign narratives and a passion account. The seven miraculous signs, he thinks, were described in shorter versions of the following passages: 2:1-11; 4:46b-54; 21:2-14; 6:1-14; 11:1-45; 9:1-8; 5:2-9, 14. The prelude to the passion account, as in the Synoptics, was originally today's reading, 2:14-16, 18-19. Verses 11:47a and 53 formed a bridge, after which came the anointing at Bethany and the entry into Jerusalem of chap. 12. Jesus' arrest, in this view, began at 18:1 and events proceeded from there in the familiar order, through to the end of chap. 20.

Fortna is of the opinion that John's "Signs Source" proved Jesus' messiahship by his works of power. Urban C. von Wahlde (*The Earliest Version of John's Gospel* [Wilmington: Michael Glazier, 1989]) finds these "signs" not associated with "the Pharisees," as "works" consistently is. Hence, the request of v. 18 for a sign authorizing Jesus to do these things is answered by, "Destroy this temple and in three days I will raise it up" (v. 19). John alone makes Jesus the subject of this verb (here and in 12:1). Elsewhere in the New Testament it is God who does the raising.

The transition between 2:12a and 4:46b seems to be a natural one. To introduce the cleansing pericope, clearly an intrusion followed by the stories of Nicodemus and the Samaritan woman, John employs one of the stereotyped editorial formulas interspersed throughout his Gospel (v. 13). Verses 14-16, derived from John's source and unaltered by him, are close to but not identical with the same material in the Synoptics. Their account culminates in Jesus' direct quotation from Isa 56:7 (cf. Mark 11:17; a shorter version is found in Matt 21:13 and Luke 19:46) with a snatch of Jer 7:11 appended. John's v. 16 *may* be an allusion to Zech 14:21, but it is more probably the composition of the author of the source to meet the situation. The evangelist's comment on the meaning of the event is contained in v. 17, where his citation of Ps 69:10 tells what the disciples made of the cleansing when they later came to believe (cf. 2:22; 12:16).

John makes Jesus' opponents "*hoi Ioudaîoi*" (v. 18), as he does characteristically. In his source it may have been "the chief priests and the scribes and the elders" of Mark 11:27 (cf. John 18:3: "the chief priests and the Pharisees"). The Judaeans are probably meant or else the Temple priesthood since everyone in the drama was a Jew, but the leading men of the south where Jesus died were remembered as unalterably opposed to the Galilean hero of the narrative.

The challenge put in v. 18 resembles that of Mark 8:11; Matt 12:38; and Luke 11:16. The Johannine source has Jesus answer in terms of a miracle of power (v. 19). "Unbelief asks for a sign so that it can dare to believe, as is clearly expressed in 6:30" (Bultmann). The destruction of the Temple and the building of a new temple will be that sign: the catastrophe followed by miraculous reversal that brings judgment to unbelievers and salvation to believers. Mark 13:2 and Acts 6:14 refer to a saying of Jesus in which he prophesies only destruction. This, coupled with the testimony reported of his appearance before priestly authority that he was responsible for such an utterance (Mark 14:58; Matt 26:61), leads to the deduction that a historical tradition underlay it.

The phrase "in three days" is a biblical expression for God's setting things right after catastrophe (cf. Exod 19:11; 2 Kgs 20:5; Hos 6:2). The evangelist interprets the "Temple" in terms of Jesus' risen body (v. 21), which for him is not completely distinct from the believers raised up with him to new life. It is possible that the author of the source was wrestling with the problem of the meaning of the destruction of the Temple (in 70 C.E.), as we know Jewish writers of the time did. He could have tied it in with the death of Jesus, the evangelist then making it an explicit reference to the resurrection. Another possibility is that the story contains an attack on the kind of adulterated worship being carried on by a venal priesthood.

Verses 23-25 conclude the narrative with a familiar Johannine motif. Many believed in Jesus as a result of the signs he performed, inadequate though this faith was (see 4:48; 14:11). Jesus has no illusions about popular acceptance of him (6:15).

რთ.ჟრ

Fourth Sunday in Lent (B)

NUMBERS 21:4-9

LM provides this lection along with John 3:13-17 on the feast of the Triumph of the Cross (September 14), as does RCL, and also on Tuesday of 5 Lent opposite John 8:21-30, but never on a Sunday. RCL corrects the omission. The skirmish of the Israelites on pilgrimage with the Canaanite king of Arad is evidently a later insertion (Num 21:1-3) since today's pericope follows immediately on the death and burial of Aaron in the vicinity of the unidentified Mount Hor, probably near Kadesh. The "way to the Red Sea" of verse 4 was the north-south caravan route well east of the Dead Sea known as the Royal Road (20:17). The plan was to skirt

Edomite territory because of the refusal of its people to grant the Israelites safe passage through it (20:14-21) which resulted in a long remembered enmity. But today's story of death in the desert from the bite of the small, venomous viper (*saraph* = "fiery," v. 6) interrupts the people's northward progress to Moab. The grumbling against God and Moses is a repetition of the same in Exodus 16:2f., when quail and manna were provided in response, and earlier in Numbers when the cry was for meat and not the deadly dull fare of cakes from manna and olive oil that brought on a second account of the surfeit of quail (11:4-23, 31-33). How Moses could have cast a serpent of an ingenious alloy is not explained. A foundry, however crude, bespeaks a lengthy settling in, like the euphemistically termed Palestinian refugee camps that became cities. But never mind. This is a story of healing at the sight of a totem. "Is the LORD's power limited?" (Num 11:23) the LORD had asked Moses before driving quail in great quantity in from the wind of the sea (vv. 31f.). And so here. The power is by no means limited, which is the point of the tale of the "serpent of brass upon a pole" of KJV (DRC: "brazen").

PSALM 107:1-3, 17-22

2 CHRONICLES 36:14-16, 19-23

This passage concludes the Chronicler's retelling of the fall of Jerusalem to the Babylonians in 586 B.C.E., recounted in 2 Kings 24–25. There (24:17) we learn that Mattaniah, the twenty-one year old uncle of King Jehoiachin, had his name changed to Zedekiah by Nebuchadnezzar, king of Babylon, who placed him on the throne of Judah. A son of King Josiah by Hamutal (2 Kgs 23:30f.; 24:18), he adopted a throne name when he was made the agent of the Babylonian king. His nephew Jehoiachin (whom 2 Chron 36:10 calls his "brother" or kinsman) had been deported to Babylon along with his family, functionaries, and chief men of the land (2 Kgs 24:15).

The Chronicler sees in Zedekiah's reign eleven years of indiscriminate resistance to the prophet Jeremiah (v. 12), King Nebuchadnezzar (v. 13), and all of God's messengers and prophets (v. 16). The eighteen-month siege of Jerusalem by the king of the Chaldeans (v. 17), i.e., the Babylonian Nebuchadnezzar, came as a result of this conduct in the eyes of the Chronicler (cf. 2 Kgs 25:1-7). The Temple, indeed the whole city, was put to the torch (2 Chron 36:19; cf. 2 Kgs 25:9). Jeremiah's counsel to Zedekiah on this occasion is famous: he should capitulate to the king of Babylon so that the people might live and not see the city become a heap of ruins (Jer 27:12, 17). Equally well known is his castigation of the prophet Hananiah for having raised false confidence in the hearts of the people and "preached rebellion against the LORD" (Jer 28:15-17). This line of public policy goes entirely counter to that of Isaiah during the Assyrian threat.

The last two verses of the present pericope (22f.) are taken verbatim from the first three of the book of Ezra. Their brief account of the restoration under King Cyrus of the Persians fifty years later keeps the book from ending in defeat and destruction with Jeremiah's prophecy of v. 21 (cf. Jer 25:9-12). The best 2 Kings can do about the problem is tell, in conclusion, of Jehoiachin's release from prison to "eat at the king's table" (25:29). After thirty-seven years of Jehoiachin's captivity (562 B.C.E.), Evil-merodach, successor of Nebuchadnezzar, set free the rightful king who had been kept a hostage all those years.

The Chronicler, through the book of Ezra, makes Cyrus out to be a believer in the LORD, the God of heaven (Ezra 1:2; 2 Chron 36:23). The addition of the doublet (vv. 22f.) was required because Ezra and Nehemiah were placed before 2 Chronicles in the Hebrew Bible. In it the last named is the book with which the "Writings" and with them the whole collection ends. The pious Chronicler stresses the Lord's compassion (v. 15) but says that his anger finally blazed forth against the people for their recalcitrance (v. 16). The key to the passage is the prophecy attributed to Jeremiah (v. 21), which makes the observance of the Sabbath, a detail absent from the book of Jeremiah, the key to the termination of seventy years under foreign dominion. Actually it was more like sixty, counting the initial siege.

PSALM 137:1-6

EPHESIANS 2:1[4]-10

God's mercy in restoring his people is the theme of this reading as of the previous one, only this time "death in sin" is a handicap experienced by the entire race over all its years of existence (lit.: "we were by nature children of wrath," v. 3). The agency of restoration is God's "favor" or "grace" (vv. 5, 7, 8) which is a totally unmerited gift (v. 8) and not a reward (v. 9). The New Testament *charis* is a development of the idea of divine favor over the more usual Septuagintal *éleos* to convey "mercy" (Heb. *ḥesed*).

The perfect participle is used in vv. 5 and 8 to express the fact that the baptized have already been saved, a strong touch of realized eschatology. The promised Holy Spirit has earlier been declared the pledge and first payment of full redemption (1:14), which means that completion lies well in the future. Here the notion is different, namely the *present* glory of Christians, which was featured in some

Hellenist circles. Thus we read: "he raised us up with him and seated us with him in the heavenly places in Christ Jesus" (v. 6). Despite the mention of "in the ages to come" (v. 7), the emphasis here is on the present authority enjoyed with Christ over angels, who are the normal inhabitants of the heavenly places of v. 6. This thought pattern is not only uncharacteristic of Paul but one that he constantly opposed, notably among the "Corinthian enthusiasts." When he speaks in his epistles of the present action of God he usually balances it off with what God will do at the End (see Rom 6:1-11; Col 3:1-4 does the same).

Verses 5 and 6 feature three *syn*-verbs: God has "brought us to life *with* Christ," "raised us up *with*," and "seated us *with*" him. This is a doctrine of fellowship with Christ rather than incorporation into him, as in the Rom 6 passage cited above and Col 2:10-13. The Pauline notion of union with Christ in his death and burial is absent. Boasting ("priding oneself," v. 9) is unthinkable to anyone who has received salvation by grace since it is all God's doing (cf. Phil 3:3; Rom 4:2; 1 Cor 1:28ff.). It is not easy to determine whether we are being called God's "handiwork . . . in Christ" (v. 10) at our creation or our redemption. As God's wisdom, Christ is as much an agent of the former as the latter. What is clear is the balance between the "good works" we are expected to devote a lifetime to, that God "prepared beforehand to be our way of life," and the gift of God that makes them possible. The preparation spoken of culminated in our being his "handiwork, created in Christ Jesus, for good works" (v. 10). Despite our responsibility to do good works, it is inconceivable that we should do them on our own or boastfully claim them as our own.

John 3:14-21

The Gospel lection, like the first two lections, has God as the healer or restorer of his people. What was done in desert days through the effective sign of the serpent of bronze, John here has God accomplish through the believer's gazing in faith on the uplifted Son of Man. The verb meaning "raise" or "lift up" does double duty for crucifixion and resurrection in John. Belief in Christ begets eternal life, not death, favorable judgment, not condemnation. Acting in truth brings one into the light and out of darkness. A total Johannine theology is available in this passage. Set against the deeds of the realm below *(kátō)* are the deeds of the realm above *(anō)*: condemnation, darkness, wicked deeds, as against God's sending his Son that the world might be saved, be light, do deeds done in God (vv. 19-21).

It is an uneven contest for John. God through the Son is already the victor.

✧ Fifth Sunday in Lent (B)

JEREMIAH 31:31-34

Gunnar Østborn, *Torā in the Old Testament* (Lund: Ohlssons, 1945), traces the theme that in the ideal future, however conceived, God or some chosen agent of God will impart Torah ("instruction" or "teaching" rather than "law"). The implication is that the new covenant (v. 31) to be formulated in days to come will be drawn up on the basis of the existing Torah. A difference will be that people will "know the LORD" without the necessity of teachers from among friends and family (v. 34).

It is not to be assumed that Jeremiah wrote these verses as part of his opposition to the Deuteronomist reform party. Some among the latter edited his prophecies; moreover, both he and they insist on the need for a "circumcision of the heart" (Jer 4:4; Deut 10:16; 30:6). The principal edition of Deuteronomy is marked by pleas for inward obedience, much as in the writings of the prophet. Jeremiah was not disaffected with written Torah so much as he was unhappy over mere words confined to the scrolls of a book or impressed with a stylus on baked clay ("tablets of stone"). He wanted written Torah to be enshrined in the heart universally and he looked forward to a time when such would be the case.

The notion here expressed by Jeremiah is found elsewhere in the Bible, notably Pss 37:31 and 40:8. The first of these verses reads, "The Law of God is in his heart, / his steps do not falter"; the second, "to do your will, O my God; / your Law is within my heart." Even if both psalms were to have been written after Jeremiah's time and under the influence of the present passage, they only establish that their authors, like him, reconciled a new covenant with written Torah. All three pericopes say that whoever now have the Law in their hearts will enjoy messianic blessings in the future.

Christians have at times mistakenly supposed, because of their belief in Christ or their knowledge of Paul's view of the abrogation of the binding force of *portions* of the Law, that in these verses Torah is being prophesied as transcended or set aside. There is no ground given by the text for such a conclusion. A better referent for Jeremiah than Paul is Ezekiel. There, a "new heart" and a "new spirit" (36:26) will be given by the Lord in place of hearts of stone to "make you live by my statutes, carefully observing my decrees" (v. 27). Any contrast between law and love is alien to Jeremiah's thought. The giving of the Law was a mark of YHWH's love. The covenant of the future envisioned by the prophet involves observance of Torah on an inner, spontaneous principle, involving both the letter and the Spirit.

PSALM 51:1-12[3-4, 12-15] OR 119:9-16

HEBREWS 5:5-10[7–9]

These verses provide what may be the New Testament's clearest picture of Jesus' suffering as one of us "in the days of his flesh" (v. 7). They contain a principle of salvation that modern soteriology is rediscovering. Once made perfect by the obedience he learned from what he suffered, Christ has become the source of eternal salvation for all who obey him (vv. 8f.). Jesus' "loud cries and tears" (v. 7) are the sign that he is facing the implications of perfect acceptance of the divine will. He saves us in both an exemplary and a more directly effective way, the obedience we are called to being in the same order as his.

The reference to God's ability to save Jesus from death and Jesus' being heard is puzzling. Evidently the author does not have the passion in mind but the "reverent submission *(eulabeías)*" of Jesus throughout his life that saved him in every instance but the last. Jesus' unique sonship (v. 8) is a primary datum for the author of Hebrews. It provides Jesus with no immunity from suffering but equips him in a special way for the high priestly office to which he is called (v. 10).

The motif of suffering followed by glory, so pervasive in the primitive *kérygma*, is evident here.

JOHN 12:20-33

The "Greeks" *(Hellénés)* of v. 20 appear but once in this Gospel, not to be mentioned again. It is warmly disputed who, exactly, they were. Only at 7:35 does John use the term elsewhere, speaking of "the diaspora among the Greeks." The Vulgate renders this *gentes,* and for many that is what is meant here, Gentiles. Others are convinced that in this passage Greek-speaking Jews are indicated in contrast to Aramaic-speaking Jews. Whoever they are, and of those some think proselytes are meant, they are in Jerusalem for a specifically Jewish reason. An approach is made to Jesus through Philip, presumably a Jew with a Greek name whose home, Bethsaida, on the north shore of the lake Kinnereth (Sea of Galilee) is in the near, Greek-speaking diaspora.

There is no suggestion in the Fourth Gospel that the heritage of Israel is to be given to the Gentiles. The disciples are never spoken of as appearing before them, as in the Synoptics. Nowhere are they held up for favorable comparison with the Jews. Jesus does not leave Jewish soil in this gospel. "Indeed the Gentiles *(ta éthnē)* are never mentioned in the gospel, and there is no . . . sign of contact with the

Gentile mission as described in Acts," (John A. T. Robinson, *Redating the New Testament* [London: SCM, 1975], 265; cf., *The Priority of John* [London: SCM, 1985]). Hence, while it is possible that non-proselyte Gentiles may be making a single appearance in the narrative at this point, it is quite unlikely that that is what the evangelist means by "some Greeks." This is not to say that John is narrowly nationalistic. He has, throughout, a cosmic perspective. Still, he never distinguishes between Gentiles who come to the light and Jews who do not. In this Gospel many Jews come to believe in Jesus (see 2:23; 7:31; 8:31; 10:42; 11:45; 12:11). We do not seem to have in the present passage a case of Gentiles seeking enlightenment while Jews do not but of Greek-speaking Jews or proselytes from Galilee in a search for the light. "To see Jesus," v. 21, connotes faith for John, not simply looking at Jesus.

He addresses himself to these *Hellēnés* as he does to all: in terms of the impending hour of his glorification, of life through death, of "loving" life and losing it versus "hating" it and keeping it (v. 25). Being a servant *(diákonos)* of the Son in John, serving him, means that the Father will respond by honoring anyone who so conducts himself (v. 26).

Jesus' soul is troubled at the prospect of suffering (v. 27). He is tempted to pray for deliverance from it, as in the prayer reported in Mark 14:36. He forbears. As in similar passages in the Synoptics (e.g., Matt 10:39; Luke 14:26f.; 17:33), he does not ask his disciples to do anything he will not do himself. The Father speaks out from the heavens, confirming the glory that will be given to Jesus in his death and exaltation. John has already given his testimony that the Spirit, like a dove, has come to rest on Jesus (1:32). Many have accepted in faith John's witness concerning him, even though it was accompanied by no "sign" (10:41f.). Now a sign is given, not for Jesus' sake but that of the bystanders (12:30). The voice like thunder sets up a debate as to whether an angel has spoken. The Johannine passage has elements of the Sinai narrative, which is in keeping with the evangelist's picture of Jesus as Messiah delivering Torah in new circumstances.

The judgment (v. 31) that has come on the world may be related to the dispute over whether or not it is God's voice that has been heard. The prince *(archōn)* of this world will be driven out as Jesus is raised up from the earth in crucifixion and exaltation. Condemnation, the evangelist is convinced, will come upon all who do not look upon him in faith. Those who *do* so view him, he will draw to himself (v. 32).

The editorial comment of v. 33 appears to be the work of the final editor of the Gospel, who has added chap. 21 and who, throughout, shows a tendency to allow little to chance. He dots all the i's, crosses all the t's, and in general reminds the reader at intervals how the story turned out.

Sixth Sunday in Lent /
(Passion Sunday or Palm Sunday) (B)

Liturgy of [Procession with] the Palms

Blessed is he who comes in the name of the LORD.

MARK 11:1[10]-11 OR JOHN 12:12-16

For a commentary on Matt 21:1-11, which closely follows Mark 1:1-11, see Passion or Palm Sunday (A).

John introduces his briefer account by saying that a great crowd at the feast heard that Jesus was coming (12:12). The Markan narrative describes the colt as one on which no one has ever sat. Matthew eliminates this but Luke retains it. All three Synoptics have the finding of the tethered colt in near-identical wording. The "fulfillment quotation" inserted by Matthew after 21:3 (Isa 62:11; Zech 9:9) has no place in Mark or Luke. Matthew makes place for it by omitting the challenge of the bystanders about untying the animal that bears a cross of black hair on its back and shoulders (Mark 11:5f.; Luke 19:33f.). For the rest, Mark's "cloaks" and "leafy branches" spread on the road are repeated by Matthew. Luke mentions cloaks only (19:36) and John identifies the branches as those of palm trees taken by those who went out to meet Jesus (12:13). The welcoming shouts of fellow-Galilean pilgrims who had preceded Jesus to Jerusalem are reported variously: "Hosha' na', O [LORD] deliver [us]" in all but Luke who adds from his nativity scene, "Peace in heaven and glory in the highest." Jesus is declared "Blessed" in the cries of all, as one who "comes in the name of the LORD!" Mark adds "Blessed is the coming kingdom of our father David" (11:10) which Matthew changes to "the son of David" (21:9), Luke to "the king who comes" (19:38), and John to "the King of Israel" (12:13), followed by a conflated version of Isa 40:9c and Zeph 3:14f., then Zech 9:9. If Jesus were thought by his followers in the north to be the hoped for anointed one, *mashiah*, hence a king, and the shouts represent a historical recollection, this was the beginning of the sealing of his fate with Pilate, who would have had no awareness of the title's meaning in Jewish end-time hope. Luke adds a rebuke of Jesus' disciples asked for by some Pharisees (19:39f.; cf. John 12:19) and John mentions a component in the crowd of Judaeans who had heard of his calling Lazarus out of the tomb (vv. 17f.). Mark ends the incident more simply by having Jesus enter Jerusalem's Temple, looking all about, and returning to Bethany (v. 11).

PSALM 118:1-2, 12-29

Liturgy of the Passion (B)

ISAIAH 50:4[7]-9A

These verses make up the bulk of the third of four "Servant Songs," generally identified as Isa 42:1-7; 49:1-6; 50:4-9; 52:13—53:12. In all four the "Servant of the LORD" seems to be Israel (cf. especially 49:3), although a case can be made for an individual representing the people as the subject of the fourth Song. In the present one, YHWH acts as a schoolmaster to the servant "morning after morning" (v. 4). The Servant is given "the tongue of the learned" to speak a word that will rouse the weary (v. 4); further, like Moses (Exod 32), he suffers contradiction (v. 7). Yet the two details together do not seem sufficient to make us see in him a giver of Torah in the last age. The Servant is "the one despised, whom the nations abhor" (49:7), someone beaten, buffeted, and treated shamefully (cf. 50:6). We have here a picture of Israel's prophetic function which can only be exercised at great cost in pain. Accepting the training in consolatory and encouraging speech that the Lord offers and refusing to rebel against him are ways Israel can express its fidelity to God. The picture of the humiliation meted out to the Servant may derive from the actual career of Jeremiah, thrown into the stocks (Jer 20:2) and a dungeon (chaps. 37–38). The Servant's trust is in God rather than idols.

God will not fail this people. It is quite certain (cf. Isa 41:11; 42:17; 45:24; 49:23).

PSALM 31:9-16

PSALM 22:8-9, 17-20, 23-24

PHILIPPIANS 2:5[6]-11

See commentary on Proper 21 [26] (A).

MARK 14:1—15:47 OR MARK 15:1-39, (40-47)

In place of either the longer or the shorter reading, a selection like Mark 15:22-27, 33-39 might better be chosen since it contains the Markan core: Jesus' death in fulfillment of Scripture, the cosmic nature of the event, and Mark's faith conviction of who he was.

The compelling reason to substitute for the readings proposed is not merely that their length precludes the preaching of a homily adequate to the problems they raise. It is rather that, in the evangelist's first-century attempt to arouse sympathy for Jesus in his innocent suffering, he almost inevitably gives the twenty-first century hearer the impression that he knows exactly where human responsibility for Jesus' death lay.

In fact, Mark does not know. He is well aware that Roman soldiery crucified Jesus, carrying out Pilate's capital sentence, and that there was some complicity of the Temple ("chief") priests (15:1, 31). But contemporary worshipers, influenced by nineteen centuries of the spurious charge, "the Jews crucified Jesus," are all too likely to hear *that*, rather than what Mark wrote. No preachers have the time to sort out what was fact and what theological development except for a brief instruction beforehand on "What to listen for."

As a vehicle for his christological concern the evangelist constructs his moving account from fragmentary historical reminiscences (he doubtless possesses a primitive narrative of arrest, appearance before some representatives of the Sanhedrin, condemnation by Pilate, journey to Calvary, and crucifixion and death) and biblical sources (Pss 22; 41; Zech 13:17; Ps 110:1; Dan 7:13). Of the two sets of sources, the biblical phrases are better suited to his theological purpose. Such historical traditions as he possesses he puts in the service of a portrait of a Christ who is to come as the victorious Son of Man (Human One), having become such by way of ignominious suffering. The latter is Jesus' Markan title for readers oriented to Jewish apocalyptic writing (14:41, 62). For the more Hellenized, "Truly this man was Son of God" (15:39). Mark has been occupied throughout to identify Jesus in the latter way (1:1; 3:11; 5:7; 15:34), but he does it by challenging readers to discipleship in the context of the prospect of the coming Son of Man.

Jesus' meal with his disciples is a Passover meal for Mark (14:12, 16), eaten after sundown on the 14th of Nisan. John locates it earlier (13:1), putting Jesus' death on the day before the first day of Passover (18:28). Mark wishes to situate

Jesus' glorification and the origins of the Gentile ministry in Galilee (14:28; 16:7). For Luke (24:47) and John (chap. 20) it is a Jerusalem mystery but for the author of John 21, a Galilean one.

Mark has two traditions on Jesus' appearance before the Sanhedrin. Of these, the one in 15:1 is likely to be historical while the "night trial" (14:55-64) is an example of Mark's intercalation or "sandwich" technique, an insertion into the story of Peter's denial in the high priest's courtyard to fill up a space of time. In 15:1, the Greek verb given in that place in the better reading is "held a consultation" rather than NIV's "reached a decision."

Mark's Christology demands an affirmation of Jesus' sonship and messiahship of God, which he puts squarely on his lips (14:62; only in this gospel does Jesus answer "I am"). Jesus as "seated" derives from Ps 110:1, "coming" from Dan 7:13, probably a conflation to meet two different parousial hopes in the primitive church. The "blasphemy" of v. 64—since Jesus has not uttered the divine name—may well be the charge on which disciples of Jesus in the Markan church are being found guilty as a result of their claims about him in relation to God.

The passion narrative is chiefly interested in making faith affirmations about Jesus in a context of the biblical-type humiliations he endured. This earnest effort has been badly misconstrued over the centuries as reporting Jewish guilt and Roman compassion (15:2-15). There is no good reason to continue the confusion in the minds of contemporary Christians.

If a parish wishes to devote a Lenten series of lectures to the way the passion narratives were formulated, it should be encouraged to do so. As proclamation, however, these portions of the gospels which were meant to arouse compassion for the innocent Jesus can serve to pour fuel on the Christian fire of anti-Jewish sentiment. Confining the Gospel reading to the thirteen verses suggested at the head of this commentary, leaving time for an exposition of the way Jesus' human obedience is the cause of human redemption, is surely the better way to go.

ᘓᘓ
Holy Week (A, B, C)

For commentaries on the lections of Monday through Holy Saturday, see under Year A.

❧ Season of Easter ❧

❧ Easter Vigil (B)

For a commentary on the readings other than the gospel, see Easter Vigil (A).

MARK 16:1-8

Assuming that we have in this pericope the conclusion of the Gospel as it came from the evangelist Mark (vv. 9-20, while canonical, being the work of another hand), we see immediately that he makes the story of an empty tomb, "the place where they laid him" of v. 5, central to his narrative. Paul's account of Jesus' being raised, presumably primitive, centers on the earliest witnesses to the event (1 Cor 15:5-7) and makes no mention of the tomb. Mark has had the highly placed Joseph of Arimathea bury Jesus according to Jewish custom and roll a stone across the entrance of the tomb (15:46). Both details render the eight verses of Mark's final chapter puzzling. Why was a further embalming with spices necessary, and why was there a tomb story at all? To complicate matters further, there is the ambiguity of who the second Mary was (see 15:40, 47, and 16:1 for the conflicting details; NAB makes her the mother of Joses and James [6:30] in the latter two verses, thereby conforming to the first, but the genitive case denotes wifehood more readily than motherhood). Also, Salome appears in 15:40 and 16:1 but is missing from 15:47.

The transition of v. 6 to v. 8 is an easy one, confirming the impression that v. 7 is an insertion into a preexistent narrative. Mark's theology requires Galilee as the place of parousial glorification or, if not that, the central place of the Christian movement. The "trembling and bewilderment / terror and amazement" of v. 8 are normal responses to the appearance of an angel (cf. Luke 1:12, 29). If this appearance to women was not part of the original narrative, it and the empty-tomb story could have been added at the same time. The announcement of the "young man" would have been central to a cultic recitation, much like the *Quem quaeritis?* tropes of medieval drama.

The mention of the stone's having been rolled back (v. 4)—a "divine passive" denoting action by God—is confirmed in John 20:1, where it occurs apart from any angelic appearance. This leads us to suppose that the stone rolled away was a detail of the earliest telling of the empty tomb story. A tradition retained in Acts (13:29) identifies Jesus' opponents as those who laid him in the tomb, leading to the speculation that legendary accretion made a certain member of the Sanhedrin a disciple of Jesus (Matt 27:57; Luke 23:50; John 19:38 describes him as a disciple "in secret" like Nicodemus). If the story of burial by Joseph is late and legendary, it leaves the account of a visit by the woman (originally Mary Magdalene alone, as in John 20:1?) intact. The disciples came back from their experiences of the risen Jesus in Galilee and received a confirmation of them from the Magdalene's story of an empty tomb. The young man in white (v. 6) is probably the rehabilitated believer who fled in 14:51f. His "He has been raised; he is not here" (v. 6) is not a report of a bodily resuscitation but of a new eschatological existence. Jesus has been resurrected from a grave to a transcendent life. It is in this mode of being that his disciples experience him. Mark has the women keep silent, a familiar theme of his (v. 8). The gospel breaks off abruptly, "For they were afraid," perhaps to heighten completion in the future by parousial encounter but more likely as an admonition to Mark's contemporaries not to fail to proclaim the resurrection out of fear of the consequences.

See the commentary on Matt 28:1-10, Easter Vigil (A), which derives in good part from this Markan pericope.

❧ ❧

The Resurrection of the Lord / Easter Sunday (B)

Acts 10:34-43

See Easter Day (A).

Isaiah 25:6-9

See Easter Evening (A).

Psalm 118:1-2, 14-24

1 CORINTHIANS 15:1-11

See 5 Epiphany [5].

ACTS 10:34-43

See Easter Day (A).

COLOSSIANS 3:1-4

As on Easter Day (A) (C).

1 CORINTHIANS 5:6-8B

As above (A).

JOHN 20:1[9]-18

As above (A).

MARK 16:1-8

See Easter Vigil (B).

❧❧

Easter Evening

All as in (A).

❧❧

Second Sunday of Easter (B)

ACTS 4:32-35

The respect that the apostles were universally accorded in Jerusalem (v. 34) is essential to Luke's idealized conception. The community members lived in peace, holding all things in common and distributing "to each according to his need from each according to his means." That, at least, was the way the socialist Friedrich Engels remembered it from his Sunday school boyhood. No one went without the necessities. It became a watchword in European communism, a utopian scheme in its origins. The apostles were the first distributors of goods (v. 35) until the number of disciples grew so large as to make the designation of assistants necessary (6:2f.). The account is so heavily romanticized that the appearance of Ananias and Sapphira (5:1-11), with its little touch of larceny comes almost as a relief in the otherwise oppressive idyll. This passage among others in early Acts has been the charter of countless idealist sects and Christian primitivists bent on doing "exactly as it was done" in Christianity's earliest days. Such has been their assumption without realizing the much later reconstruction of events that Luke was engaged in.

The narrative conveys successfully a pervasive charity and mutual support, the work of the Holy Spirit, which is truer to the Acts account than any literal attempts to replicate it.

Psalm 133

Psalm 118:2-4, 16-18, 22-24

1 John 1:1—2:2

Although tradition has called this the "First Epistle of John," the absence of any epistolary salutation and conclusion makes it seem more like a short treatise than a letter. It has certain ideas in common with John's Gospel, but the words and phrases found there often receive a different treatment (examples: "the beginning," "word," and "life," 1:1). Its main purpose seems to be to counter certain false ideas about Jesus which may or may not have taken their rise from a faulty reading of the gospel, the text of which the author may not know. The recipients of this communication are presumed not yet to have the "fellowship (*koinōnía*, life in common) with the Father and with his Son Jesus Christ"—not a Gospel of John phrase—that the writer possesses. His hope is that they may come to share it "that their joy may be complete" (vv. 3f.). The claim to have heard and seen and touched the life that was with the Father and has been revealed appears at first blush to be an intimate knowledge of "Jesus Christ come in the flesh" (4:12). This it surely is but not an actual intimacy with the pre- and postresurrection incarnate Word. "From the beginning" describes a knowledge of the life brought by the enfleshed Word that the writer has had shared with him ("the message we have heard from him," v. 5) and desires to pass on (cf. 2:24; 3:11). He knows of the reality of the divine in palpable, physical form and wishes to testify to it publicly. "Walking in the light" is his phrase for having fellowship with the God who is light (vv. 5-7) and in turn each "with one another," a company cleansed of all sin by the blood of God's Son, Jesus, again not a Fourth Gospel concept. "Doing what is true" renders the Semitic "doing the truth" of the claim of v. 6 of walking in the light; it is not, however, a claim of total sinlessness (vv. 8, 10). Acknowledgment of sins is required to bring forgiveness by that cleansing blood. Should we sin, Jesus Christ the just will be our "advocate" (*paráklēton*, 2:1) with the Father. He is the "atoning sacrifice" (*hilasmós*; cf. *hilastērion*, Rom 3:25, LXX's "mercy seat/propitiatory" of Exod 25:17; 37:6) for the sins of the whole world. The twelve verses of this lection describe the faith life of an early community convinced of what God has done for it. That deed is the revelation of "eternal life" in the one whose blood shed in sacrifice atones for a world's sin. This whole treatise is a *défi* thrown down to any of gnostic or docetic bent who think otherwise (see 1:7; 3:16; 4:6) about how the gift of eternal life has been made available to us (4:11f.).

1 John 5:1-6

It is our faith that conquers the world (v. 4), a faith that for 1 John is our acceptance of Jesus as the Christ (v. 1) and Son of God (v. 5). This faith confers divine sonship on us. Love of God and obedience to his commands, which are no burden, brings in its wake love of all who are his progeny by faith (v. 2). Some of these ideas have occurred previously in the letter at 2:13; 3:1f., 10; 4:4.

A new idea is introduced in v. 6, namely, that of Jesus' coming "in water and blood" to which the Spirit testifies. Perhaps his baptism is meant and surely his death in all its historical reality, his "flesh" having existed between these two poles (cf. the anti-gnostic 2 John 7 and 1 John's "antichrist" of 4:2f.). Less likely, the reference here is to Christian baptism and Eucharist (cf. John 6:54). The Spirit, who is truth (v. 6), testifies to the reality of Jesus both in the gospel accounts of his baptism and transfiguration and in the post-Easter spread of the Gospel, which is achieved only by the Spirit's power.

Alleluia

Give thanks to the LORD who is good, whose love is everlasting.

John 20:19-31

See 2 Easter (A).

Third Sunday of Easter (B)

ACTS 3:12-19

Abraham Lincoln once proposed to Salmon P. Chase, his Secretary of the Treasury, that the Union in its inability to pay its military creditors should produce scrip bearing Peter's words to the cripple at the Beautiful Gate: "Silver and gold I have none, but what I have I give thee" (3:6). Peter's reported speech, in extension of the healing miracle, is Luke's composition, hence contains the view found in his Gospel that the Jews handed Jesus over and disowned him while Pilate was for releasing him. The main point of Peter's discourse is not ascription of guilt but that the same God who raised Jesus from the dead healed the cripple; therefore the miracle is not to be attributed to any "power or holiness" of Peter and John (v. 12). Peter's description of God (v. 13) in relation to the patriarchs is the LORD's self-description in Exod 3:7, 15. The "glorification of his servant" is an echo of Isa 52:13 at the beginning of the fourth servant Song. God has glorified Jesus through the miracle of healing, not through raising him from the dead, which is first mentioned in v. 15. The designation of Jesus as servant (here *pais*, not *doulos*) seems to derive from an early stratum of Palestinian usage after "Jewish prayers, in which great men of God, especially David" are so denominated (Ernst Haenchen, *The Acts of the Apostles: A Commentary* [Philadelphia: Westminster, 1971]). It is Luke's way of saying "Son of God." The term will recur in the *Didachē* 9:2f., *1 Clement* 59:2-4, and the *Martyrdom of Polycarp* 14:1.

Verse 14 is a reference to the Barabbas episode in Luke's Gospel (23:17-25). In v. 15 this murderer is contrasted with Jesus, who is described as the pioneer or leader of life who gives life to all. The chief emphasis of Peter's speech is on the phrase, "whom God raised from the dead," which negates the known fact (for Luke) that the Holy and Just One was put to death in the place of a murderer. Being witnesses to Christ's resurrection is, again for Luke, the cachet of an apostle.

Peter addresses the crowd in v. 17 as "my brothers" (NRSV, "friends"), the ordinary term for Christian believers, to indicate that the ignorance that underlay the crucifixion can be mended by repentance. Some think this is a reference to the "unintended sins" of the Hebrew Scriptures (e.g., Lev 22:14; Num 15:22-31). It is, in any event, an echo of exculpation of the perpetrators that was probably part of the tradition of missionary preaching by Luke's time. See, in this connection, Jesus' word from the cross in Luke 23:24 (missing from many early MSS; also Acts 13:27 and 17:30). In the last two passages, God is spoken of as overlooking the deed because the rulers of the Jews did not "know" or "recognize" Jesus. Verse 18 reflects the common assumption of the apostolic company that all the prophets were united in prophesying the suffering of the messiah. Since this is nowhere said by any of them, the tradition must derive from coupling the identification of Jesus as the messiah with the various plights of the righteous sufferer in Hosea, Isaiah, Jeremiah, and the Psalms. The invitation to repent and turn to God (v. 19) is the climax of the speech. Only by going in a new direction can there be forgiveness of sins, new life coming from the Lord who "sends you Jesus" (v. 20).

Psalm 4[2, 4, 7, 9]

1 John 3:1-7

For a commentary see All Saints, November 1 (A).

1 John 2:1-5a

The address "my little ones" is an ordinary affectionate term used by a father to his children. The Damascus Document (Zadokite Fragment) of Qumrân employs it in the Johannine sense found at 2:14. First John has denied that anyone is sinless (1:8) and the author writes to help the reader stay clear of sin (2:1). He has a category of sin he calls "mortal" (lit.: "leading to death," 5:16f.), from which he does not think recovery is possible. All other sin is remediable through the offices of Jesus Christ as advocate (*paráklētos*, 2:1) with the Father. It is because he is just and in the Father's presence that he can succeed in the role of defense counsel. First John, like Hebrews, ties Jesus' powerful advocacy in with his death. It is an "atoning sacrifice" (*hilasmós*, v. 2; cf. 4:10). Paul in Rom 3:25 spoke of Jesus' death as "a sacrifice of atonement for all who believe," using the cognate word *hilastērion*, the LXX's normal rendering of *kaporeth*, "mercy seat" (Exod 25:17). The propitiation that heals the breach is thus a personal life freely laid down (cf. 3:16). The sure way of "knowing" Christ (in the Johannine sense, i.e., cleaving to him in faith) is keeping his commandments (v. 3). Any claim to knowledge without the obedience of love is a flagrant lie (v. 4). Keeping Christ's word means bringing to perfection the love the believer has for God, which originated in God's love for the believer (v. 5a).

It is much disputed whether the *agápē* of the Johannine literature is confined to the brotherhood (a gnostic, dualist circle, in Ernst Käsemann's view; see *The Testament of Jesus* [Philadelphia: Fortress Press] 40, 46f.) or is extended to all the world. Dodd thinks that "the brothers" of 3:16 (NRSV, "one another") is to be interpreted in light of John 4:14 which calls the Son "the Savior of the world."

Alleluia

As under (A).

Luke 24:[35] 36b-48

The commentary on Luke 24:13-55 found on 3 Easter (A) provides helpful background for today's reading. The two Emmaus road disciples have returned to Jerusalem to recount their experience of the risen Lord to the Eleven (vv. 33ff.), telling how they had come to "know him in the breaking of bread." That *klásis toû ártou* (v. 35) had become a technical term for the table fellowship of Christians by Luke's time. Joining it to the narration of appearances of the risen Christ occurs also in Luke 24:41f.; Acts 10:41; and John 21:9-14.

Verses 36-43 are concerned with proving the truth of the resurrection, while 44-49 are an instruction on Jesus as suffering and risen Messiah derived from the Hebrew Scriptures composed of "the Law, the prophets, and the psalms" (synecdoche for the "writings") of v. 44. The mention of "broiled fish" in v. 42 is an indication of the Galilean origins of this narrative (cf. John 21:1-14) but vv. 33 and 47 situate it in Jerusalem. Fuller suggests that it may be the second appearance of Jesus of 1 Cor 15:5, namely, to the Twelve, here "pedantically corrected to eleven" by a pre-Lukan link (*The Formation of the Resurrection Narratives* [New York: Macmillan, 1971], 114). Luke, like Mark and Matthew, uses this appearance, not for a Church-founding purpose as Paul has done but for a mission-inaugurating one (cf. v. 47).

The motif of doubt, absent from Paul, is introduced into this narrative as in Matt 28:17; John 20:25, and the addition to Mark at 16:11, 13, 14. Joined to it is the note of physical proof of the resurrection, something quite contrary to the eschatological character of Christ's "spiritual body" of 1 Cor 15:44 which Paul labors so hard to underline in extension of his resurrection kerygma found earlier in that chapter (vv. 4-8). This indicates the development which the narratives of Jesus' appearances have undergone (cf., for example, Matt 28:9), which is much more realistic than the narrative of Jesus' resurrection of the first seven verses, told in apocalyptic terms. Clearly Luke wishes to identify the risen Lord of the church in Acts with the earthly Jesus who could be touched and seen and who ate fish. In place of the triumphant climax of "proof" that may have existed in the pre-Lukan source, Luke inserts the Christ kerygma of vv. 44-49.

In 4:18-21, Luke has Jesus expounding Isa 61:1 as referring to himself. This attempt of the earthly Jesus was evidently not successful, for minds must be opened once again (v. 45) to the meaning of the Scriptures as at 24:27. Verses 26 and 46 are very close in intent, the title "Christ" and the word "suffer" being the common elements. Luke's concern is not with history but with salvation history, hence the actual location of the appearances is of less importance to him than that the commission to preach penance to all the nations (v. 47) should have originated in Jerusalem.

The "companions" who accompanied the eleven of v. 33 have been forgotten by v. 48, so intent is Luke upon centering on the apostles as "witnesses" (cf. Acts 1:8, 22). The ministry, death, and resurrection of Jesus have been interpreted by Jesus speaking as the risen one, as the eschatological fulfillment of prophecy. It must now be preached, worldwide.

❧❧ Fourth Sunday of Easter (B)

ACTS 4:5[8]-12

Detained overnight in jail by the Temple guard, presumably for preaching that "in Jesus there is the resurrection of the dead" (4:2), Peter and John appear before a representative high priestly group to face interrogation. The apostles' offense is their anti-Sadducee proclamation of a resurrection in the flesh (cf. Acts 23:8). This alignment of forces is essential to Luke's historical picture. He holds throughout that the Christians were opposed not by the Pharisees but by one group only, the "sect of the Sadducees" (*haíresis*, Acts 5:17). Actually, the latter were not a sect or group but those aristocratic circles that kept aloof from the popular Pharisee movement toward reform and renewal.

It cannot be established whether Luke has any exact information about an appearance of Peter and John before an official body. He does know something of the composition of the Sanhedrin or Great Council, the elders tending to be Sadducees but also possibly some scribes and Pharisees (v. 5). The same confusion persists here as in the gospels over Annas, whose high priesthood had run from 6 to 15 C.E. Joseph called Caiaphas, his son-in-law, held the office around the years 17 to 36 C.E. Perhaps all that Luke intends to convey is the uniting of all religious power figures and mentalities against the apostolic community.

Peter is filled with the Holy Spirit (v. 8), as had been promised in Luke 12:11f. He makes a spirited defense to authority in response to the charge of healing (ibid.). Peter's point is not only that a good deed is not fitting as a charge but that restoration or healing is the very matter that Jesus has come for. He whom God raised from the dead has rendered "this man before you in good health" (v. 10). Psalm 118:22 is quoted in v. 11, as has already been done in Mark 12:10

(//Luke 20:17). Here, however, Luke follows another tradition. Men have rejected Jesus as Scripture foretold. (In the context of the psalm, it is the people Israel that is being described.) God has responded by making him a person of greatest importance. Only in Jesus' name is salvation to be found. The healing of the cripple and of all humanity is attributable to that same name of Jesus and the power of God.

PSALM 23

PSALM 118:1, 8-9, 21-23, 26, 28-29

1 JOHN 3:16-24[1-2]

For a commentary see 4 Easter (B).

In the early verses of the letter, the biblical writer is lost in amazement at the gift of divine sonship in the present, yet there is more to come. He explains the undistinguished appearance of Christians in terms of the non-recognition of the Son for what he was (v. 1). Perhaps v. 2 is a response to a position which holds that total likeness to God is the condition of the believer now. If so, John is at pains to refute it, the present situation of humanity being neither one of the direct vision of God nor inability to sin (vv. 2, 8). Remaining in the Son who takes away sins and in whom there is nothing sinful (v. 5) is the best guarantee of not sinning (v. 6). At the same time, being like God and seeing him as he is are future realities, not present ones (v. 2).

ALLELUIA

As under (A).

JOHN 10:11-18

This pericope follows the selection for the fourth Sunday of Easter in Year A, commented on there. The key to the long allegorical similitudes of John 10 is Ezek 34 in which Israel's rulers, indicted as false shepherds, are deposed in vision and replaced by a Davidic shepherd king. John finds in the Jewish leadership of his time and place hireling shepherds with whom the good (literally: "honorable," "beautiful," *kalos*) shepherd is contrasted. For John, Jesus is the one Messiah deliverer. He gives his life. Hired hands run away in face of persecution. Wages are their only concern (v. 13), not the welfare of the sheep.

Mutual knowledge of the kind that characterizes Father and Son marks sheep and shepherd. It is the Johannine "knowledge" that is the same as "seeing." Who are the "other sheep"? The readiest answer proposed is the Gentiles but, as was pointed out in these pages under 5 Lent (B), these are no concern of the fourth evangelist. Probably they are the Jews who at the time of the writing have accepted Jesus but not on John's terms. The vision of "one flock, one shepherd" may be taken as an eschatological fulfillment of Ezek 34:23 which speaks of one supreme shepherd of God's flock, "my servant David."

The climax of the discourse is the statement of Jesus' freedom in laying down his life (vv. 17f.), a freedom that takes the form of obeying a command or mission given him by the Father. This freedom in "laying down" and "taking his life *(psychē)* up again" will divide Jesus' hearers in the way that Johannine discourses do.

＊＊

Fifth Sunday of Easter (B)

ACTS 8:26-40

Peter and John have been sent to Samaria by the other Jerusalem apostles to follow up on the evangelizing of Philip (8:14). For a brief commentary on what went on there see Acts 8:5-8, 14-17 on 6 Easter (A), which stops short of the account of the attempt of Simon the magician to receive the power of the Spirit with an offer of money and his subsequent request for prayers (vv. 18-24). Peter and John have returned to Jerusalem as today's lection begins (v. 25). Philip's journey to Gaza is southwesterly rather than to the south, on a road nowadays frequently blocked to Palestinians against free access to family members in the occupied territories and even to work in Israel. The castrated Ethiopian is apparently a Jew and well paid in the court of the *Kandákē*, queen of Ethiopia, to have had his own vehicle driven by another and to possess a scroll of Isaiah. Reading aloud to oneself was common in the ancient world, hence Philip's hearing him as he puzzles over Isa 53:7f. (vv. 7b-8 in the LXX with only two variants from the critical text). The eunuch's request for guidance is not based on incomprehension but on who might be prophesied in the book, which is of course Luke's interest throughout the writing of Acts. A previous verse (1) of the Isaian Servant Song is quoted in John 12:38,

v. 9 in 1 Pet 2:22, and a snatch of Isa 52:7 in Rom 10:16; but otherwise the New Testament does not make much use of these poems of a humiliated one. The Ethiopian courtier would have been denied access to Temple worship for his mutilated state if Deut 23:2 (LXX) were being enforced (see, however, Isa 11:11; Zeph 3:10), but this is not Luke's concern at the moment. He is interested in the fulfillment of prophecy. Believers in it as fulfilled in Jesus Christ were candidates for entry into the Lukan church, and so the anonymous royal official, in becoming one of them, is baptized. What his life might have been upon his return to Ethiopia is a matter of conjecture but Luke would have seen in him an evangelizer of his people, just as Philip is next reported on as such to the people of Azotus (v. 40). From this point on in Acts the spread of the Gospel to Gentiles by Jews in their diaspora cities will be featured, as was its spread like wildfire in Jerusalem (see, e.g., 2:41, 47; 6:7). For a theory that the rapid spread of the Gospel in the first three centuries was the work of diaspora Jews, not Gentiles, see Rodney Stark, *The Rise of Christianity* (San Francisco: HarperCollins, 1997).

ACTS 9:26-31

In Paul's account of his ejection from Damascus, he says he was let down the city wall in a basket by the ethnarch of King Aretas IV of Nabatea (2 Cor 11:32f.). This leads us to conclude that the king ruled Damascus through a governor at that time. The tradition that Luke possesses has forgotten the enmity of this monarch— the father of the wife of Herod Antipas whom Antipas repudiated in favor of Herodias—to Saul for his missionary activity in the Damascus area, and ascribes the plot to his customary later enemies, "the Jews" (vv. 23ff.). Luke wants to put the seal of approval on Saul by having him consort freely with the apostles in Jerusalem. This accords ill with Paul's later solemn declaration in Gal 1:18ff. that he visited Jerusalem for the first time three years after his Arabia-Damascus stay, there meeting Cephas and James but no others. "I was still unknown by sight to the churches of Judea that are in Christ. They only heard it said that 'the one who formerly was persecuting us is now proclaiming the faith he once tried to destroy'" (Gal 1:22f.). Luke's narrative requires the intermediary offices of Barnabas, however, and the preaching activity of Saul in Jerusalem where he early incurs Jewish wrath (Acts 9:29). Saul is thus bundled off to Tarsus via Caesarea (v. 30), whereas by his own account he makes his way back to his native Cilicia with no help or even knowledge of the Judaean community (Gal 1:21).

Verse 31 is a familiar Lukan-type summary of the church at peace, enjoying "increase in numbers and the consolation of the Holy Spirit."

PSALM 22:25-31[26B-28, 30-32]

1 JOHN 4:7-21

For a commentary see 6 Easter (B) and 7 Easter (B).

1 JOHN 3:18-24

This epistle has been speaking against the failure to love (v. 14) and closing one's heart to one's fellow believer in need (v. 17). The present passage proposes deeds of love rather than words as the way to know we are "from the truth" (v. 19). God's knowledge of our hearts and his greatness are sufficient to overcome any reproach of conscience within us (v. 20). "God is with us," is literally "we have boldness before God" (v. 21). Pleasing him and keeping his commands, specifically believing in his Son and loving one another (v. 23), ensure our receiving from God all that we ask. This fidelity to his commandments is the certain way to abide in God and have God abide in the one who obeys them (3:24; cf. 4:16).

ALLELUIA

As under (A).

JOHN 15:1-8

The Hebrew Scriptures in several places use the figure of vines and vineyards to refer to Israel (see Ps 80:8-15; Jer 2:21; Ezek 15:1-18; 19:10-14). The Synoptic Gospels do the same, especially at Mark 14:25, and parallels: "I will never again drink of the fruit of the vine until the day when I drink it new in the reign of God."

The Messiah Jesus, by the shedding of his blood, makes possible the true people of God. The agricultural processes of trimming and pruning (vv. 2f., 6) are ways to describe the fruitfulness the Father has brought about in Jesus' disciples. Paul uses a similar figure in the grafting of wild olive branches into the trunk of the olive tree (Rom 11:17). Jesus' word of truth is the means of pruning away what is useless (v. 3). Living on in Jesus (v. 7; cf. v. 4) provides assurance that whatever is asked will be given, that God will be glorified in the fruitfulness of Jesus' disciples (v. 8).

Sixth Sunday of Easter (B)

ACTS 10:44-48[25-26, 34-35]

This chapter contains a story of the first Gentile coming to believe in Jesus. Cornelius is a Roman army officer with a hundred men under his command (v. 1). He is "God-fearing," a technical term for someone not a full proselyte (i.e., a circumcised Gentile who observes the whole Law) but a respectful participant in synagogue study who espouses the Jewish worldview and ethos. He is garrisoned in the harbor town of Straton's Tower, renamed some decades earlier as *Kaisareía Sebastē* by Herod the Great to honor his patron Augustus. Caesarea the August was the year-round residence of the Roman prefect Pontius Pilatus until his deposition in 36 C.E. The narrative that precedes today's reading tells of Peter made aware by means of a vision that the line between fit *(kosher)* and unfit foods has been erased. One immediate consequence is that table fellowship with Gentiles which was frowned on for observant Jews because it might entail unconscious eating of proscribed foods is now allowed to participants in the table fellowship of Christ such as Peter. We know from Paul that it was Peter's practice to eat with Gentiles when he came to Antioch (Gal 2:12), even when others came "who were from James," i.e., Christian Jews from Jerusalem; this even though Peter later lost his courage and fell into pretense (v. 13).

Cornelius respectfully drops to his knees (vv. 25f.), but Peter resists the gesture, as Paul is later reported having done at Lystra (14:15). Luke stresses Peter's affability in the midst of this family gathering. Today's reading resumes with Peter's discourse, which begins with a declaration that God is not a respecter of persons (v. 34). The word literally means a "face taker," a term not unlike our "name dropper." The notion of God's total impartiality occurs in Deut 10:17; 1 Sam 16:7; and Wis 6:7. The same phrase as here occurs in Rom 2:11 and Gal 2:6. Peter's point is that God looks at respect for himself and righteous deeds irrespective of ethnicity in the hope of finding a person acceptable (v. 35).

The reading omits Peter's kerygma, which is on the same model as Paul's at Pisidian Antioch. It resumes with the Spirit's action, which follows upon the close of the exhortation to repentance for the forgiveness of sins (v. 44). The circumcised Jews in Peter's party are surprised that the Gentiles are speaking in tongues (v. 46). Peter sees no barrier to their baptism in water (v. 47). And so it is done "in the name of Jesus Christ," the formula familiar to Luke (v. 48). The narrative illustrates the Lukan theology of peaceful coexistence of Jews and Gentiles in the primitive Church. Paul's account in his epistles conveys considerable strain, as does the story of Stephen in Acts 6–7, which Luke nonetheless incorporates.

PSALM 98[1-4]

1 JOHN 5:1-6

For a commentary see 2 Easter (B).

1 JOHN 4:7-10

The love that John hymns has its origin in God, not at the plane of earth. Its clearest manifestation is the sending of God's Son for our sins (vv. 10, 9). The Son came that we might have life through him (v. 9). The loveless man is the man not possessed of God-knowledge (v. 8). God and love are the one (v. 8). Because love is something of God, we should love one another (v. 7). Love for one another is the author's great concern. He never says that love is God, only that God is love.

In these four verses we have a perfect compendium of Johannine theology.

ALLELUIA

As under (A).

JOHN 15:9-17

Today's Gospel reading continues last Sunday's, saying the same sublime things without employing the allegory of the vine and the branches. The Son loves his disciples with the Father's love for him and is faithful to his Father's commands with the fidelity he exacts of his disciples. A revelation is being made in the Son to bring about the fullness of eschatological joy *(charà)*. What is revealed is the way of friendship, not of servitude. A perfect friend will lay down his life for another. Election intends to have fruitfulness as its outcome. The great command is mutual love.

❧✍

Ascension of the Lord (B)

Thursday after 6 Easter.

ACTS 1:1-11; EPHESIANS 1:17-23; PSALM 47[2-3, 6-9] OR
PSALM 93; LUKE 24:44-53

For a commentary on two of these readings see under (A); on Luke 24:44-53 see
under (C).

MARK 16:15-20

Mark 16:9-20 gives every evidence of having been written by someone other than
Mark. William R. Farmer, *The Last Twelve Verses of Mark* (Cambridge and New
York: Cambridge Univ. Press, 1974) considers the question still open, after reviewing the external and internal evidence. They are often called "the longer ending"
in contrast to a shorter one of two verses found in certain MSS (and given in NAB,
NEB, NRSV, and JB). Non-Markan though they are, vv. 9-12 have been considered
canonical from early times. Besides the occurrence of the canonical ending in
numerous earlier codices, it is testified to from the mid-second century on by Justin,
Irenaeus, and Tatian among others. Eusebius and Jerome in the fourth century say
that it is missing from almost all the better MSS. Codex Washingtonensis ("W"
in the Freer Gallery of the Smithsonian Institution) has a second or third-century
insertion between vv. 14 and 15 that softens the condemnation of the eleven. In
it Christ explains the mystery of the atonement in the first person.

The canonical ending has often been designated the first harmonized version of
material from the four Gospels (and Acts). It may be helpful to indicate here the parallels of all the verses, not just the final six of today's reading. The Markan verse
numbers follow in parentheses: (9) appearance to Mary Magdalene, John 20:16, from
whom Jesus had cast out seven devils, Luke 8:2; (10) her bringing the news to the
eleven, John 20:18—although Mark is alone in having her companions "mourning
and weeping"; (11) the disciples' unwillingness to believe the women, Luke 24:11;
(12) the manifestation of Jesus to two disciples walking toward Emmaus, Luke 24:13-
32; (13) the report they brought to the other disciples, Luke 24:33-35—although the
renewed disbelief of the latter is proper to Mark; (14) Jesus' appearance to the disciples, Luke 24:36-41; John 20:19-21; Matt 28:16-20—Luke says "they thought they
were seeing a ghost" and are upbraided by Jesus for it, but his scolding is severest
in Mark for the lesser matter of doubting witnesses to the resurrection; (15) the command to preach everywhere, Matt 28:19f.; (16) the necessity of baptism, Matt 28:19;
(17f.) the signs that shall accompany the gospel, Acts 1:8, including the gift of speaking in tongues, Acts 2:4; (18) immunity from snakebites, Acts 28:5; exorcism, Mark
9:37; healing, Mark 6:13; (19) the ascension of Jesus, Luke 24:51, and his exaltation at his Father's right hand, Acts 2:33; (20) a summary of the spread of the gospel

from the glorification of Jesus as Lord and Christ down to the time of the writing. The commonly accepted view of this canonical ending as an artificial summary of the appearance stories in the other Gospels has been challenged by scholars like C. H. Dodd and Maurice Goguel, who compare its chronological sequence of appearances with those in 1 Cor 15:5ff. Dodd thinks that its author is composing freely from tradition, with supplementary material from Matthew and Luke (*New Testament Studies* [Grand Rapids: Eerdmans 1968], 128–31). He points out the following distinguishing characteristics: (1) the appearance to the eleven occurs while they are at table, a difference from Luke and John; (2) the Emmaus story is situated at table but to *two* disciples; (3) bread and fish are distributed to *seven* disciples in John 21:13; (4) only here does the risen one reproach the disciples for their disbelief in testimony to his risen state.

The purpose of the Markan list of persons to whom Jesus appears is not the same as in 1 Corinthians 15, viz., to authenticate the resurrection kerygma, but to prepare the way for the great commission in vv. 15-18, which is not paralleled in wording in the other Gospels. The statement of the ascension in v. 19 is the only one to echo 2 Kgs 2:11 and Ps 110:1.

All in all, then, the Markan ending contains independent traditions on the ascension, the missionary charge, and the command to baptize; and it summarizes appearances of Jesus from the other Gospels in its own fashion.

❧ ❧

Seventh Sunday of Easter (B)

ACTS 1:15-17, [20AC], 21-26

Acts 1:2-8 sums up the appearances of Jesus and the reconstituting of the apostolic group that is to act as witnesses to Jesus "in Jerusalem, in all Judaea and Samaria, and to the ends of the earth" (v. 8). The passage looks back to the twelve he had selected from among his disciples to be his apostles (cf. Luke 6:13). The twelve are witnesses of the resurrection, though clearly the number that could be so designated was larger than twelve, as the account of the choice of Matthias over Joseph Barsabbas shows (vv. 22f.). Luke's interest, here as elsewhere, is to forge a link between Jesus in his lifetime and the Church's beginnings and continuation in history. The names of eleven are given (v. 13), whose special significance is that they are not at the moment twelve.

The defection of Judas has destroyed the eschatological symbolism of the number of the tribes that would befit a mission to Israel. Since nothing is done later to replace the martyred James (see Acts 12:2), we can only conclude that while he is removed from the work of the others, he is not removed from their number. The flaw of Judas's departure was that it made him a nonwitness of the resurrection, hence the chain between religious and ethnic Israel and the newly reconstituted Israel was incomplete. Soon after Pentecost, Luke lets the Twelve disappear from the stage. They are still intact as a group in 6:2; hence presumably the Twelve are meant in 4:33, 36; 5:2, 12. In 6:3-6, the Twelve are obviously superior in Church organization to the seven, who just as obviously are leaders "of a divergent, or at least of a distinct, wing of the church" (C. K. Barrett, *The Signs of an Apostle* [Philadelphia: Fortress Press, 1970]). Barrett points out that when the apostles are mentioned again in 8:1, 14, 18; 9:27; 11:1; 15:2, 4, 6, 22, 23; 16:4, a closed group is indicated, distinguished at times from "the brothers" (11:1; cf. 1:15) and at other times from "the elders" (cf. the citations in chaps. 15 and 16 above).

The Psalms quotation which LM retains (109:8; it omits the quotation of Ps 69:26) speaks of the total repudiation of an anonymous sufferer. Another has taken his "office" (*episkopē*, v. 20c, the LXX term in Ps 100:8 for *pᵉkuda*) or responsibility, besides widowing his wife and orphaning his children. The apostles utter a prayer asking God to help them choose a replacement *(topos)* for the apostolic ministry of Judas (v. 25). In the drawing of lots *(klērous)* the choice falls on Matthias (v. 26). *Klēros* is the Greek word that has given us "clergy" but there is no connection with games of chance. The derivation is closer to the "allotted portion" of Ps 16:5, the "Dominus pars hereditatis meae" of the Vulgate in the now suppressed rite of clerical tonsure. The LORD is the psalmist's lot, his inheritance, and his cup, just as the Lord Jesus becomes the lot of apostle, cleric, and Christian believer.

PSALM I

PSALM 102:1-2, 11-12, 19-20

1 JOHN 5:9-13

The commentary of 2 Easter (B) ends with a brief word on v. 6. Verses 7 and 8 were expanded by a later hand to give them trinitarian significance. RCL provides the omitted phrasing in a footnote and NIV does the same, identifying late Vulgate MSS as the culprit. NAB simply omits the *comma ioanneum*, the clause that appeared as vv. 7b-8a in both DRC (1610) and KJV (1611), following faulty Greek (Erasmus, under pressure) and Latin texts: "in heaven: Father, Word, and Holy Spirit, and these three are one. And there are three who give testimony on earth."

The insertion attempted to make the doctrinal point that the three persons are coequal but its parallelism fails to account for whom the testimony in heaven might be given to. The writer knows that God has testified to the Son on earth (v. 9), not to Godhead itself. Those who believe in the Son of God have this testimony in their hearts, while any who would deny it make a liar of God (v. 10: cf. 2:22). What is testified to is that eternal life is in God's Son (vv. 11f., a recapitulation of the life that was with the Father, 1:2; 2:25) and is our present possession (5:13). The latter verse is a summary of all that has gone before, even though many editors and translators (Nestle-Aland, NRSV, NAB, NIV) reckon it the beginning of an epilogue.

1 John 4:11-16

Mutual love among believers is the corollary of God's initial love for us (v. 11). The biblical denial that anyone sees God and lives (Exod 33:20) is repeated here (v. 12) in preparation for affirming the believers' dwelling *(menei)* in God and God in them (vv. 12, 15, 16). Anyone's acknowledging (*Hos eàn homologēsē*, v. 15) that Jesus is the Son of God brings this mutual indwelling. The recognition of Jesus' sonship results in a knowing and believing in God's gift of love *(agápē)*, a love that is none other than Godhead itself (v. 16). The love is not inchoate but one brought to perfection (vv. 12, 17).

Alleluia

As under (A).

John 17:6[11b]-19

See 7 Easter (A) for a commentary on vv. 6-10.

John 17, Jesus' final discourse to those near to him, is interested in his glorification (vv. 1, 5), just as the prologue had been (cf. 1:14). In the Johannine community everyone is commissioned to authority and discipleship (cf. 17:18ff.). Unlike the situation in Luke-Acts, in John the theological significance of the apostles as a distinct group is not to be found. The word "apostle" in its technical sense does not occur in John. Jesus gives his peace and the breath of the Holy Spirit to his "disciples" (20:20ff.). An office is conferred, but on a wider group than the Twelve. "The world-wide commission and mission of the church and the duty of every individual believer to participate in it are all presupposed" (Käsemann, *The Testament of Jesus*). The call to discipleship includes being sent into the world as Jesus was sent (cf. v. 18). Christian life as such is mission. It is mission to the world, an alien realm (vv. 16ff.). Like Jesus, his disciples are pilgrims and sojourners below, visitors from a heavenly sphere of existence.

The Father is asked by Jesus to protect his friends from the evil one (v. 15). No one was lost in his careful watch over them except "the one destined to be lost," literally, "the son of ruin/loss"—in "fulfillment of Scripture" (v. 12). This providential view of the defection of Judas is not unlike that of Acts, where the guide of "those that arrested Jesus" is likewise seen to have been prophesied in Scripture (cf. Acts 1:16-20).

The reason for the revelation represented by the "word" Jesus spoke and will speak (vv. 14, 20) is that his disciples may share his joy completely (v. 13). This joy will be at the same time a unity among all believers, who will be united in Father and Son as they are in each other (cf. v. 21).

❧❧

Day of Pentecost (B)

ACTS 2:1[11]-21 OR EZEKIEL 37:1-14

See Day of Pentecost (A).

For a partial commentary on Ezekiel see Easter Vigil (A) and 5 Lent (A), which, however, does not speak of the sinews, flesh, and skin of the slain (vv. 6, 8, 9).

PSALM 104:[1], 24-34, [27-30], 35B

Veni, Sancte Spiritus.

1 CORINTHIANS 12:3-7, 12-13

See Pentecost (A).

ROMANS 8:22-27

For a commentary see Propers 10 [15] and 11 [16] (A).

JOHN 15:26-27; 16:4B-15

This Gospel had spoken of "another Advocate" who would be with Jesus' disciples forever, making him the initial Advocate (14:16; cf. 1 John 2:1), and had identified this person as the Holy Spirit (14:26). *Advocatus* is a faithful translation of *Paráklētos*, both meaning someone called to one's side presumably for counsel and strength. In English we use "attorney," "lawyer," and "solicitor" for the Romance languages' *avocat, avvocato, abogado*, but in the U.S. there is also a Judge Advocate General. KJV had rendered the word "Comforter," an interpretation of the Spirit's function, while DRC simply transliterated it as "Paraclete," which then entered Catholic vocabulary and is retained in JB. This one who will be sent from the Father will be the "Spirit of truth" testifying on Jesus' behalf (15:26), placing on the disciples the obligation to do the same (v. 27). Verses 4b-11 explain the silence of Jesus on these matters because unnecessary while he was with his disciples and his departure as the condition of the Advocate's coming. The "sin" the Spirit will convict the "world" of is failure to believe in Jesus, "righteousness" what true justness before God consists in, namely belief in the absent Jesus, and "judgment," the condemnation of Satan who will be driven out by the "lifting up from the earth" of Jesus in crucifixion and resurrection (see 12:31f.). The commentary for Trinity Sunday (C) on John 16:12-15 speaks briefly of what subsequent theology derived from this passage on the interrelation of Father, Son, and Holy Spirit.

JOHN 20:19-23

For a commentary see 2 Easter (A)

❧ Season after Pentecost ❧

❧❧ Trinity Sunday / First Sunday after Pentecost (B)

ISAIAH 6:1-8

For a commentary see 5 Sunday (C).

PSALM 29

DEUTERONOMY 4:32-34, 39-40

This reading is taken from the concluding part of Moses' first address of three, represented by the Levitical author as having been spoken east of the Jordan, on the brink of Israel's entry into Canaan (1:1—4:43; 4:44—28:68, the heart of the seventh-century Josian reform; 29:1—30:20). Chapter 4 is practical and hortatory in tone, coming as it does after a review of events between the deliverance of the commandments on Mount Horeb and the defeat of the Amorites, Edomites, Moabites, and Ammonites. Heshbon and Bashan are the last to be conquered, along with their kings Sihon and Og. Moses climbs Mount Pisgah, to be told there: "Look well, for you shall not cross over this Jordan" (3:27). He reviews, instead, the statutes and ordinances he is teaching the people to observe. His chief message is that in the new land, with its complex civilization, this nomadic people is not to forget the revelation made at Horeb and fall into idolatry. Abandoning the covenant will bring quick destruction in Canaan by the LORD, a jealous God.

Verse 31 describes the LORD as a merciful and remembering God. The verses that follow (32-38) spell out his deeds of mercy, unparalleled in human history. Who has ever heard of such prodigies as those reported in the theophany of

Horeb—the voice of God from the midst of fire without the destruction of the people addressed (v. 33), the snatching of Israel from the power of Egypt which is terrified by the strength of YHWH's outstretched arm (v. 34), the delivering over, by
the conquest of more powerful nations, of Canaan as a heritage, "as it is today"
(v. 38, the latter phrase betraying the lateness of authorship)?

This great display of divine power and solicitude had but a single purpose: to
fix in Israel's heart the truth that the LORD is God and there is no other (vv. 35,
39). Heretofore, other gods and their representations were forbidden (Exod 20:3).
Nothing was to be made to rank with the LORD (Exod 20:23). Now for the first
time he is described as the only God. The claim will be reiterated two chapters
later in what is to become the opening phrases of the daily prayer, the Sh^ema: "Hear,
O Israel! The LORD is our God, the LORD alone!" (Deut 6:4).

The framers of the lectionary wish to underline the conviction of Christians
that they have not deserted Israel's ancient, monotheist faith. Despite the mystery
of Son and Spirit there is for them no plurality of gods nor any plurality in God.
The LORD is one. There is no other (v. 39). Moreover, the revelation of his oneness has as its consequence the lodging of stern ethical and cultic demands (v. 40).

PSALM 33:4-6, 9, 18-20, 22

ROMANS 8:12[14]-17

See Proper 11 [16] (A) for additional commentary.

The second reading is a splendid example of what later came to be designated trinitarian thought. For Paul, the Spirit of God is a Spirit of adoption of
men and women along with Christ, whose sonship and daughterhood of God is
primary. Christ's status as heir is such by right of proper sonship, ours a matter
of becoming heirs with him (v. 17). There was no scheme of legal adoption in
the biblical period. It was an arrangement of the Hellenistic age, having largely
to do in the Middle East with inheritance. The context of Paul's remarks has
been life "according to the flesh" (vv. 12, 13), meaning life lived apart from God.
The natural consequence of such foolish autonomy is death (v. 13), its con-
comitant, slavery (v. 15). In opposition to it Paul puts life in the Spirit. The Spirit
has been received (v. 15) but the gift is not yet perfect in its effects. In its fullness it is something to be looked forward to. Now we possess the Spirit as first
fruits (v. 23). If we suffer with Christ we shall be glorified with him (v. 17). Hence
the testimony that the Spirit renders along with our spirit (v. 16) is to an eschatological event already made present in some measure. "Children of God" that

we are (v. 16), we can address God as "Abba!" the Aramaic word (Hebrew: *ab*) for father in Mark 14:36 and Gal 4:6. Paul may derive it from Jesus' own usage, if he knows the tradition of Jesus' address to God as Father in the prayer he taught (Luke 11:2; Matt 5:9).

Father, Son, and Spirit work together to achieve the adoption of the human race in the New Testament. They constitute a mystery of human salvation and describe God at work, not as God is within Godhead.

ALLELUIA

As under (A).

JOHN 3:1-17

For a commentary see Trinity Sunday (A); 4 Lent (B).

MATTHEW 28:16-20

In illustration of the point made at the end of the commentary on Romans above, there is mention of the Father and the Son and the Spirit in conjunction with the immersion in water which will signal the disciples to be drawn from all nations. The "mountain to which Jesus had summoned them" (v. 16) is in Galilee, as part of the evangelist Matthew's intent to designate this locality as the center of origin of the Christian movement. The doubts of some seem to persist (cf. John 20:24-29) as they worship the risen Christ (v. 17) and receive the command. He is not described as to his person, as he was in the transfiguration narrative (Matt 17:1-8). He speaks, that is all. His words form the only proper conclusion we have to a gospel, Mark and John having been given endings by other hands who thought the Gospels not well enough concluded and Luke supplying only a bridge to Acts.

In virtue of his full authority (*exousía* = *moshel*, as of the messianic king, Zech 9:10), pointed to by the "therefore" of v. 19, Christ tells the eleven disciples to go and make disciples of all nations. This charge to approach the Gentiles has not occurred previously in Matthew. It comes with Jesus' glorified state as Messiah. Neither is there any mention in the Synoptic Gospels of Jesus' disciples baptizing (cf., however, John 4:1-2). Baptism elsewhere in the New Testament is performed in the name of the Lord Jesus (Acts 2:38; 8:16). Hence it is supposed that we have here a Church formulation rather than a phrase from the lips of Christ. The trinitarian formula is found in *Didachē* 7:3, a writing that, in the form it has reached us, knows Matthew's Gospel or its sources. Christ's teaching is summarized as "everything that I have commanded you," an echo of the farewell speeches of Moses in Deuteronomy. These commandments could include the injunction to partake of the eucharistic meal (26:26ff.) and all his teachings of mutual love, justice, and forgiveness. Christ's promise that he will be with his disciples always, "to the end of the age" (v. 20)—for Matthew the enduring period of the Church—makes clear that this is a testament, a farewell speech. As in 18:20 there is the assurance that Christ will be in the midst of his Church, sustaining the actions its members take.

Here again, as in Paul's letter to the Romans, Christian life under the one God has a "trinitarian" character (to use the much later term deriving from Tertullian (*trinitas*; in Theophilus and writers in Greek after him, *triás*).

❧ ❧
The Body and Blood of Christ (B)
Thursday after Trinity Sunday but Commonly Celebrated on the Following Sunday

EXODUS 24:3-8

This pericope is an Elohist tradition (E) inserted between two Yahwist (J) ones, vv. 1-2 and 9-11. E resumes with vv. 12-15a. The result of the combination is the appearance of a ratification of the covenant in two stages, the first in a sprinkling of blood and the second in a meal. In the J tradition the people are not to come near the Lord since they are represented by Moses and the seventy elders. In E, although a similar awe is reported (cf. 20:18), Moses and the people are solidified in a blood rite in which he acts as their priest (v. 6). The present narrative follows that of the designation of Moses by the people as their spokesman (20:19) and their being told to construct an altar of earth or unhewn stone (vv. 24ff.).

The "words and ordinances" (v. 3) reported by Moses to the people are the E material that makes up chaps. 21 and 22 plus chap. 23 with its inserted passages (vv. 4-5, 6-9, 10-19, 22b-24 J; 27 J; 29-31a all from J). The spirit of respectful awe that characterized the people in 20:20 is found again in their declaration that they will do everything the Lord has told them (v. 3). The "book of the covenant" (v. 7) is presumably "all the words of the LORD" (v. 4) that Moses wrote down, i.e., the collection of laws contained in 20:23—23:33.

The altar and twelve pillars, which signify the twelve tribes (contrast the reprobated Canaanite pillars, 23:34), were erected at the foot of the mountain in order to prepare for the act of slaughter. In ancient Israel the priests did not do the slaughtering but offered up the blood of bulls by splashing it on the sides of the altar, placed the meat on top of the wood and embers on the altar, and burned the whole offering (viz., made a "holocaust," cf. Lev 1:5-9). Moses associates certain young men with him in the priestly act of offering (v. 5). The institutionalization of priesthood through Aaron's sons has not yet been achieved. The symbolism of blood sprinkled on the altar and the people while the "book of the covenant" is being read is self-evident. The rite solemnly ratifies the acceptance by the people of the terms of the covenant. The people are sealed in fidelity to the written words, just as they are to the LORD to whom sacrifice has been offered in blood on the altar. The "blood of the covenant" (v. 8) is the blood that symbolizes ratification of the covenant (cf. Zech 9:11).

The inner disposition of the Israelites is described as one of utter fidelity to the prescriptions of YHWH that are written in the book of the covenant. The sprinkled, sacrificial blood stands for this fidelity as a sign.

Psalm 116:12-13, 15-18

Hebrews 9:11-15

Most scholars doubt that this book was intended for Hebrew-speaking Christians, thinking Hellenists or God-fearers of the diaspora far more likely as the intended recipients. The title of the epistle (which actually is a theological treatise) is deduced from its contents. Its author knows the LXX version of the Bible thoroughly and wishes to relate Jesus to Temple priesthood and sacrifice. The case is usually made for post–70 C.E. authorship, on the supposition that the Christian author is accounting for the succession of Levitical priests by Christ in the providential plan. Some, however, see in the Christology of the book, with its stress on Jesus' being made perfect in humanness through what he suffered (cf. 2:10; 5:9; 7:28), indications of pre-70 authorship. This would date the work before the composition of the canonical Gospels, all of which betray signs of a "pressure" of Jesus' divine status on his human, something that Hebrews does not except by indirection (chap. 1). Its broad allusions to the former in 1:2-13 are quite sufficient. There are also Platonizing touches discoverable within it that have made most commentators relate its authorship to Alexandria.

Hebrews is intent on the effect of Jesus' death (cf. v. 15) through the shedding of his blood (v. 12), hence the fittingness of this reading on the feast of the Body and Blood of Christ. The "perfect tent not made by hands" (v. 11) is the heavenly abode of God (cf. Acts 7:48) where Jesus now dwells. He has entered as high priest into the sanctuary (v. 12) located there. The good things "that have come" (v. 11) is a better reading than "yet to come," following p⁴⁶, Vaticanus, and other MSS against Sinaiticus and Alexandrinus. This indicates the author's concern with the benefits of an eternal redemption (v. 12) that have been made available by Christ's priestly activity.

The author's argument in vv. 13f. is a simple one of the rabbinic type *qal vahomer*, lit.: "light and heavy" (in the West, a fortiori). If Temple sacrifice (cf. Lev 16:14) has as its function the removal of ritual defilement, how much more potent is the blood of Christ that "purifies our conscience" *(syneídēsin)* from dead works to worship the living God!" (v. 14) whose deed is rendered effective "through the eternal Spirit." Christ is offerer and offered, priest and victim. He is such effectively because his *pneûma* is *aiōnion*, everlasting, indeed the Spirit of God itself; hence the redemption he achieved is everlasting. The argument of Hebrews seems to be that ritual sacrifice achieves ritual purification whereas the deep personal involvement of Christ, in which eternal Spirit has a part, reaches deep into human consciences to set them free of personal sins. "Dead works" are not any works but deeds done apart from God's *pneûma*. Thus set free, the Christian can "worship the living God" (v. 14), a not unexpected figure of speech in a document so cultically oriented.

Verse 15 identifies the precise role of Christ as "mediator of a new covenant." His death accomplishes deliverance from "transgressions" committed under the "first covenant" (cf. Exod 24:7f., understood), that those called may receive the promised eternal inheritance. These two stages appear to be an echo of Jer 31:32, now made explicit in terms of faith in Christ. Deliverance has prepared the way for promise, ransom for inheritance. Jesus' priestly action, therefore, is a boon in two parts, the first of which is the necessary link with the initial Mosaic covenant.

ALLELUIA

As under (A).

MARK 14:12-16, 22-26

Vincent Taylor (*The Gospel according to Mark* [London: Macmillan, 1952]) found two streams in the Markan passion narrative, one that is fairly continuous, characterized by classical Greek words and Latinisms, the other made of narratives and shorter passages filled with possible Semitisms. The latter (B, as he terms it) is intercalated into or appended to A. In this schematization, vv. 12-16 by their detail and use of the term "disciples" suggest that they are a later addition to the A narrative, although Taylor will not say with certainty that they were absent from it as it was first framed. He assigns vv. 22-25 to the Semitic B narrative ("blessed and broke . . . the bread," "this is my body," "this is my blood," "blood of the covenant," "poured out for many," "Amen"; "fruit of the vine" and "reign of God" in the vow of v. 25); vv. 26-31 he assigns to A.

The phrase "two days before the Passion and the festival of Unleavened Bread (azýmōn = matzoth)" is puzzling. This is not normal usage for the day of preparation on which paschal lambs were slaughtered and offered (cf. Exod 12:6), normally 14 Nisan. It has been suggested that the Aramaic tradition that lay behind the Greek had said "the day of preparation." The narrative at vv. 13f. hints at a greater familiarity of Jesus in a Jerusalem setting than Mark would have us believe. There is nothing preternatural about the sign. Jesus knows a peculiarity of someone who may either be a friend or have a public accommodation for hire. The guest room (katálymá mou, v. 14, Luke's word for a traveler's lodge at 2:7) is situated above the ground (anágaion, v. 15). At Passover time thousands of families and companies of villagers would be making similar arrangements.

A lengthy Passover meal with its ritual order (sĕdĕr) is not reported, only the liturgical formula of what has become the commemorative Christian meal. It cannot be determined from Mark whether a true Passover supper is being described, although some like Joachim Jeremias maintain it. Bread is broken and a blessing offered "while they were eating" (v. 22), not before as is customary at Jewish meals generally. Moreover, the blessing over the cup follows immediately, not as if it were one of the four interspersed through the Passover meal. The two verbs used for blessing (eulogēsas, v. 22 and eucharistēsas, v. 23) are not different in meaning; both translate barak. It is God who is blessed rather than the food for his goodness in a particular action: in ordinary meals, that goodness takes the form of bringing forth food and drink from the earth; at the Passover, deliverance from Egypt; at the Christian eucharist, saving us through the death and resurrection of the Son.

The phrase "this is my blood of the covenant which is poured out for the many" is a clear reference to Exod 24:8, including the way the first Christians conceived Jesus' death as priestly and atoning. The phrase "for the many" (v. 24) is an echo of Isa 53:6 and 12, even though the exact prepositional phrase does not occur. The Nazirite-like vow of abstention from wine until a deed is done (v. 25) resembles the vow tradition that underlies Luke 22:16, 18. This, coupled with the cup–bread–cup order in Luke, is part of the evidence that has led some to think that this eschatological saying of Jesus with its future orientation was primitive in the Christian meal and the retrospective aspect of a body given and blood shed a later development. All this would have happened in the two decades between Jesus' death and Paul's account of the tradition he had received by the time he wrote 1 Corinthians (see 11:23-29). By this time the meal is looking back to the night on which Jesus was handed over, even while it remains a proclamation of the death of the Lord "until he come."

The songs of praise sung (v. 26) are the *hallel*, Psalms 114–18, 115–18 according to another usage, with the acclamation *Halleluiah* interspersed between each half-verse; again, such is the case if a Passover meal is being described by Mark.

❧❧
Proper 4 [9] / Ninth Sunday of the Year (B)
Sunday between May 29 and June 4, inclusive
(if after Trinity Sunday)

1 SAMUEL 3:1-10, (11-20)

For a commentary see 2 Epiphany [2] (B).

PSALM 139:1-6, 13-18

DEUTERONOMY 5:12-15

For a commentary see 9 Epiphany [9] (B).

PSALM 81:1[3-8A], 10[-11]

2 CORINTHIANS 4:5[6]-12

See 9 Epiphany [9] (B).

MARK 2:23 — 3:6

See Ninth Sunday after Epiphany [9] (B).

❧ ✌

Proper 5 [10] / Tenth Sunday of the Year (B)
Sunday between June 5 and June 11, inclusive

1 Samuel 8:4-11, (12-15), 16-20, (11:14-15)

Samuel's sons Joel and Abijah proved little better than the sons of Levi, although their sins of taking bribes and perverting justice are reported almost pro forma in v. 3. The elders charge Samuel with old age and ineffective parenthood, but their real desire is for a king like those of their pagan neighbors. The LORD is onto their game and tells Samuel that it is not he who is being repudiated but Israel's God, and that it has been going on ever since their deliverance from Egypt (v. 8). Samuel relays the LORD's reasoned judgment that the voice of the people be listened to, but first that the ways of kings be conveyed in their commonest manifestations. It is a marvelous catalogue of the conduct of ancient despots and, mutatis mutandis, modern ones (vv. 11-17). In our day people seldom ask for strong leadership. Sometimes, however, they have autocratic governance forced on them: in State and Church a mailed fist in a velvet glove but soon enough a glove of mail. The directives may be more unimaginative than cruel, resulting from a rigidity of character, but the effect is much the same.

RCL offers a choice between this lection and Gen 3:8-15, for a commentary on which see [Mary's] Immaculate Conception [in Her Mother's Womb], December 8. Both tales are powerful lessons on the reward of folly, specifically the man's garden experience of disobedience for which he blames another, while the first is a reminder of the perils of choice in an uninformed electorate. The latter also speaks to the harsh conditions under which workers and others labor. It might be well in some years to spell out what the Genesis story does and does not teach, in others the hazards of a lack of vigilant inquiry into *all* that a candidate stands for. God delivers no people from its wrongheaded choices (v. 18); they must live with them. The story in 1 Samuel is about Israel's turn from an upright priest-judge to a monarchy. The disobedience of "the Man" *(ha 'ādām)* has far more dire consequences.

Psalm 138

Genesis 3:8[9]-15

See Immaculate Conception (December 8).

Psalm 130:[1-8]

2 Corinthians 4:13 — 5:1

Paul is defensive of his conduct in this letter in response to the one who has "caused pain" among the community members in Corinth by accusing Paul of causing pain to him (1:23—2:4). Paul's vacillating spirit was evidently one of the charges (1:17). There seem to have been worse, all in the order of weakness in leadership. One suspects envy of Paul's gifts as the root of the problem, one of these gifts being the capacity to bruise another's psyche. The unhappy individual has, in any case, succeeded in dividing the local church, and Paul's apologia for his conduct attempts to heal the breach. Any who preach on this reading need to supply the background. Otherwise, attentive hearers might take it to be concerned with the resurrection body only and miss out on discussion of the problem of flaws in church leadership, male and female. Clay jars are easily shattered, something that our metal and plastic container-conscious generation may not immediately appreciate (4:7). Glass would better illustrate Paul's point to us, for he is contrasting human weakness with the power of God. A careless hand can send a goblet crashing to the floor. Our mental frame does not easily bear the weight of the divine glory as it is expected to.

The apostle wishes to go on record as realizing the problem, especially in his case. He sees himself as continually dying in order to give the life in Christ he has been commissioned to share (vv. 11-12). A snatch of a psalm occurs to him as particularly apt: "I kept faith, even when I said, 'I am greatly afflicted'" (116:1). The psalmist is speaking in Hebrew of fidelity to Israel's God. Paul employs the Septuagintal, "I believed, and so I spoke," because that verb contains the noun *pistis*, which for him means faith in a future resurrection with Christ. This brings him to meditate on "this slight momentary affliction"—the unhappy incident that has affected him and all in Corinth—as of little consequence relative to the "eternal weight of glory that lies ahead" (v. 17). Temporary pain is a preparation for endless happiness. Paul could not have known of Shakespeare's "mortal coil." He does know of a mortal tent that must be shuffled off. Happily, a finer clothing lies ahead for him and all who share his faith. The present gift of the Spirit, literally a down payment *(arrabōna, 5:5),* is their guarantee. Congregations that have been divided by a heavy clergy hand may well deserve an apology rather than need an apologia. The better way to go is for both minister and people to keep their eyes on the prize, Pauline style.

ALLELUIA. JOHN 14:6

I am the way, the truth, and the life says the Lord; no one comes to the Father except through me.

MARK 3:20-35

If today's lection from 2 Corinthians highlights the tension between Paul and one of his churches, this Markan pericope does the more basic thing of recalling Jesus' being at odds with his family. LM not only contains the account and is followed in this by RCL but spreads it over three weekdays in the second and third weeks of Year A. It proposes the verses about doing the will of God as superior to being related to Jesus (31-35) as suitable for feasts of saints and the profession of vows of men and women who live by religious rule.

Before that edifying Markan conclusion, however, there occurs what has to be the authentic reminiscence of fears for Jesus' sanity by his extended family and the attribution of his powers to Satan by those opposed to his teaching. Had neither been the case, no such unfavorable stories would have been devised. "He has gone out of his mind" (v. 21) represents a verb that reads literally, "he is out of himself," *exéstē*. The family's attempt to restrain him does not suggest bizarre behavior on Jesus' part. His miraculous powers and profound teachings would have been enough to jolt his familiars, especially if his baptism by John in Judaea represents a longer period when he was off the Galilean scene and was remembered only as a local craftsman. The charge that he casts out demons by the prince of demons, Beelzebul ("lord of the height"? "lord of the house"? Second Kgs 1:2 gives "Beelzebub," "lord of the flies"). All are derisive descriptions of the ancient adversary like early North America's "Old Scratch" or "the Old Harry." The charge would be called by modern psychologists "projection." Jesus parries the thrust by pointing out the illogic of Satan's working against himself (vv. 23f.). His "house divided" metaphor (vv. 25f.) was employed in the U.S. slavery debate by at least three others before Lincoln quoted v. 25 in his unsuccessful run for the Senate in 1858: "I believe this government cannot endure permanently half slave and half free." Dwight Eisenhower, who grew up in a Jehovah's Witnesses household before he went off to West Point, gave v. 27 as his favorite biblical quotation when asked by the now-defunct *Look* magazine, presumably realizing that the house plundered by Jesus acting for God belonged to "the strong man" Satan.

Why there could be an unforgivable sin in light of God's universal will to forgive has always puzzled those who encounter it in the Gospel. Mark can only be describing the perverse mentality of his day that attributed an evil origin to Jesus' good words and deeds. The sin cannot be forgiven because, in Mark's view, it persists without any desire for forgiveness. If there be any such sin over the ages, rooted not in ignorance but with full knowledge and intent, God alone can know.

JOHN 14:6

PSALM 116:1-2

◆◆

Proper 6 [11] / Eleventh Sunday of the Year (B)
Sunday between June 12 and June 18, inclusive

1 SAMUEL 15:34—16:13

For a third Sunday now RCL provides semi-continuous readings from 1 Samuel. There will be one more next Sunday. Verses 32-33 do not occur in any public reading, not only because they are so violent but because they are so uncharacteristic of all else we are told of this priest-judge. Having deplored Saul's sparing of Agag's life, he hews him in pieces, rendering Agag's mother childless, as his sword had done to the women of Israel. This is the same tit-for-tat killing in global wars and executions that the media report on every day. The Bible describes some moral maturing of our race in other areas—but not in this one. Judaism, Christianity, and Islam have by and large made no progress in the matter, at least as regards the convictions of most of their adherents. A few isolated religious groups and some secular states have progressed—to the shame of Christianity generally.

After the defeat of the Amalekites (15:20), Samuel and Saul never meet again (v. 35), but the prophet grieves for the lost king he thinks Saul to have been. He is sent by God to find a successor among the sons of Jesse the Bethlehemite. Understandably he fears for his life at the king's hands as he embarks on the search. The city elders are apprehensive of his mission and are placated by the God-inspired ruse that he has come only to offer a sacrifice. The first three of Jesse's eight sons whose names are given are passed over, Eliab, the first, because his appearance and his height mask a heart that does not please the Lord. This makes 16:12, in which appearance seems to count for much, all the more puzzling. Its insertion by another hand might explain it—that of an admirer of the exploits of the shepherd king. For a commentary on 1 Sam 16:1-13, which tells where the story fits into Judah's history, see 4 Lent (A).

EZEKIEL 17:22-24

It is evident why RCL lets this lection for 11 Sunday in LM stand as an alternative. It makes the same point in parable form as the tale of the choice of David; moreover, the movable date of Easter can cause [11] (B) to be of infrequent occurrence for Catholic worshipers. Most modern Bible translations set the passage in type as poetry, although NIV does not. Lest the previous poetic allegory of vv. 3-8 go misunderstood, the author provides the key in vv. 11-21. The great eagle (v. 3) is Nebuchadnezzar, king of Babylon (v. 12), who descends on Jerusalem and carries off a "royal offspring," Jehoiachin, and "the chief men of the land" (v. 13) while the shoot that becomes a vine with branches (vv. 5-6) is Judah flourishing in a foreign land. The other great eagle (v. 7) is Cyrus, king of Persia, who has supplanted the Chaldean conqueror. The poem ends with the query whether, transplanted back to its homeland, this "noble vine" (v. 8) "will thrive" (v. 10). All of the above is background to this morning's poem. The tender sprig from the topmost cedar planted "on the mountain height of Israel" (vv. 22f.) is the prophet's projection (since Ezekiel is still in exile as he writes) of a restored people led by a Davidic scion. Planted in Judah's homeland, it will grow to spread its boughs to afford shade and nesting for every kind of winged creature (cf. Jesus' parable of the mustard seed, Mark 4:31-32; Matt 13:31-32; Luke 13:18-19, which grows into a shrub in the branches of which the birds of the air—inheritors of God's reign—will nest; see the Gospel passage below). The Lord will exchange the low tree for the high and the dry tree for the green (v. 42; cf. Hannah's song, 1 Sam 2:6-8 and Mary's, Luke 1:51-53), a parable of sure and certain hope for the Church of the West and the East in a wintry season for both.

PSALM 20

PSALM 92:1-4[2-3] 12-15[13-16]

2 CORINTHIANS 5:6-10, (11-13), 14-17

For a commentary see Proper 7 [12] immediately below.

Mark 4:26-34

Besides stipulating this reading for today, LM proposes it for Friday of the Third Week of the Year in Years A and B. Mark groups four parables of Jesus in what has become chap. 4. He places him in a boat at the shore's edge, undoubtedly because Jesus often used such a pulpit so that his voice would carry over the water (4:1). The brief tale of the sower, which Mark has allegorized differently than in Jesus' actual telling (the seed as the word variously received rather than the marvelous spread of God's reign apart from human doing), and the metaphor of a lamp on a lampstand. Both precede the simile of the sprouting and growth of the seed (vv. 26-29) and the mustard seed that becomes "the greatest of all shrubs" (vv. 30-32). The first, often called "The Seed Growing Silently," is found in Mark only. The clearest memory of Jesus' teaching is that he proclaimed not himself but the reign or rule of God *(basileía, mălkuth)*. Samuel's resistance to the popular outcry for a king like those of their pagan neighbors was based on the tradition that the LORD alone was Israel's king. Jesus was a traditionalist. He wished his people to return wholeheartedly to acceptance of that gentle rule. His "kingdom parables" are the indisputably authentic ones. This reign over the Jewish people of south and north would be a work of God. It would overtake the people inexorably. The metaphor of growing things like grain and trees and bushes illustrates it best. In that figure the good earth receives the seed and lets sun and rain and seasons do the rest. And so with God, a God who rules silently over our rebellious wills.

❧ ❧
Proper 7 [12] / Twelfth Sunday of the Year (B)
Sunday between June 19 and June 25, inclusive

I Samuel 17:(1A, 4-11, 19-23), 32-49

For a commentary see 4 Lent (A).

The Samuel-Saul cycle (chaps. 1–15) is over. David has been anointed king by the priest-judge, but without the reigning king's knowledge (chap. 16). Young David is taken on as Saul's armor-bearer, but along with his skills as a warrior he has gifts on the lyre. These enable him to cope with Saul's psychosis, "an evil spirit from the LORD that tormented him" (16:14). Early in the story the Philistine threat to the "Hebrews . . . all Israel" (13:3f.) is recounted, with its larger-than-life champion, Goliath of Gath. This tribe from the coast knows how to temper iron in a forge and so it controls the weaponry that it will sell—swords and spears—to Saul and his son Jonathan only (13:22). The narrative portion in parentheses sets the stage for the encounter of the shepherd lad with the Philistine giant. David sheds the armor with which Saul has clothed him as too heavy and constrictive of his movements. How the Israelites, unskilled in metals, came to have a bronze helmet and coat of mail is not explained. What all hearers who know the tale will recall is that David goes into combat armed with but a staff and five smooth stones from the brook. His sling is twirled around his head before the missile is released, much as the young Palestinians of the *intifada* were seen doing on television against the heavily armed Israelis. Saul's admonition to David is a "Vaya con Dios" in Hebrew (17:37). The older warrior greets the younger with a curse in tones dripping with scorn. He is answered with a counter-challenge heavy not with weaponry but with theodicy. David's response spells out the superiority of Israel's God, not simply to Goliath's strength in weapons, but to the gods of the Philistines. If vv. 45-47 are not well read they should not be read at all, for they alone are the point of the story, not the stone firmly planted in the champion's forehead.

PSALM 9:9-20

1 SAMUEL 17:57—18:5, 10-16

This follow-up to the more familiar tale of David's laying low the Philistine champion ("baseborn" in DRC, "bastard" in the Knox translation following the Vulgatis *spurius*, proving the uncertainty of the meaning of *ish habbenim*) goes in swift strokes from Saul's first identification of David, Jonathan's immediate bonding with him, and David's successes in command of Saul's army (vv. 5, 13). The awe of Saul at David's military exploits was punctuated by his first psychotic seizure and attempt on the young man's life. But the victories continued, resulting in the growing allegiance of the people to David.

PSALM 133

JOB 38:1[8]-11

The closest parallel to this biblical book in ancient Near Eastern literature is the Akkadian text from ca. 1000 B.C.E. known as "The Babylonian Theodicy," a dialogue about human suffering and divine justice. There the sufferer is answered by one friend only, not three troublesome comforters with an Elihu added in (chaps. 32–37). The present pericope occurs early in the Theophany or YHWH speeches (38:1—42:6), the fourth part of this unevenly divided five-part book. Neither the dialogues of chaps. 3–31 nor the Elihu speeches use the divine name found in 38:1. It occurs in the prologue and epilogue (the first and fifth parts) and in the fourth part at 40:1, 3, 6, and 42:1.

In 31:35-37 Job has cried out, "Oh, that I had one to hear me, . . ." followed by "Oh, that I had an indictment written by my adversary," the more familiar KJV rendering being "a book." The fact that the LORD answers him and not Elihu here (v. 1) strengthens the hypothesis that the latter's speeches are an interpolation. The divine answer "out of the storm" is a detail associated with theophanies (cf. Ps 18:7-14; Zech 9:14; Exod 19:16-19) and perhaps derives from the cult of the weather god.

The LORD has quelled the sea in 7:12 and 26:12. Here he challenges Job in terms of his own power in binding up the newborn and vigorous infant sea god in swaddling bands (v. 9). The motif does not appear elsewhere in Near Eastern epic writing, although the Mesopotamian and Ugaritic creation myths have the waters defeated and held back by victorious opponents. In the former, Marduk slays the sea dragon Tiamat, creates the primeval seas from him, and holds them back in place with a bar. The Ugaritic Ba'al defeats the sea god Yam and holds him captive. In Job YHWH placed limits on the sea and "set bars and doors" (v. 10). The command to the waves, "thus far shall you come and no farther," has taken hold in the popular imagination in the legend of King Canute but in fact it derives from v. 11. G. K. Chesterton, a journalist who knew the Bible, wrote in a column of his beloved wife Frances: "You are the deity who says to these preposterous locks of hair, 'Thus far shalt thou grow and no further'" (the KJV and DRC adverb).

PSALM 107:1-3, 23-32

2 CORINTHIANS 5:14-17

The "love of Christ" (v. 14) is almost certainly a subjective genitive here: Christ's love for us. The context of these remarks is Paul's career of attempts to persuade men in his role as apostle. If any Christians are inclined to boast of him as someone caught up in ecstasy (v. 13), he will by no means discourage it. God, who knows what we are (v. 11), is the reason, in any case, behind external appearances and what lies in the heart (v. 12). The love of Christ is the impelling, driving force in Paul's life (*synéchei* = Latin *urget*, the Greek verb being found elsewhere only in Phil 1:23, "I am hard pressed"). Christ's love is proved by his death (cf. Rom 5:8; Gal 2:20) "for all" (v. 15), an axiom found in the tradition at 1 Cor 15:3. "One has died for all, therefore all have died" is the literal rendering of v. 14. Paul repeats the phrase in v. 15, then gives the reason for this death with Christ, which is obviously a mystical and not a physical death: "so that those who live [their physical status] might live no longer for themselves, but for him who died and was raised for them." Christ died to sin. Those who have done the same live not self-ishly as Adam did but "in indebtedness and obedience to Christ" (C. K. Barrett). His risen life to God is the paradigm of the selfless lives of the baptized, which ideally have Christ as their center.

As a consequence (v. 16), from the death and upraising of Christ (v. 15), from now on (v. 16) Paul looks upon no one, not even Christ, "from a human point of view" (*katà sárka*, v. 16). This phrase has been taken by Bultmann and others to mean a ruling out of consideration the historical, earthly Jesus. In fact, however, Paul rejects by the phrase the making over of Christ as a messiah in any human image. He confesses his erroneous view of Christ before his conversion and says that he now sees him and all humanity in a new eschatological way, as a "new creation" (v. 17). Of Jesus' earthly days nothing is being affirmed; the *sarx* of the phrase is an unredeemed race of men, its condition before the death and uprais-ing of v. 15. Verse 17 states positively what v. 16 has put negatively. Paul cele-brates the new act of creation (*kainē ktísis*, v. 17) constituted by God's act in Christ. The old age has passed (cf. Rev. 21:4) and a new one has come to birth. The Chris-tian still has to live amidst the old creation but does so in terms of the new; in T. S. Eliot's phrase, "no longer at ease."

ALLELUIA. LUKE 7:16

A great prophet has risen in our midst, God has visited his people.

2 CORINTHIANS 6:1-13

See Ash Wednesday (A, B, C).

MARK 4:35[40]-41

This chapter is given entirely to parables, including those of the sower (vv. 3-8) and its allegorical explanation (vv. 13-20), the seed growing on its own (vv. 26-29), and the mustard seed (vv. 31f.). A brief sayings collection, which Matthew and Luke will employ in other contexts, acts as a bridge between the first and sec-ond parables (vv. 21-25). The pericope of the stilling of the storm (vv. 35-41) is used by Mark as a challenge of Jesus to the disciples' faith in "the mystery of the reign of God" (v. 11), which for the evangelist is bound up with Jesus' person and his power (v. 41). It does not stand on its own, however—the chapter division coming from Stephen Langton, the medieval archbishop of Canterbury—but forms a unity with the deeds of power in chap. 5. These are the expulsion of the legion of unclean spirits in Gerasa, the healing of the hemorrhaging woman, and Jesus' victory over death in the case of Jairus's daughter. As such, the stilling of the storm initiates that group of four (or three) miracle stories more than it concludes the Markan day of parables. The insertion of the healing of the woman with a menstrual flow (vv. 25-34) into the story of the resuscitation of Jairus's daughter (vv. 21-24, 35-43) is an example of Mark's intercalation technique, the sole clue between inner and outer being the child's age, twelve years, and the length of the woman's suffering.

Jesus' power over wind and wave is part of the larger confrontation basic to Mark's Gospel in which Jesus takes on the cosmic powers of evil, replacing chaos and death with divine order and life. The normally placid Lake Kinnereth (Sea of Galilee) resembles in its brief squalls the Mediterranean lashing the coast—the "deep" of the Bible, which typifies all that is inimical to humankind. The Markan penchant for detail is evident in the narrative. The "great windstorm" of v. 37 terrifies even the seasoned fishermen (v. 38). Jesus' word of power (v. 39) resembles in its sovereignty that of the God of Israel (cf. Pss 65:7[8]; 77:17; 107:25-30; Job 12:15). His "rebuking" the wind is the same verb as that used to describe Jesus' dealing with the demons in 3:12 and 9:25 and closely parallels the wording of the exorcism in 1:25.

The challenge of Jesus to his disciples in v. 40 is the first of a series in Mark (cf. 7:18; 8:17f., 21, 32f.; 9:19). They have been confided in at 4:11 and 34 over the meaning of parables but have not yet (v. 40) arrived at faith. At this point in the Gospel, faith in Jesus is taken to be the same as faith in God.

❧ ✍

Proper 8 [13] / Thirteenth Sunday of the Year (B)
Sunday between June 26 and July 2, inclusive

2 SAMUEL 1:1, 17-27

David's friendship with Jonathan and his marriage to Michal, both of whom managed to save his life from the crazed and murder-bent Saul, Samuel's death, David's temporary going over to the Philistine king of Gath, and Saul's and his sons' death on Mount Gilboa have all been narrated in 1 Sam 16–31. The second book opens with David's defeat of the Amalekites accomplished and his mourning for Saul and

Jonathan begun. David mourns in a poetic lament of great beauty. Especially poignant are the phrases about the death of Saul, whom in his saner moments David must have respected and whose kingly office the biblical author has David always hold in honor. King Saul and his sons are called "the glory of Israel." Their slain bodies lying on the field of battle are not to be reported to the Philistine women lest they exult over the victory (v. 20), nor is the mountainous site ever again to flourish since it witnessed the defilement of the shield of Saul the mighty (v. 21). Saul and his son Jonathan are united in death in a love that, while living, the Bible scarcely witnesses to (vv. 23f.). But that is the way with eulogies: *nil nisi bonum.* In his temporary victories over Philistia, Saul is remembered as having clothed the women of Israel with luxurious apparel. "Where have all the garments gone?" the lamentation mighty have asked (v. 24). The weapons of war have perished—all too temporarily. What is imperishable is the memory of the love David bore to Jonathan—"passing the love of women" (v. 26). Our prurient age seems to know little of same-sex love without a sexual component. History down to our day has known millions of them.

PSALM 130

WISDOM 1:13-15; 2:23-24

In these early chapters the postexilic sage writing in Greek a century before Jesus' birth argues the question of reward for the just and punishment for the wicked, two states determined by having recourse to wisdom or spurning it. Verse 13 is redolent of the Deuteronomic charge to choose life (30:19c), while v. 14 is more philosophical in tone than anything found in Torah. What God creates is life-sustaining; there is nothing in common between man's home, the earth, and the abode of the dead (v. 14). God's justice is deathless and leads to deathlessness (v. 15). The influence of 2:18 on the passion narratives seems evident ("If the just one be the son of God he will help him / and will deliver him from the hand of his foes"). The railing continues in vv. 19ff., but the wicked have not counted on God's hidden counsels. The effect of being created in his image (cf. Gen 1:26f.) is incorruption / imperishability, *aphtharsía*, and God means to bring it about. Only primordial tragedy has set the divine plan in disarray. It is impossible to know if the author has in mind Gen 3, in which case the tempting snake is here first identified as the devil, or the story of Cain's murder of Abel in Gen 4. John's Gospel (8:44) thinks like Wisdom but provides no clue as to *how* the devil brought death to man from the beginning.

The case has been made, with the aid of the silence of Wisdom on bodily resurrection, for the author's interest in spiritual death like that of Revelation (2:10 and 21:8) and his corresponding interest in a blessed immortality (3:4), i.e., with Israel's God. While the latter is undoubtedly his concern, it seems from 3:1-12 that he is wrestling with the problem of real death and the subsequent fate of the just and the wicked.

LAMENTATIONS 3:23-33 OR PSALM 30:[2, 4-6, 11-12A, 13B]

2 CORINTHIANS 8:7-15

Despite the way they have tried his patience, Paul's prevailing sentiment toward the Corinthians is affection and respect. He is not being ironical in v. 7 any more than he was in his opening prayer of thanks in 1 Cor 1:4-7. The Corinthians possess the riches of faith and speech and knowledge they do because he brought them the gospel in the first place. Why they should seek any of these gifts from another source both eludes and pains him.

The context of his remarks is the collection for the Jerusalem church, a matter in which Titus is Paul's agent. The latter holds up for emulation the generosity of the Macedonians who are none too well off themselves (8:1-5). The chiastic figure of riches and poverty in Christ's life resembles the hymn of Phil 2:5-11 and is not too unlike the paradoxes of wisdom and folly, strength and weakness in early 1 Corinthians.

Paul then turns to practical advice. He is not proposing any giving that leaves the donors unable to provide for their own needs (vv. 13ff.). Everything will balance out, he suggests, if the churches continue in a spirit of mutual support. If the economics of this proposal do not satisfy, Paul is ready with a biblical citation (v. 15; Exod 16:18). The manna miracle provided a sufficiency all around. Only the greedy saw their manna hoarded for the next day turn wormy and corrupt.

ALLELUIA. JOHN 17:17B AND A

Your word, O LORD, is truth; make us holy in the truth.

MARK 5:21-43

The basic Markan story is about Jesus' mastery of man's enemy, death, with a word. The pericope corresponds admirably to the reading from Wisdom. Mark's inclusion technique accounts for the miracle within a miracle (vv. 24-34, flanked by 22-24 and 35-43). The girl first reported ill (v. 23) is later described as dead (v. 35) as a result of Jesus' delay. Faith (meaning perfect trust) is named as the condition of the cure in both instances (vv. 34, 36). Jesus is powerful with the power of God for those who will acknowledge it. He acknowledges the departure of "power" from him (v. 30) akin to the "portion of spirit" possessed and transmitted by the ancient prophets. Dialogue turns the fearful and trembling woman (v. 33) into a person of faith, even as Jesus proposes to the father belief in place of fear (v. 36) to ensure the resuscitation of the twelve-year-old girl. Usually when Mark intercalates one narrative within another there is a fairly evident relation between the two (as in the withered fig tree and the Temple area barren of heartfelt worship). Here the clue is minimal: the child's age and the length of the woman's suffering.

🙈 🙈

Proper 9 [14] / Fourteenth Sunday of the Year (B)
Sunday between July 3 and July 9, inclusive

2 SAMUEL 5:1-5, 9-10

This narrative has David named king by acclamation of "all the tribes of Israel" (v. 1), with no mention of the scheming and perilous friendship with the king that marked his years as young pretender. That is the way the history of strong leaders is rewritten. Reading carefully between the lines reveals him to be one who has a few more virtues than the rest. The enthronement by acclaim takes place at Hebron, because "the stronghold of Zion" with its wall called "the Millo" is still in Jebusite hands. There is no Jerusalem as the Israelite capital yet. David's occupation of it is spoken of in a phrase or two but, as in most conquests, there may have been many lives lost (vv. 6-8). These verses, omitted from a public reading, reflect little credit on David and his military force. It may be politic to avoid mention of the physically ill-favored but that is not a sufficient reason for suppression of the text. The substance of the Jebusite taunt shouted over the wall was something like "Our weak can better your strong." That may be a remembered cry from tribal warfare among the Semites, but the chronicler uses it to introduce the Israelite stratagem of ascent through the water shaft on the hill of Ophel to attack the vulnerable blind and lame within. He does more. He employs it as the mythic cause of the disqualifying physical conditions that would later keep any Aaronite offspring from offering food in God's house (v. 8; see Lev 21:16-21). This premium on physical perfection is something to be ashamed of in our day, but no apology is needed for ancient taboos, only an explanation of the prevailing mentality of Bible times. David's occupation of the city of another people has its counterpart in the modern displacement of Palestinians from their orchard farms and homes of many centuries. For that reason, the conqueror mentality can profitably be preached upon: seizure without title search.

PSALM 48

EZEKIEL 2:1[2]-5

This passage describes the restoration to normalcy of the priest Ezekiel after his vision of chap. 1, experienced in Babylonian exile some time after the year 597. It is the beginning of the commission of the LORD to this "son of man" (i.e., mortal creature) to be a teacher of his people. They may be rebellious (v. 5) but he must be obedient (v. 8) and even courageous in the face of contradiction and rebellion (v. 6).

The pericope should be preached on in the context of the rebelliousness of Christians to their Lord and his heavenly Father. Otherwise it will have proved itself an unwise choice of the framers of the lectionary. The passage makes eminent sense as a paradigm of everyone's call by God to speak the truth in a prophetic spirit to refractory listeners in one's own circle.

PSALM 123[1-4]

2 CORINTHIANS 12:2[7]-10

This is part of what is probably Paul's "severe letter" (see 2:1-4) to the Corinthians (10:1—13:10). In the present passage he feels compelled to boast of his weaknesses whereby the power of Christ is brought to perfection in him. It is in his native powerlessness that he is strongest (v. 10). The rapture of fourteen years before (vv. 2ff.), which he feels he must boast of as a deed of God and not of himself (v. 5), was a great turning point in Paul's life. It brought an end to whatever dream he may have entertained of "power, predominance, and conspicuous success" (Dodd). From this point on, all that has mattered is the grace of Christ ("my grace," v. 9) which is sufficient for Paul despite mistreatment, distress, persecutions, and difficulties (v. 10).

We have no clue as to Paul's "thorn in the flesh" (v. 7). The ordinary word for stake, thorn, or splinter, *skolops*, is here used figuratively for some recurrent misfortune calculated to keep Paul low. An impairment of vision (see Gal 4:13ff.), epilepsy, malaria, and stammering have all been proposed—none with any compelling reason, but with the Galatians passage perhaps the most indicative.

The "exceptional . . . revelations" of v. 7 answer to those of Ezekiel above—in both cases for transmission to the people in their interests and not as private endowments.

Alleluia. See Acts 6:14b

Open our hearts, O Lord, to listen to the words of your Son.

Mark 6:1-[6]13

The third reading continues the theme of the first two of gifts to the prophetic teacher, in this case wisdom and miraculous deeds, for the sake of those whom he will teach. Jesus' family circumstances are well known to the villagers in his home region (v. 1). Matthew will change "the carpenter" (v. 3) to "the son of the carpenter" (Matt 13:55). Naming a man by designating his mother is unusual Jewish practice. Here it may refer to the traditions surrounding Jesus' birth.

"They took offense at him" (v. 3) is Mark's laconic comment on this display of power by a familiar. A saying attributed to Jesus in the *Gospel of Thomas* combines two logia from the canonical Gospels: "No prophet is acceptable in his village, no physician heals those who know him" (31).

The inability of Jesus to heal any more than a few because of his distress at the lack of faith of those of his own region (vv. 5f.) is often cited as proof of the primitive and unretouched character of the tradition Mark here employs.

✿✿

Proper 10 [15] / Fifteenth Sunday of the Year (B)
Sunday between July 10 and July 16, inclusive

2 Samuel 6:1-5, 12b-19

The ark of God has been safe in the house of Abinadab on the hill in Kiryat Yearim and watched over by his son Eleazar all through the military engagements with the Philistines (1 Sam 7:1). If Saul's son of the name Abinadab is meant, he dies with Jonathan and another son on Mount Gilboa (31:2). David knows where the ark is lodged and sends for it, bringing it in jubilant musical procession to Jerusalem. Two sons of Abinadab, Uzzah and Ahio, accompany it, "David and all the house of Israel" dancing to songs and five types of musical instruments as it progresses. The tale of Uzzah's being struck dead by the LORD, angry at his having touched the ark (6:6-9), is omitted from the RCL. The similar account of the death in battle of the sons of Eli, Hophni and Phinehas, is explained by their greed, something contemporary hearers might easily resonate to. The likelihood, however, that the story of a taboo and the action of a short-tempered deity in response to disobedience regarding it will make any sense to moderns is slim indeed. Where the ancients would have recognized the holiness of an object to convey the supreme holiness of God, today's hearers might simply be scandalized at an irrational and capricious deity, considering him well succeeded by the Father of meek and gentle Jesus, as the heretic Marcion did. The omission means that an opportunity to explore the sacred status of objects in all the religions of the world has been lost.

The unread verses tell of David's transfer of the ark from the house of Abinadab to that of Obededom, fearful to bring it as its custodian into the city. Seeing Uzzah lying dead beside the ark might well have had that effect! David ultimately decided to bring it from Obededom's house into "the city of David," dancing in a holy frenzy at every step. "All the house of Israel" accompanied him in this performance with shouts and trumpet blasts. David's wife Michal, daughter of Saul, looked on, however, from her window within the city and seeing him leaping and dancing, "despised him in her heart" (v. 16). The young king is undeterred and places the ark inside the tent prepared for it, offers burnt sacrifices, and distributes food among the people. Cold Anglo-Saxon blood affects its revulsion at the outcries of charismatic Christians in procession. The smug, inward noting of "idolatry" is one response of Norteamericanos to a *cofradía* of men and boys in the streets of Cuzco led by a brass band, all carrying banners celebrating the feast day of some obscure saint. Michal would have been quite familiar with the display of religious emotion. Her spouse's participation was not what merited her scorn. She claimed it was exposing his muscular flesh to the eyes of the servant girls in his retinue (v. 20), but Michal was no champion of male modesty. She was, rather, a wife jealous that any but she could look on her husband admiringly. His response provides a reason to read to the end of the pericope. He knew that the LORD had chosen him to succeed her father, and he meant to abase himself endlessly if it were needed to show himself to be the king over the slave girls in his kingdom (v. 22).

PSALM 24

AMOS 7:7[12]-15

Jeroboam II, king of Israel, ruled ca. 783–43. The activity of Amos is placed toward the end of his reign (ca. 750). It seems to have been a brief enough career; its termination is recorded in Amos 7:10f. Tiglath Pileser III would come to the Assyrian throne in 745, hence Amos was right in speaking of impending doom. In the first half of the eighth century, however, Assyria had been weak and the two kingdoms, Israel and Judah, prosperous as a result.

Bethel was an ancient shrine going back in its foundation to Jacob's time (see Gen 28:10-19). It was the last town of consequence in the northern kingdom on the road to Jerusalem. Today there is (or was) a tiny Muslim village on its site and a modern synagogue for settlers and a military encampment named, fittingly enough, Beit El. Jeroboam II (931–10) tried to set it up, along with Dan in the far north, as a rival shrine to Zion in Jerusalem. Amaziah, its priest, thinks that Amos is guilty of lèse majesté by prophesying the king's violent death and Israel's exile from its land (v. 11). He takes the utterance to be politically seditious and a sufficient reason for ejecting Amos to his southern (cf. 1:1) homeland. The form of address, "visionary" *(ḥozeh),* is not pejorative, but the assumption that Amos earns his living by prophesying is (v. 12). Amos denies the imputation by describing himself as a herdsman-farmer. The biblical sycamore (*shikmim*, v. 14) is a kind of mulberry tree the fruit of which requires bruising to encourage ripening. Amos says he is not a prophet or "the son of a prophet" or, as NAB renders it, a member of "a company of prophets" whose religious authenticity was much in doubt.

The "was" of v. 14 is supplied, there being no verb of any tense in the Hebrew. Amos's point is that he received his call to prophesy while going about his ordinary rural tasks. He has no personal stake in prophecy, as Amaziah hints against him. It is the Lord's doing that he is engaged in it. All it will net him is reproach and expulsion from the territory of Israel.

PSALM 85:8-13

EPHESIANS 1:3-14

This epistle, a theological manifesto, is concerned with "the catholicity and divine origin of the church" (*PC*, 980), rather than the parousia. The document progresses toward notions like the building of "a holy temple in the Lord" (2:21), "the measure of the full stature of Christ" (4:13), and "the whole body . . . [which] grows in / builds itself up in love" (4:16) rather than the imminently expected return of Christ.

For a commentary on vv. 3-12, see [Mary's] Immaculate Conception [in her Mother's Womb] (December 8).

The link between the life of the baptized believer hymned in vv. 3-14 and the future consummation of that "glorious heritage" (v. 18) is found in the last two verses of today's pericope, 13f. It is the seal (sphragís) of the promised Holy Spirit given as a pledge of our inheritance (v. 14). The "first installment" of NAB is its rendering of arrabōn, leading to the twofold eis: "toward redemption as God's possession . . . to the praise of his glory." The first installment, which promises future payment in full, is already present to the Christian in the seal of the Spirit.

ALLELUIA. SEE EPHESIANS 1:17-18

May the Father of our Lord Jesus Christ enlighten the eyes of our hearts, that we may see how great is the hope to which we are called.

MARK 6:[7-13] 14-29

Jesus' instructions to the Twelve are followed quite closely by Matthew (10:1, 9-11, 14) and Luke (9:1-6). The latter two differ slightly as to equipment for journeying and add the healing of diseases to Mark's exorcism in v. 7 and Luke's omission of the preaching of repentance and exorcising from Mark, vv. 12f. The mission of the twelve has been prepared for in 3:14-19. The message of repentance they preached (v. 12) must have been related to Jesus' gospel of 1:14f. The instructions, including the sensitivity about money—the "bag" of v. 8 may be a begging bag—reflect later apostolic practice. So does the symbolic shaking of dust from the feet (cf. Acts 13:51) and anointing of the sick with oil (cf. Jas 5:14; in Luke 10:34 the context is different). These details indicate a set of guidelines for Palestinian preachers of the post-Easter period set in the context of Jesus' lifetime. His sending them is not in doubt but rather the specifics of his instruction. C. K. Barrett thinks that Luke in retaining something like the original Q form of the charge in 10:5-42 proves the case for lateness (*The Signs of an Apostle* [Philadelphia: Fortress Press, 1970], 32). Sending out messengers in pairs was a regular custom in Judaism, although it cannot be demonstrated to be as early as the Hebrew Bible. It was both a protective measure and an application of the legal clause of Deut 17:6; 19:15, originally juridical, which ensured the trustworthiness of two witnesses and provided a spokesman with a confirmatory partner. The prohibition of two tunics (v. 9) probably meant no cloak over a robe and would have made sleeping out overnight a hardship.

Josephus writes in praise of the Essenes (*Jewish War* 2.125 [2.7.4]): "They carry nothing whatever with them on their journeys, except arms as a protection against brigands. In every city there is one of the order expressly appointed to attend to strangers, who provides them with clothing and other necessities."

✌✌
Proper 11 [16] / Sixteenth Sunday of the Year (B)
Sunday between July 17 and July 23, inclusive

2 SAMUEL 7:1-14A

For a commentary see 4 Advent (B).

PSALM 89:20-37

JEREMIAH 23[1-6]

The prophet first deplores the weakness of Judah's kings (vv. 1-4) and then pronounces an oracle, probably to the discredit of Zedekiah (598–87) whom Nebuchadnezzar put on the throne in place of the young man's uncle Jehoaichin (cf. the commentary on 2 Chron 36:14-17, 19-23, for 4 Lent). Jeremiah's contempt for Jehoaichin, who ruled during 598 only, was near total. His view of Zedekiah was not much better. In place of the latter, whose throne name means "The Lord is just" will come a "righteous shoot" (v. 5), a future king whose justice will be such that Judah and Israel will be able to give him the name, "The LORD our justice" (v. 6).

See Ezek 34 for an extended parable on governance and leadership under the figure of "shepherds who mislead and scatter the flock of my pasture" (Jer 23:1).

PSALM 23:1-6

EPHESIANS 2:11[13-18]-22

Verses 14-16 are a christological hymn that Heinrich Schlier thinks reflects the gnostic concept of a redeemer who destroys the hostile wall between the Godhead and those who are to be redeemed. As to the setting of the hymn, those "who once were far off" (v. 13) are the Gentiles, in a reference to Isa 57:19, where peace and healing are promised to the far and the near. Christ's blood is the reconciling agent between Jew and Gentile (cf. Col 1:20-23; Rom 5:10f.). The "dividing wall of hostility" (v. 14) may be Torah observance, a wall at once standing between Jew and Gentile and between man and God. Perhaps a barrier between heavenly and earthly realms is meant (cf. *1 Enoch* 14:9). The writer of Ephesians sees Christ, not as the end or fulfillment, but the abolisher of the Law (v. 15), a word choice impossible for Paul without qualification. "He has evacuated the Law of its full force" conveys *kataregsas* better. Jews and Gentiles come to the Father together in the Spirit as "one new humanity" in Christ. The Mosaic commands and precepts are taken by the author to be instruments of division of Jew from Gentile.

Paul sees the one God justifying the circumcised and the uncircumcised alike on the basis of faith (Rom 3:29f.). He flatly denies, however, that he is abolishing the Law by means of faith. "On the contrary, we are confirming the Law" (v. 31).

"One new humanity," "one body," "one Spirit"—all indicate that there is to be no enmity or alienating division in the redeemed community that is the Church.

ALLELUIA. MATTHEW 11:25

Blessed are you, Father, Lord of heaven and earth; you have revealed to little ones the mysteries of the kingdom.

MARK 6:30-34, 53-56

Mark is not followed by Matthew (14:13f.) or Luke (9:10f.) in reporting the impossibility that the disciples experienced in finding time to eat. Similarly, he alone has Jesus issuing the invitation to "come to a deserted place all by yourselves and rest a while" (v. 31).

The disciples have been away from Jesus preaching (6:12f.) and Mark must get them back on the scene. It is also essential to his story of the feeding with loaves and fish that it occur in a deserted place (cf. vv. 31, 32, 35) like the desert of the exodus. Finally, people must be there in numbers to witness it (v. 33). This initial pericope of five verses is a mere link for Mark between his narrative of the beheading of John and the feeding of the five thousand. Once it was chosen by LM, it was corresponded to by the reading from Jeremiah; both speak of a leaderless people "without a shepherd." The phrase is found in Num 27:17 and Ezek 34:5. RCL provides a further link in the Markan story, having passed over Jesus' walking on the sea (vv. 45-52), by providing a closure to the series of incidents; Jesus back at

Gennesaret (modern Ginosar) beleaguered by petitioners for cures. "And all who touched [his cloak] were healed" (v. 56).

∾❧∾

Proper 12 [17] / Seventeenth Sunday of the Year (B)
Sunday between July 24 and July 30, inclusive

2 SAMUEL 11:1-15

RCL hearers can appreciate the story of David's lust for Bathsheba and his murderous betrayal of Uriah once in three years, whereas only weekday Mass-goers encounter it in LM (Friday, Week Three, Year B, which means every even-numbered year).

The Hittites were a non-Semitic people who had a huge empire in what is now eastern Turkey and northern Syria in 1900–1650 B.C.E. and again in 1430–1200. The numerous references to this people in Genesis are to the earlier period. In King David's time (ca. 1000) the empire would thus have been in decline for some two centuries. Joab is first heard of as one of three sons of Zeruiah or Serviah (2 Sam 2:13; 3:18), who is David's sister (1 Chron 2:16). As the chapter opens, Joab is away from Jerusalem conducting springtime warfare against the Ammonites, whose mercenaries, the Arameans, David has lately defeated (2 Sam 10). The king is at leisure in Jerusalem communicating with Joab at the battlefront by messenger (11:6) and letter (v. 14). He spies a beautiful woman bathing on a nearby roof, learns her name and that of her husband, and in the manner of kings sends for her, undeterred by her married state. Once he discovers she is pregnant by him David begins scheming to make her his wife along with the six he had married or had children by while still in Hebron (see 2 Sam 3:2-5; 1 Chron 3:1-4). Ten more offspring from his Jerusalem period are named in the passage that follows the latter and nine of these plus two more are listed in 2 Sam 5:14-16.

Uriah is either a proselyte of the religion of Israel or follows that people's custom by abstaining from sex with his wife on the eve of battle (11:11; cf. 1 Sam 21:6). This sensitivity and the king's plying him with drink before sending him into the thick of the skirmish to be killed discloses the depth of David's perfidy. It is not only sin but the cruelest kind of betrayal of trust, compounded by a hypocritical comment on the carefully engineered outcome (v. 25).

PSALM 14

2 KINGS 4:42-44

This brief tale from the Elisha cycle has a famine in the land as its setting (v. 38) and follows immediately upon a story of some noxious food rendered harmless by the prophet's throwing meal into the pot that contains it. The present narrative tells of the multiplication of barley loaves made from the first fruits, which are normally the portion of priests. The hundred men in this case may have been cultic prophets associated with Elisha at a shrine. Baalshalisha in ancient Ephraim is in modern Shomeron, southwest of Nablus.

PSALM 145:10-18

EPHESIANS 3:14-21

The pseudonymous author of this Pauline letter addressed to Gentiles (3:1) had provided a moving prayer of thanks for the new believers in the province of Asia and adjacent territories (see 1:15-23). It is resumed here in 3:13 and continues to v. 21. The prayer is marked by an appeal to the Father's richness in glory to see to it that Christ shall dwell in human hearts through faith by the strengthening power of the Spirit. This is a faithful echo of Paul's awareness of God as triune in act (see 2 Cor 13:13; Rom 1–6; Phil 2:1). The phrase for "inner being" (*tòn esō ánthrōpon*, v. 16) is found in Rom 7:22 and in another, cognate phrase translated "our inner nature" in 2 Cor 4:16. The fourfold dimension of v. 18 would seem to be the measure of both Christ's love and the fullness of God that follow in v. 19. This exuberant speech is characteristic of the letter throughout, expanding Paul's epistolary prose in ever richer rhetorical fashion. Note that love surpasses knowledge, a Pauline theme, and that God's unimaginable "power at work within us" (v. 20) is exercised not only in Christ Jesus but in the Church (v. 21). Ephesians has contributed much to ecclesiology but also to the Church's life of prayer and devotion.

EPHESIANS 4:1-6

The writer has designated himself a "prisoner for Christ Jesus" in Eph 3:1. Colossians 1:10 has a parallel phrase to the exhortation, "lead a life worthy," not of "the calling you have received" but of "the Lord." Verses 2f. bear a close resemblance to Col 3:12-15. There love is the bond that sustains perfection whereas here it is peace—a major concern of the author. As in 2:16, the starting point is "one body" (v. 4), which doubtless means the Church, but can also refer to the cruci-fied body of Christ that brought us into one.

The closest parallel to vv. 4-6 is 1 Cor 12:4-11, which speaks of a diversity of spiritual gifts. There are six examples of things that are "one" leading up to the seventh, "one God and Father of all" (v. 6). It was a familiar Rabbinic device of the time to heighten the unity and the uniqueness of God by enumerating things that were one and reflected the divine oneness. Thus: "One people, one Temple, one God." The groupings were usually of three, five, or seven members. Mention of Spirit, Lord, and God is no doubt intentional. It is not so certain that body con-sciously goes with Spirit, hope with Lord, and faith and baptism with God, although a case can be made for it.

The concluding phrase, "who is above all and through all and in all," is an echo of Stoicism (via Hellenist Judaism), which saw divinity everywhere. The "all" is a genitive and dative plural so it is impossible to tell if "everything" or "every-body" is intended. Probably the former, on a parallel with 1:23 where Christ fills "all in all," rendered in NAB as "all things in every way."

ALLELUIA. LUKE 19:38

Blessed is the king who comes in the name of the LORD: peace on earth, and glory in heaven!

JOHN 6:1[15]-21

This multiplication of loaves and dried fish is one of Jesus' signs (v. 14) for John. It led not only to speculation that he might be the eschatological prophet hinted at in Deut 18:15 but also to the threat to carry him off as king. C. H. Dodd (*Historical Tradition in the Fourth Gospel* [Cambridge: Cambridge Univ. Press, 1963], 199–216) sees in John 6:1—7:1 a shadow of the Markan order in 8:1-8. At the same time, this feeding corresponds in some respects, including the numbers, to Mark 6:34-44. The next incident in both is the walking on the water (John 6:16-21; Mark 6:47-51). John 6, situated in Galilee, comes puzzlingly after chap. 5, which has Jerusalem as its setting. Attempts have been made to put chap. 6 after chap. 4 and before chap. 5, but it seems clear that the evangelist wrote in this order for theological reasons, whatever order he may have found in his source.

This sign is reported to have taken place close to the second Passover of Jesus' public career (v. 4; for the first see 2:13, for the third 12:55). The dating may be chronologically based, but it clearly has theological significance, as his subsequent words, "while he was teaching in a synagogue at Capernaum" (v. 59), underscore.

The Passover commemorated the desert experience. John's Jesus describes himself as the true manna come down from heaven (vv. 31-35, 51, 58).

The verbs of v. 11, "took," "gave thanks," and "distributed," are those of the Last Supper accounts, but matters are complicated by their applicability to any Jewish meal. Similarly, John's "gather up" and "be lost" (v. 12) are his normal verbs for the gathering and perishing of men (cf. 11:52; 17:12).

The people conclude from the sign that Jesus is the king-messiah.

❧ ☙

Proper 13 [18] / Eighteenth Sunday of the Year (B)
Sunday between July 31 and August 6, inclusive

2 SAMUEL 11:26—12:13A

Once David has learned that his murderous plan has succeeded, he sends word to Joab at the front not to be discouraged at the death of his warrior Uriah (11:25), describing it callously as what modern warfare has termed civilian deaths, "collateral damage."

Bathsheba engages in pro forma mourning, whatever her sentiments were (vv. 26f.). The story is of David, not of her. The son of his adultery is delivered safely but, in the event, will live only a week (12:15b-19). Today's lection proceeds with a tale of remorse, not self-induced but the result of the conviction of David's sin by his prophet-counselor, Nathan. We first hear of Nathan in the passage where a word of the LORD impels him to convince David that he must build a "house." There is a calculated ambivalence about that word throughout chap. 7; it means both a building to shelter the ark and a royal dynasty. In today's pericope, Nathan's business is to face the king with the horror of his act. He fabricates a tale that is a powerful mode of teaching in both Testaments. David is portrayed as missing the point. He goes so far as to propose a fourfold restitution to the fictitious family and death for the rich man who robbed the poor one of his children's pet lamb. The parallel with David's deed is so evident that he cannot have missed it, but unless he is portrayed as doing so there is no story. His rabid indignation is required out of ignorance that he is the target of the narrative's irony. The story-telling skill of the Deuteronomist or whoever edited these chronicles has made this the best-known *j'accuse* in the world familiar with the Bible: "*Thou art the man!*" The catalogue of God's gifts to David with which the story ends heightens his ingratitude and makes it a parable of all the turbulence of the royal house for generations to come.

For a word on the concluding verses see Proper 6 [11] (C).

PSALM 51:1-12

EXODUS 16:2-4, 9[12]-15

The story of the manna and the quail occurs also in Num 11:4-35, quite different as to detail. This leads to the theory of an independent Moses saga as the source of both narratives. (Cf. Exod 15:22-27; 17:1b-7; and Num 20:2-13 for two treatments of the theme of finding water.) Most of this chapter is from P, but vv. 4-5, 13b-15a, 27-30 are probably from J, although some scholars catalogue today's pericope as E material.

The Israelites are described in 16:1 as having been on their desert journey one month since their departure from Egypt. The desert of Sin (Zin? See Num 13:21) is south of the Negev and northeast of Kadesh-barnea—if the shorter, due eastward route of the exodus is assumed rather than the longer, southward journey toward traditional Mount Sinai. The "bread from heaven" of v. 4 is not the allegorized "spiritual food" of 1 Cor 10:3, "heaven" being simply "sky" in Exodus. The sufficiency for a single day of v. 4 was later elaborated on (v. 5) in an edifying lesson geared to Sabbath observance. "Fleshpots" were for the cooking of meat and came to connote a sybaritic existence only in the minds of moderns for whom "flesh" in any context vaguely connotes sex. The murmuring theme (vv. 3-4) occurs everywhere in the Exodus accounts.

Manna and quail are natural phenomena of the northern Sinai desert, the former being an excretion of plant lice resembling a resinous gum called bdellium (Num 11:7) or else coriander seed (cf. Exod 16:31). The quail are migrant birds from Europe that arrived exhausted on Egyptian shores and were easily netted. The mention of quail inclines us still further toward a northern location for the Desert of Sin on the Sinai peninsula.

The J account of the quail in Num 11:31-34 seems to have been incorporated into Exod 16:13a by the P author. The flakes left on the ground by the morning dew prompted the question, "*Man hu*?" Aramaic for "What this?" (reminiscent of *New Yorker* editor Harold Ross's marginal query to nonspecific writers, "Who he?"). The etymology proposed by the J author is improbable. "Manna" was doubtless the traditional local name of the providentially available food.

The tale is one of nature's bounty, interpreted by the entire believing community (v. 1) in terms of the special care exerted by its LORD on their behalf.

Psalm 78:23-29[3-4, 23-25, 54]

Ephesians 4:1-16

For a commentary on vv. 1-6, see Proper 12 [17] immediately above. Verses 7-10 liken a couplet from Ps 67:18 (LXX; MT: 68:19) to Jesus' descent to earth and ascent to heaven, applying the slaves taken in war to the gifts consequent on human redemption—twelve of them, viz., the various ministries in the church listed in 1 Cor 12:28 in aid of achieving maturity/full stature in Christ. Paul had not called Christ the head of the body as here (v. 15; similarly, Col 2:19), but the proper functioning of each part of the body (v. 16) is surely Pauline (see 1 Cor 12:14-26).

Ephesians 4:17, 20-24

Verse 17 is a turning point in the epistle, taking it in an ethical direction without any desertion of the earlier doctrinal themes. The two are fairly closely integrated. The Gentiles (meaning pagans) are warned against, as peoples dwelling in mental futility (v. 17) and alienation from God (v. 18). "Old self" (v. 22) is literally "old human being *(ánthrōpos)*" in parallel with the "new human" of v. 23. The appeal of Ephesians is to fidelity to the days when "you learned Christ" (v. 20), as presumably happened when "you were taught in him, as truth is in Jesus" (v. 21). The new person is the whole body of Christ, Jewish and Gentile, that "person who comes to maturity, to the measure of the full stature of Christ" (v. 13). No specific ethical crisis is contemplated, contrary to the usual case in Pauline letters. We have here a general exhortation to Gentiles to a life lived in Christ. "Deceitful desires" (v. 22) are to be left behind, to yield to a life according to the likeness of God marked by justice and piety (v. 24). Both qualities stem from truth *(alētheia,* vv. 21, 24).

Note that the incorporation into Christ of Ephesians is not quite as complete as that of Rom 5:12-19 and 1 Cor 15:20-28. In this epistle Christ remains distinct from his people who "grow up in every way into him" (Eph 4:15).

Alleluia. John 1:14 and 12b

The Word of God became a man and lived among us. He enabled those who accepted him to become children of God.

JOHN 6:24-35

In the Capernaum discourse John identifies Jesus as the "real heavenly bread" (v. 32), true manna for the life of the world (cf. v. 33). The familiar Johannine typology is present. What went before in Israel's history was a foreshadowing. The occurrence in the life of Jesus is genuine, authentic *(alēthinós)*. The sign, the work provided by God to authenticate Jesus, is Jesus himself. "It is on him that, the Father, God has set his seal" *(toûton gàr ho patēr esphrágisen ho theós,* v. 27).

☙ ❧

Proper 14 [19] / Nineteenth Sunday of the Year
Sunday between August 7 and August 13, inclusive

2 SAMUEL 18:5-9, 15, 31-33

RCL has opted to include this story of a father's love for his rebellious son without having enough Sundays to tell all that went into the relations between David and Absalom. The son is first encountered as the avenger of his sister Tamar for their firstborn brother Amnon's rape of her, although their father had counseled Absalom unsuccessfully against violent action. This furious brother has his men murder Amnon and he then flees the court for three years—while David pines for him despite his evil conduct (13:37-39). Joab arranges for Absalom's return and a father-son reconciliation by getting a widow of Tekoa to spin a thinly disguised account of a fratricide, with most in her family clamoring for revenge against the murdering brother. David finally sees through this fiction: "Is the hand of Joab with you in all this?" (14:19). Absalom returns and after two years usurps the throne, requiring David to flee. A certain Ahithophel gives the miscreant Absalom bad advice about how to smoke out David and his men and destroy them, which he is inclined to accept. Then another counselor Hushai comes along and proposes what Absalom takes to be a better plan, not knowing that he means to deliver his forces over to the king. And so it happens. The rebel's troops are routed in the forest of Ephraim by David's army divided into three groups, with his order to "Deal gently for my sake with the young man Absalom" (18:5). Great was the slaughter of "the men of Israel," Absalom's forces, that day by "the servants of David" (v. 7). Absalom's freak accident under the thick branches of a great oak leaves him hanging by his head. Ten of Joab's young armor bearers surround him and kill him, all of this leading up to the report of Absalom's death to the king. The Ethiopian messenger takes this for good news, but David takes it for bad. This lection must be well read, not over dramatically, or not at all. If preachers choose to develop it they must summarize what went before it in the manner above, that is, briefly and in well-chosen words. Otherwise the poignancy of the father's grief over this thoroughly worthless son will be lost. It is no wonder that the early preachers of East and West found in the tale a foreshadowing of God's love for a sinful humanity which no human hates could diminish.

PSALM 130

1 KINGS 19:4-8

Elijah is in flight for his life because of Jezebel's threat to destroy him (vv. 2-3). The rains have come and YHWH's honor has been vindicated. The prophet is nonetheless a fugitive in the southern desert. After a day's journey from Beersheba he is accosted by a *melek* of the LORD, a term of the J and E writers that the LXX renders *ággelos* to describe the presence of God in human form. He is roused from his despair by this messenger and twice prevailed upon to eat. In the strength provided by the hearth cake and water he proceeds on foot to Mount Horeb (such is the designation of D and E; J calls the mountain Sinai).

PSALM 34:1-8[2-9]

EPHESIANS 4:25[30]-5:2

The Holy Spirit of God is personified here more than elsewhere in the epistle (see 1:13, probably an echo of Ezek 11:1; NAB 9:24f.) and likewise a hint of baptismal practice. The exhortation, coupled with mention of the Holy Spirit "with the promise of whom you were sealed" (1:13), indicates that a baptismal homily may have been the setting. The "day of redemption" is the last day. We might have expected "salvation" rather than "redemption" in a letter from Paul's hand.

Lists of vices and virtues like those of vv. 31 and 32, a convention of the ancient world, are to be found in Rom 1:29ff.; Gal 5:19ff.; 1 Cor 6:9f.; Eph 5:3-5; outside Pauline writings, in 1 Pet 4:3 and Rev 21:8. The lists are not typical of the Hebrew Scriptures or Rabbinic Judaism but were adopted from the Stoics by way of Hellenist Judaism.

The charge to be imitators of God resembles Paul's counsel to imitate him (cf. 1 Cor 4:16 and 11:1). The phrase "beloved children" (5:1) has been used in 1 Cor 4:14 with reference to Paul's fatherhood; here it appears to be as children of God. There are echoes of Christ's giving himself in love, in the phrases of Eph 5:25 and in Gal 2:20.

Ephesians 5:2 employs the LXX's language of sacrifice, "a fragrant offering." which occurs in Exod 29:18, whereas in Phil 4:18 Paul uses it to refer to the gifts that Epaphroditus has brought him from the Philippian community.

Alleluia. John 6:63b and 68b

Your words, Lord, are spirit and life, you have the words of everlasting life.

John 6:35, 41-51

Verse 42 is usually taken to be a Synoptic parallel (cf. Mark 6:3; Matt 13:55; Luke 4:22), not unlike that of 4:43ff. The fourth evangelist does not know of a tradition about the virginal conception of Jesus or, if he does, he does not advert to it. His opponents in this exchange situated in Galilee are "*hoi Ioudaîoi*," the usual designation for Jesus' hostile opponents in Jerusalem. Public readers would do well to read "the crowd" in vv. 41 and 52, since that is what is meant, not Jewish people generally, as can be mistakenly deduced from the translation of *hoi Ioudaîoi*, as "the Jews." Here as elsewhere in John "the Jews" are claimants to that title which they deny to Jesus believing Jews. The "murmuring" of the crowd is the normal LXX word for the grumbling of the period of the exodus.

The Father's drawing of people to Jesus (v. 44) resembles a later rabbinic phrase in which God attracts people to the Torah (cf. the parallel phrase in v. 65). The raising up of believers on the last day will have a similarity in 12:32, where Jesus lifted up from the earth in crucifixion/exaltation draws all to himself.

"They shall all be taught of God" (v. 45) would appear to be a slightly different rendering of Isa 54:13 than the Masoretic and Septuagint readings, which speak of "all your sons." Verse 46 puts Jesus in a position superior to Moses, as 1:18 has done. "Your ancestors," like "your law" (8:17) and "your father Abraham" (8:56), resembles the psychic distancing of an angry father in today's world who speaks to his wife of "your son." The phrases are not to be credited to the earthly Jesus, being rather the polemic speech of the evangelist in his day.

The "belief" of v. 47 is acceptance of Jesus as God's son, the only one who has "seen the Father" (v. 46). "Eating" (i.e., believing in) him brings deathlessness; *zōēn aiōnion* (v. 47) is the life proper to the final *aiōn* or age. "My flesh for the life of the world" (v. 51) is the body of Christ raised up from the earth. To look upon it in faith is to live forever. He is the manna (cf. Exod 16:15), the lifegiving nourishment of the last age.

The prospect of eating flesh, taken literally, would be as shocking to hearers of Jesus' day as to us—the more especially as it had connotations of the cultic practices of pagans. John employs his familiar technique of uncomprehending audience reaction to provide the opportunity for a further word from Jesus. In responding, Jesus is made out to be even more insensitive to Jewish reaction. "Drinking his blood" (v. 53) is doubly repulsive because of the specific Mosaic prohibition of eating meat from which the blood has not been removed (Lev 3:17; 17:10). "Flesh and blood" is a Hebraic idiom for human nature, whole and entire. Total acceptance of Jesus in faith is surely intended, with possible further reference to a two-part eucharistic meal known to the Johannine community. Raymond E. Brown and others think so, considering vv. 51-58 to have been originally part of the Last Supper scene but placed here to duplicate the Bread of Life discourse. There may also be veiled mention of the blood of the covenant of Sinai (cf. Exod 24:8), in line with "my blood, the blood of the covenant" in Mark 14:24(//Matt 26:28; Luke 22:20; 1 Cor 11:25).

The "eating" *(phágēte)* of v. 53 becomes "feeding" *(trōgōn)* in v. 54, but we cannot be sure whether a difference is intended by the second, cruder verb. It may be graphic speech to connote the taking in of Jesus in his entirety by the believer, whose daily feeding upon him places the Christian above his fathers nourished by the manna of old, or else an expression of consuming his body in the Lord's Supper.

❧ ✦

Proper 15 [20] / Twentieth Sunday of the Year (B)
Sunday between August 14 and August 20, inclusive

1 KINGS 2:10-12; 3:3-14

Bathsheba ("Daughter of Abundance") lost in death the first son she bore David, but a second survived infancy and was called Jedidiah, meaning "Beloved of the LORD." David is reported as having proposed Solomon (*Shelomoh*, 2 Sam 12:24f.), but this must have been his throne name: "of his welfare," short for something like, "The LORD is guardian of his welfare"). The dying David is credited by the Deuteronomist with giving Solomon some pious advice about keeping the LORD's commandments (1 Kgs 2:3f.) but also a little bloody counsel regarding Joab and Shimei (vv. 5f., 8f.). This he carried out with dispatch early in his reign (vv. 28-33; 36-46, Shimei's crime having been breaking parole). David spoke as he lay dying of Solomon's wisdom (vv. 6, 9), but in light of that worthy's career it must have been mere intelligence transformed into wisdom by the alchemy of court history. Solomon literally stole the election from his brother Adonijah by declaring himself king, abetted by the scheming of his mother, Bathsheba, with the priest Zadok, the prophet Nathan, and the hatchet man Benaiah. This elder brother, son of Haggith, had claimed the throne by right while the aged and confused David still lived (1 Kgs 1:5-10). The successful ruse that led to the palace *coup* entailed Nathan's proposing to Bathsheba that she have Adonijah ask the king if he could have the beautiful young companion of his old age Abishag to wife. This threat to Adonijah's succession put the cat among the pigeons. It was preceded by obsequious visits by the schemers to the addled old king, telling him he had always meant Solomon to succeed him (1:11-27). And so it is written up in this chronicle.

PSALM 111

PROVERBS 9:1-6

Wisdom has appeared in 1:20-33 and 8:1-21 as a good woman issuing an invitation (cf. Isa 53:1-3). Here she appeals for a hearing on the grounds of her priceless worth and her prime place in the created order of the world. She and Folly "are personified as rival hostesses inviting men to very different kinds of banquets" (R. B. Y. Scott, *The Way of Wisdom in the Old Testament* [New York: Macmillan, 1971, 83]). The injunction, "Keep my commandments, and live" is found elsewhere in Proverbs at 4:4; 7:2 (cf. 11:19; 12:28), and is not unlike Amos's charge, "Seek the LORD and live" (5:4, 6) or "seek good and not evil, that you may live" (5:14). The note in NAB on these seven verses provides a helpful summary: "Wisdom offers the food and drink of divine doctrine and virtue which give life. Unstable and senseless folly furnishes the stolen bread and water of deceit and vice which bring death to her guests."

The house of Wisdom (v. 1) may be an ordinary dwelling but pillars ordinarily marked palaces or the homes of the mighty, while the number seven suggests cosmic significance. Wisdom, after all, was present at the creation as the LORD's model and craftsman (cf. 8:22-31). Rabbinic tradition has the cosmos resting on either twelve or seven pillars; the *Pseudo-Clementine Homilies* speak of seven. The Babylonian planetary deities have also been proposed as the exemplar. Wisdom in such case would supplant Ishtar, the "queen of the heavens."

It is the simple, those who lack understanding, whom Wisdom invites (cf. vv. 4, 16).

She has no message for the wise or the arrogant.

PSALM 34:9-14[2-3, 10-15]

EPHESIANS 5:15-20

Verses 15-16 bear a resemblance to Col 4:5, which warns against dealings with outsiders, while vv. 19-20 largely reproduce the content of that book at 3:16-17. We learn nothing of the circumstances of the writing from the phrase "these are evil days" (v. 16) since it is a standard one with moralists. Folly, ignorance, drunkenness, and debauchery are deplored. Celebration in song and gratitude to God in Christ are praised.

"Make the most of the time, because the days are evil" (v. 16) is the *Ransoming the Time* of Jacques Maritain's book title, recalling Horace's watchword, "Carpe diem!"

JOHN 6:51-58

Consult the commentary for the previous Sunday, especially its next-to-last paragraph. Few new ideas are introduced in these verses except the command to eat Jesus' flesh and drink his blood delivered three times (vv. 53, 54, 56). The chain of the transmission of life *(zōē)* is direct: from the Father to Jesus, the Son; from the Son to the one who "feeds on him" (in NRSV, simply "eats"), "his flesh," or "this bread (vv. 56, 57, 58). The insistence of the evangelist on the quality of the eating (1970 NAB's and *Amplified NT*'s verb "feed on" as was indicated in last week's commentary being equally capable of the translation "munch" or "gnaw," vv. 54, 56, 58), has led some to see an unquestionable reference to the eucharist here, others a polemic against gnostic denials of the reality of Jesus' humanity. Either may be the case but a taking in of the person of Jesus in faith may also satisfy the text. The insistence on "eating" and "drinking" him, however, indicates how his remaining (abiding) in the believer and the believer in him is to be accomplished.

❧❧

Proper 16 [21] / Twenty-first Sunday of the Year (B)
Sunday between August 21 and August 27, inclusive

1 KINGS 8:(1, 6, 10-11), 22-30, 41-43

First Kings 6–7 provide an account of Solomon's building of the Temple and its interior furnishing, then of the construction of his own dwelling. The first project took seven years, the second thirteen. Sandwiched in among the details is an admonition to the king couched as a word of the LORD. If the ordinances and all the divine commandments are kept, God will remain faithful to every promise made to Israel and its Davidic dynasty. This people will not be forsaken (6:11-13). The prayer attributed to Solomon in 8:22-30 and continuing to v. 53 is a declaration uttered in the name of the people that their part of the covenant made with David will be kept. There is much spinning of rhetorical wheels in vv. 22-30, which makes it regrettable that none of the pleas for forgiveness of specific social sins in vv. 31-40 is read out publicly. At least the prayers of "foreigners" in the land emanating from "this house" are asked to be heard (vv. 41-43), an indication that the Deuteronomist author knew his people then (and now) to be themselves foreigners in the land of others.

PSALM 84

JOSHUA 24:1-2A, 14[15]-18

The parallel between this chapter and chap. 23 is evident, and even more so than with 8:30-35 (cf. Deut 11:29 and 27:2-26, where these ceremonies are prescribed). The present description of the promulgation of the covenant at Shechem seems to be out of place, since chap. 23 has reported a valedictory of Joshua. In this chapter only the place and the participants are named. In 8:30f. the Law written by Moses is inscribed on an altar of unhewn stones which is built on Mount Ebal. Half of the Israelites face it while the other half face Mount Gerizim to the south; the valley in which Shechem is situated lies in between. The death and burial of Joshua will be told twice, in 24:29-31 and again in the Deuteronomic book of Judges at 2:6-9. Shechem seems to be a historical covenant-site after the conquest, related to the presence of a Canaanite temple of covenant there (cf. Gen 12:6) known variously as that of Ba'al ("Ba'al of B*e*rith," Judg 9:4) and of El ("b*e*rith," Judg 9:46). Placing the people on Ebal from which they gaze at Gerizim betrays a later, anti-Samaritan editorial hand. The subsequent deemphasis of Shechem as a place of sacrifice and emphasis on Mount Zion in Jerusalem is likewise a matter of anti-Israelite or anti-Ephraimite bias on the part of editors from the southern tribes, Benjamin and Judah.

The reminiscence reported of Joshua in v. 12 harks back to Gen 11:26-28 with its mention of Abram's father, Terah, and his brothers, Nahor and Haran. Verses 3-12 review the conquest and culminate in v. 13 which praises the stability and agricultural accomplishments of the Canaanites, vineyards and olive groves—now an Israelite possession. The choice the patriarch offers is between the LORD whose cult derives from the polytheism of Abram's ancestors in Ur and the local gods of the Amurru or Amorites (lit.: "Westerners," as the Syrians and Mesopotamians called them).

Since the Israelite's God brought them out of slavery, watched them safely through the desert, and drove the Amorite dwellers in the new land out before them, the people elect to serve this God as their own (cf. v. 18). They will never forsake the LORD for other gods, they say (v. 16). Such are the terms of the covenant to which they commit themselves in the new, God-given territory.

PSALM 34:[2-3]15-22[16-23]

EPHESIANS 6:10-20

It is regrettable that last Sunday's reading from Ephesians common to LM and RCL ends where it does, namely, at 5:20. For v. 21 is the introduction to a passage on harmony in the household based on the commandment, "Be subject to one another out of reverence for Christ." This mutual deference of each community member to all others, which is by no means a subjugation on the order of slavery domestic or other, is a formula for harmony in human relations. It makes sense of the way a family of the baptized is to conduct itself (5:22—6:4) and proceeds to the master-slave relation that was the employer-employee relation of the ancient world (vv. 5-9). Family organization in that world, Jewish or pagan, assumed the headship of the father in decision making as well as providing for a family's needs. Whether *hypotassómenoi* (5:21) is translated "be subject" or "be subordinate," it is bound to connote domestic tyranny to modern women who neither know nor care how first-century family life was ideally organized. The elimination of 5:21-32 from the RCL, even as an alternate reading, removes from its hearers a powerful passage on the mutual love of the married correlated with the love of Christ for his Church. The latter may be the chief reason it is not read, namely, a weak sense of the Church in modern congregations, coupled with the tragic reality in the lives of many Christian wives: "He's no Jesus Christ to me."

Beginning today's lection at 6:10 may raise in the attentive worshiper's mind the question, "Finally, what?" For the passage proposes reliance on strength in the power of the Lord Jesus (v. 10) through persevering prayer of supplication (v. 18) to meet all the challenges of life that have just been spoken of (4:17—6:9). Contemporary Christians of both sexes may well have a greater problem with the baleful "cosmic powers of the present darkness" than women do with the preceding passage. Are there such diabolic legions patrolling the cosmos? Further, the militarist imagery of vv. 13-17, a development of 1 Thess 5:8, may not be to the taste of active peacemakers. The figures of speech may not be ours but the various sieges people of today experience themselves to be under are no less powerful for all that. Nameless anxieties trouble them. Some paranoia is real. Whatever the origins of the struggle many are engaged in, they need protection, they need help. As a prayer familiar to many has it, "May the divine assistance remain always with us." Call on God in prayer, Ephesians counsels. Be ever on the alert. And see that you pray for one another (v. 18). The author asks for prayers that he may make known the mystery of the gospel with boldness (*parrēsía*, v. 19; cf. its use in Acts 4:29; 28:31; 2 Cor 3:12; Heb 4:16; 1 John 4:17; 5:14). The same audacity must mark a frontal attack on the evil powers seen and unseen that threaten the living of a Christian life. Such boldness is not alone a matter of human strength. It is a gift of God that must be asked for.

EPHESIANS 5:21-32

The morality of the "new person" includes a conjugal morality of mutual deference and service. Reverence for Christ is proposed as the reason (v. 21). The Pauline ordering of the cosmos is apparent here: Lord Jesus : Church :: man : woman, the wife appearing in a relation of submission to her husband as the Church is to Christ (vv. 2f.). The philosophical notion of a cosmic marriage between spirit and matter is probably influential here. The relative positions of the sexes would be intolerable to contemporaries were it not for what follows, namely, the constant solicitude demanded of husband for wife (vv. 25-29). The imagery of vv. 26f. is that of the preparation of an oriental bride for marriage, something that was not the groom's task but performed by other women. The author wishes, however, to feature the idea of Christ's service to his Church. The giving over of himself, followed by the sanctifying and purifying of believers in the Word-energized waters of baptism, requires the figure of a groom immediately engaged in preparing his spotless bride. Christ's care for his church is the reality that governs the rhetoric (vv. 29f.).

Paul has the concept of Christ as a second Adam (cf. Rom 5:14f.; 1 Cor 15:21). The exegesis of Gen 2:24 proposed in vv. 31ff. is that the clear reference to human marriage has a symbolic sense. It is a "foreshadowing" (*mystērion*; Vulgate, *sacramentum*) of Christ's union with the church, which would be Eve to his Adam.

Some see in this passage a veiled response to a gnostic system like that of Valentinus featuring heavenly eons in male and female pairs. The author of Ephesians gets back to his main point in v. 33, which is that of the mutual respect and support of spouses.

Alleluia. John 8:12

I am the light of the world, says the Lord; whoever follows me will have the light of life.

John 6:56[60]-69

John reports Jesus as largely having failed in his Galilean ministry, except for Peter's confession of faith in him (6:68f.), which probably derives from traditional material. The people murmur as they had done against Moses in the desert (v. 61). Jesus proposes his ascent to "where he was before" as an even greater test of faith in him than the feeding at the lakeshore and the challenge to believe what he evoked from it. John provides his special view of flesh as "useless" when contrasted with the spirit and life represented by Jesus' words (v. 63). This seems to be a precaution against the reader's understanding the eating of flesh and blood in any gross sense. Access to Jesus, which is belief, is a gift of the Father (v. 56). The Twelve have received the gift (v. 69). The "holy one of God" means simply the Christ for John, but it does have a Synoptic ring (cf. Mark 1:24).

❧✦

Proper 17 [22] / Twenty-second Sunday of the Year (B)
Sunday between August 28 and September 3, inclusive

Song of Solomon 2:8-13

How does Solomon figure in this tale of young rustic love? Toward the end the bride to be addresses her strong husband to be as if he were that fabled sovereign, as she deeds over to him her dowry of a thousand silver pieces. She is the vineyard of great value, watched over by caretakers until now, guarded by a wall and a door protective of her chastity. But its fruit is to be his once the dowry is paid and their love consummated (8:9-12; cf. 1:6). This love poem beloved of the postexilic Jewish people takes the form of a playlet. Roles are identified in the NAB editing of the text as B, Bride; D, Daughters of Jerusalem, her attendants; and G, Groom. Today's passage is among the most familiar and best appreciated. The bride hails the advent of her athletic young lover as he comes bounding down the mountainside and stands peering through the lattice work at this dusky, well-protected maiden. He summons her to come out and join him in a springtime bursting with fragrant blooms, the soft cooing of doves a bass treble to the humming of bees. There is no chance she is free to answer his call. This, after all, is the ancient Middle East. It is also a poem of love and desire. He calls her his dove and although she is housebound by watchful parents he must voice her restraints poetically. Dove-like she is "in the clefts of the rock"; in the parallel of all such Hebrew imagery she dwells "in the secret recesses of the cliff." It is often said that the Rabbis were embarrassed by the exuberant eroticism of the poem and so made it a parable of the Lord's love for Israel, the virgin bride of God. The Church Fathers did the same, only this time it was Christ and the Church. But the claim of embarrassment and Grundyism is nonsense. The poem was ready-made for such metaphorical application since both Testaments already spoke of the union in terms of conjugal love. The *shir shirim* (a Hebrew intensive, meaning "*The* Song") offers many opportunities for preaching at weddings. Note well that the word pictures on the lips of both players are their fantasies. There is no union of bodies yet. The bride reminds herself of it in a mantra to the daughters spoken not once but three times (2:7; 3:5; 8:4). The time for the stirring up of love between two Christians or Jews comes immediately after a lifetime commitment has been publicly spoken.

PSALM 45:1-2, 6-9

DEUTERONOMY 4:1-2, 6[8]-9

The first three chapters of Deuteronomy have been devoted to a recapitulation of the final wanderings of the Israelites. The narrative has taken them from Kadesh–barnea (south of Beersheba in the Negev or southern desert) to the Moabite and Ammonite highlands east of the Jordan River. The journey is described as a matter of thirty-eight years (cf. 2:14), so as to get them into the promised land under Joshua's leadership in forty. Chapter 4 spells out the moral of the story of safe passage told in the first three chapters. In the present passage Moses, who has been the speaker, tells Israel that fidelity to the LORD's statutes and decrees is the condition of possessing the new land. Such observance alone can guarantee life there. The implication is that the Canaanite-held territory will become holy if the

LORD's commandments are neither added to nor subtracted from but only adhered to. The Deuteronomist's stress on Torah as a collection of precepts rather than globally as the instruction of God which accompanies the covenant is, of course, a postexilic development.

Wisdom and intelligence, understood as canny prudence, were much prized in Egypt and Mesopotamia. It was from these cultures that Israel had derived its notion of wisdom *(ḥokmah)*. The incoming conquerors are therefore described as superior to the pagan nations in these endowments—somewhat anachronistically, since the full flowering of the wisdom concept came after the exile. The proximity of God, the intimacy between the LORD and his people are featured in vv. 7-8, as they will be again in 30:10-14. The book of the Law is fully available; it is not something up in the sky or across the sea. All that this people has to do is carry it out. The distinguishing features of the decrees and statutes is their justice (4:8). Everything about them bespeaks the wisdom, the moral superiority, and loving care of Israel's God.

The Bible has no author to rival the Deuteronomist in hymning the glories of the Law.

PSALM 15[2-5]

JAMES 1:17-27

For further commentary, See Propers 18 [23] and 19 [24] immediately below.

In the puzzling introductory phrase, the Father who gives gifts from above is the changeless deity of Stoic philosophy, not the constantly active God of Israel. Yet, as the source of benefits to humanity, God is distinguished from the heavenly bodies he has created, in a familiar Hellenist Jewish apologetic convention. Because of the context some scholars think that being brought to "birth by the word of truth" (v. 18) has to do with the act of creation only, or at most with the instruction constituted by Torah—if the epistle had a Jewish prehistory. The weight of opinion, however, favors reference to the new birth that results from acceptance of the Gospel. This view is reinforced by reference in v. 18 to "us" as first fruits (cf. Lev 23:11; Rom 8:23; 1 Cor 15:20, and the comment on the *aparchē* of 1 Corinthians under 6 Sunday (C). The much argued "implanted word" (v. 21) has the power to save, but only if hearers becomes doers (v. 22). Failure to act on this word is self-deceit. The teaching, as often in James, is redolent of words of the Lord: here the parable of the wise man and the fool who built respectively on rock and sand as they did or did not put Jesus' teaching into practice (cf. Matt 7:24-27).

Doing the works of mercy and "keeping oneself unstained by the world" constitute "pure and undefiled religion" (v. 27). Again, we are reminded of Jesus' pronouncement of final judgment in Matthew on the basis of deeds (25:31-46); also, the word of 1 John on loving God, through the brother, one sees (4:20). This concern with ethical choices has distressed some Pauline faith-alone purists by its "Jewishness" but it is part of the fabric of New Testament teaching. Jesus never deserted *halakah*, the way of conduct, as a means to please God. Both he and Paul, like many rabbis before them, were insistent of purity of intent.

Alleluia. John 1:27

My sheep listen to my voice, says the Lord; I know them and they follow me.

Mark 7:1-8, 14-15, 21-23

Mark explains Pharisee ritual washing to his Gentile audience (vv. 3-4), something that Matthew omits in the parallel place (15:1-9) as needless for his readership. Both describe the repudiation of certain aspects of the oral tradition of the elders (vv. 3, 5), i.e., the teachers of the previous century. This repudiation characterized Hellenist Jewish Christianity and probably went back to a word of Jesus himself. The citation of Isa 29:13 in vv. 6-7 is probably the evangelist's doing. God's "commandment" (v. 8) is presumably the deliverance of Torah and is distinguished from "human tradition" (v. 8). This distinction the Pharisees did not honor because of their conviction that that oral Law, which was a modern interpretation of ancient material, was on an equal footing with the written Law.

The exchange is made the basis of an explicit teaching of Jesus (although he is totally unlikely to have been its author) that rescinds dietary observance (vv. 14-15). Only that which comes out of a person's mouth—spelled out in a Hellenist catalogue of evils (v. 22)—renders him impure (v. 23). The latter two verses probably reflect early Church teaching but there is no reason to think that Jesus did not speak on the subject of Rabbinic practices concerning food. We know from other places in the Synoptics his support of the Law of Moses. The distinction between what God intended and what men have made of it is at the heart of many of the conflict stories reported of him.

The Christians would do ill to think of Jesus as the first or the only Rabbinic teacher to stress interiority in matters of Mosaic observance. What is clear is that he did so consistently and that a tradition that had as its final outcome desertion of all such observance was traced to him.

Proper 18 [23] / Twenty-third Sunday of the Year (B)
Sunday between September 4 and September 10, inclusive

PROVERBS 22:1-2, 8-9, 22-23

Wise counsel, normally of the mature to the immature, delivered in proverbial form was a commonplace in the ancient Middle East, shared by Hebrews, Babylonians, and Egyptians alike. From time immemorial these colorful epigrams had been traded around desert campfires by the men reckoned sages in the community. The biblical collection is divided into thirty-one chapters and touches on every moral dilemma and character trait. It does so wittily and with rich insight into the human talent for self-deception and frailty of judgment. By our standard it can be considered a handbook for upright living. At the moments when it seems most cynical or calculating, it will come up with an axiom conveying humanity's total dependence on God, a lively awe before whom is the beginning of wisdom.

A comparison of the Englishing of proverbs in today's reading in NRSV, REB, NAB, and JB shows them to be so weighed down with syllables that the effect is quite lost. An attempt to retain it might be:

> A good name is better than riches,
> > respect more than silver and gold.
> The rich and the poor are alike in this:
> > the Lord gives breath to them all. (1-2)
>
> Sow injustice to reap disaster,
> > wait for the rod of wrath to fall.
> The proffered hand will earn a blessing
> > that shares the bread with eaters all. (8-9)
>
> Blame not the victim for his state
> > nor crush the needy at the gate.
> Be sure, the Lord will plead his cause,
> > your life for his by heaven's laws. (22-23)

Hebrew poetry did not know rhyme but relied on the parallel and pithy phrase. Wordiness was no part of its art.

PSALM 125

ISAIAH 35:4-7A

See commentary under 3 Advent (A).

Psalm 146:7-10

James 2:1[5]-10, (11-13, 14-17)

It has been hotly debated whether the gold-ringed man is a Christian in Gentile circumstances or Jewish, or a wealthy pagan who visits the Christian assembly envisaged (v. 2) as a law-court or a gathering for worship or study. Bo Reicke's speculations about the alignment of the Jewish poor with Roman patricians have received a wide hearing but not wide acceptance (Anchor Bible commentary on James). The assumption in possession on this reading is that *synagōgē* (v. 2) means the religious assembly, even though the arguments in favor of a Jewish court of law are not unimpressive. The point of the passage is clear. Some Christians are practicing "acts of favoritism" (lit.: "acceptance of persons," v. 1). The discriminatory tactic is reprobated by the author as being no better than the maneuverings of corrupt judges.

This world's poor are fated to be rich—but in faith and as heirs of the kingdom, according to James. Martin Dibelius (*From Tradition to Gospel* [New York: Scribner, 1935]) introduced into the world of scholarship eighty years ago the notion of *Armenfrommigkeit (Armenstolz),* a piety of the poor testified to by James. James's audience was thought to be forerunners of those Christian Jews later known as Ebionites, the "poor" used as a technical term for self-description by some early Christians. A doctoral dissertation by my student Francis Kelly at Temple University on the question seems to dispel any such notion. It shows, contrariwise, that early Christianity, like Judaism, did not propose poverty as an ideal to be sought but viewed it as an evil to be relieved. It favored simplicity of life and deplored riches because of the evils attendant on amassing them.

Here the stress of James is not on exploitation of the poor by the rich, as seems to be the case at first blush (see vv. 6-7). The offense instead is dealing unfairly with respect to the various baptized for reasons of unequal social status. All are viewed as equal by James, as had been the case with all who stood before Mosaic Law. The Rabbis fulminated against favoritism. So, too, does James (v. 9).

Alleluia. John 14:6

I am the way, the truth, and the life, says the LORD; no one comes to the Father except through me.

Mark 7:24[31]-37

This reading obviously corresponds to the first one from Isaiah with its multiplication of signs of the messianic era. It is not only the framers of the lectionary who have the correspondence in mind; the evangelist seems to as well. The geography of v. 31 has been likened to a journey from New York to Philadelphia by way of Boston. If "Sidon" were a misreading for "Bethsaida" (and there is scant textual evidence for it), the situation would be relieved somewhat but not greatly. Mark may wish to keep Jesus out of Herod Antipas's territory, but his contrivance of the "secret" (cf. vv. 33, 36) until he is ready to reveal Jesus as the Messiah and Son of God in the narrative of the trial, passion, and resurrection would sufficiently account for Jesus' sequestration.

Matthew uses the Markan summary of 7:37 in 15:31 but does not tell the healing story. The detail of the saliva has caused uneasiness, as if some magic were being attributed to Jesus. John 9:6 has Jesus using a mud paste to cure a blind man. The action may be taken as a parable in sign rather than word such as Israel's prophets employed. At the same time its occurrence in pagan healing narratives as well as Jewish is undeniable. This fact does not diminish the impact. Jesus inaugurates the messianic age for Mark by works of healing. The deaf hear and the mute speak at the hands of one who does all things well (*kalōs*, lit.: "beautifully," "admirably," v. 37).

❧ ✼ ❧

Proper 19 [24] / Twenty-fourth Sunday of the Year (B)
Sunday between September 11 and September 18, inclusive

PROVERBS 1:20-33

The proverbs in this collection were attributed to Solomon, not because he was wise (he may or may not have been) but because he was a king whose reign was marked by expansion and magnificence. Mae West is reported to have said to a woman who marveled at the size of a diamond on her finger, "Oh, my goodness!" "Honey, goodness had nothing to do with it." So with Solomon's throne-based wisdom. But the sayings are wise even if the man was not, of whom the Bible records the unraveling of his character with the success of his reign. "*Mishle*" is the first word of this collection and *mesh^alim* can mean proverbs, parables, or riddles (see v. 6). Their purpose as gathered here is to teach "shrewdness to the simple, knowledge and prudence to the young" (v. 4). Parents teach children the ways of wisdom (v. 8). The young heed the promises and lures of sinners to their peril (vv. 11-19). Mother and father *do* know best in trying to school their offspring against the snare of base gain (v. 19). Wisdom is personified as a woman because the noun is feminine in the Hebrew and Greek—Latin too. She goes public in her appeal and offers her words to all. If they fail to heed them she is not above taunting people in their folly and the calamity it leads to (vv. 20-27).

Wisdom is a harsh teacher, not a soft one. Those heedless of her appeal may regret but not repent their folly when they see what it has brought them to but she has no time for them. "Let them stew in their own juice," might be a modern translation of v. 28. The chief reason knowledge, which is wisdom's bedrock, is despised is that it is not based on *yirăth YHWH*—the fear of the Lord, but not craven fear. It is the awe before the Lord that is the only fitting response to the presence of Israel's God. Such feelings of awe Rudolf Otto identified as a trembling *(tremens)* and at the same time a gripping *(fascinans)* of the devotee faced with the Holy, a simultaneous attraction and repulsion. He described this holy awe as a kind of dread, an eerie feeling in the presence of the divine. The book of Proverbs says that dread of disaster is the one thing wisdom effectively cancels out. Those who listen to wisdom's voice will dread nothing but will dwell secure (v. 33).

Psalm 19 or Wisdom 7:26—8:1

Isaiah 50:4c[5]-9a

Zion complains in her state of defeat:

> The Lord has forsaken me;
>> my Lord has forgotten me (49:14).

The Lord responds in 50:1-4 that, although for its sins and crimes Israel's mother has been divorced and the nation's children sold to creditors (the Chaldeans), his hand is not too short to ransom. Verses 4-9 are part of the third Servant Song, a response in faith to the present adversity of the exiled people.

The servant people or its paradigmatic individual Jew knows it has not lost the role of teacher. Consolation is a daily task but one that can be discharged only after a faithful hearing of what the Lord has to say (v. 4); the Servant can claim perseverance (vv. 5, 7) in the face of humiliating treatment (v. 6). The latter verse may be patterned on the personal sufferings of Jeremiah. It probably contributed to the accounts of mockery in Jesus' trial narrative.

The Servant's trust in God is so firm that he volunteers to take on all challengers (vv. 8–9a). The Lord will hear his voice and make an end of them—wear them out like a garment (cf. Ps 102:27), consume them like a moth. In a word, his vindication of his Servant will be complete.

PSALM 116:1-9

JAMES 3:1-12

This is a Christian book of proverbial wisdom addressed to "believers" *(adelphoi)* in the Lord Jesus Christ (v. 1), a term translated throughout NRSV as "brothers and sisters" (1:2; 2:1, 5, 14f.; 3:1, 10, 12; 4:11; 5:19). Today's lection opens with a warning that the teacher's office should be confined to the few because its obligations are so serious. One thinks immediately of the ill-trained or untrained Christian educator or the preacher who does not study, as for preaching. "Making mistakes" is a weak translation of the repeated verb of v. 2, if only because so many public figures in our day explain their grand theft or acts of major injustice by saying "I erred," when far more than a mistake in judgment is involved. NIV does better in rendering *ptaíō* with "are at fault," REB with "go wrong," both suggesting moral delinquency. The list of "mistakes in speaking" that follows is about serious sins of the tongue, not involuntary misstatements. The images chosen in each proverb are memorable: the bit in a horse's mouth, the rudder of a ship, the spark in the forest; all huge consequences that come from small causes. The tongue is characterized even more directly: as a fire originating in the flames of Gehenna, a world of malice, a member capable of defiling the whole body, of setting ablaze the whole course of life (v. 6, NRSV, "the cycle of nature," for the literal "wheel of birth").

The human species is the potential master of much lower animal life but seems to have no corresponding power to master the tongue. It can and does bless but it also curses. It resembles no known spring that wells up fresh and brackish water. No tree or vine produces anything other than its fruit in kind. "Salty speech" is a weak figure in English for mildly irreligious vocabulary. James makes salt water which can kill a person dying of thirst a metaphor for evil speech, cruel speech, destructive speech. The pericope is powerful and cries out to be preached on.

JAMES 2:14-18

James returns to his theme of the necessity of testifying to religious faith with deeds. Faith that is professed without being practiced has no power to save one (v. 14).

A "brother" or "sister" is a Christian believer. The offhanded dismissal, "Go in peace," has inclined some to think that liturgical dismissal is in question. Ordinary well-wishing in the Jewish manner, however, would satisfy the requirement of the phrase. Clearly what is required is a solicitude in fact, not just in word. The author calls such faith without works dead (v. 17). The context of v. 18 is unequal, stacked as it is against the person of faith alone in his stance of moral superiority. He is challenged as one having faith without works whereas the other, representing the author's point of view, has a faith to declare that underlies his works. James is solidly in the Jewish tradition when he claims the need of deeds in proof of faith. Neither does he contravene Paul, who is by no means disinterested in an ethical life in favor of the other person. Paul resists works only when they are made the subject of a boast in lieu of or necessary complement to saving faith in Jesus Christ.

Was James writing a polemic against Paul or against a Pauline position originating in the Gentile Christian world? Possibly the latter, but not if his letter preceded Paul's first epistle (1 Thessalonians), as some think. A twofold understanding of *pistis* has been proposed as the solution: in James the Hebraic sense of trust (*ᵉmunah*) but in Paul of Hellenic belief in a saving deed. Such a variant understanding may be the case in part, but it does not seem required as a way out of the difficulty. Paul's "faith working through love" as that which counts for something (Gal 5:6) should be acceptable to James. Paul never uses the words "faith alone" in sequence. James does (2:24), only to deny its efficacy as saving. He attributes salvation to works—but not to works alone.

The two writers are engaged in emphasizing different matters. Neither denies what the other affirms. Paul would challenge James on the sense in which works justify and doubtless elicit from him a soteriology he would find woefully deficient. But Paul cannot be shown to favor a faith unaccompanied by works as saving, the matter James is at such pains to deny. He does so only if his individual statements are taken out of the context of his entire teaching on the subject.

ALLELUIA. JOHN 14:23

Whoever loves me will hold to my words, and my Father will love them, and we will come to them.

MARK 8:27[35]-38

Mark's Caesarea Philippi account differs from Matthew's (16:13-20, Proper 16 [21]) in having Jesus describe himself as "I," in omitting mention of Jeremiah, in not attributing to [Simon] Peter faith in the "Son of the living God," and, above all, in failing to use the confession of faith ecclesially as a means to underscore Peter's subsequent role. Mark makes a continuing point of the "secret" aspect of Jesus' sonship of God, v. 30 (Matthew will follow him in this, 16:20). The Gospel writer, not Jesus, is the one who enjoins silence on the disciples as part of his narrative technique.

In both evangelists, the prophecy of suffering is used as the setting for an elenchus of sayings on the self-abnegating life of the Christian (cf. Mark 8:34-38). These are already church sayings in Mark, but vv. 35-37, which are eschatological, could well have originated with Jesus.

This pericope forms a turning point in Mark's Gospel and concludes the first half. We are wrong in concluding anything about what the confession of faith meant in Jesus' career. Mark has no interest in a historical sequence, only in a faith narrative—the framework of which is entirely his doing.

❧☙

Proper 20 [25] / Twenty-fifth Sunday of the Year (B)
Sunday between September 18 and September 24, inclusive

PROVERBS 21:10-31

For a commentary, see Proper 28 [33] (A) above.

PSALM 1

WISDOM 1:16—2:1, 12-22

A look back at the comment on the early verses of this book in Proper 8 [13] (B) is suggested. The unjust covet death as the possession they deserve (1:16), erroneously supposing that after the smoke and spark of life is extinguished there will be no accounting of their wickedness (2:1-2). They look upon the just person with contempt since his life is a reproach to them (vv. 12-16). Verses 17-18 may well be the source of the taunt of Matt 27:43, since it is utterly unlikely that Jesus ever said in life "I am the Son of God" (cf. Wis 2:13, 16b, 18). Verses 19-22 give similar evidence of having contributed to the passion narrative.

WISDOM 2:12, 17-20

The earlier portion of this chapter spells out a full-scale program of hedonism, the claims of might over right and youthful vigor over infirm old age. Needless to say, the author considers this to be anything but right thinking (cf. 2:1). It serves as a backdrop, however, for his sketch of the just one, that "child of the LORD" (v. 13b) and "son of God (v. 18a) who seems to be the eternal victim of the man of power but in fact is his moral superior. The titles were ordinary designations for the pious in that period.

The antithesis spells out a parable of human life in general but its graphic character made the early Church conclude that it contained specific prophecy. The mocking of the bystanders at the cross in the passion narratives derives from v. 18, although not exclusively from there. Another contributor is the poetry of the righteous sufferer, developed long before in sources such as Jer 20 and Lam 3.

The chapter concludes with the reflection that the shameful death to which the wicked consign the just man (cf. v. 20) will not be lasting. Man was formed by God to be incorruptible (v. 23). Wages and a prize lie in store for the innocent (v. 22). In the hidden counsels of God they will be given to them to thwart death, which was brought on by the envy of the devil (v. 24). The latter notion is related to a rabbinic midrash that makes the serpent of Genesis the devil and the seducer of Eve, by whom she begot Cain.

JEREMIAH 11:18-20

Immediately before this passage there is the charge laid against the kingdoms of north and south that they have made offerings to Ba'al (11:10, 13, 17). The LORD's "beloved" has done this (v. 15), the green olive tree that the LORD had planted (vv. 16, 17). It is no wonder that the priests and prophets at the court of King Jehoiakim clamored for Jeremiah's death (26:7-9). Today's poetic portion begins with an address to the LORD by the prophet (with "O LORD" supplied from v. 20), saying that the latter had made known to him the people's evil deeds and telling what God has in store for them as a result (11:18, referring back to vv. 14-17). MT and LXX both have vv. 18-23 following v. 17, but John Bright deals editorially with the interruption constituted by 12:1-6 by placing it between vv. 17 and 18 (*Jeremiah* [AB; Garden City, N.Y.: Doubleday, 1965], 83–84.). NAB acted on the widely held suspicion of displacement by printing 11:19-23 between 12:6 and 7 where it was probably to be found originally. The phrase of the prophet comparing himself with a gentle lamb (v. 19) occurs in the better known Isa 53:7b, while the plot to "destroy the tree with its fruit" (NAB, 7b: "in its vigor") will be echoed in the book of Wisdom by the plots against the just man who reproaches the wicked for their sins (Wis 2:12-20). Jeremiah calls on the LORD to respond to all such schemes with a fitting retribution (v. 20). We have not been told up to this point (11:21) that the priests of Anathoth from among whom Jeremiah came (1:1) were the townsmen who seek his life. The men of that village (three miles north of Jerusalem) are ticketed for punishment and disaster possibly because the writer needs a fitting place on which the divine wrath is to fall (vv. 22f.).

PSALM 54[3-6, 8]

JAMES 3:13[16]—4:3], 7-8A

Jealousy and strife bring a variety of evils in their train. Wisdom produces a harvest of justice, peace, and every other virtue. Cravings (v. 1) produce inner struggle in the individual (cf. Rom 7:19 for a statement of the same axiom). Frustrated desires lead to murder and violent quarreling. The "asking" and "receiving" of v. 3 seem at first to be describing a better means of acquiring goods than murderous plunder but on inspection prove to be the suggestion of recourse to prayer. The antinomy in the writer's mind is that between God and world or God and devil. Submission to the divine will (vv. 7-9) will elevate the lowly, put the devil to flight, turn tears into laughter, and in general restore the balance of a disordered universe.

ALLELUIA. JOHN 15:15B

I call you my friends, says the Lord, for I have made known to you all that the Father has told me.

MARK 9:30-37

This pericope contains the second prediction of the passion in Mark, as last Sunday's reading did the first. (The third will occur in 10:30ff.) All three include reference to his rising again (v. 31) not—as elsewhere in the Synoptics—his being raised up (John 20:9 also has "rise"). The evangelist's secrecy theme (v. 30) is explained by Jesus' desire to instruct his disciples in particular (v. 31). This shorter prophecy than that of 8:31 introduces the notion of the Son of Man's being "delivered over"/"betrayed" (v. 30; cf. Acts 2:23; Rom 8:32), which connotes the plan and foreknowledge of God more than any handing over of Jesus by means of the deed of Judas or his captors. As on the previous occasion, Mark portrays the disciples as stunned at the disclosure—uncomprehending more than resistant. Whatever their actual thoughts on Jesus' death (if indeed he prophesied it) we cannot know. Mark's literary construct conceals this from us even while seeming to reveal it.

A series of sayings on discipleship follow (illustrative of the suffering principle?). The first two deal with ambition and humility, although the saying in vv. 36f. does not follow especially from that in v. 35. The Aramaic word *ṭalyā* which does duty as both "servant" and "little child" (*diakonos* and *paidíon*) has been proposed as the link. Later sayings in the collection are linked up by a word such as "salt" or "fire." A greater puzzle than the contiguity of vv. 35 and 36 is the separation of v. 37 from 10:14f., not only because of the children theme but because the two sets of sayings have in common a word unique in the gospels meaning "taking in his arms" (9:36; 10:16).

✍ ✍

Proper 21 [26] / Twenty-sixth Sunday of the Year (B)
Sunday between September 25 and October 1, inclusive

ESTHER 7:1-6, 9-10; 9:20-22

This is the only reading from Esther in RCL, while LM employs it on a Sunday not at all, only on Thursday of 1 Lent. It was and is a popular favorite with Jews for, despite its grisly ending with the hanging of Haman and his sons (9:25), it tells of the destruction of plotters who tried to kill all the Jews in the Persian empire (3:6, 8f.). Called in Hebrew *Purim*, a Babylonian word that means "lots," it purports to tell the origins of the feast of that name kept on 14 and 15 Adar, mid-February to mid-March (9:8-23). Originally, the story says, lots were cast on the thirteenth to establish the date of the Jews' destruction (3:7, 12f.). Through the scheming of the Jewish Queen Esther (a Persian throne name; her given name was Hadassah) and her uncle Mordecai at a royal banquet, the plot of the Jew-hating foreigner in the king's court, Haman, was uncovered. He—and not the Jew Mordecai—was hanged (7:10). Today's reading tells of the second day of the banquet when, after copious drinking, Ahasuerus (Xerxes) asks Esther what her petition is and she, who has rigged it all, asks for amnesty for her people and death for the wicked Haman. The only reason to justify preaching on this romantic tale of vengeance is to let Christians know how the life of the Jews as a people has been threatened many times before the Nazi era. It is a classic tale of a pogrom that did not happen, a forerunner of those in the eighteenth and nineteenth centuries that did. Christians should know the origins of Jewish feasts besides Passover. This one is the most joyous in the calendar, because it celebrates the people's freedom by the courageous act of a woman. It is a children's feast, as Hanukkah originally was not (but has become lately through its proximity to Christmas). The Esther scroll *(megillah)* is read in synagogues on this feast, giving the Jewish slang expression sometimes heard on television, "the whole megillah," in sportspeak, "the whole nine yards."

PSALM 124

NUMBERS 11:4-6, 10-16, 24-29

The best-known anecdote in the American experience paralleling Moses' reply is that of Abraham Lincoln, who said, when apprised of Ulysses Grant's drinking habits, that he wished the rest of the Union generals drank the same brand of whiskey. Moses responds briskly to the protective Joshua that "spirit" is a gift of the Lord freely given, and his only regret is that it is not universal among the Israelites. About its distribution beyond the seventy elders (if that is where the missing Eldad and Medad fell), Moses has no problem.

The appointment of the seventy comes in the wake of the people's complaints to Moses about the surfeit of manna (11:6) and the shortage of meat (v. 13). The Lord provides a company of authorities to share responsibility with Moses, even as he promises food so abundant that it will come out their nostrils (v. 20) and thereby remove the cause of complaint. The manna story is paralleled in the E-tradition (this is P, as is three-fourths of the book of Numbers) in Exod 16:3-35 and in the account of the selection of the elders in Exod 18:17-27, where Jethro makes the suggestion. "Spirit" is conceived in the early period as divisible, a kind of *mana* (in the Polynesian, Melanesian sense) whereby spiritual power is concentrated on individuals. In Israel, prophets who had a portion of spirit from God were at times moved to frenzied behavior (1 Sam 19:20-24). Here its primary result would be wisdom for judgment but the seventy thus endowed also prophesied (vv. 26, 29).

We are not told why Eldad and Medad were detained in the camp and were not in the assembly. If ritual uncleanness were the explanation, Joshua would have an additional reason for his scruple. Their absence from "around the tent" (v. 24) would, however, suffice. Joshua tries to protect Moses' office and reputation in the manner of aides everywhere and is repulsed for his pains. Moses has a far less protective view of his office, a proof of his greatness. He sees himself as a channel of God's spirit and not an exclusive one at that. The tale is one of incalculable importance for the exercise of power in God's name over all succeeding ages.

PSALM 19:7[8, 10]-14

JAMES 5:[1-6]13-20

Like any Jewish writer schooled in that people's Scriptures, the author of James expects good works to be the fruit of wisdom (v. 13). Envy and ambition beget another kind of wisdom, "earthly, unspiritual, demonic" (v. 15).

This excoriation of the rich, not because they are rich but because they defraud the poor (the other ways to get rich are relatively few) is in the best tradition of the eighth- and seventh-century prophets. The just Lord hears the cries of the farm workers, who are unorganized. The owners have not stopped at litigation and murder. The language of the corrosive effects of wealth may be stereotyped but it is no less powerful for that. There has been no justice for the impoverished and exploited just ("decent, hard-working people," we would say). They will receive justice, says James, in the last days (v. 3). He is by no means proposing, however, that in principle justice be deferred until then. In wrath he wants it now.

The conclusion of this short book tells of the pastoral practices of some ethnically Jewish early Christian churches in the diaspora (see 1:1). Community prayer led by *presbyteroi*, accompanied by anointing for those who are ill, has developed into the sacrament of the sick among Catholics and Orthodox and a ritual by some Protestants but not named a sacrament (vv. 14f.). Prayer for the recovery of a seriously ill member is, needless to say, universal. The sufferers should themselves pray (v. 13). Ritualized mutual forgiveness is likewise a practice of this community. The origin of that sacramental practice seems to have been the confession to a bishop of the sin of denying Christ in the Decian persecution of the mid-third century, with an appropriate public penance imposed. Some Protestant groups confess grievous wrongdoings publicly in an effort to be faithful to James, but the practice has serious community-wounding consequences. Some Christians who live by vow have long had the practice of a "chapter of faults," "chapter" meaning the assembled community and "faults" being infractions of the religious rule and minor offenses against charity. These public declarations of weakness prove the wisdom of asking in utter privacy for forgiveness of grievous sin from another human acting in God's name, but more importantly of the person(s) sinned against if that is possible.

The summarized story of Elijah's answered prayers regarding the weather (vv. 17f.; cf. 1 Kgs 18:1, 41-46) would have reminded hearers of the power of God if it did not tell them that the certain effect of their prayers was guaranteed. Their mutual concern for those who stray from the truth as the "cover of a multitude of sins" has long remained in Christian memory as proverbial wisdom. A visitor to a drought-stricken area hearing public prayers for rain Sunday after Sunday will realize that Elijah's prayer has not been forgotten. God opposes the proud. . . . But gives grace to the humble (4:6) occurs in the same wording in 1 Pet 5:5, in both cases with "God" instead of "the LORD" but otherwise an exact quotation of Prov 3:34 from the LXX, not the MT. "All the more grace" promised in that same v. 6 aids submission to God's will and resistance to the devil. Proximity to the divine puts the diabolic to flight (vv. 7-8a).

ALLELUIA. JOHN 17:17B AND A

Your word, O Lord, is truth; make us holy in the truth.

MARK 9:38[43, 45, 47-48]-50

Verses 44 and 46 of the Vulgate do not occur in the Greek, so the editors of the lectionary are proposing no omissions. The dependence of the first three verses of the pericope on Num 11 (see above) is obvious. In vv. 27, 38, 39, 41 the phrase "in my name" is common to all and ties them together (the prepositions are *epi*, *en*, *epi*, a matter of no consequence; the same is true of the modifiers, "my," and in v. 41 simply *en onómati*). Whether the deed is receiving a child, exorcising demons, or giving a cup of water "because you bear the name of Christ" (v. 41), it is good because of its personal ascription—in that wording undoubtedly the work of the Church, not a saying of Jesus—and will not go unrewarded. Contrariwise, the scandalizing of simple believers is an offense deserving of drastic punishment. No play on words remains in Greek, but similar-sounding Aramaic words for stumbling stone and millstone (v. 43) may be assumed.

The punitive sayings of vv. 43-47 are inserted by Matthew into the Sermon on the Mount in a context of lustful gazes (5:29f.). The speech is figurative as attested to by the existence of an actual Gehenna, a blazing refuse-dump in the valley of Hinnom south of Jerusalem. The warning is nonetheless serious. The worm and the fire of v. 48 derive immediately from Isa 66:24, where the fate of the corpses of God's enemies is in question.

Taking figurative language literally (severing limbs, plucking out eyes, anticipating worms or fire) is destructive of its meaning. Taking it seriously is understanding its meaning.

❧❧

Proper 22 [27] / Twenty-seventh Sunday of the Year (B)
Sunday between October 2 and October 8, inclusive

JOB 1:1; 2:1-10

This brief lection from the classic treatment of the suffering of the innocent does no more than introduce the terms of the drama. It must be referred to later if a preacher chooses to deal with the book on any of the next three Sundays. Clearly Job is a fiction, since no Jew ever thought of Israel's LORD as in equal contest with Satan, least of all participating in a wager with him. Job is described as a man of Uz, so far to the east of the land of Israel that he may be presumed by the hearers of the tale to be a pious pagan. Who else would question the justice of Israel's God so openly? The book is a challenge to the prevailing popular religion—even biblical religion up to that point—that God routinely rewards the good and punishes the wicked.

Satan as a wanderer on the earth doing mischief where he can is an ingenious conception (2:2). The LORD thinks he knows a man of impregnably upright character and presents Job as such (v. 3). Satan takes up the challenge by saying that virtue persisting through continued attacks on physical well-being is the chink in everyone's armor. Verse 4 about giving all that one has for one's life makes sense only in light of Job's losses in chapter one: his flocks and herds, camels, adult children and their spouses, all have been destroyed. Job has only one treasure left, his life. God allows Satan to capitalize on the full measure of Job's suffering short of taking his life itself. "Skin for skin" is not easy to interpret. Since it is Satan's taunt, it has to mean that one will risk everything of one's selfhood to preserve one's life. It is delivered in a tone of, "We shall see about *that*!" Job's wife has to fulfill her role in the play (for that is the kind of writing the book is) speaking as Everyperson: "Why not acknowledge you are time's fool and God's too? Die with the sneer on your lips about God's providence that alone makes sense in your situation." He refuses.

Psalm 26

Genesis 2:18-24

Genesis 2:4b-24 are part of the J account that centers on humanity (cf. "the earth and the heavens," v. 4b; "the heavens and the earth of 1:1 betrays a cosmic concern). God has formed the man out of the clods in the soil (v. 7), settled him in the garden of Eden to till and tend it (v. 15), and allowed him to eat of the fruit of any tree except that "of knowledge of good and evil" (v. 7). The present passage attempts to account for the names, i.e., the different species of beasts and birds and the origin and purpose of marriage. The "partner" to man is literally a "help" alongside him. The traditional "help meet for him" in early translations (KJV; DRC rendering the literal "like unto himself") has resulted in creating the word "helpmate." The chief help the author has in mind is bearing children, which no other creature can do.

The distinguishing feature of the "living creatures" of v. 19 (E. A. Speiser, *Genesis* [AB 1; Garden City, N.Y.: Doubleday, 1964]), thinks this phrase a later gloss because it does violence to Hebrew syntax in this position) is that, despite their variety, none is a "help suitable for him" (v. 20). The unsuitability is remedied. A rib *(selaʻ)* taken from the first human *(ha ʼadam)* is built up into a woman, who is brought to the man (vv. 21f.). The poetic couplet of v. 23 relies on the similar sounds of the Hebrew words for "woman" *(ishsha)* and "man" *(ish),* different as to their consonantal make-up and unrelated. The English "woman," derived from "wife of man," actually makes the point better philologically. The two become one "body" (lit.: "flesh," *bāsār*) through union, a fitting arrangement in the author's mind since they had originally been the one creature, man and rib.

The concrete, earthy character of this Yahwist (J) account betrays its origins from Mesopotamian sources, as the presence of loanwords for "well up / rise" (v. 6) and "Eden" (v. 8), found in both Akkadian and Sumerian, help to establish. There are numerous details in common, like the harlot who mates with Enkidu the hunter in the Gilgamesh Epic, making him forget the wild beasts of the steppe (Tablet 1.4). Yet the Priestly account can also be shown to derive from Mesopotamian traditions about the beginnings of the world. Despite the differences of emphasis in the P account of Genesis 1 and the J account of Genesis 2, "the traditions involved must go back . . . to the oldest cultural stratum of Mesopotamia" (Speiser).

The motif of the tree of knowledge (v. 17) likewise betrays certain Mesopotamian links. There is nothing strange in the biblical authors' use of these concepts, since each is writing a primeval history which is a preface to a story that comes to life in Mesopotamia. That land alone provides the necessary historical and cultural records.

PSALM 8[128]

HEBREWS 1:1-4; 2:5-12[9-11]

By an editor who appended 13:22-25, this treatise has been made to look like a letter from Paul. But in fact it has no epistolary character, rather a homiletic one. Its anonymous author writes the best Greek of any New Testament book and in a rhetorical style that points to Alexandria. The prose prologue (vv. 1-4) places God's Son in relation to all the prophets who preceded him and is a Christology not of Word or of Spirit but of Platonic realization of "God's very being" (v. 3). The work of the one who is the perfect "reflection of God's glory" has been to "make purification for sins." This having been done, he now sits at the right hand of God's majesty, where he is not to be confused with any angelic courtier around the throne.

The subjection of all things to Jesus is not a matter of present experience (v. 8) as it will be in the vision of the end that Paul spells out in 1 Cor 15:25-28. Hebrews has that much in common with Paul. More than Paul, however, Hebrews centers on the role of Jesus as "leader" (v. 10) or pioneer in the human necessity of becoming perfect through suffering. Glory and honor have come to him because he underwent death (v. 9). By that same path fellow humans will follow him in obedience (cf. 5:8f.), coming at last to where he is through the "veil" of his flesh (cf. 10:20). Jesus is not exempted from the route of pain to glory any more than his "brothers" are (v. 11).

Hebrews quotes Ps 8:6f. verbatim from the Septuagint, omitting only 7a. J. A. T. Robinson points out the almost universal English rendering of *brachy ti* (Vulgate, *mŏdicō*) by "for a little while," under the influence of subsequent Christology (*The Human Face of God* [Philadelphia: Westminster, 1973], 159ff.). But nothing in the adverbial phrase requires this translation connoting time. It is rather a matter of degree, as the normal translation of the identical psalm verse (8:4) indicates: "little less than a god / the angels." Robinson espouses Westcott's view that *brachy ti* is used here of magnitude and not of time, as the unambiguous Hebrew bears out. The KJV and DRC had it right, as does the NIV; all the other modern translations have it wrong. The point is important in conveying the Christology of Hebrews accurately. Its author is not saying that Jesus started higher than the angels and for a brief space was lower but that "in him (and as yet in no other man) we see fulfilled the ultimate *destiny* of man" (Robinson, 160). Christ *became* superior to them "when he . . . sat down at the right hand of the Majesty on high" (1:3).

Jesus' present enthronement (v. 9) marks him out for future supremacy over all. Meanwhile, he has the fatherhood of God as his possession along with all those whom he sanctifies (v. 11). This expresses a common lot between Jesus and the rest of humanity while preserving his distinctiveness which neither Paul nor the evangelists achieve as well.

A weakly attested reading gives *chōris* for *cháriti*, hence "apart from" rather than "by the grace of God (v. 9). This could speak of a work by Jesus not done through God's gracious will but on his own or even abandoned by God on the cross (as a mistaken interpretation of Mark 15:34 would have it). In terms of sense, it seems unlikely that this was the primitive reading.

ALLELUIA. SEE ACTS 16:14B

Open our hearts, O LORD, to listen to the words of your Son.

MARK 10:2-16

This account of Jesus' opposition to divorce does not appear in the Q material, hence it is not in Luke. Rudolf Bultmann and B. H. Streeter find Mark's version awkward, artificial, and inferior to Matthew in terms of Jewish usage. Mark's account seems to Bultmann to have been thoroughly rearranged from an earlier controversy story. First comes the Mosaic legislation permitting divorce (v. 4, quoting Deut 24:1). This is put on the lips of the Pharisees, strangely, who may be presumed to have known it well. Even stranger is their question (v. 2) whether divorce is permissible—a difficulty they could not possibly have had in that form. Jesus puts Moses' concession down to their hard-heartedness (v. 5) and cites against them the unequivocal divine will (vv. 7f.) expressed in Gen 2:24. Verse 9 sums up Jesus' teaching; vv. 11f. make it fully explicit, as if enunciating a fundamental law for the disciples who will act as missionaries to Jews and Gentiles alike.

Jesus' final comment, given to the disciples "in the house," is a positive regulation laid down for the wider church. Mark has in view only Christian readers and hearers; for them he sets out the Lord's teaching which unequivocally prohibits divorce followed by remarriage. It is highly likely that this final logion (vv. 11f.) had an existence independent of the story, which is complete without it (cf. Matt 5:32 and Luke 16:18 for its attestation in Q). Some, like Dungan (*The Sayings of Jesus in the Churches of Paul* [Philadelphia: Fortress Press, 1971], 109), think that the final saying had an independent circulation *"as an abstract of this story as a whole."*

Matthew's dependence on Mark or Mark's on Matthew in this narrative cannot be settled on form-critical grounds. What is clear is Mark's intention to answer his own question for the Church, "Shall there be divorce at all?" as Jews understand it, with a strong no. The question was one that arose in Hellenist churches, as is clear from the absence of all the Palestinian Pharisaic overtones found in Matthew's account. The special mention of the woman "who divorces her husband" (v. 12) gives proof of this, since only Gentile women and very rich Jews could initiate divorce. Mark's version is frequently taken to be more primitive than Matthew's because Matthew's "exceptive clauses" (at 5:32 and 19:9) are taken to be interpretative relaxations in a Jewish milieu. Whether they place lesser demands on those who dismiss or leave their partners than in the Markan form is another question. The bulk of New Testament scholarship seems to think so, and with this conclusion Orthodox and Protestant church practice is in accord. Catholic practice did not follow scholarship in the matter so much as the apparently more restrictive of the two New Testament teachings.

A modern view that has had currency among Catholic exegetes particularly is that the *porneía* of Matthew's two clauses is the woman's adulterous conduct that justifies dismissal but that Matthew has the man's remarriage no more in view than Mark does. Some have held *porneía* to mean an incestuous union that would constitute a clear exception. In other words, two closely related Jews, now followers of Jesus, would have *had* to be divorced.

As to the next pericope on Jesus and the children (vv. 13-16), it need only be said that, except for 9:36f., no passage in early Christian or pagan literature attends to children in particular. The separation of this narrative from the other of the previous chapter has already been remarked. See Proper 20 [25] (B) on Mark 9:36f., above. The child, in trusting openness, becomes the norm for all acceptance of the reign of God by the more suspicious and sophisticated adult.

✌✌

Proper 23 [28] / Twenty-eighth Sunday of the Year (B)
Sunday between October 9 and October 15, inclusive

JOB 23:1-9, 16-17

Eliphaz, Bildad, and Zophar each charge Job not once but twice with his stubbornness to admit unconscious wrongdoing. He frames a reply the substance of which is, "I have done no wrong." Eliphaz' most recent accusation is specific as to Job's social injustices (22:5-11) but, as there is no evidence for them, it is a case of an illogical deduction from his sufferings to what must have been his sins. The last charge before today's pericope is that Job obviously thinks God so far off in the heavens that his wickedness is not seen (vv. 12-20). "Capitulate, why don't you? Delight in the Almighty as you have not done and all will go well with you again" (vv. 21-30). Job responds by expressing the regret that the Lord is nowhere to be found that he may be confronted (23:2-8). He does not expect the God of power to contend with him, only to hear his case and thus acquit him forever (vv. 6f.). This stance before God is one of terror, a word that at root means fear or fright, certainly not the violent actions that cause terror. If the Almighty has terrified Job, it is because the Lord has filled him with a sense of littleness in the divine presence. But creaturely inadequacy is not the same thing as moral fault. Job is not smitten with shame. The case is that a sense of the awful majesty of God has overtaken him. His heart is faint before the glory of the Lord, as it will be with anyone who contemplates God's mighty works. An arithmetic balance between deeds and retribution in this life, good or bad, is not one of those works.

Psalm 22:1-15

Amos 5:6-7, 10-15

The voice of this prophet of Tekoa in Judah is heard seven times over the three years of RCL but sequentially only on Proper 10 [15] and 11 [16] of Year C. LM employs the book on the first of these but in Year B, then again on [25] and [26] C, in no case using the present pericope. Amos prophesied in the north, hence to "the house of Joseph" (v. 6) or "the remnant of Joseph," which had Bethel as its cult center. The patriarch Joseph, father of Manasseh and Ephraim, did not give his name to a tribe (Gen 48:13f.) but passed on the name of Ephraim instead (v. 20). Fulminating against the corruption that marked the prosperous reign of Jeroboam II (786–746), Amos tells the people to seek the Lord if they would have life. If they keep on perverting justice, "turning it to wormwood" (Old English *vermod*, the bitter plant from which absinthe is extracted), a devouring fire will break out against Bethel. The prophet speaks obliquely of himself as the one rejected (v. 15). This does not keep him from cataloguing the people's sins: trampling on the poor, extortion, ostentatious living, bribes. How twenty-first century! But the oppressors will take little pleasure from their magnificent houses and fine wines. The Lord knows their excesses. At that point the prophet lowers his voice: "Hate evil and love good; establish justice that God may be gracious to you" (v. 15).

Psalm 90:12-17

Wisdom 7:7-11

Beginning at 6:22 the author has been speaking as if he were a king in search of wisdom, exhorting kings and judges to seek it. Assuming the persona of Solomon but without ever mentioning his name, he says he is no better than the rest in his common humanity (7:1-6) but he should be set apart by the search for wisdom (vv. 7ff.). The prayer and plea of v. 7 evoke the tale in 1 Kgs 3:5-15 of Solomon's dream at Gibeon, where he begged for "an understanding mind to govern your people, able to discern between good and evil" (3:9). Solomon's wealth, particularly his possession of gold, is highlighted in 1 Kgs 10:14-17, 21-23. In immediate context, however, there is placed (by an editorial hand?) his pursuit of wisdom, v. 24. That juxtaposition, by way of contrast, is central to the present pericope. Gold, silver, health, beauty—even the great treasure of light itself in the ancient world unillumined except by torches—are as nothing compared to prudence and wisdom.

The bloom is taken off the rose somewhat by the practical conclusion (after all, a king is a king) that all good things and uncounted wealth come in wisdom's train (v. 11). Proverbs 8:21 has said the same. Uneasy, evidently, lies the unwise head that wears a crown, whereas the possession of *ḥokmah* finds the king in the counting-house, counting out his money. Yet such rewards were insignificant compared to the supreme benefit of "friendship with God" (Wis 7:14). R. B. Y. Scott (*The Way of Wisdom in the Old Testament* [New York: Macmillan: 1971], 219) observes that the author's "only wish now is that his thoughts and words should be worthy of his theme" (see vv. 15f.).

Psalm 90:12-17

Hebrews 4:12[13]-16

The author has been engaged in a disquisition on fidelity and infidelity, obedience and disobedience, with Jesus proposed as the supreme example of both virtues. For his completion of the work God gave him to do, Christ enjoys the heavenly "rest" of the LORD himself (Gen 2:2; cf. Heb 4:4). It was not given to the Israelites of old, even though it was promised them (cf. 3:18f; 4:6), because of unbelief. Psalm 95, on which these two chapters are a commentary, especially the recurring vv. 7b-8 (cf. Heb 3:7, 15; 4:7), represents a renewal of the promise in David's day (4:7). "So then, a Sabbath rest still remains for the people of God" (v. 9). Failing in faith, in imitation of the unbelief of the people of old, is the great sin that this Christian author warns against.

In today's reading of five verses, self-deceit likewise is warned against. All lies bare and open before God (v. 13) who judges the reflections and thoughts of the heart by the sword of his word (v. 12). God's "word" here is his communicating power, not particularly the *logos* of the Johannine prologue nor the rational element behind the creation nor even the Hebrew scriptures. It is God's speaking to his people in prophecy and act (cf. Rom 9:6), a communication the substance of which is eminently conveyed by preaching (cf. 1 Cor 14:36; 2 Tim 2:9). The sword figure seems to derive from Wis 18:15f. Ephesians speaks in allegory of "the sword of the spirit" (6:17) and Revelation (19:15) of a sharp sword coming from the mouth of "the King of kings and Lord of lords." The all-seeing eye of God is the theme of Job 34:21f.; Pss 90:8; 139:2-6, 16.

The sword of God's word is alive and active (v. 12). Its penetration and division of "soul from spirit, joints from marrow" is a way of describing penetration to one's innermost being. Nothing physiological is intended, least of all a real separation of the members named. Perhaps the closest New Testament parallel to this passage is found in Simeon's words to Mary in Luke 2:35. For Hebrews, God's word represents "the dynamic activity of the omnipresent God" (Hugh Montefiore, *A Commentary on the Epistle to the Hebrews* [New York: Harper and Row: 1964], 89).

ALLELUIA. SEE EPHESIANS 1:17-18

May the Father of our Lord Jesus Christ enlighten the eyes of our hearts, that we may see how great is the hope to which we are called.

MARK 10:17-[30]31

The detail of the journey (v. 17) is used by Mark as a link with what has gone before. The mention of kneeling and the form of address, "Good teacher," betray obsequiousness, a stance that Jesus will not allow (v. 18; Matt nervously changes this to "Why do you ask me about what is good?" 19:17). The story underscores Jesus' respect for the various commandments—cited from Deut 5:16-21, with "do not defraud" summarizing the last two and the one on parents placed at the end. At the same time, Mark wishes to put becoming a follower of Jesus (v. 21) above perfect observance. Detachment from riches is a condition of such discipleship (v. 21). This enunciation leads to a special explanation to the disciples in Markan fashion (v. 23). Verse 25 comes before v. 24 in some MSS, the probable order. God is so powerful that he can save even the rich (v. 27). Peter's plaintive declaration of insufficient funds (v. 28) was probably a separate saying originally that here serves as a link to still another independent logion (vv. 29f.). The "hundredfold" of v. 30 represents the conviction of the Markan church that its members had made a good bargain. Adhering to Christ was infinitely rewarding; compared with it, any wrench experienced by separation from family or property was as nothing.

✺✺

Proper 24 [29] / Twenty-ninth Sunday of the Year (B)
Sunday between October 16 and October 22, inclusive

JOB 38:1-7, (34-41)

Was a whirlwind something like a Kansas twister? NAB calls it a "storm" (v. 1). Whatever the case, it was a show of meteorological power out of which Job was the pawn of fate, to be given an oral examination, a "final." God has dealt him four hundred blows and he sees no justice in it. Only bad things have happened to him who knows he is good people. He thinks he is wise with self-knowledge and wise in the ways the Scriptures say God always acts. This cannot be true, Job maintains. It is a fraud. The wicked prosper, the just suffer, and nothing in the holy writings has prepared Job for it. In his presumed wisdom (v. 36) he is about to be shown a holy fool. The barrage of questions is relentless. Have you laid out the measurements of the earth like a good builder, God asks, worked by the fading starlight of dawn (vv. 4-7)? Do you summon the rain-laden clouds which you can number and bid the lightnings flash at will? What is your gift for making tons of mud by tipping water baskets of leather at the dust below? Describe your skill at tracking prey in the wild to provide meat for the cubs in their lair. The young ravens stalk the ground awaiting the return of their scavenger parents. If they find anything, is it you who supplied it?

Job is properly mute before the questioning. It begins to dawn on him that he is not God running the universe to the satisfaction of all but him. The so-called YHWH speeches (38:1-41:26) are calculated to make a fool of him—but a holy fool, since they are the beginning of wisdom. Job's capitulation is by and large credible

(42:1-6), but the epilogue appended by another hand than the author's (vv. 7-17) destroys the whole point of the book.

Psalm 104:1-9, 24, 35c

Isaiah 53:4-12[10-11]

These verses are part of the fourth "Servant of the Lord" oracle, Isa 52:13—53:12. The first (42:1-4) describes a just and gentle figure who acts like a king, the second and third (49:1-7; 50:4-11) someone cast more in the prophetic mold. Here the Servant is to be exalted above the kings of earth (52:15) after a humiliation (v. 14) that ends in his death (53:8ff.). It is likely that Second Isaiah had in mind the "death" of Abraham's seed in undergoing Babylonian exile, which is still a reality as he writes. Thus the "wicked" and the "rich" of v. 9 would be the pagans among whom the exiled believers dwelt.

The crushed Servant will in the future see his seed ("offspring," v. 10), long-lived as a result of his proffering his life (lit.: "spirit," v. 10) as a sacrifice of reparation ("offering for sin"), a word that means first an offense. It then comes to signify the means by which the offense is righted and finally a sacrifice of reparation. Confusion in the Bible between this expiatory rite and a "sin offering" is nearly total. We must say, at least, that the offense referred to here is a measurable one and that Second Isaiah is proposing the life of the Servant as a compensation for the people's sins. The Servant (the exiled portion of the people?) acts on behalf of all the rest. To "see the light" (v. 11) means to enjoy happiness, as a footnote in NAB observes; but it and NRSV indicate that "light" must be supplied to the Hebrew from the LXX and Qumrân. The Servant, described as "my just servant" in Hebrew, through his knowledge (i.e., experience, suffering) will render many just.

"He shall bear their iniquities" is again an expression of the author's conviction that the servant's humiliation and death act as a reparation for sin.

Psalm 91:9-16

Psalm 33:4-5, 18-20, 22

Hebrews 5:1-10

Believers in Jesus Christ risen shortly came to appropriate to him the paradoxical title Messiah *(Christós),* knowing that as the Anointed of God he fulfilled the end-time projections of the postbiblical apocrypha better than the hoped-for deliverer from political oppression. A learned Christian, probably an Alexandrian from his polished literary style, did a similar thing in conceiving Jesus the Galilean layman in the image of Israel's high priest but now transcending all earthly categories of the Jerusalem scene. It is impossible to discern whether the Temple has been destroyed or is still in use at the time of the writing, despite NRSV's present-tense rendering of 9:8 by "as long as the meeting tent is still standing." The author has no interest in the question. He takes his data from the Septuagint and from the practice of offering sacrifice and sprinkling blood on the mercy seat and the altar in the Holy Place on Yom Kippur (see Heb 9:6, 12f.; cf. Lev 16:15-19, as both are described there). Previous to today's lection Hebrews has described Jesus Christ as a faithful high priest (in 2:17; 3:1 and 4:14). He is now being distinguished from all others who have held that office. They being weak, human, and wayward must offer sacrifice for their own sins (v. 3). Not he, for although human and weak like the rest he is neither ignorant nor sinful (see John 8:46; Heb 4:15; 2 Cor 5:21; 1 Pet 2:22 for the unbroken tradition on Jesus' sinlessness) but compassionate for sinners in his gentleness (v. 2).

He is known not to be of Aaronite stock, but his calling to the priestly office by God is no less assured (vv. 4f.). His is the higher vocation: divine sonship and priesthood in Melchizedek's line (v. 6), the latter attribution traceable to Ps 110:4. In his recall of Gen 14:18-20, a courageous poet had raised a muted cry against those among the hereditary priests unworthy of their trust by having recourse to a non-Hebrew king to whom Abraham gave one-tenth of all his possessions. The poet-psalmist must have delighted in hearing it sung many times in the worship place where it had immediate application. Hebrews uses the tale from the life of the revered patriarch Abram to establish its claim that Jesus, not a priest of Aaron's line, could qualify as a priest nonetheless, much as dimly remembered patriarchal history had done with Melchizedek.

Jesus' humanity meant that he was vulnerable to suffering, to which he responded normally, namely, with loud outcries and tears. He knew that in response to his prayers God could save him from death but the answer came to him in an unequivocal no. It was Jesus' human sonship that taught him to obey. The author names suffering as his teacher. It did more for him than that; it shaped him in perfection. In this way Hebrews acts as the teacher of Christians. At a certain point all must let go of life, some like Jesus after a siege of tortured pain. God lets our physical self go its fragile way but at the same time gives it strength to endure suffering and even grow to the stature of Christ by means of it. It is quite in order for us to cry out, unlike Jesus as we are, in uncomprehending protest at the divine decree.

HEBREWS 4:14-16

The author at this point resumes his theme that Jesus is the faithful apostle and high priest who founded a house of faith (cf. 2:17—3:6). He was tested through what he suffered (2:18). This makes him sympathetic toward us and a model for all who are tempted as he was (2:18; 4:15). The phrase "yet without sin" (v. 15) does not negate the fact that Jesus was "subject to weakness" (5:2). It does concur in the theological judgment of all the New Testament writers who consider the question—this cannot be a historical judgment except through remembrance of his goodness—that Jesus never sinned (cf. 2 Cor 5:21; 1 Pet 2:22; Heb 7:26); that he was an unblemished victim (cf. 1 Pet 1:19; Heb 9:14). For Jesus' temptation to have been real, he must have known it "from within the existential meaning of human sinfulness . . . [while] not consenting" (John Knox, *The Humanity and Divinity of Christ* [Cambridge: Cambridge Univ. Press, 1967]); otherwise, he was not tempted as ordinary mortals are. To feel the pull of evil one must see it, under some aspects at least, as more attractive than the good. The "set" of Jesus' will therefore "remains constant in its direction . . . [although like a battle-weary soldier] physically—even mentally—he may consent to the relief he longs for" (C. F. D. Moule, *The Origin of Christology* [Cambridge: Cambridge Univ. Press, 1977]).

Confidence is recommended to those who approach the "throne of grace" (located in the sanctuary" of 10:19; "exalted, above the heavens," 7:26; where God "rests from his labors," 4:10). Mercy, grace, and help are available there "in the time of need" (v. 16).

ALLELUIA. 1 SAMUEL 3:9; JOHN 6:69B

Speak, O LORD, your servant is listening; you have the words of everlasting life.

MARK 10:35-45

The third of Mark's three predictions of the passion has intervened since last Sunday's reading. Matthew has the mother of the sons of Zebedee speak for them (20:20), but Mark is never protective of the disciples; if anything, the contrary.

Matthew also eliminates the phrase about being baptized with Jesus' baptism (Mark 10:39), retaining only mention of the cup. The placement of this story of selfishness after Jesus' reiteration of his need to suffer is surely intended by Mark as part of his having the disciples consistently miss the point. Verses 35-40 seem to be the original unit, with 41-55 woven out of individual logia appended to it as Mark's commentary.

Verses 38f. seem to say that martyrdom has a priority in the kingdom (Jesus' "cup" being death) but it may only mean to highlight the disciples' need to suffer like the master as the precondition of glory, the very point made by Hebrews above.

Luke's use of the sayings of Mark 10:42-44 (Luke 22:24-27) shows that they were originally concerned with authority and service in the community. The final Markan word on Jesus' life as a ransom for "the many" (the *rabbim* of Isa 53:11) closes the pericope on a soteriological note.

☙ ❧

Proper 25 [30] / Thirtieth Sunday of the Year (B)
Sunday between October 23 and October 29, inclusive

JOB 42:1-6, 10-17

Some have speculated that the author of this work of genius had to situate the story in Uz from its name in Edomite territory or perhaps Arabia of the Nabateans if pious Jews were to stomach the challenge to the LORD it posed. That would account for this clothing of the penitent Job in dust and ashes at the end. His troublesome comforters are given names from Edom: Eliphaz a Temanite, Bildad a Shuhite, and Zophar a Naamathite. When the youthful Elihu appears he is identified as a Buzite. He reacts angrily at the failure of the older men to condemn Job for his untraditional position on reward and punishment in this life for the way one has lived. Job's repentance, so briefly stated, can be taken as pro forma (42:5f.) but it does not strain the imagination as much as the epilogue that follows (vv. 7-17). That piece looks like the work of a pious continuator bent on showing that Job's defiance of God's treatment of him was in no way blameworthy (vv. 6, 8). In the exaggerated terms of his rehabilitation it may even be a spoof of the position the book is calling in question. God *does* let bad things happen to good people for divine unfathomable purposes. The answer to the mystery of why it should be lies in a deeper mystery still: the very Godhood of God.

PSALM 34:1-8, (19-22)

JEREMIAH 31:7-9

Here we have a vision of the return from exile, which forms part of the "Book of Consolation," made up of chaps. 30–33, of which chaps. 30–31 are a distinct part. Jacob (Israel) stands for the exiled people, specifically the northern tribes. Deliverance has come. The remnant of Israel will be brought back from the land to the north (v. 8) across the fertile crescent. The throng shall include the diminished (blind and lame) and the increased (childing mothers). Sorrow marked their going (v. 9). Their return shall be on a level road with the wadis full of water at the their feet. It has to be so since the LORD is Israel's father and Ephraim—son of Joseph—is his "firstborn" (NRSV, "dear son"), a term of affection for the northern kingdom (cf. v. 20).

Verses 2-6 and 15-22 of this chapter seem to have been addressed by Jeremiah to northern Israel early in his career when Josiah was pressing his reforms in the north (622 B.C.E.; cf. 2 Kgs 23:15-10). Verses 7-9 may have been composed in similar circumstances and modified later to refer to the exiles living in Babylon. They bear a striking similarity, in any case, to the later chapters of Isaiah. In particular here is a relation between vv. 8-9 and Isa 35; 40:3-5, 11; 41:18-20; 42:16; 43:17; 44:3f; 48:20f.; 49:9-13.

PSALM 126[1-6]

HEBREWS 7:23-38

For a commentary on the last six verses, see Proper 26 [31] (B).

HEBREWS 5:1-6

Having declared Jesus the perfect high priest because of his sympathy with us in our weakness and his being himself tempted (4:14ff.), the author goes on to discuss the office theoretically. He does so in idealized terms from sources such as Exod 28:1; Num 18:7; Lev 4:3-12; 9:7; 16:6, 11. It is almost as if he knew nothing of the debased process of selection of high priests in his day or was totally disinterested in current Jewish views of the office. The author concentrates exclusively on the high priest's representative function in worship. He ignores completely his role as presiding officer of the Sanhedrin if he held it in Jeremiah's time. The words for "gifts" and "sacrifices" (v. 1) are used interchangeably in the LXX, so no case can be made for a description of cereal offerings in contradistinction to blood sacrifice. Hebrews is interested in expiatory sacrifices "for sins," a phrase used in the plural with respect to Yom Kippur only (Lev 16:16, 21, 30). The transition from the selection process (v. 1), which de facto is confined to Aaronite stock (Num 18:1-7), to the sympathetic stance of the non-Aaronite Christ (v. 2) is imperceptible. Erring sinners (v. 2) are literally the "ignorant and wayward," a single class of unconscious offenders whose sins need expiatory sacrifice for remission. Leviticus 4:3-12 describes the offering of a bullock in cases where the priest himself is an inadvertent sinner (i.e., a transgressor of ritual taboo); there is mention of a priest's sacrifice for his own sins as well as those of the people in Lev 9:7, while 6:11 speaks of the necessity of his doing so in a context of the annual observance of the Day of Atonement. All of the above is background for Heb 5:3.

For v. 4, cf. Exod 28:1. The offense of Korah the Levite, Dathan, and Abiram, described at length in Num 16, was their leadership of 250 Levites who aspired to the priestly office on the ground that the whole nation was holy (v. 3). The ground did not sustain them (cf. vv. 31f.). The author of Hebrews, like the Hebrew scriptures, requires a divine vocation for the priestly office. Since he is presumably aware of Christ's non-priestly origins, he situates his calling to the office of high priest in two psalm verses, 2:7 and 110:4. It is God who calls him "Son" (v. 5; cf. 1:5), then designates him a priest forever in a Melchizedekian sense (v. 6).

Whence did Hebrews derives its central theme of Jesus as high priest? Other New Testament authors use Ps 2:7 in support of Jesus' special sonship of God (cf. Acts 13:33; also, the verse's probable use as underlying Mark 1:1; 9:7; Matt 3:17; Luke 3:2). The author of Hebrews acts like a conscious innovator in the way he develops the argument of Christ's priesthood in chap. 7 (see also 6:20). Yet he may have been started on his train of thought—Christ as a priest like the pre-Aaronite Melchizedek—by meditating on the use of Ps 110:1 in Mark 12:36 (//Matt 22:44; Luke 20:42). There the verse is attributed to Jesus, arguing in behalf of his own status as a son of David who is at the same time his "lord." The author of Hebrews might have gone on from this tradition to examine the implications of v. 4 of the psalm. It is clear from 10:5 that he thinks Jesus' whole career one of a call to sacrifice. The non-Aaronite priesthood of Jesus was separated by a world from the usurping Hasmonean prince exercising the priestly office whom the author of Ps 110 probably had in mind. No matter. The words are right to describe Jesus Christ so far as the author is concerned because it is he who is being directly addressed by God in v. 4.

ALLELUIA. MATTHEW 11:25

Blessed are you, Father, LORD, of heaven and earth; you have revealed to little ones the mysteries of the kingdom.

MARK 10:46-52

Mark seems to have come upon a story in the tradition in which Jesus was already leaving Jericho (not the ancient city but a town near it, rebuilt as a Roman garrison by Herod the Great). This would account for the strange "came" and "were leaving" of v. 46. The characters in the first level of tradition in the healing narratives are nameless. This causes some to think that an original story came to be connected with a known figure in the Markan church, Bartimaeus of Jericho. The awkward introduction of the parenthetical explanation of the meaning of the name probably identifies it as an early textual gloss. The point of the story is the messianic title "Son of David" (vv. 47, 48) coupled with that of the man's alacrity in becoming a follower of Jesus (vv. 50, 52). The "healed" *(sésōkén)* of v. 52 is studiedly ambiguous for "cured" and "saved." It is attributed to the beggar's "faith" *(pistis),* again ambivalently his trust in Jesus' power to heal him and the state of the later disciple regarding Jesus as the Christ (cf. Mark 5:34//Luke 7:50; 17:19; Mark 2:5). The element of personal trust in these healing narratives is probably historical.

The pericope is transitional in Mark between the unit of the third prediction of the passion (10:33-45) and the entry into Jerusalem (chap. 11). Jesus is the sight-giving Son of David whom Markan church members are following. He is also the one who suffers, as they must suffer, in Mark's studied correction of the false Christology abroad that viewed Jesus only as a "divine man" *(theíos anēr),* or thaumaturge.

❧✣❧

Proper 26 [31] / Thirty-first Sunday of the Year (B)
Sunday between October 30 and November 5, inclusive

RUTH 1:1-8

The MT places Ruth among the Writings, between the Song of Songs and Lamentations, but it occurs where it does in the LXX and consequently the Vulgate because it begins by saying that all took place "in the days when the judges ruled" (1:1). Ruth doubtless merited inclusion among "the scrolls that soil the hands"—

the rabbinic expression for writings so holy that they affect the holder by physical touch—not so much for its charm as a tale of married love but because it concludes with a partial genealogy of King David of the tribe of Judah (4:17-22). Matthew derives his briefer tracing of the line from Boaz to David from the book of Ruth in 1:5f., while the Lukan genealogy gives Boaz a different immediate pro-genitor (at least as to spelling, Sala for Salmon) but then similarly proceeds from Obed to Boaz to Jesse to David, going on to name not Solomon but Nathan as David's son (who precedes Solomon in 2 Sam 5:14 and 1 Chron 3:5). While David is a descendant of Boaz, the fact of his Moabite ancestry through Ruth is its more important detail. Moab was a land of "plains by the Jordan opposite Jericho" (Num 26:63) but also hills, including Mount Nebo, where Moses died (Deut 34:5). At one point in the forty-year journey of the Israelites, the men took Moabite women to wife and were thereby drawn to worship the god of that pagan people, the Ba'al of Peor (Num 25:1), but the strictures against Moab had evidently receded in the days of the judges. Matthew's genealogy of Jesus, as is well known, includes the foreigner Ruth along with Rahab and Tamar, respectively described as a prostitute of Jericho (Josh 2:1) and the seducer of her father-in-law, Judah, who had failed to give her to his son Shelah in her long widowhood (Gen 38:12-26).

The lengthy reading from Ruth calls for little comment, on the proverbial principle that good wine needs no bush. It is a story admirably told about the bonding of two women. Naomi foresees that the young widows have in her no marital prospects. Orpah concurs and remains in Moab. Ruth clings to her mother-in-law and opts to go to Judah with her. The detail that matters to the narrator is that Naomi's God and people will be Ruth's (v. 16). As so often in these Scriptures, this is a tale of many ethnic strands that become one people by the worship of the one true God. Centuries later the heavy influx of Gentiles was more than the people could endure.

PSALM 146

DEUTERONOMY 6:1-9

The previous chapter has contained the commandments delivered in the covenant of Horeb. These are to be observed faithfully in the land of Canaan, which Israel is about to conquer (vv. 1-3). There, milk and honey will flow on condition of perfect observance. The promise of the LORD will be fulfilled if the terms of the covenant are kept.

The commandments delivered on Sinai were not simply to be kept in the heart (v. 6). They were to be talked about with children, discussed while carrying on every waking activity (vv. 7-9). Even more was done about them in the much later period of the Rabbis.

"Hear *(Sh^ema')*, O Israel!" introduces the expressed conviction that "The LORD alone" (6:4) is Israel's God, to be loved totally and exclusively. The four Hebrew words of the formula can be rendered in various ways. Of these, the best known alternative to that of NAB and NRSV (which *Tanakh* of the Jewish Publication Society of America also follows) is perhaps NIV's "The LORD our God, the LORD is one." BJ has "*est le seul Yahvé,*" leading JB to propose: "Yahweh, our God, is the only Yahweh." TEV goes with: "The LORD—and the LORD alone—is our God!" REB adopts still another position: "The LORD is our God, the LORD our one God." Whether the Hebrew text means to emphasize God's unity or God's uniqueness, it is clear that identifying Israel's God by his proper name is paramount and that he is the exclusive object of the people's devotion. This creedal statement, as it rightly or wrongly is frequently called, means to distinguish the LORD from all the gods of Canaan. The command to cleave closely to him ("heart," "soul," and "might" expressing the ideas of interior will, person, and intensity) is to be taken to heart (vv. 5f.).

The passages Deut 6:4-9; 11:13-21; and Num 15:37-41 came to be written on small scrolls and recited daily as the *Sh^ema'*. In later times they, along with Exod 13:1-10, were inserted in leather boxes worn on wrist and forehead, or in a cartridge affixed to the doorpost, in literal fulfillment of vv. 8f. Compare the related passage, Deut 11:18-20, on Proper 4 [9] (A).

PSALM 119:1-8

PSALM 18:2-4, 47, 51

HEBREWS 9:11-14

For a commentary see Body and Blood of Christ (B).

HEBREWS 7:23-28

The commentaries on the four readings from Hebrews in the previous month should be consulted, especially that on Heb 4:14-16 of Proper 24 [29], where Christ's sinlessness despite his temptations is discussed, and that of Proper 25 [30], where the first half of the text (5:1-6) underscores the personal sins of the ordinary high priest.

Today's passage refers to Christ's unique status (v. 23) as high priest continuing forever (vv. 24f.), while returning to the theme of his sinlessness (v. 26; cf. 4:15 and, elsewhere, 2 Cor 5:21; 1 Pet 2:22). A new idea is introduced in v. 27, namely, the definitive character ("once for all") of his self-offering. The necessity the ordinary high priest labors under of offering sacrifices for his own sins as well as those of the people, found in v. 27, has been alleged in 5:3. Here mention of Christ's exempt status is repeated. It is the people's sins that do not require remission by his repeated offering. His self-offering did not take away any sins of his own, since this Son appointed priest was "made perfect forever" (7:28). The "oath" is that of Ps 110:4, succeeding the Law which sets up a priesthood marked by weakness. The parallel of the line of argument here with that of Paul in Gal 3:19-22 and Rom 5:20-22 is inescapable, though without the Law's function of increasing offenses or locking all things under the constraint of sin.

There is no biblical mention of the high priest's offering sacrifice daily (v. 7) but only on the Day of Atonement (Lev 16:16; see 23:28; 25:9). The Septuagint rendering of Lev 6:13, however, has the priest sons of Aaron making a cereal grain-offering "continually" *(dià pantós)*, while v. 12 in the Hebrew describes fat burning on a wood fire made fresh by a priest every morning (followed by NRSV; in *Tanakh* vv. 5-6). Philo reports a tradition of daily sacrifice by the high priest; Ben Sirach has Aaron a richly vested priest offering sacrifice twice daily (45:14).

ALLELUIA. MATTHEW 24:42A AND 44

Be watchful and ready; you know not when the Son of Man is coming.

MARK 12:28-34

Frequently Mark describes Jesus as having taught the crowds but, except for the parables of chap. 4, not much of his teaching is reported in the first nine chapters. Not until 9:33, with the second of the three predictions of the passion behind him, does Mark provide any sizable blocks of teaching besides the parables. From that point on teaching begins to proliferate, especially after the entry into Jerusalem at the beginning of chap. 11. Chapter 12 features the parable of the tenants and the exchanges with the Pharisees and Herodians over tribute to the emperor and the Sadducees on the resurrection of the body.

Today's pericope does not report struggle but agreement. A scribe, presumably of Pharisaic bent, has found Jesus to have answered the Sadducees "well," predictably enough. The link in v. 28 to what precedes it is awkward, but it is doubtless Mark's way of following one story with another. The question was usual enough in rabbinic circles, where the search for the weightiest commandment of the Law was constant. Jesus responds by reciting the opening phrases of the *Sh^ema'*, Israel's daily prayer. The phrase, "all your *mind*" *(dianoías sou)*, is not found in the Hebrew text or the LXX, which at Deut 6:5 has *dynameōs* for "strength" rather than Mark's *ischýos*. The two details lead to the speculation that this version of Deut 6:5 came from a church that was following some other Greek biblical text than the LXX. How Lev 19:18 (v. 31) is a "second" commandment is not clear. Matthew takes the pains to explain that the second is "like" (22:39) the first, hence presumably on an equal footing, while Luke runs them together uninterruptedly (10:27). Mark's comment in v. 31b has the same net effect: the two are inseparable. Yet he alone of the three evangelists precedes his answer with the summons to reflect on the LORD as the source of the possibility of love, whether of himself or of one's neighbor.

Jesus' Jewish contemporary Philo places the two together as "duties" (*Special Laws* 2.63). The commandments are found side by side in the *Testaments of the Twelve Patriarchs* (*T. Iss.* 5:2; 7:6; cf. *T. Dan.* 5:3; *T. Zeb.* 5:1; *T. Benj.* 3:3). In rabbinic times the conjunction was a commonplace. We cannot know how original Jesus was in placing the two together, nor is it important. What is important to Christians is that they live by them.

Verse 32 is the sole instance in the gospels of a teacher agreeing with Jesus except for John 3:2. Jesus' favorable view of the scribe's response contradicts Mark's usual opinion of teachers of the Law (cf. 2:6f.; 3:22; 7:1ff.; 12:38ff.). While these details have led some to think that the story arose in the Church, its unusual character tells in favor of its genuineness.

Jesus and the scribe concur in the importance of love over ritual requirements, a biblical theme (cf. 1 Sam 15:22; Hos 6:6; Isa 1:11; Prov 21:3); they are followed by many of the Rabbis. In approving the scribe's answer, however, Jesus does not say that he is under God's rule. He is not far from that rule or reign. There is still a gap, which in his response of v. 34 Jesus invites the scribe to close. This means that the reign Jesus envisages does not lie in an eschatological future but can be achieved now. As Eduard Schweizer remarks, "salvation and judgment are accomplished when one meets Jesus" (*Jesus* [Richmond: John Knox, 1971]).

✧✧✧
Proper 27 [32] / Thirty-second Sunday of the Year (B)
Sunday between November 6 and November 12, inclusive

RUTH 3:1-5; 4:13-17

The story continues by one giant leap and then concludes with another. Presiders or readers in a worship service of more leisurely pace may wish to include some of the tale proposed for omission by the lectionary. The wealthy and prominent Boaz has shown signs of uncommon favor to this new field hand. He disregards her status as a foreigner because he has been told of all she has done for her Israelite mother-in-law (2:11). Naomi in turn has apprised the young widow that Boaz is "one of our nearest kin" (2:20). Ruth then lies chastely at the feet of Boaz as he sleeps after a hard day of winnowing barley, who responds positively to her request to cover her with his cloak as a sign of conjugal commitment (3:1-10). But first a matter of importance must be dealt with. A closer kinsman of the dead Chilion was known to Boaz as having the right of first option to inherit a parcel of land from Naomi's deceased husband. When that worthy learns he will have to acquire Ruth as a wife in the bargain he immediately loses interest (vv. 11-13). His wife may have had none of it.

Boaz then takes the symbolic action of exchanging sandals with that next-of-kin to confirm acquisition of the land of Naomi and her sons. It was a different custom from the one that marked the obligation of a brother to marry the widow of his dead brother and raise up an heir to his property (Deut 25:5-10; cf. Matt 22:24 and parallels). Should he refuse, the elders of the city could then remove the sandal of the woman's brother-in-law (Heb. *gis*, Lat. *levir*) and spit in his face.

The first child Ruth conceived by Boaz came to birth as Obed who was grandfather to David (unless some generations are missing in the genealogy (vv. 13-18). Equally important is the delighted cry of the women attending the birth that Naomi now had a "restorer of life and a nourisher of [her] old age" (v. 15). She began immediately to nurse the child at her breasts (v. 16). All too often male preachers, like the Bible itself, give scant attention to the women of Israel in both Testaments. Not so the author of the book of Ruth.

PSALM 127

1 KINGS 17:8[10]-16

Zarephath, the Sarepta of the LXX and Vulgate, is the first Phoenician city to yield up its treasures—an event of 1970 under the expert hand of James Pritchard of the University Museum of the University of Pennsylvania. It is about ten miles south of Sidon on the seacoast and some fifteen miles north of ancient Tyre. Elijah is introduced as the adversary of King Ahab (874/3–853) and threatens the king with drought (17:1) because Ahab has married Jezebel, daughter of the king of Sidon and erected a statue of the chief deity or Ba'al of that country, Melkart, in Samaria (16:31f.).

The Elijah cycle comes to us unedited by the Deuteronomist's hand, probably from before the mid-eighth century period of Amos and Hosea. The miraculous element of the tales is part of their fabric. It shows forth the LORD's power in his servant Elijah, who will challenge the Phoenician cult and culture that threatens that of Israel. The prophet is probably in flight from Ahab when we first encounter him, hence his hiding in the Wadi Herith. Ravens, no friend to other species, feed him. A Phoenician woman, no friend to Israelites, does the same. She even accedes to his demand to feed him before herself and her son, and in her obedience ensures the life of this unlikely trio for a year (v. 15). The drought was doubtless the cause of the famine and the widow's starvation. She is promised flour and oil in unending supply until the rains come (v. 14).

PSALM 146[7-10]

HEBREWS 9:24-28

The author reiterates his point (see the commentary on Heb 7:27, Proper 26 [31]) that Christ is a high priest who was offered up but once (*hapax*, v. 28). As the death of humankind is unrepeatable, so is his. But whereas judgment faces the normal individual after death (v. 27), in Christ's case there will follow his return to save; not to take away the sins of the many—that has already been done—but to bring final salvation.

MARK 12:38-44

We can find as severe a condemnation of the conduct of religious functionaries in Jewish sources as in vv. 38-41. Mark clearly means to distinguish, however, between the usual mode of behavior of the self-consciously religious and those who follow in the footsteps of Jesus (cf. Mt 23:1-7; Lk 11:43; 20:45ff.) There is some grammatical evidence that v. 40 had circulated as a separate saying but had been appended to 38f. in a pre-Maran source.

The same is true of 41-44, although the transfer from a public occurence to an admonition of the disciples in 43a is probably an editorial addition. Mark sees in the widow's generosity an example of Jewish piety of the poor like that of most in the crowd. They heard Jesus with delight (v. 37), in contrast to leaders of the type described in vv. 38ff.

Stories like that of the widow's mite are told in many traditions. Note that she could have kept one of the coins, but did not. A *lepton* ("two small copper coins") is something like one tenth of a cent, indicating her marginal status if two were "all she had to live on."

❧ ❧

Proper 28 [33] / Thirty-third Sunday of the Year (B)
Sunday between November 13 and November 19, inclusive

1 Samuel 1:4-20

The once childless Hannah conceives and bears a son. Samuel is the name she gives him, because "I have asked him of the Lord" (v. 20). It is Shaul that means "asked of God." Shmuel is literally "name of God." Did the biblical writers not know the basic etymology of their own tongue? Of course they did. But as with native American name-giving, their greater interest lay in what was happening at the time of conception or birth. For this they set obvious word meanings aside.

Elkanah's greater love for his childless wife than his childbearing one could not be adequately expressed by giving Hannah double portions but he could not grasp this. His view of himself as making up for her barren womb is a classic expression of male opaqueness (v. 8). The Nazirite vow she uttered at the doorpost of the temple is told as binding for a lifetime on any son she should bear. Normally, a vow such as this was made until what was prayed for came to pass. This was the case with Paul's reported Nazirite vow in Acts 18:18. It was otherwise in the case of the son of Manoah's wife. Samson as he was called was fated not to put a razor to his head all his life long (Judg 13:5; 16:17) and the tragedy of his infidelity is well known. It was his mother to be who was not to have any wine or strong drink or impure food (vv. 4, 7, 14). For Hannah it was her son whom she vowed to abstain from alcohol along with his unshorn locks (1 Sam 2:11). It is instructive that a writer of the time could have portrayed the wife of a regular pilgrim to the shrine at Shiloh as suspect of being addled by drink. Were housewives known to be tipplers of wine in that era? Or does the storyteller need the detail to account for Elkanah's misinterpretation of Hannah's silent prayer—therefore, were prayers usually voiced? This is a tale about the conception of the priest-judge Samuel and so we should not stop to ponder the details. Eli the priest does not tell her that she will conceive but expresses it optatively as a pious wish or prayer (v. 17). One year later it comes to pass.

1 SAMUEL 2:1-10

DANIEL 12:1-3

The book of Daniel is concerned with "a calamity so great . . . [as] has never before been done under heaven" (9:12), the humiliation of Jerusalem by "a little horn [on the ram that was Greece] which grew exceedingly great toward the south," namely, Antiochus IV (8:9; cf. vv. 23-26). The interruption of Temple sacrifice achieved by his desecration (cf. 11:31) ran from 168 to 165 B.C.E., according to 1 Maccabees (1:54 and 4:52). Gabriel, the first angel to be mentioned in the Hebrew canon by name (Dan 8:16), explains to Daniel the meaning of his visions. Michael, the second (10:13), is "one of the chief princes" of Israel. Persia (v. 13) and Greece (v. 20) have their own protective princes. Chapter 11 describes conflict between the king of the north, Antiochus, and the king of the south, Ptolemy, son of the Egyptian monarch who was the brother of Antiochus, Seleucus IV (d. 175). It peaks in its description of Antiochus's blasphemies, which include desertion of the gods of his fathers for other gods (vv. 36-39). Verses 40-45 presumably describe the resolution of the struggle, but at this point the author deserts history for eschatology. There was no such overwhelming of Egypt as v. 40 describes, nor do we know what the pitching of the palatial tents between the Mediterranean and Mount Zion (v. 45) signifies. It may have been the beginning of the siege of Jerusalem. We do know that Antiochus IV "came to his end" (v. 45) in Persia, a matter concerning which the author has either no knowledge or no interest. He does care, however, about the fate of the victims of the unparalleled distress he describes (12:1).

Michael shall take care of his people "at that time." Those who escape, "everyone found written in the book" (v. 1), are presumably the Jews who remain faithful. There is no implication, however, that the heroic dead in the Maccabean uprising are unfaithful. They are projected as living forever in the flesh while the betrayers of the cause live on in shame (v. 2). The "wise" who "lead the many to justice" (v. 3) are the national heroes who counseled and took part in the resistance.

Undoubtedly, life after death is being spoken of here, but without any detail as to its conditions. The Jewish Scriptures have been largely silent on the point until now (Isa 26:19 and Ezek 37 are probably only prefigurative of the last age). Their fear of foreign mythologies about rising deities may have been influential. But here there is a clear statement of faith in the lot of those who took part in the resistance to the Greeks. They will awaken to everlasting life or to shame and contempt in relation to their deeds (12:2).

Psalm 16:[5, 8-11]

Hebrews 10:11-14, (15-18), 19-25

This passage returns to the theme of the last two Sunday's readings and those of the preceding month. A new argument is proposed in support of the preeminence of Christ's priesthood. He is seated, as in Ps 110:1 (cf. David's posture in 2 Sam 7:18). The temple priests stand (cf. Num 16:9). The visual lesson provided by the cathedral church at Aachen comes to mind, the "triple church" where a seated Charlemagne observed from his throne the activity of the bishop standing at the altar below him. The positioning is a matter of significance.

Jesus has performed his priestly work once and finally, and sits at the right hand of God (v. 12). He continues as a priest; that role will last forever (cf. 7:16f.). He exercises his priestly function now by renewed intercession (cf. 7:25; 9:24). Enemies are placed beneath his feet (v. 13) as in the footstool metaphor of Ps 110:1. Paul in 1 Cor 15:24-28 uses a similar figure to describe Christ's victory at the end, even if verbally he relies on Ps 8:7 rather than 110. There, a more general dominion of man over nature is described. The enthroned Christ need not move about like the Aaronite priests, since his work is done. It is not as though the sanctified (v. 14; cf. 2:11) had been perfected in every respect, even though from the standpoint of Christ's sacrifice, a perfect act, they are. The perfection lies in Christ the cause rather than in the effect on the sanctified. The same idea recurs in v. 18. The forgiveness of sinners in Christ means that no further offering will be required on his part, not that none will be necessitated on theirs.

Alleluia. Luke 21:36

Be watchful, pray constantly, that you may be worthy to stand before the Son of Man.

MARK 13:1-8[24-32]

Interestingly, this Sunday in Year C proposes Luke 21:5-19, which derives from Mark 13:1-11, but LM uses only the Lukan version of the disciples' awe at the magnificence of the Temple to introduce the Synoptics' so-called end-time discourse of Jesus. It is placed on what had been the last Sunday of the Church year before Christ the King intervened. Mark either knows that the Romans have destroyed the Herodian structure or that the army of Vespasian and his son Titus is at the gates. Whichever the case his main concern is to warn believers in Christ in his corner of the diaspora that claimants of the mantle or even the person of Jesus are not to be believed. There may be rumors of war abroad with all its turbulence and destruction but the Christian prophet Mark is perfectly assured that this is *not* the time of the coming of Jesus in glory. Kingdoms in conflict, earthquakes, famines: we have seen them all many times since Jesus' ascension in glory. When his *parousía* is imminent, Mark teaches, we will know the signs.

The evangelist describes the end-time but his real interest is in the Church living in his own age. "In those days" of vv. 17 and 24 is a favorite Markan phrase (cf. 1:9; 8:1) that serves as a link between narratives but does not connote proximity in time to what preceded. There will be suffering *(thlipsis)*, presumably in Judaea and somehow related to the "desolating sacrifice/abomination" (v. 14), a phrase rendered in TEV by "the Awful Horror." The same version personifies the neuter noun as "where *he* should not be," although *deî* is impersonal. Evidently the horror is taken to be that of an individual's presence. Caligula's desecration of the temple by erecting statues of himself is most often presumed here (his actual throne name, 37–41 C.E., was Gaius; "Caligula" means "Little Boots"). In the midst of cataclysm, the Son of Man will appear. His coming will be sudden, like the burst of summer in Palestine (v. 28). Encountering him is not a matter for distant generations but for this one (v. 30).

The apocalyptic setting of the passage is not so important as the coming of the Son of Man. His assembly of his chosen "from the ends of the earth to the ends of heaven" (v. 27) is a detail from Deut 30:4f. and Isa 60:4ff. (cf. Mic 4:1f.). The ingathering is of the chosen, as in 12:25, not the resurrection of all the dead or the judgment of the good and evil. In contrast to other apocalypses of the period like the *Assumption of Moses*, there is no mention of the annihilation of enemies. The goal of the prophetic narrative is the great power and glory of the Son of Man, in which the dispersed will be joined with him in ultimate fellowship with their God.

Verses 28f. are a parable which, in its original independent form, was not referring by "these things" to what has preceded in vv. 24-27. "All these things" of

v. 30 (which is seemingly a separate saying) may refer to Jesus' activity (cf. 9:1). In any case the *tauta* and "becomes/takes place" *(génētai)* of the two logia is what brought them together. Similarly, v. 31 has been joined to v. 30 only because of the catchword "pass away." Verse 31 is similar in meaning to Matt 5:18 except that here it is Jesus' words that have the staying power, a development beyond the Matthean attribution of such perdurance to the Law.

Verse 32 was also a separate saying originally. It is in a quite different spirit from 29f. and is unique in Mark for its mention of "the Father" and "the Son." If it is a genuine saying of Jesus—as its reference to limits to his knowledge hints—it is his only Markan reference to himself as the Son (12:6-8 being an insertion of Jesus into one of his stories). Whatever the case, it sets him apart from other mortals and puts him in company with the angels in his ignorance. If, on the other hand, Jesus cannot be thought of as calling himself the Son, the saying could be one of the early Church to express the fact that it had no word from him about when these things would happen. The gathering of the chosen to the Son of Man, in its circumstances, was an absolute mystery of God.

❧.❧

Proper 29 [34] / Reign of Christ or Christ the King / Thirty-fourth, or Last Sunday of the Year (B) Sunday between November 20 and November 26, inclusive

2 Samuel 23:1-7

David's purchase of the threshing floor of Araunah the Jebusite in order to build an altar to the LORD may be the best remembered story of this book as it brings the chronicle of the shepherd-king toward a close (24:18-25). Less well remembered are his "last words," a literary conceit that places an elegy of the person's deeds on the lips of many of Israel's greats. The passage is termed an oracle (lit.: words whispered), the biblical word commonly used for prophetic utterances. David is called God-exalted, God-anointed, and the favorite of the Strong One of Israel (v. 1). Language of great beauty is employed to hail David as a spokesperson for God and a just ruler over the people. All these things Christians believe of Jesus as they celebrate his reign under God. The chief feature of the poem may be the celebration of the dynasty David founded rather than his personal exploits (v. 5). The covenant God gave him was thought at the time of the writing to be everlasting (v. 5; cf. 7:8-16). It came to an end with the bitter defeat by Chaldea as Judah went off. into exile leaving only a remnant to till the soil (25:8-12). But this people, called "a treasured possession out of all the peoples . . . a priestly king-dom and a holy nation," continues to this day (Exod 19:5-6) and its daughter, largely Gentile, hails an offspring of David as its sovereign under God who is king over all the peoples.

PSALM 132:1-12, (13-18)

DANIEL 7:9-10, 13-14

A "son of man" means an individual human being in Hebrew. The author wishes to distinguish the one like a man in his visions (who stands for Israel) from the beasts who had preceded him (the empires of the Babylonians, Medes, Persians, and Greeks, vv. 3-7). The manlike figure comes on the clouds of heaven, an indication that something suprahuman is intended. To him the Ancient One, Israel's God, turns over people of every sort. Later it is the "holy ones" of that same God who receive the kingship (see vv. 18, 22). The author of Daniel does not connect the angelic-like man with the concept of messiah. The reference to kingship should provide a link, however (*m*ᵉ*shiaḥ* = anointed king). An eschatological appearance is intended, of one who is a man but who has a representative function both with respect to Israel and Israel's God. Later Jewish apocalypses like *1 Enoch* and *4 Ezra (2 Esdras)* featured in detail visions and revelations given to "the one of the time before time," "my son," "my elect one," and "the man." The activities of Daniel's "one like a son of man" are restrained in comparison. He is chiefly the recipient of "domin-ion and glory and kingship" (v. 14) from "the Ancient One": Israel made sover-eign among the nations. For a further commentary see Transfiguration (August 6).

PSALM 93[1-2, 5]

REVELATION 1:4B[5]-8

Verse 4 has introduced the letters to the seven churches. John, the author, is God's servant (v. 1). The letters come as a message from the LORD (cf. Exod 3:14, LXX, for the present participle with a masculine article, *ho ōn*, to render "he who is") and from Jesus Christ (v. 5). "Enduring witness" is from Ps 89:37[28] referring to the moon in the sky, "firstborn" from the same psalm at v. 27 [38]. The author leaves them in the nominative, not bringing them into line with the genitive of "Jesus Christ" as good style requires. Paul, whose epistles some commentators think Revelation was familiar with, uses the phrase "firstborn of many broth-ers" (Rom 8:29) and "first fruits of those who have fallen asleep" (1 Cor 15:20). Colossians 1:18 uses the same words as Revelation, "firstborn of the dead." The "highest of the kings of earth" is, again, from Ps 89:27 [28]. The psalm is speak-ing of David. Revelation modifies it to describe Christ as Lord of the living and the dead. The author has God freeing us by his blood in a past action; his con-tinuing love is expressed by the present tense.

Verse 6a quotes Exod 19:6, and 7a quotes Dan 7:13, both in Theodotion's version rather than the LXX. Verses 5b and 6 are a doxology to Christ who is cred-ited with making us "a kingdom, priests," a work of the LORD in Exodus. Matthew 26:28 and Heb 10:19, like v. 4, have theologies of the saving character of Jesus' blood, as do 1 Pet 1:19 and 1 John 1:7. Theodotion describes the one like a son of man as coming "amid *(metà)* the clouds," LXX "on *(epí)*" them. Verse 7, after quoting one brief line from Dan 7:13, immediately turns to Zech 12:10, 14, para-phrased and used selectively, for its picture of a sufferer who has been run through by a sword or spear and is bitterly lamented. John 19:37 likewise quotes a por-tion of v. 10, "They will look upon the one whom they have pierced." "So it is to be. Amen *(naí, amēn)*" are words saying the same thing in Greek and Hebrew. "Amen" will become a proper name of Christ in 3:14 but here it is more the strong affirmation of the saving work of God that occurs in 2 Cor 1:20.

The separation of "God" from "the Almighty *(ho pantokrátōr)*" that occurs in v. 8 is unusual in Revelation (cf. 4:8; 11:17; 15:3; 16:7; 21:22). The author will use the first and last letters of the alphabet to describe God again in 21:6 and per-haps of Jesus in 22:13 (see v. 16). He repeats himself in v. 8 from v. 4, "the LORD God, who is and who was and who is to come," as if to enclose his Christology within two brackets that declare Israel's faith in the everlasting nature of its God.

ALLELUIA. REVELATION 2:10C

Be faithful unto death, says the Lord, and I will give you the crown of life.

JOHN 18:33B-37

The fourth evangelist does here what he does throughout, namely, hang a profound theological reflection on a peg of history. The peg is the fact derived from the tra-dition that Jesus was sentenced to death by Pilate. Despite the apparent trustwor-thiness of John in certain other details of the passion narrative, the fact of sentencing appears to be the sole *datum* behind this exchange. One other proba-ble historical reminiscence is Pilate's question, "Are you the king of Judaea / the

Jews?" (v. 33) found in Mark's more primitive stratum at 15:2 and Luke 23:3. The title has no subsequent history in the church but since it had a nationalist political connotation, it could have derived from historical tradition. Only John troubles to answer the charge that Jesus' kingship—the *basileía* that he preached and the term *basileús* that enthusiasts attributed to him—was nonpolitical.

Verses 34, 36, and 37 are clearly Johannine developments. Verse 35 contains the theme of "handing over" so dear to the Synoptics. In 24, John has Jesus distinguish between the Roman and the Jewish notions of kingship, the latter with its profoundly religious component. "My kingdom" (v. 36) does not accord fully with the Synoptics' "kingdom of God." "Only those who belong to the truth can understand in what sense Jesus has a kingdom and is a king" (R. E. Brown).

Pilate declares Jesus not guilty (v. 38b; cf. 19:6) but inexplicably hands him over to be crucified (19:16). John must be concluding thereby that Pilate is not "of the truth." Pilate's favorable view of Jesus in John has often been identified as part of the Christian apologia before the empire. It is far more likely, however, that John is employing Pilate as a symbol of the vacillating "world." At first he accepts Jesus when, paradoxically, the Johannine *Ioudaîoi* do not, but ultimately the worldliness of power prevails.

❧·❧

All Saints (B)
November 1 or the First Sunday in November

WISDOM 3:1-9

The first reading for Proper 8 [13] (B) in LM is from the first two chapters of this deuterocanonical book, which is not found in every pulpit Bible. That fact is noteworthy, for the proposal that *it* be read with Isa 24:6-9 as an alternative is something of an ecumenical landmark. See Proper 23 [28] (A). The closing sentence of that commentary from earlier this year (which see) correctly identifies the author's concern with the immortality of the soul in the Hellenist manner rather than the resurrection of the body. The two ideas are by no means contradictory and Jews of the Pharisee persuasion held both. The passage is a favorite choice for Christian funerals when the person recently dead is known to have lived a righteous life (3:1). Especially pertinent in light of the recent feast of the Reign of Christ is the assurance that "the LORD will reign over them for ever" (v. 8). The pericope is so laudatory of the departed that going on to read v. 10 could provide a jarring note. The "ungodly" are surely in for some heavy weather in the life to come. This poses a problem for congregations whose faith remains intact that heavenly glory or total reprobation are the only two possibilities at death. Gone is the day when the living cheerfully assumed who would be among the damned. (Well, not entirely. The "blessed assurance" folk are still with us.) Belief in a purgation of the lingering effects of an evil life atoned for "between the stirrup and the ground" or however death came on does not mark non-Roman congregations likely to proclaim this Scripture. It is worth noting, however, that the Hellenized Jews of 100 B.C.E. were convinced that a God of justice who tested some and found them worthy (vv. 5f.) was not about to let the wicked off that easily. But to read on to vv. 10-12 at certain funerals might bring end to future contributions from surviving loved ones.

ISAIAH 25:6-9

See Proper 23 [28] (A).

PSALM 24

REVELATION 21:1-6A

See New Year's Day (A, B, C).

JOHN 11:32-44

John 11:1-45 is commented on under 5 Lent (A), which see. There it is the last of the readings from John on Sundays 2 through 5 that a congregation may employ in any Lent when adult candidates are preparing for baptism or entry into a new communion (John 3:1-17; 4:5-42; 9:1-41; 11:1-45). All four narratives tell somehow of new life in Christ and are prefigured by the first readings (which should not be abandoned if these are chosen). The life of the world to come envisioned in Wis 3:1-9 and Isa 25:6-9 does the same.

MATTHEW 5:1-12A

See 4 Epiphany [4] (A).

Thanksgiving Day
Fourth Thursday in November (United States)
Second Monday in October (Canada)

JOEL 2:21-27

For a commentary see under Proper 25 [30] (C).

PSALM 126

1 TIMOTHY 2:1-7

For a commentary see under Proper 20 [25] (C).

MATTHEW 6:25-33

For a commentary see under Epiphany 8 [8] (A).

YEAR C

❧ Season of Advent ❧

❧❧
First Sunday of Advent (C)

JEREMIAH 33:14-16

This passage is from the final chapter of the "Book of Consolation" (chaps. 30–33), which spells out how things shall be after the return from the exile in 538. It is part of a dynastic oracle that builds on that of Nathan (1 Sam 7:11-16) and adds the notion of perpetual sacrifice by a Levitical priesthood (v. 18). Today's reading, with which the complete passage (vv. 14-26) opens, is the rephrasing by a postexilic author of Jer 23:5-6. See Proper 11 [16] (B). There the prophet was playing on the throne name Zedekiah (598–87), which means "The LORD is just," by promising a wise Davidic king in time to come who would fittingly be called, "The LORD our justice. . . ." In the original oracle the predicted king was the subject of such attribution. Here the subject is Judah and Jerusalem (v. 16). The "righteous Branch" of the two passages (23:5; 33:15) resembles Isa 11:1, which describes a green "shoot" and "bud" (a different Hebrew word from "branch") sprouting from the stump and root of Jesse.

The endowments of such a sovereign are listed in Isa 11:2-5. His preeminent justice in judging described there (vv. 3b-5) is a theme developed at length in Ps 72:1-4, 12ff.

PSALM 25:1-10[4-5, 8-10, 14]

1 THESSALONIANS 3:9-13[12—4:2]

Paul has already thanked God copiously for the Thessalonian community with its work of faith and hope and love (1:2f.) but also for its imitation of him and of the Lord (v. 6). He repeats his thanks for the joy they give him and prays constantly that he may see them once again. Paul's prayer is that God may restore whatever is lacking in their faith. Timothy has returned from a visit to Thessalonica lately and reported that their faith and love are firm, that they have resisted the tempter in Paul's absence from them (v. 6). His hope is that God and Christ will direct him to Thessalonica again. The prayer of Paul that follows for abounding mutual love asks for hearts that are blameless in holiness before God at the coming *parousía* of Christ "with all his saints" (v. 13). The last phrase is doubtless an echo of the one describing the holy ones who accompany the one like a son of man in Daniel's vision (see Dan 7:13, 18, 21, 25), the faithful Jews in the Maccabean revolt. Paul makes his love for his believers the norm for theirs (v. 12) as is his frequent practice. They have learned from him how they ought to live and please God (4:1); they must do so yet more. His "instructions" of v. 4:2 mean strict orders in ordinary Greek, but there they stand for Paul's preaching.

Alleluia. Psalm 85:8

Lord, let us see your kindness, and grant us your salvation.

Luke 21:25-36[25-28, 34-36]

Luke's apocalyptic discourse in vv. 25-26 parallels Mark 12:24-26 and Matthew. Verse 28 is special to him. He omits the falling of the stars from heaven found in the other two, speaking instead of signs in the "the sun, the moon, and the stars" (v. 25). Isaiah 13:10 seems to be the source of cosmic disturbance for all three Synoptics. Psalm 65:7[8] provides Luke, uniquely, with his image of the roaring sea and the waves. The fright seems to derive from the next verse of the psalm, where "those who live at earth's farthest bounds"—and not Judaea only—are in fear. G. W. H. Lampe (*Peake's Commentary*, 839) suggests that the "gateways of the morning and the evening," i.e., two stars, are the *astra* of Isa 34:4 in the LXX— a part of the "host of heaven" that shall rot away (in the Hebrew).

The climax of the passage occurs after the signs of v. 25, with the coming of the Danielic Son of Man "in a cloud" (Mark 14:62), "with the clouds," resembling Theodotion's "with clouds," following the LXX. The singular "cloud" in Luke may be the middle of a series of three, in which the usage as to number occurs in the Transfiguration (9:35) and Ascension (Acts 1:9) accounts as well. Luke omits the apocalyptic detail of the angels sent out to gather the elect from the four winds and puts in its place a word of comfort about the certainty of impending redemption (v. 28).

Again, Luke's conclusion to the discourse is special to him in its present form. It probably draws on Mark's exhortation to watchfulness (13:33-37) without including its parable. Such a parable has already been used by Luke in a form he might have deemed sufficient (12:35-40). Isaiah 24:18 probably lies behind Luke's image of a self-indulgent people caught in a trap (vv. 34f.) or snare, which would require Isaiah's "pit."

❧.❧

Second Sunday of Advent (C)

BARUCH 5:1-9

A poem of consolation for Jerusalem and her captive children runs from 4:5 to 5:9, coming after another poem characteristic of the later sapiental school, which equates Wisdom with the Torah (3:9—4:4). It is impossible to date the one from which today's pericope comes. Most choose the Maccabean period as that in which the whole collection was composed. (The prayer of 1:15—3:8 derives strongly from Dan 9:4-19; Belshazzar is made Nebuchadnezzar's son in both books.) Clearly, the catastrophes of a later time are being described as if they took place in the days of Jeremiah's well-known secretary, Baruch. Some have even opted for the period after the sack of Jerusalem in 70 C.E., the two Persian kings being thought code names for the father and son, Vespasian and Titus. Thus, submission to Rome (the "distant nation" of 4:15?), in the interests of peace, may be the course of action counseled in 1:12: "We shall live under the protection of King Nebuchadnezzar of Babylon . . . and . . . his son Belshazzar, and we shall serve them many days, finding favor in their sight." If written after 70, however, the detail of sacrifice on "the altar of the LORD our God" (v. 10) is an anachronism.

The sins of Israel are the cause of God's destructive wrath (4:5-13), but God promises deliverance (vv. 18, 21, 27, 29). Jerusalem is told to look to the east for liberation (vv. 36f.), a reconstruction of the events of 538 B.C.E. The latter happenings pervade the remainder of the poem (5:1-9), since its details depend heavily on Isa 35:1-2; 40:4; 49:22-23. Jerusalem is to dress in her finest, no longer the clothes of mourning. Her children were once led off captive on foot but now they come back borne on thrones. The *Psalms of Solomon* 11:2-7, probably from the first century C.E., contains phrases in common with this portion of Baruch: "Stand on a high place, Jerusalem, and look at your children, / from the east and the west assembled together by the LORD; . . . He flattened high mountains into level ground for them; . . . / God made every fragrant tree to grow for them. . . . / Jerusalem, put on (the) clothes of your glory, / prepare the robe of your holiness" (trans.

R. B. Wright, *The Old Testament Pseudepigrapha*, ed. James W. Charlesworth [New York: Doubleday, 1985], 2:662).

The whole poem is an exhortation to hope. The Roman liturgy uses this deuterocanonical book in Advent with a view to the song of Zechariah in Luke 1 and the east as the provenance of Matthew's astrologers (2:1) who follow the star at its rising (v. 3), all portents of joy for Jerusalem.

PSALM 126:1-6

MALACHI 3:1-4

For a commentary see Presentation of the Lord (February 2).

LUKE 1:68-97

Zechariah's song, known from the Vulgate and the Latin liturgy as the *Benedictus* (1:68), is Luke's composition or adaptation to balance out Mary's in his Jesus-John diptych. Verse 66 asks a question about the infant John's future and verses 76-79 answer it. Verse 68 echoes the many psalms that hail the God of Israel as its redeemer (19:14[15]; 78:35; 111:9). The horn of the people's salvation (v. 69; cf. Ps 18:2[3]; 1 Sam 2:10, KJV/NAB) bespeaks the bull's strength and fertility, a symbol of the Lord's. The image of the horn *(kéras)* and of daybreak *(anatolé* [v. 78]) more fittingly refer to God's work in Jesus than in John. This is not surprising since the song is about the fulfillment of God's promise in him through the prophets (v. 70), of whom John is but another (v. 76).

PHILIPPIANS 1:3[4-6]-11

Verses 3-11 are the prayer of thanksgiving with which Paul customarily sets the tone of what is to follow by reviewing recent happenings—often deeds of the recipients of the letters—for which he is grateful to God. He says he prays constantly and joyfully for the Philippians (v. 4) because of the way they promote the gospel in "partnership" with him (v. 5). The *koinōnía* spoken of may be either financial or by way of fellowship; it probably connotes both. Later in this letter the apostle will mention Epaphroditus, whom the Philippians have sent to take care of his needs (2:25). Elsewhere he writes of the unique generosity of this Macedonian community in supporting him (4:15-16), and his willing acceptance of that support (2 Cor 11:9). Since he constantly underscores his fiscal independence in his dealings with the other churches, the Philippian case must be an exception in his mind: not "support" so much as taking part in a common enterprise.

NRSV, NAB, and all English translations render v. 3 as though the remembrance *(mneía)* is Paul's of the Philippians, but the *hymōn* that modifies it could just as well be subjective as objective, i.e., their keeping him in mind. We know from elsewhere in the letter that he is thankful for that.

The "first day" of v. 5 is that of the Philippians' initial coming to believe and is contrasted with the "day of Jesus Christ" (v. 6), the hoped-for consummation of faith.

It is unclear which imprisonment Paul refers to in vv. 7, 13f., and 17. Ephesus and Caesarea both had praetorian guards (cf. v. 13), like the traditional favorite, Rome. Whatever the case, he writes of his lively hope that he will be rejoined to the Philippians (vv. 8, 26). He prays for their growth in love accompanied by understanding and insight so that they may value the things that matter (v. 10), again "up to the day of Christ." The eschatological assize is never far from Paul's thoughts. He wishes to find his converts laden with the fruits of justice when that day comes, with God's glory and praise as necessary concomitants.

ALLELUIA. LUKE 3:4 AND 6

Prepare the way of the LORD, make straight his paths: all humanity shall see the salvation of God.

LUKE 3:1-6

The third evangelist is alone in setting his Gospel in the context of contemporary events. His dating by Tiberius's fifteenth year makes it 28–29 C.E. Pilate was *praefectus*—later the title was changed to *procurátor*—from 26 to 36. The Galilean Herod is Antipas, a half-brother to Herod Philip. Both are sons of Herod the Great. "Tetrarch" is a title that once designated rule over the fourth part of a kingdom but it was not so in this case. The empire divided Palestine in 6 C.E., ten years after the old tyrant's death, into three parts: Galilee and Perea (east of the Jordan and south of the lake), the area well east of the lake designated "Ituraea and Trachonitis" by Luke, and the prefecture of Judaea under a Roman of equestrian rank who looked to a senatorial legate in Syria as his superior. Historical sources confirm all this but are silent on any Lysanias of Abilene (west of Damascus, lying between Ituraea to the west and Trachonitis to the east). A century before, that territory had had a king so named; this would be another Lysanias.

There was no "priesthood of Annas and Caiaphas," but the former (6–15 C.E.), father-in-law of the latter (18–36 C.E.), continued to wield such influence that Luke's phrasing is understandable.

John's preaching is in the prophetic mold (cf. Jer 1:2). He calls for reform of life and proposes an immersion in water as the sign of repentance. Luke seems to follow Mark in his quotation of Isa 40:3, lengthening it to include vv. 4-5. This fits in with his universal concern ("all flesh"); perhaps "all the region around the Jordan" (v. 3) is a similar trace. For Luke as for the other synoptists John is the forerunner of Jesus in a christological pattern they all find important.

❧ ✿

Third Sunday of Advent (C)

ZEPHANIAH 3:14-20

This book of prophecy dates to the closing years of the seventh century. Its author is much influenced by Amos and Isaiah. The first two chapters speak of the destruction of all humanity (1:2-18) and, specifically, judgment on the heathen nations (2:1-15). The third chapter holds out hope for a righteous remnant, "a people humble and lowly" (3:12). The concluding verses of the oracle that make up the bulk of today's reading are thought to be by another hand than Zephaniah's. They celebrate the LORD's presence in Israel's midst and call for rejoicing; the sentiments are very much in the mold of Second Isaiah and various enthronement psalms. The joyous conclusion to the book, probably derived from the period of the restoration (sixth-fifth centuries), serves the purposes of an Advent liturgy admirably, however little it may accord with the somber note struck by the earlier prophetic oracles.

ISAIAH 12:2-6

PHILIPPIANS 4:4-7

For another commentary on this passage, see Proper 22 [27] (A). In Greek the Pauline injunction to rejoice in the LORD is the LXX's eschatological greeting, *Chairete en Kyriō*. Earlier (v. 1) Paul called the Philippian community his joy and his crown. He enjoins its members to display their gentleness ("kindness," NAB; "good sense," JB; "moderation," "modesty" KJV; *modestia vestra*, ineradicably "modesty" in DRC, to a generation brought up on the Vulgate). It is the one sure sign that the Lord Jesus "is" (or "draws"; the Greek has no verb) near—again, a reference to the final age.

Joy and rejoicing are recurrent themes in this epistle (cf. 1:18f.; 2:17f., 28; 3:1; 4:10). The incomprehensible nature of God's peace is the fact that it is bestowed in the midst of difficulties. It is given "in Christ Jesus," that is, in the mystery of our salvation through his cross and resurrection.

ALLELUIA. ISAIAH 61:1

The Spirit of the LORD is upon me, who has anointed me to bring glad tidings to the poor.

LUKE 3:7[10]-18

For a commentary on vv. 7-9, see 2 Advent (A) with the discussion of its parallel, Matt 3:7-10.

Verses 10-14 are not found in the other evangelists' accounts of the preaching of John. They immediately remind the reader of the picture of sharing in the Jerusalem community in early Acts. The "two coats" of v. 11 may depend on the logion of Matt 5:40, which uses the same word along with one for the outer garment, proposed as the sign of more generous giving. (Luke preserves the Matthean gesture of divesting in 6:29 but in reverse order: coat-shirt rather than shirt-coat.) Tobit 4:16 may be the source for both. The tender conscience of the chief tax collector Zacchaeus reported in 19:8 is the standard proposed in v. 13, just as the soldiers of v. 14, probably Herodian, are enjoined to conduct themselves like the God-fearer Cornelius (Acts 10:1ff.).

Mark's "one more powerful than I" (1:7) is made explicit by Luke in v. 16. He spells out the mood of popular anticipation somewhat as John does in 1:20f. This may be a polemic against a still flourishing sect of baptizers, although not necessarily so (see Acts 18:25 for John's baptism as the only one known to Apollos, despite his having been "instructed in the Way of the Lord"). Josephus's reference to the preaching and the execution of John (*Antiquities* 18.116–19) confirms how influential he was. All four evangelists place Jesus above him as a result of their faith conviction, but whether in terms of a direct apologetic is hard to say. Verse 16 is a conflation of Markan and Q elements (Mark 1:7f.; Matt 3:11); v. 17 is from Q (Matt 3:12). The theme of the purification of Israel by the refiner's fire occurs in Mal 3:2f.; of stubble in a blazing oven in 3:19 (MT, hence NRSV, 4:1).

The final verse, 18, is a summary proper to Luke. He has John preaching good news to the people, an indication of his desire to associate the Baptizer with the new age (cf. 16:16). At the same time, Luke notes John's imprisonment at this point, unlike Mark (6:17f.) and Matthew (14:3f.), to clear the stage for the appearance of Jesus. Hans Conzelmann has called attention to Luke's epochal scheme (cf. Acts 10:37; 13:24f.) in which he puts the activity of John in the age of the prophets (*The Theology of St. Luke* [New York: Harper, 1960], 22–27). The "centre of history" is the age of Jesus' preaching. It takes place largely in Galilee, Jerusalem being the scene of the inauguration of the third age of world history (Luke 24:47ff.; Acts 1:1-11). Luke in 24:6 alters Mark 16:7//Matt 28:7 to make Galilee the scene of a former prophecy of Jesus, not the geographic center of the new age as Mark does (see Conzelmann, 202–206). Luke will reintroduce John into his narrative at 7:18, but his summary at vv. 29f. tends to support Conzelmann's contention that, despite Jesus' lavish praise of John, Luke means to situate him in the former epoch rather than "die Mitte der Zeit," the central age of Jesus Christ.

❧ ❧
Fourth Sunday of Advent (C)

MICAH 5:2-5A

This eighth-century prophet was active in the reigns of Ahaz (733–21) and Hezekiah (720–693). Only the first three chapters of the book are thought to be authentically his. Chapters 4–5 date to the exile and the postexilic period; the same is true of part three (chaps. 6–7), with the possible exception of 6:6—7:4 as genuinely Mican material. Today's passage seems to refer to the exile as past in speaking of the "giving up" of the people and the return of "the rest of his kindred" (v. 3) but reverts to the eighth century in its mention of the Assyrian threat (vv. 4f.). The thrust of vv. 1-3 is in the direction of a restored monarchy of the line of David, an ancient family that had its origins in Bethlehem-Ephrathah. Ezekiel 34:21f. and Amos 9:11 contain similar promises of a restoration of the fallen "booth" or "hut" (*sukka*) of David. The LORD will abandon Israel and Judah until a woman has borne such a ruler, says the oracle (v. 3).

The "seven shepherds" and "eight men of royal rank" are the bold defenders of Israel against Assyria, the numerical progression being a biblical device to show strength (cf. Amos 1:3).

The lectionary probably retains v. 4 [3], which derives from the earlier period because it has the word "shepherd" in common with the Davidic prophecy.

Matthew 2:6 employs the Micah prophecy in a form that is neither that of LXX nor the MT. The Bible has featured Bethlehem's insignificance in Judah, despite which a great principle of leadership emerges from it. Matthew reads quite the opposite: "You . . . are by no means the least" (v. 6). Krister Stendahl shows in *The School of St. Matthew* (Philadelphia: Fortress Press, 1968), 99–100, how this text, one of eleven "formula quotations," adapts biblical material in the *pesher* or interpretative tradition used also by the Qumrân sect. The concluding phrase in v. 6, "who is to shepherd my people Israel," is added from 2 Sam 5:2 (LXX), although v. 4 [3] of Micah suggests the same idea in other words: "he shall . . . feed his flock by the strength of the LORD." Matthew's interpretation of the Micah text clearly has a specific object, namely, to point out the fulfillment in Christ. He is not at all deterred from putting such a reading in the mouths of "all the chief priests and the scribes of the people," since he is convinced of the truth of the interpretation.

LUKE 1:47-55 OR PSALM 80:1-7[2-3, 15-16, 18-19]

HEBREWS 10:5-10

In v. 5 the author of Hebrews quotes Ps 40:7-9a in the LXX (39), which reads, "but ears you readied for me" (v. 7), changing it to "a body you prepared for me," as better suited to his purpose. There is a very small possibility of a textual error: *sōma* in place of *ōtía* (one Syriac MS has the marginal correction *ōta*, also "ears"); nor is the suggestion of synecdoche helpful here, i.e., the whole substituted for the part. It seems a clear case of alteration in the *pesher* tradition. The verb for "you have taken no pleasure" (Hebrews) in place of "you did not will" (LXX) is a minor matter; the variant reading "you did not desire" occurs in the MS tradition of both Psalms and Hebrews. The psalmist has declared himself ready to do God's will as superior to all blood sacrifices, and Hebrews attributes the sentiment to Jesus in the flesh. The "book" is either Torah or the whole collection (*Tanakh*, an acronym for *Torah, Nebiim, Ketubim*). All Scripture speaks of Jesus for the author of Hebrews.

Verse 8 is a rearrangement of Ps 40:6 [7] with an eye to 1 Sam 15:22, naming the four main classes of Levitical offerings as the psalm verse does. Verse 9a is from Ps 40:7f. [8f.] and declares the obedience of the man Jesus to be preferable to Temple sacrifice. In its reading of Jer 31:31ff. (9b) it is less nuanced than Paul in Romans (9:3-6; 11:1f., 14, 32), bearing a closer resemblance to his "new covenant" in 2 Corinthians. The author of Hebrews is quite convinced that Christ has abolished (*anairei*, v. 9) the first covenant and established the second by his blood (cf. 9:15-28). In 10:19, 29 the effective agent of redemption is Christ's blood.

Here (v. 10) it is his body, an echo of the *sōma* of v. 5, which is at the same time a Hebraic means of designating his entire person.

ALLELUIA. LUKE 1:38

I am the servant of the LORD: may his will for me be done.

LUKE 1:39-45, (46-55)

This pericope follows immediately that employed as the gospel in the feast of The Immaculate Conception. It is a part of the longer reading proposed for the feast of The Assumption (Luke 1:39-56). In Luke's theology, Jesus is "Lord" from before his birth (1:43). The infancy and boyhood narratives of the first two chapters indicate what Jesus will become through what he already is. When he passes through death to glory and is made Lord and Christ he will be no other than he was proclaimed to be at the beginning.

The story of the meeting of Mary and Elizabeth is part of Luke's John-Jesus diptych, the Baptist being identified as a prophet and witness to Jesus from before his birth. Luke may have in mind the oracle of Gen 25:23 in which the elder twin in Rebekah's womb, Esau, is fated to serve Jacob, the younger.

The "hill country" *(oreinê)* of Judah (the Romans called it Judaea) is indeterminate (v. 39). 'Ain Karem is a centuries-later attribution of no special merit except for its natural beauty. The baby's leaping in Elizabeth's womb may derive from the call of Jeremiah: "Before I formed you in the womb I knew you, / and before you were born I consecrated you, / I appointed you a prophet to the nations" (Jer 1:5). The spirit of prophecy, the Holy Spirit, is active throughout the Lukan account. Elizabeth acts as a prophet in praising the faith of Mary, her younger kinswoman (v. 45).

For a commentary on the "Magnificat," vv. 46-55, see Assumption of the Blessed Virgin Mary (August 15).

❧ Season of Christmas ❧

❧❧
Nativity of The Lord / Proper I (C)
Mass at Midnight

ISAIAH 9:2-7. PSALM 96[1-3, 11-13].
TITUS 2:11-14. LUKE 2:1-14, (15-20)

As in (A).

❧❧
Nativity of The Lord / Proper II (C)
Mass at Dawn

As in (A).

❧❧
Nativity of The Lord / Proper III (C)
Mass during the Day

ISAIAH 52:7-10. PSALM 98[1-6].
HEBREWS 1:1-4, (5-12)

❧❧
First Sunday after Christmas Day /
Sunday in the Octave of Christmas (C)
The Holy Family of Jesus, Mary, and Joseph

1 Samuel 2:18-20, 26

This story from Samuel's boyhood is chosen to prefigure that of Jesus' puberty told in today's Gospel. The ephod was a linen garment as indicated, perhaps apronlike, to be worn during service in the sanctuary. It was simple in its earliest usage but later seems to have acquired metal components and even to have been revered as a cultic object (Judg 8:27). Today's story is of a lad living away from home who had not escaped his mother's anxious care. The priest Eli expressed gratitude to the parents on their annual visit for having made a gift of their son to the Lord (v. 20). Samuel's growth in stature and favor with the Lord and the people ("in nature and grace" in older translations) is copied by Luke about Jesus in 2:52.

Psalm 148

1 Samuel 1:20-22, 24-28

For a commentary on 1:4-20 see Proper 28 [33] (B). Hannah waits until the child is weaned, then offers an appropriate sacrifice and leaves him with Eli at Shiloh to be dedicated to the Lord.

Psalm 84:2-3, 5-6, 9-10

Sirach 3:2-6, 12-14

As in (A).

Colossians 3:12-17[21]

As in (A).

Alleluia. Colossians 3:15a and 16a

Let the peace of Christ prevail in your hearts. Let the word of Christ dwell in you richly.

I JOHN 3:1-2, 21-24

For a commentary see Fourth and Fifth Sundays of Easter (B).

LUKE 2:41-52

This is the sole narrative in the Gospels about Jesus' boyhood, and it takes place in Jerusalem, not Nazareth. The pilgrimage feast of Passover, one of the annual three, is the occasion. Luke's purpose is to underscore Jesus' giftedness in youth and where his primary loyalty lay. The mix-up is thoroughly realistic as neighboring families from Galilee set out for home, Jesus' mother thinking he is with his father, the boy's father with his mother. In fact, he is "in his Father's house / about his Father's business" (*en tois*, the definite article, with the substantive understood by the first hearers of this Gospel). In any case, seated among the teachers in a Temple-area alcove is where he belongs, doing what he is doing. He is a questioner first, then a respondent to the elders' questions causing amazement by his answers. The brief description is true to Rabbinic practice of debate over the meaning of biblical texts. The mother's anxiety is expressed in anger, like that of any mother today who would rescue a child from darting between parked cars and then give it a healthy swat and a scolding, in relief it has come to no harm. Jesus' explanation for his tarrying behind is described as beyond their understanding (2:50). The evangelist means to give an early hint of what this child is destined to be. Mary's "treasuring all these things in her heart" (2:51 is a repetition of 1:29 and 2:19) is Luke's way of describing the thoughtful wisdom of this profound young woman.

JOHN 1:1-14

For a commentary see Mass during the Day (A).

❧❧

January 1 / Holy Name of Jesus (C)

NUMBERS 6:22-27

For a commentary see under (A).

PSALM 8

GALATIANS 4:4-7 OR PHILIPPIANS 2:5-11

As in (A).

LUKE 2:15-21

As in (A).

❧❧

January 1, when observed as New Year's Day

ECCLESIASTES (QOHELETH) 3:1-13

PSALM 8

REVELATION 21:1-6A; MATTHEW 25:1-6

All as in (A).

❧❧

Solemnity of Mary, Mother of God
January 1—Octave of Christmas

NUMBERS 6:22-27

For a commentary see under (A).

PSALM 67:2-3, 5-6, 8

GALATIANS 4:4-7

As in (A).

LUKE 2:15-21

As in (A).

ALLELUIA. HEBREWS 1:1-2

In the past God spoke to our Fathers through the prophets; now he speaks to us through his Son.

LUKE 2:16-21[41-52]

All as in (A).

ৰা.ঞ
Second Sunday after Christmas (C)

JEREMIAH 31:7-14

ECCLESIASTES 24:1-4, 12-16

PSALM 147:12-20

WISDOM 10:15-21

EPHESIANS 1:3-14[18]

ALLELUIA. 1 TIMOTHY 3:16

Glory to Christ, proclaimed to the Gentiles, belived in throughout the world.

JOHN 1:[1-9], 1-18

All as in (A).

❧ Season of Epiphany ❧
(Ordinary Time)

❧❧

Epiphany of the Lord (C)

ISAIAH 60:1-6

PSALM 72:1-7, 10-14

EPHESIANS 3:1-12[2-5, 5-6]

ALLELUIA. MATTHEW 2:2

We have seen his star in the east; and have come to adore the LORD.

MATTHEW 2:1-12

All as in (A).

❧❧

Baptism of the Lord [1] (C)
First Sunday after the Epiphany

ISAIAH 43:1-7

This beautiful poem of the LORD's compassionate concern for Jacob/Israel follows on a description of the people's flight in exile (42:14-25). It does not occur randomly in Deutero-Isaiah but is "skillfully stitched into place and just as care-fully structured" (Carroll Stuhlmueller, C.P., *NJBC*, 21:20, 335). Israel is God's servant, God's messenger, but as one blind walking in darkness and deaf (vv. 16, 18f.), neither seeing nor hearing what is there to be observed (v. 20). The peo-ple that has received the LORD's glorious teaching has been robbed and plun-dered by "the spoiler," presumably Chaldea, Jacob's conqueror. The sin, the disobedience of Israel, was the reason that the LORD in anger could do no other (vv. 24f.). But now the God who created and formed this people will prove the depth of divine affection. "I have called you by name, you are mine" (43:1b). Jacob/Israel can come to no harm from flood or fire: "You are precious in my sight, and honored, and I love you" (v. 4a). That Egypt, Ethiopia, and Seba have served as the ransom price to reclaim Israel does not give the poet a second thought (vv. 3b, 4b). In his sight they are nothing, Israel is all. But no harm is done because it is all a pleasant fiction to illustrate how great is YHWH's love for this people. The pagan empires in all directions are ignorant of the divine command they have received to yield up tiny Israel, give it its freedom. This poem is a good indication of the way the one God and the Jewish people are conceived as absolutely correlative in the Jewish mind. That any one Gentile people or great numbers of them could claim the LORD as *their* God as well, they cannot com-prehend. Despite this, the whole Christian and Muslim worlds see themselves, that is, every member born to them, as objects of the same overpowering love and care. It is a continuing difference between Israel and the nations that expe-rience this election.

ISAIAH 42:1-4, 6-7

As in (A).

PSALM 29[1-4, 9-10]

1 CORINTHIANS 12:1-11

See Second Sunday of the Year (C), immediately below.

ACTS 8:14-17

For a commentary see 6 Easter (A).

ACTS 10:34-38

As in (A).

ALLELUIA. SEE MARK 9:6.

The heavens were opened and the Father's voice was heard: this is my beloved Son; hear him.

LUKE 3:15-17, 21-22

For a commentary on vv. 7-18 see 3 Advent (C).

RCL fleshes out the LM lection by adding to vv. 1-6 vv. 15-17, and 21-22. The latter two closely resemble Matt 3:16f., and both give evidence of deriving from Mark 1:10f. The differences from Matthew are that, after Jesus was baptized, he "was praying" (Luke 3:21), a characteristic Lukan touch; when the heaven was opened the Holy Spirit descended, not that Jesus saw "the Spirit of God descending and alighting on him," as in Matthew (3:16; cf. Luke 3:22); the latter verse in Luke speaks of the dove uniquely "in bodily form"; and lastly, the voice that came from heaven addresses Jesus, "You are my beloved Son" (as in Mark 1:11) rather than Matthew's, "This is my beloved Son" (3:17). These seem to be stylistic rather than substantive changes among the three Synoptics. John does it all quite differently beginning with John's, "I saw the Spirit descend as a dove from heaven" (1:32ff.).

MATTHEW 3:13-17

As in (A).

❧❧

Second Sunday after the Epiphany / Second Sunday of the Year [2] (C)

ISAIAH 62:1-5

The entire chapter can be taken as a single poem in the collection known as Third Isaiah (chaps. 56–66; see commentary on Isa 56:1, 6-8, Proper 15 [20] (A). Each of these five verses may also be viewed as separate. The affinities with the poem that makes up chap. 60 are evident. See commentary on Isa 60:1-6, Epiphany of the Lord (A). The similes of the dawn and a burning torch are complementary to

the light images of 60:1-3, 5a. The "new name" of v. 2b has been given in 60:14cd;
two of them, in fact. Ezekiel has likewise renamed the new Jerusalem, "The Lord
is there" (48:35). The city is a crown and a diadem. It is also "My delight" (Heb.
Hephzibah) and its land "married" (Heb. *Beulah*), v. 4b. The theme of marriage
between the Lord and his virgin bride occurs in Hos 2:4-7; Jer 3:1, 8f.; Ezekiel
16. "The one who rebuilds you" (*banai*, v. 5a) in an emended vocalization of the
Masoretic Text to read "your sons," yields the awkward figure of Jerusalem
espoused to her own offspring. God is a bridegroom (*ḥāthān*) who takes joy in
Zion his bride.

Psalm 36:5-10

Psalm 96:1-3, 7-10

1 Corinthians 12:1[4]-11

The Corinthian community is torn over "spiritual gifts" (*pneumatika*, v. 1, with
charísmata from v. 4 understood). Paul in this epistle supplies a radical criterion
for discriminating among them: it is the Spirit of God bearing witness to the Lordship of Christ (vv. 3f.). In the "Holy Spirit" (v. 4) alone can one acknowledge
in speech that "Jesus is Lord," sometimes called the first Christian creed. Various other spirits are available, Paul intimates, to account for ecstatic utterances
like the puzzling "Let Jesus be cursed," *Anáthema Iesoûs* (v. 3a), which Christians might cry out in the assembly while moved by a perverse spirit resisting
the ecstasy they felt coming upon them.

Having dealt with the criterion for judging inspired ecstatic speech, Paul moves
on to a general discussion of gifts and persons. "One and the same Spirit" (v. 11)
whose sole purpose is the "common good" (v. 7) is responsible for putting them
all into operation in everyone (v. 6), distributing them individually as the Spirit
sees fit. The varieties of gifts are likewise the Spirit's doing (vv. 4, 5, 6). "Activi-
ties/forms of service" (v. 5) are here probably any services, not ministerial functions; "works" (v. 6), the ways in which divine power is applied. A "manifestation"
of the Spirit is just that (v. 7); one receives such a manifestation to put this gift of
the Spirit in the service of all.

Further gifts are an utterance of wisdom and one of knowledge (v. 8). This gift of
discourse in two situations varies more as to Paul's word use than in reality. The

"faith" of v. 9 cannot be the saving *pistis* found in all believers but must be related to the special gift of 13:2 that can "move mountains," i.e., work miracles. "The gift of healing" (v. 9) and "miracles" are given to different persons, just as one can utter prophecy, *prophēteía* (v. 10, i.e., intelligible speech as spelled out in chap. 14), another things said unintelligibly in tongues and still another *hermēneía*, interpretation of the utterances. All these [gifts] have been given by the one Spirit, not to divide the community but to bring it into unity through diversity (v. 10).

ALLELUIA. 1 SAMUEL 3:9; JOHN 6:69B

Speak, O Lord, your servant is listening; you have the words of everlasting life.

JOHN 2:1-11

The Cana miracle is the first of Jesus' "signs" (v. 11). John seems to forget his own count (4:54) unless he is using the word "signs" in a sense that escapes us. Despite ingenious attempts by scholars like M.E. Boismard (*Du Baptême à Cana*, 1956) to plot a symbolic six-day week of Jesus' activity (see 1:29, 35, 43), there is a good likelihood that "on the third day" is primarily intended as the biblical designation of divine activity (cf. 4:43). The sign is calculated to reveal Jesus' "glory" so that his disciples may believe in him. Such is the announced purpose of the Gospel (20:30f.) as it comes from the hand of the last editor but one (who added chap. 21). Even with the working of this sign, it is not Jesus' "hour" (v. 4) as his raising up on the cross will be (19:27). The "woman" addressed in this first sign anticipates the "woman" of the last sign (19:26). Surely the address is symbolic, since no man spoke to his mother that way. Jesus' question to his mother in v. 4, literally, "What to me and to you?" occurs in biblical Hebrew in just this form to express a difference between two persons (see Judg 11:12; 1 Kgs 17:18), for John, her solicitude in a human dilemma and his intent in the context of his calling. Operating thus at two levels is a favorite Johannine device.

   C. H. Dodd cites three treatises of Philo of Alexandria in which wine instead of water is seen as the symbol of joy, perennial grace, and sober intoxication of spirit. In one of the three the Logos is the cupbearer at the drinking party *(symposion)*. He also sees in the six stone waterpots of ritual purification signs of the old order, to be replaced by the wine of teaching, not water, in the new order (*The Interpretation of the Fourth Gospel* [Cambridge: Cambridge Univ. Press, 1953], 298–99). The levels of meaning intended by the evangelist are multiple here, as throughout.

❧❧
Third Sunday after the Epiphany /
Third Sunday of the Year [3] (C)

NEHEMIAH 8:1-3[4A], 5-6, 8-10

The framers of LM (largely European, one Canadian) cannot have known of any special reasons for omitting v. 3 from public reading when they were at work on their task of selection. At that time Vatican funds had been invested in the development venture responsible for the Watergate complex (Vulgate: *porta aquarum*) on the Potomac. Public disclosure of financial irregularities in the construction resulted in the Holy See's withdrawing its financial stake. All this occurred well before the "third-rate burglary" into the offices of the Democratic National Committee, as President Nixon tried to dismiss the caper of which he was well aware.

Unlike the modern situation, the open space before the Water Gate in Ezra's fourth century witnessed the full disclosure of a document of record: the Law in its Deuteronomic form. The "Chronicler" responsible for 1 and 2 Chronicles is the author of the two books of postexilic history known as Ezra and Nehemiah. They have had a complex literary history, their contents having once formed a single book that became two distinct recensions in the transmission process. Ezra is described as a scribe of the exiled people in Persia, possibly a court secretary for Jewish affairs, sent to Judah to promulgate an already existing Law (Ezra 7:14, 25f.). His mission may be placed at about 400 B.C.E. in the reign of Artaxerxes II, who came to the throne in 404. His chief responsibility in Judah was to enforce the prohibition of mixed marriages for Jews which had been in force since Zerubbabel's time (Ezra 9–10). The law promulgated in Nehemiah 8 is not the Priestly Code, as scholars once thought, nor the entire Pentateuch (Wellhausen's view), but the D strand in the Pentateuch, or perhaps a combination of JED.

The old people wept for joy at the restoration of their people's great treasure, the Law. The celebration of it at the end of the feast of Booths (modern *Simḥath Torah*; see Deut 31:11) is reported in vv. 8-12. A description of this autumn feast, which is Deuteronomic, not Priestly, follows. The scene is one of joyous religious renewal after the repudiation of foreign wives and a fitting penance for that offense have been achieved.

Modern Christians do well to grasp the exultant spirit that marks the possession of Torah, even to this day. It is not a burden or a curse for the pious Jew, but all that is liberative and restorative.

PSALM 19[8, 9, 10, 15]

1 CORINTHIANS 12:12-31A

Paul teaches in this section that all in the church are a body and that the body is that of Christ (v. 27), who is Lord (v. 3). The context of the passage is the dispute in Corinth over the possession of spiritual gifts. Paul engages in his elaborate figure of the diversity of parts in the human body and their mutual dependence to hammer home the lesson that not all can do everything. His rhetorical questions in vv. 29f. call for negative answers, possibly as a refutation of certain Corinthian "spirituals" who are claiming omnicompetence. No one can do anything except in the one Spirit (v. 13) who, in the sign of baptism, made many diverse types of persons to be one body of believers. Differences remain in the Corinthian church ("Jew," "Greek," "slave," "free"), but they must now contribute to a higher unity, as in the functioning of parts of a body. Their having been "made to drink of the one Spirit" (v. 13) requires this.

The body figure is an old one in rhetoric (cf. Plato, *Protagoras* 330A). "And so it is with Christ" (v. 12b) contains a surprising leap, collapsing the lengthy argument that culminates in v. 27. All who are "in Christ" are members of the body that has its purpose and direction from him. Verses 14-20 spell out the necessity of distinction of function, while vv. 21-25 stress complementarity with an excursus into the less important (lit. "weaker," v. 22) and less presentable (vv. 23f.) parts, the latter made by Paul the occasion of a rationale for clothing (v. 23). In v. 26 he deserts his figure for the reality of members as actual people who suffer, are honored, and rejoice.

Having made his case for the essential nature of supportive contrariety, the apostle then deals with offices, the big three first, which deal with the all-important ministry of the word (v. 29). "Apostles" is impossible to identify specifically from other Pauline usage beyond itinerant proclaimers, while "prophets" and "teachers" are stable members of local communities. Perhaps prophets are the bearers of revelation as contrasted with teachers who spell out its implications for Christian life. In modern parlance these would be, respectively, preachers and theologians. NRSV and NAB attribute the gifts of second rank to persons, but in Paul they are the gifts themselves: "miracles," "gifts of healing," "forms of assistance," "forms of leadership," "various kinds of tongues." The third and fourth resemble what later emerged as the offices of deacon and bishop, both of them local ministries in contrast to the traveling ministries of apostles. C. K. Barrett notes that "Gifts of a self-assertive kind, *direction* and *tongues*, which appear to have suited the Corinthian taste, are placed at the end of the list (*The First Epistle to the Corinthians* [New York: Harper and Row, 1968], 296).

As rhetoric, Paul's presentation is marked by small inconsistencies and *non sequiturs*. As pastoral counsel to a troubled church, it is impeccable.

Alleluia. Matthew 11:25

Blessed are you, Father, Lord of heaven and earth; you have revealed to little ones the mysteries of the kingdom.

Luke [1:1-4]; 4:14-21

The identity of Theophilus (v. 3; cf. Acts 1:1) is unknown. He is more likely to have been the actual patron of Luke's two-volume work than an anonymous "lover of God"—something like the "gentle reader" of nineteenth-century fiction. The high-born title of address, "most excellent" *(krátiste)*, accords with the presumption of wealth. The first four verses, in the form of a prologue in classic rhetoric, announces the purpose of the entire work, resumed with the opening verses of Acts as a simple reminder of the flow of the narrative. The "fulfillment" of v. 1 may mean no more than that the events took place, but the accomplishment of divine promise is more likely, especially in light of chaps. 1–2. The stress in "eyewitnesses and servants of the word" (v. 2) is on the transmission of apostolic testimony. The latter term connotes official church designation of some sort (cf. 4:20; Acts 25:16; it is the Gospel word for the apprehenders of Jesus in Gethsemane, John 18:3, and the retinue of a household, Matt 26:58). Luke has investigated matters "carefully from the very first," namely, the progress of God's word from Jerusalem—for him the place of origin of the revelation made in Jesus Christ (Luke 1:5-23)—to Rome (Acts 28:14). Theophilus has been "instructed" in these matters previously rather than merely informed. In any case, the "truth" provided in the writing to follow (which NAB translates "certainty," REB "authentic knowledge," and JB "authentic teaching") is intended to confirm Theophilus in his present state of knowledge. The testimonies of the next two chapters in particular "spring from and seek to elicit shouts of joy and hymns of praise on the part of the devout community, which knows itself dependent on God's saving power. The term *proof* is alien to that milieu" (Paul Minear, *To Heal and to Reveal: The Prophetic Vision According to Luke* [New York: Seabury, 1976]).

Luke effects the transition from the first of his epochs, the time of the Law and the Prophets up to John, to the second, the ministry of Jesus, in the sermon in the synagogue at Nazareth (4:16-30). "Their" synagogues (v. 15) conveys Luke's psychic distance from the Palestinian reality, whereas the popular acceptance of Jesus in Galilee comes from the tradition. Luke's word picture of a postexilic synagogue is accurate—a layman with something to say being asked to comment on a reading from Scripture—but its position as programmatic for all that Jesus does (cf. Mark 6, Luke's source) is all-important. H. C. Kee calls the sermon and its immediate sequel Janus-like: "The passage looks back to the Old Testament, whose prophecies are seen as being fulfilled in Jesus, and it looks forward to the events of Jesus' ministry, in which the fulfillment itself takes place" (*Jesus in History*, 2d ed. [New York: Harcourt Brace Jovanovich, 1977], 193).

Isaiah 61:1-2, the passage chosen to be read, inaugurates one of the great eschatological poems of the Hebrew collection. The speaker, Third Isaiah, describes himself as anointed for his prophetic mission of announcing glad tidings to the poor. Luke 3:21f. has described just such a figurative anointing of Jesus by the Spirit. For Luke, all that the Isaian author has proposed as the work of the final age, Jesus will do. Of special importance is the concluding phrase "the year of the LORD's favor" (v. 19) because it fits in so well with Luke's periodization scheme. History unfolds for him in accord with that divine plan which the prophetic scroll announces. Luke links up prophecy and fulfillment in v. 21 in the person and ministry of Jesus.

✆ Fourth Sunday after the Epiphany / Fourth Sunday of the Year [4] (C)

JEREMIAH 1:4-10[17-19]

We know nothing of the circumstances of Jeremiah's upbringing in a priestly family in Anathoth of the land of Benjamin (1:1). We may presume that it was pious. He never married, according to 16:1-4, as if he had some intimation of disaster "in this place" too great for a wife and children to bear. He was probably somewhat younger than King Josiah, who came to the throne as an eight-year-old boy in 640. The incident of his call as a prophet occurred in the thirteenth year of Josiah's reign (v. 2), hence 628. The almost fifty years of King Ashurbanipal on Assyria's throne were drawing to a close, to yield to a neo-Babylonian dynasty. Nineveh would be destroyed in 612 and the Assyrian empire ended by Nebupolassar in 606. Nebuchadnezzar, who figured so prominently in Jeremiah's book of prophecy, came to rule in the Chaldean capital, Babylon, in 604. Jeremiah lived on until that sovereign's conquest of Jerusalem (587), following which he was carried off to Egypt despite his strong protest (43:7f.).

Jeremiah's initial protest that he was too young to prophesy (v. 6) was probably compounded by fear of the "awful cost of prophetic office" (John Bright). The LORD dismissed his scruples (vv. 7f.), telling the young priest that he had made him "a fortified city, / an iron pillar, a bronze wall, against the whole land" (v. 18). Despite these assurances, Jeremiah never seemed fully at ease in the prophet's role. In part this was because of the extreme distaste he felt for the company of prophets who, as a class, soothed with soft words those who despised the word of the LORD (cf. 23:16-22). He was conscious, however, of a divine call that went back to before the time of his birth and he accepted it. He had no course but to answer it and so, all his life long, he spoke the word that the LORD had spoken to him (cf. 23:21).

PSALM 71:1-6[15 AND 17]

1 CORINTHIANS [12:31]—13:1-13

The Corinthians put a high value on speaking in tongues (whether a pagan practice "baptized" or one introduced by the apostle), while Paul regarded it as one of the lowest of the gifts. Prophecy and teaching ranked well ahead of it, following the important norm he proposed of service to the community. But now the apostle comes to the "still more excellent way" (v. 31), namely, *agápē*, other-regarding love. Since the introduction of chap. 13 by v. 31b is awkward and the transition between vv. 31a and 14:1 smooth, some have come to think chap. 13 an independent unit. A few scholars attribute authorship to another hand, but most suppose it to have been composed by Paul and inserted here because so apposite to the situation at Corinth. Verse 14:1 seems to distinguish love from the "spiritual gifts" as if every Christian should have it no matter how individuals might otherwise be endowed.

Verses 13:1-3 contrast love with other gifts and attitudes; vv. 4-8a describe it largely but not entirely by the way of negation; vv. 8b-13 contrast love in its future fullness with its present immature and partial state. In v. 1 Paul reverts to the question in the previous chapter of speaking in tongues (12:3, 10, 28, 30), something he will say he can do "more than all of you" but is indifferent to. The "tongues of angels" perhaps describes such unintelligible speech. "Gong" (lit. "brass" or "copper") and "cymbal" may have once referred to pagan worship but have become by Paul's time a figure for meaningless noise. Prophecy, knowledge, and the faith that works miracles (v. 2) are great gifts, but they can be equally hollow if they are not exercised in love. "Understanding all mysteries" is probably a way to describe grasping the church's eschatological situation, just as giving relief to the poor and practicing self-dedication are colorful figures for religious zeal. "Giving my body over to be burned" perhaps has Dan 3:19f. in mind, if *kauthēsomai* is the better reading than "so that I may boast," *kauchēsomai*; but neither makes much more sense than the other. Without love, all endowments and activities come to naught.

The description of love turns out to be not something abstract but the concrete behavior of a person who loves (vv. 4-7). "Love bears" (v. 7) is literally, "love endures, supports *(stégei)* all things." This may be related to the saying of Simeon the Just in *M. Aboth* 2:1 that the world is supported by three things: Torah, Temple-worship, and the doing of kindnesses *(gemiloth = agápē?)*. Only God's love is indefectible, yet Paul describes it as it is found in humanity. It never ends (lit. "falls," v. 8) in the sense that perseverance under the Spirit's guidance brings with it the dependability of God.

Prophecies, knowledge, and tongues (vv. 8f.) are all imperfect revelations of God. When the complete comes, the partial will go, the imperfect yielding to the perfect (v. 10). Our knowledge of God now is indistinct like that in a mirror (v. 12)—no mercury-backed glass in the ancient world but polished metal or alabaster. Paul thinks of our present state of God-knowledge as that of childhood with adulthood to come, not as something already here as some Corinthians conceived it. As God knows us, we shall know God. Love will last (v. 13) because, unlike faith and hope, it of the three is the property of God.

Alleluia. Luke 19:38

Blessed is the king who comes in the name of the LORD: peace on earth and glory in heaven!

Luke 4:21-30

Luke's source is Mark 6 (Luke 4:24//Mark 6:4), but he places the incident at the beginning of Jesus' public activity instead of later on as programmatic for his ministry (see last Sunday's commentary on vv. 14-21). Luke describes the popular acceptance of Jesus in his hometown synagogue as favorable (vv. 21-22a), not merely a cause for wonderment (cf. Mark 6:2b). The proverb and challenge of v. 23 are peculiarly Lukan. He answers the opposition that Jesus aroused by having him cite God's deeds to non-Israelites through Elijah and Elisha (vv. 25ff.; cf. 1 Kgs 17:8-16 and 2 Kgs 5:1-14). This implicit criticism of Israel's lack of faith angers his audience, whose members threaten violence. A walk from the center of Nazareth southward to the nearest "brow of the hill on which their town was built" should have cooled the indignation of the townsfolk—the distance is about a mile and it is not properly a brow—but Luke's intent is theological, not geographic. Thus early in his narrative, he wishes to describe Jewish rejection of Jesus as a prelude to Gentile acceptance in "the year of the LORD's favor" (v. 19).

Verse 31 picks up from 14f. and is parallel to Mark 1:21. Luke has indicated in vv. 16-30 how his story will come out, hence he can proceed to the actual beginnings of Jesus' Galilean ministry.

❧❨

Fifth Sunday after the Epiphany / Fifth Sunday of the Year [5] (C)

ISAIAH 6:1-8, (9-13)

Last week featured the call of Jeremiah to the prophet's office, this week that of Isaiah more than a century earlier. The death date of King Uzziah of Judah was 742. Isaiah expresses an initial reluctance to fulfill the prophet's office on the ground of being unfit in speech (v. 5). His "guilt" and his "sin" are ritually purged away by a glowing coal from the temple altar (vv. 6f.). The proclaimer of the gospel in the Roman Rite prays for fitness of speech in Isaian terms, now in English but for centuries in Latin: *Munda cor meum, ac labia mea, omnipotens Deus, qui labia Isaiae prophetae calculo* [a coal] *mundasti ignito. . . .*

Presumably the oracles of the first five chapters were written after this majestic, inaugural vision. It is described as if taking place in the Temple (v. 1), the house of the Holy One of Israel. The LORD is seated on a throne like an oriental king. Seraphim (lit. "burning ones") do not appear elsewhere in the Bible. Their winged condition and their sacred song reveal them as angelic creatures in the heavenly court. The incense smoke and the shaking edifice convey the awesomeness of the Sinai theophany (cf. Exod 40:34). The threefold chant of the seraphim highlights the LORD's perfection of holiness (i.e., separateness); the title "LORD of hosts" earlier referred to God's character as warrior, from the days when the Ark accompanied Israel's armies into battle, but now it suggests the angelic hosts in full array.

One of the seraphim flies from the golden altar of perfumes (cf. 1 Kgs 6:20f.; 7:48; 2 Chron 26:16) in front of the sanctuary *(debir)*, the only altar inside the temple, putting an ember to the prophet's mouth. Thus cleansed, he is in a condition of readiness to do the Lord's bidding as designated spokesman (v. 8). That Isaiah experienced the vision while the majestic Temple liturgy was in progress is a historical circumstance that cannot be verified. It is safer to assert merely that the prophet-to-be framed his terrifying vision of the King (v. 5; cf. Exod 33:20) in his deity's earthly dwelling place.

This commission of Isaiah occurs as the prelude to the Immanuel prophecies (6:1—12:6), which touched on the events of the Aram-Ephraim crisis of 735–33 (see 1 Kgs 15:29; 16:19) in which Ahaz disregarded Isaiah's advice and sought an alliance with Tiglath-pileser III of Assyria.

A poem follows the prose account of Isaiah's vision of the seraphs in the Temple, one of whom touches his lips with a purifying live coal as he is sent on his prophetic mission. When the prophet says "*Hineni* (Here I am)," the LORD responds with a charge so cryptic that it has been misunderstood by Christians more than it has been understood. "Blind my people, make them deaf to your message, lest [NRSV, 'so that they may not'] they look, listen, comprehend, and turn and be healed" (v. 10). It is a case of Jewish irony, of course. The one thing the Lord wishes above all is that the people heed the message delivered through Isaiah, but it is put negatively as if to say: "All right. *Don't* listen, you might learn something!" The three Synoptic evangelists quote vv. 9f. (Mark 4:12 followed by Matt 13:14f. and Luke 8:10) as an explanation of why Jesus' teaching in parables is not being understood. That Semitic technique of instruction may have escaped Gentile crowds unfamiliar with it or Jews resistant to it, but Jesus, like any teacher, has no desire whatsoever not to be understood. Christian scholarship of the last two centuries has nonetheless mistakenly dubbed it "the blinding text" as if it were Jesus' intention to obfuscate by parabolic teaching. For a more extended discussion see under Matt 12:1-23 on Proper 10 [15] (A). Luke not surprisingly quotes the Isaian text to conclude his book of Acts, where Roman Jews come to Paul's lodgings "in great numbers" and are divided into acceptors and rejecters of his message. This allows Luke to conclude his two-volume work by once more repeating his theme that Gentiles largely received Paul's teaching and Jews largely did not. See Rodney Stark, *The Rise of Christianity: How the Obscure Marginal Jesus Movement Became the Dominant Religious Force in the Western World in a Few Centuries* (San Francisco: HarperSanFrancisco, 1996), on the probable reasons for the spread of that faith largely among Jews of the diaspora between 50 and 300, *contra* what the book of Acts and Paul's epistles have led Christians to suppose.

PSALM 138:[1-5, 7c-8]

1 CORINTHIANS 15:1-11

Paul inserts a traditional reading of the kerygma ("I *handed on* to you as of first importance what I in turn *had received*," v. 3) for the benefit of his innovating

Corinthians, as if to link them up with the churches of Damascus and Antioch in which he had confirmed the tradition he received by revelation (cf. Gal 1:12). His introductory terms *parélabon* and *parédōka* in v. 3 are equivalent to the Hebrew rabbinical terms *qibbel min* and *masar lᵉ*. What follows is marked by numerous non-Pauline words, among which are the Greek for "for our sins," "he was raised," "on the third day," and "the twelve." All of these are terms that the Synoptics incorporated from the tradition. Paul cites anew the gospel he has preached (v. 1) lest the Corinthians believe "in vain" (v. 2). Their faith would be purposeless if it did not include the conviction that Christ was raised up so that the dead might be raised up in turn (vv. 15f.). The conviction of the Corinthian spirituals that they were already sufficiently risen in baptism, hence had no need to be raised up at the *parousía*, elicits the traditional account of the appearances of the Risen One to the appointed witnesses.

Important to observe in the earliest written account we have of the appearances is the omission of any mention of the empty tomb (although, notice that "he was buried," v. 4); of appearances to the women; and of an angelophany. Paul's account uses the divine passive, "he was raised" (v. 4), which Mark, the next one to write, will also employ ("he has been raised up," 16:6). All the linguistic evidence points to a creedal formula worked up by a Hellenist Jewish community, perhaps at Damascus, from a tradition that goes back to the earliest Aramaic-speaking church. It consists of vv. 3b-6a, 6b seemingly being Paul's editorial comment. The witnesses are in two groups of three: Cephas, the Twelve, 500 believers; then James, all the apostles, and Paul. Throughout, the verb used is, "was seen" (vv. 5, 6, 7, 8). This, coupled with Paul's verb in Gal 1:16 ("[God] was pleased to *reveal* his Son to me"), has led to the conclusion that the kerygma describes the disclosure by God of the eschatologically resurrected *Christós*.

Fuller's theory that the first three appearances (vv. 5-6a) were concerned with the Church as eschatological community and the second three (vv. 7-8) with the inauguration of the apostolic mission of the Church has not found immediate favor (see R. E. Brown, Karl Donfried, et al., *Peter in the New Testament* [Minneapolis: Augsburg, 1973], 34–35). There is nothing geographic about the appearances, although we may connect Cephas and the Twelve with Galilee; the 500, James, and the apostles with Jerusalem; and Paul with the revelation he experienced wherever that was (1 Cor 9:1). They are spread over at least three years, lending support to the notion of resurrection and ascension as a single mystery separated only by Luke for narrative purposes (cf. Acts 1:3, 9).

Paul describes his own call to witness the risen Christ under the figure of a monstrous late birth (v. 8). In v. 9 he reports the only sin he ever seems conscious of, persecuting God's church (cf. Gal 1:13; with Stendahl and others we take his graphic account of human weakness in Rom 7:15-25 to be nonautobiographical). Besides Paul's having seen Christ last of all (v. 8), he calls himself the least of the apostles, even though he has worked harder than any of them (vv. 9, 10). This self-deprecation and elevation is possible only because he is so confident of his status as an apostle (1 Cor 1:1; Gal 1:1, 15f.; 2:7f.). It is God's grace or favor (v. 10) that has achieved this role and subsequent evangelizing activity in him. His concession in v. 11 that "I or they" may have brought the apostolic preaching to them supports the view that Cephas may also have preached in Corinth (see 1:12) or, if not that, emissaries from Cephas or James. Paul wishes to stress above all the harmony of the apostolic preaching and to eliminate claims of spiritual parentage as a cause of strife in the Corinthian church.

ALLELUIA. JOHN 1:14 AND 12B

The Word of God became a man and lived among us. He enabled those who accepted him to become children of God.

LUKE 5:1-11

Luke places the call of Simon, James, and John in the setting of a miraculous catch, unlike the more prosaic accounts of the call of the first disciples in Mark (1:16-20) and Matthew (4:18-22). Jesus has already met Simon in the preceding chapter at the healing of his mother-in-law, a narrative that comes after the call in the other Synoptics. The remarkable similarity of this account to Simon Peter's miraculous catch of fish in John 21:1-13, even to some identical vocabulary, has been observed. The two evangelists have preserved the same miracle story independently rather than borrowed from one another. Luke's account has undergone more development in certain details (nets almost breaking, v. 6; two boats almost sinking, v. 7), while in others (the enumeration of 153 fish) John's is more developed. It is impossible to settle whether the story first arose in Jesus' ministry or as a post-resurrection appearance. Inclining us toward the latter are the "O Lord" of v. 8 and Jesus' "Do not be afraid" of v. 10b (cf. Matt 28:10; Luke 24:37f.). If such is the case, then Luke acts here as Matthew seems to do in 16:16b-19 by forming the Petrine dialogue from post-resurrectional material. That he has changed the locale is clear from v. 8, where Simon's kneeling and his "Leave me, Lord" are details that originally doubtless took place on land rather than in a boat.

Luke makes the abundant catch of fish a symbol of Simon's future catching of people, a prefiguring in Jesus' lifetime of the missionary activity of Peter in Acts. Simon has caught nothing by his own power during the night (a symbol of darkness,

Luke 5:5, even though these are the hours when fishermen ply their trade). By day and in the power of Jesus Christ this sinful man has an abundant catch. James and John will also catch men (v. 10) but, in directing the Lord's promise to Simon alone, Luke is preparing for the dominant role he will have in Acts.

❧❧

Sixth Sunday after the Epiphany / Sixth Sunday of the Year [6] / Proper 1 (C)

For instructions on the readings of today and the Sundays through the 9 Epiphany and Transfiguration Sunday see under (A).

JEREMIAH 17:5-[8]10

The contents of this chapter are a kind of editor's miscellany, including poetry and prose on Sabbath observance (vv. 19-27, probably not from the prophet's own hand), declamations against persecutors (vv. 14-18), on true wisdom and on the LORD who is its source (vv. 5-13). More specifically, the present pericope (vv. 5-10) is a bit of wisdom poetry very close in spirit to Ps 1. Verses 9-10 reflect on the deceits of the human heart and v. 11 is a proverb on unjust acquisitions.

The great sin of "flesh," here meaning human nature (although like the Latin *caro* it also means meat in the Semitic tongues), is that it trusts in people and not in God. This misplaced confidence makes it like a scrubby bush in the desert. Were humanity to trust in the LORD, the "fountain of living water" (v. 13), its leaves would stay green in every season; fruit would adorn its branches even in time of drought.

PSALM 1[1-4, 6]

1 CORINTHIANS 15:12[16]-20

This continuation of last week's reading brings us to the reason why Paul has reviewed for his new believers the gospel he preached to them when he was in Corinth. Some are saying that there is no resurrection of the dead (v. 12). Their rejection of the belief is not on the Sadducean principle (viz., that the five books of Moses which alone they reckoned as Scripture did not teach it) or because of a Greek sense of horror at a notion of eternal life that would involve the body.

They reject the future resurrection of the dead because they think they already experience it as present.

The Christian preaching, at least in the condensed form reported by Paul, has not incorporated a promise of individual resurrection or immortality as Greek promises of salvation did. The former is there by implication from the fact of the death and resurrection of Jesus Christ. As an anticipation of the eschatological reality for all the just, his resurrection made eminent sense in the Jewish circles where it had originated. In Corinth it needed to be spelled out, as Paul has recently learned to his woe. The preaching of Christ raised from the dead, a matter common to all the apostles (vv. 11f.), demands the corollary of resurrection for all believers. The apostolic preaching would be pointless (v. 14) if, having proclaimed something about God's deed in Christ, it said nothing about what he meant to achieve in Christians. Paul's starting-point is that the Corinthians' present experience of risenness is illusory.

The "some of you" (v. 12) who hold this position may conceivably be believers in immortality, Greek-style, rather than in the Jewish reading of the mystery. Hans Lietzmann, for example, held that Paul simply misread their faith. A rereading of 4:8, however, reveals his scorn for their present state of satisfaction as already rich and reigning as kings. His charge against them is precisely that they "limit [their] hopes in Christ to this life only" (v. 19). The mentality of two Christians named Hymenaeus and Philetus is made explicit in 2 Tim 2:17f: they "have gone far wide of the truth in saying that the resurrection has already taken place." Paul himself teaches new life in Christ as a resurrection in some sense (see Rom 6:5-11; 2 Cor 5:15; Gal 2:19f.; also Col 3:1-4). In 1 Cor 15 he is dismayed that his strong figurative language has not been taken literally and that his teaching on bodily resurrection has not been understood as *future*.

Verse 16 sums up the three verses omitted from the reading. If we had done the writing, we might have framed the argument in reverse: "If Christ was not raised, then the dead are not raised." Paul makes the center of gravity the resurrection of the dead. If that is not to happen, then Christ's resurrection "did not take place" in the sense that it was a pointless display of God's power. Paul's sole argument against his opponents is the absurdity of a God who has acted to no purpose.

He goes on to threaten the Corinthians with the practical consequences of their misconception. The faith on which they pride themselves as saving is futile (v. 17) in that it does not remit their sins. It has been reposed in a risen Christ whose risenness does not ensure their own in the future. But there is no such risen Christ as that. Therefore their faith is misplaced; it is not saving. It leaves them still in a condition of sinfulness. Paul faces them with the hypothetical reality of sin's victory, not faith's victory. As if that were not enough he taunts them with the lack of hope of rising which would be the present state of their dead (v. 18). He then faces them with the absolute wretchedness of their own condition in terms of their theology (v. 19). They are bearing the dying of Jesus in their bodies (2 Cor 4:10) without the prospect of the life of Jesus being revealed in them—at least in no lasting way that outlives this life.

Having taken the Corinthians to the brink of despair by his logic, Paul then snatches them back by proclaiming the true gospel. Christ is raised and precisely as "first fruits"—the early harvest that anticipates the raising up of all the dead (v. 20).

Note that Paul's argument does not make salvation depend on the historical fact of the resurrection but on right faith in what God has accomplished in this mystery.

ALLELUIA. JOHN 6:54B AND 69B

Your words, Lord, are spirit and life, you have the words of everlasting life.

LUKE 6:17, 20-26

Luke's sermon is on the plain (v. 17), where the people remained behind while Jesus selected his disciples in prayer on the mountain (v. 12; cf. Mark 3:13-19, where likewise the mountain is the place of revelation as to who his associates will be). The "mountain" in Luke is a place where the people cannot come (9:37). It is a place of communion with God, leading to the Mount of Olives (22:39; Mark and Matthew situate his agony only at "a place called Gethsemane"). The "level stretch" of Luke consequently attains a special character as the place of meeting with people. Jesus' disciples, Galileans, are described as accompanied by a large crowd from Judaea and Jerusalem, Tyre and Sidon (v. 17). This may be a reiteration from 5:17 of the area covered by Jesus' ministry.

He presents four states of blessedness ("macarisms") in the second person, derived from his Q source. Matthew seems to have added other beatitudes from another place. Verse 20b parallels Matt 5:3; vv. 21a, Matt 5:6, but with the Jewish reference to righteousness eliminated; vv. 22f., Matt 5:11f. Luke has the title Son of Man (v. 22) and adds the blessing for weepers who will laugh (v. 21b), probably another version of the mourners who will be comforted (Matt 5:4). The woes (vv. 34ff.) are his own and consist in an exact role reversal of those mentioned in the beatitudes. He has done the same thing about the bringing down of God's enemies from their thrones in the "Magnificat," Mary's song (1:52ff.). The framing of the woes is a little clumsy, as the resumption of the narrative in v. 27 shows.

It is not easy to make a case for Luke's deemphasis of futurist eschatology from this passage, or to speak of his disinterest in poverty as an ideal. Quite simply, he retains the teaching of Jesus as he finds it in Q, editing it only slightly for a Gentile readership. The overturning of all received values is a historical theme in Jesus' preaching of God's reign and not merely a Lukan theme.

✍
Seventh Sunday after the Epiphany / Seventh Sunday of the Year [7] / Proper 2 (C)

GENESIS 45:3-11, 15

This touching narrative is the dramatic high point of the Joseph cycle as this highly placed Jew in the Pharaoh's court reveals his identity to his brothers. LM does not have it on a Sunday, only on Thursday of Year A (odd-numbered years) in the Fourteenth Week *in anno*. RCL worshipers are the richer for the inclusion. See also its occurrence in Proper 15 [20] (A). Joseph identifies himself twice (vv. 3, 4). He is completely forgiving of his brothers' deed against him and is large-hearted enough to see the providential hand in his rise to power in Egypt (v. 8). His siblings tried to rob him of life. He has been spared so as to preserve life for his family and the many other Hebrew survivors (v. 7). Knowing mysteriously that there are five more years of famine in prospect in Egypt (v. 11; see the Pharaoh's two dreams to this effect, 41:1-8, which Joseph interpreted), he has the brothers summon their old father Jacob with all his possessions and livestock to the land of Goshen northeast of the Nile delta. There they will have enough grain to survive as a result of Joseph's careful administration (see 39:4ff.; 41:33-41). The vignette ends with embraces and tears all around, including large ones for Benjamin, the youngest and Joseph's full brother, born of Rachel, who died at his birth (35:18f.).

The story has often been told in recent times of John XXIII, born Giuseppe Roncalli, who received a delegation of prominent Jews early in his bishopric of Rome with the words, "I am Joseph, your brother." The greeting did not ring hollow for they remembered how many Jewish lives he had schemed to save when he was the apostolic nuncio to Bulgaria and Turkey. One might have wished that all Christians had embraced all Jews as their siblings over the centuries, but nothing like that has been the case. It took the Shoah to begin to make it happen.

PSALM 37:1-11, 39-40

1 SAMUEL 26:2, 7-9, 12-13, 22-23

The lectionary makes judicious omissions in the earlier part of this story which do nothing to slow its tempo. Then, by leaving out vv. 14-21, it alters its tenor completely. The taunts of David—a man fighting for his life—shouted across the ravine, his curse of the evil counselors of Saul who have exiled him from his people and from God, and Saul's compunction over having acted the fool in David's regard are details omitted at a high price. What remains is merely an edifying tale featuring David's respect for the divine office of kingship and his readiness to forgive. Surely no lector will destroy the narrative by eliminating the latter part with such memorable phrases as: "For the king of Israel has come out to seek a single flea like one who hunts a partridge in the mountains" (v. 26b).

The tale told here in chap. 26 may well be another version of that in chap. 24. Both describe David's betrayal by Ziphites (cf. 23:19; 26:1) and speak of Saul's picked force as being of three thousand men. David's awe at the prospect of harming the king is repeated (see 24:11; 26:11). So is Saul's admission that David will succeed him (24:21; 26:25)—in the second case, in the form of a blessing on all the young man's endeavors.

Clearly the shape of this narrative is determined by its outcome. It is official military history sanctioned by the soldier-king who achieved the coup. Hence, David's youthful awe at Saul's kingship may be a much later device to encourage respect for his own. It is hard but not impossible to read between the lines of the stories in the David cycle and come to some conclusions about the complex characters of the two men. Surely 1 Samuel reports on one of the most delicate struggles for power in history, complicated—as is so often the case—by religious sentiment, possibly even by faith.

PSALM 103:1-4, 8, 10, 12-13

1 CORINTHIANS 15:35-38, 42-50[45-49]

The first four verses of this lection (35-38) provide the reality in nature that will serve as Paul's analogy for burying the dead in the earth (42-49). He thinks the challenge to the possibility of resurrection of the body on the last day to be pure folly, or at least he says so (v. 36). Seeds planted in the earth seem to be the easy case but, since crops come up every spring but no one has ever known of a person to come up from the grave, Paul's charge of "Fool!" appears overly harsh. He goes on, however, to give a basic lesson in plant biology. The bare seed is not the full-grown wheat. It has to be buried in the ground in apparent death to become such. This reminds Paul that species beget species, a springboard to say that there are different intensities of heat and light of the heavenly bodies. Then he is into the difference in what comes up from what goes down leading to his main point, namely, that a body of flesh will be succeeded by a body of glory. Aha! That body will be like the body not of the first Adam but of the Last, who arose a spirit body capable of giving life.

Genesis 2:7 has: "And so the man became a living being" *(nephesh ḥayyah).* Paul adds "first" to Adam because he will designate Christ as the last Adam in the same verse (45). He also adds the name "Adam" to the "human" *(ánthrōpos)* of the LXX, a duplication. The first man was merely a *psychē zōsa,* an animate creature. Christ by contrast is a *pneûma zōopoioûn,* a man of spirit who enlivens in the Spirit (cf. John 6:63). The adjective "natural" *(psychikón)* in v. 44 has preceded the description of Adam as *psyché.* He is the begetter of a race of ordinary humanity while Christ leads off a humanity indwelt by Spirit. Earth and dust are the components of the unredeemed race whereas the principle of redemption comes from heaven (v. 47). This twofold parentage results in two progenies that are respectively "of the dust" and "of heaven" (48). Redeemed people of the earth that we are, we bear the likeness or image of both the man of earth and the man of heaven (vv. 48f.).

Paul perhaps drew on rabbinic developments of a cosmic or heavenly man who was to be complementary to the father of the race. Here, as so often in the use of Christ as antitype, the apostle is able to specify the myth by supplying an actual historical resurrection (see Rom 1:4). The Lord qualifies perfectly as justifier of the eschatological hope for all because, as Spirit-filled, he becomes the archetype of those who will be raised up on the last day. It is the Spirit they already possess in measure who will accomplish this. Paul's main theme in this chapter is *bodies,* not the moral likeness of the just to Christ. Hence he describes the different kinds of bodies there are (cf. Phil 3:21), with special reference to the future reality of the resurrected body. It is this reality that some in Corinth deny.

ALLELUIA. JOHN 8:12

I am the light of the world, says the Lord; whoever follows me will have the light of life.

LUKE 6:27-38

Luke's development of the love of one's enemies is derived from Q (cf. Matt 5:44; 39–42; 7:12; 5:46f., 45, 48; 7:1f.). His special material which is not contained in Matthew includes: "Do good to those who hate you; bless those who curse you" (v. 27), where also Luke has "abuse" for Matthew's "persecute" (v. 28); he omits mention of going two miles rather than one (Matt 5:41) and the Matthean equation of the Golden Rule with "the law and the prophets" (Matt 7:12). Where Matthew has even Gentiles doing as much, Luke has sinners (Luke 6:33//Matt 5:47); Luke also changes greeting your brothers in public to doing good to others.

Verses 34f. are proper to Luke, with an echo at the end of Matthew's rain upon "the just and the unjust" (5:45). Luke asks for a compassion like that of the Father (v. 36), whereas Matthew wishes disciples to be perfect. Lastly, the graphic figure of a full measure of grain poured into one's garment is proper to Luke only.

In general, the supposition regarding this passage is that Luke has "Gentilized" Q for his purposes just as Matthew has "Rabbinized" it for his. The spirit of Jesus shines through both, namely, doing more than is asked or expected.

❧❦❧

Eighth Sunday after the Epiphany / Eighth Sunday of the Year [8] / Proper 3 (C)

SIRACH 27:4-7

These four proverbs are all on the same theme, namely, as the "damsel" by the firelight said to Peter, "Surely thy art *one* of them; forspeech bewrayeth thee" (KJV). With examples from the colander that separates grain from chaff, the clay fired in the kiln, the fruit of a tree that discloses its cultivation, the point is made that speech betrays a person's character. Speak well of no one until you are justified in doing so. None of the four proverbs says how much speech must be heard before a fair judgment can be passed. A fifth proverb might encapsulate the idea.

ISAIAH 55:1-13

For a commentary see Proper 10 [15].

PSALM 92:1-4, 12-15[2-3, 13-16]

1 CORINTHIANS 15:51-[54]58

By "a mystery" Paul means a hidden truth to which he has been given access about what will happen at the end (cf. Rom 11:25). This lection is a continuation of his vision of the way Christ will hand the kingdom, over which he must reign, to God the Father (15:24-28; cf. 1 Thess 4:13-18). "All we" who will not die but be changed are the Christian believers and others like them to whom he has brought the gospel. The change will come instantaneously at the trumpet's sound and the perishable body will put on imperishability. The Greek mind could take in the body's freedom from decay (*aphtarsía*, vv. 43, 51) more readily than immortality or deathlessness (*athanasía*, v. 53). The perishable, mortal body will put on both of these new qualities at the last day, of this Paul is sure (v. 54). He is so certain that victory has overcome death by Christ's triumph (v. 54b; cf. Isa 25:8f.) that he can use a half-remembered phrase from Hosea (13:14) in an opposite sense than the one the prophet intended. There the sting of death is used as a threat by the LORD whose eyes at the time "are closed to compassion" because of Israel's flirtation with false gods. Paul believed death's sting removed—but not entirely. Sin remains. Its power resides in the Law, which for Paul is always a means to identify what is sin and what is not. He never denies it that primary function, which must have been the way he thought of it from his youth onward. Victory over sin comes from another source or rather through another person, who has done what the Law could not do, namely, removed the sting of sin and its consequence, death (v. 57). Confidence in this victory requires a human response: steadfastness in "the work of the Lord" (v. 58), a holding fast to the saving deed of Christ.

ALLELUIA. PHILIPPIANS 2:15A; 16A

See that you are inncoent, shining like lights in the world as you hold on to the word of life.

LUKE 6:39[-45]49

Jesus' saying about the unreasonableness of one blind man leading another (v. 39) occurs in Matt 15:14 in a context of the Pharisees as blind guides, Matthew's contemporary opponents of the gospel. There was no sensitivity in the ancient world to what were until recently called the physically handicapped. Verse 40 has its parallel in Matt 10:24f., which contains the slight twist that "it is enough for the disciple to be like his teacher," settling for similarity over mastering the teaching fully (Luke 6:30). The speck and the log/beam/plank saying appears almost verbatim in Matt 7:3-5. That evangelist has removed the Lukan impossibility of seeing the log in one's own eye (v. 42). The inability of a bad tree to bear good fruit (6:44a), which may have been prompted by Sir 27:6, is expanded as Matt 7:17-20; 12:33, the form in which it has become better known. Luke 6:45 (cf. Matt 12:35) seems to derive more directly from the Sirach proverb. Verse 46 about calling on Jesus as "Lord, Lord" is likewise much expanded in Matt 7:21-23, which turns it into a rejection of certain disciples at the judgment whom that evangelist considers unworthy. Contention in the paradise of the early church even among prophets and exorcists! The remaining image of houses built safely and unsafely as reflecting lives faithfully and unfaithfully lived in response to Jesus' teaching (Luke 6:46-49) is found in Matt 7:24-27 in close but not identical wording. One thinks of expensive homes demolished by mudslides in our day and apartment buildings threatened by angry seas.

❧☙

Ninth Sunday after the Epiphany / Ninth Sunday of the Year [9] / Proper 4 (C)

1 KINGS 8:22-23, 41-43

The special importance of the prayer attributed to Solomon is the content of the last three verses of the lection, after all that is said of God's majesty, the newly completed Temple with the solemn oaths sworn there, and the prayers of petition uttered in it in times of drought or famine (vv. 23-40). The prayer must have been written while the magnificent structure stood. It could not have been part of the final editing of the book done in the Babylonian exile. The hope expressed represents an early outreach to the Gentile world. Foreigners are expected to come in awe and pray "toward [not in] this house," having heard of the LORD's mighty hand and outstretched arm. The Israelite author of the prayer cannot imagine that the Temple would not incline a foreigner to believe in the God of Israel, the one true God.

PSALM 96:1-9

PSALM 117:1-2

GALATIANS 1:1-12[1-2, 6-10]

RCL employs readings from this letter on the same six successive Sundays starting today, which is the Ninth Sunday of the Year, as it is for LM. The letter has an aggrieved tone throughout. Paul has learned that some churches in the Roman province of Galatia (1:2b; *which* churches he does not say) have adopted a "different gospel" than the one he first brought them. The initial indication of his displeasure comes with the omission of a thanksgiving to God for their fidelity after the salutation, as in all his other extant letters. He gets immediately into recording his astonishment that these churches have been led astray by teachers who have come after him, perverters of the gospel as he calls them (v. 8). He declares such false evangelists *anathema*, "accursed" in English, the word in the LXX for the "ban" *(ḥerem)*. Some in Galatia must be accusing him of presenting the gospel in such a way as to win human approval (v. 10). One must read on in order to learn what this can mean. Paul's insistence on his having received the gospel direct, that is, from Jesus Christ and not from any human intermediaries (v. 11), may mean that the charge of "trying to please people" (v. 10) is rooted in his claim of special privilege among the evangelizers who had not known Jesus in his lifetime. But as we read on and learn from this one source of the few and interrupted contacts Paul had with the Jerusalem apostles, we discover that he did not insist on Titus's circumcision in Jerusalem, and begin to see how he was thought to be currying human approval. The accusation of the later "false apostles" must have been that Paul tried to please Gentile new believers by telling the men that they did not need to be circumcised or adhere to portions of ritual Law (see 2:7ff.; 10-14).

ALLELUIA. JOHN 3:16

God so loved the world that he gave his only Son, that all who believe in him might have eternal life.

LUKE 7:1-10

Luke has this narrative in common with Matthew (8:5-13) but not Mark, while John develops its main lines quite differently (4:46b-54). It is sometimes described as "a miracle at a distance" and most often singled out as the way one person who speaks authoritatively recognizes another who can achieve an effect by a word of command. John calls the petitioner an "official" in the empire *(basilikós)*. The person near death is variously a slave *(doulos*, Luke), a servant *(pais*, Matthew), and the man's son *(huiós*, John). No oppressed people has ever been on warm terms with the occupier's army. The position of Palestinian Jewry vis-à-vis Rome was no different. But all who are under another's heel know which of its functionaries are antagonistic to them and which not; some conquerors in turn realizing that they are "only there to do their job." That the commander of a hundred men would have gone so far as to build a meeting place for impoverished Jews was not unthinkable. Many a British officer in the days of the *raj* in India and the United Nations command in our day did—and does—"liberate" enough material and person power to relieve the needs of local people who never invited the foreign troops to take over in their land. Western liturgies have incorporated the Vulgate's demurrer at communion time: "Domine, non sum dignus ut intres sub tectum meum, sed tantum dic verbo et sanabitur anima [spirit, not slave or son] mea" (7:6b). No questions have been raised as to who is worthy enough for the Eucharistic Christ to enter one's body except by those who think worthiness an ill-fitting word, nor how much healing is achieved by such a reception. It is the right prayer for the right time.

🙟🙠

Last Sunday after the Epiphany / Transfiguration Sunday (C)

Exodus 34:29-35

One cannot think of a better choice than this pericope for a feast on which Jesus' face "changed in appearance" as he was praying on a mountain. Proximity to deity was the reason for the holy glow in the two cases, centuries apart. The veil is the important detail in this one. It keeps Moses from addressing fellow Israelites with the same familiarity as when he speaks with God. The basic reason seems to be that the shining of his face is such that their eyes need protection from its brilliance, of which he seems unaware (v. 29). That is the way it is with the saints. They know well the holiness of God. They are the last to claim any of it as their own.

Psalm 99

2 Corinthians 3:12—4:2

NRSV translates the glory of Moses' face as that which has now been "set aside" (*katargouménou*) each time it appears in vv. 7, 11, and 13. NIV and NAB, along with RSV, prefer "is fading." Such was Paul's idea, and it is not a good one, in the first place because Exodus does not say so. He wishes to contrast the greater glory, for which he devises the phrase "the ministry of the Spirit," with the lesser glory that he thinks cannot have been permanent (v. 11). Things get worse as the apostle proceeds to today's reading. In his discouragement at the small number of fellow Jews who heed his preaching, he sees in the image of the veil on Moses' face a foreshadowing of the incapacity of the Israel of his day to recognize the truth of Christ when the old covenant is read out. Only when one turns to the Lord (Jesus) is the veil removed (v. 16). Any number of biblical images could have served to illustrate the improved condition of Jew and Gentile alike when they heard passages of the LXX read in public worship. Christ makes a huge difference for all who believe in him but the "hardened minds" of Moses' contemporaries were no part of that picture. Most modern worshipers are ignorant of an Israel portrayed in medieval statuary as a maiden blindfolded, but they know a bad attitude attributed to Jews when they hear one. This lection casts an evil shadow on any Christian Sunday and has no place in lectern or ambo without a thirty-minute lecture explaining that Paul's outlook on Jewish nonacceptance of Christ has had no relevance since the year 150 or so.

LUKE 9:28-36, (37-43)

For commentary see 2 Lent (C) and, on Matt 17:1-9, 2 Lent (A).

Luke (37-43a) and Matthew (17:14-21) seem to derive this healing story from Mark (9:14-20), who provides more details than either. The narrative follows the Transfiguration on a mountain in all three as if to stress that family woes continue despite the revelation of Christ in glory. Jesus is approached by a man out of the crowd who begs him to heal his son, his only offspring, but whether he is a boy or man we are not told. The chief symptoms are convulsions. Matthew says "he is moonstruck" *(seléniázetai),* hence the NAB and older renderings identify him as a lunatic; NRSV and NIV call his malady epilepsy, either because of the violent symptoms (see Mark 9:17; Matt 17:15) or because the medical knowledge of the day attributed its seizures to the phases of the moon. Mark has Matthew's self-destructive symptoms but confines his analysis to saying that the son has a mute and deaf spirit (Mark 9:17, 25). The son has a demon in Matthew (17:18), a demon and an unclean spirit in Luke (9:42). The point of the story is that even as the troubled youth was brought to Jesus, he healed him with a rebuke to the unclean spirit. Luke has the crowds in awe of God's majesty while the other two Synoptics make the healing an occasion for faith "the size of a mustard seed."

Tenth Sunday after the Epiphany /
Tenth Sunday of the Year [10] / Proper 5 (C)

1 Kings 17:8-16, [17-24]

See Proper 27 [32] (B) for a commentary on vv. 10-16. That story of the meal and the oil not running out until the rains came in response to the prophet's prayer is followed by another, namely, of the revival of the son of the Sidonian widow. She speaks of "the LORD your God" to indicate that Yhwh is not her deity. Moreover, she is suspicious of this man of another religion, like many a modern individual in the presence of a strange clergyman (v. 18). Has he come to do harm? Is not the death of her son quite enough trouble? (See v. 18.) The prophet asks for the lifeless body of the son, lays it out on his own bed, and then utters a prayer for the boy's resumed breathing (vv. 19f.). The threefold stretching of Elijah's body upon his is ritualized and may not be dismissed as a case of cardiopulmonary resuscitation (v. 21). Clearly a wonder is being reported. The church fathers delighted in their homilies to liken the spread-eagled Elijah to Jesus on the cross who restored sinful humanity to life by contact with every human limb and sense, encompassing our humanity completely. By the effect of Jesus' prayer like Elijah's, we know him to be a man of God whose mouth speaks a word of truth (v. 24).

Psalm 146

Psalm 30[2, 4-6, 11-13]

Galatians 1:11-[-19]24

Last Sunday's lection continues this morning without interruption, linked by the repetition of vv. 11 and 12. Paul's autobiographical review has to feature his youthful commitment to the pieties of Pharisaism (which has fidelity to the oral Law at its core) because such fidelity on his part some in Galatia are calling in question. Verse 15 echoes Jeremiah's prenatal vocation, like Paul's, to preach to "the nations" *(ha goyim, en toîs éthnesin)*. Only God's revelation of the Son with a direct charge could have persuaded Paul that the special signs of Jewishness ("the traditions of my ancestors," v. 14) were not to be imposed on a Gentile world. His self-declared route into Arabia (the land southeast of Israel, not the land mass named by the Saudi clan for itself early in the twentieth century), and then north to Damascus, is at odds with Acts 9:26-30. There was no immediate contact with the Jerusalem apostles in Paul's account. His first visit after time spent in Nabatea and Syria (both Gentile territory) occurred when the revelation of Christ was three years behind him. A home visit to his native Cilicia came after his brief encounter with Cephas and James. It is evident that Paul wishes to stress the fact that his movements are directed by Jesus whom he calls "the Lord," not by men whom he views as peers in his apostolic calling. When he describes himself as the subject of rumor and report in the Judaean churches (vv. 22-24) he is distancing himself from a home base as many missionaries have to do. With the imposition of hands the one God, Son, and Spirit becomes the author of every apostolic calling.

Alleluia. Luke 3:16

I baptize you with water but one mightier than I will baptize you with the Holy Spirit and with fire.

Luke 7:11-17

Anyone who stands on the high ground at the south end of Nazareth can see the plain of Esdraelon (also called Jezreel) falling away like a carpet of grain at one's feet and the village of Nain in the distance. The present writer had the good fortune to be present in the village church on the one day of the year the Eucharist is celebrated to commemorate the Gospel miracle. The villagers are entirely Muslim, but the church, which is not ancient, is testimony that the village was not always so. The Franciscan friar who presided came from Nazareth, but no matter. Is not Issa who by his word and his touch gave a mother's only son back to her celebrated as the next to last of the prophets in the Holy Qur 'an? There is no better way than this to observe the miracle in a way that goes back to the Middle Ages and before—probably even before the time of the Prophet, when the land was Christian. Luke alone provides this story, but shortly he will tell of the resuscitation of Jairus's daughter (8:49-56), which it closely resembles.

❧ Season of Lent ❧

❧ Ash Wednesday (C)

As in (A).

❧ First Sunday in Lent (C)

DEUTERONOMY 26:1[4-10]-11

Earlier in Deuteronomy, a similar historical summary of reasons for belief has occurred in 6:20-25. The present rite of thanksgiving for harvest with the credo it contains (vv. 5b-10a) comes at the end of the laws section of Deuteronomy (12:1—26:19). The law enjoining the presentation of the first fruits is probably very early; here it serves as the introduction to the faith statement concerning deliverance from Egypt and blessedness in the new land.

"Some first fruits" are to be brought to the presiding priest in the central sanctuary in acknowledgment of the LORD's bounty. In v. 10 the worshipers themselves deposit the offerings rather than the priest, as in v. 4.

The declaration of vv. 5b-10a is thought to be very old. It summarizes the contents of Genesis through Judges. The individual Israelite's "father" (v. 5) is Jacob who bestowed his name on the people. NAB suggests in a footnote that "Aramean" either refers to the origin of the patriarchs in Aram Naharaim (cf. Gen 24:10; 25:20; 28:5; 31:20, 24), the region around Haran on the River Balikh, modern Turkey, or is used merely in the sense of "nomad." Of importance here is the joining of history to harvest festival or, as G. Henton Davies describes it, "the combination of rite and creed [which] sets the pattern for Israel's feasts." Jews are not fond of the Christian word "creed," understandably. A better description of vv. 5b-10a might be "a summary of God's beneficent intervention in Israel's history."

474

PSALM 91:1-2, 9-16

ROMANS 10:8B-13

In vv. 5-13 a contrast is set up between the righteousness that comes through the Law and that which is based on faith. Deuteronomy 30:11-14 refers to God's command to Israel, and speaks in praise of its accessibility and the ease with which it can be carried out (v. 13). Paul accommodates this passage by making the Deuteronomic *mitsvah* the word of faith that he preaches (v. 8). The creedal formula, "Jesus [Christ] is Lord" has already appeared in 1 Cor 12:3 and Phil 2:11. Here it is made the central affirmation of faith. Paul is not contrasting profession of Jesus' Lordship "on the lips" with belief in his resurrection "in the heart." The two are complementary aspects of the one mystery of Christ. The same is true of "justification" and "salvation" (v. 10) in this context. They are not successive steps or stages but part of a chiastic, i.e., X-shaped, rhetorical device to convey a single reality; thus: confess–believe, believe–confess (vv. 9f.).

Paul quotes the Deuteronomist in a version close to but not identical with the LXX (v. 8 = Deut 30:14). Deuteronomy "is full of the notion that God's relations with his people rest on grace" (C. K. Barrett), so it is doubtful that fulfillment of God's "word" is understood by the Deuteronomist as mere observance of a command. Paul has quoted Lev 18:5 in v. 5, which says of God's statutes and ordinances that "the one who carries them out will live by keeping them." He employs this nomistic understanding of fulfillment (as again at Gal 3:12) to summarize in the Law's own words what he understands the Law to mean. Even though the Levitical author's view of the Law is that it is life-giving, Paul feels that he must contrast Leviticus unfavorably with Deuteronomy, making the former speak of the "justice / righteousness that comes from the Law" but the latter of "justice that comes from faith." Since Baruch 3:29 interprets Deut 30:11-14 to refer to heavenly wisdom, Paul is on solid ground in applying these verses to Christ, who for him is the wisdom of God.

The "word of faith" (v. 8) is the gospel as Paul preaches it. It is immediately available to those to whom it has been brought. It is the occasion for a faith that justifies, a creedal confession *(homología)* that saves. Neither Jew nor Greek has the advantage over the other since this gift of faith is available indiscriminately to both. Paul in v. 13 concludes with the triumphant declaration from Joel 3:5 that all who call on the name of the Lord—viz., with faith in Christ—will be saved.

Verse before the Gospel. Matthew 4:4b

One does not live by bread alone but by every word that comes from the mouth of God.

Luke 4:1-13

The Markan temptation narrative is brief (1:12f.) and is characterized by signs of eschatological consummation—community between man and beast, ministering angels, "the desert as the place of Yahweh's marriage with Israel as well as the Satanic temptations" (H. Flender, *St. Luke: Theologian of Redemptive History* [Philadelphia: Fortress Press, 1967]). Matthew begins the tendency to use it as instructive for the Christian under temptation. Luke, drawing on Q like Matthew, goes further in providing community members with an example for their own behavior. He omits the details of the devil's taking Jesus up a very high mountain (v. 5//Matt 4:8) and the ministry of angels (v. 13//Matt 4:11), possibly because these are messianic signs. Instead, Luke portrays Jesus as the new Adam (cf. 3:38), prototype of every Christian in temptation and in victory over it. Satan tempts Jesus less as the Messiah (see Matthew's heavy dependence on Deut 6 and 8 and Ps 91 for Israel's failure where Jesus the Messiah succeeds) than as an ordinary man by subjecting him to "every temptation" (v. 13). Luke has Satan leave Jesus alone "until an opportune time" (v. 13). That time comes in 22:3 when Satan takes possession of Judas, and at the supper table when Jesus commends the disciples for standing by him in his "trials" (v. 28).

Luke places the second and third scenes in reverse order from Matthew, putting the parapet of the Temple last. Perhaps it is his preoccupation with Jerusalem that accounts for the choice of that site as the climax of the exchange of scriptural texts. Jesus vanquishes the devil as he must, being the Son of God (vv. 3, 9).

❧ ❧

Second Sunday in Lent (C)

Genesis 15:1[5]-12, 17-18

The nobility of Abraham's character has been underscored in the previous chapter. He will not take "a thread or a sandal-thong" in spoil from the king of Sodom (14:2) whom he has successfully defended against Chedorlaomer king of Elam and his three allies (see 14:23). Bera king of Sodom made the famous offer of booty to the Hebrews if he might have all the civilian captives. In its Vulgate rendering this became a Christian charter of missionary zeal. "*Da mihi animas, cetera tolle tibi*" (14:21, "Give me souls and you may have all the rest"). Abram's determination not to profit by the military skill he displayed in behalf of his nephew Lot, who was living in Sodom at the time, is made by the Yahwist author to lead into the LORD's offer of a covenant.

Verses 4 and 5 are from the E narrative but all the rest of today's reading is J material. The promise of a son for Abraham, hinted at in 13:16, is reiterated in Gen 22:17; 28:14 (where, as in 13:16, the dust of the earth is substituted for the stars of the heavens); Exod 32:13 and Deut 1:10. Abram "put his faith" in the LORD, who credited it to him as "an act of righteousness" (*tsedaka*, v. 6). His right attitude toward God, in other words, gave him title to the fulfillment of God's promise. He will have his own, boundless issue as his heir and not have to fall back, childless, on his steward, Eliezer of Damascus (v. 3).

The LORD authorizes the possession of Canaan by Abram (v. 7) and suggests as a sign of it a covenant to be cut (vv. 10f.) with Abram (see v. 18). This mysterious, symbolic action is illumined somewhat by Jer 34:18ff., where violators of the pact are promised they will be split like the calf and their corpses left for the beasts and birds of prey (cf. Gen 15:11). Abram undergoes a trance like the sleep of Adam as darkness falls, fascinated by the mystery before which he trembles in awe (v. 12).

The brazier and the torch that pass between the divided parts of the carcasses (v. 17) are a consuming fire that represents the LORD who repeats his promise (v. 18), saying that Abram's descendants (lit. "seed") will possess the land from Egypt to the Euphrates. Righteousness is basically his—a gift to humankind. The LORD passes symbolically through the covenant thus cut to show unmistakably that he means to keep it.

PSALM 27[1, 7-9, 13-14]

PHILIPPIANS 3:17—4:1

Paul has no hesitance in proposing himself and those who are faithful to his example as guides for the conduct of the Philippians (v. 17). As Christ lives in Paul, so should he live in Paul's new believers. The Apostle deplores any departure from this standard (v. 18), somewhat in the way that 1 John does in describing members who leave the ranks of believers (2:18f.).

Verse 19 has often been popularly taken to describe gormandizers, but the belly as god is perhaps a Pauline euphemism for lustful conduct—or it may be a scornful reference to kosher diet imposed on Gentiles. What lies ahead for such offenders is *apóleia*, utter "destruction." It is possible that the "things of this world" are material benefits but equally that we have in the term a contrast with the "heavenly," namely, the gifts available in Christ through faith. The earthbound among the Philippians are, in that sense, fools from Paul's point of view. They are not friends of the cross of Christ but its enemies since they do not accept it in faith (v. 18).

Christians have their true citizenship in heaven, Paul says, since it is from there that Christ shall come to assert his Lordship (v. 20). The language is political in that Christ is viewed as the redeeming emperor. His power (v. 21) will be exercised only in such a way, however, as to transform our bodies from their present "humiliation" (*tapeínōsis*, the word rendered by "lowliness" in Mary's Magnificat) into conformity with Christ's "body of glory" (cf. 1 Cor 15:35-49; 2 Cor 5:1-5). That last phrase of v. 21 resembles the picture of final consummation in 1 Cor 15:24-28.

In the intensity of his exhortation to the Philippians to stand firm in the Lord he calls them "beloved" twice in the same sentence (4:1). They can be his joy and crown in the last age only if they live heavenly, not earthly lives, i.e., in the Lord.

Luke 13:31-35

Jesus headed for Jerusalem, says Luke, because the days for his departure *(éxodon)* were "fulfilled / about be accomplished" (9:31). As he proceeded southward (13:22) he was approached by some Pharisees who, in the only friendly reference to them in the Gospels (but see Luke 7:36; 14:1), warn him that Herod Antipas, tetrarch of Galilee, wished to take his life. No reason is given why he would wish to do so. One can only speculate a fear of Jesus' popular acceptance by great crowds. Jesus calls him a fox and says he means to continue with his work of exorcising and healing over a biblical three days, meaning until the work is done. None of the writing prophets of the Bible was killed in Jerusalem, so the proverbial utterance of v. 33 is a puzzle. Were other prophetic voices known to have been silenced there by violence? The metaphor of a hen and chickens may reflect unsuccessful attempts to advance the Gospel in Jerusalem in the decades after the Resurrection. The "house that is left to you" has to be the Temple, spared another forty years.

Verse before the Gospel. Matthew 17:5

From the cloud came a voice that said: "This is my beloved Son; listen to him."

LUKE 9:28-36

Luke substitutes eight days for the six of Mark's interval, probably to relate it to the resurrection by making the eighth day the beginning of a new week. He expands the basically Markan transfiguration narrative (Mark 9:2-8) by having Moses and Elijah, who "appear in glory," discuss the "departure" *(éxodon)* he was about to fulfill in Jerusalem (v. 31). His account looks forward to Jesus' anticipatory glorification on another mount than this one, that of Olives (19:37), his agony in the same place (19:45), and his ascent into heaven from there (Acts 1:12). In Luke's Gospel there is a heavenly apparition (22:43) as in the Transfiguration; also his disciples—not named in Luke, unlike Mark and Matthew—who sleep during his agony, sleep here before awakening to the vision (v. 32; no parallels).

The disciples are caught up into the cloud and are afraid (v. 34; again Luke only). They keep silence about what they have seen (v. 36; cf. vv. 21f., referred to by some as the "passion secret in Luke").

"Listen to him" (v. 35) was the injunction concerning the Moses-like prophet of Deut 18:19. Jesus for Luke is this prophet.

❧❧
Third Sunday in Lent (C)

ISAIAH 55:1-9

For a commentary see Propers 13 [18] and 20 [25] (A).

PSALM 63:1-8

EXODUS 3:1-8A, 13-15

Morton Smith has written that "The Old Testament is primarily concerned with the cult of the god Yahweh. It undertakes to show how this cult was established, [and] to outline the rules for its practice. . . . In sum, the purposes of the Bible are to tell the worshipers of Yahweh what they should do and to persuade them that they had better do it" (*Palestinian Parties and Politics that Shape the Old Testament* [New York: Columbia Univ. Press, 1971]). Smith goes on to remark that even if we accept the Bible's story that all Israel came out of Egypt, that story also knows of the mixed multitude that accompanied the Israelites, the peoples— Midianites and Moabites—who became associated with them in the desert, and of the others enumerated in v. 8—who joined them after their entrance into the promised land.

Verses 1-5, 7, 13-14 have been identified as Priestly, vv. 6, 8-12 as Yahwist, and vv. 15-20a as Elohist. Jethro, the Midianite priest of P, seems to be the Reuel of 2:16, 18 (J or Yahwist), who some scholars think was originally Hobab the Kenite (see Num 10:29; Judg 4:11) of the clan of Reuel. Midian in ancient sources is the strip of land along the east side of the Gulf of Aqaba south of modern Elat, today the northwestern extremity of Saudi Arabia. It is the only area in the entire region where there have been active volcanoes in historical times. This would tell in its favor as the location of Sinai (cf. Exod 19:16, 18) except for the fact that so many other indications favor the Sinai peninsula.

The mountain Horeb (v. 1) of E and D is evidently the Sinai of J and P where the Law was given (cf. 19:10-23). As has been pointed out in this commentary, this mountain is unlikely to have been the massive peak near the tip of the Sinai peninsula singled out as Jebel Musa since the fourth century of the Christian era. The actual Mount Sinai probably lay northwest of the Gulf of Aqaba on the northern part of the peninsula, modern Jebel Helal, with the nomadic Midianites found in the region of Kadesh-barnea east of it. They seem to have had no scruple worshiping the LORD along with the Israelites at the "mountain of God" (cf. 19:1-12) and may even have brought from their homeland the tradition of volcanic activity at a sacred peak.

An angel of the LORD (*malak* = "messenger," v. 1) is a characteristic of E but appears here in J. The word for a thornbush *(sĕnĕ)* resembles Sinai, perhaps as an intended ingredient of the theophany. The phenomenon known as St. Elmo's fire, in which pointed objects seem to emit static electricity during a storm, may have underlain the original narrative. In any event, fire or lightning is the sign of the Lord's activity (cf. Gen 15:17; Exod 13:21; 19:16), made more remarkable by the fact that here the bush goes unconsumed (v. 2). The occurrence is mentioned again in the Bible only at Deut 33:16, in the blessing of Moses spoken over Joseph. Jesus refers to the LORD's self-identification as God of the patriarchs as in "the story about the bush" (Mark 12:26//Luke 20:37) since there was no citation by chapter and verse in his day.

Moses "is afraid to look at God." He hides his face and removes his sandals as a sign of his awe (vv. 5f.). God (*Elohim*, a generic term for deity) is self-described as the same one whom Abraham, Isaac, and Jacob acknowledged. He will bring to completion the deliverance of the Israelites from Egyptian oppression (vv. 7f.). The name God gives to Moses will serve as proof of his intention: "I am who am" (*ehyeh asher ehyeh*, 14a) or, more simply, "I am" (*ehyeh*, 14b). Earlier (v. 12), the same verb form has connoted God's intent to be with this people, which leads some to render the divine name as "I will be [with you]." The hope in such a translation is to convey a sense of dynamic presence rather than metaphysical self-existence. The latter Greek concept was contributed to much later by the Septuagintal translation, *ho nōn*, the "Being" or "One who is." The word play on the Hebrew verb "to be" *(hayah)* is an example of the familiar popular etymology of the Bible. The actual origins of the name YHWH are unknown but are at least traceable back to "Yah" or "Yahu." Some take this to be an onomatopoeic shout to acknowledge divinity.

This passage marks the first occurrence in E of the proper name of God, "The LORD," whereas J represents it as having been known and used before the flood (cf. Gen 4:26).

PSALM 103:1-4, 6-8, 11

1 CORINTHIANS 10:1[6]-13

Paul is here issuing a warning to the Corinthian church against presumption, the great offense he finds its members guilty of. In adopting the style of a Hellenistic synagogue homily, he presumes a sufficient knowledge of Rabbinic midrash in some readers to refer to the extra-biblical legend of the LORD's having followed Israel as a rock (*tsur = petra*, v. 4; cf. *t. Sukkah* 2.11). Even if this is lost on most, he expects them to know the basic exodus symbolism of sea and cloud, manna, water struck from the rock (i.e., a potable spring in a sun-baked mud flat), and poisonous snakes (cf. Exod 16–17; Num 20; Deut 8:3). Food, drink, and rock are all "spiritual" (*pneumatikònēs*, v. 4), meaning symbolic. Paul exhorts his new believers not to "desire evil," his term for idolatry and lewd conduct. For "being desirous" he uses the verb and noun found in the LXX at Num 11:4, 34; Ps 78:29f. to describe the craving of the Israelites for meat in the desert: *epithyméō, epithymía*.

The Masoretic text contains the story of a plague in Num 16:36-50 after the tale of the destruction of Korah, Dathan, and Abiram, which the LXX does not have. NAB and BJ follow the latter as the older textual tradition, RSV and NEB the former, hence including at vv. 47ff. the account of the 14,700 who were felled for murmuring in sympathy with the three who infringed on priestly prerogatives. This is the reference to being "destroyed by the destroyer" found in 10:10, which might prove puzzling to anyone except those schooled in the problems of textual criticism. Hearers or readers familiar with the traditions of the KJV or DRC should recognize the reference immediately as occurring in the MT and the NRSV.

Paul thinks of his own time as "the ends *(tà télē)* of the ages" (v. 11), conse-quently that period of history that all biblical events were meant to illumine. The Corinthians should read the Exodus accounts of disobedience and grumbling with great care, he writes, with a view to finding warnings there on their own perilous condition.

Verse before the Gospel. Matthew 4:17

Repent, for the kingdom of heaven is at hand.

Luke 13:1-9

No other New Testament Gospel has this material, although some have speculated that Jesus' cursing of the fig tree (Mark 11:12ff., 20f.//Matt 21:18f., 20ff.) origi-nated from a parable like the one that Luke tells here. It is impossible to identify this bloody suppression of a Galilean revolt by Pilate with any of the several such events reported by Josephus. Luke's normal care with sources, however, has led most commentators to suppose that he is reporting a historical reminiscence. The same is true of the accident at the tower of Siloam, presumably near the pool of that name below David's city on Mount Ophel, the terminus of Hezekiah's aque-duct leading from the Gihon Spring.

The point Jesus makes about the innocence of victims of violence and acci-dent resembles his declaration in John 9:2f. that neither the blind man nor his parents were guilty of a sin that caused the blindness. It is also related to his con-sistent treatment of the possessed as if they were guilty of no wrong. The theme of chap. 13 is the fate of Jerusalem and the Judaean people, starting with a call to repentance (vv. 1-5) that leads into a parable (vv. 6-9). Luke likes to set say-ings of Jesus in a dialogue situation as he does here in v. 1. The audience raises the question of God's justice: Luke has Jesus elevate the discussion to the level of personal response, charging the hearers with the same phrase at vv. 3 and 5 (only the tense of the verb "repent" is different). "All" will perish similarly unless they repent—not merely all who hear him on this occasion but an unlimited popu-lation. Even if Jesus had in mind only his Jewish hearers both here and in the parable (which derives from Isaiah's song of the vineyard, 5:1-7), Luke broadens it out to the Christian community. Jerusalem has already been destroyed at the time of the writing, so the threat of judgment in the absence of repentance is a threat to all.

As the chapter continues, so does the theme of accepting or rejecting salva-tion. The question in v. 23 is a Lukan formulation. The "you" of v. 28 is the hearer/reader, not the "heirs of the kingdom" (Greek: "sons") as in Matt 8:12. The chapter concludes (vv. 34f.) with a reminder to the Christian readers of Luke's day that what happened to Jerusalem for putting to death the prophets (although the Old Testament records none; see Matt 23:35 with its unidentified Zechariah son of Barachiah, a confusion perhaps between the Zechariah of 2 Chron 24:20-22 (seemingly Lk's choice), Zechariah son of Barils in Josephus' *War*, 4:334 (Matthew's) and the prophet of Zech 1:1, of whose death nothing is recorded) can happen to them. They can avoid God's judgment only if they learn a lesson from the past and repent.

✌ Fourth Sunday in Lent (C)

JOSHUA 5:9-12

The sanctuaries of early Israel such as Shiloh, Gilgal, and Shechem were the repositories of ancient narratives. It is thought that the stories of the conquest contained in Joshua had their origins there. Verses 2-8 contain the account of the circumcision of the men and boys born during the forty years of journeying in the desert. This is obviously a cultic tale which has as its object the prescription of fitness (removal of the "disgrace of Egypt") for all males who would worship in the new land. "Gilgal" probably means "circle of stone shafts" (like those at Stonehenge, although not nearly so massive and for a commemorative rather than an astronomic-religious purpose). As a note in NAB points out, the name is connected by popular etymology with "I have removed," *gallothi* in Hebrew (v. 9). The circle of stones from the river that make up the memorial at the shrine (cf. 4:5) are matched by another twelve commemorative stones in the river bed (4:9), one for each of the Israelite tribes.

Gilgal is thought to have been northeast across a wadi from ancient Jericho. The author of the early portion of Joshua has a priestly interest in feasts as well as sanctuaries. He ties the observance of Passover in with the entry into Canaan, a natural and possibly even historical link, since the motifs of the crossing of the Sea of Reeds and the River Jordan are so similar. The manna of the old epoch ceases abruptly (v. 12) as the unleavened cakes and the parched grain of the new epoch begin (v. 11). The Israelites are described thereby as entering immediately into a stable agricultural life. This may not be so fanciful if, in fact, they adopted a spring agricultural festival of the Canaanites as the symbol of their deliverance and safe entry into Canaan. The "time of harvest" of 3:15 is a month straddling

March and April, Nisan in New Testament times but in the earlier calendar Abib, the first month of the year.

The Hebrew word for Passover *(pesaḥ)* is made up of the same three letters as the verb for "leap" or "hop" and "limp" (see 1 Kgs 18:26). This has led to the speculation that a pre-Israelite feast marked by dancing might have given its name to the festivities.

Psalm 32

Psalm 34:2-7

2 Corinthians 5:16-21

The love of Christ on behalf of all has changed Paul's perspective on everything (v. 14). He has had to desert the "human point of view" (*katà sárka*, v. 16) that he once had on everyone, even Christ. The reference is undoubtedly to his days as a persecutor (Gal 1:23) when he thought of Jesus as under the curse of having been crucified rather than as a deliverer from the power of a curse (see Gal 3:13). Now that he is "in Christ," Paul is sure that he is part of a renewed creation (*kainē ktísis*, v. 17). The new epoch succeeds the old; the latter has passed into history. The inscription on the great seal of the United States, *Novus Ordo Seclorum*, while not biblical, partakes of this epochal mode of Semitic thought.

It is God who has achieved the change in history, not people. The believers' lot as a result of the change is a "ministry of reconciliation" (v. 18), a service role that follows from God's work of reconciling a sinful humanity to God's own self. This God did by abandoning the role of injured party. Human trespasses were simply not reckoned any longer (v. 19). It is clear to Paul that humanity continues the task of reconciliation by a similar disregard of offense. "We are ambassadors for Christ," he writes (lit. "we exercise a representative function," v. 20), with "God making his appeal through us." The apostle is thinking in the first place of himself and others with a charge like his. Therefore he calls upon the Corinthians to be reconciled to God, as presumably some are not (v. 20b). After that has been achieved, the continuing work of representing Christ will be theirs.

The concreteness of the final verse of this pericope is a striking and deservedly famous Pauline utterance. God made the personally sinless Christ "to be sin who knew no sin" so that we might become the righteousness of God in him. "Sin" here is not personal offense so much as the condition of alienated humanity. Righteousness is the condition of reconciled humanity. Christ assumed the one so he might give us the other. Needless to say, he does not remain "sin" but in his exaltation becomes the depository of the divine justness insofar as it can reside in a human being. Through him it is given to all.

Verse before the Gospel. Luke 15:18

I shall get up and go to my father and say, "Father, I have sinned against heaven and you."

Luke 15:1-3, 11-32

Luke features the journey motif in his Gospel and, along with it, that of the hospitality accorded to Jesus. Jesus is the wanderer in whose guise God visits his people (cf. 1:7; 7:16; 5:27-38; 19:9; 24:13-55). The complaint of "Pharisees and scribes" (v. 2) against Jesus' welcoming tax gatherers and sinners (v. 1) underlines the soteriological aspect of the guest motif. "Fellowship with Jesus means forgiveness of sins and newness of life" (Flender).

The principle in two-edged parables is that the main trust lies in the second part. Verses 11-21, the wastrel son, and 22-32, the father's treatment of the elder, resentful son were undoubtedly originally two parables in Luke's source. Linguistically, he has made them both his own.

The custom prevailed in the ancient world of deeding one's property to one's heirs while keeping the rent from it as income during one's lifetime. The younger son achieved this settlement from his father but also the control of his inheritance, rather than having to wait until the father died. The phrase spoken to the elder son, "all that is mine is yours" (v. 31), would reflect the normal arrangement, while that with the younger son (v. 12b) the abnormal. The elder son's lively imagination, in his anger, supplies a career of loose living to the younger for which he may not have any evidence (v. 30). All we are told is that he was reduced to the supreme indignity of tending pigs for a Gentile master. Relative to this, eating carob pods was as nothing.

The father's initiative in forgiveness is the operative detail in the first part of the parable (v. 20bc). He does not stop to discuss the son's confession of faults but cites his return as in itself sufficient cause for new clothing, a ring (sign of authority in the household), and the order for a celebration (vv. 22ff.).

In Jesus' telling the parable would have been a tale of the repentance of the social outcast directed at the self-righteous observants of his day. Luke always sees the Christian mission directed first to the Jews, then to the Gentiles. We are therefore right in finding in the younger son's unstable behavior—his "death" and lostness—an image of the condition of Gentiles vis-à-vis Israel, the elder brother, who is with God without interruption and whose patrimony is always his by right. The story is another and perhaps the best illustration of the theme Luke puts so strongly on Jesus' lips: that God can forgive and accept whom he wishes, when and how he wishes.

❧ ❧

Fifth Sunday in Lent (C)

ISAIAH 43:16-21

The Chaldeans of v. 14 are of the tribe that settled in Lower Mesopotamia during the period of Assyria's domination, founding the Neo-Babylonian kingdom. The context of this passage is Israel's anticipation of deliverance from Babylon (late sixth century) as something actually accomplished. Verses 16f. rehearse the Reed Sea episode during the exodus. In what follows, the Jews are invited not to dwell overly on those marvels from the past (v. 18) since the LORD intends to do a new and greater thing (v. 19), namely, deliver the people from Babylon and send them back through the desert (vv. 19f). This new exodus will make the first one pale by comparison as a desert road is laid down (see 35:8ff; 40:3f.) and springs and rivers make it green with vegetation 35:6f; 41:18). God's providential care will be such that inimical birds and beasts will be subdued and the desert itself—unlike the Sinai peninsula of old—will be transformed into a rich land. The sign of fulfillment of this marvel will be greater still: the transformation of Israel into a people of praise (v. 21).

The powerful imagery of Second Isaiah, never literally fulfilled, was of course realized in the conquest of the desert that lay under the Fertile Crescent. The restoration of God's people to their homeland validated the wildest claims of poetic imagination.

PSALM 126[1-6]

PHILIPPIANS 3:4B[8]-14

Paul writes this letter from prison in some unknown city that has an army garrison (see 1:7, 13, 17). The tone of 1:1—3:1 is one of rejoicing that the gospel is being proclaimed, whatever the motivation in some quarters. He is sure that in

Philippi, at least, the motives are beyond question. In 3:2, however, the letter takes a sharp turn, creating the suspicion that from here to 4:9 another missive has been inserted (otherwise, why the "finally" of 3:1?), with 4:10-20 expressing gratitude to the community for gifts received as part of still a third letter. These problems need not be solved before an adequate treatment of today's portion can be dealt with by preachers. They need only know that putting the Philippian recipients of this letter on notice as threatened by "dogs" and "workers of evil" is a different theme from all that has gone before and will follow. The apostle has heard of enforced circumcision of Gentile new believers here as in Galatia and refers to it scornfully as mutilation *(katatomé, not peritomé),* claiming that "we are the circumcision . . . [who] do not put our confidence in the flesh" (v. 3). The word *sarx,* he then sees, can have a double meaning in his regard: the flesh of the foreskin and the more usual signification of any life that would attempt independence of the Spirit of God. Having made the disclaimer of reliance on the flesh, however, Paul is prompted to review his pedigree as a Jew (vv. 4-6; cf. Gal 1:14; Acts 22:3; 23:6). If there is anyone, he maintains, who has a right to tell Gentiles they need not adopt this special sign of Jewishness, it is he.

The abrupt break or seam at verse 2 suggests that the passage from it to v. 21 is from another letter so different is it in tone from what precedes and what follows. Verses 4:1-9 similarly seem to be the conclusion of still a third letter.

John Henry Newman's novel *Loss and Gain* (1848) is about a fictional character who experiences the Pauline loss (v. 8) of all things that brings indescribable gain in the form of knowledge of Jesus Christ as Lord. Paul's careful weighing of alternatives (twice in v. 8: "I regard/consider") leads him to conclude that everything—but chiefly any trust in righteousness based on legal observance—is "rubbish, garbage" *(skýbala,* plural) in contrast to this wealth. Paul seems to be challenging the two chief claims made by some in the Philippian community: that in favor of observance of aspects of the Law and that of special knowledge, as justifying. God alone justifies through faith (v. 9), in Christ's sufferings no less than in the power of his resurrection (v. 10). Sharing in his sufferings constitutes being "in Christ," Paul's well-known formula of mystical union. This shared knowledge of sufferings is experiential. Being formed in the pattern of the Lord's death is the precondition for attaining to his resurrection (vv. 10f.).

The "justice" Paul possesses (v. 9) is his right relation with God. None of this is of his doing or earning. God holds out the mystery of his Son's dying and rising to be shared in by a lived faith. On condition of the latter, not of circumcision or perfect conformity, the believer may hope ultimately to achieve personal resurrection from the dead.

The apostle hastens to add that he does not yet possess resurrection but looks forward to it (v. 12a). This is an echo of the problem of the Corinthian enthusiasts examined in the commentary for 6 Epiphany [6] (C). Paul claims that he has not as yet "been perfected" (*teteleíōmai*, 12), probably a word taken from gnostic vocabulary. Using the language of what today's world of sports would call track events, he contrasts grasping the award—a laurel wreath at the finish line—with being grasped (*katelēmphthēn*, v. 12) by Christ. He is still in the race, his thoughts not at all on his progress up to this point but on the prize that lies ahead: an "upward call" (*anō kléseōs*, v. 14) to be "in Christ Jesus." This awareness of the award alone constitutes spiritual maturity (v. 15). Only those who have such maturity can aspire to the title coveted in Graeco-Roman gnostic cults, "the perfect." Paul claims it for some of his new believers and himself, an approach to perfection in Christ.

JOHN 12:1-8

For a commentary see Monday in Holy Week (A).

VERSE BEFORE THE GOSPEL. JOEL 2:12-13

Return to me with your whole heart. Rend your hearts, not your garments, for gracious and merciful is he.

JOHN 8:1-11

This is one of the justly famous passages of the New Testament, yet it has an unusual textual history. It is bracketed in NRSV, NAB, and TEV, with a note in NIV to the same effect, because it is missing from John in the best manuscripts. Others have it after Luke 21:38. Its lateness or interpolation does not make it an inauthentic tradition. No doubt the story has been inserted here because of Jesus' declaration in 8:15 that he passes judgment on no one, or v. 26, where he says he forbears from making statements in condemnation.

The similarities to the story of Susanna and the elders are evident (Dan 13 in the LXX). There the young Daniel would have "no part in the death of this woman" (v. 46) but examined the two witnesses separately and caught them at their perjury (v. 61). Nowhere is the woman taken in adultery in John 8 exonerated from the guilt of her shameful deed. Jesus is not flouting the Law or its, by then, archaic prescription for adultery, the death penalty. He is interested more in the motives of her accusers. For her there is compassion and the admonition not to commit this sin again; for them, judgment on their hypocrisy.

One of my early memories is of H. B. Warner in *The King of Kings* tracing in the dust the Aramaic words for "lust," "extortion," and "greed," which turned into English forthwith—in movie-magic style. As each one was completed, another man slipped into the crowd, dropping the stone he held. It was pure DeMille, but the memory remains.

Sixth Sunday in Lent / Passion Sunday or Palm Sunday (C)

Liturgy of [Procession with] the Palms

LUKE 19:28-40

This passage so closely resembles Mark 11:1-11 that the commentary on it under Liturgy of the Palms (B) should be consulted; also Matt 21:1-11 (A). The Lukan differences from Mark are so few that this evangelist can be presumed to have copied Mark's account verbatim. Luke makes a few interesting changes, none of any consequence; eliminates the Lord's promise to "send [the colt] back here immediately" (Luke 19:31//Mark 11:3); changes Mark's "he sat upon it" (11:7) to "they set Jesus on it" (19:35); and alters the chant of the welcoming pilgrims already arrived by calling Jesus "the King who comes" (19:38) rather than simply "he"; he further replaces Mark's v. 10 with a couplet that resembles the angels' song in his nativity narrative and adds a rebuke by onlooking Pharisees to Jesus' disciples (19:39) that is paralleled in John (12:19). The latter does not have the well-remembered phrase on Jesus' lips that if the crowds were silent the very stones would cry out (Luke 19:40). Luke Timothy Johnson points out "echoes of the saying in 3:8, that God could raise up children to Abraham 'from these stones'" and brings attention to a number of "stones sayings" that follow: 19:44; 20:18; 21:5-6; 24:2 (*The Gospel of Luke* [Sacra Pagina 3; Collegeville, Minn.: Liturgical, 1991], 298, n. 40). Matthew at this point (21:16) quotes Ps 8:2, "Out of the mouths of babes and infants . . ." (LXX).

PSALM 118:1-2, 19-29

❦❧

Liturgy of the Passion

ISAIAH 50:4-9A

For a commentary see Proper 19 [24] (B).

PSALM 31:9-16

PSALM 22:8-9, 17-20, 23-24

PHILIPPIANS 2:5-11

For a commentary see Proper 21 [26] (A).

VERSE BEFORE THE GOSPEL. PHILIPPIANS 2:8-9

Christ became obedient for us even to death, dying on the cross. Therefore God raised him on high and gave him a name above all other names.

LUKE 22:14—23:56 OR 23:1-49

Luke relies on traditions (he probably possesses a primitive narrative of arrest, appearance before some representatives of the Sanhedrin, condemnation by Pilate, journey to Golgotha, and crucifixion and death) and biblical sources (Pss 21; 41; Isa 50:6; 53:12; Hos 6:1ff.; 10:8b, 11f., 14; Amos 8:9). Such historical sources as he possesses he puts in the service of a portrait of Jesus as an innocent sufferer "counted among the wicked." He seems to have a tradition on the primitive Eucharist superior of that of Mark and Matthew, likewise one that omits the Markan inquiry by priests at night and also that gives the political charges before Pilate that probably led to Jesus' condemnation by Rome (23:2).

I accept the theory that Luke edited a special passion source at his disposal with the aid of Mark rather than revised Mark in the light of his source. Luke has Jesus eating with "the apostles," not "the twelve disciples" (Mark 14:17; Matt

26:20) and introduces in vv. 15-18—probably from his source—Jesus' twofold vow of abstention from food and drink until the reign of God has come. The eschatological concern of the vow recalls Paul's primitive sense of the eucharistic meal which is to be eaten by Christians "until he come" (1 Cor 11:26). The signs of food and drink will be fulfilled only when the *basileía* arrives. Verses 19b-20 have long been disputed textually, not because the manuscript attestation is weak but because they were thought to be an interpolation of 1 Cor 11. Through the researches of Heinz Schürmann in particular they have come to be widely accepted as genuine. Both they and Paul's supper account are thought to derive from the same source, of which Luke's version is presumed to be the earlier. The place of origin hazarded is Antioch, somewhere between 30 and 40. Part of the reason why vv. 19b-20 were thought nongenuine was the supposition that later copyists, nervous over the sequence cup-bread in vv. 17-19a, inserted 19b-20 to supply the more familiar bread-cup sequence. Luke probably did this on his own, however, having first provided the eschatological development he was more interested in.

Verses 24-27, the disciples' dispute over precedence, seems to come from the special Lukan source; similarly 28-30 and 31-33 (but cf. Mark 8:33; John 21:15-19), with v. 34 a later Markan addition to the narrative as v. 22 had been. Verses 35-38 are entirely peculiar to Luke, looking back as they do to 10:4 when everything was different with the disciples as regards preparedness for their mission.

Jesus' suggestion about a disciple's selling his coat to buy a sword must be a metaphor to describe coping with hostility to the gospel. Taken as referring to a future time of privation and opposition it is completely serious. Jesus terminates the literal misconstruing of his meaning by the disciples impatiently ("Enough!"; certainly not "Two are enough"). His healing action in vv. 49ff. makes this abundantly clear. Conceivably the puzzling sword saying of v. 36 was a logion of Jesus, but more likely an early apostolic practice that Luke refutes by reporting the Master's peaceful spirit. We have some extrabiblical data on the way traveling Jewish teachers went armed.

The story of the agony in the garden (vv. 39-46) is non-Markan, all but 46b (cf. Mark 14:38) and perhaps vv. 41f, where the wording is not in Mark's style.

Verses 52b-53a give every indication of being a Markan insertion (from Mark 14:48f.) into a non-Markan source—Luke 22:47-54a—about the arrest of Jesus, although word study would indicate that Luke did his editing with Mark before him (thus 47a//Mark 14:43).

Luke's denial of Jesus by Peter (22:54b-61) suggests reliance on Mark chiefly (cf. 14:54, 66-72). It is an evening occurrence in both Gospels, but Luke will not let it serve as the framework for a night inquiry by the priests as Mark does. See the commentary on Mark's passion narrative on Passion Sunday or Palm Sunday (B). Luke's two challengers to Peter subsequent to the servant girl (vv. 58,

59) are males in Greek, unlike the parallel places, and the piercing look of Jesus in 61a is likewise proper to him. His own editorial activity could account for this without the need to posit a special written source. The mocking scene (vv. 63ff.) appears to derive from elsewhere than Mark 14:65, although the vocabulary shows that Luke has made it his own. It is much more likely that the men guarding Jesus mocked him, as in Luke, than that the priests should have done so (cf. Mark 14:65).

Aside from the probable dependence of v. 69 on Mark 14:62 and v. 71 on 63b (with mention of blasphemy omitted), Luke's account of a morning appearance of Jesus before "their council" (v. 66) is so different from Mark 14:53-65 that dependence on another source seems likely. David Flusser in *Jesus* (New York: Herder and Herder, 1969) concludes that while Luke does not hesitate to report the delivery of Jesus to Pilate by Jewish authorities, he is working from materials that precede Mark's dramatized attempt at popularization. Such is also the burden of D. R. Catchpole's *The Trial of Jesus* (Leiden: Brill, 1971).

In 18:32 Luke has had Jesus prophesy his deliverance to the Gentiles only. When the evangelist places Jesus before the Roman prefect (23:1-5) the dialogue is peculiarly Luke's except for v. 3; this he derives from Mark, taking the equivocal response of Jesus as not leaving the meaning open (Mark's and Matthew's technique) but as denying the charge, for shortly Pilate will declare that he has "not found this man guilty of any of your charges against him" (v. 14). Verses 6-16, the examination before Herod, is Luke's special composition, one that will be echoed in Acts 4:27. Luke shows some knowledge of Johannine tradition throughout, as for example Pilate's threefold declaration of Jesus' innocence (23:4, 15, 22//John 18:38b; 19:4-6).

It is hard to tell whether Luke's account of Barabbas is his own or a modification of Mark. Chances favor the former, with v. 25 perhaps a version of Mark 15:15 finishing off the section with a carefully constructed summary. The historicity of the Barabbas tale is all but impossible to establish. Pilate's offer to release a convicted insurgent—and we know nothing of a practice of amnesty at Passover—is highly improbable on the face of it. Yet some report of a man who went free while the innocent Jesus died has lingered in the popular memory.

Pilate passes sentence on Jesus in Luke alone ("gave his verdict," 23:24), yet even here the burden of guilt is transferred to the shoulders of Jewish leadership: He "handed Jesus over as they wished" (v. 25).

The journey to the cross (vv. 26-32) is non-Markan except for the first verse, which derives from Mark 15:21, the drafting of Simon of Cyrene. Luke's crucifixion narrative (vv. 33-49) is similarly his own except for these insertions from Mark: 23:34b, 38, 44f., 49. The word of Jesus from the cross in 34a is textually doubtful and may have been inspired by Acts 7:60. Mark is Luke's source for the burial narrative (vv. 50-54), "without any clear sign of a second source except a knowledge of Johannine tradition" (Vincent Taylor, *The Passion Narrative of St. Luke* [Cambridge: Cambridge Univ. Press, 1972], 101). Luke has the women take a more active part in the interment of Jesus than the other evangelists (v. 56), perhaps as a means to forge a link with 24:1.

The passion narrative is chiefly interested in making faith affirmations about Jesus in a context of the biblical-type humiliations he endured. This earnest effort has been badly misconstrued over the centuries as a historical report on Jewish guilt and Roman compassion (22:70—23:22). There is no good reason to continue the confusion in the minds of contemporary Christians.

If a congregation or parish wishes to devote a Lenten series of lectures to a form-redaction-critical treatment of the passion narratives, it should be encouraged to do so. As proclamation, however, these portions of the Gospels can only serve to pour fuel on the Christian fire of anti-Jewish sentiment. The much wiser thing to do on this day is preach on Jesus' entry into Jerusalem, while choosing for the Gospel lection Luke 23:26-56 if the worshipers expect it. The tradition of reading "the long Gospel" is very old but it stems from a time when the people were not made a party to celebration of the *triduum sacrum*, the paschal "three days."

ᴥᴥ

Holy Week

ᴥᴥ

Monday of Holy Week (A, B, C)

ISAIAH 42:1-9

See Baptism of the Lord (A).

PSALM 36:5-11

HEBREWS 9:11-15

See The Body and Blood of Christ (B).

JOHN 12:1-11

See 5 Lent (C).

❧☙ Tuesday of Holy Week (A, B, C)

ISAIAH 49:1-7

See 2 Epiphany [2] (B).

PSALM 71:1-14

1 CORINTHIANS 1:18-31

See 3 Lent (B).

JOHN 12:20-36

See 5 Lent (B).

❧☙ Wednesday of Holy Week (A, B, C)

ISAIAH 50:4-9A

See Proper 19 [24] (B).

PSALM 70

HEBREWS 12:1-3

See Proper 15 [20] (C).

JOHN 13:21-32

This is John's expanded narrative of the sign of betrayal (v .26) found in Mark 14:20; Matthew 26:23; Luke 22:21. The disciple whom Jesus loved lay close to Jesus because the Jews ate reclining, Greek-style, uniquely at Passover. Only John attributes Judas's motivation to the impulse of Satan (v. 27), coupled with the charge that, as custodian of the common purse (v. 29), he was a thief (12:6). Medieval England called this day Spy Wednesday.

Holy [Maundy] Thursday and Good Friday

See under (A).

❧ Season of Easter ❧

❧❧
Easter Vigil
(A, B, C; in RCL intercalated with those of LM)

See the Service of Readings, Easter Vigil (A).

ROMANS 6:3-11

As in (A).

PSALM 118:1-2, 14-24[16-17, 22-23]

LUKE 24:1-12

"The women who had come with him from Galilee" (23:55) is the subject of the sentence in 24:1. They have prepared spices and perfumes before the Sabbath (23:56), which they now bring. They find the stone rolled back, but no body. The question put by the "men" about searching for the Living One among the dead does not occur elsewhere in a gospel (but cf. Isa 8:19). Verse 6a, NRSV 5c (//Mark 16:6b) is missing from Codex D (sixth century) and many MSS of the Vulgate. Unlike Mark and Matthew, where the "young man" or "angel" directs the women to bring the disciples the message that Jesus is going before them to Galilee, Luke has the men reminisce about the passion prediction (v. 7; cf. 9:22, 44; 18:34f.) Jesus made "while he was still in Galilee" (v. 6). The place of glorification and the starting-point of the message is Jerusalem (cf. 24:49), for Luke as for John (chap. 20). The other Synoptics and the author of John 21 situate it in Galilee. The same point of fulfillment of prophecy will be made in the Emmaus story later in this chapter at vv. 25-27, 32-35. The "sinful men" *(hamartōloi)* of v. 7 are no doubt the "pagans" (*ánomoi*) of Acts 2:23, "Gentile sinners" (one word, like "damnyankees") who in Luke's view did the bidding of the Jewish leaders.

The women act as bearers of a message to the disciples in Luke and Matthew (28:8). In Mark they say nothing to anyone out of fear (16:8). John alone has Mary Magdalene report to the men what the risen Lord has told her (20:18).

"Mary, the mother of James" (v. 10; cf. Mark 15:40; 16:1) is "Mary of James" in Greek. The other possibility is that she is the daughter of a man so named, but not the wife. As to identifying the James in question, he may be "the younger" of Mark 15:40, but it is impossible to know. Only Luke reports on Joanna, here as in 8:3. Verse 10b seems to conflate with the tradition on "the Eleven and the others" (v. 9), another tradition on the "apostles."

Verse 12 is missing from the Western text of Luke. If genuine, it reflects a tradition that John also has (20:3-10). Verse 24 presupposes something like it, while v. 34 reports an appearance of Jesus to Peter not otherwise recorded in the Gospels but found in the tradition Paul passes on in 1 Cor 15:5.

It is characteristic of Luke's risen-life account that he has everything take place not only in Jerusalem but on the same day (see vv. 1, 13, 36, 50), possibly for reasons of later community liturgical observance. His report of Jesus' appearances "over the course of forty days" (Acts 1:3) is not at odds with chap. 24 of the Gospel, because it is a symbolic biblical forty days. It simply fills up the time until the Pentecost he wishes to report on in 2:1. Luke-Acts stresses the exaltation of the Lord to God's right hand rather than his character as risen.

❧❧

Resurrection of the Lord / Easter Sunday (C)

See Easter Sunday (A).

1 Corinthians 15:19-26

For a commentary see 6 Epiphany (C). The pitiable condition of these whose hope is for this life only (v. 19) is countered by the certainty that, as death came for all through one man, so in Christ all shall be brought to life.

Isaiah 65:17-25

For a commentary see Proper 28 [33] (C).

✎ Easter Evening

All as in (A).

✎ Second Sunday of Easter (C)

Acts 5:[12-16] 27-32

This is one of three summaries of community and apostolic activity found in early Acts, the others being 2:42-47 and 4:32-35. They are not unlike certain summations of Jesus' healing activity in Mark (e.g., 6:56). Benoit thinks vv. 12b-14 of the present pericope the work of a redactor (thus also 2:43ff. and 4:33). In his theory, 12b is taken from 2:46a and 3:11; 13 from 2:47a; and 14 from 2:47b. If he is correct, Luke is somewhat absolved of the ambiguity of who "they" (all, *hápantes*) are in v. 12. NAB opts for the apostles rather than the people as the natural subject of the sentence; the same would apply to "them" in v. 13. Who, then, are the others of "no one else" *(tōn dé loipōn oudeìs)?* It would be easier to identify them as Jerusalemites motivated by fear if the ones they "did not dare join" were, not the apostles but the whole church. But the next verse, 14, describes many who were not thus inhibited and who did become believers. Torrey thought that "no one else" meant none of the elders as contrasted with the common people. The NAB rendition hints at a holding back of ordinary church members from associating themselves actively with the apostles in their "signs and wonders" (v. 12), which are an answer to the prayer of 4:29f. The problem may be caused by an early corruption of the text, *loipōn* not having been the original reading.

The power of Peter here is balanced by the attribution of a similar gift of healing to Paul (19:12). Whenever a shadow falls (*episkiásē*, v. 15) in the New Testament it is a work of divine power (cf. Luke 1:35; 9:34; Mark 9:7). What God once did for Mary in her conceiving and for Jesus in his transfiguration is now at work in the apostles in their ministry. See the discussion of charismatic healers in Judaism, particularly the first-century C.E. Galilean *ḥasid* Ḥanina be Dosa, in Geza Vermès' *Jesus the Jew: A Historian's Reading of the Gospels* (Philadelphia: Fortress Press, 1981), 72–80.

For a commentary on vv. 27-32 see 3 Easter (C).

Psalm 118:[2-4], 14-29

Psalm 150

Revelation 1:4-8

For a commentary see Reign of Christ [34] (B).

Revelation 1:9-13, 17-19

Jesus Christ as the one who was once dead but now lives "forever and ever" (v. 18) accounts for the occurrence of this reading on the Sunday after Easter. His appearance in glory to the visionary author John, exiled on Patmos because he "proclaimed God's word and bore witness to Jesus" (v. 9), is not unlike his appearances to the chosen witnesses in the gospels and to Paul (Gal 1:16; 1 Cor 15:8; 2 Cor 12:2-5). It more resembles the last-cited Pauline rapture than any other New Testament account, although the apocalyptic details of vv. 13-16—in the spirit of Ezek 1:26; 9:2; 43:2; and Dan 7:9; 10:6—are nowhere to be found in the christophanies of the risen life.

After a prologue (vv. 1-3), the author of Revelation provides a covering letter (vv. 4-11) for the epistles to the seven churches in the province of Asia (modern Turkey across from Istanbul), which will follow (chaps. 2–3). It is from this introductory epistle to the Christians of Ephesus, Smyrna, Pergamum, Thyatira, Sardis, Philadelphia, and Laodicaea that today's reading is taken. The cities lie clockwise around a Roman road that is still discoverable, e.g., at the ruins of Sardis and Laodicaea. The cities are not far separated. I did all but Thyatira (modern Akhisar) to the north in a day out of Izmir (Smyrna) by car and could have done them all without stopping if this doubtful achievement were to have made any sense. A visit to earthquake-buried Ḥonaz (Colossae) near Laodicaea but, much more, a disastrous road-diversion to the ruins of Aphrodisias consumed many hours. Philadelphia is Alasehir, Ephesus near Selçuk—the former a Muslim town lately prosperous, the latter a treasure-house to be returned to again and again. Only Pergamum and Sardis rival it as excavations, but neither for size or splendor; Latakia, however, for area excavated.

The title John adopts for himself is not apostle, overseer, or elder but "brother," and this because he has a share with fellow-Christians in the distress *(thlipsis),* kingly reign *(basileía),* and endurance *(hypomoné)* that are their lot (v. 9). Patmos is an island of six by ten miles which lies some thirty-seven miles WSW of Miletos. Despite its proximity to the Turkish coast, it belongs, like most of the offshore islands, to Greece. Nearby Naxos, Kalimnos, and Cos outshine it as tourist attractions. It was a penal colony for political prisoners in Roman times. We know of a campaign of emperor-worship in Ephesus during Domitian's reign (81–96). Even so, the martyrdom of Antipas of Pergamum (2:13) is hard to set in any known context.

The author dates his ecstasy (lit. "I was in spirit") on the Lord's day as a cachet of its genuineness (v. 9). The number seven, already introduced with reference to the churches, will be a constant in this book. It appears early as referring to the lampstands (*lychníai*, v. 13, the biblical *menoroth*), which in v. 20 are to be identified as symbolic of the churches.

"One like a Son of Man" in Dan 13 refers to a human figure who represents Israel, as contrasted with the beasts who are other empires. Noncanonical apocalyptic literature made a specific individual of him. The author probably has Dan 19:9ff. in mind, as the seer falls prostrate and is raised up reassuringly (cf. Ezek 1:28—2:1). For "I am the First and the Last" (v. 17; cf. v. 8), see Isa 44:6 and 48:12, where it is Israel's God who makes the claim. Here and in 2:8; 22:13 the title is transferred to Christ, victorious over death and the nether world (*hádou* = *shĕôl*, the abode of the dead). Matthew 16:18 uses the same figure for death, *hádēs*, but there Peter's keys do not admit to it but to the "reign of the heavens (i.e., God)." Christ in glory has this power in that, at the end, he will unlock the doors to every tomb and release the faithful dead from their imprisonment. Verse 19 contains the seer's charter to inscribe in this book all that he has seen or will see.

ALLELUIA. JOHN 20:29

Blessed are those who have not seen and have believed.

JOHN 20:19-31

For a commentary see Second Sunday of Easter (A).

Third Sunday of Easter (C)

Acts 9:1-6, (7-20)

Weekday worshipers who regularly hear selections from LM will encounter Acts 9:1-20 on Friday of 3 Easter but not on a Sunday. RCL corrects this omission but may not be doing hearers a great favor because it accords ill with Paul's own early acquaintance with the Jesus movement. All this may have happened but, if so, he does not record it in places where he might. He willingly acknowledges and repents of his earlier persecution of the movement's adherents but with no indication of his being commissioned by Jerusalem's high priest, least of all bringing any who are committed to the Way (*hē hodós*, the earliest designation in the diaspora we know of) to the capital as prisoners in bonds (9:1-12). From Paul's letters we deduce that Syria was the place of his first harassment of a church community (probably in Damascus; perhaps Antioch). But Luke's story of his coming to believe in the risen Christ will forever be more fixed in Christian memory than his own, subdued account (Gal 1:11-24; cf. 1 Cor 9:1; see 2 Cor 12:2-4, which may describe a later experience). This is especially the case because of Luke's graphic style, which repeats 9:19 in 22:3-18 and 26:12-18 with various embellishments. Preachers are able to distinguish the lively narrative style of Acts from Paul's fairly bloodless account without diminishing in the least his claim that he had received a revelation direct form Jesus the Lord. They should also avoid Paul's being thrown from his horse in popular embellishment ("he fell to the ground," v. 4); if on a beast it would have been an ass. "The road to Damascus" becomes the locale only if Paul and "the men traveling with him" originated in Jerusalem and vv. 19f. are historical. Debunking the historical likelihood of an event, especially in a sermon, has no merit whatever. Employing Paul's own laconic account of so great an event has every merit.

Acts 5:27-32, 40b-41

The framers of the lectionary seem more interested in the ill-treatment of the apostles at the hands of the Sanhedrin "for the sake of the Name" (v. 41) than in their spirited and intelligent defense by Gamaliel (vv. 33-39). No lector alert to the reality of Jewish-Christian tensions should follow their lead and omit these seven verses. The historical dependability of Acts, a book that very much "looks" like history, is a doubtful matter at many points. Hence the introduction of the name of the much respected Pharisee Gamaliel and the historical reminiscence attributed to him should by no means be omitted, if only to serve as a corrective for the stereotyped concept of "Pharisee" that stalks the Gospels. In Luke certain Pharisees warn Jesus of Herod Antipas' enmity (cf. 13:31), while in Acts the alliance of Pharisees and followers of Jesus is quite explicit (cf., besides the present passage, 15:5; 23:6-9; 26:5f.).

Gamaliel is Gamaliel I (fl. 10–40 C.E.), the leader of the Jerusalem Pharisees and, according to the Talmud, grandson of Hillel. The Judas of Galilee he speaks of (v. 37) is probably Judas of Gamala, a town east of the Golan Heights, who in the census under Quirinius, at the beginning of Coponius's term as the first prefect of Judaea (6 C.E.), joined with a Pharisee named Zadok to resist paying taxes to Rome (see Josephus, *Antiquities*, 18.1.1). These are the roots of the religious party of the Zealots, so that the statement of 37b is hardly true. Two of Judas's sons were crucified under the Romanized Jewish procurator Tiberius Julius Alexander (46–48); the last son Menaḥem captured Masada from the Romans in 66; and the latter's nephew Eleazar was the legendary captain of that mountain fortress who led in holding out until 73, when all were slaughtered. Of the identity of the Theudas referred to in v. 36 we cannot be sure. Either he is the self-proclaimed prophet of the procuratorship of Cuspius Fadus, 44–46 C.E. (Josephus, *Ant.* 20.5.1), whose story Luke anachronistically inserts here, or the unknown bearer of a name common in those times. Theudas may be a shortened form of Theodoros, "gift of God" (Heb. Mattithýa = Mattathias), in which case a visionary of the latter name described in *Ant.* 17.6.2 becomes a candidate. But this is pure speculation.

The actual, formal attention of the supreme council of Judaism to the Christian movement within a year or two of Jesus' execution is problematic. Stephen is described as summoned by this tribunal (6:12-15; 7:54). So is Paul (22:30—23:30). All of the accounts labor under the same difficulties as those in the Gospels of Jesus' appearance before the Sanhedrin and its presiding high priest. Here, as in that case, a historical reminiscence of official Jewish displeasure over a long period should suffice to account for the summonings in legal form that Luke describes. It is impossible at this distance to distinguish the historical reality—whatever it may have been—from Luke's determination to make the Sanhedrin "responsible for *that* man's blood" (v. 28).

The claim of the apostles to a higher obedience (v. 29) has already appeared in 4:19. G. W. H. Lampe (*PC*, 892) wonders whether Luke has Plato's *Apology* 29D in mind. The speech of Peter in vv. 29-32 is an echo of the longer one reported in 3:13-26. Both are early *kērýgmata* that deal with Israel's history and its fulfillment in Jesus Christ as one continuous narrative. The "tree" of v. 30 is a stake of execution and derives from Deut 21:22 (*'ēts* = *xylon*). "Savior" is confined to Luke-Acts in New Testament usage, as a title congenial to the Greek world. Jesus is a "leader" (*archēgós*) here but the word is translated (probably incorrectly) as "Author [of life]" in 3:15. In both cases the connotation is of a Moses-like figure who initiates a journey from death to life. Hebrews 2:10 brings the two concepts together in the phrase "leader [in the work] of salvation"; Jesus is the "leader/pioneer" *(archēgós)* of our faith in Heb 12:2. Bringing Israel to "repentance and the forgiveness of sins" is God's gift through Jesus and also the entire purpose of the gospel, in Luke's view (v. 31). The apostles and the holy Spirit testify jointly to this reality.

"This speech persuaded them" (v. 39b), followed immediately by a report of flogging, recalls the behavior of Pilate (Luke 23:14ff., 22c; for the practice as a contemporary form of punishment, see 2 Cor 11:24; Acts 22:19).

The complicated question of the historical dependability of the various traditions in Acts referred to above may require skepticism as to a formal action by Jerusalem's highest authority. It does not impugn confrontation of any sort. The intervention reported of Gamaliel is consonant with all we know of a respected sage, the more so as this one represents the Pharisee outlook in a body where priestly Sadducees were probably in control.

PSALM 30[2, 4-6, 11-13]

REVELATION 5:11-14

The ministering thousands (v. 11) in this vision of a heavenly liturgy derive from the description of the court of the Ancient One in Dan 7:10. Those purchased from every race and tongue, people and nation (see Dan 3:4, 7) in the new community of believers are a kingdom of priests in the manner of Exod 10:6. They call out in praise of the slain Lamb *(arníon,* v. 12; 28 times in this book) the imperial acclamation *Axios!,* "Worthy!" Before the One seated on the throne (vv. 7, 13), there is the Lamb who is standing (v. 6). He may be the Passover lamb (Exod 12:5) or the slaughtered innocent of Isa 53:7f., but he is more than that. His seven horns (v. 6) make him a ram at the very least (a symbol of power in Dan 8:3 even if Alexander the Great, the he-goat, takes the measure of the ram with two horns, Media and Persia). There is the further possibility that a ram of Jewish apocalyptic literature is intended, a strong leader of the flock of Israel. Revelation 14:1 would support this interpretation.

All creation, every possible category of creature (v. 13), sings the praises of God and the Lamb. Christ has won the victory and sits beside his Father on the throne (3:21). The four living creatures (cf. 4:6b-8) and the twenty-four elders (cf. 4:4) coupled in 5:14 fall down in worship. The symbolism of both is obscure.

The safest thing to say is that the totality of God's people (the twenty-four priestly courses? a reference to some non-Jewish mythology?) and of the world's empires bow low before the Lamb and hymn his victory. The "new song" (v. 9) they sing celebrates him who has come to make all things new (cf. 21:1, 5).

Alleluia

Christ has risen and makes all things new; he has shown pity on all humanity.

John 21:1-19

The "disciple whom Jesus loved" (21:20) is the great authority-figure for the author of this final, appended chapter. This disciple is the dependable witness, even in writing, to "all these things" that happened to Jesus—only a fraction of which the author recorded. We do not know why the composer of chap. 21 (who is seemingly the redactor of the whole Gospel; cf. 12:23; 19:26; 20:2) gave his independent witness to appearances of the risen Jesus in Galilee. The author of the first twenty chapters has situated his three christophanies in Jerusalem. Probably the author of chap. 21 simply possesses certain traditions—found scattered around the Synoptics in other forms (cf. Luke 5:1-11; Matt 16:17-19; Luke 22:31f.; 24:31, 34f, 41b-43; Mark 14:29ff.)—and preserves them in tribute to the great hero of his community whom Jesus loved (*ho mathētēs hon ēgápa ho Iēsous*).

This disciple is described in v. 20 as one of the seven present (cf. v. 2) in such a way that he seems to be one of the unnamed "two others" rather than a son of Zebedee, viz., John. Jesus has performed two of his Johannine "signs" in Galilee but in the Fourth Gospel the time he spends there is minimal. Only chap. 6 has the lake as its locale, specifically the Tiberias-Capernaum crossing where small modern ferries ply the choppy waters.

The unsuccessful night of fishing resembles what is told in Luke 5:4-7. "As at 20:8, [the beloved disciple] is the quicker in perception, but as at 20:6, Peter is the more impulsive in action" (C. K. Barrett, *PC*, 868). The size of the catch which did not tear the net (v. 11) is put down by some as a trustworthy remembrance because meaningless in itself. These commentators scarcely reckon with the numerological symbolism *(gematría)* of the Johannine school. Jerome volunteers the information that 153 species of fish were listed by the natural historians of his time. Or again, it is a "triangular" number arrived at by adding the digits from 1 to 17; but 10 and 7, equaling 17, are signs of perfection in the Jewish world. Most likely of all, perhaps, is converting the letters of certain words in Ezek 47:10 into numbers. Thus, *Gedi* in Hebrew yields 17 and *Eglaim* 153. It can be done in Greek only by finding variant spellings in the MSS. Whatever the explanation, the number is allegorical for all the new believers. We can be sure, at least, that these fishers of men are making a catch of "sizable fish" (v. 11) while doing no harm to the net that takes them.

The distinction between lambs and sheep in vv. 15, 16, 17 (*arnía, próbatá, próbatá*) and the verbs for pasturing and tending (*boske, poímaine, boske*) do not seem significant. The thrust lies rather in the threefold challenge, the verbal variation being incidental. The same is true of the verbs *agápăn* and *phileîn*. This profession of love elicited from Peter rights the offense of his threefold denial (18:17, 25, 27). He is told, moreover, that he can now follow Jesus (*Akoloúthei moi*, v. 19) even to martyrdom—apparently the tradition on his end which the author has—as once he was told he could not follow Jesus (cf. 13:36ff.).

The poetic form in which v. 18 is cast by NAB, following Brown and others, betrays the conviction that it is a hymnic fragment.

❧❧

Fourth Sunday of Easter (C)

ACTS 9:36-43

This story of the resuscitation of the dead Tabitha (Aram., "gazelle") closely resembles that of the restoration of the daughter of Jairus to her father (Luke 8:41f., 49-56, nearly identical in wording to Mark 5:22ff., 35-42), as is often the case of an event or miracle in Acts patterned on one told of Jesus in Luke's Gospel. In naming the Joppa native Tabitha, Acts omits Mark's mode of address, "Talitha" (Aram. "little girl"), but the similarity is evident. Tabitha has given her name to ten million cats, Dorcas to fewer sewing circles for the missions and the poor (see v. 39). Christian Gisèles/Giselas outrun them both (no pun intended), as do Arabic Gazalas, all named for the fleet-footed gazelle. The Lydda of the story is modern Lod, site of the international airport. The once sizeable Palestinian harbor town of Jaffa has been dwarfed by Tel Aviv, built near it. As to the story, it is one of many in Acts showing that some of Jesus' miraculous powers were shared with the early apostles. Paul confirms this by speaking of the "signs and wonders" that accompanied his ministry and that of others (see Rom 15:19; 2 Cor 12:12 adds "mighty works").

PSALM 23

ACTS 13:14, 43-52

The occurrence described in this reading is Luke's theological interpretation of the increasing gentilization of the churches of Paul. It is not to be presumed literally historical, except in the sense that his source could well have recorded turbulence in the Jewish community of Phrygian Antioch. Luke uses this as the setting of a definitive shift of Pauline interest by way of declared policy (vv. 46f.). What evolved over many years, despite Paul's consistent and unremitting efforts to preach Christ to fellow Jews, Acts describes as a matter of Jewish rejection of salvation and correlative Gentile acceptance. It is hard to think of a passage that is pastorally less apt for public reading, as all must identify the excitement caused by Paul here as elsewhere as divisive—but hardly decisive in the way described. We may not underestimate the impact on Paul and Barnabas of their early discovery of Gentile interest in the Gospel. They were doubtless unprepared for the paradox of resistance in synagogues and a friendly hearing by the wider populace ("the whole city," v. 44). Yet, the modern Christian needs to be more critical than Luke in his estimate of what is going on here.

The diaspora Jew Paul had long borne the burden of the day's heat. His patient, plodding efforts with converts of v. 43, probably a mixture of many "devout" worshipers and far fewer circumcised proselytes) were well known to him. So was the enthusiasm of a day in a Greek populace with which he was well familiar. The agitation of the Jewish community reported in v. 50 would be fully understandable if, after a week's reflection, its members saw the social threat represented by Barnabas and Paul. An equal place in the Jewish community for proselytes, God-fearers, and straight-out Gentiles more numerous than Jews would have destroyed the fabric of religious community life. The Jews are therefore to be applauded for perception rather than reviled for lack of faith. The speech framed for the apostolic pair by Luke (vv. 46f.) is the early Christian understanding of Isa 49:6. Israel's enlightenment of the nations has, ever since the time of the Second Isaiah, been understood by Jews in terms of themselves as a moral and religious influence on the non-Jewish world through Torah. Verses 48-49 are a summary of apostolic activity in liturgical form.

This narrative occurs toward the beginning of the first of three missionary journeys of Paul which Luke has constructed. The immediate progress from Perga on the seacoast to the northern plateau where Antioch lies is unexplained. The author's far greater interest is in God's grace (v. 43) and its action. For him it begets contradiction of God and violent abuse (*antélegon . . . blasphēmoûntes*, v. 45) on the part of some; delight, praise, and belief (*échairon kaì edóxazon . . . kaì epísteusan*, v. 48) on the part of others. Leading personages of both sexes in the Jewish community are cast in the role of *provocateurs/-ses*.

PSALM 100:1-3, 5

REVELATION 7:9[14B]-17

The crowd from every "nation and race, people and tongue" of v. 9 have previously appeared in 5:9, having originated in an older Aramaic text of Dan 3:4 (according to R. H. Charles). Palm branches are a symbol of victory after war; the long white robes (*stolàs leukàs*, v. 9) are identified as possible baptismal vesture. It has been observed by many that the substitution of "Lamb" for God in vv. 9, 10, and 14 would be all that would be necessary to transform this from a paean celebrating Jewish martyrs into a Christian one, on the assumption that "white" (v. 14) is a generic term to convey purification.

The problem of the lack of information on any widespread early persecution of Christians has been referred to in the commentary on Rev 1:9-19 (see 2 Easter [C] above). The "great trial" (v. 14) is probably an eschatological rather than a historical conflict, especially if the original version of the chapter is Jewish. The washing of garments (v. 14) occurs in Gen 49:11, a washing to the whiteness of wool in Isa 1:18. The shelter God will give (v. 15) is an echo of the "made his dwelling among us" (*eskénōsen*, John 1:14) of the Johannine prologue. Both have been connected with the cloud above the propitiatory (cf. Lev 16:2) but the tent of Dwelling that God pitched in the midst of his people (cf. Exod 26) seems the likelier biblical type.

Freedom from thirst and the sun's heat (v. 16) is bliss for parched Israel (cf. Isa 49:10), freedom from hunger a reminiscence of the privations of the exodus. The Lamb as shepherd (v. 17) evokes Ezek 34:23, among many biblical places, while the springs of flowing water are from Jer 2:13 and the wiping away of every tear from Isa 28:8. "Springs of life-giving water" are literally "waters of life," a phrase that recalls all that the Fourth Gospel does with "running water" (*hýdōr zōn*, John 4:10).

ALLELUIA. JOHN 10:14

I am the good shepherd says the Lord, and I know mine and mine know me.

JOHN 10:22[27]-30

The Feast of Dedication (Greek *tà egkaínia*; Heb. Ḥanukkah) celebrates the recapture of the Temple from the Seleucid Greeks by Judah the Maccabee and his brothers. He ordered the construction of a new altar, sacrifice on which resumed on 25 Kislev. Songs and instrumental music marked the ritual of dedication along with incense and many lamps to light up the Temple (1 Macc 4:47-56). Much later the name Feast of Lights was given it, while the attribution of a Christmas-like character to it (gift-giving and the like) came only with the proximity of Jewish children to Christians celebrating Christ's Nativity. For centuries many Rabbis withheld approval of this feast because it celebrated a violent human act and not God's intervention to restore the Holy Place to Jewish use. None of this, however, touches today's lection, which makes nothing of the feast other than that Jesus was there to celebrate it. The direct challenge by certain Judaeans (v. 24) about his messiahship probably comes from long after his lifetime like much of the polemic in this Gospel. Jesus' volunteering of his "works" as testifying to him (v. 25) is a building-block of the testimony in his favor as in a law court that is an important feature of the book of John.

Using the figure of YHWH as the shepherd of Israel so familiar from the Bible, John creates with swift strokes a picture of the bond between Jesus and his flock. The evangelist's pointing out that Ḥanukkah occurs in winter (v. 22), specifically December, is a detail that, like many in John, assumes ignorance of Jewish customs. The shepherd Jesus gives sustenance, the life of the final age (*zṓēn aiónion*, v. 28), and protection. He gives what he has been given by the One with whom he is intimately united. No one can snatch this gift of life away. One supposes that this latter is a polemical aside, telegraphed by the evangelist to any outside the Johannine circle who would come between God and God's elect in Jesus.

❧❧

Fifth Sunday of Easter (C)

ACTS 11:1-18

Luke undoubtedly knows that his hero Paul was not requiring new Gentile believers in Christ to keep the kosher-food laws. He may also have heard that Peter had not abided by them while in Gentile company. He has a story to account for Peter's departure from a strict biblical command that did not envision widespread numbers of non-Jews espousing the religion of Israel. It is first told as a vision Peter had on a rooftop in Joppa at the very moment two slaves and a soldier were approaching him sent by the God-fearer Cornelius (*phoboúmenos tòn theòn*, Acts 10:2, a technical term for an uncircumcised Gentile committed to the religion of Israel). Peter comes to Caesarea with them and then delivers a proclamation *(kérygma)* in summary of God's message to Israel about Jesus (vv. 34-43; for the use of the word see Luke 11:32). The assembled company of Gentiles receives the Holy Spirit, prompting them to accept the message and be baptized, to the amazement of the onlooking Jews (vv. 44-48). In today's lection the account of Peter's vision is repeated in the first person rather than the third (11:5-10; cf. 10:9-16) in response to a challenge by some circumcised believers in Jerusalem. The voice he had heard telling him three times that non-kosher food was from God, hence should not be called profane or unclean (10:14; 11:8-10), is now relayed as, "The Spirit told me to go with them and not to make a distinction between them and us" (11:12). Luke gives a truncated version of the Baptist's prediction that, with Jesus, "You will be baptized with the Holy Spirit" (v. 16; cf. Luke 3:16). Did Luke know of Paul's confrontation of Cephas in this matter (Gal 2:11-14)? This narrative does not permit us to say. It is one story of the many that could be told of Jewish evangelizers throughout the diaspora telling Gentiles they could be baptized without being held to the special laws of Judaism to the displeasure, not simply the amazement, of certain baptized Jews. Mark puts it baldly, "Thus [Jesus] declared all foods clean" (7:19). This could hardly have been a revolutionary statement of Jesus' lifetime but a decision of the church Mark was familiar with. Whatever the case, the Gentile admission into the religion of Israel on these terms, unlike the proselyte movement, must have caused great pain on both sides.

PSALM 148

ACTS 14:21-27

At Lystra in Lycaonia Paul and Barnabas had been accorded divine honors by the native pagan populace as a result of the cure of a man crippled from birth (14:11-13). Despite their vigorous demurrers, they were apparently thought by some Jews from Antioch and Iconium to the west to have acceded to it. These reacted violently (v. 19). The stoning reported of Paul could be the one which he himself says he received (cf. 2 Cor 11:25). Derbe (vv. 20f.) was to be the farthest east he would penetrate into Asia Minor. With Barnabas he could have elected to return overland to Syria from which they had set out. Instead they retraced their steps westward to check on the progress of their new believers (v. 22). Entering "into the reign of God," like "persevering in the faith," means for Luke living the life of the new age. It is something achieved only after many trials, whether for the Christian (see Luke 21:16-19) or for Christ (Luke 24:26). Paul's use of the concept of

God's reign *(basileía)* is infrequent (cf. Rom 14:17; 1 Cor 4:20). When he does employ the term, it is as something popularly misconceived: "eating and drinking" and "talk" rather than what is in fact, the justice, peace, and joy given by the Spirit or the Spirit's power.

The installation of officers in the local communities is done ritually (v. 23), by way of a solemn charge. These elders *(presbýteroi),* chosen on the Jewish model, need not have been senior persons; wisdom was the chief requirement. Testimony to a similar practice in Ephesus will be found in 20:17; in v. 28 they are called those who keep watch *(episkópus),* with the task of shepherding. In Paul's letters, the only reference to such local incumbents is the mention of *epískopoi* and *diákonoi* in Phil 1:1. This sparseness of reference has created the problem of the exact nature of local congregational government in his lifetime. The deutero-Pauline letters are specific about personal qualifications but do not remove the uncertainty of who was designated to do what (see 1 Tim 3:1-13; Tit 1:5-8). In the two latter references the titles *epískopoi, presbýteroi,* and *diákonoi* appear but not in any one place. All that can be fairly deduced is that the latter class included women and that the monoepiscopate, so-called, was not a feature of the Pauline churches.

Verses 27f. describe the report of the two apostles to the congregation *(ekklēsía)* that had sent them out. A point is probably being made of their unawareness of any obligation to make a report to the church of Jerusalem. In any case, it serves as an introduction to the tension reported between Judaea and Antioch in the next chapter. The "door of faith" recalls Paul's language (cf. 1 Cor 16:9). No explanation is offered as to why the pair set sail from Attalia without returning to visit Salamis and Paphos in Cyprus (13:4-12).

PSALM 145:8-13

REVELATION 21:1[5A]-6

This passage is a vision of renewed heavens and a renewed earth. It is important to be clear that Jewish apocalyptic eschatology concentrated on an age to follow this one after cataclysmic purification. The popular and incorrect view is that such literature featured the destruction of humanity or the end of the world (i.e., universe). Only one passage in the Qumrân scrolls can be adduced that envisions the "end" as an actual destruction by fire (1QH 3.29–33). The whole tenor of this style of writing was one of redemption and hope for a new life on earth. Thus, the "sea [the abyss, the human's enemy in ancient mythology] was no longer."

The new Jerusalem of this chapter is probably not the dwelling-place of God transferred to this sphere but the center of Christ's activity during some millennial period to come or the community of believers present in the world—on the assumption that they will respond to their lofty vocation. The bride image, descriptive of Israel faithful to her husband YHWH, sustains the latter view, for it was very much a hoped-for reality of earthly existence.

Verse 3 derives from Ezek 37:27; 4a from Isa 25:8; 4b less directly from Isa 35:10. Portions of vv. 4-5 recall 2 Cor 5:17 strikingly.

ALLELUIA. JOHN 13:34

I give you a new commandment, love one another as I have loved you.

JOHN 13:31-35

These verses introduce the soliloquy of chaps. 14–16 and the prayer of Jesus with which it closes, the latter an epilogue that balances off the prologue of 1:1-18.

The glorification spoken of in v. 31b is an anticipation of Jesus' sufferings, which for John are none other than his glory. Some have suggested that the specific reference is to the just concluded washing of feet as a sign of all that is to follow; or it may be that Judas's deed, which will set all the rest in motion, is intended. This means that the glory that is to come "soon" (v. 32) need not signify resurrection but the mystery of crucifixion and glorification taken as one.

John's "children" (*teknía*, v. 33) are the believers of his community, who are reminded here, as at 7:33; 8:21; 20:29c, that belief includes separation from the glorified Christ who is not seen.

The "new commandment" is such in its role as the sign of the new age. The injunctions to love in Lev 19:18 and Matt 5:44 have not been superseded by a further one. That general command is lived out in the Johannine church, with Jesus' love for his disciples now established as the norm of all interpersonal loves (vv. 34f.). It is the badge of discipleship.

The "Jews" of v. 33 are our familiar out-group of the Fourth Gospel—all who, unlike the Johannine circle, do not accept Jesus. John's community is likewise made up of Jews. Many hold that John, unlike the Synoptics, has no interest in an outreach to the Gentiles.

❧ ❧

Sixth Sunday of Easter (C)

ACTS 16:9-15

This is the story of Paul's first entry onto the European continent. It should be remembered that the church in Rome had come to birth without his efforts, for one often reads that this was the introduction of the gospel to Europe. In a familiar Lukan scene, a vision given to Paul provides the impetus. Verse 16:10 is noteworthy as the first of the "we" sayings, whether it means that Luke accompanied Paul on this journey or simply employed a literary device to tell a travel tale ("You are *there*"). The company sails from one port city to another with no mention of a stop-off at Samothrákē. Visitors to the Louvre will remember the statue called "Winged Victory" found on that island. Neapolis is Kavalla nowadays. One can go to the ruins of Philippi on a road that leads to Dráma, but Paul would have to go around the low-lying mountains. Finding "the river outside the city gate" (v. 13) is impossible. There might have been a stream flowing into the Anglitis at the time, but if so it has long since been silted in. One nice touch is that the tiny village at the edge of the extensive, buried city—less than one-quarter of which was unearthed by French archeologists early in the twentieth century—is named Lydia (vv. 14f.; 40).

ACTS 15:1-2, 22-29

Luke's account of the "council of Jerusalem" is notoriously difficult to square with Paul's version of what seem to be certain of the same events and, indeed, with anything we know of the mentality of Jerusalem Christians. Peter's speech (vv. 7-11) and James's (vv. 13-21) are pure Lukan discourse, as evidenced by the improbable exegesis of LXX texts by James. The narrative is probably a fusion of two accounts, one of a dispute on circumcision and the other about food laws in cases where kosher-observing and nonkosher-observing Christians mingled in the same churches.

A delegation made up of Paul, Barnabas, and others went up (southward, since everything is "down" from Mount Zion) from Antioch to Jerusalem to discuss differences over circumcision practice with regard to Gentile converts to the Christian way (cf. vv. 1f.). This journey seems to be the one described by Paul in Gal 2:1-10, on the occasion when he sought and achieved a favorable settlement on his decision not to circumcise Titus or Gentiles like him. Paul describes the visit as the result of a revelation, but he includes the detail from Acts about provocation by infiltrators from Judaea, whom he calls "false claimants to the title of brother" *(pseudadélphous)*. The sole stipulation on that occasion, according to him, was care for the poor (Gal 2:10). Acts 15 has nothing to say about this. Moreover, the occasion was only Paul's second visit to Jerusalem by his clear recollection (cf. Gal 1:18; 2:1), whereas Acts 15 makes it the third (cf. Acts 9:26; 11:30). The so-called famine visit by Barnabas and Saul in 11:30 contains an echo of Paul's Galatian testimony about care for the (Judaean Christian) poor.

Since Peter's acceptance at Caesarea of the uncircumcised to baptism and his promulgation of full table fellowship with them thereafter (cf. Acts 10 and 11) seems not to have convinced all Pharisee and priestly Christians in Judaea, Luke requires a formalization of the understanding like the one he records. The practice of Paul, which he says in his letters that he follows, indicates that he either came away with a wholly different understanding or, more likely, that there was no letter drafted like that of vv. 23-29.

We should have no difficulty in classifying it as a Lukan construct, since the speeches of Peter, Paul, and James are already in that category. All represent theological charters, as it were, for the settlements that were subsequently arrived at over a long period. This is not to say that there is no possibility of historical reminiscence of a delegation to the church at Antioch, which included the Judaeans Judas and Silas (v. 22).

The pairing of "apostles and elders" (v. 23) is significant in light of last week's discussion of v. 23. It is Luke's way of describing both those roving bearers of the message outside any jurisdiction and the officers of the local church, a distinction made even in Jerusalem. Since Antioch is named in the greeting rather than Damascus or Tarsus, it can be seen as the recognized center of Gentile Christianity, as previously in Acts (cf. especially 13:1-3). Verse 24 distinguishes between the official status of the letter-writers and the unauthorized character of those who created the initial dissension in Antioch (cf. 15:1f.). Judas and Silas are the accredited interpreters of the authentic Jerusalem spirit, here understood to be that voiced by Peter and James earlier in the chapter and in chap. 10. The coupling of the Holy Spirit with the human makers of the decision (v. 28) bears the cachet of Lukan theology. The four out of seven traditional Noachian precepts of the settlement, repeated from v. 20 are the only burden imposed on Gentile converts.

The probable Old Testament sources for the four prohibitions enjoined, ritual rather than ethical, are: meat sacrificed to idols (Lev 17:8f.), blood remaining in meat (Lev 17:10ff.), the ritual slaughter of animals (Lev 17:13), and sex within close degrees of kinship (Lev 18:6-18). These four occur among the seven proposed by later rabbis as a *derek ereṣ* (law of the land), which bound all the descendants of Noah until the Law was given and the resident aliens among the Jews thereafter. The seven prohibitions constituted a minimum for the Torah-oriented community.

This was probably incomprehensible to later Christians, with the result that the variant Western text of Acts omits "what is strangled" from v. 20, and many MSS add the Golden Rule in the prevailing negative form. *Porneía* is omitted from some texts as out of place among dietary rules, or understood as prohibiting unchaste conduct generally rather than the Levitical incest taboo. Similarly, the prohibition against blood comes to be taken as a forbidding of bloodshed, i.e., murder, in line with later Church discipline.

Paul is well familiar with the problems arising from eating foods not slaughtered ritually or sacrificed to idols (cf. Rom 14:14-17; 1 Cor 8:9-13; 10:23-30 and the corresponding commentaries on Rom 1:12 [7-19], Proper 19 [24], Year A, and 1 Cor 10:16-17, The Body and Blood of Christ, Year A). He does not give counsel as if the decree of Acts 15 bound him, although if it were drawn up in any such form he could argue that the problems in Corinth and Rome were different from those of Antioch, Syria, and Tarsus.

The settlement on foods recorded in Acts is probably documented in some Jerusalem church source which Luke has come upon. It does not accord with Paul's practice but Luke, the great reconciler, makes it do so. As to the one great reconciling element in Paul's mind, the relief of the Judaean poor, Luke seems to have no documentation on that.

PSALM 67[2-3, 5-6, 8]

REVELATION 21:10, 22 — 22:5

This vision of a Jerusalem descending from on high takes its departure from the bride figure of v. 2 (cf. v. 9) but concentrates on a city of precious stones. The author is undoubtedly influenced by Ezekiel, whose chap. 40 seems to have four gates, one facing in each direction. They become twelve named for the twelve tribes in 48:30-35. Ephesians has a similar conception, namely, of a temple made up of believers which rises "on the foundation of the prophets and the apostles" (2:20). The twelve names of the twelve tribes and the tutelary angel for each in Revelation are details that connote the perfect character of the believing community, at least in conception. The New Jerusalem is a perfect cube (vv. 15f.), making the same point. This city is an earthly reality but it partakes of the heavenly nature of the abode of God from which it derives (v. 10).

The city that is the Church in ideal needs no Temple: God the Almighty and the Lamb are that; neither is there any sun or moon needed. The Lamb is its great luminary. No wicked persons populate it, only the cleansed. It is a city of perpetual day, not of night, and the Gentile nations and their kings come streaming into it. The earthly Jerusalem is distinguished among the great capitals of the world by not being situated on a river. The heavenly one is, however, situated on one (22:1), much like the stream that flows from beneath the Temple envisioned in Ezek 47. There, the son of man was shown a great many trees on both sides of the rising river (v. 7); here they bear twelve kinds of fruit whose leaves are for the healing of the nations (22:2). The servants of the Lamb will worship God, whose face they look upon. They are better termed slaves *(douloi)* than servants, since the Name will be on their foreheads in the familiar tattoo of slavery (v. 4), even as the heavenly messenger is self-described as a fellow-slave *(sýndoulós, v. 9)*. The LORD God shines in this depiction of the free city as its everlasting light. What a vision is here of the Holy Church of God come down from heaven!

ALLELUIA. JOHN 14:23

Whoever they are who love me will keep my word, and my Father will love them and will come to them.

JOHN 14:23-29

The fourth evangelist cannot get over the marvel of faith in Jesus as the Messiah of his faith community. The opposite reality of a "world" that has not accepted him is likewise never far from his thoughts. This pericope comes in answer to a problem posed as a personal difficulty of the disciple Judas (not Iscariot) but doubtless very real in John's time: How is it that Jesus has revealed himself to those who believe in him but not successfully to a hostile world?

The answer proposed is in terms of being true to Jesus' word (v. 23) and the love common to the Father, Jesus, and the believer that comes as the fruit of this fidelity. The word of Jesus is from the Father, just as he is from the Father. Both God and Jesus will come to dwell with anyone who accepts the word (v. 23).

The Holy Spirit of God will be sent by the Father as *Paráklētos* (counselor or advocate) in a surrogate position for the departed Jesus. His function will be to instruct (v. 26) and to remind *(hypomnései)* with respect to all that Jesus told the disciples, not to bring new teaching.

Jesus gives as his parting gift a deep and abiding *shalom*—not, presumably, the thoughtless word of farewell that is on the lips of people constantly. His is quite the opposite of the world's "Peace."

There is no place in the believer's heart for distress or fear at separation from Jesus (v. 27). The separation is temporary (v. 28a). True love will rejoice that Jesus is with the Father, where he belongs. The Father is "greater" (*meízōn*, 28c) in the sense that he is before Jesus as before all; his will must prevail.

The revelation of Jesus' impending departure serves as a preparation for belief. There must be no hesitancy in faith because he is away from his friends. Just as later in 20:29, the non-seeing believer is praised here above the one who, like Thomas, sees.

JOHN 5:1-9

This Synoptic-like healing miracle occurs on the Sabbath (vv. 9, 16; cf. 9:14) during an unspecified feast. It does not appear on a Sunday in LM but is part of a longer reading on the Tuesday of 4 Lent (5:1-3a, 5-16). Many tourists and pilgrims to Israel have been shown the scattered stonework of the pool by the Sheep [Gate] (see Neh 3:1, 32; 12:39) called Bethesda (or in some MSS Bethzatha), which lies below the roadbed of the Old City on the property of the Missionaries of Africa (formerly *Les Pères Blancs*), now a seminary for Eastern rite candidates for the priesthood. Bethesda (*Beth 'Esdatayin*, an Aram. pl.) seems the better reading because that spelling, long suspected as original, was found on the Copper Scroll of Qumrân to describe a double pool northeast of the Temple Area. When President Franklin Roosevelt went touring in an open car to choose the site for the National Institutes of Health in the 1930s, he asked his assistant Harry Hopkins, "What place is this?" and was told the farmland was in Bethesda, Maryland. He then said, "Good! What better place for healing!"

Verses 3b-4, influenced by v. 7, occur in KJV, DRC, and the ASV, following some late fourth-century Greek MSS—but not the earliest. The significance of the man's illness "for thirty-eight years" is not known, despite this evangelist's penchant for numerology. That it is somehow allegorical for that number in Deut 2:14 seems unlikely. If by "signs" *(sēmeía)* in this Gospel Jesus' miracles alone are meant (2:1-11; 4:40-54; 5:1-9; 6:4-15, 16-21; 9:1-40; 11:1-44), this is the third. Reckoning the two of chap. 6 as distinct makes their number to be seven but if as one they are six, culminating in Jesus' resurrection from the dead as Jesus' seventh and greatest of signs.

The Ascension of the Lord (C)
Thursday after the Sixth Sunday of Easter

ACTS 1:1-11

Luke 1:1-4 is a preface to Luke-Acts in its entirety, addressed to the unidentified, highly placed *(krátiste)* Theophilus. Acts 1:1-5 is a preface to this book only, which reviews certain materials found in Luke 22. Among these are Jesus' being taken up to heaven (v. 2; cf. Luke 22:51; his appearing to "the apostles" over the course of forty days (v. 3; Luke 22:15f., 30f., 36), his suffering *tò patheîn* (v. 3), of which he spoke in Luke 22:25ff. and 44-47; and his meeting (eating) with his disciples (v. 4; cf. Luke 22:41-43), at which time he told them not to leave Jerusalem (v. 4; cf. Luke 22:49). The order of events in the preface to Acts is obviously different but this does not alter or minimize the importance of the events, namely, as links between Luke's "first account" *(prōton lógon,* Acts 1:1) and his second. Jesus' life, death, and glorification prepare for his Father's promise (Luke 22:49; Acts 1:4f.) to be sent down: "power from on high" (Luke) or "being baptized with the Holy Spirit," which will bring "power" (Acts). The detail of forty days (v. 3 does not appear in Luke. This sacred space of time (cf. Gen 7:12; 8:6; Exod 24:18; 1 Kgs 19:8) gives ample room for the demonstration "in many convincing ways" (v. 3) of his state as living *(zōnta).* Luke's Gospel, conversely, seems to describe Jesus as leaving the Eleven after having blessed them (24:51) on the evening of the day he was raised up (see vv. 9, 13, 36, 50 for indications of the sequence). The difference is of no consequence; least of all is it to be settled by recourse to the theory of Jesus' earthly visitations from his new home in heaven. The two things being affirmed are the reality of his being taken from his friends into glory and his conversations with them about God's reign (v. 4), which for Luke will begin with the parousia. For him the life of the Spirit-directed Church is a separate matter. The affirmations against gnostic docetism (Luke 24:43; Acts 10:41) were probably later developments. "All that Jesus did and taught" (v. 1) describes Jesus' earthly life, while the risen-life instruction (lit., "command," from *enteilámenos)* he gave the chosen apostles (v. 2) corresponds to Luke 24:44. It is in their chosenness "through the Holy Spirit" (v. 2) that they have been given authority to teach in the ways that will follow in Acts.

Luke's word for Jesus' taking up in v. 2 *(anelémphthē)* has already been used in its noun form in his Gospel (9:51) for the same purpose. It seems to derive from the LXX of 2 Kgs 2:11, where Elijah—a type of Christ for Luke—is taken up in a chariot of fire.

Only in Mark 13:11 and its parallel in Matthew (not Luke, interestingly) does Jesus speak of the Spirit in the Synoptics. In Acts 1:5 and again in 11:16, a saying attributed to John the Baptizer (Matt 3:11; Luke 3:16) is put on Jesus' lips. Luke will later have Paul make the same distinction in Ephesus between the water-baptism of John and the Spirit-baptism of Jesus (Acts 19:1-6) as is made in v. 5.

The apostles' query about when Israel will have the *basileía* restored to it (v. 6) is answered in terms of undivulgeable mystery (v. 7) and missionary command (v. 8). Mark 13:32 (par. Matt 24:36) contains a logion of Jesus like that of v. 7, which Luke had not used in his Gospel, saving it for here. It is calculated to relieve disappointment in the Christian community over the nonrealization of the parousia (cf. 1 Pet 3:3ff.). By Luke's time the question is not even to be raised; a new relationship to the world has been arrived at: life in the holy community. The notion of witnessing to Jesus, viz., to his resurrection, is common throughout Acts. Jesus' sending of the apostles "to the ends of the earth" (v. 8) will only mean getting Paul as far as Rome in this book, but it is at least a divine sanction on his mission. Peter and John travel as far as Samaria.

There is no final blessing by Jesus in Acts, as in Luke 24:50 (cf. Sir 50:20f.). He is taken up swiftly in the sight of the apostles (v. 9); they are witnesses of the ascension. Livy tells of Romulus being swept up in a cloud, while the intertestamental book of Enoch has that prophet say the same of himself. The two men in white (v. 10) resemble those in Luke's empty-tomb account (24:4). They administer a rebuke intended for the whole Church. All expectation of the imminent return of Jesus is to be reprobated. It is a reality of the future, but one that has about it no precise connotation of time.

PSALM 47[2-3, 6-9]

PSALM 110

EPHESIANS 1:15[17]-23

Ephesians after its initial greeting begins with a blessing of God (v. 3) in vv. 3-14—the traditional Jewish *berakah*—and moves on to a thanksgiving in vv. 15-23 (*eucharistōn*, v. 16). The anonymous author, usually known as "the Ephesian continuator," doubtless includes both forms because the use of each was Paul's practice at various times. The technique, while redundant, is nonetheless to be found in Dan 2:20 and 23. The hope expressed in the present passage is that the wisdom bestowed on Gentile Christians (v. 9) may be effectively received by them (v. 17). A heritage has been given, the wealth of which (v. 18) is made up of wisdom and understanding (v. 9). This inheritance (v. 14) is not yet fully given but exists at present by way of pledge or first payment *(arrabōn),* to be rendered in its entirety when the full redemption *(apolýtrōsis)* of God's personal possession—his people (cf. 1 Pet 2:9)—has been bestowed. Such time will be after the parousia. The acceptance of the inheritance by believers is required if it is to be a completed reality. That Christians may know the hope to which they are called, the "eyes of their hearts" must be enlightened (v. 18). God's power in the believer is likened to the strength he showed in Christ when raising him from the dead and seating him at God's right hand (v. 20). The importance of v. 20 is that it distinguishes between the resurrection and the subsequent exaltation of Christ, something that Paul does not do. He thinks in terms of a single act of glorification while Luke-Acts resembles Ephesians in its division of the mystery into two episodes.

Mention of the Ephesians' faith (v. 15) is a Pauline touch, but this theological treatise in epistolary form does not much resemble the communication of someone who has lived quite a while among the recipients. Paul knew this congregation as well as any and did not need to learn of its faith by hearsay.

The anti-gnostic or anti-angelic-hierarchy tone of Colossians is caught here in vv. 21-23 and again in 6:12. Christ is high above the choirs of angels. Four of the traditional intertestamental nine are here named: *archaí, exousíai, dynameîs,* and *kyriótētēs* (Col 1:16 has "thrones" in place of "virtues," *dynameîs*). The headship of Christ is over his body, the Church, here (vv. 22f.), whereas in 1:10 it has been over all things in the heavens and on earth, over principalities and powers in Col 2:10. The important declaration of faith in Christ (as in Col 2:9) is that he has been made the *plérōma* of him who fulfills everything in the universe, namely, God. Colossians says that in Christ the *plérōma* of God dwells in bodily form. Both writers mean to challenge all Gnostic and angelic hierarchies that lay claim to *plérōma* status and put in their place the ascended, exalted Christ and him alone.

HEBREWS 9:24-28; 10:19-23

For a commentary see Proper 27[32] and Proper 28[33] (B).

ALLELUIA. MATTHEW 28:19A, 20B

Go and make disciples of all nations. I am with you always to the end of the age.

Luke 24:44[46]-53

Christ's concluding charge to his disciples has him interpreting to them the prophetic message of the Scriptures (v. 45), just as he did to the two at Emmaus (v. 27). Verse 46 has already appeared in longer form in 9:22. Penance and the remission of sins must be preached worldwide in the name of Christ (v. 47; cf. Mark 13:10) because he has suffered and is risen. The latter is the content of the Gospel, the former its practical consequence. Jerusalem, not Galilee, is for Luke the *locus originis* of the new faith. It is the place where the disciples do the witnessing they must now proclaim (v. 48). The promise and power of God from on high has come down like the Spirit on all flesh and specifically to this city (v. 49).

Direct mention of Jesus' being taken up (v. 51) is referred to again in Acts 1:2 as the link between the two books. Luke's Gospel ends as it has begun, in Jerusalem's Temple (vv. 52f.). He is ready to begin the complementary narrative of how the Gospel was first lived and then carried abroad. He will proceed from its fate in Jewish circumstances to Gentile to make his point that the transfer was providential, in the sense of totally foreseen by God. Luke's great theme is that the Jews had their chance and, as we might say in terms of a contemporary hermeneutic, blew it. The Christian must read him with caution.

❧ ✦
Seventh Sunday of Easter (C)

Acts 16:16-34

The "spirit of divination," as KJV calls it, is a *pneûma pýthōna* (v. 16), so named because such a serpent was believed to guard the Delphic oracle. She was a clever old woman behind a crack between two rocks who gave questioners ambiguous answers they could interpret as best suited them. The unfortunate but equally clever slave-girl of Philippi was a money-maker for her master. The Lukan author makes her out to be demon possessed by attributing to her exact knowledge of who Paul is and his mission, much as in the exorcism stories about Jesus in his gospel (4:41; 8:28-39). This story serves as the occasion of a Gentile-Jewish fracas that result in the beating and imprisonment of Paul and Silas. The custodian of some reconstructed rooms from the ruins in Philippi solemnly assures modern visitors that "this" open-faced cell was Paul's. The account of the freeing of the pair as the result of an earthquake (vv. 25-34) is the same as that of "the apostles" imprisoned by the high priest but freed by an angel (5:17-26), only told with much more detail. Its point is the coming to faith and baptism of the jailer and his entire family.

Psalm 97

Acts 7:55-60

The speech that Luke puts on Stephen's lips ends with a direct, harsh accusation addressed to the Sanhedrin (Acts 6:12) and the high priest (7:1), whom he associates with their fathers, the murderers of the prophets (v. 52). Told that their offense is failure to observe the Law (v. 53), they are understandably enraged (v. 54; cf. Ps 35:16). The commentary on Acts 8:5-8, 14-17 for 6 Easter (A) speaks of the reported action of the infuriated mob (vv. 57f.) as bearing no relation to anything we know from the Mishnaic tractate *Sanhedrin*. In that document, compiled with the rest around 200 C.E., the "place of stoning is twice the height of a man." The victim is laid supine and finished off with a stone "dropped on his heart" by either a first or a second "witness." The mention of "witnesses" in v. 58 suggests a juridical process in an otherwise extra-legal account.

Today's pericope is as much about Stephen's vision in vindication of his witness to Jesus, the Just One, as it is about the circumstances of his death. Possession of the Holy Spirit has been named earlier as characteristic of him (6:5). Here (v. 55) it is the condition of his being strengthened for death. A vision of divine glory before execution is conventional in Jewish accounts of martyrdom. Acts uses it to confirm the fact of Jesus' standing at the right hand of God (v. 56). See Luke 22:69, where he is seated; the phrase betrays Luke's ignorance of the Jewish term "the Power" for God, similar to "the Glory" in v. 55.

Luke is familiar with the designation "Son of Man," as we know from his Gospel. He does not employ it anywhere in Acts but here (v. 56), perhaps to signalize the transition from a Jewish to a Gentile Church. The question has been raised whether Luke has in mind an advocate's role for Jesus, patterned on that of God in Job 16:19: "Even now, behold, my witness is in heaven, / and my spokesman is on high." Jesus' reception of Stephen, standing, recalls Luke's view of immediate glorification promised to the repentant brigand in Luke 23:43.

The similarities in the deaths of Jesus and Stephen are evident (cf. Luke 23:46 and 34a if it is genuine; also the detail of the witnesses' garments, 34b). The role of the Sanhedrin in Stephen's death, as in that of Jesus, is entirely problematic. So too is the intimation of blasphemy in both cases (Mark 14:64; "holding their hands over the ears," Acts 7:57). *Sanhedrin* 1:5 of the Mishnah speaks of one's being a false prophet as an offense actionable before this body; 4:5 of witnesses in capital cases; 6:4 of blasphemy and idolatry as two capital cases. The uncertainty as to whether Rome had withdrawn capital punishment from the jurisdiction of the Sanhedrin in the days of the prefects of Judaea is well known. For an extended discussion see Paul Winter, *On the Trial of Jesus* (New York: de Gruyter, 1974), 9–10, 13–14.

PSALM 97[1, 2B, 6-7C, 9]

REVELATION 22:12-14, 16-17, 20-21

Jesus pronounces what is more promise than valedictory as this book comes to a close with his solemn commitment to come soon (22:12, 20). He declares himself the Alpha and the Omega (v. 13), a title previously claimed by the Lord God seated on the throne (1:8; 21:6). Jesus declares a variety of workers of evil unfit for the city (v. 15). It is the standard vituperative vocabulary of the period employed by pagan and Jewish moralists. Verse 16 largely repeats 1:1.

This is the concluding passage of the revelation given by God to Jesus Christ, reported by John on Patmos (1:1). Verse 12 is repeated from v. 7, and four of Jesus' six titles are taken from those of God in 21:6 (cf. 1:8, 17; 2:8; Isa 44:6). Jesus promises that the end will come soon (*tachý*, v. 12). In eschatological perspective this is not a precise time word and may just as well mean swiftly or suddenly. Upon his return he will act as judge.

The dire warning against tampering with the words of this book is the other side of the coin of blessing on anyone who keeps the words (1:3). The bride who is the Church come down from heaven (21:2) issues an invitation in concert with the Spirit that says, "Come!" "Come to the waters," Isaiah's summons, had been to all who were thirsty (55:1). Jesus does the same, offering the water of life as a gift. The poetry is peerless. It conveys the high titles applied to Jesus in the time of persecution that Revelation was concerned with. It lets the hearer know what to expect in the final age. Better still, it conveys what life in the heavenly Jerusalem on this earth is meant to be.

The seer, John, is Jesus' messenger (*ággelos*, v. 16) who has given his witness regarding the state of the churches (v. 16). The title "Root of David" occurs in 5:5, while "Morning Star" *(ho astēr ho proïnós)* without its adjective "bright *(ho lampros)* appears in 2:28. Those who have washed their robes (cf. Gen 19:11) and may enter the city are presumably the martyrs, or perhaps merely the just of 3:4, 7:14. The figure of the tree of life from Gen 2:9; 3:22 is cited here for the only time in the New Testament. These writings in general show little interest in the "sin of our first parents" which looms so large in catechetical history (cf. John 8:44?; 2 Cor 11:3; in another category are 1 Cor 15:22, 45; Rom 5:14f.).

God's spirit speaks through the visionary authors (v. 17). The spirit is not alone in issuing an invitation to drink of the waters of life. It is also uttered by the bride of the Lamb (cf. 19:7b-8), the community of God's saints. The life-giving water is traceable to Isa 55:1 and occurs frequently in the Johannine literature. *Uisge beatha* and *eau de vie* are the *hýdor zōēs* of v. 17 but clearly distinguishable from the biblical draught: they are not free *(dōreán)*, although they may at times be duty-free.

Christ promises a speedy (sudden?) advent and the author of the book confirms this with a grateful "Amen." He concludes with a phrase in Greek (*érchou Kýrie Iēsoû*, v. 20) which we know in transliterated Aramaic from 1 Cor 16:22 and also from the *Didachē: Maran atha*, "Our Lord, come!" This was evidently a liturgical phrase used in Greek-speaking churches as a remnant, like *Kyrie eleison*, *Hosanna*, and *Sabaoth* in the Roman Rite.

Verse 21 provides the farewell blessing which seems to be missing from all seven letters to the churches of chaps. 2–3.

Alleuia. John 14:18

I will not leave you orphans. I will come back to you and your hearts will rejoice.

John 17:20-26

Verses 9-19 of Jesus' final apostrophe to the Father upon completing his work have been a prayer for the needs of the disciples. In these concluding verses (20-26) he prays for all who believe in him through the disciples' witnessing word. This prayer is one for unity among believers (v. 21) and for their acceptance of Jesus' legacy of love (v. 26). The bond of personal interpenetration between Jesus and the Father is proposed as a model for unity among believers. Jesus' prayer is that they may be in God and him, as he and God are in each other (v. 21). More than that, the presence of believers to God and Jesus (*"en hēmîn"*; the *hen* of "[one] in us," v. 21, is found in Sinaiticus but is lacking in the other earliest MSS) is the sign proposed by Jesus "*that* the world may believe that you sent me." In other words, nothing can convert a hostile world but its experience of Christians who are in God and Christ.

Jesus possesses a fullness (1:16) and a glory (1:14; 8:54) from the Father that he is able to transmit to others. This glory *(dóxa)* was God's gift to him "before the foundation of the world" (v. 24). Here he would have them see it (*theōrōsin*, v. 24), whereas a few phrases above he says he has given it (*dédōka*, v. 22). The Vulgate renders the gift as *claritas* rather than *gloria*, a divine luminosity bestowed first on Jesus, then all who associate themselves with him in intimacy with the

Father. Jesus lives in his friends and God lives in him (v. 23); therefore God lives in them. This, it is hoped, will bring to completion a unity (*hína ōsin teteleiōménoi eis hén*, v. 23) among them, with no distinction drawn as to who is one with whom: the Father, Jesus, all believers. The picture is one of mystical union in faith of God and humanity, with Jesus as the first beneficiary of a plan that originates in the depths of godhead.

Jesus wills that where he is those whom the Father has given him may be along with him (v. 24) to see his glory. This is all part of the futurist thrust of Johannine eschatology which some would deny to it. Massey Shepherd draws attention to the opinion that this prayer with which chap. 17 concludes is an exposition of the succinct Lord's Prayer in Matthew and Luke, and observes in both "a curious lack of reference to the Spirit."

God is a just (*díkaie*, v. 25) Father for Jesus, the source of all justice (Heb., *tsedāka*). John knows Jesus as primarily a Moses-like prophet who reveals God to Israel, but now in the fullest way possible (cf. 1:17f.; 17:26). Ever at the Father's side (lit. "deep in his bosom," 1:18), he has been sent (17:25) by God to reveal God's name (v. 26). His work of revealing will not cease. It will continue, so that the Father's love for Jesus may continue as life in Jesus' friends.

❧ ✍

Day of Pentecost (C)

ACTS 2:1-[11]21

For a commentary see under (A).

GENESIS 11:1-9

If this lection is chosen the second one should be Acts 2:1-21, because the latter is almost certainly Luke's way of saying that, with the outpouring of the Holy Spirit (2:4), the multiplicity of tongues begun at Babel (Gen 11:6f.) has come to an end. All the peoples can now speak the one language of faith (Acts 2:7-11). This is the last tale in the pre-Abramite first eleven chapters of Genesis, which are told to account for the origins of things. The Judahites in their sixth-century, fifty-year exile in Babylon became acquainted with a people whose tongue they could not understand. A tower in Hebrew is *migdāl* but in Akkadian, the ancient Semitic language of Mesopotamia, it is a ziggurat (*ziqquratu*, from the verb "to tower high"). Earlier in Genesis, Cain was the first to build a city (4:17), not a good thing in the eyes of a nomadic people. But in today's story the people of Babel in the plain of Shinar already have a city. The pious Hebrews of a later day tell of ancestors who migrated eastward and were shocked at the planned city under construction. In its midst are temple towers of brick and bitumen, not the stone and mortar they are used to (11:3f.). For the double sin of pride in attempting such a structure and its purpose the worship of a false god, the LORD had to punish this people. As it lay in ruins a millennium later the Israelites devised a tale—or edited an ancient one—that accounted satisfactorily for the confusion of tongues. "Look, they are all one people, and they have all one language" (v. 6a). It is worth considering not what unity but what global mischief might come of such a state of affairs, in light of the disunity among many peoples of the same tongue.

PSALM 104:[1]24-34, 35B

ROMANS 8:14-17

For a commentary see Trinity Sunday (1 Pentecost) (B).

1 CORINTHIANS 12:3-7, 12-13

SEQUENCE

Veni, Sancti Spiritus.

ALLELUIA

Come, Holy Spirit, kindle in the hearts of your faithful the fire of your love.

JOHN 20:19-23

For commentaries on the above two readings see Pentecost (A) and 3 Easter (A).

JOHN 14:8-17, (25-27)

For a commentary on John 14:1-[12] 14 see 5 Easter (A). If love for Jesus takes the form of keeping his commandment, the Father will send his disciples another Advocate (presumably Jesus himself is the first). This Spirit of truth will be with them forever (vv. 16f.). The Spirit is spoken of again as the Teacher of "all things," the reminder of all that Jesus taught (v. 26). Peace is Jesus' gift to his disciples who, after his glorification, became the Church. John 20:19-23 has rightly been called "the Johannine Pentecost." The gift of the Spirit, which is the gift of Christ's peace, was not given after fifty days as in Acts but it was promised in the supper discourse and given on the evening of the day of resurrection behind closed doors. God never retracts a promise, whether made to Abraham and his offspring according to the flesh or to a Gentile world according to the spirit. The church, like the Jewish people, is heir to every promise ever made. But there are always conditions in the realm of free response. Synagogue and Church must ask themselves in every age whether the promise has been understood and, if so, whether it has been given free and unconditional answer.

❧ Season after Pentecost ❧
(Ordinary Time)

❧❧
Trinity Sunday / First Sunday after Pentecost (C)

Proverbs 8:1-4, 22-31

Wisdom (*ḥokmah*, f.) speaks throughout this chapter from v. 4 on. Ruling, governance, and justice are within her province (vv. 15f.). Wealth and prosperity follow in her train (v. 18) for those who walk the path of duty and righteousness (v. 20).

Wisdom had the status of a creature for the Jews, not an eternal one but a manifestation of the creative act of God at every stage in human history. The phrases "of long ago" (v. 22) and "of old" (v. 23) convey the primeval, a notion taken up in the subsequent phrases which describe the formation of the earth (vv. 24-26). Wisdom was there before there were depths or springs, mountains, clods of earth, or fields. She was with God at the foundation of the heavens and the pillars of the earth (vv. 27f.) and at the decreeing of the tides (v. 29). Wisdom is from God and at God's side (v. 30) but she becomes the companion and the playmate of humankind (v. 31).

The recurring phrases "when," "before," and "while as yet" of verses 24ff. are to be found in the Babylonian creation epic *Enuma elish*. The adoption of the mythology of this composition is nearly total, but when it comes to causality the author of Proverbs is firm. The Lord made all through the agency of wisdom. Wisdom preceded the creation, but very clearly she came after the creator God.

Psalm 104:24-34; 35b

Psalm 8:4-9

Romans 5:1-5

In the previous chapter Paul has begun his development of Abraham's justifying faith. Abraham hoped "against hope" that he would be the father of many nations as he had been promised (4:18). His faith in his role for the future was credited him as justice (see Gen 15:6; Rom 4:3) just as ours will be credited to us as justice "if we believe in him who raised Jesus our Lord from the dead" (Rom 4:24). It is conventional to say of the latter verse and v. 25 (e.g., Martin Buber, Rudolf Bultmann) that Hebrew *ᵉmunah* is trust in the person of the Lord whereas Pauline *pistis* is faith in a fact, a deed that God has done in Jesus Christ. Paul would probably be shocked to learn of any such difference and say that he was incapable of thinking like a German professor. He seems to be at pains to show how the Christian believer and the patriarch Abraham are identical in all respects as regards faith in God's promise. Note that 4:24 does not praise the deed of the resurrection or ask faith in *it* but in the one who did it. Paul cares more for the faith of the Christian in a God who will yet act than in a God who has acted.

Justification by means of faith is already, however, a reality for Paul. It means peace with God for the believer (cf. Col 1:21) achieved through Christ the reconciler (5:1; cf. 2 Cor 5:18f.). The present condition of the Christian is grace; with respect to the future it is hope for a share in God's glory. Christ is the person who has made both possible, faith the condition to which God has successfully invited us through him (v. 2). "The immediate results of Christ's work are ours through faith" (T. W. Manson, *PC*, 944).

The road to hope may be a rocky one. Paul traces it by means of stages, the stopping-points of which are affliction / endurance / tested virtue / hope (*thlîpsis / hypomonḗ / dokimḗ /elpís*, vv. 3f.). The hope is not a frustrating kind because the gift of the Spirit fills our hearts with love (v. 5). *Agápē* for Paul is what to do until the Messiah comes.

Alleluia. Revelation 1:8

Glory to the God who is, and who was, and who is to come.

John 16:12-15

If God's wisdom is the principle of the creation (see Proverbs, above) and justifying faith together with hope and love the proper response to God's work of salvation (see Romans, above), the guidance of the Spirit of truth is the personal assurance that trust in God through Christ has not been misplaced (John 16:13).

This pericope has a long history in Trinitarian debate, notably—and regrettably—in the "filiōque" controversy ("All that the Father has belongs to me" taken as the fullness of Godhead transmitted to the Son, who in turn "sends [the Paraclete] to you," 16:7, as he could not do unless he had him, any more than the Father could send him "in my name," 14:26, unless the Paraclete proceeded from the Son). This report on ninth-century debates, resurrected in the thirteenth and fifteenth at Lyons and Ferrara-Florence with new emphasis, would no doubt confuse the fourth evangelist. He would probably point out that he had spoken only of what would take place among people in the world, not about what went on eternally in the Godhead. But he would assent vigorously to a common possession of a message from God by Jesus and the Spirit of truth. The latter would not deviate from it by a hair's breadth.

While this passage says nothing directly about Trinitarian theology it says everything about Jesus' message as God's own truth. Jesus will be glorified by the Spirit's total fidelity to his message (v. 14). Since Jesus' teaching has had God as its source, any spirit that is of God can do no other than adhere to it fully (v. 15).

While there is current debate about the suitability of the words "infallibility" and "indefectibility" with respect to human possession of the "all" that is "announced" (*pánta hósa . . . anaggeleî*, v. 15), it is clear that John is interested in the question from another point of view. His concern is the divinity of the source, the transmitter of all that is proclaimed—Jesus—and its guarantor the Spirit. He assumes but does not say that faith will receive the message in proportion as the message is given.

<hr>

⁊⋅⋅⋅⋅⋅⋅⋅⋅⋅
The Body and Blood of Christ (C)
Thursday after Trinity Sunday but Commonly Celebrated on the Following Sunday

GENESIS 14:18-20

Benjamin Disraeli's quip about the Honorable Member who resembled a mule that has neither pride of ancestry nor hope of posterity is too well known for rehearsal. Does it have any application to Melchizedek, whose activity is recorded as mysteriously as that of "a bird flying through the night"? Probably not, since the pious Yahwist author makes all the use possible of the historical fragment he possesses. If the designation reached the J author as *melek Shalem*, "king of Salem," it is clear why he should have wished to have the father of the Jews blessed by the king of this Jebusite city on the slope of Mount Zion. A note in NAB suggests that the original reading may have been *mĕlĕk shĕlōmō*, "a king allied to him." We do not even know with certainty that ancient Salem was the site of Jerusalem. The operative concept in J's use of the Melchizedek story comes from Ps 133:3: "For there [the mountains of Zion] the LORD has pronounced his blessing, life forever."

Melchizedek venerates his Canaanite deity El-elyon, "The Most High God." The Genesis author has the priest-king invoke on Abram a blessing of his God, designating him "the creator of heaven and earth." He also makes El-elyon responsible for Abram's victory. There is the possibility that Abram acquired the notion of God as creator from this Canaanite deity, just as he worshiped him under the title El-shaddai, the name of another Canaanite deity (see 17:1 where the title is translated "the Almighty"; it may mean "the mountain god" but we do not have certainty on this). The designation "the LORD" dates to Moses' time (see Exod 3:13ff.), despite the Yahwist's claim (in Gen 4:26) that it was used before the flood. Psalm 91:1 puts the two ancient titles *elyon* and *shaddai* together in the service of YHWH: "You who dwell in the shelter of the Most High, / who abide in the shadow of the Almighty, / Say to the LORD . . ." Two other divine titles follow, "refuge" and "fortress," the latter giving us the place-name Masada.

The Yahwist wants to portray the king of Salem as subservient to the patriarch Abraham. He reveals him as a learner about the creator who wins victories for those who trust in him.

For a note on the matters that precede and follow this pericope, see 2 Lent (C), Gen 1[5]–12, 17–18 and Proper 12 [17] (C).

PSALM 110:1-4

1 CORINTHIANS 11:23-26

It was mentioned in the commentary on Luke 22–23 on Passion or Palm Sunday (C) that more recent opinion considers Luke's account of the Last Supper and Paul's in this pericope to have derived from a common source (Antioch practice in the years 30–40?), with Luke's version probably the earlier. Previously, many thought Luke 22:19b-20 an interpolation from 1 Cor 11:24-25a because of the similarity in wording, not for any lack of textual attestation of the passage in Luke.

For a commentary on the words of institution in Mark (14:22-26) see The Body and Blood of Christ (B).

Paul uses in v. 23 the rubric on dependable transmission of tradition that he will employ again in 15:3. "From *(apò)* the Lord" probably means from oral or

Church tradition about the Lord, not direct revelation to Paul. "I received" *(parélabon)* is the Rabbinic formula *qibbel min;* "what I handed on" *(parédōka), masar l^e*. First Corinthians alone of the four accounts of the supper situates it "on the night he was handed over." This may be word play, *paredídeto* echoing the recently occurring *parédōka.* It may also be a chronological precision. Those who follow Mlle. Annie Jaubert in her chronology of the last days of Jesus' life *(The Date of the Last Supper* [Staten Island: Alba, 1965]), in which the supper is placed on Tuesday night, because the verb "handed over" does not warrant the conclusion from the Mark/Matthew accounts that he ate with his friends the night before he died. The Roman canon's *"pridie quam pateretur"* is not biblical (the Vulgate for Paul is *"tradebatur"*); it seems to be a deliberate straddle, since Jesus' *patheîn* could be taken as either his death or all that led up to it.

Jesus' three actions upon taking the bread in hand are blessing God *(eucharistésas),* breaking the bread *(éklasen),* and saying *(eîpen)* the words. The Markan and Lukan traditions have Jesus also giving *(édōken)* the bread and cup to his friends. Verbs for bless, break, and give occur in both of Mark's accounts of the multiplication of the loaves (6:41 and 8:6), on which the supper account is patterned or vice versa. The presumption is that actual eucharistic practice in the churches provided the vocabulary for both. Paul's familiar liturgy, like Luke's, has Jesus' body being given—without that Lukan verb—"for you," in contrast with the Mark/Matthew blood shed "for many" (see Mark 14:24; Matt 26:28). Paul's remembrance phrase, attached to both bread and cup, occurs in Luke in connection with the bread only (22:19b). *Eis tēn emēn anámnēsin* is the Hebrew *l^e zikkaron,* "in memorial"—better than "remembrance" or "memory." For this is not merely a command to recall but to perform a memorial rite.

The meal as proclamation of the Lord's death "until he come" (v. 26) is an echo of its presumably primitive status as eschatological in emphasis (cf. the wording of Jesus' vow of abstention in Luke 22:16, 18). It is widely supposed that Christians ate this forward-looking meal in connection with Jesus' death and resurrection and composed the liturgies of which we possess New Testament fragments only later.

SEQUENCE

Lauda, Sion, Salvatoris

ALLELUIA. JOHN 6:51

I am the living bread come down from heaven. Whoever eats this bread will live forever.

Luke 9:11b-17

This feeding of the multitude, the only one in Luke, parallels the first one in Mark (6:30-44) and Matthew (14:13-21) more closely than the second. Luke situates it in relation to Bethsaida (v. 10), as they do not. His account could be an edited version of Mark's; no independent source is demanded. The identity of vocabulary between this miracle narrative and the Last Supper accounts explains the iconographic representation of the eucharist in catacomb art. There, fish and wicker baskets are just as prominent as loaves, with the cup often missing. The "breaking of bread" *(hē klásis toû artoû)* is an early name for the Christian eucharist *(katéklasen*, v. 16, the same in Mark 6:41; Matt 14:19 gives the participle *klásas)*.

Luke changes Mark's groups (lit., garden plots) of "hundreds and fifties" *(prasiaì prasiaì katà hekatòn kaì katà pentékonta*, Mark 6:40) to "groups of fifty or so." Mark probably got the phrase from Jethro's plan for the government of the people by upright judges (see Exod 18:21). The story was likely influenced in the telling by Elisha's feeding of a hundred men with twenty barley loaves (2 Kgs 4:42ff.), but it must have had some historical basis in Jesus' career. The actual event was no doubt viewed as an anticipation of the banquet of the end-time, as evidenced by the development in John 6.

For a commentary on what immediately precedes this pericope in Mark 6:30-34, see Proper 11 [16] (B), as well as the treatment by John of what is apparently the same incident (ibid.).

❧❧
Proper 4 [9] / Ninth Sunday of the Year (C)
Sunday between May 29 and June 4, inclusive (if after Trinity Sunday)

1 Kings 18:20-21, (22-29), 30-39

The last reading from this book that worshipers following RCL have heard was the prayer of Solomon (1 Kgs 8:22-23, 41-43) on Proper 4 [19] (same as 9 Epiphany [9] in the years it occurs). A commentary on it was provided under Proper 16 [21] (B). Solomon is now dead (1 Kgs 11:41-43) after a tumultuous reign toward the end of which he took many foreign wives who turned his heart away after other gods (vv. 1-5). He was challenged by Hadad the Edomite and Rezon king of Damascus (vv. 14-25) and far more seriously by Jeroboam, son of an Ephraimite servant who engaged in open rebellion (vv. 26-40). The secession of the ten northern tribes under this man led to his twenty-two year reign (14:20) during which

Solomon's son Rehoboam succeeded him on the throne of Judah (14:21). First Kings lists the kings of the south and north in the years after the schism, namely, Abijam, Asa, and Jehoshaphat in Judah and Nadab, Baasha, Elah, Zimri, and Omri in Israel. The last named (876–869; called "twelve years" by a scribal error, 16:23) is given short shrift by the Judahite author but extrabiblical sources, chiefly Assyrian and one stele from Mesha, testify to the most distinguished rule by Omri of any of the kings of Israel. This brought his son Ahab to the throne in Samaria (869–850) while the aged Asa was drawing his long reign in Jerusalem to a close (913–873). Omri had arranged a marriage of convenience for Ahab to Jezebel, daughter of the pagan king of Sidon. The contest reported in today's lection is between Israel's God represented by Elijah and the Ba 'al or chief deity of the Sidonians whom the weak-kneed Ahab worshiped (16:31). There is a famine in the land (18:2) and the challenge on a southeastern peak of the Carmel range is to see whether God or a god will send rain. An altar is prepared, a bullock is placed on it, and Elijah proceeds to taunt the pagan priests for their morning-long, ineffective outcries in prayer. The prophet rebuilds the altar destroyed after their defeat and soaks its wood thoroughly. At his prayer, not surprisingly, fire comes down and consumes the offering, wood and all. He then dispatches the four hundred fifty priests of Ba 'al. Pilgrims to Galilee should ask tour guides to show them the reconstructed Canaanite altar of stones at *Mukraḥa*, chest-high, round and twenty or more feet in diameter.

PSALM 96

1 KINGS 8:22-23, 41-43

For a commentary see Ninth Sunday after the Epiphany [9] (C).

PSALM 96:1-9

GALATIANS 1:1[2, 6-10]-12

Paul is angry over the reports he has received concerning some in these churches, so angry that after his salutation he omits his customary thanksgiving to God for all God has done among them. What is evil about the present age? In the apostle's periodization of history he is describing all of world history from Adam up to the present. Only in the new age that has dawned with Christ are we set free for lives of grace and peace. He, Paul, is the one who called the baptized of the unnamed Galatian cities to this new life and some among them have turned, not away from him which he could endure, but to a different gospel (v. 6). Since there is no other, the resort can only be to a perversion of the good tidings (*eu-aggélion*; Old English, *gōd-spel*) he has brought. It takes a while for him to specify what this falling away from the truth can be, so excited and disturbed is he. Before getting to that, he levels a curse *(anáthema)* at any who have promulgated a contrary message. Not even an angel from heaven dare do this!

Some in Galatia must have been saying he preached as he did to curry favor with people (v. 10). Only the modification of strict demands could bring such a charge, surely not stringency in the practices he called for. And so it will prove. He is being charged with not requiring non-Jews to live like Jews as part of belief in the Jew Jesus. It would be like demanding contemporary Protestants or Catholics to adopt a discipline or pieties that are no part of Christian life. So it was with circumcision, the kosher laws and the like that some have been demanding of Paul's Gentiles. His defense of his gospel not requiring this is that it did not originate humanly. He had it direct from a revelation of Jesus Christ (v. 12).

Alleluia. John 3:16

God so loved the world that he gave his only Son, so that all who believe in him might have eternal life.

Luke 7:1-10

This is a story about a Jew being asked to call on Israel's God for the healing of the slave of an officer in the occupying army. It could have happened as described then or now, but it would be an uncommon occurrence. Luke makes it believable by adding to the source he has in common with Matthew the detail that the officer loves the Jewish people and has built a meeting place (*synagōgē*, v. 5) for them. Some highly placed military do win the confidence of the peoples they are charged with keeping under control by just such measures: public works that a subject people's government does not have the will or the funds to provide. Both evangelists (although Matthew uses fewer words) describe it as a healing at a distance, when a touch or some other physical gesture is more usual. A centurion had one hundred legionaries under his command in wartime but seldom in peace. There were 3,000 in a Roman legion at full strength, 5 cohorts of 600 each, and 6 centuries. The officer expects a healing by a word of command because he is used to giving orders and expects it in others who have authority. He has already identified Jesus as someone with authority over the forces of nature. "*Sed tantum dic verbo*," "Say but the word and my slave will be healed." Matthew calls him a lad, *paîs*. "Go! And he goes, Come! And he comes. Do this! Do that!" That is the way things work in this man's army. There is no time for debate or argument. So it is with the power God has given to Jesus. The divine command is transmitted to Jesus instantaneously and from him to us. The trouble is, we say, "Heal" or "Spare" or "Accomplish," to God, but we know we cannot give orders. We have to wait and see what God makes of our prayers.

🐟🐟

Proper 5 [10] / Tenth Sunday of the Year (C)
Sunday between June 5 and June 11, inclusive

1 KINGS 17:8-16, (17-24)

See Proper 27 [32] (B) for a commentary on vv. 10-16. That story of the meal and the oil not running out until the rains came in response to the prophet's prayer is followed by another, namely, of the revival of the son of the Sidonian widow. She speaks of "the LORD your God" to indicate that YHWH is not her deity. Moreover she is suspicious of this man of another religion, like many a modern individual in the presence of a strange clergyman (v. 18). Has he come to do harm? Is not the death of her son quite enough trouble? (See v. 18.) The prophet asks for the lifeless body of the son, lays it out on his own bed, and then utters a prayer for the boy's resumed breathing (vv. 19f.). The threefold stretching of Elijah's body upon his is ritualized and may not be dismissed as a case of cardiopulmonary resuscitation (v. 21). Clearly, a wonder is being reported. The Church fathers delighted in their homilies to liken the spread-eagled Elijah to Jesus on the cross, who restored sinful humanity to life by contact with every human limb and sense, encompassing our humanity completely. By the effect of Jesus' prayer like Elijah's we know him to be a man of God whose mouth speaks a word of truth (v. 24).

PSALM 146

PSALM 30[2-6, 11-13]

GALATIANS 1:11[19]-24

ALLELUIA. LUKE 7:16

A great prophet has arisen in our midst, God has visited his people.

LUKE 7:11-17

For commentaries, see Tenth Sunday after Epiphany (C).

❧☙
Proper 6 [11] / Eleventh Sunday of the Year (C)
Sunday between June 12 and June 18, inclusive

1 KINGS 21:1-10, (11-14), 15-21A

King Ahab had been humiliated by Elijah's God—who should have been his God—when we last heard of him two Sundays ago. He will die in a battle with the king of Aram (Syria) in a case of mistaken identity (22:29-40), but not before he wins a temporary victory over that King Benhadad's troops (chap. 20) and hears his death foretold by a prophet for letting that worthy escape with his life (20:35-43). As we resume the story it might help to review the portions of this book read on Propers 4 [9] and 5 [10] and look forward to the one on Proper 8 [13].

The greed of a man in power has seldom been better portrayed. The determination of his wife, however, was required to achieve what he could not have achieved on his own. The story opens with the supposition of Ahab common to kings and the super-rich that money can buy anything (v. 2). He is wrong. He has not taken into account a poor man's attachment to the soil his ancestors owned and worked for centuries. This is not a tale of a vineyard so much as of countless generations of human lives. "I will give you the vineyard of Naboth the Jezreelite," Jezebel said. Her plot is a simple one: a public fast promulgated in the king's name, Naboth libeled publicly for blasphemy and lèse-majesté by two thugs, and he then executed by stoning without trial. The queen is calm. Her plan carries. Not so the king. Ahab has taken possession of Naboth's vineyard but the prophet meets him there and faces him with the enormity of his crime (vv. 20-23). As the dogs licked up Naboth's blood, Elijah promises, so will they do with Ahab's. Jezebel's corpse will meet the same fate, escaping becoming carrion for the vultures only by dying in the city (see 22:35; 2 Kgs 9:30-37). Thus was the theft of ancestral land vindicated.

Psalm 5:1-8

2 Samuel 11:26—12:[7]-10, 13-15

Reading Nathan's charge to David, "You are the man!" could be meaningless to hearers except that the king's covetous, murderous conduct is recalled in the succeeding verses. The use the author makes of David's lapse is instructive. The king has chosen to live by the sword; his house will therefore die by the sword, or at least be plagued by its persistent presence.

The *dénouement* of this tale is brief. David repents and for this is told that he will not have to pay with his life. The price exacted is the life of the adulterously conceived child.

Jesus taught his hearers not to make easy correspondences between human tragedy and moral fault as its cause (Luke 13:1-5). The tendency is so deeply ingrained, however, that not even the Savior succeeded in eradicating it. There may be no swift one-to-one retribution such as 2 Samuel envisions but the author's instinct is sound that sees violence as the breeder of violence. A morally callous society, or even household, proliferates callousness.

Psalm 32:[1-2, 5, 7, 11]

Galatians 2:15[16, 19]-21

Chronologically, v. 16 is Paul's first recorded statement on the conflict between justification (i.e., being declared not guilty because no longer guilty) by faith in Christ and by "works of the law." Paul means by that phrase the "special laws" (the phrase is Philo's) that spell out the signs of Jewishness—in this context as non-applicable to Gentiles. Already the statement of v. 16 is an axiom with him. He will later provide reasons why he holds it but no reasons are needed or compelling for an axiom. The deed of God in Jesus Christ has eliminated any element of uncertainty for Paul.

Just how he died to the Law, *through the Law*, to live for God (v. 19a) is unclear. His later statement that the end *(telos)* of the Law is Christ is a clue of sorts (Rom 10:4). Accepting the Law in a spirit of Abrahamic faith—which Paul's struggles with observant Jews of the diaspora and the Jerusalem church have led him to as his chief argument—has left him open to the grace of God made manifest in Jesus Christ (Rom 3:21-26). The fact of Christ's crucifixion probably gives an even better indication (v. 19b). Faith in this deed of God was for Paul the watershed. One way he argues the question is to identify the Law as self-destructive because it was temporary in God's design (3:15-18). It was at best a means to identify transgression (Rom 4:15) and when transgression was removed by faith in the cross its usefulness was over. Still, how any of this came about "through the Law" is a puzzle. Perhaps God had made fidelity to it during the Mosaic interim a condition of the sending of the Son. The mystical death of all believers with Christ is the key, that much is clear (v. 19; cf. Rom 7:4ff.). Can it be that, since the mode of this death which is a blessing for all has been described by the Law as a curse (Gal 3:13; cf. Deut 21:23); "death to the Law" has therefore come *through* the law?

Paul continues to live his life "in the flesh" but it is now a "life lived by faith" (v. 20). Christ's self-abnegating love for others has made his living in Paul a reality (ibid.). To expect that fidelity to the Law will bring justification now that Christ has died is to regard the gift of God, conflated with "grace" in most translations, as needless or, again in modern translations, that "Christ died for nothing" (v. 21).

ALLELUIA. JOHN 15:15B

I call you my friends, says the Lord, for I have made known to you all that the Father has told me.

LUKE 7:36—8:3

Luke seems to be accommodating a narrative he has from Mark (14:3-9//Matt 26:6-13), which the first two evangelists use as anticipatory of Jesus' burial, to illustrate forgiveness (v. 47), a leading Lukan *motif*. "The parable (vv. 41ff.) does not exactly fit the case. The woman does not love because she has been forgiven but vice versa" (G. W. H. Lampe, *PC*, 831). Luke wishes to compare her favorably in the need for forgiveness she experiences with Simon who is unaware of his need.

Women companions of Jesus and the Twelve are a feature of the Galilean ministry (see Mark 15:40f.). Their benefactions are highlighted here (8:3), as in Mary Magdalene's possessed/psychotic state (note: *never* in the Gospels her sinfulness).

Proper 7 [12] / Twelfth Sunday of the Year (C)
Sunday between June 19 and June 25, inclusive

1 KINGS 19:1-4, (5-7), 8-15A

Tracking Ahab and Jezebel to their deaths last Sunday has meant that the story of Elijah's flight from the queen's wrath and the refuge he sought in a cave on Mount Horeb has been passed over. We return to it this morning. She learns of the slaughter Elijah has ordered of the priests of her Sidonian god Ba'al, and she is furious (18:40; 19:1-3). The second leg of the prophet's journey from Beersheba to "the mount of God" is one of a biblical forty days and forty nights (v. 8; cf. Gen 7:12; Exod 24:18; Matt 4:2; Acts 1:3). He has the strength for it only from a jug of water and cake of meal placed near him by an angel as he sleeps under a broom tree. Once arrived at the cave for shelter he is challenged by the LORD for his presence there. He answers self-righteously that the LORD now has only him as a defender since all the others in the northern kingdom have apostatized, thrown down the priestly altars, and killed the prophets. The LORD will call him on it, speaking not in a rock-splitting voice nor out of wind and fire but a "sound of sheer silence" (v. 12). The "still, small voice" of older translations has become a tiny whispering or murmuring sound in modern ones. This passage does not contain the once equally familiar "cloud no bigger than a man's hand rising out of the sea" (18:44), which was the sign of the end of the drought over which the contest with the pagan priests had been staged. Today's pericope repeats YHWH's challenge to the fugitive Elijah and his boastful response verbatim (vv. 9b-10, 13b-14). The LORD passes judgment on the claim by first disregarding it entirely and sending Elijah on a threefold prophetic errand (vv. 15-17) and then observing curtly that seven thousand remain in Israel who have not bowed the knee to Ba 'al or kissed his image (v. 18). Paul finds that declaration apposite to remind the Gentile believers in Rome that there is a Jewish remnant of believers "chosen by grace . . . God's people whom God foreknew" (Rom 11:2-5). Christians need this frequent reminder with respect to the Jewish people who have not bowed the knee to any but the true God. It is a salutary text, besides, for the many Christian groups of all the ages convinced that they alone have preserved the true faith.

See also Propers 14 [19] (A) and 14 [19] (B).

PSALM 42 AND 43

ISAIAH 65:1-9

The first twelve verses of this chapter are an oracle that is hardly judgmental, while the remainder (vv. 13-25) is an oracle of salvation culminating in the promise of "new heavens and a new earth" (v. 17) and the peaceful coexistence of the wolf and the lamb along with the lion, ox-like, munching straw (v. 25). Could the Judahites upon their return after fifty years in Babylon have resumed pagan cultic practices like those described in vv. 3-4a? Thoroughly disregarding the prohibition of swine's flesh is a more believable offense (v. 4b). And who can these "holier than thou" people of v. 5a be? Surely Jewish sectaries of some kind, perhaps a group committed to gnostic-tinged purity laws of their own devising.

The Persians had been their deliverers and are now their political masters. Has anything of the spirit-matter dualism of that land raised its head for Trito-Isaiah to deplore? One clear answer to these questions seems to be that the prophet is using preexilic language to criticize the laxity in observance of the postexilic community. The LORD is ready all day long to be sought out but is not being called on by a rebellious people (vv. 1-3). They may expect repayment of their iniquities (v. 7a) which are patterned on the iniquities of their ancestors (v. 7b). But the LORD means to repent of the harsh judgments leveled on some, or at least "not destroy them all" (v. 8c). A familiar proverb is quoted to illustrate this change of heart. One says when new wine is thought to be present in a cluster of grapes: "Don't destroy it; there's good in it" (v. 8a, *Tanakh*). So, "I will bring forth offspring from Jacob. . . . My chosen ones will take possession; my servants shall settle there" (v. 9). The people may be unfaithful. God is ever faithful.

See also 1 Advent (B).

PSALM 22:19-28

ZECHARIAH 12:10-11; 13:1

There is no indication of who the unnamed sufferer of this mysterious passage is. The "spirit of compassion and supplication" is a divine blessing on the Jerusalemites, bestowed somehow in connection with the victim. He has been thrust through by the very people who mourn him, an indication of a blunder or an impetuous act immediately regretted. The similarity of this verse to the developed Isa 52:13—53:12 is evident. If Hadadrimmon is a place near Megiddo, the speculation is that the grief expressed at the death of King Josiah may be intended (see 2 Chron 35:22-25). Since the word is composed of two names of the Canaanite storm god, the reference may be to his annual celebration and the weeping and wailing on that occasion.

As mentioned above, Proper 9 [14] (A), the last six chapters of Zechariah are a collection from various hands other than the composer's of the first eight and are done in an entirely different spirit. Finding a common thread for these oracles is virtually impossible.

Were it not for the use made of v. 10 by John 19:37, it is doubtful any place would have been found for this reading from Zechariah in the lectionary. Like Jesus, the pierced victim has met his end through folly or stupidity and his true worth has been discovered only later.

Psalm 63:2-6, 8-9

Galatians 3:23[26]-29

The earlier part of this chapter contains an argument intended to convince the reader of the superiority to the Law of the faith that justifies. The Law is likened to a disciplinarian or monitor who is a slave bringing the freeborn child to school (vv. 23ff.). With Christ came justification through faith (v. 24). This means an end to the Law's constraints (v. 23) and a new condition as "children" (lit., "sons") of God (v. 26). Baptism into Christ, the sign of faith, has meant "clothing your-selves with Christ" (v. 27), a possible reference to a white garment. The unity of all in the new condition (v. 28), as a practical reality, is something that the male, Gentile freeman has had no reason to challenge since. The female response is not so enthusiastic, that of the enslaved Christian less so, and of the Christian Jew totally inaudible. Possessing the faith of Abraham which makes one an inheritor of the ancient promise is, says Galatians, the same as belonging to Christ (v. 29).

The glorious vision of oneness in faith (v. 28) and hence lack of any disabil-ity through circumcision, social condition, or sex is one that should give the mod-ern baptized pause. One wonders if any will inherit the promise if what are described as conditions essential for all, namely, the absence of the threefold social distinction, continue to go unfulfilled.

Alleluia. John 17:17b and a

Your word, O Lord, is truth; make us holy in the truth.

LUKE 8:26-39

Luke follows Mark 5:1-20 quite closely in telling the story of the unclean spirits in a man of Gerasa. Jesus casts the spirits into a herd of swine that was summarily drowned in the lake. Matthew reads Mark's detailed account and notably abbreviates it (8:28-34). He makes the country around Gadara the site which is likewise in pagan territory across Lake Kinnereth. Both locations thus account for the very existence of a herd of pigs and the unconcern of the Jewish narrator for any economic loss to the herdsman-owner. Matthew doubles the demoniac from one man to two but eliminates the self-identification as "Legion" (Luke 8:30, following Mark 5:9). The occupying Roman army was fair game for satire and scorn, hence, from a Jewish viewpoint no harm was done. The demons (plural in Luke) had driven the man to live "in the tombs," a favorite refuge for the mentally disturbed of that age. His strength was prodigious, his awareness of Jesus' holiness acute. All three Synoptics present this event not so much as a pitched battle between good and evil as a petition by one of disordered life for order in his mind and world. He knows that if Jesus answers his request for healing there will be some cost ("Do not torment me," v. 28), but healing is what he wants. The story distinguishes clearly between the crazed or troubled self ("many demons," v. 30) and the untroubled or restored self ("sitting at the feet of Jesus . . . [the man] begged that he might be with him," vv. 35, 38). Jesus' command that he "return home and declare how much God has done for you" (v. 39; cf. Mark 5:19) is a departure from Mark's normal injunction of Jesus to silence addressed to the fellow Jews he healed. The erroneously termed "messianic secret" (for the secret is about Jesus' sonship of God rather than his messiahship) is a narrative technique of the evangelist rather than a historical reminiscence. The explanation probably is that the healed man was a Gentile, the first one reported by Mark to believe in Jesus and proclaim him publicly. It is the same in Luke. In the early churches from which these three Gospels came, Gentiles were beginning to be a component. A remembered outreach of Jesus to them, a man who was the opposite of an exclusively ethno-centered Jew, would have meant much. The fear of the crowd upon witnessing such a marvel and wanting Jesus to be on his way is by all means a realistic touch. Proximity to extreme holiness might terrify any of us.

ALLELUIA. JOHN 10:27

My sheep hear my voice; I know them, and they follow me.

LUKE 9:18-24

There is no mention of Caesarea Philippi in Luke's account of this incident, which is paralleled in Mark 8:27-30 and Matt 16:13-20. For a commentary on Mark, see Proper 19 [24] (B); for Matthew see Proper 16 [21] (A).

Mark 6:45—8:26 and its matching passages in Matthew are not found in Luke, except for Mark 8:12b-15 (//Luke 11:29; 12:1). The Lukan pericope that immediately precedes this one is that of the multiplication of the loaves (the first multiplication in Mark and Matthew). Luke has Jesus praying "alone" while his disciples are "near him" (v. 18). He follows Mark in having Jesus speak of himself as "I," not Matthew's "Son of Man." The inquiry is about the view of the "crowds," not "people" as in Mark followed by Matthew. The response in v. 19 repeats what has been said in vv. 7f. For the rest, Luke is faithful to Mark with two exceptions: he changes Mark 8:29, "the Messiah" *(ho christós)* to "the Messiah of God" (v. 20) and, perhaps significantly, omits the rebuke of Peter in which the latter is described as "Satan" (cf. Mark 8:32f.). This may reflect his desire to save the reputation of the leader of the Twelve. An interest in avoiding distraction from likening the fate of the suffering disciple to that of the suffering Jesus would, however, explain the omission just as well. Mark 8:34 may contain a real invitation by Jesus to martyrdom as the cost of discipleship. If it is figurative there, Luke makes it such beyond doubt by adding "daily" (v. 23) to the injunction to take up one's cross. As in Mark, only the loss of one's life for Jesus' sake (Luke omits "and the gospel's") will result in saving it (v. 24).

Jesus commands silence regarding Peter's conviction that Jesus is the Messiah, precisely because he "must" *(deî)* suffer, die, and be raised (vv. 21f.). This gives the concept of messiahship a meaning it has not had. Hence, presumably, continued use of the term "messiah" would cause confusion. Luke simply follows Mark 8:30f. here.

➴➴

Proper 8 [13] / Thirteenth Sunday of the Year (C)
Sunday between June 26 and July 2, inclusive

2 KINGS 2:1-2, 6-14

For a commentary see Last Sunday after the Epiphany (Transfiguration Sunday) (B).

PSALM 77:1-2, 11-20

1 KINGS 19:15-16[B], 19-21

Elijah's succession in prophecy by Elisha is described in this passage (ca. 850 B.C.) but, more importantly, the later transition of kingship in Israel is hinted at (v. 16). Ahab continued as king in Israel until 853 when Ahaziah (cf. 1 Kgs 22:52ff.—2 Kgs 1:2-18) succeeded him for a year. Next came Ahab's other son Joram (852–41), then Jehu after his successful revolt against Ahaziah of Judah and Joram of Israel in 841 (see 2 Kings 9). The anointing of Elisha in 1 Kgs 19:16 is described at length in 2 Kgs 2:1-18, together with Elijah's departure in a flaming chariot (v. 11). The anointing of Jehu previous to his military victory over the house of Ahab was done prophetically by a guild prophet at Elisha's direction and is recounted in 2 Kgs 9:1-10.

Today's reading is concerned with the initial choice of Elisha. The twelve yoke of oxen with which he is plowing are surely symbolic. So, in another sense, is Elijah's throwing of his cloak over his chosen successor (2 Kgs 2:13-15). Since Elisha's severance of his ties with his farming past could not have been more final (v. 21), Elijah's response to the younger man's request to bid his parents farewell is puzzling. What he says in Hebrew is: "Go back again, for what have I done to you (or, to do with you)?" This may have been his forceful way of saying: "Leave them if you understand what I have done in naming you my successor."

PSALM 16[1-2A, 5, 7-11]

GALATIANS 5:1[2, 5, 7-11], 13-[18]25

Eleuthera (Greek: "freedom") is the name of an island in the Bahamas given to it as part of the Spanish legacy. It is surprising that the term or its Latin equivalent, *libertas*, does not figure more significantly in place-names in this country. There is Libertyville, Illinois, and New Freedom, Pennsylvania, also a town called Liberty in fifteen states and a Freedom in five—all small. The epistle speaks ringingly of another kind of freedom.

Paul has told his "allegory" of Sarah and Hagar in support of his conviction that returning to subjection to the Law (5:1) is an abjuring of the freedom that comes with being offspring of Abraham, a blessing that has been achieved for Gentiles through Christ (3:14). He "freed us for freedom" (5:1) is a Hebraism; the point is made strongly because the yoke is not to be resumed. Paul suggests in the eleven intervening verses, which do not occur in LM, that some persons other than Jewish observants are proposing circumcision to the Galatians. The latter do not seem to Paul to be sufficiently aware of the full burden of keeping the Law that goes with circumcision (v. 3). He angrily proposes castration such as the eunuchs of the cult of Cybele, goddess of fertility, engage in (v. 12; see Phil 3:2f.). Surely his tone is heavily sarcastic.

At v. 13 Paul seems to fear that the freedom he so much advocates may be mistaken for the absence of any inhibition whatever. "Flesh" (i.e., humanity left to itself) needs to be directed and the proper governor is love or faith working through love (vv. 6, 13). Without such a directing factor a terrifying number of aberrations may ensue (vv. 19ff.). Love means mutual service for Paul. It is the perfect expression of life in the Spirit. Lest he be understood to teach that the Law has no meaning and cannot be kept, he sums up his understanding of it in terms of Lev 19:18 (v. 14). On balance he comes out on the side of freedom from the Law for those who are led by the Spirit (v. 18)—at least for the recipients of this letter, who seem to be preponderantly Gentiles (4:8).

The catalogue of vices that Paul provides here as elsewhere (vv. 19-21; cf. 1 Cor 5:10-11; 6:9-11; 2 Cor 6:6-7; 12–20; Rom 1:29-31; 13:13) resembles those assembled by Stoic philosophers and even Essene Jews found in a Dead Sea Scroll (1QS 4:2-6, 9-11). Note that these are called "works" *(erga)* of the flesh while the next list (vv. 22f.) enumerates the "fruit" *(karpos)* of the Spirit. It is a catalogue of virtues of a Spirit-directed life in the spirit that counters the flesh. Paul certainly expects good deeds to flow from this virtuous life, but not that living so become a subject of conceit by some and envy by others (v. 26). He has not stigmatized all passion and desire, a healthy component of the human make-up, but only those flesh-induced passions and desires (of which deviant sex is but one and covetousness/greed the greatest) that believers in Christ Jesus have crucified (v. 24).

ALLELUIA. 1 SAMUEL 3:9; JOHN 6:68C

Speak, LORD, your servant is listening; you have the words of everlasting life.

LUKE 9:51-62

This pericope inaugurates Luke's "special section," which continues to 18:14. It does not depend on Mark's order. Even though there are scattered parallels with Mark throughout, those with Matthew are more numerous. Material unique to Luke is found in chaps. 10–18, much of it in parables. The first five verses of this reading and vv. 60-62 are not part of any other Gospel. Luke alone develops the picture of Jesus as Elijah; the others put John in this rôle.

Luke speaks of Jesus' "being taken up" (v. 51), an echo of Elijah's mode of departure (2 Kgs 2:1, 11). The Greek text has "when the days drew near/were fulfilled," conveying the idea of a providential plan. Samaritan resistance to pilgrims to and from Jerusalem (v. 52f.) was a feature of the life of that time. The proposal of calling down fire is an Elijah touch (v. 54; cf. 1 Kgs 18:24, 36ff.), probably Luke's. It receives no encouragement from Jesus (v. 55).

Verses 57-60a have their parallel in Matt 8:19-22. The second of these two sayings of Jesus (v. 60) leads to another like it (v. 62). As has been remarked in the commentary on 1 Kings 19, above, Elisha's "looking back" seems to be so slight a matter as not to provide the model for this logion. It would appear that Luke possesses that of v. 62, spoken by Jesus independently of any reference to Elisha, and then provides v. 61 as an imprecise introduction to it because of vague similarity. Luke, too, may have had trouble deducing Elijah's meaning in v. 20!

⚜ ⚜

Proper 9 [14] / Fourteenth Sunday of the Year (C)
Sunday between July 3 and July 9, inclusive

2 Kings 5:1-14c

For a commentary see Proper 10 [5] (B).

Psalm 30

Isaiah 66:10-14

The collection of poems known as the Third Isaiah (chaps. 56–66) was compiled between the mid-sixth and mid-fifth centuries B.C. Little is known of the history of the community of Jewish Palestine in that period. The books of Ezra-Nehemiah suggest poverty and a certain confusion in the religious life of the people. Today's reading beginning at v. 7 proposes salvation for Jerusalem (Zion) in terms of an instantaneous birth (vv. 7-9). Continuing the metaphor, the poet suggests that this mother city taken for dead will once again nourish at her abundant breasts. "Salvation will come suddenly (lxvi 7–9) and will be the result of the tender care of Yahweh (lxvi 10–14)" (John L. McKenzie, *Second Isaiah*, AB 20[Garden City, N.Y.: Doubleday, 1968], lxix).

The description of prosperity as a river has occurred in 48:18—a natural figure for life in a parched land. The gathering of the Gentiles to share in the riches of Israel after judgment is a theme of Third Isaiah. The "wealth of nations," familiar as Adam Smith's title (v. 12), will flow like a rushing torrent. In v. 12c the birth metaphor is returned to. The people of the new Jerusalem will be like babes carried on the hip and fondled on the lap. YHWH as a nursing mother is a tender and uncommon biblical image. Sight of the vision will invigorate the bodies (lit. "bones," v. 14a) of the onlookers, who will respond like vegetation in the presence of moisture. The array of similes is dizzying in a collection not noted for its restraint.

All that has preceded leads up to an apocalyptic judgment in which the LORD's servants, viz., the poet and his ethically sensitive fellow Jews, will be separated from the enemies of the LORD (v. 14b) by a Persian-type conflagration (v. 15) or, in the title made famous by Henryk Sienkiewicz, "by fire and sword" (v. 16).

PSALM 66:1-9[3-7, 16, 20]

GALATIANS 6:(1-6), 7-16[14-18]

The epistle has featured a vigorous polemic against the introduction of circumcision into a presumably Gentile Christian community by itinerant preachers who have "bewitched/cast a spell over" the "foolish Galatians" (3:1). Foreskins are being made the subject of a boast (v. 13), like scalps in the fabled days of tribal warfare against the settlers. Paul deplores this pernicious rivalry to which the Galatians are falling prey. They seem to have no notion, any more than do their proselytizers, that circumcision is either the sign of the full acceptance of the Mosaic Law or else it means nothing. There are certain signs in our day that have been similarly uprooted from their contexts, like the "bikers'" ominous iron cross or the Confederate flag, more innocently the rosary beads in the cars of drivers who have never called on Mary to intercede with her Son. None of these, however, serves as a satisfactory modern example of the binding power of covenant circumcision evacuated of its significance. Paul finds the Galatians' folly in the realm of signification complete.

Verses 1-6 follow upon last Sunday's lection and should not be omitted in a public reading this morning. (LM regrettably does not have them.) They contain invaluable pastoral counsel. Paul may consider himself to have been over-harsh in his strictures against those Galatians taken in by "another gospel" and so be proposing a means of community reconciliation. His advice to the Spirit-guided about restoring to the community one found in a transgression (*paráptōma*, v. 1) is so much milder than his command to eject a man in an incestuous relation (1 Cor 5:3-5) that he must have far less grievous offenses in mind. The proposals the apostle puts forward are noteworthy: they must bear one another's burdens (*tà bárē*, v. 2) and share their goods with those who have taught them (v. 6; cf. 1 Cor 9:11, 14), both of them ways to fulfill "the law of Christ," a phrase found only here and in 1 Cor 9:21 (cf. Rom 8:2). "Their own loads" (*phortíon*, v. 5) are daily responsibilities that are the work of each one and should be a source of pride. This admonition is not unlike those delivered to lazy shirkers who are not workers (1 Thess 4:11; 2 Thess 3:10ff.). The warning to "those who are nothing" to stop "thinking they are something" is an echo of 1 Cor 1:26 and 3:18, phrased somewhat differently. Paul is at his best giving practical counsel for daily living.

If those who have already accepted the gospel have a sign, it is the cross of Christ. For Paul this is the only legitimate subject for boasting (v. 14). In taking on its challenge he—and presumably they—have been separated from the *kosmos* and its sinfulness. Being created anew (i.e., as a "new creation," v. 15) is all that matters. This results in adoption of the cross as one's faith symbol. Neither circumcision, its absence, nor anything else continues to be of symbolic worth.

Paul then utters a blessing on those who follow such a rule of life and in so doing designates as the "Israel of God"—the only New Testament occurrence of the phrase—the new people that believes in the power of the cross. He clearly means to set aside the Jewish-Gentile difference and with it the sign distinctive of Jewish existence as effective (not as a continuing sign of peoplehood). Paul does not hold circumcision in contempt—far from it. It is merely that as a saving sign it has been succeeded by a more effective one that transcends peoplehood. Faith in the cross creates an Israel made up of Jews and Gentiles.

It is not clear exactly whom Paul wishes "from now on not to make trouble for me" (v. 17). The most likely subjects are the Galatians, whose stupidity he does not wish to have brought to his attention in the future. He may, however, be issuing a wider challenge, namely, to any Jew who cares to fault him for the low estimate he seems to be putting on a scar in the flesh. He can boast greater scars than circumcision that proclaim his sufferings in the service of Jesus Christ. These "brand marks" (*stígmata*, v. 17) are the signs of ownership in a slave's body, not the same as the "marks of the nails" of John 20:25 in the story of Thomas. Paul is referring to the rigors of his mission (cf. 2 Cor 4:8-12; 6:4-10; 11:23-28), not least of them "that daily tension pressing on me, my anxiety for all the churches" (2 Cor 11:28). There is no thought here of the medieval phenomenon of the wounds of Christ reported of St. Francis of Assisi and others.

Paul concludes with his usual blessing, asking the Lord's grace or favor (v. 18) on the quite thoroughly chastised Galatian community.

Alleluia. See Ephesians 1:17-18

May the Father of our Lord Jesus Christ enlighten the eyes of our hearts, that we may see how great is the hope to which we are called.

Luke 10:1-[11]12, 16-[17]20

The mission of Luke (vv. 1-12) is Q material, having its parallels in Matt 9:37f.; 10:16, 9, 10a, 11ff, 10b, 7f, 14f. (see Proper 6 [11] [A], which comments on Matt 9:36—10:8). Only Luke has the sending of the seventy, a better-attested reading than seventy-two. This and other details identify the passage as a reworking of Q to describe the Gentile mission. The Jews commonly thought of the nations of the earth as seventy or seventy-two in number, following Gen 10 (certain ambiguities occur in vv. 24f.). This accounts for the designation of the LXX. It was done in Gentile lands by and for Jews who lived there. Moses chooses seventy elders for judgment in Exod 24:1 and Num 11:16. The sending "in pairs" (v. 1) will reappear in Acts in the mission of Peter and John to Samaria (Acts 8:14), of Barnabas and Saul (13:2) and Paul and Silas (15:40) to the Gentiles. Luke 10:1-12 should be compared carefully with Luke 9:1-6; there, the mission of the twelve is closer to Matthew than the mission of the seventy. The wider appointment of disciples is set in a Samaritan town (9:56) and is probably meant by Luke to typify the mission to the Gentiles, which will come later, with Samaria serving as a borderland leading out to the Gentile world (see Acts 1:8). For a parallel to v. 2 see John 4:5, likewise in a Samaritan setting.

Matthew follows the injunction to carry no money and go without extra clothes and sandals with a citation of his principle of support for preachers: "For laborers deserve their food" or a worker "is worth his keep" (Matt 10:10). In separating the two ideas and adding the advice not to salute anyone on the way, Luke (10:4, 7b; cf. 2 Kgs 4:29) changes the tenor of the saying from one of need to urgency. His advice to eat and drink what the host provides (v. 7) does not appear in Matthew; it may reflect an active disregard of dietary inhibitions by preachers in Gentile lands. That the principle of their support is thought by Paul to be an ordinance of "the Lord" (here the Church?) is clear from 1 Cor 9:14 (cf. v. 7), despite the freedom he experiences not to accept such help.

The Greek of v. 9 is different from that of v. 11 when it says that the reign of God draws near "to you." The first declaration is in a context of healing and is consolatory; the second "in protest against you," is judgmental.

Verses 17-20 are uniquely Lukan, his hallmark being the eschatological "joy" (chará) with which the seventy return. In Isa 14:12 the king of Babylon is addressed as "morning star, son of the dawn" and described as having fallen from the heavens. Luke makes the *Lucifer* that translates Venus in the Vulgate of Isaiah (Heb. *heilel,* "morning star") "Satan," leading to that worthy's having the name in Christian usage. The Christian denomination of Satan as Lucifer stems from the third century and is influenced by the account of the war in heaven in Rev 12:7-10. It totally ignores that book's designation of Jesus as the "morning star" (22:16; not *"Lucifer"* in the Vulgate, however, but the *stella matutína,* which in turn is applied to Mary in the Litany of Loreto). Venus is rendered by the more usual term *phōsphóros* in 2 Pet 1:19.

John's Gospel will speak in this connection of the driving out of "the ruler of this world" (12:31). The promise that the faithful Jew may tread on snakes with impunity derives from Ps 91:13. Something like it occurs in the "canonical" ending assigned to Mark (16:18), which speaks of the handling of serpents and the drinking of deadly poison as proofs of apostolicity of mission. Mark 16:17 is probably taken from Luke 10:19. Exodus 32:33 and Dan 12:1 speak of a heavenly book of record, accounting for "your names written in heaven" of v. 20.

❧ ❧

Proper 10 [15] / Fifteenth Sunday of the Year (C)
Sunday between July 10 and July 16, inclusive

AMOS 7:7-17

For a commentary see Proper 10 [15] (B).

PSALM 82

DEUTERONOMY 30:9[10]-14

"This book of the Law" that Deuteronomy describes as so accessible was the book of the Josian reform, whatever its content (many think chaps. 12–16 and 28, perhaps as much as 4:44—30:20). The LORD's "commandments and decrees" (v. 10) are reduced to "this command" (v. 11), which is the injunction to elect life and prosperity over death and doom (v. 15), to choose between the blessing and the curse (v. 19). The passage is a favorite one of Rabbis, spoken in praise of Torah and the ease with which it can be fulfilled. Christian preachers frequently apply it to love, not often to life.

The importance of today's pericope is its setting. Written as if spoken by Moses on the brink of entering Canaan (see 31:1), chap. 30 tells the members of the scattered people how to repent wherever they may find themselves. It does this under the guise of enjoining a fidelity in the new land that will guarantee prosperity. Since the chapter was composed long after the conquest of Canaan, it more realistically envisions a Jewish people trying to keep the Law in a variety of lands and settings. The basic promise is that on condition of repentance this covenanted people can always look forward to an ingathering from dispersion which its LORD will achieve (vv. 3-5). If there is a biblical charter for the state of Israel, as the strict observants believe, these verses constitute it. The orthodox rabbinate of that country, in any case, is zealous to see that Torah is kept in terms of this passage, now that the Jewish people are back in *ereṣ Yisroel* in numbers.

PSALM 25:1-10

PSALM 69:14, 17, 30-31, 33-34, 36-37

COLOSSIANS 1:1-14 [15-20]

For a commentary on Col 1:11[12]-20 see Reign of Christ or Christ the King (C).

Despite the conclusion of this letter (4:7-17), which places Paul in prison somewhere with Aristarchus (v. 10) and in regular touch there with Tychicus (v. 7), Onesimus (v. 9), Luke, and Demas (v. 14), there are numerous turns of phrase betraying authorship by another hand, despite Paul's having seen and vouched for the letter's content (4:18). Among these are "the hope laid up for you in heaven" (v. 5) and "the word of truth" (ibid.), found also in Eph 1:13, a treatise apparently based on Colossians and 2 Tim 2:15. There are many cognate features common to the latter three texts, as well as 1 Timothy and Titus, and a striking similarity between the concluding greetings and Phlm 23–25 and Col 4:7, 9, 10, 12, 14, 17 (five names in common, only Tychicus, Jesus called Justus, and Archippus missing from Philemon). Pairs of nouns, the second in the genitive case, begin to occur early in Colossians: "the knowledge of his will" (v. 9); "the knowledge of God" (v. 10); "the strength of the power of his glory" (v. 11). They will come tumbling out in Eph 1:5-14 and passim. Finally, for a Laodicean church that has not seen Paul face to face (2:1) there is concentrated attention paid to that church (4:13, 15, 16), presumably by Epaphras (see 1:7; 4:12) since Paul's knowledge of the faith and love of the Colossian church is a matter of hearsay with him (1:4).

These six verses have been subjected to extensive analysis of every sort. The scrutiny reveals a hymn in two strophes, vv. 15-18a and 18b-20. The hymn probably has pre-Christian origins. The first strophe makes Christ the agent of God in creation, the second God's agent in the work of cosmic reconciliation. This reconciliation is possible because "all the fullness" of God resides in him (v. 19). The author's main point, however, is that the Colossian community is part of that larger body over which Christ has the headship, "the Church" (v. 18), and that its members are safely delivered from the dominion of any angelic or demonic powers that may reside in the universe (vv. 16f.). It has been conjectured that if this is a hymn, some phrase like "Praise the Lord" or "Praised be Christ" would have stood at the head (so Wayne Meeks and others).

Philo, the Alexandrian Jew, spoke of the *Logos* as the image and the firstborn of God (see v. 15). The creation of all things by God "through" and "for" Christ (v. 16) has a Stoic ring, in phrasing like that of 1 Cor 8:6a (where all things are "for" God only; in 6b, "through" Christ, through whom we exist; cf. Rom 11:36).

Christ is the firstborn of all creation (v. 15) and also of a redeemed progeny (the "firstborn from the dead," v. 18). As if to challenge the pretensions of any other *plérōma* (v. 19), the epistle attributes fullness to Christ twice, specifying it in 2:9 as the fullness of deity that dwells in Christ "bodily." "The Church" (v. 18) was probably added to "his body" in a primitive poem that would have conceived the cosmos in that role.

It was on the cross that everything in the heavens and on the earth was reconciled to God in the person of Jesus (v. 20). There, peace was made in his blood.

This hymn makes greater claims for Christ than anything in the undisputed Pauline corpus. It is true that 1 Cor 8:6 reaches a zenith in describing his intimacy with God, a passage that prepares for this one. In the Pauline letters the Church is one body with Christ (1 Cor 12:12, 27; Rom 12:5), whereas here (v. 18) and in Eph 1:22 Christ is head of the body.

He is the "beginning" who will "come to have first place in everything" (v. 18; cf. Rev. 22:13). The claim that he is "before all things" (v. 17) may with equal force refer to place, time, or rank. While many commentators favor a temporal sense, no apodictic argument can be made that the author is claiming preexistence. The firstness of Christ with regard to the universe is total. God does not now look upon the world, whether as created or redeemed, apart from this man in glory, "his beloved Son" (v. 13).

ALLELUIA. 1 SAMUEL 3:9; JOHN 6:69B

Speak, O LORD, your servant is listening; you have the words of everlasting life.

LUKE 10:25-37

Second Chronicles 28:9-15 tells an interesting story of four Ephraimite leaders and a prophet of Samaria named Oded who resisted the savagery with which certain men of Judah were slaughtered and other men and women taken captive. They opposed those who returned from the war, saying that the holding of the Judahites as slaves would make them even more guilty in the LORD's eyes. The conquered of Judah were then brought before the whole assembly, whereupon:

> Then the men just named [Azariah, Berechiah, Jehizkiah, and Amasa] proceeded to help the captives. All of them who were naked they clothed from the booty; they clothed them, put sandals on their feet, gave them food and drink, anointed them, and all who were weak they set on asses. They brought them to their kindred at Jericho, the city of palms. Then they returned to Samaria (v. 15).

The wording is at least suggestive of verbal origins in Luke's narrative.

His introduction to the parable of the good Samaritan probably derives from Mark 12:28-31. If so, it is much edited. The lawyer asks how to gain everlasting life, not which is the first commandment of all. In Mark Jesus answers. Luke has him throw the question back to the lawyer, who responds by combining Deut 6:5 with Lev 19:18 in what was presumably a well-known convention of the period. Luke also has Jesus omit Deut 6:4, the phrase with which the *Shema'* opens: "Hear, O Israel! The LORD is our God, the LORD alone!"

The good Samaritans of 2 Chronicles returned the captives to Jericho, with the weak ones mounted on beasts of burden. The Samaritan in Jesus' story does the same. The tribesmen around Samaria, the old northern capital, had fallen low in Judaean esteem by Jesus' day. Their chief offense was that they had returned from Assyria centuries before, unwilling to worship with the Judahites of the south. Conservative of their traditions, they had kept worshiping at Mount Gerizim when the victorious David decreed that the one shrine of the nation was to be in Jerusalem. By 200 B.C. or so their expulsion and ostracism at Judaean hands was made by their acceptance of a synagogue built by the Greeks.

The parable is elicited by the lawyer's desire to "justify himself" (v. 29), although nothing in his earnest conduct up to this point has prepared us for this. The meaning of the technical biblical term $r^e a'$ ("neighbor / fellow countrymen") was a matter in dispute in Rabbinic circles and a legitimate subject of inquiry. Luke may have included the story to show the superiority of the outlook of Jesus and his missionaries regarding "sinners" to that of the priests and Levites of Judaism. These had a legitimate scruple with regard to proximity to corpses, a matter made explicit in the Bible regarding persons under Nazirite vow (Num 6:9-12) and extended to the general laws of ritual purity for priests.

Whatever Luke's sources or motives, he reports a rhetorically perfect tale. It lives in memory as a parable of giving help when help is needed. It redounds to the everlasting discredit of official religionists. It has also paradoxically affixed the adjective "good" to a despised people—an authentic expression of the spirit of Jesus.

❧ ✍
Proper 11 [16] / Sixteenth Sunday of the Year (C)
Sunday between July 17 and July 23, inclusive

AMOS 8:1-12

Amos may be a shepherd or herdsman (1:1) and dresser of sycamore trees (7:14; *shikmim*, a kind of mulberry), but this does not hinder the compiler of the book from making him the author of some of the Bible's richest rhetoric in condemnation of injustice. He has just finished prophesying the northern kingdom's doom at the hands of Assyria and its people's going into exile (7:17) when he launches on a catalogue of their sins of greed during the prosperous reign of Jeroboam II (783–43). The "basket of summer fruit" of the prophet's vision (vv. 1, 2) is a pun on the word for "the end" that immediately follows, normally a term for God's final day of judgment but in context a dramatic end to divine concern for the northern kingdom's welfare. The ruin of the poor by the greed of the rich is the theme of the entire passage. The heavy irony of waiting for the end of the monthly festival day with its cessation of commerce (v. 5) is reminiscent of the anxious wait in the film of the 1940s *Tight Little Island* (made from Compton MacKenzie's *Whiskey Galore*) for the Presbyterian Sabbath to be over so that the Hebridean islanders can rifle the shipwrecked vessel of its cargo.

The price-fixing of vv. 5b-6 goes on in our day, likewise the once-common practice of the shopkeeper with his thumb on the scale and the modern half-full box of cereal explained in print by its contents' "settling in transit." The ancient practice of Amos's accusation puts one in mind of higher prices for gasoline and everything else in ghetto neighborhoods. Shoplifting is the lame excuse. There is more theft at the pump. The hypocrisy is total. But the LORD has sworn that none of this profiteering will be forgotten. The time is surely coming (v. 11), that day (v. 9) when earthquake, flood, and famine shall overtake the land and songs of celebration become dirges of lament (vv. 8-12). There will be much to-ing and fro-ing in search of a reassuring word of the LORD (v. 12; cf. the frantic "Look there!" or "Look here" of Luke 17:23; Matt 24:23) but the people will not be given it. Samaria's beautiful people prefigure Hollywood's except that the names of the gods are different, but both "shall fall, never to rise again (v. 12).

See also Proper 20 [25] (C).

PSALM 52

GENESIS 18:1-10A

"The terebinth of Mamre, which is at Hebron" (13:18) not surprisingly no longer stands, but the well that watered it is easily found, off the Jerusalem–Hebron road. The well is enclosed by the massive masonry of Herod the Great. The J narrative here given seems to follow chap. 13 directly, while the P account with which chap. 17 concludes resumes at chap. 21. This pericope contains the promise to Abraham that through a son he will beget a host of nations (vv. 10, 18) which is found seven other times between chaps. 12 and 21. The tale is told as an epiphany of the LORD, something that is revealed to Abraham only in v. 14.

The three mysterious visitors are a favorite subject of Eastern iconography, where they are usually represented with aureoles as manifestations of Father, Son, and Holy Spirit. In the text, "the LORD appeared to Abraham" (v. 1), but the LORD does not speak until v. 13. Meanwhile, Abraham deals variously with one (vv. 3, 10) and all three (vv. 2, 4, 5, 8, 9) of his human visitors. As they go on to Sodom (v. 16; two of them? v. 22) the LORD stays on behind (vv. 17-22). The story has obviously undergone some modification at this point.

The thrust of the tale is not merely the assurance of a son that is given but also Sarah's laugh (v. 12; see 17:17 for Abraham's laugh), to account for the naming of Isaac. The familiar popular etymology of the Bible derives the name *Yitsḥak* (21:3) from the form of *tsaḥak* that occurs in 17:17, "he laughed"; 18:12 has another form of the verb to describe Sarah's doing the same. Sarah denies having laughed (v. 15), a charming vignette of who is allowed to do what around this tent.

The limitless power of the Lord is stressed in v. 14, while the divine promise of a blessing through Abraham's offspring is reiterated in v. 18. Not the least detail of the account is the warm hospitality of the nomad *sheikh* Abraham, who is described throughout as magnanimous and trusting.

Psalm 15[2-5]

Colossians 1:15[24]-28

The commentary on 1:1-14[15-20] of last Sunday, Proper 10 [15], coupled with that on the Reign of Christ or Christ the King (C) should provide background material for today's lection, while the latter explores vv. 15-20 in some detail.

Even if certain passages and phrases in this letter are not characteristically Pauline, the present pericope tells in favor of Paul as responsible for it. If he wrote it in his own person as 4:18 affirms, it was from prison and in conjunction with the letter to Philemon (cf. 4:7ff., 17). Joy in suffering (v. 24) is a characteristic theme of Paul. The second part of v. 24 contains a classic puzzle. Since the writer cannot be implying to the Colossians that the sufferings of Christ were in any way insufficient (Christ's victory being described in 2:8-15 as complete), his own "completing what is lacking in Christ's afflictions" (v. 24) must have some other meaning. The usual conjecture is that a divine plan for the spread of the gospel is being hinted at in which the indignities suffered by its servants like Paul are patterned on Christ's. No quota of sufferings that must be made up is necessitated by the text, however. The apostle's suffering for the sake of his body which is the Church (v. 24; cf. v. 18) simply accompanies the preaching of a salvation that was achieved through suffering.

A divine commission *(oikonomía)* made the writer a servant of this Church (v. 25), he says. The mystery spoken of (v. 26) is not something arcane, like the pagan mysteries that were hidden from all but the devotees of the cult deity (cf. Rom 16:25; Eph 1:9). Rather, the *mystērion* is God's eternal plan, only lately revealed, whereby the Lord means to live in the Gentiles through Christ. "Christ in you" is the mystery (v. 27). The Colossians' present grace will be their future glory if they continue in hope. There is no other Christ to proclaim but this one, the Christ now in glory, in whose image all are called to be mature (v. 29, *téleios*, a term from the Greek religions for a fully initiated member).

There should be no hesitancy in seeing Colossians employ standard religious vocabulary in the service of what has been newly done in Christ. Protestant theologians—with Albert Schweitzer as a notable exception—tend to deny to the phrase "in Christ" or "Christ in you" any implication of mystical union. Their supposition that a loss of personal individualism is entailed would account for this. More likely, however, it is because mysticism is taken as a threat to the way justifying faith functions. The Catholic is more at home with the assumption that Paul and his school are propounding a genuine Christ mysticism, a union with him by grace that has no automatic elements and does not imperil his personhood or the believer's. Schweitzer was eloquent in this position.

ALLELUIA. MATTHEW 11:25

Blessed are you, Father, LORD of heaven and earth; you have revealed to little ones the mysteries of the kingdom.

LUKE 10:38-42

The parable of the good Samaritan features compassion (v. 37). This next narrative features discipleship under the aspect of two forms of service. John knows of the tradition regarding these sisters and situates their home in Bethany (11:1). Luke has Jesus and his disciples vaguely "on their journey" (10:38), "on his way to Jerusalem" (9:53) after a rebuff at the hands of Samaritan villagers.

Martha receives a reproach from Jesus but it is not clear exactly why—whether because she is "anxious and upset" (v. 41; the first verb is the root of the adjective "solicitous" reprobated in Matthew's Sermon on the Mount), or because she is not sitting and listening like Mary.

Mary, in any case, receives Jesus' praise for having chosen the "good part." The latter word can mean a serving, and probably does here—the option chosen by *The Amplified Bible* to convey a play on meal preparation words: *mérimna*, "worry/anxiety" and *merída*, "portion."

🙠🙢

Proper 12 [17] / Seventeenth Sunday of the Year (C)
Sunday between July 24 and July 30, inclusive

HOSEA 1:2-10

Amos was a man of Tekoa in the south who delivered prophetic judgments at Bethel, a northern shrine. Hosea was a native of the northern kingdom active in the last days of Jeroboam II. It is impossible to learn from the collection that bears his name whether he was a priest or cult prophet or where he fit into things in life. It is assumed that his wife, Gomer, had multiple liaisons in their marriage, but the naming of their first child Jezreel ("God sows"), for a valley in which Jehu bloodily brought the dynasty of Omri to an end, creates the suspicion that the prophet needed to illustrate Israel's multiplied infidelities with such a marriage, a metaphor common throughout the prophetic writings. Could the poet have invented such an unfortunate woman? It is entirely conceivable, as we know from many other fictions in biblical and world literature. The poetry of vv. 2b and 4bc lend strong support to the theory.

A daughter is born to the union and named Not Pitied, an expression of the divine love withheld from faithless Israel (v. 7). The next child is a boy, Not My People, likewise explained in the text as a repudiation of the north while Judah, the south, notably under Hezekiah (ca. 715–687; v. 1), is promised pity and salvation by God, although not by military means (v. 7b). The reference may be to the withdrawal of Sennacherib's troops from Jerusalem in 701 as contrasted with the fall of Samaria to Assyria in 721. People following LM in its use of NAB will observe that here as elsewhere it engages in some text critical work. The Hebrew, followed by a later hand, included the hoped-for but never achieved reunion of the two kingdoms under one head, NRSV 1:10-11 (see 2:21-23 for the less assured content of these verses). Recognizing this as an inauthentic interpolation, NAB proceeds to 2:4 (MT and NRSV: 2:2). This changes the subsequent verse enumeration throughout the chapter, the rearrangement of the text being done on the basis of sense. NAB here gives the ordinary Bible reader the benefits of some text-critical scholarship by indicating that the optimistic reunion of north and south (1:10-11) represented pious hope rather than realistic expectation.

PSALM 85

GENESIS 18:20-32

The story of the Levite's concubine who was ravished unmercifully by the men of the Benjaminite city of Gibeah after they had first beaten on the door of the pair's host and asked for the Levite himself (Judg 19:22-26) suggests that the naming of sodomy for Sodom may be a matter of historical chance. The details of the earlier part of the Judges narrative are so close to this narrative that it seems to be the one tale of two cities.

Ezekiel names pride, prosperity, and callousness toward the poor as the sins of Sodom (16:48-50). In Jeremiah, Sodom and Gomorrah are guilty of adultery, lies, and siding with the wicked. Isaiah accuses the two Dead Sea towns of unspecified decadence (1:10; 3:9). It is very likely that their tragic end (by sulfurous eruption; see 19:24, 28) led to the attribution of every shameful crime to these towns, given the mentality of that protohistoric past.

The LORD muses about checking on the evil reports he has heard of Sodom and Gomorrah (vv. 20f.) but does not go there. He stays with Abraham while the two men/angels (lit. "messengers") proceed ahead (18:22; 19:1). The remarkable exchange of vv. 23-32, much like the haggling that goes on in a Middle Eastern bazaar, is not only a tale of the influence of the patriarch Abraham with God. It is also a wrestling with the problem of evil. The J author wonders how much wickedness the divine trade will bear. The ten just men in the midst of a sea of iniquity are a parable of later Israel surrounded by wicked neighbors. The inexorability of catastrophe (19:13f.) is another instructive lesson.

A by-product of this bargaining session, one of the most memorable of all the biblical "strivings with God," may be the *minyan* (lit. "numbering"), the prescribed minimum of ten men for Jewish public prayer, found as early as the Dead Sea Scrolls. The Mishnaic tractate *Sanhedrin* 1:6 cites Num 14:6, 38, twelve tribes, less Joshua and Caleb, although why the subtraction is unclear. But the main points of the tale are the candor of YHWH who hides nothing from his trusted friend Abraham (v. 17) and the justice of the one who is "judge of all the earth" (v. 25).

PSALM 138:[1-3, 6-8]

COLOSSIANS 2:6[12-14]-15, (16-19)

Early in this epistle there has been enunciated the *motif* of rescue from darkness to light in the kingdom of God's Son. The forgiveness of sins is the reality synonymous with both of these figurative concepts (1:13f.). This same pardon reappears in v. 13, but now the antithesis is between the body of sin and flesh buried in the waters of baptism and the new life of the baptized in company with Christ (2:12f.). The baptismal symbolism has been developed by Paul in Rom 6:3-6. A difference is that there the risen life lies in the future, whereas here it is conceived as present.

The development of a spiritual understanding of circumcision was not new with Paul. Other Jewish writings had it. For the healing of uncircumcised flesh, he proposes baptism. In the graphic figure of v. 11 this rite strips away not only

a piece of skin but the whole human reality insofar as it is subject to "the elemental spirits of the universe and not . . . to Christ" (v. 8). The burial in water
accomplishes nothing in itself, of course. It is ultimately an effective sign only if it
stands for the faith of the baptized in God's forgiving power.

The "record that stood against us" is nailed to the cross, a description of
humanity's status as dead in trespasses and subject to legal demands (vv. 13f.). The
nailing of Christ to the cross was like the posting of a counterclaim to all previous claims. He is placarded triumphantly, and the "rulers and authorities" are made
public examples of for all to see. They are led off in a victory train—paraded
through the streets like the sorry captives of a worsted army (cf. Ps 69:19).

ALLELUIA. LUKE 19:38

Blessed is the king who comes in the name of the Lord, peace on earth and glory
in heaven!

LUKE 11:1-13

Luke's introductory verse situates Jesus' instruction on how to pray in the midst
of his own prayer. It is peculiar to him as is the parable of the friend at midnight (vv. 5-8). The prayer of Jesus has its parallel in Matt 6:9-13; the last five
verses of this pericope are paralleled in vv. 7:7-11. Both are assigned in Matthew
to the sermon on the mount. Only Luke has spoken of the disciples of John as
"praying" (5:33); Mark (2:18) and Matthew (9:14) confine themselves to a
report of fasting.

The prayer of Jesus is probably from Q material, Matthew having added the
phrases, "Our" and "in the heavens" (6:9), "your will be done on earth as it is in
heaven" (v. 10), and "rescue us from the evil one" (v. 13). All are Judaic and would
have a familiar ring in the ears of Matthew's church. A case can be made for the
elimination by Luke of such phrases as not being usual for Gentile readers. His
retention of the very Jewish remainder, however (including the baffling *epioúsion*—
"for the morrow"?—not found elsewhere in Greek literature), tells against the theory of an edited Lukan version of a long Q original.

It has been pointed out that the prayer is eschatological in its entirety. It asks
for the coming of God's rule or kingdom (v. 2), for bread on a continuous basis
given each day (*epioúsia kath' hēméran*, present participle of *epeîmi*, the "coming
[day]" = *māḥār*, "tomorrow"); for the forgiveness of sins (v. 4); and that the petitioners be not led to the final testing (v. 4). All are futurist Jewish concepts. Some
hold that the eschatological urgency of Matthew is missing from Luke, who is

reporting a form that is in daily Christian use and that reflects the concerns of the world. This can only be deduced from Matthew's more general Jewish-eschatologizing tendency, however, not from the wording of the prayer in the two gospels. Luke retains the same types of phrases as are found in Matthew and other Jewish prayers of the first century and following—simply not as many of them.

The key to the parable of the shameless friend is the phrase "how much more" of v. 13 (the Rabbinic *qal vaḥomer*, "light and heavy" = *a fortiori*). Luke makes the "good gifts" of Matt 7:11 read "the Holy Spirit," which for him is God's greatest gift. In line with this, two Greek MSS of the New Testament have in place of Luke's "hallowed be your name," "may your Holy Spirit come upon us and cleanse us."

Luke replaces Matthew's loaf/stone example with one of his own, egg/scorpion (leaving fish/snake in place). This makes us wonder if some similarity of the Aramaic words underlies Matthew's choice of objects that escapes Luke. The eel, snake-like in appearance, could be taken for a fish and all the commentators speak of a scorpion's ability to role up in a ball. But an *egg*?

The sayings about knocking and asking (vv. 9f.) are identical in Matt 7:7f., hence presumably come from Q.

❧❧

Proper 13 [18] / Eighteenth Sunday of the Year (C)
Sunday between July 31 and August 6, inclusive

HOSEA 11:1-11

"Israel" in this moving passage means the Hebrews in v. 1, called out of Egypt as son of God. Ephraim, in other contexts called Israel, denotes the northern kingdom that is the object of the prophet's censure (vv. 3, 8, 12). The image of a people as an infant child guided by a parent by "cords" or "bands" (once called "leading strings") to assist the child in learning to walk is a touching one (v. 3). So too are the other images of early child care in verse 4b. But the object of much love and kindness has grown to be an ungrateful adult. "Return to Egypt" means an enslaved condition, this time under Assyria whose "sword rages in their cities" (vv. 5f.); but the people are bent on turning away from their God (v. 7). The LORD muses that he cannot turn Ephraim/Israel over to destruction like the two cities that suffered the fate of Sodom and Gomorrah (see Deut 22:29). He has relented. God will not come in wrath as an ordinary mortal might. When he roars like a lion the dispersed of Israel will come from the west and Egypt to the south, fluttering like sparrows, like doves captive in Assyria. Back, back will the LORD bring them to dwell in their homes once again (vv. 10f.).

PSALM 107:1-9, 43

ECCLESIASTES (QOHELETH) 1:2, 12-14; 2:18[21]-23

The writer of this insightful treatise portrays himself as having come abreast of all wisdom and knowledge ("king over Israel in Jerusalem," in that sense) and the human activity that accompanies the pursuit. It is like "a chasing after wind," he now concludes (vv. 12-14). The "vanity" of these verses has nothing to do with preening (Chesterton, on a novelist who was his contemporary: "He was worse than proud. He was vain") but is equivalent to the Latin *in vanum*, "to no purpose." The Hebrew superlative of v. 2 is literally "breath of breaths" (like the construction *servus servorum* or *parthenos parthenōn*). The pope does not serve other servants; Mary is not a virgin among the rest. Both are at the top of their class. "*Utter* purposelessness" is the meaning of the biblical phrase.

Hard work is a bore. Leaving its fruits to indolent heirs is worse (v. 22). Lying awake nights thinking about the inequity of the scheme is worst of all (v. 23).

This is the only theme of the Preacher (better, Teacher) and it is a profound one. The game would not be worth the candle but for the truth of 12:13f.

PSALM 90:3-6, 12-14, 17; PSALM 49:1-12

COLOSSIANS 3:1[5, 9]-11

Verse 1 echoes 2:12 from last Sunday's reading in its description of the life of the baptized as an already risen life. The "things that are above" of vv. 1 and 2 are both *tà ánō*, deeds proper to the abode of Christ who is spirit, and are contrasted with "things on earth" (vv. 2 and 5) or "nature" (*tà mélē*, v. 5; lit. "members") "whatever" (lit. "parts" or "members") of you that are earthly. These can lead to vices like the five catalogued in v. 5 and those in v. 8. (Compare with them the five virtues of v. 12.) The vices are to be "put to death" (v. 5).

The pre-baptismal "old self" (v. 9) has been replaced by the new (v. 10) which is constantly refashioned according to "knowledge" (see 1:9, 10; 2:2, 3). Being "clothed with Christ" (Gal 3:27) and "conformed to the image of [God's] Son" (Rom 8:29) are the Pauline phrases that lie behind this passage, with a backward glance at God's "making humankind in our image, according to our likeness" (Gen 1:26). If the Colossian error is a gnostic one, Christian life is being proposed as the true *gnōsis*. The whole "image" figure has Stoic overtones, not biblical only.

Galatians 3:27ff. and Philem 15–19 have sentiments similar to those of v. 11 about the end to all social and sexual distinctions that comes with life in the Lord. "Foreigner" is literally *bárbaros*, i.e., a non-Greek, while Scythians were an untutored nomad tribe from the east who by their cruelties exemplified the breed especially. Christ for the author is "all and in all" (v. 11). Paul has used this rhetorical phrase, which does not cry out for too careful scrutiny, when speaking of God's victory at the end (1 Cor 15:29).

Alleluia. John 1:14 and 12b

The Word of God became a man and lived among us. He enabled those who accepted him to become children of God.

Luke 12:13-21

This material is found exclusively in Luke. The carefully stipulated inheritance laws in Israel have evidently been violated, and the brother who asks Jesus to arbitrate is the victim. Jesus refuses the arbiter's mantle (v. 14). His comment to the crowd (v. 15) sounds like an independent logion warning against greed that Luke or his source has inserted here. As quoted, the saying stands as a reproach to both brothers, the cheated and the cheater.

Luke, who leaves very little to the imagination, appends the saying of v. 21 as a comment on the parable. The opposition is between those who pile up riches "for themselves and who are not rich toward God."

Understanding Christian life as a kind of riches that cause no loss of sleep (see Eccl 2:23), the homilist has a rare opportunity in these three readings to trace a unity that is really there.

✎✎
Proper 14 [19] / Nineteenth Sunday of the Year (C)
Sunday between August 6 and August 13, inclusive

Isaiah 1:1, 10-20

RCL, in its diligent search for important biblical passages not read out on a Sunday, proposes Isaiah's initial declaration of his identity and vision concerning

Judah's sins (LM has 1:10, 16-20 on Tuesday of 2 Lent but not on a Sunday or feast day). The prophet announces the years of his service under four kings of Judah stretching from 783 to 687. Using Sodom and Gomorrah as surrogates for his errant people (v. 10), he charges them with carrying out Temple sacrifice in an iniquitous state of heart (v. 13). The slaughter and burning of beasts and the clouds of incense (to cope with the stench) are declared futile in God's eyes (v. 13), hateful to his soul (v. 14). The festivals calculated by the lunar calendar are burdens the LORD is weary of hearing (ibid.). It became conventional for nineteenth-century European students of the Scriptures, in which they were followed in the twentieth by those in the U.S., to find in the ethical teaching of the prophets a total repudiation of Temple ritual. Baptist scholar Samuel E. Balentine attributes the trend, in good part, to confessional bias of Protestant scholarship (*The Torah's Vision of Worship*, OBT [Minneapolis: Fortress Press, 2000]. Among many others, on p. 3 he quotes Harold H. Rowley's *Worship in Ancient Israel*: "the quality of worship is to be found in the spirit even more than in the forms, for worship belongs to the heart rather than to the act"). Preachers on this powerful passage need to be on guard lest they fall into the trap of their forebears, repudiating Temple sacrifice as if it were all show and hateful to God. It is the state of the heart in which the act is performed, not the act itself, that the LORD finds reprehensible (v. 15). Repentance for sin, not an end to blood sacrifice, is the demand of the all-holy God (vv. 15f). Its only proof will be justice for the oppressed (v. 17). Scarlet sins can be removed to the whiteness of snow, crimson red to the appearance of wool (v. 18). Judah can go in either of two directions, expecting in turn a prosperous land or Assyria's sword (v. 20).

PSALM 50:1-8, 22-23

GENESIS 15:1-6

This brief pericope is a specification of the promise earlier made by the LORD that the land should be that of Abram and his offspring (see 13:14-17). There, they should be as numerous and uncountable as the dust of the earth; here, as the stars in the heavens. The patriarch is told by God not to fear, but for what deed is his reward to be very great (15:2)? Looking to what went immediately before, it might be Abram's raising a force of 318 men to recover the kidnapped Lot and his plundered goods from the four kings (read desert chieftains) led by Chedorlaomer of Elam (14:1-16). It is more likely, however, that the reward will be for "believing the LORD" that the son born to a slave in his household should not be his heir but one born to his childless wife (vv. 4, 6). Some preachers are tempted to deal with v. 6, "And he believed the Lord; and the Lord reckoned it to him as righteousness," in Pauline terms of the sixteenth-century disputes of the West, about which the Christian East, reading Genesis in the LXX's Greek, knows nothing. See the commentary on the portion of Gen 15 that follows today's on 2 Lent (C) for some background on the vocabulary employed.

Tanakh, which has no stake whatever in Christian debates, renders v. 6, "And because he put his trust in the Lord, he reckoned it to his merit." This translation would be a stumbling block to certain eyes, but *tsedaka* can mean many things. In modern Hebrew it is a charitable gift, as to the United Jewish Appeal. It can also mean uprightness of conduct—justice by God's standard—or, as here, a reward for a good deed. That deed is an expression of total trust in the Lord. If the divine covenantal promise (whose ritual sealing is described below in vv. 7-20) is that Abram would yet have an heir by his true wife, he believes it—at the moment, God knows how.

See also 2 Lent (C).

Psalm 33:12-22

Wisdom 18:6-9

The theme of chaps. 11–19, a midrashic homily on the exodus, is announced in 11:5: "Through the very things by which their enemies were punished / they themselves received benefit in their need." The children of Israel, in other words, profited by the phenomena which, in the form of plagues, were destructive to Egypt. The theme is developed in five segments that feature contrast or opposition: 11:6-14; 11:15—16:15; 16:16-29; 17:1—18:4; 18:5—19:22. These panels are concerned successively with water from the rock, quail, manna, the pillar of fire, and, in the final instance from which today's pericope is taken, the glorification of Israel by the drowning of Pharaoh's troops. The five matching woes ("plagues") of the Egyptians were the Nile running red, the various insects and animals, the storms, the darkness, and the destruction of the firstborn sons. These final nine chapters constitute a homily that may have been delivered on Passover.

Moses was seeing the preparation of ritually slaughtered lambs for the Passover meal on the night of the tenth plague (Exod 12:21-28; Wis 18:9). In this fidelity to "the divine Law" (v. 9), Israel's chanting "the praises of the ancestors" (ibid.) was mingled with the "discordant cry" and "piteous lament" (v. 10) of the despoiled enemy. "At the destruction of the firstborn they [Egypt] acknowledged that the people [Israel] was God's son" (v. 13).

The antitheses pointed out in Wisdom, it should be noted, are by no means so clearly drawn in Exodus but reflect the preacher's art.

PSALM 33:1, 12, 18-22

HEBREWS 11:1-2, 8-19

The biblical examples of faith—actually, fidelity—given in this chapter follow an exhortation to continue trusting in the mediatorial offices of Christ despite suffering (see 10:10-14, 29), not "willfully persisting in sin" through apostasy (10:26). Habakkuk 2:4, which Paul employs in Rom 1:17, is used here in support of the relation between faith and justification (10:38).

The "substance" of things hoped for of former translations has become "assurance" or "realization" in modern renderings and the "conviction" of things not seen (11:1, NRSV) is retained as "evidence" in NAB from KJV and DRC. God as deliverer is that unseen object of hope. A catalogue of "ancestors who received approval" follows. The lectionaries omit the verses that mention the creation, Abel, Enoch, and Noah, coming directly to Abraham the father of faith. His obedience in leaving Haran is mentioned first (v. 8; cf. Gen 12:1-4), then his nomad status in Canaan where, with his son-in-law and later his son, he dwelt as a foreigner. Abraham's support and stay was the conviction that a "city that has foundations" (v. 10) lay in the future for him, the "Sabbath rest" of 4:9. Sarah's faith is conspicuously absent in Genesis. In Hebrews it is Abraham who by faith receives the power of procreation / to generate (lit. "the deposit of seed") according to NRSV, NAB and NIV (v. 11). He is clearly the "one person" of v. 12; but the phrasing understood in this way is so little related to a woman's part in conception that "Sarah herself was barren," viewed as parenthetical or taken by some to be a marginal gloss, is probably erroneous. The KJV, DRC, and *Amplified Bible* all have *her* receiving strength to receive seed, a position supported by Myles M. Bourke in *NJBC*: "by faith Sarah herself received power for the sowing of seed." The biblical promise of a numerous progeny (cf. Gen 15:5; 22:17; 28:14; 32:12; Exod 32:13) is repeated (v. 12). The patriarch described himself to the Hittites at Hebron as a "stranger and an alien" when it came time to bury Sarah (Gen 23:4). The author of Hebrews has extrapolated the latter term to all the patriarchs (vv. 13-16) in support of his argument that they looked forward to a better, i.e., a heavenly homeland (vv. 14, 16). Abraham's crowning act of faith is his offering up of Isaac, who is the key to the promise (v. 17). The phrasing of v. 19 "even, to raise someone from the dead," is almost certainly prompted by the raising up of Christ. Abraham's willingness to sacrifice and God's sparing of the boy was done "figuratively," that is, as a symbol or type (v. 19). See the commentary on the "binding of Isaac" and on Gen 22:1-14 more broadly under 2 Lent (B).

ALLELUIA. JOHN 6:64B AND 69B

Your words, Lord, are spirit and life, you have the words of everlasting life.

LUKE 12:32-40[48]

Verses 32, 35-38, 41, and 47-48 are uniquely Lukan; v. 33 occurs in Matthew (6:19f.) in quite different form, as does v. 46. There are exact parallels in Matthew to v. 34 (6:21), vv. 39f. (24:43f.), and vv. 42-45 (24:45-50).

Two different but similar parables occur in this pericope, each of which has a complicated redactional history: the Gatekeeper (12:35-38//Mark 13:33-37) and the Servant Entrusted with Supervision (12:42-46//Matt 24:45-50). In the first, the master has gone "abroad" in Mark, not just to a wedding, and only one man watches to let him in. In Luke, "you" in the plural (v. 36) must be like the men waiting, who open to him. This change has been made because of the parousial significance Luke gives it, a matter confirmed by the addition of v. 37b. Masters do not wait on servants in that fashion (see Luke 17:7f.); Christ the *Kyrios* does, as in Luke 22:27 and John 13:4f. In its original setting, the parable was a charge to be watchful, like the injunction of Jesus in the garden: to "keep awake" (Mark 14:38) and to pray so as to be ready for the coming eschatological trial or test. Whether spoken in the first instance to disciples or scribes, it has been thoroughly allegorized by the early Church. In Matthew the parable disappears and only the injunction to watchfulness remains (24:42; cf. 25:13). Luke makes Jesus' reward of selfless service to his own at the final banquet central (see 12:37b).

The second parable is likewise given a parousial interpretation in Luke, whatever its earlier, simpler meaning. The slave of the Matthean telling (24:45) becomes a steward in Luke (v. 42). It has particular application to the apostles, not to all (v. 41); a special responsibility ("put in charge of his slaves," v. 42; "in charge of all his possessions," v. 44; "he knew what his master wanted," v. 47) falls on those to whom it is directed; they will be punished severely for failure (vv. 46c, 47, 48bc), presumably in the judgment.

Joachim Jeremias sees in this parable as Jesus told it a stern warning to the religious leaders and teachers of his time, while the early Church saw in the delay ("My master is long in coming," v. 45) a reference to the parousia. The master was Christ who would return to judge adversely those who abused their charge.

✎.✎

Proper 15 [20] / Twentieth Sunday of the Year (C)
Sunday between August 14 and August 20, inclusive

Isaiah 5:1-7

For a commentary see Proper 22 [27] (A).

Surprisingly, this is the second of only two readings stipulated from this prophetic book as RCL makes its way through the First Testament on the Sundays after Pentecost to The Reign of Christ. That is probably because the Sundays of Advent, Christmas, and the other seasons make so much use of it, as does LM in its traditional, type-fulfillment scheme.

Psalm 80:1-2, 8-19

Jeremiah 23:23-29

RCL indicates with an asterisk the passages it deems more suitable in the "pattern of paired readings" (see the other description of it immediately above). This is the case with the brief Jeremiah lection proposed as an alternate in relation to the Lukan lection below. Fire on the earth and division, whether among prophet-teachers or in households, is the link.

Jeremiah maintains that the word of the LORD he is sure he possesses has power like that of a hammer to break a rock (v. 29). His God is everywhere, filling heaven and earth. There is nothing fugitive about him, nothing hole-and-corner about his word. The court prophets Jeremiah opposes he stigmatizes as dreamers. When Martin Luther King Jr. proclaimed loudly at the Washington Monument on August 28, 1963, "I have a dream," he knew it was no figment of imagination but a word of the LORD. So do Hananiah and Co. prophesy (28:1-17). They trade in straw, Jeremiah in wheat. Let them dream on and speak it (23:28). Theirs are attractive dreams, the forth-teller for God says, but they serve to let the people of Judah forget the name of Y<small>HWH</small>. Their ancestors were lulled into similar forgetfulness and turned to the worship of the *ba 'alim* of Canaan.

PSALM 82

JEREMIAH 38:4-6, 8-10

The prophet's offense in the eyes of King Zedekiah's counselors is that he keeps telling the people the unpalatable truth that Babylon is stronger than Judah and hence should be capitulated to. The four men listed in 38:1 have a "better-dead-than-Red" attitude that they keep pressing in terms of optimism and victory. Jeremiah's "disloyalty" consists in his political realism. The entire sequence resembles the rhetoric of U.S. foreign policy in Southeast Asia in the Kennedy through Nixon administrations and in Central America throughout the Reagan-Bush years.

The "Pashhur, son of Malchiah" of v. 1 is the emissary sent by the king to the prophet in 21:1, not the harassing chief of the Temple police of the same name ("son of Immer") in 20:1. For background to today's reading, consult the commentaries on Jer 20:7-9 (Proper 17 [22] A) and Jer 20:10-13 (Proper 7 [12] A).

The important thing in Jeremiah's message is that he speaks for life for his people, not death with honor (read: "the defense of political blunders at all cost") by "sword, by famine, by pestilence" (v. 2). Verse 4 is a key statement in code language of the doublethink of the princes.

The story is much too interesting to make stopping the public reading at v. 10 attractive. If, however, the whole chapter is read, or a passage that stops with v. 16 or v. 23, the entire homily should then be devoted to the problems raised. Not least of them is that posed by the concurrence of Jeremiah in not reporting his entire conversation with the king.

The reliance of the passion narratives of the gospels on this chapter cannot go unnoticed. In particular, the portrait of Pilate probably relies on that of the weak Zedekiah (esp. v. 5), Joseph of Arimathea on the compassionate Ethiopian eunuch Ebedmelech (v. 7), and above all Jesus' response to the council in Luke 22:67f. on v. 15, where Jeremiah says: "If I tell you, you will put me to death. . . . If I give you advice, you will not listen to me!"

PSALM 40:2-4, 18

Hebrews 11:29—12:[1]-4

This treatise illustrates the faith it has defined in 11:1 by proceeding methodically from its exercise by the first four patriarchs (vv. 17-22) to Moses' faith, in a short summary of his career that culminated in a faith-inspired observance of Passover (vv. 23-28). Today's lection goes from Joshua to the prophets. All suffered torment and death (vv. 33-38), but to none was given what God had promised. That was reserved for "us" whom God elects to "make perfect," namely, the "something better" of faith in what God has done in Christ (v. 39).

This "cloud of witnesses" (12:1), a title used by Dorothy Sayers for one of her Lord Peter Wimsey detective stories, refers to the men and women of faith detailed in chap. 11. Their example should inspire Christians to lay aside all that hinders their progress (v. 1) and press on to the finish line of the race (v. 1). Sin "that clings to us" is NRSV and NAB's rendering of *euperístaton*, "entangling," the better attested reading; *euperíspaston*, "distracting," is found in P[46], a Chester Beatty papyrus at Ann Arbor. The figure envisions a runner who is clothed rather than near-naked, the custom of the time for all but Jews. The image of the footrace recalls its use by Paul (1 Cor 9:24, 26; Phil 2:16) and the author of 2 Timothy (4:7f.). Jesus is spoken of as if he were starting-gun, tape, and distance in between; the begetter/author/leader (*archēgòn* [cf. 2:10; Acts 3:15]) and perfecter of our faith (v. 2). Proposing Jesus as a model of patiently endured suffering (vv. 2bc, 3) is a characteristic of this letter, as it will be of the Pauline-inspired 1 Peter (1:11, 13; 4:1f., 12-19). Jesus is seated in glory at God's right hand (v. 2; cf. 1:3), sitting in the LORD's presence being a prerogative of Davidic kings (see 2 Sam 7:18; Ezek 44:3).

The (Alexandrian?) Hellenist Christians to whom the treatise is addressed are reminded that, unlike Christ, their fight against sin has not yet been carried to the point of shedding blood (v. 4). This would serve to date Hebrews before the Neronian persecution of 64 C.E., if its readers were familiar with events at Rome.

Alleluia. John 8:12

I am the light of the world, says the Lord; whoever follows me will have the light of life.

Luke 12:49[53]-56

Verses 49f. are peculiar to Luke, while 51ff. have their Q parallel in Matt 10:35f. The images of fire and baptism (cf. Mark 10:38) are undoubtedly judgmental, with special reference to the judgment of the LORD on the priests of Ba 'al when

Elijah—a type of Jesus, not the Baptist for Luke—had his God cast fire on the earth (cf. Sir 48:1-3; 1 Kgs 18:36ff.). Here Luke pictures Jesus willing that the fire be ignited and his being "under stress" (v. 50) until the bath in pain of his death should be over. There may be some reference back to the baptism of John, with its imagery of judgmental fire (cf. Luke 2:16f.; Matt 3:11f.).

Luke changes Matthew's "bringing" *(baleîn)* peace to "giving" it *(doûnai)*— rendered "bringing" by NRSV nonetheless—probably to avoid repeating the *baleîn* he has taken from Sirach, "casting fire," immediately above. He likewise makes the Semitic figure "a sword" in Matt 10:34 read "division" (v. 51), perhaps to avoid conveying a posture of violence for Jesus. Luke allows a sword image in 2:35 where there is no danger of misinterpretation and is alone in transmitting a mysterious sword-saying of Jesus in the garden (22:36ff.). For him this must be figurative, since in 22:49ff. Jesus counters his disciple's swordplay with an act of healing.

Verse 53 makes all the family hostilities over the person of Christ reciprocal, doubling the phrasing of Matt 18:35. The change is stylistic and not significant. Luke omits, "One's enemies will be those of one's own household" (Matt 10:36), possibly as redundant.

❧❧

Proper 16 [21] / Twenty-first Sunday of the Year (C)
Sunday between August 21 and August 27, inclusive

JEREMIAH 1:4-10

Some autobiographies are gripping, others are a bore. Faithful Jews, Christians, and Muslims care deeply about the accounts of the ways God's servants, the prophets—male or female—were called. Isaiah tells his story as it happened in vision (Isa 6:1-13). Here we have a report on Jeremiah's call and commission. A prophet to the nations *(ha goyim)* is he to be? He will find it hard enough to convince fellow Judahites that he has been given "the word of the LORD" (Jer 1:4). At first he pleads youth and lack of skill in public delivery (vv. 5-8). He is told to forget it. There is a touch to his lips and he receives the gift of words (v. 9), empowered to do, in an agricultural figure, what farmers and kitchen-gardeners do: pluck up and plant; and builders: tear down and build up (v. 10). Is this to be a local enterprise in the kingdom of Judah? Not at all. "Nations and kingdoms" will experience Jeremiah's influence (v. 10a).

The poet of these verses knew well the prophet's later career, even to history's losing track of him as he went into Egypt in exile (chaps. 43–44). This passage can embolden the fainthearted. How many in the service of the gospel but not by any means all clergy, commended years afterward for careers of remarkable achievement, say: "There was nothing especially remarkable about it. I was just faced with a need and I spent the rest of my life trying to meet it." Jeremiah, queried on his calling, might say the same. "I didn't know I could do what I was called to do. Evidently, God helping me, I could—and did."

See also 4 Epiphany [4] (C).

PSALM 71:1-6

ISAIAH 58:9B-14

For a commentary on the earlier part of this lection see 5 Epiphany [5] (A). Verses 10-12 spell out the LORD's rewarding response to those who meet the needs of the hungry and the afflicted. Faithful observants of the Sabbath as the LORD's holy day will be "set astride the heights of the earth" (v. 14). Regulars at Sunday church the same.

PSALM 103:1-8

ISAIAH 66:18-21

Modern translations set these verses in prose, but John Bright and H. H. Rowley think they are verse, like the material that precedes and follows them, with a prose gloss of nations (v. 19) and animals (v. 20) added. They represent, in any event, a culmination of the breadth of YHWH's interest in the Gentiles, which was hinted at in 56:3-8; 60:3-7; and 62:2. This pericope serves as a capstone to Third Isaiah, Second and Third Isaiah together, and indeed the whole book. The "sign" the LORD will choose (v. 19) is the fugitives or survivors (of the apocalyptic slaughter?) who will go forth to the peoples of Tarshish (Spain? Sardinia?), Put (Somalia? Libya?), Lud (Assyria? Lydia in Asia Minor? Egypt?), Mosoch (Meshech) and Tubal (the Ural mountains north of Assyria and southeast of the Black Sea), and Javan (= Ionia; Greece). The list is a selection taken from Gen 10:4, 6, and 22, where Put is said to descend from Ham, Lud from Shem, and the remaining four from Japheth. Appearing in Trito-Isaiah it resembles a list of Native American tribes made by a modern white who has heard the names but knows little else, and about patterns of migration nothing at all. If the scattered peoples "have not heard of my [YHWH's] fame" (v. 19), it is equally clear that his worshipers have barely heard of theirs.

Not only shall emissaries proclaim the LORD's glory to these distant lands (v. 19); their inhabitants shall come bringing "all your kindred, fellow Jews," to holy Zion. They shall come on every conceivable beast and conveyance (v. 20). As the Israelites bring their offerings in clean vessels, so shall their scattered members be brought. The "some of them" (v. 21) to be chosen as priests and Levites have to be Gentiles, as a reward for their service as intermediaries and offerers. This verse would make no special sense if it referred to Jews.

Commonly the passage is taken as a gloss in its entirety but it is very much in the spirit of v. 23b, "All flesh shall come to worship before me, says the LORD." It is in any case "one of the most spacious views of religion and mankind which is found in the entire Old Testament" (John L. McKenzie, *Second Isaiah*, AB 20 [Garden City, N.Y.: Doubleday, 1968], 209).

PSALM 117:1-2

See Proper 17 [22] (C) immediately below.

HEBREWS 12:18-29

See Proper 17 [22] (C) immediately below.

HEBREWS 12:5-7, 11-13

The quotation from Prov 3:11f. that makes up vv. 5bc and 6 reminds believers that "discipline" is a sure sign that one is a child of the Lord. This notion is expanded in vv. 7-11, which resemble certain parts of Elihu's speeches in Job. There, God chastises man on his bed of pain and brings him back from the grave so as to instruct him (33:19-33); he "delivers the afflicted by their affliction, / and opens their ear by adversity" (36:15); "Exalted is God in his power; / who is a teacher like him?" (36:22).

Discipline (vv. 5, 6, 8) is the proof that one is a genuine offspring. Omission of it is a proof of illegitimacy. How much more will not the "Father of spirits" (12:9; cf. Num 16:22; 27:16), whose plan it is to ready them for a share in his own holiness (v. 10), do the same and give them thereby the "peaceful fruit of justice" (v. 11)?

The last two verses, 12 and 13a, are echoes respectively of Isa 35:3 and Prov 4:26 in Greek. They counsel not only improving the self but the environment as well, a caution to modern moralists who want people to "shape up" without seeking any alleviation of the conditions that make it impossible.

ALLELUIA. JOHN 10:27

My sheep listen to my voice, says the Lord; I know them, and they follow me.

LUKE 13:10-17

Not much from this chapter in Luke occurs in LM on Sunday besides this and vv. 22-30 on [21] (C). This is not surprising, because parallels in Mark and Matthew have the rest of Luke's content, all but the first seventeen verses which are proper to him. Both lectionaries propose 13:1-9 for 2 Lent (C), where its context is the repentance proper to the season. Preachers should not disregard Jesus' important word that there is no relation between death from patriotic action against Rome the oppressor, or an industrial accident, and punishment for sin. This disclaimer is unique in the Synoptics, but compare John 9:2f. The noteworthy detail in today's healing miracle is not the power of God through Jesus' touch but the indignation of the synagogue leader—Dickens would have called it a beadle's mentality—that Jews should heal on the sacred, seventh day. His admonition to the crowd is nothing short of laughable but there are religious functionaries like this everywhere. "Come back on the days scheduled for miracles." Only a family whose loved one's body has been turned away at the cemetery gates because the paperwork is not in order, or because the gravediggers have gone home at five, can appreciate the mad irony of the situation. Jesus knew from experience a world of strained-at gnats and swallowed camels. This lection is not the occasion for beating up on long dead "hypocrites" but living church personnel at whose hands many Christians have suffered. The laity are the chief victims but the clergy are not exempt from the same pain at the hands of those who "do it by the book."

ALLELUIA. JOHN 14:6

I am the way and the truth and the life. No one comes to the Father except through me.

Luke 13:22-30

This pericope is an arrangement of Q material quite different from Matthew's and occurs as part of Jesus' Lukan journey toward Jerusalem (cf. v. 22) that began at 9:51 (cf. vv. 9:57; 10:38; 13:33; 17:11; 18:31). Verses 23f. have a rough parallel in Matt 7:13f.; v. 25 faintly resembles Matt 25:10ff., the parable of the improvident virgins; v. 27 matches Matt 7:23 and vv. 38f., Matt 8:11f., where it refers to the centurion. The final saying about the first and the last (v. 30) occurs in Matthew at 19:30 and 20:16.

Luke makes everything in the passage refer to the religious leaders of Israel, to confront whom Jesus is going to the holy city. They will be ejected from the messianic feast (v. 27, quoting Ps 6:9a) and be replaced by people from the four corners of the earth (v. 29), specifically the Gentiles of v. 30. These are Luke's candidates for the first who will be last.

🔊🔊

Proper 17 [22] / Twenty-second Sunday of the Year (C)
Sunday between August 28 and September 3, inclusive

Jeremiah 2:4-13

Chapter 1 had contained Jeremiah's first prophecy that disaster should break out on the land of Israel from the north (1:14). He may foresee the coming of the Chaldeans from Babylon but for the moment he sees the infidelities of the northern kingdom as a threat (vv. 15f.). He tells his people to stand as firm as a bronze wall against any relapse into paganism by Judah's kings, princes, or priests (vv. 17ff.). It sounds much like a call to the peasants *(los campesinos)* of Latin America to resist their ruling class, *norteamericano* business interests, or dominant military. The word of the LORD has come to Jeremiah three times (1:4, 11, 14) before it is enunciated twice in today's lection, 2:1, 4), the latter word of accusation at great length. If the English term *jeremiad* is meant to describe a sustained lament or prophecy of doom, this is one. It culminates in two evils committed by the people which, in fact, are the one: they have deserted a pure gushing spring which is their LORD and opted instead for cracked cisterns—the old and faulty sewer pipes of our day (v. 13). In between, a rich word picture of Israel's history is provided that goes from release from Egypt by the LORD through all the desert wanderings to the possession of the land—which the priests and prophets have then polluted by adopting the worship of the local ba'als. Jeremiah's charge may be overblown but his language is such as to leave no doubt. He makes an interesting observation in cultural anthropology. Ancient peoples do not desert their gods at whim (vv. 10-11). If you could check it over centuries from east (Kedar, a tribe in the Syrian desert) to west (Cyprus) you would find a perfect stability in the relation. Only Israel has changed its "glory" (the LORD) for profitless things. Modern congregations need to identify the search going on in the culture for gods in their own image and liking.

PSALM 81:1, 10-16

SIRACH 10:12-18

Jews and most Protestants, depending on the editing of their Bibles, are deprived of the wisdom of this Jerusalem sage whose misfortune was to have his grandson Jesus write up his wisdom in Hebrew and then translate it into Greek for diaspora Jews (Prologue; 50:27). That fact is probably what made the Rabbis of Iavneh and later in two locations in Galilee lose interest in it. The early collection of proverbs on pride, today's alternate lection (for congregations that have it in their pulpit Bible), shows why the book was a favorite in early instruction for adult baptism and also why the medievals listed pride first in their seven capital or deadly sins. "Capital," from *capita*, were the seven headings under which all deviations from moral rectitude occur, since from one of the seven all the particular sins derive. In Sirach, however, the case is other. Old Sirach does not say that all sin is spawned by pride but by forsaking the LORD. That apostasy is, for him, the primordial sin and pride is its offspring (vv. 12-13a). The apostate may expect dreadful, God-induced calamities (v. 13b) which the next four verses spell out (vv. 14-17). Waste and destruction of rulers and their lands will fall upon the unredeemed proud, a fate that Sirach's people of power normally assign to "the lesser breeds without the Law." God has no choice but to erase their memory from the earth (v. 17). The summing up is instructive. Whatever brought pride into being, it cannot be called a creature of God; no more can violent anger (v. 18). Both have to be human products and mean ones at that.

PROVERBS 25:6-7

Jesus of Nazareth, like Jesus ben Sira two hundred years before, not only knew many proverbs but frequently taught in them as well as parables, as the Synoptic Gospels richly attest. The well remembered, "Friend, move up higher" (Luke 14:10), of the host's command to the wedding guest who took the lowest place is a faithful echo of today's proverb: "It is better to be told, 'Come up closer,' than to be humbled [in the king's presence]." Luke downgrades the king of the ancient epigram to the father of the bride.

PSALM 112

SIRACH 3:17-18, 20, 28-30

A brief *Haustafel* or table of domestic duties in proverb form, chiefly the duties of children toward their parents, precedes today's reading. The arrogance of those who despise and anger their parents leads to advice about humbling oneself. Little needs to be said about these verses, which praise in succession humility (vv. 17-18), a sense of one's own limitations (v. 20), careful listening to epigrammatic wisdom (v. 28), and the atoning effects of almsgiving (v. 29). The higher placed one is, the more attentive should one be to thoughts of self-abnegation. Yet 10:27 serves to restore a possible imbalance:

> My son, with humility have self-esteem;
> prize yourself as you deserve.

Sirach certainly numbers himself among the sages whom v. 28 commends. His grandson tells us in the prologue that the old gentleman wrote these lines "in the nature of instruction and wisdom" so that others might profit from his counsel "in living in conformity with the divine Law."

PSALM 112; PSALM 68:4-7, 10-11

HEBREWS 13:1-8, 15-16

This treatise ends with words of encouragement (v. 22) and exhortation (vv. 1-8); to mutual love, care for the imprisoned, chaste marriage, and avoidance of greed. A plea for the virtue of hospitality defines the form mutual love must take (see John Koenig, *New Testament Hospitality*, OBT [Philadelphia: Fortress Press, 1985]). Obedience to the community's leaders is counseled (vv. 7, 17), whose business it is to keep believers clear of strange teaching and practice (vv. 9-11). Jesus' blood shed in sacrifice is made the antitype of Temple sacrifice (vv. 10-13), one that can continually be offered through him as a sacrifice of praise as his name is confessed (the *sacrificium laudis* of the Roman eucharistic canon of the Mass).

HEBREWS 12:18-19, 22-24A

The author proceeds from a reprobation of Esau as an immoral *(pornos)* and godless person—who is helpful, however, as a horrible example of irreversible choice (vv. 16f.; cf. 6:4-6)—to an evocation of the Sinai theophany. The awesome phenomena of old (see Exod 19:16, 19) do accompany the present call of Christians (vv. 18-21). God does not now speak so fearsomely that he must be enjoined to address the people through a mediator as of old (v. 19; cf. Exod 20:19). The contrast is between the terms of the present covenant, sealed in the "sprinkled blood" of Jesus, and those of the covenant delivered on Sinai (v. 24). There, even the mediator Moses declared he was terrified and trembling (v. 21; cf. Deut 9:19, where he speaks of his fear at the LORD's anger, namely, after the incident of the golden calf). Verse 22 anticipates the final assembly in the heavenly Jerusalem, with angels and men intermingled. In v. 23 "the spirits of the just made perfect" assemble without fear before "God, the judge of all."

The "assembly of the firstborn who are enrolled in heaven" recalls Luke 10:20, hence may refer to the entire company of Christians who have been faithful. The angels of v. 22 are less likely; slightly more so, the "just made perfect," those Hebrew saints who are inheriting the promises (cf. 6:12).

Abel's blood cried out from the soil to be revenged (Gen 4:10), while that of Jesus' "gives us confidence to enter the sanctuary" through the curtain of his flesh (Heb 10:19).

ALLELUIA. MATTHEW 11:29

Take my yoke upoon you and learn from me, for I am meek and humble of heart.

LUKE 14:1, 7-14

The first fifteen verses of this chapter are special Lukan material. This is Jesus' only recorded meal as the guest of a Pharisee, even though Luke has Jesus make it the occasion of a rebuke of Pharisees and experts in the Law (v. 5). After a Sabbath cure of a man with dropsy (vv. 2-6), he tells a *parabolé* about the choice of places at table (vv. 7-11). It is more an instruction than a story. Jewish folk wisdom featured the notion of taking the lowest place at table, including this teaching from Prov 25:6f:

> Do not put yourself forward in the king's presence,
>> or stand in the place of the great;
> For it is better to be told, "Come up here,"
>> than to be put lower in the presence of a noble.

Mark 12:39 (//Luke 20:46), in which Jesus rebukes those who take the first places at banquets, has its parallel in a saying attributed to a late 1st century Rabbi Simeon ben Azzai. In its original form the logion may have been merely a reproach of selfish conduct, but Luke's appending of v. 11 about the humbled and the exalted, and the mention of the resurrection of the just in v. 14, indicate that he is using both counsels of Jesus on banquet protocol (vv. 12f. suggest inviting those who cannot repay you) to illustrate the eschatological situation.

An examination of the occurrence of the proverb, "Everyone who exalts himself shall be humbled, while the one who humbles himself shall be exalted," in its various settings (Luke 14:11; 18:14; Matt 23:12) and its cognate, Mark 9:35, "Whoever wants to be first must be last of all and servant of all," is instructive. In Matthew and Mark the context is the role reversal that will mark life in the reign of God, while Luke alone uses the saying as descriptive of the way things will be at the end. The call for modest behavior at formal dinners in Luke and the proposal of a plebeian guest list when one acts as host are thus introductions to "an 'eschatological warning,' which looks forward to the heavenly banquet, and is a call to renounce self-righteous pretensions and to self-abasement before God" (Joachim Jeremias, *The Parables of Jesus* [New York: Charles Scribner's Sons, 1963], 193).

᷍᷍
Proper 18 [23] / Twenty-third Sunday of the Year (C)
Sunday between September 4 and September 10, inclusive

JEREMIAH 18:1-11

When Shakespeare's Hamlet says to his friend Horatio, "There's a divinity that shapes our ends, / Rough-hew them how we will" (5.2.1), he was expressing belief in a providential design that any medieval Dane or Renaissance Englishman might have held. Augustine's *Civitas Dei* looked for a similar pattern in the rise and fall of nations. Jeremiah was doing much the same centuries before the other two. He did not think the house of Israel a plaything in divine hands, a misshapen piece of mud to be reformed on the potter's wheel (vv. 3-6) or a clay pot to be reduced to shards. He was convinced, however, that the fate of a nation is somehow in God's hands to be built and planted or plucked up and destroyed at the divine will (vv. 7-9). The change in the providential design is not a matter of marionettes on the world's stage but of a people's choosing to do evil or listen to God's voice (v. 10). The evil that God, the potter, is shaping against all Judah and Jerusalem is the impending incursion from the east. The proof that the prophet does not think his people a helpless puppet manipulated by a capricious God lies in the way his long-remembered metaphor ends. The people of Judah are charged with turning from their evil way and amending their doings, which means that they can do so. The Bible in both Testaments holds fast to a conviction of the freedom of the human will that God will not coerce.

Psalm 139:1-6, 13-18

Deuteronomy 30:15-20

For a commentary see 6 Epiphany [6] (A).

Psalm 1

Wisdom 9:13-18

This entire chapter is cast by its first- or second-century B.C. author in the form of a prayer of King Solomon. He asks that "the wisdom that sits by your throne" be given him (v. 4), that this wisdom "may labor at my side, / and that I may learn what is pleasing to you" (v. 10b). Wisdom is conceived as an attribute of God who has sent it as "your holy spirit from on high" (v. 17b) to "set right the paths of those on earth" and save those who "were taught what pleases you" (v. 18).

The counsel of God is contrasted favorably with the reasoning of mortals that is worthless (vv. 13f.). So much for dismissers of this late bit of "apocrypha" who think it smacks overly of philosophy. Even earthly matters are a puzzle to the earthbound. How much more must not matters of heavenly wisdom be (v. 16b)?

The body-soul contrast does not appear in the earlier Hebrew scriptures. It is not to be characterized as full-scale Greek dualism here (v. 15). Nonetheless, the *vocabulary* is more reminiscent of Plato than the Bible, which limits itself to observing that man's origins are in the dust of earth and his life cut off like a weaver's last thread or the taking down of a shepherd's tent (cf. Pss 103:14; Job 4:19; Isa 38:12).

Verse 13 derives from Isa 40:13; together they provide the conclusion to Paul's diatribe on the mystery of the election of the Gentiles at the end of Rom 11: "For 'who has known the mind of the LORD? Or who has been his counselor?'"(v. 34).

Psalm 90:3-6, 12-14, 17

Philemon 1–21[9–10, 12–17]

Paul feels that he is Philemon's partner in the gospel (*koinōnós*, v. 17) but also that the slave-owner of Colossae is indebted to him for his very self (v. 19). This probably indicates that Paul instructed him in the faith. He could command Philemon to take back his runaway slave Onesimus (-os in Greek, v. 8) but instead he "appeal(s) on the basis of love" (v. 9). Paul is detained as a guest of the nation—exactly where, we cannot be sure. His imprisonment is sufficiently relaxed that it has not kept him from receiving Onesimus into the Christian community (v. 10). He now sends him back as he would his own heart (v. 12). There is no reason for LM readers to omit v. 11, since the pun on the slave's name, Onesimus as "useful," can be conveyed adequately, provided it is well read and explained afterward ever so briefly.

Paul's technique of persuasion is clever. He would have kept the slave by him in place of his master except that this might be taken by Philemon as a good deed forced upon him (vv. 13f.). Forced upon him! The troublesome runaway who may have liberated some of the proceeds (v. 18) has been changed into an emissary of love, like Cinderella's coach turned into a pumpkin. A better example might be Tom Sawyer's getting people to whitewash his fence for him and counting it an honor. The useless fugitive has become a beloved brother (*adelphós*, v. 16), the normal word for a person baptized. Paul proposes that the cheated Philemon snap up the chance to receive back in the Lord someone who is as good as Paul in the role of houseguest.

His lordly instruction to bill all charges to him (v. 18) recalls Ethel Merman's key to all hearts as a Washington hostess (ambassador to Luxembourg?) in *Call Me Madam*: "I'll take the check!" "If he has wronged you in any way or owes you anything, charge it to my account" (v. 18). One thinks of the apocryphal tale of the statue of the innkeeper on the Jericho road scanning the horizon with eyes shaded by an upraised hand, the inscription beneath reading: "And if there is any further expense, I upon my return shall repay thee."

The silence of this letter on the fact of slavery is often remarked. Yet the common view is that Paul by presenting Onesimus the slave as a brother beloved to Philemon, his owner at law, voiced an idea revolutionary in that day. Regrettably, it was many centuries before Christians recognized the evil of holding human beings as chattel.

ALLELUIA. JOHN 14:23

Those who love me will hold to my words, and my Father will love them and we will come to them.

LUKE 14:25-33

Verses 25ff. have their Q parallel in Matt 10:37f., but the remainder is pure Luke. The phrase "does not hate father or mother (v. 26) is Hebraic speech that contrasts love and hate with no shading in between. "Carry one's cross" (v. 27; Matt 10:38 has the verb "take" meaning "shoulder the cross-beam") is widely thought to be a saying of the early Church in light of Jesus' tortured ending rather than his authentic saying. This Roman form of execution was everywhere visible to the horrified Jewish eye.

The two brief parables of the builder of a tower (vv. 28ff.) and the king about to do battle (vv. 31f.) make the same point: lack of planning leads to ridicule or ruin. Luke uses the necessity of foresight in farming or making war to underscore the point that renunciation of all one's possessions is a condition of discipleship (v. 33). The tower of v. 28 (*pyrgos*) can also mean a farm building. Some are inclined to favor this rendering because of the great money outlay; in this hypothesis, a silo rather than a shaft as a lookout for crows would be indicated. The king of Jesus' parable negotiates from weakness in today's vocabulary of aggression (v. 32). Luke employs both stories to suggest negotiating from strength, which for him means divesting oneself of all that one has.

❧ ❧

Proper 19 [24] / Twenty-fourth Sunday of the Year (C)
Sunday between September 11 and September 17, inclusive

JEREMIAH 4:11-12, 22-28

By any standard this passage is a warning and a threat. The first two verses are not readily comprehensible whichever the translation. Who is the "hot wind from the desert heights" and does it come "at my bidding" (v. 12, NAB), "it is I who speak" (NRSV)? Or does it come "from them, My poor people . . . against Me *(Tanakh)?* Whether the searing wind is the people's conduct or an enemy poised, it does not come to winnow or to cleanse (v. 11c). Is not the coming of the invaders on horses and in chariots, shouting against the cities of Judah and encompassing her, a doom brought on by the people's wicked ways (vv. 13, 16, 17)? Then come the heavy charges of their folly, stupidity, and sheer inability to do what is right (v. 22). The prophet has a vision of a desolate land of the future, like the landscape in a serious film after nuclear war (vv. 23-26). The whole land shall be desolate but the LORD promises that it will not be utterly destroyed (v. 28; cf. Gen 9:11).

PSALM 14

EXODUS 32:7-[12]14

Jeroboam set up calves of gold in Dan and Bethel to split the people's religious allegiance and draw them away from Jerusalem (1 Kgs 12:28ff.). This act was reprehensible in the eyes of the Jerusalem-oriented author but, strangely, Jeroboam's artifacts were not. The story in 1 Kings may be calculated to denigrate Jeroboam even further by assuming in the reader a knowledge of today's pericope. Since no reference is made to the book of Exodus there, however, some are inclined to think that things went in the other direction, namely, that the molten images—not readily cast in the Sinai desert—got into Exodus after having originated in 1 Kings. The images were not offensive in themselves, being stands or bases to receive the invisible YHWH, much like the cherubim upholding the propitiatory (Exod 25:18ff.). Hosea fulminated against the "calf of Samaria" in the eighth century (8:5f.), the earliest dependable historical reference to a view of calves as idols in themselves.

Moses pleads for his people like Abraham of old bargaining over Sodom and Gomorrah. The lawgiver reminds the LORD of his mercies in the desert wandering to date (v. 11) and his oath to the patriarchs to make Israel a numerous people (v. 13). The LORD's blazing wrath simmers down (v. 14), presumably lest the Egyptians say that he set the people free only to destroy them in the desert.

See Deut 9:11-21 for the same story as if told by Moses.

Aaron's part in the business is puzzling. At first his complicity in making the images is total (32:1-6) but then he is exonerated by Moses for his weakness (vv. 21-24). There is an amusing touch in his explanation, more ingenious or naïve than anything Adam put forward in his defense: "They gave it to me, and I threw it into the fire, and out came this calf!" (v. 24).

One wonders how Aaron, who is usually connected with the ark of the covenant, is described here as abandoning his charismatic office and aligning himself with the enemies of YHWH. Some conjecture that his association with a golden calf in Jerusalem's later temple was originally honorific and that it became the center of a story of idolatry only in the later "apostasies" of Samaria. It would be an interesting outcome of biblical criticism if this best known of tales from the desert experience should be established as having had its origins five centuries later.

PSALM 51:1-10[12-13, 17, 19]

1 TIMOTHY 1:12-17

This reading is helpful in establishing the non-Pauline authorship of the epistle by the very way it goes about recalling Paul's career. It also contains the first of three statements in the epistle "sure and worthy of full acceptance" (v. 15; see also 3:1; 4:9; 2 Tim 2:11; Tit 3:8) which seem to be creedal, liturgical, and Church-order fragments. This one, "Christ Jesus came into the world to save sinners," is probably the center around which everything else in the pericope turns. Paul's self-denunciation is so stiff that it is doubtfully his: "Of these I myself am the worst." It is true that he strongly regrets his career as a persecutor of the Church (Gal 1:13, 23; Phil 3:6; esp. 1 Cor 15:9, "I am the least of the apostles") but in general Paul has a very robust conscience (see Rom 9:1; 1 Cor 4:4; 2 Cor 1:12; 5:10) and cannot be imagined engaging in self-abnegation so strong that it sounds like a boast. Paul calling himself arrogant (v. 13) sounds more like the word of a close observer of Paul than Paul. Praise of Christ's mercy and patience are Pauline; so is his presenting himself as a model for emulation (v. 16). But the sum is less than its parts—a Pauline anthology rather than Pauline diction.

The doxology of v. 17 mixes Hebrew and Greek elements unselfconsciously ("King of ages," "the only God," as against "immortal," "invisible") but this was not untypical of Hellenist Judaism.

ALLELUIA. JOHN 15:15B

I call you my friends, says the Lord, for I have made known to you all that I have heard from my Father.

LUKE 15:1-10[1-32]

For a commentary on the first three verses of this reading and the parable of the forgiving father, see 4 Lent (C).

Matthew 18:12f. contains the parable of the lost sheep, but makes a different point of it: "It is not the will of your Father in heaven that one of these little ones should be lost." Rather than highlighting the providential care of the simple, Luke features eschatological joy over the repentance of sinners. He will do the same with the story of the recovered drachma (peculiar to him) and the longer parable that follows. The reason for the telling is withheld until v. 32 when it emerges strongly.

Luke's interest throughout his Gospel and Acts is in the forgiveness of sins (Luke 1:77; 3:3; 24:47; Acts 5:31; 10:43; 13:38; 26:18). He adds to the spare telling of the lost sheep in Matthew the detail of the shepherd's laying it on his shoulders. A figurine with this depiction, which may well have had a non-Christian origin, was a favorite in the early Roman church. Luke, too, is alone in having the shepherd summon friends and neighbors to rejoice with him that the sheep has been found (v. 6), the same with the woman and her drachma (v. 9). This evangelist commonly pairs a male with a female character in his narratives. The two brief tales are totally true to Palestinian culture. One sheep out of a hundred would have been recognized as a stray as a result of the shepherd's daily count, and one silver coin out of ten would have been a substantial part of the woman's dowry, a hedge against reverses in the family fortunes or her widowhood. Up until the last century nomad women were captured in photos with treasured coins firmly sewn into their headdresses for festal wear. The neighborhood celebration at the recovery of the loss in each case was real. Luke expands Matthew's unadorned "rejoicing" of the shepherd as a figure of the Father's delight that a simple one *(mikrós)* not perish, into a block party before the angels of God that a sinner has repented.

❧❧

Proper 20 [25] / Twenty-fifth Sunday of the Year (C)
Sunday between September 18 and September 24, inclusive

JEREMIAH 8:18—9:1

This prophet has been heard from in his mode of censure over the past four Sundays. Today we encounter him at his sympathetic best over the plight of his people. He hears them cry out in a series of laments at their situation (vv. 19f.) and his joy is turned to grief upon the hearing. The LORD has abandoned them, they are sure. Jeremiah speaks for them in their anguish, "Is the LORD not in Zion?" but cannot forbear adding what must be the LORD's response, "Why have they provoked me to anger with their images, with their foreign deities?" (v. 19). But then the LORD is immediately back to the mode of consolation as he feels the hurt of his people. The LORD too can wonder whether there be no balm in Gilead, no physician to heal the people (vv. 21f.). Gilead was the region across the Jordan flanking the River Jabbok, rich with oaks, pines, and balsam firs, from the resin of which a healing salve was made. In a change of figure but one no less rich the poet prophet asks for a head full of tears that he may cry his eyes out for the slain of his poor people (9:1; MT 8:23). That some have been killed confirms what is said in vv. 16 and 17, namely, that the poem was written after the invasion from the north (Dan) has taken place.

Psalm 79:1-9

Amos 8:4-7

This brief, powerful oracle against oppressors of the poor echoes certain sentiments found in 2:6f. It does not seem to follow logically upon the four visions of the author (locusts, fire, plumb line, fruit basket) recorded in 7:1-3, 4ff., 7ff.; 8:1ff. Amos flays dishonest tradesmen and merchants whom he accuses of oppressing the poor. They cannot wait for the religious festivals to be over so that they can return to their fixing of weights (the shekel = 4 oz.; the loaded scale) and measures (the epha = .62 bushel or 19.97 dry qts.). The feasts were calculated by the new moon, the Sabbath by Friday sundown (see Isa 1:13; Hos 2:13) and required the cessation of movement and commercial activity.

Verse 6 refers to the selling into slavery of defaulting debtors; the sale of wheat husks is an added stroke of rapacity. Yhwh is made to swear by the "pride [gāʾōn: excellence, majesty] of Jacob" (v. 7). Since elsewhere he swears by his holiness (4:2) or by himself (6:8), we are led to conclude that this oath has the same meaning, all of the splendor of Jacob (later named Israel) having been derived from the Lord. Yhwh means never to forget the greedy assault on the poor (v. 7b). He will punish it with earthquake (v. 8), eclipse (v. 9), deprivation (v. 10), and famine (v. 11).

Amos had a deep concern over economic trends in the northern kingdom under Jeroboam II (786–46), in which the rich grew richer and the poor grew poorer.

Psalm 113[1-2, 4-8]

1 Timothy 2:1-8

The Pauline author proposes liturgical suffrages for all (v. 1). The Roman emperors (v. 2) are especially to be remembered, but also all in high positions. This verse may well be a phrase taken from a liturgical prayer. It accords with a spirit of concern for the well-being of political institutions and personages found in Rom 13:1-7 and 1 Pet 2:13-17. The vote of confidence in a stable order as divinely sustained is not to be attributed to Christian self-interest. There was the genuine conviction that God lies behind the good sovereign or magistrate who does not despotically resist him. Nor was a mere quiet life (v. 2) the aim. Such stability of men and institutions was the very condition of piety ("godliness") and dignity. Without these as a matrix, which only prayer could ensure, there could be no salvation or coming to the knowledge of the truth (v. 4).

The writer makes explicit the truth he has in mind by quoting a hymnic or creedal fragment that is probably both (v. 5). In it the uniqueness of God is strongly affirmed. Distinct from God is the one mediator between God and "the human race [*ánthrōpos* without the article], Christ Jesus." The latter phrasing is a thrust against gnostic elements that might be denying the full manhood of the mediator. This middleman is one "who gave himself as a ransom for all" (v. 6). The word for ransom, *antílytron* occurs here for the only time in the New Testament; more usual are *lýtron antì pollōn* (Mark 10:45; Matt 20:28) and *lýtrōsis* (Luke 1:68; Heb 9:12).

Paul's self-description as "herald," "apostle," and "teacher of the nations," a phrase that will recur in 2 Tim 1:11 except for mention of the Gentiles, is well-nigh unthinkable in a letter to a close associate (v. 7). Even less imaginable is the writer's protestation that he does not lie about the Gospel. The latter is obviously a modification of the phrase in Gal 1:20, where Paul strongly affirms the truthfulness of his recollection about visits to Jerusalem. Verse 7 must be taken as a declaration of the Pauline school against all opponents that Paul was not only the apostle and preacher he thought himself (Rom 11:1; 1 Cor 1:1; 2 Cor 1:1; Gal 1:1, 9) but also a thoroughly trustworthy teacher and "apostle to the Gentiles."

Verse 8 leads into the disciplinary section on women (vv. 9-15) by citing men as the proper leaders of public prayer in the *orans* position ("lifting up holy hands"). Because Paul is widely thought in our day to be a male chauvinist, the preacher should take some pains to indicate that we have in this epistle the earnest teaching of a follower of Paul, probably early second century, and not the man himself, especially 2:11f., which seems to have made its way into 1 Corinthians as 14:33b-35 because Paul has assumed in 11:5 that women *are* praying and prophesying (i.e., speaking comprehensibly, see chap. 14 passim) in the assembly.

ALLELUIA. JOHN 17:17B AND A

Your word, O LORD, is truth; make us holy in the truth.

LUKE 16:1-13

The homilist needs to know chiefly that Luke has made a collection of at least four distinct money sayings of Jesus (vv. 9-13), each having its own power whereas threaded together they lose force. This is especially true when (as seems to be the case) they are being proposed as elucidations of a parable that the evangelist gives some evidence of not understanding. Verse 9, also a saying delivered on another occasion, has some chance of being related to the point of Jesus' parable; the rest have none.

As Jesus told the story it probably ended at v. 8. It is a simple, forceful tale suggesting that the good should take a leaf from the book of the wicked. It carefully documents a well-known system of extortion. Various proposals have been made about the economics of entrepreneurship of the times that would result in the owner's admiration or acceptance of his wily manager's cleverness. The likeliest explanations but not the only ones are those that have the owner able to praise the middleman grudgingly because he himself has suffered no personal loss. A scheme whereby the owner knew the quotas agreed on before the harvest without inquiring into those levied by his manager would suit the facts best. In this case "owed" would have nothing to do with indebtedness but a rehearsal of the quota system that the manager had imposed on the tenant farmers in the first place as if the owner had set it. All he was then doing was eliminating or diminishing his profit so as to look good to them, with his own eye cocked to the future.

An explanation that sees to it that the owner suffers no loss is not essential. The owner was as deep in defrauding the laboring poor as his employee and could have appreciated a good "con" when he saw one, even though he might be its part victim. To make Jesus' point, the wilier all around the better.

🐚🐚

Proper 21 [26] / Twenty-sixth Sunday of the Year (C)
Sunday between September 25 and October 1, inclusive

Jeremiah 32:1-3a, 6-15

The final selection from this anthology of poetry and prose is part of a prose selection chronicling the Chaldean siege of Judah which is in progress and Jeremiah's detention by the king's guard as if, through prophesying the invasion, he has brought it on. Killing the messenger is a very old game (vv. 1-5). Verses 3b-4 are unaccountably omitted from the public reading but a preacher must master them to follow the story. Zedekiah did in fact speak to Nebuchadnezzar face to face (v. 4) when he fled Jerusalem, was pursued and captured by Chaldean troops, and after seeing his sons slaughtered was sent to Babylonian exile (39:1-7). The story of the imprisoned Jeremiah's buying land from his cousin in their native village Anathoth is symbolic not of his hope of return but of his conviction that his people would come back to their "houses, fields and vineyards" (v. 15b). The real estate transaction is described in detail and the deed of ownership is deposited with his secretary Baruch. And so it happened after the passage of fifty years, when the exiled best and brightest came struggling back under Cyrus the Mede called God's messiah (Isa 45:1).

PSALM 91:1-6, 14-16

AMOS 6:1A, 4-7

Mention of Zion and Mount Samaria and the complacent and overconfident leaders of a favored nation in both places immediately tells us of a warning to Judah and Israel (Ephraim), the southern and the northern kingdoms (v. 1). Normally Amos, a man of the south (1:1), does not address himself to Judah but this does not mean (as some have held) that mention of Judah's holy mountain must be a gloss. The accusation against the leaders is that, by their luxurious living, they are preparing for defeat—at Assyrian hands—by the very practices calculated to keep defeat farthest from their consciousness.

The denunciation in vv. 4-6 is a bill of particulars specifying why the Jews can expect no better treatment than their Syrian and Phoenician neighbors (v. 2), no deferment of the evil day of violent retribution (v. 4). The prophet does not have any difficulty in identifying Israel's infidelities as the cause of the hastening of that day. The "beds of ivory" (v. 4), like the houses of "ivory" of 3:15, describe the inlays that have been so prominent among the archaeological finds of the ancient city of Samaria (later Sebasteia). The imputation in vv. 4, 5, and 6 is of women, song, and wine, with roasted meats for rich fare and body culture thrown in besides. Joseph (i.e., the northern kingdom) is in deep political trouble because of its "fat cat" status (v. 6b). The perpetrators of that trouble are oblivious to it.

Yet they shall all be carted off into exile (v. 7) when the day of wrath, about which vv. 8-11 grow graphic, descends.

PSALM 146[7-10]

I TIMOTHY 6:6[11-16]-19

The first five verses of this reading (not proposed in LM), with their strong warning against the love of money as the root of all evil, especially for those deep enough in the works of religion to make "godliness" a means of personal gain (v. 5), are essential to an understanding of the concluding charge of v. 11. The whole epistle has been directed to workers in the service of the Gospel, hence the choice of "Timothy" from the apostolic age as its recipient. An important difference is that the structures of a much later Church life are evident.

Timothy is instructed to flee all harmful desires for base gain and seek everlasting life through the path of the virtues (vv. 11f.). His baptismal experience is referred to as a means to motivate him (v. 12), the "good confession" meaning profession of faith on that occasion being likened to that of Jesus before Pilate (v. 13). He must "fight the good fight of faith" (v. 12). God's "command" is his charge that believers be faithful to his revelation (v. 14) in Christ, whom God will make known at the right time (v. 15). The pericope ends in a doxology that draws on phrases in praise of God found in 1:17 (cf. 2 Macc 12:15; 13:4; Rev 17:14; 19:15), all standard Hellenist Jewish vocabulary which mixes Hebrew phrases with Greek attributes freely. No doubt it was a liturgical formula.

The normal word in the Pauline writings for Jesus' reappearance is parousía (2 Thess 2:8; 2 Tim 1:10; 4:1, 8; Tit 2:13). *Epiphaneía* is used here, but without any change in meaning. The sense of the passage is that one's Christian life must be lived free from blame or reproach (v. 14) until God sees fit to reveal the Son finally.

ALLELUIA. ACTS 15:14B

Open our hearts, O LORD, to listen to the words of your Son.

LUKE 16:19-31

This perfect Lukan parable bears the stamp of a folk tale that the evangelist, having reported it and doubtless improved on it, puts at the service of his continued invitation to repentance. He is equally interested in the failure of the offspring of Father Abraham, who have every advantage, to heed "Moses and the prophets" (v. 31). Their hardened condition, in his view, is such that no report of resurrection from the dead (Jesus' resurrection, i.e.) will move them. The poor beggar for Luke is the true son of Abraham. Luke will stress the theme of true sonship again in the case of Zacchaeus (19:9), as he has done with a woman bent double for eighteen years (13:13) and those rejected versus those accepted at the judgment (13:28f.).

Needless to say, the rich man in torment seeking comfort at the hands of Lazarus (v. 24) is an authentic touch of Jesus' teaching. His message was nothing if not a projection of the overturning of every convention and stereotype. God who sees all hearts will lay them bare at the end. God's justice is not man's justice, as Isaiah said long ago.

✍✍

Proper 22 [27] / Twenty-seventh Sunday of the Year (C)
Sunday between October 2 and October 8, inclusive

LAMENTATIONS 1:1-6

Jerusalem fell to the Chaldeans who then leveled Solomon's Temple in 587. For the survivors whether those carried into exile or those who remained as captives it was a time of national mourning. This book of poetry divided into five chapters comes from that period. It is carefully constructed, the first four chapters being acrostics in which each stanza begins with a successive letter of the twenty-two in the Hebrew alphabet while chapter five has twenty-two verses. The musical form of the dirge *(qina)* was later applied to it. Lamentations is the third scroll of five *(megilloth)* recited at feasts, this one being the sorrowful Ninth of *Ab (tishah be'Av)* commemorating Jerusalem's first and second destructions (587 B.C.E. and 135 C.E. in the Bar Kokbah revolt). "Daughter Zion," "the princess," is the city widowed by separation from her strong husband, the LORD. Judah is an exile living in slavery dispersed among the Gentiles. The pilgrimage movement is interrupted, the priests have little to do, virgins weep, and the young stalwart males are robbed of strength like pastureless rams. An explanation is attempted by pious scribal hands: "The LORD has punished [Judah] for her many sins."

LAMENTATIONS 3:19-26 OR PSALM 137

HABAKKUK 1:1-4; 2:1-4

Some have conjectured that we have here in vv. 2:1ff. the first questioning of the ways of God in Israelite literature. Later the authors of Job and the Psalms will raise it to an art. ("I cry to you and you do not answer; / I stand, and you merely look at me. / You have turned cruel to me; / with the might of your hand you persecute me." [Job 30:20f.]; cf. Pss 88; 142.) The occasion is the desperate state of Judah on the brink of Nebuchadnezzar's invasion of Jerusalem in 597 B.C. The LORD says he is raising up Chaldea to do his will (1:5-11). There is violence and injustice everywhere, and the prophet charges God with doing nothing to alleviate it. Why must Habakkuk have to see trouble and wrongdoing; why must he be required to look at this strife and contention (v. 3)? If the LORD has no intention of intervening, he could at least spare his prophet the repulsive sight of ruin.

The author then declares that he will set himself up at a guard post on a rampart to discover what response, if any, he will get from the LORD (2:1; Isa 21:6-9; Ezek 3:17 all use the same figure of the sentinel). The answer he awaits he receives (vv. 4-20). The message is to be posted publicly (v. 2). Vindication seems to tarry; he is told it will not be delayed (v. 3). The programmatic opening that sets the tone for the whole oracle states that people are divided into two groups: the rash who trust in wealth and personal resources and the just whose integrity derives from their faith, meaning trust in God's promise. YHWH will set about delivering his people from oppression from Chaldea and injustice from within, in accord with this analysis. Some rely on themselves; the just one relies on the LORD (*justus autem in fide sua vivet* [v. 4], Vulgate), better translated "by his fidelity," the subject made plural in NRSV. The presence of total trust or faithfulness (*ᵉmunah*) makes a person just or righteous, a *tsaddik*. Its absence makes him proud and unstable (v. 4) with an insatiable appetite for destruction. It is well remembered that 2:4a is the phrase that Paul isolated in Rom 1:17, and Martin Luther after him.

PSALM 37:1-9

PSALM 95:1-2, 6-9

2 TIMOTHY 1:1[6-8, 13]-14

Second Timothy is widely regarded as pseudonymous, as are 1 Timothy and Titus. The reasons include weak attestation to all three Pastoral Epistles in early canons and papyri, the nature of their polemic against heretics, the transition from the Pauline proclamation to the concept of faith as a *parathēkē* (Vulgate, accurately, *depositum*, 1 Tim 6:20; 2 Tim 1:12, 14); vocabulary divergencies from Paul, the difficulty of fitting 1 and 2 Timothy into his life situation, and the non-Pauline character of the church order described in the pastorals.

Paul had used Hab 4:1 to press home his point that the justice and fidelity of God were displayed in entrusting the gospel to us (Rom 1:17). Paul's disciple who writes this letter is addressing himself to some third generation Christian (v. 5; Timothy's grandmother a believer in Christ before him?). The point the writer makes is that faith cannot be transmitted merely as a family inheritance. Neither can it be counted on to burn with the same bright flame as when a Christian received the sacraments of initiation (or was commissioned to preach, if that is all that is meant by the laying on of hands, v. 6). A rekindling is constantly needed if the Christian is to continue in the spirit of power, love, and self-discipline that he first received (v. 7). The strength God gives should help the disciple accept the hardships entailed in the gospel, as he gives testimony about "our Lord" (v. 8) and joins the imprisoned Paul in his sufferings. Paul's words delivered in faith and love are proposed as a model of sound teaching (v. 13). This "good treasure" (again, *parathēkēn*, v. 14) is to be guarded "with the help of *(dià)* the Holy Spirit living in us." The writer knows that the one in whom he has put his trust will watch over the rich treasure he has received "until *that* day," presumably of final consummation (v. 12).

Alleluia. See Ephesians 1:17-18

May the Father of our Lord Jesus Christ enlighten the eyes of our hearts, that we may see how great is the hope to which we are called.

Luke 17:5-10

Luke derives vv. 5f. from Q (see Matt 17:20) but the remaining short parable is peculiarly his. The "sycamore" of v. 6 is a sycamine or black mulberry, not the American buttonwood. A mustard seed is like the faith that moves a mountain in Matthew, while here it commands a tree to throw itself into the sea. Large and incommensurate effects from scarcely discernible causes are the point of this hyperbole. The tufts of grass that break through and over time break up paving provide a modern parallel without the element of exaggeration, but of course in the Gospel it is a figure.

Servants act like servants, says the parable. They are not waited on but do the waiting (v. 8). Such is the fixed social order of things. No verbal bouquets are handed out when this order is adhered to. The argument is "from the lesser to the greater," *qal vᵉḥomer*, "light and heavy" or *a fortiori*, familiar from rabbinic interpretation. If slaves in domestic service serve, how much more should not God's servants go beyond routine commands to do God's bidding (v. 10)? Fortunately for Luke's argument, he can provide Jesus as the model for all as the one "among you as one who serves" (22:27).

❧❧
Proper 23 [28] / Twenty-eighth Sunday of the Year (C)
Sunday between October 9 and October 15, inclusive

JEREMIAH 29:1, 4-7

When Nebuchadnezzar came to power in Babylon some time around 605 (25:1) Jeremiah was vindicated in his consistent prophecy that the LORD would bring judgment from the north on Judah for its sins. He pointed out the folly of resistance to this powerful conqueror and for his pains was reviled by court prophets and priests alike. Their counsel to Judah's kings was to stand and fight. When King Zedekiah (594/3–587) sent emissaries to him asking the LORD what to do in light of the fact that "the king of Babylon is attacking us," Jeremiah gave the LORD's response. "See, I am giving you a choice between life and death": stay in the city and die by the sword or famine or pestilence, surrender to the Chaldeans and have life as your booty (21:2, 8f.). Today's lection is consistent with all the unwelcome advice Jeremiah has been giving kings and their courts. He is still in the capital as he writes to the exiles in Babylon, once Jerusalem has been bereft of its entire leadership class (29:1f.). His counsel is what might be expected from this politically astute public man. "Stay there and prosper. You have had the gift of life forced on you. Make the most of it." The women are to continue having Jewish children (v. 6). The men are to be industrious and make a difference in the life of Babylon (vv. 5, 7). Thus Joseph did in Egypt, and so have the Jews done in every city of the dispersion, whether Alexandria, Berlin, Moscow, or New York. Their very diligence and intelligence often netted them opposition. Jeremiah could hold out to his fellow countrymen a promise of the LORD that they would be back in seventy years (v. 10; a round figure made up of seven times ten). In the event they were back in fifty but they left a body of colonists behind that was still influential six and seven centuries later.

PSALM 66:1-12

2 KINGS 5:1-3, 7-15C[14-17]

Beginning this reading at v. 14, as LM proposes, makes it an edifying tale of not accepting a money gift for acting as an agent of God's power. Hearers need to have a better clue to the story unless it is presumed so familiar to them that they need not have it reviewed in its entirety. Beginning the reading at vv. 1-3, then 7 and following, is strongly indicated. Since, however, the venality of Elisha's servant

Gehazi will figure prominently in the tale at vv. 20-27, the refusal of Elisha to accept a gift for doing the LORD's work is especially important. In a sense, it is a sub-plot of the story. The main plot concerns the power of the God of Elisha—a point not lost on the upright Aramean commander. An important aspect of the tale is the curative power of the Jordan, which is situated in a land made holy by its association with YHWH. The mule-loads of earth are to be this land transplanted. Naaman will have to appear in the sanctuary of the god Rimmon as part of his duties as a military aide. His sincerely directed holocausts, however, will be offered on the soil of Israel to Israel's God.

It would seem unwise for the preacher to make a point of Naaman's leprosy (v. 3). Victims of the disease erroneously so designated in English (actually Hansen's disease, *not* the biblical family of skin infections) suffer enough already without their affliction being made symbolic of moral fault, as is commonly done. The healing power of God and the trust in God of the captive Jewish girl (v. 2) and the prophet (v. 10) are the important matters—they and the new faith of the soldier of the king of Aram (Syria).

PSALM 111

PSALM 98:1-4

2 TIMOTHY 2:8-15

As pointed out last Sunday, an impressive body of scholarly opinion situates the authorship of 1 and 2 Timothy in the early second century because of their similarity to documents of the subapostolic age. There is also the unlikeness of many phrases to those of Paul, despite the author's mammoth effort to re-create every known detail of his career. The "enduring" until we reign with Christ of the hymn of v. 12a and the denial and infidelity spoken of in 12f. bring to mind the harassment of Christians that we know of from Trajan's reign (98–117 C.E.) more than they do the imprisonments of Paul (cf. Phil 1:13f.).

The author reflects a knowledge of Rom 1:3f. in v. 8 and Col 1:24 in v. 10. Leonard Bernstein's sermon of the presider at *Mass*, an ingenious targumic interweaving of Epistle, Gospel, and homily, restored v. 9 to popular consciousness for some:

But you cannot imprison the word of the Lord!

Verse 11 contains one of the "sayings that are sure" found in 1 Tim 3:1; 4:9. Death with Christ brings life; perseverance in suffering assures a share in his reign. (Cf. "We are . . . heirs of God, joint heirs with Christ—if, in fact, we suffer with him so that we may also be glorified with him," Rom 8:17.) Verse 13 features Christ's inner fidelity, which is like that of God—a sole occurrence in the New Testament.

The pericope is a sober discussion of the choice between faith in Christ and life itself, with specific motivations given for perseverance and not recanting the faith under persecution. "If we deny him, he will also deny us" (v. 12b; cf. Luke 13:27).

ALLELUIA. 1 SAMUEL 3:9; JOHN 6:69B

Speak, O LORD, your servant is listening; you have the words of everlasting life.

LUKE 17:11-19

This narrative is not found elsewhere in the Gospels. Luke makes the account he has from the tradition a story of the gratitude of the outsider in contrast to the ingratitude of those in the community of Jewish faith. We have come to expect this stress of his. Jesus' very appearance along the borders of Samaritan territory (v. 11) was not without risk. The lepers keep their distance (v. 12) in accordance with the requirement of Lev 13:45 that they call out their affliction. Their skin diseases (impetigo? ringworm?) were highly infectious, as Hansen's disease is not. They address him as *Epistáta*, "Master," a secular title employed by Luke six times, usually on the lips of the disciples. Jesus intimates a cure rather than referring to it specifically. His immediate response to the lepers' plea, namely, that they should show themselves to the priests, does not conform to the specifications of Lev 13:9ff. or 49, where the priest acts as a health officer, but comes closest to 14:3, where he declares a cure an accomplished fact. But that is not the point.

The cure of ten and the gratitude of only one who was a Samaritan, is the nub (vv. 15ff.). This despised people had the five books of Moses in common with the Jews, but their claim to their own shrine at Shechem and their heritage stemming from it (see Joshua 24) had long been rejected by the southerners of Judah. Such claims and counterclaims were not of significance to Jesus in the Synoptic tradition, even though John has him acknowledge the rightness of Jewish faith (4:22) as a prelude to transcending both claims with a worship in "spirit and in truth." The healed Samaritan is reported as having achieved that transcendence.

🙩🙩

Proper 24 [29] / Twenty-ninth Sunday of the Year (C)
Sunday between October 16 and October 22, inclusive

JEREMIAH 31:27-34

For a commentary see 5 Lent (B).

That lection begins with v. 31, today's with an important promise by the LORD that after Judah has been brought low by Assyria, both it and its livestock will be rejuvenated, repopulated. The LORD declares that his people has been under the divine gaze throughout its overthrow and destruction—indeed, God claims it was his doing. YHWH will be equally vigilant to oversee its rebuilding and planting. "In days that are surely coming" the proverb about inherited guilt will no longer be bandied about. Deuteronomy had enunciated in non-proverbial fashion that neither fathers nor children would be held responsible for the others' guilt (24:16). Ezekiel repeats the Jeremian proverb (18:2) and for some reason is better remembered for it. If the Deuteronomist saw it as a precept for the present, the notion of a parent's guilt transmitted to children or their coming from "bad seed" must have been so prevalent that the prophets had to put it in a brighter future. It may have survived in weak fashion as "sour grapes" to convey resentment at another's better lot than one's own but this is more likely to be from Aesop's fable "The Fox and the Grapes."

PSALM 119:97-104

GENESIS 32:22-31

For a commentary see Proper 13 [18] (A).

PSALM 121:1-8

EXODUS 17:8-13

Joshua's name occurs for the first time in the Bible abruptly in v. 9. He is introduced as Moses' aide in 24:13 and appears in the narrative at 32:17. Not until Num 13:8 does he properly get into the story. This means that the incident is out of order and ought to come much later in the book. Moreover, the Amalekites are elsewhere described (Num 13:29; 14:25) as people of the Negev or southern Palestinian desert, not from south in the Sinai peninsula near Rephidim. This seems to be the story of a raiding party near Kadesh-barnea in the northeastern portion of Sinai as the Israelites approach Canaan.

Moses holds up his staff (v. 9; cf. 4:17) and raises his hands as a symbolic action calculated to ensure victory, similar to the postures struck by Elijah in 1 Kgs 17:21; 18:42. Joshua is totally successful in terms of the "ban" (*ḥerem* = *anáthema*, the commanded utter destruction of the Israelites' enemies; v. 13; cf. Num 21:1-3; Deut 7:1-2). Verse 16 provides a snatch of a victory song, probably sung long after. "*YHWH-nissi*" ("The Lord my banner") is victorious through the Israelites over the Amalekites down through the ages.

Early Christian iconography likened Moses' upraised hands, supported by Aaron and Hur, to the position of the hands of Jesus on the cross and of the eucharistic presider or the praying Christian as *orans*. In the Exodus account it was undoubtedly more a prophetic sign than a prayer.

PSALM 121

2 TIMOTHY 3:14−4:[2]5

Verse 14 is an argument in favor of the tradition, with a charge to observe fidelity included. The Scriptures (v. 15) known to the recipient from his infancy are the Hebrew Law, the Prophets, and Writings (cf. Luke 24:44; the acronym TᵃNᵃK became common in later Judaism, *Torah*, *Nebhiim*, and *Ketubhim*) in the LXX version as for all non-Palestinian Christians. Salvation and wisdom are available through reading them in a spirit of faith in Christ (v. 15). Only by knowing them well and interpreting them rightly can a teacher in the community be equipped for his office (v. 17). They are "inspired of God" (*theópneustos*, v. 16) and useful for instruction in faith, morals, and discipline.

The stern apostolic charge of 4:1f. to be faithful to the task of proclamation (v. 2) until the Lord returns to judge (v. 1) is laid upon the disciple Timothy. Jesus' appearing and his reign (v. 1) are realities that have in some sense already occurred. There must be an unflagging fidelity to preaching, whatever the seeming unsuitability of the occasion, until the Lord's return. It is to be done through convincing argument, rebuke, and encouragement, relentlessly but with utmost patience, in expository teaching *(didaché)*.

ALLELUIA. MATTHEW 11:25

Blessed are you, Father, LORD of heaven and earth; you have revealed to little ones the mysteries of the kingdom.

LUKE 18:1-8

Luke's corrupt judge is all his own; there are no parallels. The story resembles the parable of the persistence of the householder awakened in the middle of the night (11:5-8). Luke tells this tale in response to the uncertainty of the community regarding Jesus' return. The Lord will come to do justice if he is prayed for night and day (vv. 7f.). Again, the technique is "from the lesser to the greater," the Hebrew "light and heavy." If even an unjust judge must yield to a petitioner lest she wear him out (lit. "receive a blow to the face," v. 5, suppressed in the NRSV paraphrase), how much more will not the just and generous God do for his chosen who call on him? Luke has made of his parable a prayer for the final arrival of God's reign, whatever Jesus meant in telling it. Sirach 35:14a-15 speaks of a widow who may well provide the model for this one.

Luke's pious conclusion (v. 8b) is what he makes of this tale, illustrative of persistent prayer for the parousía.

✌✌
Proper 25 [30] / Thirtieth Sunday of the Year (C)
Sunday between October 23 and October 29, inclusive

JOEL 2:23-32

See Ash Wednesday (A, B, C) for the passage that immediately precedes this one. The first two chapters of the book, written in Judah at the onset of the fourth century, employ the plague of locusts in the land as an image of doom on the Day of the LORD unless the people repent. Beginning at 2:18 the LORD relents, sending them rich green fields and pastures in place of the barren. This reading (which is divided as 2:23-27—3:1-5 in Kittel's MT and the LXX) moves from the promised relief of famine to an outpouring of God's spirit on all humanity, the young and old alike, even slaves. There is a renewed picture of the great and terrible Day in the terms of the Sinai theophany and more. But there will be deliverance for the remnant on Mt. Zion that calls on the name of the LORD.

PSALM 65

JEREMIAH 14:7-10, 19-22

These two poems are interrupted by Jeremiah's prophecy that sword, famine, and pestilence will overtake the land (vv. 11-16). The introduction to the first, however, relates the need for repentance to the miseries the people have experienced in a great drought (vv. 1-6). It is a marvelous word picture of people and beasts dying for lack of rainfall and serves as an image of the "iniquities" and "apostasies" (v. 7) of the populace. The LORD is called on suppliantly and charged with apparent helplessness (vv. 8f.). He in answer reminds them of their sins (v. 10) and offers them the word that he weeps copiously for their victim state in war and famine but can see no wisdom shared with them by prophet or priest (v. 17f.). The people respond asking, "Why? Why? We look for peace and find only terror. Is our rejection by you to be complete?" (v. 19). Then comes the acknowledgment of their current sinfulness wedded to the iniquity of their ancestors (v. 20). Jeremiah has long hoped for the first but will repudiate the second as a rationalization for personal guilt (see 31:29f.). The people remind YHWH as the psalmist and others frequently do of his own dishonor if he breaks the covenant with them. They recall as if to him but really to themselves that pagan idols are powerless as the skies are, without divine power behind them to relieve the drought (vv. 21f.).

PSALM 84:1-7

SIRACH 35:12[17]-18

This is the passage referred to in the commentary on last week's Gospel. The God of justice, who knows no favorites (v. 12/16), is not deaf to the widow when she pours out her complaint (v. 14/17; the NAB numbering is cited first, since this is canonical Scripture for Catholics and Orthodox). Those who cause her tears to fall (v. 15/18) are undoubtedly the oppressor and the merciless and proud (vv. 20/22b-23a) who harass the weak, the orphan, and the widow. The chief thrust of this passage is the declaration of vv. 17f./21-22a that the prayer of the humble will be answered by God with justice and their rights restored to them. Verses 20ff./22b-23 have a grim retributive quality, reflected in the song of Mary (cf. Luke 1:51ff.), but to the ancient Semitic mind this was simply a means of expressing God's justice. The proud and the haughty of the verses first cited have been referred to before in 10:14-17 and 16:14. In the latter place the "sinners" (v. 6) are overtly the rebellious Korah, the people of Sodom and Gomorrah, and others from the biblical past. Actually, a veiled polemic against the Greeks of Sirach's day is probably intended.

The incorruptibility of God, the just judge (vv. 11f./14ff.) who is as impervious to sacrifice taken from the possessions of the poor as to extortion, has been featured in 34:18ff. His wrath will flare up against the oppressors of widows and orphans, destroying them and leaving their women and children in the same condition, as Exod 22:21ff. had long ago promised.

Psalm 34:2-3, 17-19, 23

2 Timothy 4:6-8, 16-18

Verses 6-8 of today's reading constitute the solemn conclusion of the hortatory material that goes to make up the bulk of the epistle. The disciple should suffer for the faith on the basis of the bond between his teacher and him (cf. 1:8, 12; 2:3-13; 3:10-12).

The notions of "being poured out like a libation" (v. 6) and of dissolution *(análysis)* in the sense of "departure" from life are reminiscent of Phil 2:17 and 1:23. Verse 7 with its three parallel clauses triumphantly reviewing the life of an apostle is a familiar part of Christian literature—almost invariably attributed to Paul. Two of the images employed come from athletic contests (cf. 1 Cor 9:24ff.; Phil 4:1). "Keeping faith *(pístin tēreîn)* was already a fixed expression meaning maintaining a trust. Günther Bornkamm has cited the words attributed to Dido, "cursum perēgi," from Virgil's *Aeneid* 4.653, as a parallel to, "I have finished the race," where the phrase refers to the course of life that the goddess Fortuna has mapped out for her.

A crown of righteousness awaits, "is reserved for" the apostle (v. 8), a verb that occurs both in imperial edicts of commendation and later in accounts of martyrdom (*Martyrdom of Polycarp* 17:1; 19:2). "On that day" is doubtless "the day of the Lord," as indicated by 2 Timothy's reference to Jesus Christ's "appearing" in the role of just judge after much eager "longing." It is the Lord who will award the faithful apostle his crown *(stéphanos),* the laurel-wreath of the successful athlete.

The immediate context of vv. 17f. is v. 16, with its mention of "my [i.e., Paul's] first defense." An early interpretation of this passage is found in Eusebius's *History of the Church* 2.2, where the fourth-century author follows a tradition that Paul was released from his two years of captivity at Rome with which Acts concludes, and that he set out on a further ministry of preaching and was apprehended a second and last time. It was during this second Roman captivity that he is said by Eusebius to have written 2 Timothy. On such a hypothesis, his earlier release would have constituted his deliverance "from the lion's mouth" (v. 17), the lion being imperial power. Against this theory is the fact that the Pastoral Epistles know of only one imprisonment of Paul. His first hearing in court, therefore, is meant to be an episode in his sole Roman trial. Alternatively, on the supposition that the epistle was written from a Caesarean imprisonment, he is portrayed as reporting on the events of Acts 23:1ff., with the Lord appearing at Paul's side (as in v. 17).

The reading in public worship need not be freighted with these complex historical considerations. It is a straightforward declaration of what the faithful messenger of the Gospel may look forward to. There is no ethical problem attaching to pseudonymous authorship, even to simulated farewells and personal messages. It was a convention of the times and is totally unrelated to our modern concept of literary forgery.

Alleluia. Luke 19:38

Blessed is the king who comes in the name of the Lord; peace on earth, and glory in heaven!

Luke 18:9-14

See next Sunday, Proper 26 [31] (C). This two-character story of Jesus conveys two general attitudes, one of self-congratulation with "nothing to declare," the other of awareness of sin and an implicit plea for the restoration of justice. The characterization of the Pharisee is so devastating that that unfortunate class of men has been type-cast in the Christian mind ever since. Jacob Neusner has pointed out that we do not have enough data on the Pharisees from Jewish sources dating to Jesus' time to generalize on them or even to distinguish among different types. Christians, meanwhile, have generalized adversely from the Synoptic data. The basic and unresolved question is, what is the relation of *hoi pharisaioi* of the Gospels to *ha p*e*rushim* of the talmudic literature? The latter may be the "separated," but from what or whom we cannot be sure. They may also be the "distinguishers" or the "precisionists." The Gospels are interested in one type of Pharisee only, the proud one who is separated not only from all that might defile him ritually, but in a contemptuous way from the "people of the land." The more righteous seekers of wisdom in Pharisee ranks are largely disregarded, their very existence being hinted at only briefly. Both the Babylonian (*b. Sota* 22b) and Palestinian (*j. Sota* 5:7 [20c]) Talmuds classify the *p^erushim* in seven types, five of which are held up to ridicule (e.g., the knee-knocking *p^erushim*, those who rub themselves against the wall to draw blood, the one bent over like a pestle in a mortar), while two types are praised (for fearing like Job, for loving like Abraham) as cited by Anthony J. Saldarini, "Pharisees" in *The Anchor Bible Dictionary* (New York: Doubleday, 1992), 5:300. The Pharisee of the Lukan parable is in neither of the latter two categories.

The Pharisee's prayer is no prayer at all but a declaration of Law observance (good!) and contempt for another (bad!). The tax-gatherer's self-accusation may very well have been true and not merely the expression of a sense of unworthiness. These functionaries, after all, had as their way of life a collaboration with the Romans against fellow Jews. In saying he is unworthy he may really be unworthy. This could mean that he goes home from the Temple justified because he intends to amend his unjust ways. That refinement is not the point, however, so much as the attitudes of the two men in the one activity, prayer.

Luke repeats his summary conclusion on the exalted and the humbled (v. 14b) from his parable of places at a feast (14:11), which in turn is based on the phrase in Mary's song that says that God has deposed the mighty and raised the lowly to high places (1:52).

❧❧❧
Proper 26 [31] / Thirty-first Sunday of the Year (C)
Sunday between October 30 and November 5, inclusive

HABAKKUK 1:1-4; 2:1-4

For a commentary see Proper 22 [27] (C).

PSALM 119:137-144

ISAIAH 1:10-18

For a commentary see Proper 14 [19] (C).

PSALM 32:1-7

WISDOM 11:23—12:2

It is possible to say in commenting on this passage that it features God's mercy (v. 23), love (v. 24), creating and sustaining of all things (v. 25) and the gradual character of God's punishments which are primarily remedial. Yet the chief thing that leaps up from the page is none of these but the unmistakably Hellenist character of the pericope. It bristles with Greek-oriented statements about God that would not have occurred to a biblical writer of a pre-Alexandrian age. Among them are: "You can do all things," "You love all things that exist," "You detest none of the things that you have made," "How would anything have endured if you had not willed it?" "You spare all things, for they are yours," "our immortal spirit is in all things." An Hebraic equivalent of some of the above might be worked out but that is not the point. The point is that the Greek world in which the author of Wisdom had his being had ontological problems (and a vocabulary to cope with them) that his Jewish forebears did not have and felt none the poorer without.

These verses are part of a digression on the subject of God's mercy (11:17—12:22) from the second of five pairs of opposites taken from the Exodus narrative. The segment on the providence of God during the exodus runs from 11:2 through 19:22, the end of the book. The present pairing sets in contrast the Egyptian worship of dumb creatures (11:15f.; 12:23-27; 15:18—16:4), for which they were struck with plagues of small animals and serpents, and the quail that, contrariwise, benefited the Israelites. The lengthy digression (11:17—12:22), of which today's reading is a part, is triggered by mention of the punishment of sin in 11:16. God's universal love for creatures is elaborated on at length in the language of Greek philosophy.

PSALM 145:1-2, 8-14

2 THESSALONIANS 1:1-4, 11—2:2

The identity of this letter's salutation to that of 1 Thessalonians aside from the dittograph found in 2b is the first detail of many that create the suspicion that a later hand has written a resolution to the problem raised in 1 Thessalonians of apprehension at the imminence of the final days. A second detail is the mention of persecutions and afflictions in the thanksgiving (v. 4) that echo the persecution spoken of in 1 Thess 1:6, to which is coupled an invocation of apocalyptic judgment on the persecutors (vv. 5-10) quite different from the tone of solicitude and confidence about Jesus' coming that marks Paul's first letter (1:4-10).

Verses 11f. are obviously a prayer for the recipients of the epistle, that they may be strengthened against the persecution and trial that will be a necessary preliminary to the Lord's coming in glory (vv. 3-10). If they fulfill God's call in faith, that day will be one of mutual glorification for the Lord Jesus Christ and them.

In vv. 1f. of chap. 2 the author—Paul or some other—attempts to allay the anxieties that 1 Thess 4:16f. could have created. Although the latter verses end with a charge to "console one another with this message," the graphic account of the coming of the day of the Lord might well have agitated or terrified Macedonian populations not accustomed to Jewish apocalyptic language. The problems of the dating and authorship of this letter stem from chap. 2 as it proceeds from here. Either Paul became aware of the fears he had aroused by his first letter and penned a second one fairly soon, naming signs and conditions that would have to be realized before the Lord could be expected back, or more likely some other Christian long after Paul, with 1 Thessalonians before him, supplied reasons for the delay of the parousía, using a quite different set of eschatological images.

Alleluia. John 1:14 and 12b

The Word of God became a man and lived among us. He enabled those who accepted him to become children of God.

Luke 19:1-10

This is another narrative peculiar to Luke. Feeling runs high against Zacchaeus in the Jericho community (vv. 2, 7). His wealth and his reputation as a sinner are closely related details. Despite Zacchaeus's protestation of innocence, more probably of occult compensation (v. 8), the story ends with Jesus' declaration that he (the "Son of Man," for Luke) has come to search out and save the "lost"—no proper description of an innocent man. The old proverb speaks of time for repentance between the stirrup and the ground. Some change of heart must have overtaken Zacchaeus while Jesus spoke, equating salvation and sonship of Abraham, or between vv. 9 and 10. Verse 10 is otherwise meaningless. On the supposition that the runty tax-gouger repented, we have a story from life that makes the same point as the parables of chap. 15.

Proper 27 [32] / Thirty-second Sunday of the Year (C)
Sunday between November 6 and November 12, inclusive

HAGGAI 1:15B—2:9

This first of the postexilic prophets dates his book to the Persian period by naming the second year of King Darius's reign (520) as the time when the word of the LORD first came to him (1:1). Today's passage dates the start of the rebuilding of the Temple (the "sixth month" would be our August/September) and names the governor of Judah at the time under Persian power and the high priest then in office (v. 14). A message to the two and the returned "remnant" is carefully dated one month later: what is left of Solomon's glorious Temple must seem like nothing but all must take courage and begin to rebuild, for the LORD of hosts is with them. His is the silver and gold and all the treasures of the earth (vv. 7f.) which, in the future, will adorn a house of the LORD more glorious than before. Haggai's prophecy proved true but not until half a millennium had passed and Herod the Great outdid the Solomonic glory. Jewish literature to this day speaks of the Second Temple period meaning these humble beginnings under Persian and Greek domination. The tyrant Herod—not especially held in honor—is thought to have done no more than complete it. The pericope is lived out in our day by Christians and Muslims in Europe and Africa who have lost everything in the wars of politicians and their armies but who have never lost faith in God to restore their fortunes. European Jewry largely abstained from the socialist-secular Zionist movement right up to the founding of the state of Israel by the United Nations, which was preceded by successful terrorism against the British. It was seen by most Torah-observant Jews as a work of man, not of God. Only in recent decades have the Orthodox begun to claim their return to the land and the Western Wall of the Temple as a fulfillment of prophetic promise like that made to Abraham down through Haggai.

PSALM 145:1-5, 17-21 OR PSALM 98

JOB 19:19, 23-27A

Because the verses immediately preceding this portion have Job complain that his intimate friends abhor him, that all pursue him in Godlike fashion, the opening lament of today's lection has found its way into Western literature as, "Oh, that mine enemy would write a book!" But neither the Hebrew text nor the LXX says that. They only record the wish that his words were inscribed on a scroll, better yet engraved on a rock with a stylus of iron (vv. 23f.). What Job wants to stand forever in lead upon stone is his conviction that his Ransomer *(go'el)* is a living God who will fulfill that office for him. The footnote apparatus of NRSV, NAB, and JB indicate the corrupt state of the Hebrew text which some translators have resolved by making it a more explicit statement of the resurrection of the dead (vv. 27-28) than the time of authorship would warrant (7th–5th centuries B.C.E.). St. Jerome's Vulgate, the work of an honest scholar but one zealous for the Gospel, renders *go'el* as "my Redeemer" who at the last will stand upon the earth—a case perhaps of an ancient writer foretelling more than he realized. However the passage originally read, it has Job despite his present wretched state (vv. 20f.) continuing to trust God. It is a mistake to read this classic of bad things happening to good people otherwise. The baffling and now immortalized "escape by the skin of my teeth" (v. 20) is a translator's guess as to what the corrupt text might mean. NAB hazards "thin lips over my teeth" and NIV "over my gums." A clue may be found in 13:14b where the common biblical expression for risking one's life occurs: "I take my life in my hand." By the law of poetic parallelism v. 14a, "I will take my flesh between my teeth," must mean something similar, namely, a grim resolve to carry on in spite of reduction to the miserable state of the clearer 19:20a, "My bones cling to my skin and to my flesh."

PSALM 17:1-9

2 MACCABEES 7:1-2, 9-14

Today's reading recounts the torture and death of the first, third, and fourth of seven sons of an anonymous Jewish mother (7:1), together with the edifying speeches made to their Seleucid Greek captors. The tale of the second brother (vv. 3-8) has doubtless been omitted from public reading because of its grisly details.

This book of Scripture was written in Greek by members of the Maccabean (priestly) party. The designation "the scrolls that soil the hands," was their colorful phrase for the books they thought the holiest. The creators of the Jewish canon did not include it for the reason of its Greek-language composition and their own anti-priestly inclinations. The other collection of the Jewish scriptures contain it, those retained in a Greek version other than the Septuagint translation. The mood of the book is pious. It proposes a theological interpretation of certain events between 180 and 161 B.C.E. and describes itself as a condensation of a work in five books by Jason of Cyrene (2:19-23) which is not extant. Second Maccabees contains much interesting history told from the standpoint of the murdered high priest Onias (Ḥoni; 4:30-34) and Judah the Maccabee (8:1–33), to the discredit of Jewish collaborators like Jason, Simon, and Menelaus and the Greek general of Antiochus IV, Nicanor. Today's pericope is from one of two pious interludes which in effect are martyrologies, chaps. 6–7 and the death of the Jewish elder Razis (14:37-46), the only suicide that the biblical literature praises. Elsewhere, throughout, there are prayers and soliloquies, including one by the dying Antiochus in Persia (9:12), his doubtful vow to become a Jew (v. 17), and a letter to the Jews that there is no reason to think inauthentic which describes his turning of power over to his son Antiochus V (9:19-27).

The denial of Jewishness by breaking the food laws (Deut 14:3-21) is given as the cause of the murder of the seven sons and their mother (7:1, 30). The "king" (7:3), improbably, carries out the execution. A strong theme of their resistance speeches is faith in a risen life in the body (vv. 9f., 14, 23, 29, 36) which was developed through the experience of the revolt with its many dead. The murdered Ḥonias and the prophet Jeremiah appear in vision to present a sword of victory to Judas (15:12-16). A second theme of the resistance speeches is a theology of Jewish guilt that has brought God's righteous wrath on the people (7:18, 32f.). A statement of the seventh brother, "for we are suffering for our sins" (7:32), seems to have supplied the words of admission of guilt by the so-called good thief (Luke 22:41).

Interestingly, the fourth brother denies resurrection to the wicked (7:14b) whereas Daniel in this same period affirms it (12:2). Second Maccabees specifies that "for you, there will be no resurrection to life!" Daniel promises "shame and everlasting contempt" for the others than the just who shall live forever.

Psalm 17:1-9[5-6, 8b, 15]

Verse 8a, "Keep me as the apple (Heb., pupil) of your eye," is puzzlingly omitted.

2 Thessalonians 2:1-5, 13-17[16—3:5]

The earlier portion of the RCL lection (vv. 1-5) is the writer's attempt to still the fears recorded in Paul's first letter to Thessalonica (4:13-17) by telling the church there that no teaching "that the day of the Lord is already here" can come from Paul (v. 2). A scenario of all that must precede that day is then provided. Some mysterious "lawless individual" must first be revealed (the "man of sin" in earlier translations from the poorer reading, *hamartías*, not the better, *anomías*). The rebellion *(apostasía)* that presumably he will lead must come first (v. 3). Daniel 11:36 speaks of "a king who exalts himself and considers himself greater than any god," probably Antiochus IV, against whom the Maccabees revolted. Searching for images to illustrate a claimant of power over God's people and hence God, the Thessalonian author seems to be resorting to this and other apocalyptic passages, notably "an abomination that desolates" (Dan 9:27). This would have been the statue of Zeus that the Seleucid Greek tyrant set up in place of the altar of sacrifice in the Temple (2 Macc 6:2). Closer to the writer's time the Roman emperor Gaius (Caligula, "Little Boots" had done something similar; see Philo, *Embassy to Gaius* 30 §203). The force that is "now restraining him" (v. 6, neuter) and "the one who now restrains (v. 7, masculine) are the subject of much speculation. Imperial Rome and its emperor? Some angelic force? The spread of the gospel itself? Whatever the case, the Thessalonian community is being told that the end is not near, contrary to anything alarmists may be telling them. The assurance is given that the Lord is faithful (3:3) and will both guard them from the evil one and direct their hearts toward the love of God and steadfastness in Christ (v. 5).

Verse 15 is a charge to "hold fast to the traditions you were taught by us, either by word of mouth or by our letter" (i.e., 1 Thessalonians); vv. 16f. are a prayer. Christ and God are jointly invoked as comforters and strengtheners in every good work and word (v. 17). Further injunction to the Thessalonians to prayer (3:1-4) concludes with an invocation of the Lord to rule their hearts (v. 5). All of this rhetoric of gratitude (2:13), encouragement (v. 15), consolation (15ff.), and prayer (3:1-5) follows the grim picture of those who, in an entirely different spirit from the Thessalonians, will follow the mysterious adversary (2:4), the man (vv. 2, 8, 9) and force (v. 7) of lawlessness who seduces to apostasy and ruin (vv. 3, 10).

Observe the play on words between "faith" in 3:2b (lit., "The faith is not of all") and "faith" in v. 3 (lit, "Faithful is the Lord"). The writer of 2 Thessalonians is convinced that his apostolic injunctions are being carried out, "the things that we command" (v. 4), another instance of expected fidelity to tradition that this is a later composition than Paul's.

ALLELUIA. JOHN 6:64B AND 69B

Your words, Lord, are spirit and life; you have the words of everlasting life.

LUKE 20:27-38

All three Synoptics have this pericope (Mark 12:18-27; Matt 22:23-33). Luke has largely been following the Markan order and wording since 19:28, which is parallel to the beginning of Mark 11, with the exception of omitting the parable-in-act of the withered fig tree.

Luke departs from Mark's original in this account of Sadducee disbelief in bodily resurrection (apart from small verbal changes) only by omitting Jesus' charge that his challengers know neither the scriptures nor the power of God (Mark 12:24; Matt 22:29). He adds the phrase "sons of the resurrection" (v. 36b) and the explication of the mystifying argument that there will be a bodily resurrection from the fact that YHWH is God of the patriarchs, "for he is the God not of the dead but of the living" (v. 38b). Luke (vv. 39f.), like Matthew (22:33), finishes off the account with a summary indication of response, whereas Mark terminates the exchange abruptly.

Our information of Sadducee beliefs ("Sadducee" after Zadok, 1 Sam 8:17; 1 Chron 12:29) is slight, although Josephus says that they deny rewards and punishments and the persistence of the soul after death (*War* 2.8.14 [165]; cf. Acts 23:8). Josephus also writes: "Sadducee doctrine is that souls perish with bodies" (*Ant.* 18.1.4 [16]), an attempt to explain the position of this group to the Greek world in terms they themselves would never have used. The silence of the Pentateuch on survival after death—the Mosaic books being the only scriptures for this conservative party—would account for their belief. The Maccabean theology which was priestly (see commentary on the first reading above) seems to have dislodged this traditional agnosticism somewhat.

We are left to conclude that the citation of Exod 3:6 ("the story about the bush," v. 37) means either that God is the contemporary of every age or that God is the God of the long dead patriarchs *now*. Luke chooses the latter meaning (v. 38).

Mark (12:25) and Matthew (22:32) are clear that neither marrying nor giving in marriage is characteristic of the resurrected state. Luke's elaboration of Mark 12:25 in his verses 34f. has been influential on the celibate life in the West. The ones who marry and give in marriage, for him, are the "sons of this age" (*aiōn* = Heb. *'olam*, v. 34); those "who are considered worthy of a place in that age" neither marry, give in marriage (v. 35), nor die (v. 36). Luke says they are "like" (lit. equal to) angels (v. 36) and are sons of God, being sons of the resurrection. The Vulgate translated *kataxiōthéntes* in v. 35, a gnomic or atemporal aorist, by *illi vero, qui digni habebuntur saeculo illo . . . neque nubent neque ducent uxores.* This translation, "those who *will be* accounted worthy of that age . . . neither marry nor give in marriage," was pressed by some Latin fathers to mean that celibate men *(illi = hoi)* have heaven in prospect. Luke abstains from any time sequence in relating worthiness of the coming age to abstention from marriage. NRSV and NAB both retain his atemporal phrase by its rendition "those considered/ deemed worthy . . . do not [marry or give in marriage]." The history of interpretation of this text, however, has Luke favoring abstention from marriage in this life in a way Mark and Matthew do not.

❧☙

Proper 28 [33] / Thirty-third Sunday of the Year (C)
Sunday between November 13 and November 19, inclusive

ISAIAH 65:17-25

So-called Trito-Isaiah or Third Isaiah (chaps. 56–66) is a collection of oracular utterances by poets back in Judah after the exile who attempt to replicate the spirit of the poet who prophesied return, Deutero-Isaiah. Today's reading eminently befits the Church year and indeed the three-year cycle as both come to a close. It celebrates a Jerusalem prosperous and at peace like any country of our time that has survived the ravages of war and a population once displaced and now returned to relative normalcy. The vision it proposes could stand for the Church at peace in any quarter of the globe: divisions among believers healed and the whole body unthreatened by religiously or politically unfriendly neighbors. The things to rejoice over are that infant mortality is down and longevity is again a possibility (v. 20). Homes newly built and fields freshly tilled are not taken over by others from the people of God who are as long-lasting as the trees (v. 22b, the cedars of Lebanon are doubtless intended). The people's work will not be fruitless; its children will grow to maturity and carry on the line. Most importantly, God will answer before he hears the people's call (vv. 23f.). The last verse, so often quoted (and misquoted), envisions a paradise that never was. Nature red in tooth and claw will be at an end, with no question of whether the lion will flourish on his diet of straw. But if the last detail is fantasy the dream that precedes it is not. Many in our time hope for a secular paradise in which science is the reigning queen. The Christian hope, like the Jewish and Muslim, is more modest. It is for the peace of God in a variety of somewheres in which the teachings of the holy books of those three related peoples are lived out seriously.

ISAIAH 12

MALACHI 4:1-2A (MT 3:19-20)

LM follows the Vulgate verse enumeration, which is also that of the LXX. Amos has foretold that the "day of the Lord" will be darkness and gloom, not the brightness and light expected by those who see in it only triumph for Israel (5:18ff.). The anonymous sixth- or fifth-century prophet whose thoughts are recorded in this book (Malachi = "my messenger") paints a picture of destruction for "all the arrogant and all evildoers" (v. 4:1//3:19). He uses the language of the Zoroastrian hymns that portray a final conflagration. In this oracle the arrogant in Israel will be destroyed like stubble thrown into a field oven at harvest time. The preaching of John the Baptizer called upon similar imagery (cf. Matt 3:12//Luke 3:17).

The sun, worshiped as a god of healing in various ancient religions, is depicted in Ps 19:5ff. as a groom emerging from his bridal chamber, a joyful giant traversing the sky and touching everything with his heat. Here the prophet says that the LORD will send not only destructive heat but healing warmth as well, the rays (lit. "wings") of a "sun of justice" for those who fear his name (v. 4:2//3:20a). It is the same sun the rising and the setting of which mark a day-long "pure offering" among the Gentiles (1:11) while Israel thinks that the LORD's table may be polluted (v. 12). The paradox of the future is that YHWH's sun, which looks upon acceptable behavior by the nations, will heal and purify all present Israelite impurities (in Temple sacrifice, 1:7f.; 2:11; in divorce, 2:14ff; in sorcery, perjury, and the defrauding of laborers, 3:5; in the neglect of the LORD's statutes, 3:7; and holding back tithes and offerings, 3:8ff.).

PSALM 98:[5-9]

2 THESSALONIANS 3:6-13[7-12]

Paul's own conduct while among the Thessalonians, namely, working for his livelihood, is put forward as the "tradition" they received from him (v. 6). The word *parádosis* puts it on a par with the deliverances of the creed handed on by the apostle (cf. 1 Cor 15:3-11). Imitation of Paul (v. 7) is a theme found in 1 Cor 4:16; 11:1; Phil 3:17. This epistle repudiates idleness (vv. 6, 11). Paul's independence of the Thessalonians by self-support echoes a conscious choice (v. 8) for he knew he had a claim on them in justice as their teacher (v. 9; cf. 1 Cor 9:12, 18). He was trying to set an example of industriousness for them to follow (cf. 1 Thess 2:9), something they have not done. Some are gadding about unoccupied except in other people's affairs, according to report (v. 11). "Not busy but . . . busybodies"—today's sidewalk superintendents—renders the Greek pun accurately, *mēdèn ergazoménous allà periergazoménous.*

Verse 10 was probably a proverb in current use; v. 12 repeats it. The emphasis is on not being willing to work. This passage is the charter of the Christian work ethic, understood as a contribution necessary for survival in the community, not as industriousness to achieve calculated temporal benefits.

Nowhere does the passage speak of the omission of contributory services as arising from expectation of an imminent appearance of the Lord. Almost all commentators infer this but 2 Thessalonians speaks only of an idle and "kibbitzing" spirit that is abroad in the community.

ALLELUIA. JOHN 8:12

I am the light of the world, says the Lord; whoever follows me will have the light of life.

LUKE 21:5-19

Luke follows Mark (13:1-13) fairly faithfully here, Matt 24:1-21 staying even closer in words but departing in order (9b and 13 are a dismembered Markan v. 13, with other special Matthean material inserted). Luke's contributions to this discourse about the end include eliminating the Mount of Olives as the locus and a query put by four disciples—listed in the interesting order Peter, James, John, and Andrew (cf. Mark 13:3); adding "plagues, dreadful portents, and great signs" (Luke 21:11 cf. v. 25); omitting mention of the necessity of proclaiming the good news to all creatures (Mark 13:10) and the Holy Spirit as speaker before tribunals (Mark 13:11, cf. Luke 12:1); substituting "words" [lit. "a mouth"] and wisdom which Jesus will supply, thereby pressing Luke's prophetism motif); adding the phrase "not a hair of your head will be harmed" (lit. "perish," v. 18). Luke is sure of the destruction of the Temple (v. 6) but also that false claimants coming in Jesus' name ("I am he!") must precede it (v. 18). He is alone in adding "The time is near" (v. 8) as another false statement, as part of his general concern with a deferred parousia. The same is no doubt true of his changing "but the end is still to come" (Mark 13:7) to "will not follow immediately" (Luke 21:9). He probably knows of the destruction of Jerusalem but that knowledge does not modify his traditional apocalyptic prose. Isaiah 19:2 provides the model for v. 10:

> I will stir up Egyptians against Egyptians;
>> brother will war against brother.
> Neighbor against neighbor,
>> city against city, kingdom against kingdom.

Verses 12-19 are concerned with the conduct of the disciples in their time of trial. A case can be made for Luke's modification of Mark in small matters but not in overall emphasis. The traditional dating of Mark just before the siege of Jerusalem and Luke after, on the basis of what the former did not need to know beforehand in order to write his chap. 13, is fairly tenuous. Luke does not appear to write from hindsight any more than Mark does from foresight. Luke 21:20 does substitute "*Hótan dè ídēte*," "When you see Jerusalem surrounded by armies," for Mark's "desolating sacrilege" (13:14), thus providing the only solid clue that he is introducing the siege of the city into his otherwise ahistorical account of disaster. His report of the testimony of disciples (vv. 12-17) may be viewed as historical.

❧ ✎

Proper 29 [34] / Reign of Christ or Christ the King / Last Sunday of the Year (C) Sunday between November 20 and November 26, inclusive

JEREMIAH 23:1-6

Throughout the First Testament, YHWH is identified as Israel's proper and only king. The anointed who lived from Saul down through the puppet rulers installed by the Persians and Greeks were no more than vice-gerents ruling as God would have them do or failing to. It is therefore no surprise that the people's shepherds were repudiated as a class. Political leaders are the intended target of that repudiation. It has been a commonplace for centuries for the Christian clergy to have appropriated the metaphor of shepherds to themselves. There is little basis for it. Priests and prophets are the biblical archetypes for clergy. Shepherds are rulers, often unworthy ones, both in Jeremiah (23:1-3), in Ezekiel's more fully developed condemnations of them (chap. 34), and in Zechariah's pointed allegory (11:4-9). Jeremiah promises better shepherds in the future (23:4), but it is doubtful that the prophecy of improved political leaders was fulfilled. The LORD alone emerges as the Good Shepherd, with the Son Jesus in the same mold (John 10:1-18). His leadership was of a quite different kind. The clerical self-image is based on the latter. It cannot be derived from the more general biblical paradigm or, if it is, the worthless clerical shepherds are happily unaware of the types they fulfill.

LUKE 1:68-79

For a commentary see Second Sunday of Advent (C).

PSALM 46

2 SAMUEL 5:1-3

David filled the vacuum caused by the death of Saul and his sons at the hands of the Philistines on Mount Gilboa (cf. 1 Sam 31) and was anointed king by the Judahites at Hebron (2 Sam 2:1-4). Saul's general Abner set up the son of Saul Ishbaal briefly as king over a variety of northerners—Jews and others—plus Benjaminites (vv. 8f). The reign of David at Hebron was confined to the people of Judah for seven years. The forces of Ishbaal under Abner and those of David under

Joab and his brother, meanwhile, continued their fighting (2 Sam 3). When Abner, offended by Ishbaal's charge of intimacy with his dead father's concubine (probably a defensive move stemming from fear of Abner's growing strength), that warrior began conversations with David that could lead to his turning all of Israel, the north, over to David peacefully (3:19ff.). David is reported as having had no part in it and mourning the death of the great warrior Abner publicly (vv. 28-39). As always in the case of David's motivations as he fought his way to the throne, it is impossible to know how much of his grief was genuine and how much his protestations of innocence meant "Gibeah papers, please copy." As to David's admiration for the military feats of Abner, however, and Abner's wisdom in being ready to desert Ishbaal's cause, there can be no reasonable doubt.

Two treacherous military leaders in Ishbaal's forces dispatched him in his sleep (4:1-7) for the alleged reason that he gave up all resistance when he heard of Abner's death (v. 1). In a spirit of lively hope, they brought the king's severed head to David, who reminded them wrathfully of the short shrift he had given informers on Saul in Ziklag (v. 10). He ordered them killed for their treasonous act supposedly done on his behalf, and had Ishbaal buried decently in Hebron next to Abner (vv. 11f.). Thus David continued to have the best of several worlds, which was the story of his life.

All this leads to today's pericope describing the enthronement of the shepherd king over Israel as well as his native Judah. The elders of Israel simply repeat the fealty to David that Abner had sensed was theirs (v. 3; cf. 3:17ff.). It needs to be borne in mind that the unification of the north and the south was a settlement achieved at the top. The alignment of the tribe of Benjamin with David (v. 19) was a natural geographic one; with "Jezreel, Ephraim . . . and the rest of Israel" (2:9) it was a case of the ruling elements siding with a winner against Ishbaal, a loser. That is why the pulling apart of the two kingdoms in Jeroboam's secession from Rehoboam, son of Solomon, comes as no surprise. The twelve tribes were never very unified in the first place, any more than were the states of Europe in Napoleon's day or Stalin's day in ours. Like the little corporal, it was David who made the difference.

The parallel account to this one of David's anointing as king over Israel, quite close in detail but with "the word of the LORD as revealed through Samuel" given as the justification, is 1 Chron 11:1-3. This pious reason is not surprising in the 5th century retelling of Israel's history. The Chronicler saw everything from the standpoint of present Temple cult and priestly dominance rather than past glories.

PSALM 122:1-5

Colossians 1:11[12]-20

Epaphras is Paul's coworker at Colossae (1:7f.) who evidently is staying on with the imprisoned Paul (4:12, 18). It may be he who has brought Paul news of the "Colossian error" (2:16-23) although he is described as having reported only "your love in the Spirit" (1:8). The aberrations in the community that Paul is worried about relate to teachings about diet and feasts as having a saving quality, the worship of angels (possibly *with* angels), and bodily austerities in "checking self-indulgence / against gratification of the flesh" (2:23).

The Pauline authorship of this epistle in its entirety is questioned because no authentic writing of Paul contains a description of Christ like that of the hymn of 1:15-20. Solutions to the problem tend to look on it as an insertion or else credit the entire forward portion of the epistle to another hand, with a variety of cut-off points suggested.

Ephesus, Caesarea, and Rome are all claimants to the title of place of origin of this captivity epistle. One thing about it that is sure is its common provenance with Philemon (cf. 4:3, 18; Phlm 9; 13). Colossae (still buried by earthquake near a totally modern Honaz) makes a triangle with Laodicaea and Hierapolis, close to a resort place with numerous salt baths and motels, in the Lycus valley. Paul writes in 2:1 as if he had not met the recipients, knowing of their faith only from Epaphras and others.

The light-darkness figure of vv. 12f. is an accommodation of the theme of deliverance from Egypt and occurs in 1 Thess 5:4-9; Rom 13:11-14 (cf. also its use in Acts 26:18 and by a follower of Paul in Eph 5:8). Paul refers to the reign of God extensively only in 1 Cor 4:20; 6:9f.; 15:24, 50; Gal 5:21; Col 1:13; 4:11; 1 Thess 2:12; and Rom 14:17f. He never speaks of the kingdom of God's Son as here, coming closest to it with a mention of serving Christ in God's reign (Rom 14:18).

The exalted Christology of vv. 15-20 is worthy of Paul but in no sense typical of him. Not only is Christ the redeemer and agent of forgiveness (v. 14), he is the one through and for whom all things, including the celestial powers, are created (v. 16). The Talmud tells of a rabbi so holy that God made all things for him, but this usage in Colossians is another conception more consciously cosmic. The fullness *(plérōma)* of God dwells in Christ (v. 19) bodily (2:9). In other Pauline letters, Christ and believers with him form "the one body" (cf. 1 Cor 10:16f.; 12:12, 27). Here, as in Ephesians (1:22f.), he is the head of the body, the Church. He not only has divine fullness among creatures but also a primacy ("first place in everything" v. 18). This firstborn from the dead is above all a reconciler (v. 20). The blood of his cross has made peace for all discordant elements on earth and in the heavens.

Clearly, Jesus is being spoken of here as a man so closely associated with God in the work of creation (v. 16) that there is a sense in which he is not a part of it. He who has the totality of deity residing in him (v. 19) is above all the cosmic powers (or elemental spirits, v. 16). One who has faith in this Jesus who has died in fulfilling the reconciling office (v. 22) has by that fact died to the cosmic forces (2:20). The alienation of the Colossians from Christ before they knew him is over (1:21). They may not release their grasp on the faith and hope that came to them with the gospel (v. 23).

ALLELUIA. MARK 11:10

Blessed is he who inherits the kingdom of David our father; blessed is he who comes in the name of the LORD.

LUKE 23:33[35]-43

Luke is remarkably close to Mark's order and selection of incidents in the passion narrative, yet he adds enough material of his own (the formal charge before Pilate, 23:2; the hearing before Herod, 23:6-12; the road to Golgotha, 23:27-32; the verbal exchange of the criminals on their crosses, 23:39-43) to make some, including the present writer, assume a Lukan passion source. Verse 35 parallels Mark 15:31f., with some changes by Luke ("leaders" for "chief priests" and "scribes" as scoffers; "the Messiah of God, his chosen one" for "the Messiah, the King of Israel"); verse 36 parallels Mark 15:36 (the title on the cross, with the brief Lukan prefix, "This is").

In Mark/Matthew the two insurgents/bandits *(lēstai)* "who were crucified with him also taunted him" (Mark 15:32; Matt 2:44) in the same way as the onlookers. Luke makes this explicit (v. 39) by reworking the phrases attributed to the leaders in v. 35. There is a possible dependence of v. 49 on 2 Macc 7:32. Jesus is asked by one of the criminals for remembrance when he comes into his kingdom (v. 42). He responds by promising that the man will be with him "today . . . in paradise"—the abode of the just. Paradise is a Hebrew loan-word from the Avestan meaning enclosure or pleasure park. It occurs in 2 Cor 12:4 and Acts 2:7; likewise, 27x in the LXX but not the MT. Its use in the Qur 'an for heaven may derive from familiarity with passages like Num 24:6.

The crucifixion narrative (Luke 23:27-48) of Luke's source need not be viewed as a Markan composition that has been modified. It can be seen as an independent and cohesive account to which Markan touches have been added (vv. 34b, 38ff., 49).

❧ Feasts of Jesus, Mary, ❧ and the Saints

❧❧
The Immaculate Conception
(Of Mary in Her Mother's Womb)
December 8

GENESIS 3:8-15, 20

The description of the sin of the man *(ha'adham)* and the woman *(ha 'ishshah)* in today's first reading is part of the Yahwist narrative that runs from 2:4b to 4:25. The human being, for this author, is "but flesh" (6:3) "with all of its possibilities of knowledge, desire, and choice, and also its possibilities of failure and error" (S. H. Hooke, *PC*, 179). The man gives names to all the beasts and birds (2:20), for the Yahwist a sign of his power; he is at the same time incomplete in his solitude, hence "Woman" is taken out of "Man" (v. 23). The passage under consideration tells of disobedience and the consequent disruption of God's design. It will end in 3:20 with the man's naming his wife Eve *(Ḥavvah),* because she is the mother of "all living" *(kol ḥai).* In other words she is a sign of hope, not merely the man's fellow culprit in an act of weakness.

The pair is in hiding among the trees when the story begins (v. 8), clothed because "the eyes of both were opened" at the eating of the fruit (v. 7). The man has hidden himself because of nakedness and fear (v. 10). The LORD God connects this self-consciousness with transgression of the command not to eat (v. 11). A sexual motif may underlie the entire tale, in which case a knowledge of "what is good and what is bad / good and evil" (v. 5) would be the godlike power of immortality through the power of begetting. This interpretation is not certain. What is certain is that moral autonomy of some sort is being sought through gaining knowledge proper to God alone (see Deut 29:29; 28 in NAB and there indicated as textually doubtful). The serpent in the Gilgamesh myth, which the Yahwist may be using, is cunning enough to steal from Gilgamesh the magic herb that renews life. Serpents were a symbol of fertility in various Canaanite cults. The one in the Yahwist's story is not the devil (that identification will come much later; see Wis 2:24) but a deceiver (vv. 4, 13) whose counsel brings not likeness to gods (v. 5) but the necessity of death (v. 19c). The story is etiological throughout, i.e., concerned with the causes of things. Like other, familiar ancient fables, it explains why snakes crawl on the ground (v. 14), why snakes are the enemies of humans (v. 15), why men are the pain and the joy of women (v. 16), and why man's hard life ends in death (v. 19).

The temptation of the man by the woman is not an especially significant detail despite what subsequent generations have made of it. It is simply a requirement of the narrative technique's three stages. There is no doubt, of course, that the woman is a companion of the man in his sin. This makes her new name, Life (3:20), all the more telling.

Verse 15 has prompted whole libraries of Christian theological argument, much of it having little to do with the Yahwist's intent. The common older tradition was that the passage had messianic significance but later scholars (John Skinner, Gerhard von Rad, Claus Westermann) concluded that it is without it, and even that man's continuing battle with snakes is all that is intended. The theological arguments of a former age were as much related to Mary as to text and context, the Vulgate having *ipsa* ("she") for the weakly attested *hi* rather than the likelier *hu* ("he"). In all modern translations the woman's offspring, "he," "it" or "they," not the woman, will strike at / bruise the snake's head. So much for the myriad representations of Mary's heel firmly planted on the head of a snake who often has a fruit in its mouth. But for Mary as new Eve in association with Christ as antitype of Adam (1 Cor 15:22; Rom 5:14), see Justin, *Trypho* 100; Irenaeus, *Adv. haer.* 3.22.4; 5.19.1; Tertullian, *De carne Christi* 17.

The seed of the woman is collective humankind, the seed of the serpent the forces opposed to YHWH in every age. Yet if David was the Yahwist's model for Adam, a royal defeat of enemies under the conqueror's foot (on the Egyptian model) may be intended. On any reading, this is an oracle of ultimate victory for the forces of life over the forces of death.

PSALM 98:1-4

EPHESIANS 1:3-6, 11-12

The opening doxology (1:3-14) attaches a cosmic significance to Christ, and therein lies its chief importance. God's choice of those who would believe in him through the mystery of the Son, was made "in the Beloved" (v. 6), "our Lord Jesus Christ"

(v. 3). The election preceded the history of the cosmos (v. 4). It was a matter of "the good pleasure of [God's] will," the "mystery of which he set forth in Christ," the result of the "purpose" of his "counsel and will" (v. 11). We therefore have received an inheritance, "destined" as we were (v. 11) to praise God's glory by being the first to hope in Christ (v. 12). The predestination to "adoption as God's children" (lit. "sons") had as its ultimate purpose praise of the glorious favor God has bestowed on us in Christ (v. 6). The entire cosmic plan is designed to show forth God's glory, *doxa* being the LXX word for *kābhōd*, a means of expressing what we would call Christ's godliness or divine nature. In origin, this eulogy of believers may be a baptismal hymn about those who have been sealed in the Holy Spirit after accepting the word of the Gospel (v. 1).

The letter is probably an encyclical one. Only doubtfully was it addressed, in its lack of particularity, to a community in which Paul had spent two and more years (Acts 19:10). This is further attested to by the omission of "at Ephesus" (1:1) from Sinaiticus, Vaticanus, other textual witnesses, and Origen. Arguments that claim authorship either of Paul or of a disciple of his (generally known as "the Ephesian continuator") depend on whether Paul could have been the author of this kind of writing, so uncharacteristic of him otherwise.

The doxology resembles Col 1:9ff. in its claim of a way of life superior to anything available through either *gnōsis* or the mediation of heavenly powers. In its stress on the eternal character of election it answers the objection in the early period of the apologists (second century) that the Church cannot be of God since it has appeared only recently. The "we" who are "the first to hope in Christ" (v. 12) are probably the members of what is conceived as the whole Church, the "you" of v. 12, the recipients of the letter, perhaps newly aggregated to it.

ALLELUIA. LUKE 1:28

Hail, Mary, full of grace, the LORD is with you; blessed are you among women.

LUKE 1:26-38

Luke has completed the first panel of his diptych which features the mysterious circumstances surrounding the conception of John, son of Zechariah. He turns now to the second panel. The archangel Gabriel had come bearing revelations in Daniel 8; 9; and 10 (where he reduced Daniel to silence, e.g., 10:15; cf. Ezek 3:26). His identification of himself to Zechariah in Luke 1:19 resembles that of Raphael in the book of Tobit (12:15).

Luke's account of Jesus' conception has as its purpose stressing his election, indeed his divine origins. Joseph is identified as Davidic, hence royal (v. 27). Elizabeth, Aaronic and therefore priestly (v. 5), is described as Mary's kinswoman (v. 36). These details heighten the claim that Jesus is Messiah in both a royal and a priestly sense (1QS 9:10: "until there shall come the Prophet and the Messiahs of Aaron and Israel").

Nazareth (v. 26) is the traditional town of Jesus' beginnings in later Gospel material. *Parthénos*, v. 27, may be the ordinary word for "girl," as NEB has it, but Luke's intent is clear, as is acknowledged by that translation's rendering of *ándra ou ginōskō* (lit. "I do not know man") by "I am a virgin / have no relations with a man" (v. 34). This is the story of one who is "Son of the Most High" (v. 32), constituted as such by the latter's power which is the same as the coming upon Mary of the Holy Spirit (v. 35). Gabriel's greeting, *Chaîre* (it would have been the Semitic *Shalom*), makes possible the word-play of *kecharitōménē*, "most highly graced (or favored) daughter" (v. 28). The wording of the angel's message is that of messianic rule (vv. 32f.). To this announcement of her election Mary answers, with a faith like Abraham's, "Let it be done with me according to your word" (v. 38).

✍ Presentation of the Lord / Candlemas Day (A, B, C) February 2

MALACHI 3:1-4

For some background on this brief but important book see Proper 26 [31] (A) and Proper 28 [33] (C). It is from v. 1 that the name of the book is taken, "my messenger" *(malachi)*. In 2:7 the priest is the messenger of the LORD of hosts in a chapter that charges him generically with failure in the conduct of his office (2:8f.), even though the charge against him is laid hypothetically (2:1-6): "If you do not listen, and if you do not lay it to heart . . ." (vv. 1f.). The coming messenger of the covenant of 3:1 seems to be some personification of a purified priesthood. The covenant of Levi, made void by contemptible priestly behavior (2:4, 8), will be restored and renewed through a particular messenger who will "purify the sons of Levi" (3:3). It is hard to know if he is a promised individual or the LORD as reformer of the institution of priesthood.

Judgment will take place at the Temple, the holiest place in the nation (3:1b). As metal is refined in fire or cloth cleansed by lye (vv. 2b-3a), so will the sacrificing priesthood be purified (v. 3b). Then will it be repristinated (v. 4) and sacrifice will be offered by a class fit to do so. Judgment will be leveled against those who practice a variety of social evils (v. 5), all of them reprobated in the Law: sorcery (Exod 22:18), adultery (Exod 20:14), false swearing (Lev 19:12), defrauding laborers (Deut 24:14), widows and orphans (Deut 24:17), and turning aside the stranger (*ger* = resident alien): in general, those "who do not fear me [says the Lord of hosts]" (v. 5bc).

Psalm 24:7-10

Hebrews 2:14-18

A rereading of the commentary on Heb 2:9-11, Proper 22 [27] (B), might be a good preparation for today's pericope, as would be those on the selections from that epistle throughout that month and November of that year; also, on the obedient sacrifice of Christ described in Heb 5:7-9 (5 Lent [B]). See also 1 Christmas (A).

Jesus is made as if the speaker in v. 12, quoting Ps 22:23, as he announces the praise of God to his brothers in the assembly. He is represented (v. 13) as trusting in God in the manner of David in 2 Sam 22:2-6 and presenting himself as a sign and portent like Isaiah and his sons in the story of the document drawn up about the younger of the two, Maher-shalal-hash-baz ("quick spoils, speedy plunder," Isa 8:3, the Immanuel of the prophecy?). The "brothers [and sisters]" of Isaiah for the author of Hebrews are Jesus and all others of flesh and blood (v. 14) with this difference, that his tasting death was for the sake of all (v. 9). God made Jesus, who was the "pioneer/leader" (*archēgós*, v. 10) in the work of salvation, perfect through suffering. This perfection was not a "good" of Jesus only. It robbed the one who has the power of death, the devil, of his power and freed humanity of its lifelong fear of death (vv. 14f.). The other children of Abraham were Jesus' beneficiaries, a thing that would have been impossible had he not "become like his brothers in every respect" (v. 17). His status as a merciful and faithful high priest before God required it.

Verse 18 is crucial to New Testament Christology and soteriology, because it leaves in no doubt the weakness and limitations essential to a man if he is to be believed in as "true man," the affirmation about Jesus of all the creeds. It is "in the fact that" (*en hǭ*, the "because" of v. 18) he himself suffered and was subjected to trial that he can be of help to others similarly tested *(tois)*. This phrase cannot be confined to physical suffering which is the least of human suffering. The second verb, *peirazeîn*, occurring in the aorist passive participle and present passive participle, is the normal biblical word for eschatological testing. Jesus has been with his brothers in their extremity, says Hebrews. He could not go any lower in experiencing the anguish of the human situation. His common lot with us in our temptation, our desolation, our alienation, is complete. That is why we dare to hail him as the conqueror of the fear of death and the brother who saved us.

ALLELUIA. LUKE 2:32

This is the light of revelation to the nations, and the glory of your people Israel.

LUKE 2:22-40

The Alleluia verse (Luke 2:32), sung as the presider or deacon approaches the lectern, does not reproduce any First Testament place exactly. Isaiah 42:6 and 49:6 content themselves with describing Israel as a "light to the nations." Luke's v. 32b echoes Isa 40:5 and 46:13 but does not literally reproduce either. The parallelism of the Lukan verse shows the manifestation of God to all in Christ:

> *light* revealed to the Gentiles,
> *glory* to your people Israel.

This last verse of Simeon's brief canticle of praise to God has been known for centuries in the West, even in secular literature, as *Nunc dimittis*. The pious old Jerusalem Jew, just and devout, is guided by the Holy Spirit to see the LORD's Messiah. He will shortly be balanced by a woman, Anna, in Luke's familiar diptych technique (vv. 36-38). Luke speaks of "their" purification after a childbirth (v. 22), even though Lev 12:2-8 requires it of the woman only, forty days after the birth of a boy, eighty days in the case of a girl. The "impurity" is ritual and has nothing to do with conduct, least of all the glory of bearing a child.

ᴥ᙭ The Annunciation of the Lord (A, B, C) March 25

ISAIAH 7:10-14

See 4 Advent (A).

PSALM 45

Psalm 40:7-11

Hebrews 10:4-10

See 4 Advent (C).

Alleluia

The Word of God became man and lived among us, and we saw his glory.

Luke 1:26-38

See 4 Advent (B).

🖎🖎

The Visitation of Mary to Elizabeth (A, B, C)
May 31

1 Samuel 2:1-10

See Proper 28 [33] (B).

Psalm 113

Zephaniah 3:14-18a

See 3 Advent (C).

Isaiah 12:2-6

See Easter Vigil (A).

Luke 1:39-57

See 4 Advent (C) and Assumption of the Blessed Virgin Mary.

❧❧
Peter and Paul, Apostles
June 29

ACTS 12:1-11

The "time" of the opening phrase is the reign of the emperor Claudius (41–54 C.E.). The harassment of the church by King Herod Agrippa I (37–44), son of Aristobolus and brother of Herodias, was probably on civil charges as the form of execution indicates. Beheading was reserved by the much later legislation of the Mishnah (*Sanhedrin* 9:1) for murderers and members of an apostate city. The book of Acts has up to this point portrayed the Jewish religious authorities as unfriendly to Christians. The text does not suggest, however, any initiation of charges by the Sanhedrin or the high priest. The historian Josephus says that Agrippa wished to be thought of as a loyal Jew. Hence, if the charges against James and Peter were religious, Agrippa would have permitted a Sanhedrin trial. This entailed the capital punishment of stoning if the finding were one of guilt. While the king might have acted arbitrarily and simply eliminated James as persona non grata, it is much more likely that he had him and Peter arraigned on charges of threatening the political stability of Palestinian Jewry. Since John the Baptist and Jesus had both been thought guilty of the same offense, the latter having forfeited his life on a civil charge in the area of political stability, it is not surprising that a verdict of guilty was secured against James on some charge such as that the apostles were proclaiming "another king," Jesus.

Acts suggests that Agrippa executed James simply to gratify public opinion (v. 3). While the capital sentence may have had that effect in certain Jewish circles, it is not to be supposed that Agrippa acted on that basis only. The author of Acts suppresses the actual charge if he happens to know it. A distinct possibility is that James, one of the two "Sons of Thunder" (Mark 3:17), offended the royal sensibilities with a public utterance like that of John the Baptizer before him about the conduct of the royal family.

That Peter was also being detained on a capital charge is probable since his guards were executed for letting him escape (v. 19). Great should be their heavenly reward if the "angel of the Lord" (v. 7) were a heavenly being and not an enterprising Christian adept at the first-century equivalent of picking locks. In any case, the two companions of Jesus were no doubt apprehended as lingering threats to the stability of the Roman-Herodian settlement, even though more than a dozen years had passed since Jesus' death. The whole sequence would be the more comprehensible if the pair had borne the burden of association with the movement for violent revolt all that time, going back to the days before Jesus called them.

Eusebius in his *History of the Church* (2.9) quotes an edifying tale from the Pseudo-Clementine *Outlines*, Book 7, to the effect that the delator of James, himself a Christian, was so moved by the apostle's testimony in court that he asked for forgiveness, received it, and was beheaded along with him.

We know that Herod Agrippa's death (reported in Acts 12:20-23) occurred in spring of 44. Hence the death of James is to be dated anywhere between the accession of Claudius and the violent demise of the king.

Acts 12:11 reverts in its account of Peter's rescue to its theme of Jewish antipathy to the Christian movement.

As to the martyrdoms of Peter and Paul, the earliest documentation occurs in 1 Clement 5:3-7 (ca. 100 C.E.) which speaks of Peter's "witness, [going to] the glorious place he merited" while Paul "bore his witness before rulers and . . . was taken up into the holy place" (*Early Christian Fathers*, ed. C. C. Richardson [New York: Touchstone, 1996]).

Psalm 34:2-9

2 Timothy 4:6-8, 17-18

The second letter of Paul to Timothy is widely regarded as pseudonymous, as are 1 Timothy and Titus. The reasons include weak attestation to all three pastoral epistles in early canons and papyri, the nature of their polemic against heretics, the transition from the Pauline *kērygma* to Christian faith as a *parathēkē* ("deposit," 1 Tim 6:20; 2 Tim 1:12, 14), vocabulary divergencies from Paul, the difficulty of fitting 1 and 2 Timothy into his life situation and the un-Pauline character of the church order described in the pastorals. For the remainder of the commentary, see Proper 24 [29] (C).

Alleluia. Matthew 16:18

You are Peter, the rock on which I will build my Church; the gates of the nether world will not hold out against it.

[B] Matthew 16:13-19

See Proper 16 [21] (A).

🙟🙝
The Transfiguration
August 6

DANIEL 7:9-10, 13-14

The visions of Daniel 7, like the king's dream and Daniel's vision of chap. 2, are concerned with the unity and finality of history. In the apocalyptic genre, however, history is not important in itself since it is fated to disappear with the coming reign of God.

The four beasts referred to earlier in the chapter (lion, bear, leopard, and ten-horned horrible) are, in the first three cases, conventional motifs from the period portraying Babylon, Media, and Persia, and in the fourth, Alexander's empire (the gold, silver, bronze, and iron-clay images of chap. 2). The ten horns are the kings of the Seleucid dynasty descended from Alexander's general Seleukos—the conqueror having died without a designated heir (the "divided kingdom" of 2:4)—while the "little horn" is Antiochus IV Epiphanes (175–63 B.C.E.), the most troublesome ruler of all for the author of Daniel.

The picture of Israel's deliverer as "one like a human being / son of man" (v. 13a) reflects the transcendent character of the eschatological savior whose image was developed in the late Hellenist, pre-Christian period. History is not his milieu, as had been the case with a kingly or prophetic person in all previous Jewish expectation of the future. The eschatological event that the vision of Dan 7 describes is cosmic and universal, not historical and national. Some of the details of the vision are derived from the description in Ezek 1 of "the likeness of the glory of the LORD" (v. 28), among them the clouds (vv. 4, 28), the flashing fire (vv. 4, 27), and "something that seemed like a human form" seated on "the likeness of a throne" (v. 26). See also Deut 33:2 and Isa 6 for descriptions of appearances of God in the heavenly court attended by thousands of ministering spirits. Fire as the sign of judgment (Dan 7:9c, 10a) suggests an Iranian source, a theory borne out by the more detailed presentation of the "son of man" in 4 Ezra 13 and the Similitudes of Enoch. The Ancient One with wool-white hair (7:9a, b) is probably so depicted to contrast the venerability of the divine Judge with the upstart kings recently—relative to him, at least—come to power.

The one "like a human being / a son of man" (qᵉbar enash) of 13a is to be distinguished from the four beasts preceding (vv. 3-8). "Son of man" is the ordinary designation of an individual, "man" being generic: "humankind." (Modern Hebrew continues to render "people" by "bᵉnei ha 'adham," lit. "sons of the human one.") Unlike the beasts, who arise from earth and sea, this manlike figure comes on the clouds. He is not spoken of as a human being but "like a human," a term that describes the various appearances of what are otherwise called "angels" (cf. Dan 8:15; 10:5, 6, 18 and the "man of God" of Judg 13:6). It is he who receives the "dominion and glory and kingship" (v. 7:14) that are accorded to the "holy ones of the Most High" in vv. 18 and 27; hence he is somehow their representative.

They seem at first to be faithful Israel, victorious under God over the four evil kingdoms (v. 18), but the fact that the one who comes "with the clouds of heaven" (v. 13) rejoins them makes it plausible that these "holy ones" are the angelic host. They stand for a dominion of God that is to be ultimate and everlasting (vv. 14c, 27c), hence by definition eschatological or metahistorical. The "holy ones of the Most High" shall receive dominion, to possess it forever (vv. 18, 23, 27). Further complications are the "manlike figure" (*gĕbĕr*, 8:15) standing before Daniel who hears a human voice crying out to Gabriel to help this "son [of man]" (*ben 'adham*, v. 16) understand the vision, and the designation of a Davidic king by the same term in the Hebrew of Ps 80:17/18 (and in Ps 146:3, "mortals" [lit. "sons of men"], who are not to be trusted).

Is something messianic indicated by Daniel's use of the term "one like a son of man"? This is not clear. The main point is that from now on the kingdom of God—and God's agent, the Son of Man—will exercise hegemony in place of the demonic world-wide kingdoms to the glory of God.

The absence of a dependence on Daniel 7 in the Son of Man sayings in Q is a puzzle.

Psalm 97:1-2, 5-6, 9

2 Peter 1:16-19

These four verses contain the main contention of this latest of the New Testament authors to write. His teaching is apostolic (note the shift to "we" in vv. 16, 18 from the "I" of previous verses); it is based on a historical revelation (vv. 17f.) that comes as the fulfillment of prophecy (v. 19); and it is not to be confused with "cleverly devised myths" (v. 16) that other false teachers are purveying (cf. 2:1, 3) —men whose lives are as morally disordered as their doctrine is false (2:10-22). "Our Lord Jesus Christ's power and coming" (1:16) is the truth the author is at pains to stress; he will return to the problem of skepticism concerning it in 3:3-7. He may be defending the reality of this hoped for event against the charge that *it* is a cleverly devised myth more than castigating the teachings of opponents as being such, although the participle chosen to describe "myth" (with *sophia* as its root) indicates that the opposition may be gnostic inclined. The claim to eyewitness status (*epóptai*, a word that also means higher-grade initiates) of Christ's majesty in the Transfiguration, v. 16, is put forward as evidence that he will return in glory.

The expected coming of Christ, his "parousia," is literally his "presence." The term comes from Greek religion and from the mystery cults and is used as a designation of the manifestation of a god. Josephus employs it to describe an epiphany of God, while the Testament of Judah contains the very phrase of 2 Pet 1:16, "power and coming," to make the same point. Christ's power in this case is his godlike might as risen Lord, his present power and future coming being the chief affirmations of this epistle. The author probably got his account of the transfiguration from traditional material, not from any of the gospels, although he comes close to Matthew's version. The locus of the event has become, by the time of the writing, the "holy mountain" (v. 18).

The "prophetic message" of v. 19 was a phrase current in Jewish usage to describe the entire Bible, not the books of the prophets only. As a whole, Scripture testified to Christ for Christian preachers. The "dark place" is the sinful world and the "day" that the dawn inaugurates is "the day that is near" of Christ's coming (Rom 13:12). *Phōsphóros* of v. 18 is Venus, the morning star, here Christ dissipating doubts and fears in the hearts of Christians (cf. Luke 1:78 and Rev 22:16 for other uses of the dawn-figure, even if not the same terminology). Traditional belief in the transformation of the cosmos at the end is retained by the Jewish-oriented author of 2 Peter but his eschatology has, for the first time, a personal orientation. Individual believers will be altered in their hearts at the coming of Christ, a notion that traditional eschatological material does not contain.

ALLELUIA. MATTHEW 17:5C

This is my Son, my beloved, in whom is all my delight; listen to him.

MATTHEW 17:1-9 (A)

See 2 Lent (A).

MARK 9:2-10 (B)

See 2 Lent (B).

LUKE 9:28-36 (C)

See 2 Lent (C).

❧❧

The Assumption of the Blessed Virgin Mary
August 15

REVELATION 11:19A; 12:1-6A, 10AB

The ark of the covenant had been lost with the destruction of the first Temple. Jewish tradition held that it would reappear in the messianic age. Its visibility (v. 19a) indicates that God through his Messiah (v. 15) has resumed his great power and begun his reign (v. 17). Those who laid the earth waste have been destroyed. It is time now to judge the dead and to reward the prophets and the saints (v. 18).

The "great portent" that follows (12:1) depicts the conflict of good and evil as a cosmic one, not one originating on earth. The apocalyptist seems to have availed himself of one form of an ancient myth transmitted in Greek, Persian, and Egyptian circles—he comes closest to the Greek tale—which describe the escape of a divine infant from a superhuman enemy at birth. Here at the beginning of chap. 12 we encounter the first appearance of a female figure in the book of Revelation.

The "woman" of chap. 12 had been variously Leto, Ormazd, and Isis in other mythologies. She may have been a sun goddess in the original myth employed, with the twelve signs of the zodiac as the stars in her crown and the moon at her feet. Since the cult of Cybele was widespread in Asia Minor, it is to be expected that the author of Revelation would be influenced by it. The statue of Cybele in the Museum of Berlin shows the moon at her left and the sun at her right; at other times the sun is a cloud that envelops her; in still another statue the twelve stars form her crown. Austin Farrer (*A Rebirth of Images* [London: Dacre, 1949]) thinks that the author intends a veiled reference to Rachel, whose son Joseph (Gen 30:23f.; 37:9f.) in his second adolescent dream saw his parents as the sun and the moon and he and his brothers as twelve stars (of the zodiac?). A further possible reference is Eve, cursed in the pain of her childbearing (Gen 3:16) and blessed in the hope of her offspring who will strike at the serpent's head (v. 15c). While the biblical imagery cannot be discounted entirely, none of it is as close in detail as are several non-Hebrew myths. Leto with child by Zeus was pursued by the dragon Python. Poseidon gave her refuge on an island where she safely delivered herself of the god Apollo.

One biblical source reveals the begetting by mother Zion of a male child who is the people Israel (Isa 66:7-9). Elsewhere the people is a woman, the bride of YHWH, who wears on her head a glorious crown (Ezek 16:12). The woman's wailing in pain as she labors to give birth (Rev 12:2) is unlike the Isaian picture of a woman who gives birth before she comes to labor (Isa 66:7, 8d). Micah is closer to the apocalyptist's imagery: "Writhe and groan, O daughter Zion, like a woman in labor; / For now you shall go forth from the city and camp in the open country" (4:10ab). The Hymns of Qumrân provide a close parallel: "She labours in her pains who bears the Man. / For amid the pains of hell / there shall spring from her child-bearing crucible / a Marvelous Mighty Counselor; / and the Man shall be delivered from out of the throes" *Hodayoth* III (*The Dead Sea Scrolls in English*, Geza Vermès, tr. [Baltimore: Penguin, 1968], 157); cf. F. Garcia Martinez, tr. (Leiden: Brill, 1996), 331.

The huge, fiery red dragon with seven heads and ten horns has been variously interpreted as the constellation Hydra that extends one third of the length of the zodiac attacking Virgo; as a symbol of the imperial purple driving the Christian community off to Pella (if that tradition is dependable); and as Daniel's fourth beast (7:7). The latter had been Alexander's empire whereas in Rev 13:1 the beast is Rome. In any case, the dragon's quarrel is not immediately with the woman but with her child. Christian Jews are probably intended by "her child as soon as it was born"—the place of the "the Devil or great dragon . . . who is called Satan, the seducer of the whole world" (v. 9) being filled by any worldly power inimical to Christians.

The passage was probably originally Jewish, as can be deduced from its reference to final victory by Michael and his angels. If a Christian hand had framed it initially the victor would have been Christ. A Christian hymn has been inserted at v. 10. "The accuser of our brothers" may be a veiled reference to the informers *(dēlatores)* who abounded in Domitian's time (81–96 C.E.), busy with their attacks on Asian Christians. Satan's overthrow is achieved (v. 9) but not before the son of the woman has been identified in terms of messianic Ps 2, which speaks (vv. 8f.) of the king's ruling all the nations with an iron rod (Rev 12:5).

PSALM 45:[11-13]10-12, [15], 16

1 CORINTHIANS 15:20-26

It is understandable why the Church should employ this passage on the feast of Mary's Assumption, since her glorification in the body, anticipatory of the resurrection of all, comes as the result of her Son's resurrection from the dead.

Paul describes him as the first to rise under the agricultural figure "first fruits" (v. 20), in which a sheaf was brought to the priest on "the day after the Sabbath" following the Passover celebration (Lev 23:11), to be waved as an offering before the LORD. This had to be done along with the offering of a yearling lamb before any grain of the harvest could be eaten. In somewhat the same way, the raising of Christ by God anticipates the resurrection of all who belong to him (cf. 2 Cor 1:22; Rom 8:23; Col 1:15-23).

Paul uses Adam as his second type of Christ, just as he will do later more explicitly in Rom 5:12-14. Men are of two kinds for Paul, those who are "in Adam," who will surely die as a consequence of sin, and those who are "in Christ," who will share in his victory over death (vv. 21f.). The apostle spells out his death-life antithesis with respect to sin and to justice in terms of slavery and freedom in Rom 6:20-23.

The resurrection will not occur in random fashion but in orderly stages. At Christ's coming (v. 23) each will rise in proper order, those who belong to Christ following him who is first fruits. Paul refers to the consummation of all as "the end" (v. 24). He assumes that a variety of demonic powers must first be crushed before Christ's dominion can be complete (see 1 Cor 2:6, 8; Rom 8:20f. for Paul's idea of this world's slavery to corruption and the "rulers of the present age," a working together of evil and death, perhaps personified as Satan). Paul may be distinguishing here, as some Rabbis did in his time, between the age to come and the age of the messiah. The hostile powers have been vanquished in part with Christ's resurrection, but their complete destruction will not be achieved until his coming and power.

Meanwhile, the Church's faith in the mystery of the Assumption (in the Eastern Churches her Dormition or Falling Asleep) is that Mary has won the victory over death, having first died and then been elevated on high, as the first in rank of those who are "in Christ."

ALLELUIA

Mary is taken up to heaven, and the angels of God shout for joy.

LUKE 1:39-56

In Luke's theology, Jesus is "Lord" from before his birth (1:43). The infancy and boyhood narratives of the first two chapters indicate what Jesus will become through what he already is. When he passes through death to glory and is made Lord and Messiah he will be no other than he was proclaimed to be at the beginning.

The story of the meeting of Mary and Elizabeth is part of Luke's John-Jesus diptych, the Baptist being identified as a prophet and witness to Jesus from before his birth. Luke may have in mind the oracle of Gen 25:23, in which the elder twin in Rebekah's womb, Esau, is fated to serve Jacob, the younger.

The "hill country" of Judah is indeterminate (v. 39). Ain Karem, now a Jerusalem suburb, is a centuries-later attribution of no special authenticity except for its merit as natural beauty. The baby's leaping in Elizabeth's womb may derive from the call of Jeremiah: "Before I formed you in the womb I knew you, / and before you were born I consecrated you; / I appointed you a prophet to the nations" (Jer 1:5). The spirit of prophecy, the Holy Spirit, is active throughout the Lukan account. Elizabeth acts the prophetess in praising the faith of Mary, her younger kinswoman (v. 45).

Mary's canticle as a whole is patterned on Hannah's song in 1 Sam 2:1-10 at the birth of her prophet-priest son Samuel. It is a tissue of Old Testament allusions. Thus v. 48b recalls Leah's exclamation at the birth of Asher (Gen 30:13), v. 50 evokes Ps 103:17 on the kindness of the LORD from all ages past (cf. *Pss Sol* 10:4); v. 51 recalls Ps 89:13/14, v. 54, Isa 41:8-10, and v. 55, Mic 7:20: "You will show faithfulness to Jacob, and unswerving loyalty to Abraham, / As you have sworn to our fathers from days of old." Verse 55 with its recall of the covenant made with Abraham (Gen 12:2f.; 15:1; 22:17f.; 24:7) links messianic hope with earliest promise.

A few New Testament MSS—some in Old Latin and Greek ones known to Origen and Irenaeus—attribute the hymn to Elizabeth at v. 46 (in which case her "lowliness" would be the reproach of her childless condition). The manuscript tradition is not strong enough to be credited, however. Besides, such attribution would upset Luke's chiastic (X-like) balance, which requires attention to the two births in the form John (1:5-25), Jesus (26-38); Jesus (39-56), John (57-80). The Magnificat remains a monument to God's unbounded mercy, which delights in the paradox of deposing the mighty and exalting the lowly. As messianic fruition comes closer, the mother of Jesus the Christ is fittingly declared blessed for ages to come (v. 48b).

Verse 56 tells us nothing about whether Mary was present for the birth of John. Luke's narrative technique requires that she be off the scene, though not necessarily literally, before he proceeds to his next frame.

❧✿

All Saints
November 1 or the First Sunday in November

Daniel 7:1-3, 15-18

Belteshazzar was the Babylonian name given to the fictional Daniel (NRSV 4:8; NAB 4:5), the heroic young Jew in Nebuchadnezzar's court. This book, written in 167–64 during the persecution of the Jews by Antiochus IV, reconstructs the period of the Chaldean conquest of Assyria and was meant to fortify the people by telling of the courage and influence of one Jew in another time and place. "King Belshazzar" (5:1) was actually the crown prince, son of King Nabonidus, in turn a descendant of Nebuchadnezzar. The tale of the drinking party from the vessels taken from Jerusalem's Temple is an introduction to Daniel's interpreting the three words on the wall to mean "number," "weight," and "divide" (5:1-9, 25-28), a prophecy of the dynasty's ending in division. The important point in today's reading is not who the four beasts are who come up out of the sea (7:1-3, representations of the Babylonian, Median, Persian, and Greek emperors), but that the saints of God Most High should receive an eternal kingship (v. 18). Christian faith and worship sees the holy ones of all the centuries prevailing with Christ over evil forces in their lifetimes and reigning with him forever.

Psalm 149

Revelation 7:2-4, 9-14

Six seals on a scroll that had been handed to the Lamb by the One who sat on the throne (Rev 5:7) were opened in chap. 6. At the beginning of chap. 8 (v. 1), the Lamb opens the seventh seal. Hence chap. 7 represents an interruption like the interruption between the sixth and seventh trumpet blasts of 9:13 and 11:15. The four angels who restrain the earth's winds (v. 1) at its four corners are from Ezek 7:2 and 37:9. The corners, not the compass-points, are normally sources of destruction as in 7:2, rather than of life (breath to dry bones) as in 37:9. The underlying concept is the apocalyptic Jewish one of spirits charged with control of the elements. In v. 1 they achieve a calm on the earth.

This calm sets the stage for imprinting the seal *(sphragís)* of the living God on the foreheads of his servants (vv. 2-4), once the land and sea and trees have been forcibly stilled. God's enemies, represented by locusts (9:4), will be commanded to spare those thus sealed, just as the Israelites who bore the bloodmark on their houses were rendered immune from being struck down in Egypt (cf. Exod 12:13). Ezekiel 9:4 with its symbolism of the Hebrew letter Taw on the brows of mourners—rendered in translation variously as a "mark/X/cross"—is probably the source of this saving sign. The "seal" of this chapter will be specified as the name of the Lamb and of his Father "written on their foreheads" in 14:1 (if the reference there is to the same group) and 22:4. The word *sphragis* emerges in the mid-second century as a term for baptism, a sealing of the faith begun in repentance, according to the researches of Franz J. Dölger (*Sphragis* [Paderborn: Schönigh, 1911]).

The completion of God's people is represented by the squaring of twelve, the number of the tribes, and multiplication by a thousand (7:4). In their own minds believers in Christ were the authentic Israel. The omission of the tribe of Dan is a puzzle, as is the listing of the tribe Manasseh where we should have expected his father Joseph (cf. Gen 48:1, 13, 14; 49:16f., 22f.). Yet Hebrew literature, including the Bible, lists the twelve tribes in a variety of namings and sequences. Judah no doubt comes first (v. 5) because Jesus descends from him. It is not certain that the celibates of 14:4, probably a figure for martyrs, are identical with the believers of chap. 7, although the number is the same.

The 144,000 are the "huge crowd" assembled from every "nation and race, people and tongue" (v. 9). The vision of vv. 9-17 is undoubtedly meant to strengthen fearful Christians against their own "great ordeal" (v. 14), an anticipation of the final apocalyptic engagement. The martyrs have survived in the sense that they have kept their faith and their honor. The white robes and palm branches are signs of a victory already achieved. Joining angels and others around the throne, the victors sing the praises of God (v. 12) in a phrase reminiscent of Ps 3:9 which says, "Deliverance/safety is from the LORD."

The entire vision could very well be Jewish, with "the Lamb" substituted for "God" in vv. 9, 10, and 14, martyrdom being signified by the phrase, their robes washed and "made white [i.e., resplendent, glorious] in the blood of the Lamb" (7:14c).

PSALM 24:1-6

1 JOHN 3:1-3

Verse 1 is an utterance of joyous amazement that God should have made those who receive the Son to be his children (cf. John 1:12). The Johannine "world" can no more recognize this sonship in us than it did in him (v. 1). Spiritual likeness to God, which is the present reality, is being identified as the cause of an even greater likeness when full light and the vision of the Son reveal him as he is. The Son is "pure" (v. 3), he is sinless (v. 5). That is why our hope is based on him (v. 3).

While it is certain that such claims of sinlessness are being made for Christ, it is doubtful that 6a means to reprobate a heretical position adhered to by some who are "in him." It is even less likely that the statement, "No one who abides in him sins" (v. 6), is itself heretical. What cannot be denied, however, is that the Johannine literature is sectarian in the sense that it reflects the convictions of a particular group distinguished from others that do not have the faith in Jesus as the Christ that is peculiar to it.

ALLELUIA. MATTHEW 11:28

Come to me, all you who labor and are burdened, and I will give you rest, says the Lord.

LUKE 6:20-31

See 6 Sunday (C).

MATTHEW 5:1-12A

See 4 Sunday (A).

◆◆

Thanksgiving Day
Fourth Thursday in November (United States)
Second Monday in October (Canada)

DEUTERONOMY 26:1-11

For a commentary see 1 Lent (C).

PSALM 100

Philippians 4:49

For a commentary see Proper 22, 27 Sunday [22] (A)

John 6:25-35

For a commentary see Proper 13, 18 Sunday [18] (B).

❧ Appendix ❧

The Lectionary of *The Book of Common Prayer*

Readings for Sundays and festivals from the *Lectionary for Mass* (Roman Catholic) and the *Revised Common Lectionary* are listed in the body of this book. For the convenience of the reader, lections from *The Book of Common Prayer* (New York: The Church Hymnal Corporation and The Seabury Press, 1979) are provided below, correlated with the table of contents. Designations of Sundays and festivals in *The Book of Common Prayer*, when they differ significantly from those of the table of contents in this book, are given first.

❧ YEAR A ❧ BCP	❧ YEAR A ❧ LM/RCL
First Sunday of Advent Isaiah 2:1-5 Psalm 122 Romans 13:8-14 Matthew 24:37-44	**First Sunday of Advent**
Second Sunday of Advent Isaiah 11:1-10 Psalm 72 or 72:1-8 Romans 15:4-13 Matthew 3:1-12	**Second Sunday of Advent**
Third Sunday of Advent Isaiah 35:1-10 Psalm 146 or 146:4-9 James 5:7-10 Matthew 11:2-11	**Third Sunday of Advent**
Fourth Sunday of Advent Isaiah 7:10-17 Psalm 24 or 24:1-7 Romans 1:1-7 Matthew 1:18-25	**Fourth Sunday of Advent**
Christmas Day I/ **The Nativity of the Lord I** Isaiah 9:2-4, 6-7 Psalm 96 or 96:1-4, 11-12 Titus 2:11-14 Luke 2:1-14 (15-20)	**The Nativity of the Lord I/** **Mass at Midnight**

✿ YEAR A ✿
BCP

Christmas Day II/The Nativity of the Lord
Isaiah 62:6-7, 10-12
Psalm 97 or 97:1-4, 11-12
Titus 3:4-7
Luke 2:(11-14), 15-20

Christmas Day III/The Nativity of the Lord
Isaiah 52:7-10
Psalm 98 or 98:1-6
Hebrews 1:1-12
John 1:1-14

First Sunday after Christmas/Sunday between December 26 and January 1
Isaiah 61:10—62:3
Psalm 147 or 147:13-21
Galatians 3:23-25; 4:4-7
John 1:1-18

Holy Name, January 1/Solemnity of Mary, Mother of God/Octave of Christmas
Exodus 34:1-8
Psalm 8
Romans 1:1-7 or Philippians 2:9-13
Luke 2:15-21

Second Sunday after Christmas Day
Jeremiah 31:7-14
Psalm 84 or 84:1-18
Ephesians 1:3-6, 15-19a
Matthew 2:13-15, 19-23 or Luke 2:41-52 or Matthew 2:1-12

Epiphany of the Lord, January 6 or Nearest Sunday
Isaiah 60:1-6, 9
Psalm 72 or 72:1-2, 10-17
Ephesians 3:1-12
Matthew 2:1-12

First Sunday after Epiphany/Baptism of the Lord [1]/Sunday after January 6
Isaiah 42:1-9
Psalm 89:1-29 or 89:20-29
Acts 10:34-38
Matthew 3:13-17

✿ YEAR A ✿
LM/RCL

The Nativity of the Lord II/
Mass at Dawn

The Nativity of the Lord III/
Mass during the Day

First Sunday after Christmas Day/
Sunday between December 26 and January 1

The Holy Family/Sunday in the Octave of Christmas/Holy Name of Jesus/Solemnity of Mary, Mother of God/Octave of Christmas/January 1—When Observed as New Year's Day

Second Sunday after Christmas Day

Epiphany of the Lord, January 6 or Nearest Sunday

Baptism of the Lord [1]/First Sunday after the Epiphany/Sunday after January 6

❧ YEAR A ✍
BCP

Second Sunday after Epiphany [2]/
Second Sunday of the Year
Isaiah 49:1-7
Psalm 40:1-10
1 Corinthians 1:1-9
John 1:29-41

Third Sunday after Epiphany [3]/
Third Sunday of the Year
Amos 3:1-8
Psalm 139:1-17 or 139:1-11
1 Corinthians 1:10-17
Matthew 4:12-23

Fourth Sunday after Epiphany [4]/
Fourth Sunday of the Year
Micah 6:1-8
Psalm 37:1-18 or 37:1-6
1 Corinthians 1:(18-25), 26-31
Matthew 5:1-12

Fifth Sunday after Epiphany [5]/
Fifth Sunday of the Year
Hab. 3:2-6, 17-19
Psalm 27 or 27:1-7
1 Corinthians 2:1-11
Matthew 5:13-20

Sixth Sunday afterEpiphany [6]/
Sixth Sunday of the Year/Proper 1
Sirach 15:11-20
Psalm 119:1-16 or 119:9-16
1 Corinthians 3:1-9
Matthew 5:21-24, 27-30, 33-37

Seventh Sunday after Epiphany [7]/
Seventh Sunday of theYear/Proper 2
Leviticus 19:1-2, 9-18
Psalm 71 or 71:16-24
1 Corinthians 3:10-11, 16-23
Matthew 5:38-48

Eighth Sunday after Epiphany [8]/
Eighth Sunday of the Year/Proper 3
Exodus 24:12 (13-14), 15-18
Psalm 99
Philippians 3:7-14
Matthew 17:1-9

❧ YEAR A ✍
LM/RCL

Second Sunday after the Epiphany [2]/
Second Sunday of the Year

Third Sunday after the Epiphany [3]/
Third Sunday of the Year

Fourth Sunday after the Epiphany [4]/
Fourth Sunday of the Year

Fifth Sunday after the Epiphany [5]/
Fifth Sunday of the Year

Sixth Sunday after the Epiphany [6]/
Sixth Sunday of the Year/Proper 1

Seventh Sunday after the Epiphany [7]/
Seventh Sunday of the Year/Proper 2

Eighth Sunday after the Epiphany [8]/
Eighth Sunday of the Year/Proper 3

❦ YEAR A ❧
BCP

**Last Sunday after Epiphany [9]/
Ninth Sunday of the Year/Proper 4**
Exodus 24:12(13-14), 15-18
Psalm 99
Philippians 3:7-14
Matthew 17:1-9

Ash Wednesday
Joel 2:1-2, 12-17 or Isaiah 58:1-12
Psalm 103 or 103:8-14
2 Corinthians 5:20b—6:10
Matthew 6:1-6, 16-21

First Sunday in Lent
Genesis 2:4b-9, 15-17, 25—3:7
Psalm 51 or 51:1-13
Romans 5:12-19 (20-21)
Matthew 4:1-11

Second Sunday in Lent
Genesis 12:1-8
Psalm 33:12-22
Romans 4:1-5 (6-12), 13-17
John 3:1-17

Third Sunday in Lent
Exodus 17:1-7
Psalm 95 or 95:6-11
Romans 5:1-11
John 4:5-26 (27-38), 39-42

Fourth Sunday in Lent
1 Samuel 16:1-13
Psalm 23
Ephesians 5:(1-7), 8-14
John 9:1-13 (14-27), 28-38

Fifth Sunday in Lent
Ezekiel 37:1-3 (4-10), 11-14
Psalm 130
Romans 6:16-23
John 11:(1-16), 17-44

**Palm Sunday/Sixth Sunday in Lent/
Passion Sunday/Liturgy of the Palms**
Psalm 118:19-29
Matthew 21:1-11

❦ YEAR A ❧
LM/RCL

**Ninth Sunday after the Epiphany [9]/
Ninth Sunday of the Year/Proper 4**

Ash Wednesday

First Sunday in Lent

Second Sunday in Lent

Third Sunday in Lent

Fourth Sunday in Lent

Fifth Sunday in Lent

**Sixth Sunday in Lent/Passion Sunday
(Palm Sunday)/Liturgy of [Procession with]
the Palms**

❧ YEAR A ☙
BCP

❧ YEAR A ☙
LM/RCL

Liturgy of the Word
Isaiah 45:21-25 or Isaiah 52:13—53:12
Psalm 22:1-21 or 22:1-11
Philippians 2:5-11
Matthew (26:36-75), 27:1-54 (55-66)

Liturgy of the Passion

Monday in Holy Week
Isaiah 42:1-9
Psalm 36:5-10
Hebrews 11:39—12:3
John 12:1-11 or Mark 14:3-9

Monday of Holy Week

Tuesday in Holy Week
Isaiah 49:1-6
Psalm 71:1-12
1 Corinthians 1:18-31
John 12:37-38, 42-50 or Mark 11:15-19

Tuesday of Holy Week

Wednesday in Holy Week
Isaiah 50:4-9a
Psalm 69:7-15, 22-23
Hebrews 9:11-15, 24-28
John 13:21-35 or Matthew 26:1-5, 14-25

Wednesday of Holy Week

Maundy Thursday
Exodus 12:1-14a
Psalm 78:14-20, 23-25
1 Corinthians 11:23-26, (27-32)
John 13:1-15 or Luke 22:14-30

Holy (Maundy) Thursday

Good Friday
Isaiah 52:13—53:12 or Genesis 22:1-18 or
    Wisd. Sol. 2:1, 12-24
Psalm 22:1-21 or 22:1-11 or 40:1-14 or 69:1-23
Hebrews 10:1-25
John (18:1-40), 19:1-37

Good Friday

Easter Vigil
Genesis 1:1—2:2
Genesis 7:1-5,11-18; 8:6-18; 9:8-13
Genesis 22:1-18
Exodus 14:10—15:1
Isaiah 4:2-6
Isaiah 55:1-11
Ezekiel 36:24-28
Ezekiel 37:1-14
Ephesians 3:12-20
Romans 6:3-11
Matthew 28:1-10

Easter Vigil

✷ YEAR A ✷
BCP

Easter Day/Resurrection of the Lord
Acts 10:34-43 or Exodus 14:10-14, 21-25;
   15:20-21
Psalm 118:14-29 or 118:14-17, 22-24
Colossians 3:1-4 or Acts 10:34-43
John 20:1-10 (11-18) or Matthew 28:1-10

Easter Evening
Acts 5:29a, 30-32 or Daniel 12:1-3
Psalm 114 or Psalm 136 or Psalm 118:14-17,
   22-24
1 Corinthians 5:6b-8 or Acts 5:29a, 30-32
Luke 24:13-35

Second Sunday of Easter
Acts 2:14a, 22-32 or Genesis 8:6-16; 9:8-16
Psalm 111 or 118:19-24
1 Peter 1:3-9 or Acts 2:14a, 22-32
John 20:19-31

Third Sunday of Easter
Acts 2:14a, 36-47 or Isaiah 43:1-12
Psalm 116 or 116:10-17
1 Peter 1:17-23 or Acts 2:14a, 36-47
Luke 24:13-35

Fourth Sunday of Easter
Acts 6:1-9; 7:2a, 51-60 or Nehemiah 9:6-15
Psalm 23
1 Peter 2:19-25 or Acts 6:1-9; 7:2a, 51-60
John 10:1-10

Fifth Sunday of Easter
Acts 17:1-15 or Deuteronomy 6:20-25
Psalm 66:1-11 or 66:1-8
1 Peter 2:1-10 or Acts 17:1-15
John 14:1-14

Sixth Sunday of Easter
Acts 17:22-31 or Isaiah 41:17-20
Psalm 148 or 148:7-14
1 Peter 3:8-18 or Acts 17:22-31
John 15:1-8

Ascension Day
Acts 1:1-11 or Daniel 7:9-14
Psalm 47 or 110:1-5
Ephesians 1:15-23 or Acts 1:1-11
Luke 24:49-53 or Mark 16:9-15, 19-20

✷ YEAR A ✷
LM/RCL

Resurrection of the Lord/Easter Sunday

Easter Evening

Second Sunday of Easter

Third Sunday of Easter

Fourth Sunday of Easter

Fifth Sunday of Easter

Sixth Sunday of Easter

Ascension of the Lord

❧ YEAR A ✍
BCP

Seventh Sunday of Easter
Acts 1:(1-7), 8-14 or Ezekiel 39:21-29
Psalm 68:1-20 or Psalm 47
1 Peter 4:12-19 or Acts 1:(1-7), 8-14
John 17:1-11

Day of Pentecost
Acts 2:1-11 or Ezekiel 11:17-20
Psalm 104:25-37 or 104:25-32 or Psalm 33:12-15,
    18-22
1 Corinthians 12:4-13 or Acts 2:1-11
John 20:19-23 or John 14:8-17

Trinity Sunday (First Sunday after Pentecost)
Genesis 1:1—2:3
Psalm 150 or Canticle 2 or 13
2 Corinthians 13:(5-10), 11-14
Matthew 28:16-20

**Proper 4, Closest to June 1 [9]/Ninth Sunday
of the Year/Sunday between May 29 and June 4,
inclusive**
Deuteronomy 11:18-21, 26-28
Psalm 31 or 31:1-5, 19-24
Romans 3:21-25a, 28
Matthew 7:21-27

**Proper 5, Closest to June 8 [10]/Tenth Sunday
of the Year/Sunday between June 5 and June 11,
inclusive**
Hosea 5:15—6:6
Psalm 50 or 50:7-15
Romans 4:13-18
Matthew 9:9-13

**Proper 6, Closest to June 15 [11]/Eleventh Sunday
of the Year/Sunday between June 12 and June 18,
inclusive**
Exodus 19:2-8a
Psalm 100
Romans 5:6-11
Matthew 9:35—10:8 (9-15)

**Proper 7, Closest to June 22 [12]/Twelfth Sunday
of the Year/Sunday between June 19 and June 25,
inclusive**
Jeremiah 20:7-13
Psalm 69:1-18 or 69:7-10, 16-18
Romans 5:15b-19
Matthew 10:(16-23), 24-33

❧ YEAR A ✍
LM/RCL

Seventh Sunday of Easter

Day of Pentecost

**Trinity Sunday (First Sunday after Pentecost)/
The Body and Blood of Christ**

**Proper 4 [9]/Ninth Sunday of the Year/
Sunday between May 29 and June 4,
inclusive**

**Proper 5 [10]/Tenth Sunday of the Year/
Sunday between June 5 and June 11,
inclusive**

**Proper 6 [11]/Eleventh Sunday of the Year/
Sunday between June 12 and June 18,
inclusive**

**Proper 7 [12]/Twelfth Sunday of the Year/
Sunday between June 19 and June 25,
inclusive**

✿ YEAR A ✿
BCP

Proper 8, Closest to June 29 [13]/Thirteenth Sunday of the Year/Sunday between June 26 and July 2, inclusive
Isaiah 2:10-17
Psalm 89:1-18 or 89:1-4, 15-18
Romans 6:3-11
Matthew 10:34-42

Proper 9, Closest to July 6 [14]/Fourteenth Sunday of the Year/Sunday between July 3 and July 9, inclusive
Zechariah 9:9-12
Psalm 145 or 145:8-14
Romans 7:21—8:6
Matthew 11:25-30

Proper 10, Closest to July 13 [15]/ Fifteenth Sunday of the Year/Sunday between July 10 and July 16, inclusive
Isaiah 55:1-5, 10-13
Psalm 65 or 65:9-14
Romans 8:9-17
Matthew 13:1-9, 18-23

Proper 11, Closest to July 20 [16]/ Sixteenth Sunday of the Year/Sunday between July 17 and July 23, inclusive
Wisdom 12:13, 16-19
Psalm 86 or 86:11-17
Romans 8:18-25
Matthew 13:24-30, 36-43

Proper 12, Closest to July 27 [17]/ Seventeenth Sunday of the Year/Sunday between July 24 and July 30, inclusive
1 Kings 3:5-12
Psalm 119:121-136 or 119:129-136
Romans 8:26-34
Matthew 13:31-33, 44-49a

Proper 13, Closest to August 3 [18]/ Eighteenth Sunday of the Year/Sunday between July 31 and August 6, inclusive
Nehemiah 9:16-20
Psalm 78:1-29 or 78:14-20, 23-25
Romans 8:35-39
Matthew 14:13-21

✿ YEAR A ✿
LM/RCL

Proper 8 [13]/Thirteenth Sunday of the Year/ Sunday between June 26 and July 2, inclusive

Proper 9 [14]/Fourteenth Sunday of the Year/ Sunday between July 3 and July 9, inclusive

Proper 10 [15]/Fifteenth Sunday of the Year/ Sunday between July 10 and July 16, inclusive

Proper 11 [16]/Sixteenth Sunday of the Year/ Sunday between July 17 and July 23, inclusive

Proper 12 [17]/Seventeenth Sunday of the Year/ Sunday between July 24 and July 30, inclusive

Proper 13 [18]/Eighteenth Sunday of the Year/ Sunday between July 31 and August 6, inclusive

❧ YEAR A ❧
BCP

❧ YEAR A ❧
LM/RCL

Proper 14, Closest to August 10 [19]/
Nineteenth Sunday of the Year/Sunday between
August 7 and August 15, inclusive
Jonah 2:1-9
Psalm 29
Romans 9:1-5
Matthew 14:22-33

Proper 14 [19]/Nineteenth Sunday of the
Year/Sunday between August 7 and
August 15, inclusive

Proper 15, Closest to August 17 [20]/
Twentieth Sunday of the Year/Sunday between
August 14 and August 20, inclusive
Isaiah 56:1(2-5), 6-7
Psalm 67
Romans 11:13-15, 29-32
Matthew 15:21-28

Proper 15 [20]/Twentieth Sunday of the
Year/Sunday between August 14 and
August 20, inclusive1

Proper 16, Closest to August 24 [21]/
Twenty-first Sunday of the Year/Sunday
between August 21 and August 27, inclusive
Isaiah 51:1-6
Psalm 138
Romans 11:33-36
Matthew 16:13-20

Proper 16 [21]/Twenty-first Sunday of the
Year/Sunday between August 21 and
August 27, inclusive

Proper 17, Closest to August 31 [22]/
Twenty-second Sunday of the Year/Sunday
between August 28 and September 3, inclusive
Jeremiah 15:15-21
Psalm 26 or 26:1-8
Romans 12:1-8
Matthew 16:21-27

Proper 17 [22]/Twenty-second Sunday of
the Year/Sunday between August 28 and
September 3, inclusive

Proper 18, Closest to September 7 [23]/
Twenty-third Sunday of the Year/Sunday
between September 4 and September 10, inclusive
Ezekiel 33:(1-6), 7-11
Psalm 119:33-48 or 119:33-40
Romans 12:9-21
Matthew 18:15-20

Proper 18 [23]/Twenty-third Sunday of
the Year/Sunday between September 4 and
September 10, inclusive

Proper 19, Closest to September 14 [24]/
Twenty-fourth Sunday of the Year/Sunday
between September 11 and September 17, inclusive
Sirach 27:30—28:7
Psalm 103 or 103:8-13
Romans 14:5-12
Matthew 18:21-35

Proper 19 [24]/Twenty-fourth Sunday of
the Year/Sunday between September 11
and September 17, inclusive

✿ YEAR A ✿
BCP

Proper 20, Closest to September 21 [25]/
Twenty-fifth Sunday of the Year/Sunday between
September 18 and September 24, inclusive
Jonah 3:10—4:11
Psalm 145 or 145:1-8
Philippians 1:21-27
Matthew 20:1-16

Proper 21, Closest to September 28 [26]/
Twenty-sixth Sunday of the Year/Sunday
between September 25 and October 1, inclusive
Ezekiel 18:1-4, 25-32
Psalm 25:1-14 or 25:3-9
Philippians 2:1-13
Matthew 21:28-32

Proper 22, Closest to October 5 [27]/
Twenty-seventh Sunday of the Year/Sunday
between October 2 and October 8, inclusive
Isaiah 5:1-7
Psalm 80 or 80:7-14
Philippians 3:14-21
Matthew 21:33-43

Proper 23, Closest to October 12 [28]/
Twenty-eighth Sunday of the Year/Sunday
between October 9 and October 15, inclusive
Isaiah 25:1-9
Psalm 23
Philippians 4:4-13
Matthew 22:1-14

Proper 24, Closest to October 19 [29]/
Twenty-ninth Sunday of the Year/Sunday
between October 16 and October 22, inclusive
Isaiah 45:1-7
Psalm 96 or 96:1-9
1 Thessalonians 1:1-10
Matthew 22:15-22

Proper 25, Closest to October 26 [30]/
Thirtieth Sunday of the Year/Sunday between
October 23 and October 29, inclusive
Exodus 22:21-27
Psalm 1
1 Thessalonians 2:1-8
Matthew 22:34-46

✿ YEAR A ✿
LM/RCL

Proper 20 [25]/Twenty-fifth Sunday of the Year/
Sunday between September 18 and September
24, inclusive

Proper 21 [26]/Twenty-sixth Sunday of the
Year/Sunday between September 25 and
October 1, inclusive

Proper 22 [27]/Twenty-seventh Sunday of the
Year/Sunday between October 2 and October 8,
inclusive

Proper 23 [28]/Twenty-eighth Sunday of the
Year/Sunday between October 9 and October 15,
inclusive

Proper 24 [29]/Twenty-ninth Sunday of the Year/
Sunday between October 16 and October 22,
inclusive

Proper 25 [30]/Thirtieth Sunday of the Year/
Sunday between October 23 and October 29,
inclusive

❧ YEAR A ✍
BCP

Proper 26, Closest to November 2 [31]/
Thirty-first Sunday of the Year/Sunday between
October 30 and November 5, inclusive
Micah 3:5-12
Psalm 43
1 Thessalonians 2:9-13, 17-20
Matthew 23:1-12

Proper 27, Closest to November 9 [32]/
Thirty-second Sunday of the Year/Sunday
between November 6 and November 12, inclusive
Amos 5:18-24
Psalm 70
1 Thessalonians 4:13-18
Matthew 25:1-13

Proper 28, Closest to November 16 [33] (A)/
Thirty-third Sunday of the Year Sunday between
November 13 and November 19, inclusive
Ephesians 1:7, 12-18
Psalm 90 or 90:1-8, 12
1 Thessalonians 5:1-10
Matthew 25:14-15, 19-29

Proper 29, Closest to November 23 [34] Reign
of Christ or Christ the King/Thirty-fourth or
Last Sunday of the Year/Sunday between
November 20 and November 26, inclusive
Ezekiel 34:11-17
Psalm 95:1-7
1 Corinthians 15:20-28
Matthew 25:31-46

All Saints' Day, November 1 or the first Sunday
in November
Sirach 44:1-10, 13-14
Psalm 149
Revelation 7:2-4, 9-17
Matthew 5:1-12

Thanksgiving Day
Deuteronomy 8:1-3, 6-10 (17-20)
Psalm 65 or 65:9-14
James 1:17-18, 21-27
Matthew 6:25-33

❧ YEAR A ✍
LM/RCL

Proper 26 [31]/Thirty-first Sunday of the
Year/Sunday between October 30 and
November 5, inclusive

Proper 27 [32]/Thirty-second Sunday of the
Year/Sunday between November 6 and
November 12, inclusive

Proper 28 [33] /Thirty-third Sunday of the
Year/Sunday between November 13 and
November 19, inclusive

Proper 29 [34] Reign of Christ or Christ
the King/Thirty-fourth or Last Sunday of
the Year/Sunday between November 20
and November 26, inclusive

All Saints /November 1 or the first Sunday
in November

Thanksgiving Day

✆ YEAR B ✆
BCP

First Sunday of Advent
Isaiah 64:1-9a
Psalm 80 or 80:1-7
1 Corinthians 1:1-9
Mark 13:(24-32)33-37

Second Sunday of Advent
Isaiah 40:1-11
Psalm 85 or 85:7-13
2 Peter 3:8-15a,18
Mark 1:1-8

Third Sunday of Adven
Isaiah 65:17-25
Psalm 126 or Canticle 3 or 15
1 Thessalonians 5:(12-15)16-28
John 1:6-8,19-28 or John 3:23-30

Fourth Sunday of Advent
2 Samuel 7:4, 8-16
Psalm 132 or 132:8-15
Romans 16:25-27
Luke 1:26-38

Christmas Day I/Nativity of the Lord
Isaiah 9:2-4,6-7
Psalm 96 or 96:1-4,11-12
Titus 2:11-14
Luke 2:1-14 (15-20)

Christmas Day II/Nativity of the Lord
Isaiah 62:6-7, 10-12
Psalm 97 or 97:1-4, 11-12
Titus 3:4-7
Luke 2:(1-14) 15-20

Christmas Day III/Nativity of the Lord
Isaiah 52:7-10
Psalm 98 or 98:1-6
Hebrews 1:1-12
John 1:1-14

First Sunday after Christmas/Sunday between December 26 and January 1
Isaiah 61:10—62:3
Psalm 147 or 147:13-21
Galatians 3:23-25; 4:4-7
John 1:1-18

✆ YEAR B ✆
LM/RCL

First Sunday of Adven

Second Sunday of Advent

Third Sunday of Advent

Fourth Sunday of Advent

**Christmas/Nativity of the Lord I/
The Vigil Mass/Christmas/Nativity of the Lord/
Mass at Midnight**

**Christmas/Nativity of the Lord II/
Mass at Dawn**

**Christmas/Nativity of the Lord III/
Mass during the Day**

First Sunday after Christmas/Sunday between December 26 and January 1

❧ YEAR B ❧
BCP

Holy Name, January 1/Solemnity of Mary, Mother of God/Octave of Christmas
Exodus 34:1-8
Psalm 8
Romans 1:1-7
Luke 2:15-21

Second Sunday after Christmas
Jeremiah 31:7-14
Psalm 84 or 84:1-8
Ephesians 1:3-6, 15-19a
Matthew 2:13-15,19-23 or Luke 2:41-52 or
    Matthew 2:1-12

The Epiphany, January 6 or Nearest Sunday
Isaiah 60:1-6, 9
Psalm 72 or 72:1-2, 10-17
Ephesians 3:1-12
Matthew 2:1-12

First Sunday after Epiphany/Baptism of the Lord [1]/Sunday after January 6
Isaiah 42:1-9
Psalm 89:1-29 or 89:20-29
Acts 10:34-38
Mark 1:7-11

Second Sunday after Epiphany [2]/ Second Sunday of the Year
1 Samuel 3:1-10 (11-20)
Psalm 63:1-8
1 Corinthians 6:11b-20
John 1:43-51

Third Sunday after Epiphany [3]/ Third Sunday of the Year
Jeremiah 3:21—4:2
Psalm 130
1 Corinthians 7:17-23
Mark 1:14-20

Fourth Sunday after Epiphany [4]/ Fourth Sunday of the Year
Deuteronomy 18:15-20
Psalm 111
1 Corinthians 8:1b-13
Mark 1:21-28

❧ YEAR B ❧
LM/RCL

The Holy Family/Sunday in the Octave of Christmas/Holy Name of Jesus/Solemnity of Mary, Mother of God/Octave of Christmas January 1—When Observed as New Year's Day

Second Sunday after Christmas

Epiphany of the Lord, January 6 or Nearest Sunday

Baptism of the Lord [1]/First Sunday after the Epiphany/Sunday after January 6

Second Sunday after the Epiphany [2]/ Second Sunday of the Year

Third Sunday after the Epiphany [3]/ Third Sunday of the Year

Fourth Sunday after the Epiphany [4]/ Fourth Sunday of the Year

<table>
<tr><td>

❧ YEAR B ❧
BCP

Fifth Sunday after Epiphany [5]/
Fifth Sunday of the Year
2 Kings 4:(8-17), 18-21(22-31), 32-37
Psalm 142
1 Corinthians 9:16-23
Mark 1:29-39

Sixth Sunday after Epiphany [6]/
Sixth Sunday of the Year/Proper 1
2 Kings 5:1-15ab
Psalm 42 or 42:1-7
1 Corinthians 9:24-27
Mark 1:40-45

Seventh Sunday after Epiphany [7]/
Seventh Sunday of the Year/Proper 2
Isaiah 43:18-25
Psalm 32 or 32:1-8
2 Corinthians 1:18-22
Mark 2:1-12

Eighth Sunday after Epiphany [8]/
Eighth Sunday of the Year/Proper 3
Hosea 2:14-23
Psalm 103 or103:1-6
2 Corinthians 3:(4-11)17—4:2
Mark 2:18-22

Last Sunday after Epiphany;
Transfiguration Sunday
1 Kings 19:9-18
Psalm 27 or 27:5-11
2 Peter 1:16-19(20-21)
Mark 9:2-9

Ash Wednesday
Joel 2:1-2,12-17 or Isaiah 58:1-12
Psalm 103 or 103:8-14
2 Corinthians 5:20b—6:10
Matthew 6:1-6, 16-21

First Sunday in Lent
Genesis 9:8-17
Psalm 25 or 25:3-9
1 Peter 3:18-22
Mark 1:9-13

Second Sunday in Lent
Genesis 22:1-14
Psalm 16 or 16:5-11
Romans 8:31-39
Mark 8:31-38

</td><td>

❧ YEAR B ❧
LM/RCL

Fifth Sunday after the Epiphany [5]/
Fifth Sunday of the Year

Sixth Sunday after the Epiphany [6]/
Sixth Sunday of the Year/Proper 1

Seventh Sunday after the Epiphany [7]/
Seventh Sunday of the Year/Proper 2

Eighth Sunday after the Epiphany [8]/
Eighth Sunday of the Year/Proper 3

Ninth Sunday after the Epiphany [9]/
Ninth Sunday of the Year/Proper 4/
Last Sunday after the Epiphany—
Transfiguration Sunday

Ash Wednesday

First Sunday in Lent

Second Sunday in Lent

</td></tr>
</table>

❧ YEAR B ✍
BCP

Third Sunday in Lent
Exodus 20:1-17
Psalm 19:7-14
Romans 7:13-25
John 2:13-22

Fourth Sunday in Lent
2 Chronicles 36:14-23
Psalm 122
Ephesians 2:4-10
John 6:4-15

Fifth Sunday in Lent
Jeremiah 31:31-34
Psalm 51 or 51:11-16
Hebrews 5:(1-4), 5-10
John 12:20-33

**Palm Sunday/Sixth Sunday in Lent/
Passion Sunday/Liturgy of the Palms**
Psalm 118:19-29
Mark 11:1-11a

Liturgy of the Word
Isaiah 45:21-25 or Isaiah 52:13—53:12
Psalm 22:1-21 or 22:1-11
Philippians 2:5-11
Mark (14:32-72), 15:1-39(40-47)

Monday in Holy Week
Isaiah 42:1-9
Psalm 36:5-10
Hebrews 11:39—12:3
John 12:1-11 or Mark 14:3-9

Tuesday in Holy Week
Isaiah 49:1-6
Psalm 71:1-12
1 Corinthians 1:18-31
John 12:37-38, 42-50 or Mark 11:15-19

Wednesday in Holy Week
Isaiah 50:4-9a
Psalm 69:7-15, 22-23
Hebrews 9:11-15, 24-28
John 13:21-35 or Matthew 26:1-5, 14-25

Maundy Thursday
Exodus 12:1-14a
Psalm 78:14-20, 23-25
1 Corinthians 11:23-26(27-32)
John 13:1-15 or Luke 22:14-30

❧ YEAR B ✍
LM/RCL

Third Sunday in Lent

Fourth Sunday in Lent

Fifth Sunday in Lent

**Sixth Sunday in Lent/Passion Sunday or
Palm Sunday Liturgy of [Procession with]
the Palms**

Liturgy of the Passion

Monday of Holy Week

Tuesday of Holy Week

Wednesday of Holy Week

Holy (Maundy) Thursday

✿ YEAR B ✿
BCP

Good Friday
Isaiah 52:13—53:12 or Genesis 22:1-18 or
  Wisd. 2:1, 12-24
Psalm 22:1-21 or 22:1-11 or 40:1-14 or 69:1-23
Hebrews 10:1-25
John (18:1-40), 19:1-37

Easter Vigil
All as in Year A except Gospel according to Mark

Easter Day/Resurrection of the Lord
Acts 10:34-43 or Isaiah 25:6-9
Psalm 118:14-29 or 118:14-17,22-24
Colossians 3:1-4 or Acts 10:34-43
Mark 16:1-8

Easter Evening
Acts 5:29a, 30-32 or Daniel 12:1-3
Psalm 114 or 136 or 118:14-17, 22-24
1 Corinthians 5:6b-8 or Acts 5:29a, 30-32
Luke 24:13-35

Second Sunday of Easter
Acts 3:12a,13-15,17-26 or Isaiah 26:2-9, 19
Psalm 111 or 118:19-24
1 John 5:1-6 or Acts 3:12a, 13-15, 17-26
John 20:19-31

Third Sunday of Easter
Acts 4:5-12 or Micah 4:1-5
Psalm 98 or 98:1-5
1 John 1:1—2:2 or Acts 4:5-12
Luke 24:36b-48

Fourth Sunday of Easter
Acts 4:(23-31)32-37 or Ezekiel 34:1-10
Psalm 23 or 100
1 John 3:1-8 or Acts 4:(23-31), 32-37
John 10:11-16

Fifth Sunday of Easter
Acts 8:26-40 or Deuteronomy 4:32-40
Psalm 66:1-11 or 66:1-8
1 John 3:(14-17)18-24 or Acts 8:26-40
John 14:15-21

Sixth Sunday of Easter
Acts 11:19-30 or Isaiah 45:11-13, 18-19
Psalm 33 or 33:1-8, 18-22
1 John 4:7-21 or Acts 11:19-30
John 15:9-17

✿ YEAR B ✿
LM/RCL

Good Friday

Easter Vigil
All as in Year A except Gospel according to Mark

Resurrection of the Lord/Easter Sunday

Easter Evening

Second Sunday of Easter

Third Sunday of Easter

Fourth Sunday of Easter

Fifth Sunday of Easter

Sixth Sunday of Easter

❧ YEAR B ❧
BCP

❧ YEAR B ❧
LM/RCL

Ascension Day
Acts 1:1-11 or Ezekiel 1:3-5a, 15-22, 26-28
Psalm 47 or 110:1-5
Ephesians 1:15-23 or Acts 1:1-11
Luke 24:49-53 or Mark 16:9-15, 19-20

Ascension of the Lord

Seventh Sunday of Easter
Acts 1:15-26 or Exodus 28:1-4, 9-10, 29-30
Psalm 68:1-20 or 47
1 John 5:9-15 or Acts 1:15-26
John 17:11b-19

Seventh Sunday of Easter

Day of Pentecost, Principal Service
Acts 2:1-11 or Isaiah 44:1-8
Psalm 104:25-37 or 104:25-32 or 33:12-15,
    18-22
1 Corinthians 12:4-13 or Acts 2:1-11
John 20:19-23 or John 14:8-17

Day of Pentecost

Trinity Sunday/First Sunday after Pentecost
Exodus 3:1-6
Psalm 93 or Canticle 2 or 13
Romans 8:12-17
John 3:1-16

**Trinity Sunday/First Sunday after Pentecost/
The Body and Blood of Christ**

**Proper 4, Closest to June 1 [9]/Ninth Sunday of
the Year/Sunday between May 29 and June 4,
inclusive**
Deuteronomy 5:6-21
Psalm 81or 81:1-10
2 Corinthians 4:5-12
Mark 2:23-28

**Proper 4 [9]/Ninth Sunday of the Year/
Sunday between May 29 and June 4,
inclusive**

**Proper 5, Closest to June 8 [10]/Tenth Sunday
of the Year/Sunday between June 5 and June 11,
inclusive**
Genesis 3:(1-7), 8-21
Psalm 130
2 Corinthians 4:13-18
Mark 3:20-35

**Proper 5 [10]/Tenth Sunday of the Year/
Sunday between June 5 and June 11,
inclusive**

**Proper 6, Closest to June 15 [11]/Eleventh
Sunday of the Year/Sunday between June 12
and June 18, inclusive**
Ezekiel 31:1-6, 10-14
Psalm 92 or 92:1-4, 11-14
2 Corinthians 5:1-10
Mark 4:26-34

**Proper 6 [11]/Eleventh Sunday of the Year/
Sunday between June 12 and June 18,
inclusive**

YEAR B
BCP

Proper 7, Closest to June 22 [12]/Twelfth Sunday of the Year/Sunday between June 19 and June 25, inclusive
Job 38:1-11, 16-18
Psalm 107:1-32 or 107:1-3, 23-32
2 Corinthians 5:14-21
Mark 4:35-41; (5:1-20)

Proper 8, Closest to June 29 [13]/Thirteenth Sunday of the Year/Sunday between June 26 and July 2, inclusive
Deuteronomy 15:7-11
Psalm 112
2 Corinthians 8:1-9, 13-15
Mark 5:22-24, 35b-43

Proper 9, Closest to July 6 [14]/Fourteenth Sunday of the Year/Sunday between July 3 and July 9, inclusive
Ezekiel 2:1-7
Psalm 123
2 Corinthians 12:2-10
Mark 6:1-6

Proper 10, Closest to July 13 [15]/Fifteenth Sunday of the Year/Sunday between July 10 and July 16, inclusive
Amos 7:7-15
Psalm 85 or 85:7-13
Ephesians 1:1-14
Mark 6:7-13

Proper 11, Closest to July 20 [16]/Sixteenth Sunday of the Year/Sunday between July 17 and July 23, inclusive
Isaiah 57:14b-21
Psalm 22:22-30
Ephesians 2:11-22
Mark 6:30-44

Proper 12, Closest to July 27 [17]/Seventeenth Sunday of the Year/Sunday between July 24 and July 30, inclusive
2 Kings 2:1-15
Psalm 114
Ephesians 4:1-7, 11-16
Mark 6:45-52

YEAR B
LM/RCL

Proper 7 [12]/Twelfth Sunday of the Year/Sunday between June 19 and June 25, inclusive

Proper 8 [13]/Thirteenth Sunday of the Year/Sunday between June 26 and July 2, inclusive

Proper 9 [14]/Fourteenth Sunday of the Year/Sunday between July 3 and July 9, inclusive

Proper 10 [15]/Fifteenth Sunday of the Year/Sunday between July 10 and July 16, inclusive

Proper 11 [16]/Sixteenth Sunday of the Year/Sunday between July 17 and July 23, inclusive

Proper 12 [17]/Seventeenth Sunday of the Year/Sunday between July 24 and July 30, inclusive

❧ YEAR B ❧
BCP

❧ YEAR B ❧
LM/RCL

Proper 13, Closest to August 3 [18]/Eighteenth Sunday of the Year/Sunday between July 31 and August 6, inclusive
Exodus 16:2-4, 9-15
Psalm 78:1-25 or 78:14-20, 23-25
Ephesians 4:17-25
John 6:24-35

Proper 13 [18]/Eighteenth Sunday of the Year/Sunday between July 31 and August 6, inclusive

Proper 14, Closest to August 10 [19]/Nineteenth Sunday of the Year/Sunday between August 7 and August 13, inclusive
Deuteronomy 8:1-10
Psalm 34 or 34:1-8
Ephesians 4:(25-29)30—5:2
John 6:37-51

Proper 14 [19]/Nineteenth Sunday of the Year/Sunday between August 7 and August 13, inclusive

Proper 15, Closest to August 17 [20]/Twentieth Sunday of the Year/Sunday between August 14 and August 20, inclusive
Proverbs 9:1-6
Psalm 147 or 39:9-14
Ephesians 5:15-20
John 6:53-59

Proper 15 [20]/Twentieth Sunday of the Year/Sunday between August 14 and August 20, inclusive

Proper 16, Closest to August 34 [21]/ Twenty-first Sunday of the Year/Sunday between August 21 and August 27, inclusive
Joshua 24:1-2a, 14-25
Psalm 16 or 34:15-22
Ephesians 5:21-33
John 6:60-69

Proper 16 [21]/Twenty-first Sunday of the Year/Sunday between August 21 and August 27, inclusive

Proper 17, Closest to August 31 [22]/ Twenty-second Sunday of the Year/Sunday between August 28 and September 3, inclusive
Deuteronomy 4:1-9
Psalm 15
Ephesians 6:10-20
Mark 7:1-8, 14-15, 21-23

Proper 17 [22]/Twenty-second Sunday of the Year/Sunday between August 28 and September 3, inclusive

Proper 18, Closest to September 7 [23]/ Twenty-third Sunday of the Year/Sunday between September 4 and September 10, inclusive
Isaiah 35:4-7a
Psalm 146 or 146:4-9
James 1:17-27
Mark 7:31-37

Proper 18 [23]/Twenty-third Sunday of the Year/Sunday between September 4 and September 10, inclusive

❧ YEAR B ✿
BCP

Proper 19, Closest to September 14 [24]/
Twenty-fourth Sunday of the Year/Sunday
between September 11 and September 18, inclusive
Isaiah 50:4-9
Psalm 116 or 116:1-8
James 2:1-5, 8-10, 14-18
Mark 8:27-38 or Mark 9:14-29

Proper 20, Closest to September 21 [25]/
Twenty-fifth Sunday of the Year/Sunday
between September 18 and September 24, inclusive
Wisdom 1:16—2:1(6-11), 12-22
Psalm 54
James 3:16—4:6
Mark 9:30-37

Proper 21, Closest to September28 [26]/
Twenty-sixth Sunday of the Year/Sunday
between September 25 and October 1, inclusive
Numbers 11:4-6, 10-16, 24-29
Psalm 19 or 19:7-14
James 4:7-12(13—5:6)
Mark 9:38-43, 45, 47-48

Proper 22, Closest to October 5 [27]/
Twenty-seventh Sunday of the Year/Sunday
between October 2 and October 8, inclusive
Genesis 2:18-24
Psalm 8 or 128
Hebrews 2:(1-8)9-18
Mark 10:2-9

Proper 23, Closest to October 12 [28]/
Twenty-eighth Sunday of the Year/Sunday
between October 9 and October 15, inclusive
Amos 5:6-7, 10-15
Psalm 90 or 90:2-8, 12
Hebrews 3:1-6
Mark 10:17-27(28-31)

Proper 24, Closest to October 19 [29]/
Twenty-ninth Sunday of the Year/Sunday
between October 16 and October 22, inclusive
Isaiah 53:4-12
Psalm 91or 91:9-16
Hebrews 4:12-16
Mark 10:35-45

❧ YEAR B ✿
LM/RCL

Proper 19 [24]/Twenty-fourth Sunday of the
Year/Sunday between September 11 and
September 18, inclusive

Proper 20 [25]/Twenty-fifth Sunday of the Year/
Sunday between September 18 and
September 24, inclusive

Proper 21 [26]/Twenty-sixth Sunday of the
Year/Sunday between September 25 and
October 1, inclusive

Proper 22 [27]/Twenty-seventh Sunday of the
Year/Sunday between October 2 and October 8,
inclusive

Proper 23 [28]/Twenty-eighth Sunday of the
Year/Sunday between October 9 and October 15,
inclusive

Proper 24 [29]/Twenty-ninth Sunday of the
Year/Sunday between October 16 and
October 22, inclusive

❧ YEAR B ❧
BCP

Proper 25, Closest to October 26 [30]/Thirtieth
Sunday of the Year/Sunday between October 23
and October 29, inclusive
Isaiah 59:(1-4)9-19
Psalm 13
Hebrews 5:12—6:1, 9-12
Mark 10:46-52

Proper 26, Closest to November 2 [31]/
Thirty-first Sunday of the Year/Sunday between
October 30 and November 5, inclusive
Deuteronomy 6:1-9
Psalm 119:1-16 or 119:1-8
Hebrews 7:23-28
Mark 12:28-34

Proper 27, Closest to November 9 [32]/
Thirty-second Sunday of the Year/Sunday
between November 6 and November 12, inclusive
1 Kings 17:8-16
Psalm 146 or 146:4-9
Hebrews 9:24-28
Mark 12:38-44

Proper 28, Closest to November 16
   [33]/Thirty-third Sunday of the Year/Sunday
between November 13 and November 19, inclusive
Daniel 12:1-4a(5-13)
Psalm 16 or 16:5-11
Hebrews 10:31-39
Mark 13:14-23

Proper 29, Closest to November 23 [34]/Reign
of Christ or Christ the King/Thirty-fourth or
Last Sunday of the Year/Sunday between
November 20 and November 26, inclusive
Daniel 7:9-14
Psalm 93
Revelation 1:1-8
John 18:33-37 or Mark 11:1-11

All Saints' Day/November 1
See Year A

Thanksgiving Day
See Year A

❧ YEAR B ❧
LM/RCL

Proper 25 [30]/Thirtieth Sunday of the
Year/Sunday between October 23 and
October 29, inclusive

Proper 26 [31]/Thirty-first Sunday of the
Yea/Sunday between October 30 and
November 5, inclusive

Proper 27 [32]/Thirty-second Sunday of
the Year/Sunday between November 6
and November 12, inclusive

Proper 28 [33]/Thirty-third Sunday of the
Year/Sunday between November 13 and
November 19, inclusive

Proper 29 [34]/Reign of Christ or Christ
the King/Thirty-fourth or Last Sunday of
the Year/Sunday between November 20
and November 26, inclusive

All Saints November 1 or the first Sunday
in November

Thanksgiving Day

❧ YEAR C ❧
BCP

First Sunday of Advent
Zechariah 14:4-9
Psalm 50 or 50:1-6
1 Thessalonians 3:9-13
Luke 21:25-31

Second Sunday of Advent
Baruch 5:1-9
Psalm 126
Philippians 1:1-11
Luke 3:1-6

Third Sunday of Advent
Zephaniah 3:14-20
Psalm 85 or 85:7-13 or Canticle 9
Philippians 4:4-7, (8-9)
Luke 3:7-18

Fourth Sunday of Advent
Micah 5:2-4
Psalm 80 or 80:1-7
Hebrews 10:5-10
Luke 1:39-49, (50-56)

Christmas Day I/Nativity of the Lord
Isaiah 9:2-4, 6-7
Psalm 96 or 96:1-4, 11-12
Titus 2:11-14
Luke 2:1-14, (15-20)

Christmas Day II/Nativity of the Lord
Isaiah 62:6-7, 10-12
Psalm 97 or 97:1-4, 11-12
Titus 3:4-7
Luke 2:(1-14), 15-20

**Christmas Day III/Nativity of the Lord/Mass
during the Day**
Isaiah 52:7-10
Psalm 98 or 98:1-6
Hebrews 1:1-12
John 1:1-14

**First Sunday after Christmas Day/
Sunday between December 26 and January 1**
Isaiah 61:10—62:3
Psalm 147 or 147:13-21
Galatians 3:23-25; 4:4-7
John 1:1-18

❧ YEAR C ❧
LM/RCL

First Sunday of Advent

Second Sunday of Advent

Third Sunday of Advent

Fourth Sunday of Advent

**Christmas/Nativity of the Lord I/
Mass at Midnight**

**Christmas/Nativity of the Lord II/
Mass at Dawn**

**Christmas/Nativity of the Lord III/
Mass during the Day**

**First Sunday after Christmas Day/Sunday
between December 26 and January 1**

❧ YEAR C ✍
BCP

Holy Name, January 1/Solemnity of Mary,
Mother of God/Octave of Christmas
Exodus 34:1-8
Psalm 8
Romans 1:1-7
Luke 2:15-21

Second Sunday after Christmas
See Year A

The Epiphany, January 6 or Nearest Sunday
Isaiah 60:1-6, 9
Psalm 72 or 72:1-2, 10-17
Ephesians 3:1-12
Matthew 2:1-12

First Sunday after Epiphany/Baptism of the
Lord [1]/Sunday after January 6
Isaiah 42:1-9
Psalm 89:1-29 or 89:20-29
Acts 10:34-38
Luke 3:15-16, 21-22

Second Sunday after Epiphany [2]/
Second Sunday of the Year
Isaiah 62:1-5
Psalm 96 or 96:1-10
1 Corinthians 12:1-11
John 2:1-11

Third Sunday after Epiphany [3]/
Third Sunday of the Year
Nehemiah 8:2-10
Psalm 113
1 Corinthians 12:12-27
Luke 4:14-21

Fourth Sunday after Epiphany [4]/
Fourth Sunday of the Year
Jeremiah 1:4-10
Psalm 71:1-17 or 71:1-6, 15-17
1 Corinthians 14:12b-20
Luke 4:21-32

Fifth Sunday after Epiphany [5]/Fifth Sunday
of the Year
Judges 6:11-24a
Psalm 85 or 85:7-13
1 Corinthians 15:1-11
Luke 5: 1-11

❧ YEAR C ✍
LM/RCL

The Holy Family/Sunday in the Octave of
Christmas/Holy Name of Jesus/Solemnity
of Mary, Mother of God/Octave of
Christmas/January 1—When Observed as
New Year's Day

Second Sunday after Christmas Day

Epiphany of the Lord, January 6 or
Nearest Sunday

Baptism of the Lord [1]/First Sunday after
the Epiphany/Sunday after January 6

Second Sunday after the Epiphany [2]/
Second Sunday of the Year

Third Sunday after the Epiphany [3]/
Third Sunday of the Year

Fourth Sunday after the Epiphany [4]/
Fourth Sunday of the Year

Fifth Sunday after the Epiphany [5]/
Fifth Sunday of the Year

YEAR C
BCP

Sixth Sunday after Epiphany [6]/Sixth Sunday of the Year/Proper 1
Jeremiah 17:5-10
Psalm 1
1 Corinthians 15:12-20
Luke 6:17-26

Seventh Sunday after Epiphany [7]/ Seventh Sunday of the Year/Proper 2
Genesis 45:3-11, 21-28
Psalm 37:1-18 or 37:3-10
1 Corinthians 15:35-38, 42-50
Luke 6:27-38

Eighth Sunday after Epiphany [8]/ Eighth Sunday of the Year/Proper 3
Jeremiah 7:1-7(8-15)
Psalm 92 or 92:1-5, 11-14
1 Corinthians 15:50-58
Luke 6:39-49

Last Sunday after Epiphany (Transfiguration Sunday)
Exodus 34:29-35
Psalm 99
1 Corinthians 12-27—13:13
Luke 9:28-36

Ash Wednesday
Joel 2:1-2, 12-17 or Isaiah 58:1-12
Psalm 103 or 103:8-14
2 Corinthians 5:20b—6:10
Matthew 6:1-6, 16-21

First Sunday in Lent
Deuteronomy 26:(1-4), 5-11
Psalm 91 or 91:9-15
Romans 10:(5-8a), 8b-13
Luke 4:1-13

Second Sunday in Lent
Genesis 15:1-12, 17-18
Psalm 27 or 27:10-18
Philippians 3:17—4:1
Luke 13:(22-30), 31-35

Third Sunday in Lent
Exodus 3:1-15
Psalm 103 or 103:1-11
1 Corinthians 10:1-13
Luke 13:1-9

YEAR C
LM/RCL

Sixth Sunday after the Epiphany [6]/ Sixth Sunday of the Year/Proper 1

Seventh Sunday after the Epiphany [7]/ Seventh Sunday of the Year/Proper 2

Eighth Sunday after the Epiphany [8]/ Eighth Sunday of the Year/Proper 3

Ninth Sunday after the Epiphany [9]/ Ninth Sunday of the Year/Proper 4
Last Sunday after the Epiphany (Transfiguration Sunday)
Tenth Sunday after the Epiphany [10]/ Tenth Sunday of the Year/Proper 5

Ash Wednesday

First Sunday in Lent

Second Sunday in Lent

Third Sunday in Lent

❧ YEAR C ❧
BCP

❧ YEAR C ❧
LM/RCL

Fourth Sunday in Lent
Joshua (4:19-24); 5:9-12
Psalm 34 or 34:1-8
2 Corinthians 5:17-21
Luke 15:11-32

Fourth Sunday in Len

Fifth Sunday in Lent
Isaiah 43:16-21
Psalm 126
Philippians 3:8-14
Luke 20:9-19

Fifth Sunday in Lent 483

**Palm Sunday/Sixth Sunday in Lent/
Passion Sunday/Liturgy of the Palms**
Psalm 118:19-29
Luke 19:29-40

Sixth Sunday in Lent/Passion Sunday
(Palm Sunday)/Liturgy of [Procession with]
the Palms

Liturgy of the Word
Isaiah 45:21-25 or Isaiah 52:13—53:12
Psalm 22:1-21 or 22:1-11
Philippians 2:5-11
Luke (22:39-71), 23:1-49, (50-56)

Liturgy of the Passion

Monday in Holy Week
Isaiah 42:1-9
Psalm 36:5-10
Hebrews 11:39—12:3
John 12:1-11 or Mark 14:3-9

Monday of Holy Week

Tuesday in Holy Week
Isaiah 49:1-6
Psalm 71:1-12
1 Corinthians 1:18-31
John 12:37-38, 42-50 or Mark 11:15-19

Tuesday of Holy Week

Wednesday in Holy Week
Isaiah 50:4-9a
Psalm 69:7-15, 22-23
Hebrews 9:11-15, 24-28
John 13:21-35 or Matthew 26:1-5, 14-25

Wednesday of Holy Week

Maundy Thursday
Exodus 12:1-14a
Psalm 78:14-20, 23-25
1 Corinthians 11:23-26, (27-32)
John 13:1-15 or Luke 22:14-30

Holy [Maundy] Thursday

Good Friday
Isaiah 52:13—53:12 or Genesis 22:1-18 or
    Wisdom 2:1, 12-24
Psalm 22:1-21 or 22:1-11 or 40:1-14 or 69:1-23
Hebrews 10:1-25
John (18:1-40); 19:1-37

Good Friday

❧ YEAR C ❧
BCP

Easter Vigil
See Year A

Easter Day/Resurrection of the Lord
Acts 10:34-43 or Isaiah 51:9-11
Psalm 118:14-29 or 118:14-17, 22-24
Colossians 3:1-4 or Acts 10:34-43
Luke 24:1-10

Easter Evening
Acts 5:29a, 30-32 or Daniel 12:1-3
Psalm 114 or 136 or 118:14-17, 22-24
1 Corinthians 5:6b-8 or Acts 5:29a, 30-32
Luke 24:13-35

Second Sunday of Easter
Acts 5:12a, 17-22, 25-29 or Job 42:1-6
Psalm 111 or Psalm 118:19-24
Revelation 1:(1-8), 9-19 or Acts 5:12a, 17-22,
   25-29
John 20:19-31

Third Sunday of Easter
Acts 9:1-19a or Jeremiah 32:36-41
Psalm 33 or Psalm 33:1-11
Revelation 5:6-14 or Acts 9:1-19a
John 21:1-14

Fourth Sunday of Easter
Acts 13:15-16, 26-33, (34-39) or
   Numbers 27:12-23
Psalm 100
Revelation 7:9-17 or Acts 13:15-16, 26-33, (34-39)
John 10: 22-30

Fifth Sunday of Easter
Acts 13:44-52 or Leviticus 19:1-2, 9-18
Psalm 145 or 145: 1-9
Revelation 19:1, 4-9 or Acts 13:44-52
John 13:31-35

Sixth Sunday of Easter
Acts 14:8-18 or Joel 2:21-27
Psalm 67
Revelation 21:22—22:5 or Acts 14:8-18
John 14:23-29

Ascension Day
Acts 1:1-11 or 2 Kings 2:1-15
Psalm 47 or Psalm 110:1-5
Ephesians 1:15-23 or Acts 1:1-11
Luke 24:49-53 or Mark 16:9-15, 19-20

❧ YEAR C ❧
LM/RCL

Easter Vigil

Resurrection of the Lord/Easter Sunday

Easter Evening

Second Sunday of Easter

Third Sunday of Easter

Fourth Sunday of Easter

Fifth Sunday of Easter

Sixth Sunday of Easter

Ascension of the Lord

❮ YEAR C ❯
BCP

❮ YEAR C ❯
LM/RCL

Seventh Sunday of Easter
Acts 16:16-34 or 1 Samuel 12:19-24
Psalm 68:1-20 or Psalm 47
Revelation 22:12-14, 16-17, 20 or Acts 16:16-34
John 17:20-26

Seventh Sunday of Easter

Day of Pentecost
Acts 2:1-11 or Joel 2:28-32
Psalm 104:25-37 or 104:25-32 or 33:12-15, 18-22
1 Corinthians 12:4-13 or Acts 2:1-11
John 20:19-23 or John 14:8-17

Day of Pentecost

Trinity Sunday (First Sunday after Pentecost)
Isaiah 6:1-8
Psalm 29 or Canticle 2 or 13
Revelation 4:1-11
John 16:(5-11), 12-15

Trinity Sunday (First Sunday after Pentecost)
The Body and Blood of Christ

Proper 4, Closest to June 1 [9]/Ninth Sunday of the Year/Sunday between May 29 and June 4, inclusive (if after Trinity Sunday)
1 Kings 8:22-23, 27-30, 41-43
Psalm 96 or 96:1-9
Galatians 1:1-10
Luke 7:1-10

Proper 4 [9]/Ninth Sunday of the Year/Sunday between May 29 and June 4, inclusive (if after Trinity Sunday)

Proper 5, Closest to June 8 [10]/Tenth Sunday of the Year/Sunday between June 5 and June 11, inclusive (if after Trinity Sunday)
1 Kings 17:17-24
Psalm 30 or 30:1-6, 12-13
Galatians 1:11-24
Luke 7:11-17

Proper 5 [10]/Tenth Sunday of the Year/Sunday between June 5 and June 11, inclusive (if after Trinity Sunday)

Proper 6, Closest to June 15 [11]/Eleventh Sunday of the Year/Sunday between June 12 and June 18, inclusive (if after Trinity Sunday)
2 Samuel 11:26—12:10, 13-15
Psalm 32 or 32:1-8
Galatians 2:11-21
Luke 7:36-50

Proper 6 [11]/Eleventh Sunday of the Year/Sunday between June 12 and June 18, inclusive (if after Trinity Sunday)

Proper 7, Closest to June 22 [12]/Twelfth Sunday of the Year/Sunday between June 19 and June 25, inclusive (if after Trinity Sunday)
Zechariah 12:8-10; 13:1
Psalm 63:1-8
Galatians 3:23-29
Luke 9:18-24

Proper 7 [12]/Twelfth Sunday of the Year/Sunday between June 19 and June 25, inclusive (if after Trinity Sunday)

❧ YEAR C ☙
BCP

Proper 8, Closest to June 29 [13]/Thirteenth Sunday of the Year/Sunday between June 26 and July 2, inclusive
1 Kings 19:15-16, 19-21
Psalm 16 or 16:5-11
Galatians 5:1, 13-25
Luke 9:51-62

Proper 9, Closest to July 6 [14]/Fourteenth Sunday of the Year/Sunday between July 3 and July 9, inclusive
Isaiah 66:10-16
Psalm 66 or 66:1-8
Galatians 6:(1-10), 14-18
Luke 10:1-12, 16-20

Proper 10, Closest to July 13 [15]/Fifteenth Sunday of the Year/Sunday between July 10 and July 16, inclusive
Deuteronomy 30:9-14
Psalm 25 or 25:3-9
Colossians 1:1-14
Luke 10:25-37

Proper 11, Closest to July 20 [16]/Sixteenth Sunday of the Year/Sunday between July 17 and July 23, inclusive
Genesis 18:1-10a, (10b-14)
Psalm 15
Colossians 1:21-29
Luke 10:38-42

Proper 12, Closest to July 27 [17]/Seventeenth Sunday of the Year/Sunday between July 24 and July 30, inclusive
Genesis 18:20-33
Psalm 138
Colossians 2:6-15
Luke 11:1-13

Proper 13, Closest to August 3 [18]/Eighteenth Sunday of the Year/Sunday between July 31 and August 6, inclusive
Ecclesiastes 1:12-14; 2:(1-7, 11), 18-23
Psalm 49 or 49:1-11
Colossians 3:(5-11), 12-17
Luke 12:13-21

❧ YEAR C ☙
LM/RCL

Proper 8 [13]/Thirteenth Sunday of the Year/Sunday between June 26 and July 2, inclusive

Proper 9 [14]/Fourteenth Sunday of the Year/Sunday between July 3 and July 9, inclusive

Proper 10 [15]/Fifteenth Sunday of the Year/Sunday between July 10 and July 16, inclusive

Proper 11 [16]/Sixteenth Sunday of the Year/Sunday between July 17 and July 23, inclusive

Proper 12 [17]/Seventeenth Sunday of the Year/Sunday between July 24 and July 30, inclusive

Proper 13 [18]/Eighteenth Sunday of the Year/Sunday between July 31 and August 6, inclusive

❧ YEAR C ❧
BCP

Proper 14, Closest to August 10 [19]/Nineteenth
Sunday of the Yea/Sunday between August 6
and August 13, inclusive
Genesis 15:1-6
Psalm 33 or 33:12-15, 18-22
Hebrews 11:1-3, (4-7), 8-16
Luke 12:32-40

Proper 15, Closest to August 17 [20]/Twentieth
Sunday of the Year (C) Sunday between August
14 and August 20, inclusive
Jeremiah 23:23-29
Psalm 82
Hebrews 12:1-7, (8-10), 11-14
Luke 12:49-56

Proper 16, Closest to August 24 [21]/
Twenty-first Sunday of the Year/Sunday
between August 21 and August 27, inclusive
Isaiah 28:14-22
Psalm 46
Hebrews 12:18-19, 22-29
Luke 13:22-30

Proper 17, Closest to August 31 [22]/
Twenty-second Sunday of the Year/Sunday
between August 28 and September 3, inclusive
Sirach 10:(7-11), 12-18
Psalm 112
Hebrews 13:1-8
Luke 14:1, 7-14

Proper 18, Closest to September 7 [23]/
Twenty-third Sunday of the Year/Sunday
between September 4 and September 10, inclusive
Deuteronomy 30:15-20
Psalm 1
Philemon 1-20
Luke 14:25-33

Proper 19, Closest to September 14 [24]/
Twenty-fourth Sunday of the Year/Sunday
between September 11 and September 17, inclusive
Exodus 32:1, 7-14
Psalm 51:1-8 or 51:1-11
1 Timothy 1:12-17
Luke 15:1-10

❧ YEAR C ❧
LM/RCL

Proper 14 [19]/Nineteenth Sunday of the
Year/Sunday between August 6 and
August 13, inclusive

Proper 15 [20]/Twentieth Sunday of the
Year/Sunday between August 14 and
August 20, inclusive

Proper 16 [21]/Twenty-first Sunday of the
Year/Sunday between August 21 and
August 27, inclusive

Proper 17 [22]/Twenty-second Sunday of
the Year/Sunday between August 28 and
September 3, inclusive

Proper 18 [23]/Twenty-third Sunday of
the Year/Sunday between September 4 and
September 10, inclusive

Proper 19 [24]/Twenty-fourth Sunday of
the Year/Sunday between September 11
and September 17, inclusive

✍ YEAR C ✍
BCP

Proper 20, Closest to September 21 [25]/
Twenty-fifth Sunday of the Year/Sunday
between September 18 and September 24, inclusive
Amos 8:4-7, (8-12)
Psalm 138
1 Timothy 2:1-8
Luke 16:1-13

Proper 21, Closest to September 28 [26]/
Twenty-sixth Sunday of the Year/Sunday
between September 25 and October 1, inclusive
Amos 6:1-7
Psalm 146 or Psalm 146:4-9
1 Timothy 6:11-19
Luke 16:19-31

Proper 22, Closest to October 5 [27]/
Twenty-seventh Sunday of the Year/Sunday
between October 2 and October 8, inclusive
Habakkuk 1:1-6, (7-11), 12-13; 2:1-4
Psalm 37:1-18 or 37:3-10
2 Timothy 1:(1-5), 6-14
Luke 17:5-10

Proper 23, Closest to October 12 [28]/
Twenty-eighth Sunday of the Year/Sunday
between October 9 and October 15, inclusive
Ruth 1:(1-7), 8-19a
Psalm 113
2 Timothy 2:(3-7), 8-15
Luke 17:11-19

Proper 24, Closest to October 19 [29]/
Twenty-ninth Sunday of the Year/Sunday
between October 16 and October 22, inclusive
Genesis 32:3-8, 22-30
Psalm 121
2 Timothy 3:14—4:5
Luke 18:1-8a

Proper 25, Closest to October 26 [30]/
Thirtieth Sunday of the Year/Sunday between
October 23 and October 29, inclusive
Jeremiah 14:(1-6), 7-10, 19-22
Psalm 84 or 84:1-6
2 Timothy 4:6-8, 16-18
Luke 18:9-14

✍ YEAR C ✍
LM/RCL

Proper 20 [25]/Twenty-fifth Sunday of the Year/
Sunday between September 18 and September 24,
inclusive

Proper 21 [26]/Twenty-sixth Sunday of the
Year/Sunday between September 25 and
October 1, inclusive

Proper 22 [27]/Twenty-seventh Sunday of the
Year/Sunday between October 2 and October 8,
inclusive

Proper 23 [28]/Twenty-eighth Sunday of the
Year/Sunday between October 9 and October 15,
inclusive

Proper 24 [29]/Twenty-ninth Sunday of the
Year/Sunday between October 16 and
October 22, inclusive

Proper 25 [30]/Thirtieth Sunday of the Year/
Sunday between October 23 and October 29,
inclusive

✿ YEAR C ✿
BCP

Proper 26, Closest to November 2 [31]/
Thirty-first Sunday of the Year/Sunday between
October 30 and November 5, inclusive
Isaiah 1:10-20
Psalm 32 or 32:1-8
2 Thessalonians 1:1-5, (6-10), 11-12
Luke 19:1-10

Proper 27, Closest to November 9 [32]/
Thirty-second Sunday of the Year/Sunday
between November 6 and November 12, inclusive
Job 19:23-27a
Psalm 17 or 17:1-8
2 Thessalonians 2:13—3:5
Luke 20:27(28-33), 34-38

Proper 28, Closest to November 16 [33]/
Thirty-third Sunday of the Year/Sunday
between November 13 and November 19, inclusive
Malachi 3:13—4:2a, 5-6
Psalm 98 or 98:5-10
2 Thessalonians 3:6-13
Luke 21:5-19

Proper 29, Closest to November 23 [34]/
Reign of Christ or Christ the King/Last Sunday
of the Year/Sunday between November 20 and
November 26, inclusive
Jeremiah 23:1-6
Psalm 46
Colossians 1:11-20
Luke 23:35-43 or 19:29-38

The Presentation of the Lord (Candelmas Day),
February 2
Malachi 3:1-4
Psalm 84 or 84:1-6
Hebrews 2:14-18
Luke 2:22-40

The Annunciation of the Lord, March 25
Isaiah 7:10-14
Psalm 40:1-11 or 40:5-10 or Canticle 3 or 15
Hebrews 10:5-10
Luke 1:26-38

The Visitation of Mary to Elizabeth, May 31
Zephaniah 3:14-18a
Psalm 113 or Canticle 9
Colossians 3:12-17
Luke 1:39-49

✿ YEAR C ✿
LM/RCL

Proper 26 [31]/Thirty-first Sunday of the
Year/Sunday between October 30 and
November 5, inclusive

Proper 27 [32]/Thirty-second Sunday of
the Year/Sunday between November 6
and November 12, inclusive

Proper 28 [33]/Thirty-third Sunday of the
Year/Sunday between November 13 and
November 19, inclusive

Proper 29 [34]/Reign of Christ or Christ
the King/Last Sunday of the Year Sunday
between November 20 and November 26,
inclusive

The Immaculate Conception (of
Mary in Her Mother's Womb), December 8

The Presentation of the Lord (Candelmas
Day), February 2

The Annunciation of the Lord, March 25

The Visitation of Mary to Elizabeth, May 31

YEAR C
BCP

Peter and Paul, Apostles, June 29
Ezekiel 34:11-16
Psalm 87
2 Timothy 4:1-8
John 21:15-19

The Transfiguration, August 6
Exodus 34:29-35
Psalm 99 or 99:5-9
2 Peter 1:13-21
Luke 9:28-36

All Saints, November 1 or the First Sunday in November
See Year A

YEAR C
LM/RCL

Peter and Paul, Apostles, June 29

The Transfiguration, August 6

The Assumption of the Blessed Virgin Mary, August 15

All Saints, November 1 or the First Sunday in November